Lincoln Steffens

The System

Journalism 1897 - 1920

The Archive of American Journalism

Lincoln Steffens

Henry Stanley

Theodore Roosevelt

Richard Harding Davis

Ida Tarbell

Ray Stannard Baker

Nellie Bly

H.L. Mencken

Ambrose Bierce

Stephen Crane

Jack London

Mark Twain

Ernest Hemingway

Horace Greeley

Lincoln Steffens

The System

Journalism 1897-1920

The *A*rchive ▲ *St. Paul, Minnesota*

Note on Sources

All articles are complete and unabridged, with headlines, subheads and formatting that match those of the original publication. Note that minor edits have been made to correct obsolete spelling and punctuation. Students and researchers: these are "public domain" texts that can be freely copied, reproduced and distributed without permission or cost. Please credit The Archive of American Journalism as your source.

The Archive LLC
9269 Troon Court
Woodbury, MN 55125.

Article selection and original Introduction Copyright ©2014 by Tom Streissguth

Cover Image: Senator Robert M. LaFollette, July 5, 1924. From the Library of Congress, National Photo Company Collection.

Library of Congress Control Number: 2014949765
ISBN: 978-0-9907137-3-9
Printed in the United States of America

Acknowledgments

For their encouragement and suggestions, sincere thanks to Mark Lerner, Gordon Hagert, Pier Gustafson, Phil Gapp, Jonathan Peacock, John Hatch, Marian Streissguth and our original founding supporters:

William F. Zeman
Phil Gapp
Walter Crowley
Adele Streissguth
Richard Prosser
Abhilash Sarhadi
James McGrath Morris

Contents

Introduction

The Modern Business Building
Scribner's Magazine/July, 1897
3

Life in the Klondike Gold Fields
McClure's Magazine/September, 1897
34

The Conduct of Great Business - The Business of a Newspaper
Scribner's Magazine/October, 1897
46

Theodore Roosevelt, Governor
McClure's Magazine/May, 1899
68

Governor Roosevelt—As An Experiment
McClure's Magazine/June, 1900
85

The Overworked President
McClure's Magazine/April, 1902
93

A Labor Leader of Today - John Mitchell and What He Stands For
McClure's Magazine/August, 1902
106

Tweed Days in St. Louis
McClure's Magazine/October, 1902
111

The American Man on Horseback
McClure's Magazine/December, 1902
129

The Shame of Minneapolis
McClure's Magazine/January, 1903
143

Pittsburgh: A City Ashamed
McClure's Magazine/May, 1903
161

Philadelphia Corrupt and Corrupted
McClure's Magazine/July, 1903
187

Jacob A. Riis - Reporter, Reformer, American Citizen
McClure's Magazine/August, 1903
210

Chicago: Half Free and Fighting On
McClure's Magazine/October, 1903
222

The New School of Journalism
The Bookman/October, 1903
246

New York: Good Government to the Test
McClure's Magazine/November 1903
255

The Political Leaders Who are Selling Out the state of Missouri
McClure's Magazine/April, 1904
270

Illinois: A Triumph of Public Opinion
McClure's Magazine/August, 1904
296

Wisconsin: Representative Government Restored— The Story of Governor LaFollette
McClure's Magazine/October, 1904
326

Rhode Island: A state for Sale
McClure's Magazine/February, 1905
356

New Jersey: A Traitor state
PART I.—THE CONQUEST
McClure's Magazine/April, 1905
385

New Jersey: A Traitor state
PART II.—HOW SHE SOLD OUT THE UNITED STATES
McClure's Magazine/May, 1905
418

Ohio: A Tale of Two Cities
McClure's Magazine/July, 1905
449

A Servant of God and the People
McClure's Magazine/January, 1906
484

Everett Colby, "The Gentleman From Essex."
McClure's Magazine/February, 1906
509

Ben Lindsey, The Just Judge
McClure's Magazine/October – December, 1906
535

Rudolph Spreckels: A Business Reformer
American Magazine/February, 1908
619

W. S. U'Ren, The Lawgiver
American Magazine/March, 1908
642

Midnight in Russia
McClure's Magazine/May, 1918
666

Report of Lincoln Steffens
The Nation/October 4, 1919
684

John Reed: Under the Kremlin
Freeman/November 3, 1920
693

Sources

For Further Reading

Online Resources

Introduction

The suitcase bomb detonated at the corner of First Street and Broadway at 1:07 AM. The timer had failed; three hours early, 17 sticks of dynamite brought an entire floor of the *Los Angeles Times* building down on the heads of dozens of late-shift workers, and started a fire that burned 21 people to death. The motive? A labor union's demand for a minimum wage of $.50 per hour, and the stubbornly anti-union stance of *Times* owner Harrison Gray Otis.

Before the ashes of the *Times* building had cooled, Otis took to editorial pages across the country to denounce union violence and demand the gallows for the perpetrators. Random arrests, police beatings, and extra-judicial executions of union leaders may be excused, but this was cold-blooded murder, in the opinion of Otis, and the perpetrators must hang. The California justice system was ready to oblige when an investigation by Detective William J. Burns turned up three suspects: union agitators Ortie McManigal, John McNamara, and James McNamara. Ortie turned state's evidence for a light sentence, leaving the McNamara brothers to face the music.

On the scene arrived defense attorney Clarence Darrow and Lincoln Steffens, star journalist and muckraker, revealer of political and business corruption across the nation. By this time Steffens had a reputation as a tireless investigator and a left-leaning literary agitator; he never seemed to tire in pursuit of stories that served his higher purpose: inspiring elected leaders to act on the Golden Rule and truly represent the common interest. In a series of 16 powerful articles that made his reputation and that of *McClure's* as a champion of Progressivism, Steffens applied a keen sense of the dramatic and a florid writing style to the people he met and the cause he championed.

> There were J. B. McNamara, who was charged with actually placing and setting off the dynamite in Ink Alley that blew up part of the Times building and set fire to the rest, bringing about the death of twenty-one employees, and J. J. McNamara, J. B.'s brother, who was indicted on some twenty counts for assisting at explosions as secretary of the Structural Iron Workers' Union, directing the actual dynamiters. He was supposed in labor circles to be the commanding man, the boss; he looked it; a tall, strong, blond, he was a handsome figure of health and personal power. But his brother, Jim, who looked sick and weak, soon appeared as the man of decision. I had never met them before, but when they came out of their cells they greeted and sat down beside me as if I were an old friend.

Darrow and Steffens considered the accused as heroes in the spirit of John Brown, who likewise committed violent crimes in the interest of a noble aspiration: the abolition of slavery. "Direct action" such as Brown's raid on Harper's Ferry, and the suitcase bomb in downtown Los Angeles, was unfortunately still necessary in the unequal battle between downtrodden labor and greedy management – this was war, and the representatives of the working man and woman were disadvantaged combatants.

The evidence against the brothers was strong; the district attorney would have no trouble getting a conviction. Always ready to match wits with a courtroom opponent, Darrow thought the best the McNamaras could hope for was a mistrial, but Steffens persuaded the brothers to plead guilty and hope for the best from the light, merciful hand of American justice. A guilty plea would avoid a trial and appeal, in Steffens' view, to the better natures of the enemies of labor.

James McNamara was skeptical, but the gallows loomed, and eventually the brothers agreed. Steffens negotiated with prosecutor John D. Fredericks. In exchange for the plea of guilty, there would be no confession, no death sentence, and no further prosecutions for the bombing. The appointed day arrived in the court of The Honorable Walter Bordwell, who heard the McNamaras' plea, took Steffens' offer under consideration, and then sentenced James McNamara to life, John McNamara to 15 years. From the bench Bordwell denounced Steffens for his hypocrisy as well as his anarchism and brought the gavel down.

"You see," muttered James McNamara to Steffens, before leaving the court in chains. "You were wrong, and I was right."

Steffens could make no reply. For once, he had nothing to say; and wouldn't have much more to publish. His career as a muckraking journalist was unofficially over.

After a failed attempt at fiction, Steffens had begun reporting at the *New York Evening Post* in 1892. In 1902 Samuel McClure took him on as a staff writer at *McClure's*, where Steffens joined a masthead already loaded with literary star power: Ida Tarbell, Theodore Dreiser, Frank Norris, Ray Stannard Baker, Jack London, Upton Sinclair, Willa Cather. Steffens made a splash with his first lines for the magazine, a description of political shenanigans in St. Louis that is widely credited as the first example of that probing investigative journalism known as muckraking:

The visitor is told of the wealth of the residents, of the financial strength of the banks, and of the growing importance of the industries; yet he sees poorly paved, refuse-burdened streets, and dusty or mud-covered alleys; he passes a ramshackle firetrap crowded with the sick and learns that it is the City Hospital: he enters the Four Courts, and his nostrils are greeted with the odor of formaldehyde used as a disinfectant and insect powder used to destroy vermin; he calls at the new City Hall and finds half the entrance boarded with pine planks to cover up the unfinished interior.

Steffens showed no favoritism to the cities and states he covered. His theme was constant and dependable: graft, bribery, the corruption of the political system, the schemes of the fixers and boodlers who populated the stately city halls and marbled state houses, and sold out the interests of the citizens to business interests and the all-powerful profit motive. He uncovered scandals in Minneapolis, Pittsburgh, Philadelphia, Chicago. He found corruption in New Jersey and Cincinnati. The misdeeds in the name of machine politics astonished him, but even worse, in his view, was the complicity and apathy and resigned acceptance of the public. He saw the System, always with a capital S, as the enemy of everything America stood for, and corrupt politicians as traitors to the country and the ideals of its founders.

Steffens picked no political sides in these matters; he condemned both parties and he found ample material at all levels: local city councils, state governments, and the US Congress. The stories provided drama, conflict, and suspense, and presented endless variations on the common theme: voters poorly served by the men who demanded their votes. In Rhode Island, Steffens found party hacks and lawmakers rigging elections and simply buying off the voters. In St. Louis, it was an ongoing war of reformers versus elected thieves who took no interest whatsoever in the public interest. In Minneapolis, Steffens described a mayor whose racket turned an entire police department into a private bank for friends and co-conspirators, and the noble crusade of a courageous individual determined to do right. In Philadelphia, it was the public's abject surrender to an overpowering, systematic destruction of representative government, in the birthplace of representative government.

The sheer detail in these articles will astonish readers who get their political infotainment in 300-word blogs, 140-character Tweets and sketchy, short-lived media investigations. Steffens arrived in his target city, notebook in hand, and spent weeks interviewing anyone and everyone who had connections or something to say. He dug deep into the mechanics of bribery and graft, and laid it all out in exhausting, double-columned detail, with names, dates, and amounts. He described the machinations and the negotiations, and the endless double-dealing. He uncovered secrets long hidden from, or covered up by, the local press; he named sources without fear of retribution, and he made accusations while leaving no doubt as to his personal sentiments toward the characters he was exposing. Taken together, his articles form a great chronicle of American municipal corruption, the most thorough ever compiled.

Steffens had no patience for demagogues or their convenient labels: Democrats and Republicans, anarchists, conservatives, and Socialists all drew the attention of his baleful literary eye. Nevertheless, he found several men who were doing good: a courageous juvenile court judge in Denver, a brilliantly talented businessman in San Francisco, and a few politicians – a very few – including the senator and Progressive presidential candidate from Wisconsin:

> *[Robert] LaFollette from the beginning has asked, not the bosses, but the people for what he wanted, and after 1894 he simply broadened his field and redoubled his efforts. He circularized the state, he made speeches every chance he got, and if the test of demagogy is the tone and style of a man's speeches, LaFollette is the opposite of a demagogue. Capable of fierce invective, his oratory is impersonal; passionate and emotional himself, his speeches are temperate. Some of them are so loaded with facts and such closely knit arguments that they demand careful reading, and their effect is traced to his delivery, which is forceful, emphatic, and fascinating.*

The establishment and the System derided Steffens and dismissed his muckraking as just another example of the decrepit modern journalism that could never pass for genuine writing. Nor did Steffens get much respect from the other side; his naiveté angered Socialists, as did the absurd idea that the Golden Rule and the tenets of Christianity, and the noble ideals of the founding fathers, had anything to do with business, or labor, or government, or any other serious matter. Radicals like Emma Goldman and *Masses* editor Max Eastman had no time for Steffens' ideas of reform, and after the *LA Times* trial labor leader Olav Tveitmoe made this trenchant observation: "I will show him there is no Golden Rule, but there is a Rule of Gold".

And there was retribution. The trial of the McNamaras effectively ended Steffens' career in magazines. He lost interest in *McClure's*, but couldn't get his own publications off the ground. World War I did nothing for the muckraking market; the public was bored by magazine exposés and the fine details of municipal corruption; nationalism and the anti-Socialist militancy of the Red Scare triumphed. Steffens tried an investigation into the oil business, following up on Ida Tarbell's sensational book-length expose of Standard Oil, but had no takers for the work. William Randolph Hearst made an offer, and a good one, but Steffens knew what writing for the Hearst organization meant – well-paid hackdom in the service of one man's political ambitions. He drifted to California, contributed the occasional newspaper piece, semi-retired to an artists' colony by the sea in Carmel, wrote general interest pieces for a small-town newspaper published by his wife, raised a daughter, and passed quietly into journalism history.

The System

Journalism 1897 - 1920

Scribner's Magazine
July, 1897

The Modern Business Building

THE skyline of New York is changing so rapidly that the American traveler who goes abroad can recognize with more certainty the profiles of the foreign cities he approaches than that of his own metropolis as he sees it from the deck of the steamer on his return. It may be his first visit to Europe; he may know London, Rome, and Paris only from views of them in old prints. But, if he has an eye for such things, his first glimpse of St. Paul's, St. Peter's, or Notre Dame will tell him to what place he is coming, for all the world knows these pinnacles, has known them for centuries. They are as conspicuous and characteristic in the silhouettes of their cities as they were when they were built. One of the Dutch governors of New Amsterdam, seeking in spirit some familiar earthly habitation, might find old Amsterdam, for it cuts the same figure in the sky today that it did when he left it, but the last dead boss of New York, if by any chance he should get away from where he ought to be, would search the horizon in vain for the face of his city. The features his eye would seek are there: Old Trinity still stands, its steeple, like the spires of the old cathedrals, uplifted high above the earth; but its solitary prominence is gone. The modern office building has risen higher than the head of the cross, and the church has lost its distinction. The enterprise of business has surpassed the aspiration of religion.

New York, in this, as in so many other things, is but the archetype of American cities. Chicago, Boston, Philadelphia, St. Louis, even Washington—they all are rising bodily, constantly, fast, and their climbing skylines are writing with reckless realism across the heavens the same great story of material progress. It is time to read this writing of the walls. It may mean more than the increase of wealth, the growing power of capital, the might of skilled and disciplined labor. These have their own value, and have been the cause of national pride, but now they are the scapegoats of reactionary discontent. Men hate them. Is there nothing better back of these things?

The papers that have preceded this one have been answering the question. It was brains and character, the writers showed, that initiate, organize, and develop such enterprises as the department store, the modern hotel, the factory, and the bank; and this is the story of the skylines. They do not tell it so simply as the other businesses, because they are less familiar, but they make it more conspicuous when told, and they leave it in a more enduring form for the future to read. A great building may be a failure financially without disappearing, like a mismanaged store or banking company. It will remain, bearing in its form and plan the traces of its uses, which may be finally the only remnants of the other creations of modern business enterprise, the only legible chapter of the common tale. With this in mind some men build, giving what is called the monumental building; and corporations, seeking, however, the more immediate form of fame—advertisement—put up structures on a scale of expenditure that precludes the possibility of a fair, direct income in rent. The prophecy that the present will be known hereafter as the period of high building in the United States is not absurd, for while other countries have great banks and factories, department stores and hotels, none of them has "skyscrapers." The modern high building, whether it be ugly or beautiful, whether it express pleasant or disagreeable traits and truths, is distinctively of this day and this country, and. containing all the other modes of enterprise, it is comprehensively typical.

The men who are raising these new structures are rebuilding cities. That is the scheme of magnificent proportions which the broken skylines sketch out roughly for the imagination to fill in, and the sharp angles of the outline that offend the sense of form now give aesthetic pleasure to the mind by their suggestion of problems solved and to be solved. For mind sympathizes with the efforts of brain labor. The sudden peaks that scrape the sky are not so hideous when the complication of difficulties they overcome is realized. Then it is the gaps of blue sky between that seem unlovely; and they, too, have an appeal for toleration, since the art of high building is new and crude, and these spaces are opportunities for the builders of tomorrow to perfect the architecture of today.

To the minds that are "rebuilding American cities" the work does not appear on the grand scale suggested by that phrase. New York and Chicago have not, as London had in Prince Albert and Paris in Baron Haussmann, a representative of the community to mark out a design and to carry through a scheme to which all of the parts should conform. Here the individual is supreme, and, thus far, unchecked. Even the architects, who have to care for the interest of beauty, do not often strive for unity and proportion in the completion of a block, to say nothing of a street or a district of the city they are making over. Each man builds for himself, according to his own taste; and Greek seldom meets Greek.

But that is one of the problems still to be solved, and there is time yet if the willingness to cooperate, found in two or three of the greater architects, spreads through the profession and meets a responsive spirit among the other callings engaged in modern construction. Heretofore the architect has not always been the master mind, and his considerations have not been the only ones that weighed. The financier, the real estate expert, the engineer, the machinist, the contractor or builder, and the business manager have all worked with the architect, and sometimes one, sometimes another, has been the predominating influence. Capital and labor have also played important parts. But capital, though an essential, is a small element, and receives little of the reward; as an investment, an office building ranks with and pays not much more than a gilt-edged bond. Labor is the most expensive factor, getting from eighty to ninety per cent, of the total cost of construction, but, like capital, it does none of the brainwork. And the subject of this article is the brains that go into high buildings; we have to do with capital as the financier handles it, and with labor as the contractor directs it. For the rest, our interest is in the foresight, the imagination, the thought, the originality, and the knowledge of these and other experts in this business.

Originally the demand for high buildings presented a purely financial problem. Owners of property in the business parts of cities found they could rent more space than their buildings of two, three, and four stories contained, and they wanted new buildings of five or six stories, or additional floors above the old roof. To finance this operation was easy, and any intelligent carpenter or mason could do the job. After awhile, however, the need in the larger cities for space in the centres where business was most progressive and profitable passed beyond the capacity of the six-story buildings, and a better man than the master-mason was needed.

"Downtown," as the great city marketplaces are called, became overcrowded. It could grow and expand as a whole, but certain parts of it could not move. Some lines of business had taken possession of ground space enough to accommodate them when they settled, and others grouped themselves close around till they hemmed one another in. Then traditions and the habits of customers fixed the limits more and more definitely, making changes almost impossible. To cross a street might mean failure, and the turning of a corner would not be thought of. The wholesale dry goods firms of New York succeeded in getting out of Cedar, William, and Pine Streets, but it was done with fear and trembling after years of hesitation, and nobody was certain for many months after the moving that a fatal mistake had not been made. Every effort of the jewelers of Maiden Lane to leave their street has been unsuccessful. Their rent is high, the location is not convenient, and other businesses would pay well to be so near the financial centre, but the jewelers are afraid their customers would not find them elsewhere than in Maiden Lane, and that street as an address is invaluable to the firm that writes to the country with it on its letterhead. Then, for a last example, there is "Wall Street;" how far can the stockbrokers go from Wall Street?

Confined on all sides round, the only way out was up. Limited as to the ground, business sought the air. It had to be done; but how? That was the question. To pile more stories on the sixth was useless, since no one would climb up to them; the young brokers and lawyers might be willing to do it, but their customers would not follow. The problem became mechanical, and the financier and the architect were as helpless as the mason.

The passenger elevator was the solution. It was a clumsy hoist moved by a hand windlass when inventive genius began to study its possibilities, and no one could have foreseen in any of its earlier forms that it was to be to modern building what the steam engine is to transportation, a revolutionary agent. Steam-power was applied to it in 1866. The result was an apparatus with so many faults that it presented dearly all the necessities for success. It was slow, jerky, and dangerous. To overcome these defects the experimenters turned to hydraulic power, in the water-balance elevator. A car was carried up by the weight of a water-vessel filled at the top of the shaft, and was let down by emptying the water at the bottom. Speed and smoothness of motion were thus secured, but the control was doubtful, and though the accidents that occurred were not fatal, they were wet and disagreeable. Absolute safety was first achieved in the direct-acting ram hydraulic elevators; but they, too, were slow and, for high structures, impracticable, since the cylinder had to be sunk as deep below ground as the shaft rose high above it. Having safety, however, the makers clung to the hydraulic power till they eliminated one by one all the defects of their machine. Meanwhile electricity was applied successfully, and now there are several systems that satisfy all the requirements of the highest buildings and the most impatient of human beings.

With the elevator, long before it was perfected, rose all that made the problem of high building—high rents, high prices for ground space, and high hopes. There was great risk in the first application of the elevator to the office building, but it is capital that is timid, not the financiers, the brains that handle it; they are cautious, but daring. They saw that the new device for lifting passengers to the unbuilt upper stories brought the unclaimed space above the costly ground within easy reach, but no one could foresee how the tenants and their customers would take this mode of transit, nor was there any basis for estimating the rents that would be paid. The whole financial question rested on these unknown elements.

The prices charged for a given space in one of the earliest buildings called high in New York will show how speculative and how far astray were the first reckonings on the effect of the elevator. The building was finished in 1868, and the manager let a suite on the top floor for $850 a year. He raised the rent the next year to $1,250, and, thinking the limit reached in that figure, signed a contract for a five-year lease. Bound by his agreement, he had to refuse offers rising gradually to $4,500, which he got readily at the end of the sixth year. People became accustomed to the elevator as their fathers did to the steam-cars, and now the top stories of high buildings bring in more rent than the middle floors. There are men called "high livers" who will not have an office unless it is up where the air is cool and fresh, the outlook broad and beautiful, and where there is silence in the heart of business.

The first builders, trusting that something like this would come to pass, drew the elevator shaft in their plans, and put up eight-story buildings regardless of the gasping skepticism of the crowd. On every trip of the car was an unseen passenger, the value of property in the financial and other centres where the commercial fight was thickest. A lot that was worth forty dollars a square foot rose to fifty, sixty, seventy-five dollars, and owners of low buildings in good locations found themselves receiving an income, fair for half a million, on what was worth a million. They were tempted to sell or rebuild. Those who could afford it held on for a further rise, encouraged by the slower but equally certain advance of rents. Many sold, however, and the new owners had bought to make the property pay, or, if they sought primarily a permanent location for their business, they listened to proposals to improve the property into an independent paying investment.

This was the financial problem, and it is the same today that it was twenty years ago, and it will be the same twenty years hence. In general terms its purpose is to make a good security also a good investment; to buy something that has a value above its earning powers because it is first-class security for a loan, like a government bond, and is in demand as a perfectly safe investment for trust funds, and then try to make it pay as a business enterprise. In most of our greater cities a man can borrow money at nearly as low a rate on real estate in the financial centres as he can on high-class bonds, and the difference is disappearing. The bonds have the advantage of their divisibility; the holder of a million dollars' worth can hypothecate them in any number of parcels at even rates, while the owner of a piece of real estate of equal value has to put a mortgage on the whole to secure a loan however small, and the first lien lowers the value of all subsequent mortgages. To obviate this difficulty, companies are incorporating to fund real estate so that its value can be handled in the form of stocks and bonds, just as the securities of railroads and manufacturing companies are handled in the financial markets.

Thus stated, the financial aspect of the high-building problem may look like another perpetual motion quest. But the financiers, fortunately, do not take that view of it, and their approximations to the solution have been productive at every step. They began the rebuilding of cities the moment the elevator led the way, exercising little mental power in exact calculation, but showing all the more courage and experimental curiosity. Perhaps there was some recklessness in the first ventures. They spent large sums of money, and could not tell whether they would get back any fair portion of it. It has been said that the earliest builders were corporations, the custodians of other people's money; but the exceptions where individuals, however few, entered the field, some in New York and many in Chicago, indicate that it was a natural, general movement, caused by the chase of brains after the rent-ridden rise of real estate values.

In Chicago the great fire of 1871 forced property owners to reconstruct from the ground up. Having had some experience with values that outstripped the capacity of their old buildings, they rebuilt either temporarily or as permanently as they knew how. They meant to erect structures so cheap that they could be torn down without much loss, or so high that they would be up at any height to which land values might ever rise. They did not build quite as wisely as they thought, it turned out, but they found out how to do it, and as the demand continued to grow, and architects kept on building, the Chicago builders long held their lead in the solution of the structural problems.

The first "high" buildings, which were from eight to eleven stories high, served only to increase the demand for higher construction, for values kept pace with their growth and the elevator did not stop. It could go on up to any height, and the success of these buildings proved conclusively that tenants would not balk. The financial outlook was clear, but capital waited on the ingenuity of the builders.

From 1865 up to about 1875 the architects planned for solid masonry walls and heavy beams and pillars. The walls carried the weight of the floors and supported themselves. With each additional story, therefore, the walls at their base had to be increased in thickness and strength, so that as the demand for height grew and was satisfied, the lower structure became more and more bulky and costly. The material that went into these sustaining parts was enormous in amount and expensive in quality. It is estimated that the material in a certain high building, erected in 1869, would supply masonry for six modern buildings of its size.

Then, too, most of the high buildings were put up in the streets where ground space was so valuable that even rich men and large corporations could not afford to have very much of it, and one lot or two was so small a space that the thickness of the fattening walls cut appreciably into the rentable room. There came a time when to go higher with the solid masonry method was to lose more income at the bottom than was won at the top. Adding the ever-increasing cost of the foundation and the walls, the financiers saw that their upward course was coming to an end; the beckoning elevator, with its load of rents, had to be disregarded.

There was no time, of course, when either financiers or architects confessed that progress was checked. Nor did the problem set forth here ever appear with the definiteness that it has in the retrospect. Men were working on particular buildings; they were studying out devices to overcome the minor difficulties that beset them, and they made progress slowly, step by step. They began early to use metal, for instance. Probably there is not a building anywhere that rises eight stories without cast-iron or steel somewhere in its frame. It was applied as floor beams, as pillars, later for all interior columns, and by and by was recognized as the key to the building problem. But it was new to architects as a means, and was not the material contemplated in the art they had studied; hence they hesitated.

Another expert was needed, if the art of building was to go on supplying the insatiable demands of the real estate market—someone who understood the laws of metals. The engineer was the man. The architect, seeing him spinning his suspension bridge, recognized that his was the knowledge wanted, and called him down to consultations about the building of houses. It was a new problem to the engineer, and he had to study its requirements; but it was a promising field, too, and he stayed. He studied architecture, and the architectural engineer was the result. In some conspicuous instances his conversion was so complete that his origin is almost forgotten, and he ranks among the leaders of his adopted art. But while the engineer was mastering architecture, the architect was working into the mysteries of engineering, and among the famous builders of any large American city today there are examples of the combination in three ways—the architect who has made himself an engineer, the engineer turned architect, and the firm with one member an architect and another an engineer.

The union of the two arts extended the substitution of metal for masonry. The architect, blocked by the widening base of his brick walls, was taught that a slender pillar of iron could carry as much as his fattest mound. All that stone and brick were needed for was to protect the iron from fire and corrosion. In the superstructure the masonry need be no thicker than was required to give the framework rigidity. So they built, throwing more and more of the real work on the iron, and leaving off ever-increasing amounts of masonry.

Without following the transition through the minuter changes, the movement may be divided into two periods, that of the double and that of the single construction. After all the saving of space that seemed possible in the details of pillars and girders, the building of high structures had risen only a story or two, and the demand for more of the free air and light continued. The next step was a brilliant one; the engineer suggested that iron could be made to carry the floors. This would relieve the walls of any weight but their own, and would reduce still further the space they must occupy all the way down the building. There would be two distinct structures—the iron frame, which would be independent and complete in itself, and a shell of masonry around it, closing it in to keep out the weather. They were fastened together, these two buildings, and supported each other somewhat, but theoretically either would stand alone so long as there was no wind or other side pressure.

When done, this revolutionary method of construction stood the test that was considered sufficient by the eager men who were trying to solve the modern architectural problem, and the financiers backed them for more. The price of lots in the neighborhood of the new buildings rose with them, in part because of them. The very solution of the old problem entailed a fresh one. The permanent financial question was revived in altered proportions. The builders overcame the difficulties of details, perfected their construction, and forged ahead a story or two by minor savings. But as the buildings grew in height even the separate walls, which had to bear only their own weight, increased at the base again, and presented the same old obstacle, a wall so thick on the most valuable floors that the rentable space was encroached upon to an extent that cut off below the gains in income above.

Why not let the iron frame that had carried the floors so easily take also the weight of the walls? It meant running the floor beams out under the masonry, a little strengthening of the columns, and it presented a pretty problem in handling wind-pressure. But these were matters of mathematics and engineering, not of rentable space. On the contrary, there would be a saving of room everywhere. It was tried on a small scale in New York in 1881, again on a whole building in Chicago in 1883, and during the next few years was gradually accepted everywhere as a profitable method of high construction on a narrow foundation. Steel was substituted for iron; hot steel rivets closed the connections and secured perfect rigidity, and gusset plates took the lateral pressure not distributable to the floors and interior columns. The steel cage assumed the whole burden of the skyscrapers. The walls became a veneer, panels to protect the metals and the tenants from fire and weather. A Chicago architect recently began at the top, and put on his walls in succession downward to show that it could be done, and last year a builder in New York, whose supply of lower story stone was delayed by the cutters, closed in his upper floors while he waited.

Some architects are still afraid of the Chicago method, as the steel cage construction is called, and lean heavily when they can on their masonry, but for the lofty tower on a small base the steel cage is inevitable. No one can tell how long it will stand the test of time. There are 1,950 tons of steel in a building 370 feet high, which weighs in all 15,000 tons, and the metal will surely corrode; but how long before its sustaining strength will be vitiated to the danger point is a question that no one can answer empirically, and the present generation of builders is not likely to know how well or how badly it has builded.

They can be sure of this, however, that they have solved their problem; they have reduced the cost of construction from about $5 to 37 cents a cubic foot; they can build as high as the elevator can go, and the elevator knows no limit. Legislation may interfere. The architects and builders themselves have invited legal restrictions to the height of buildings in several of the eastern states. Otherwise, there is nothing in sight to check the rise of the skylines of the great cities. The financier talks of foundation costs and the increasing space required for elevators to serve more than thirty stories. All this means that the problem is back with the financier again, and that to go on would make necessary the combination of capital for the purchase of a large enough ground space to start with to give room for a solid bottom on which to build and plenty of inside room for the numerous elevators, local and express. A building thirty stories high has dug a hole for itself in New York; and, at the time of this writing, in the same city, the plans for fifteen buildings of fifteen stories or more were filed in the Building Department. One heard much grumbling about overdoing, and there was the rub; the builders had outstripped at last the rise of rents, which were handicapped by hard times.

But whether they go higher or not is a question beyond the present theme. The point is that they can. There are engineers who can lay the foundations for fifty stories; there are architects who can plan the construction; there are builders who can realize the conception, and financiers who can manage the scheme. In short, brain can do its work when capital is ready and if the law permits.

The brain that is engaged in this business directly is divided into more than a hundred trades, each one of which has been developing its particular branch with the same strenuousness, boldness, and ingenuity that have characterized the architectural engineering. The architect himself has been laboring with a thousand considerations not even hinted at in this article. He has been studying out such other general problems as ventilation, light, economy of space, convenience, proportion, besides attending to special applications of all his principles, and those of all the other trades that entered the building with his, and add to the ever-varying problem. The engineers have been pondering such essentials as joinings and strains and foundations. In Chicago, where there is no hard pan within reach, they devised a floating "raft" of steel and concrete to lie flat on the shifting sands below the lake level, and on that they can build with such perfectly even distribution of weight that when the whole structure of twenty or more stories settles it sinks plumb. The elevator-builder has achieved such precision that the number of cars put into a building is determined by the cubical contents of the structure. The plumber has applied to his art the principles of sanitary science. The machinist has fitted his enormous plant to the dimensions of the cellar, and has plotted with the elevator man to use for the improved heating system the exhaust steam from the power engines to warm the tenant after it has lifted him to his floor and lighted his room. The heater man has arranged so that all the tenant has to do is to set a gauge opposite the degree Fahrenheit at which he would like to have the temperature of his room kept, and the machinery automatically keeps it there.

So it is with the roofer and the tile man, the master mason and the carpentry man (no longer a mere carpenter), the manufacturer of hardware and the locksmith; the patent spring on the door closes it quickly, but prevents a slam, and the locks are exclusive for each door, with a master-key for the janitor. In one case, an armory, a set of locks was made with a private locker for each man, a master-key for all, and for each company another master-key that would not open a locker in any other company room.

"I didn't realize there were so many trades in the world as I found I had to deal with when I undertook to finance this building," said the president of a corporation that had built a skyscraper. "But what amazed me most was the thought and the forethought and the cleverness that have gone into even the smallest things connected with a building, and the complicated perfection to which everything has been brought."

This financier, it happens, is one who attempted to manage the construction as well as the financing of his company's building, and, like many another expert manipulator of capital who has thought he could build an office building to pay, simply because he could put up a country house or run a railroad, he has paid heavily to learn that it is a distinct business, requiring special knowledge and training. Just who the head expert should be—the real estate man, the architect, the builder, or the manager—has not been settled unanimously even in the trade, probably because the business is so new. Each of these can give good reasons why he should control, and in practice, first one, then another, appears as the master mind who hires the special service of the others. Again, all four and the engineer and the owner are combined successfully in one person; but in such a case the comprehensive talent builds to sell, not to rent, which is quite a different business.

The rule that is working out most satisfactorily to the investor, who knows only that he wants a building that will pay good interest on his capital, is to choose his experts, and form them into a committee, over which he himself presides to see to it that the best executive mind directs the work, while the considerations of the other specialists are regarded in proportion to their importance from the owner's point of view; or, if the owner cannot attend to it, to leave it all either to the real estate man who is to manage the building as a business after it is constructed, or to an architect who has built buildings that pay. Corporations appoint a committee of their directors, to which are added, one by one as they are chosen, the architect, the builder, and the manager. Individuals go first to the man they happen to know personally—architect, builder, or real estate man—and whichever is the first on the field is apt to keep the ascendancy to the end. This accidental procedure is operating so steadily to the advantage of the real estate man that he is coming to be the chief of builders.

He is the first and the last adviser of the investors; they go to him to buy the ground, or, if they have it, to discuss what to do with it to make it pay, and they consult with him, when the building is ready, about leases, tenants, rent-collecting, and the details of management. Indeed, it is he who often suggests the whole enterprise. Knowing the value, the probable income, and the capacity for paying improvements of property, he goes to the owners with propositions to tear down and rebuild, and if unsuccessful in this attempt to drum up trade, he seeks for the property a purchaser who will listen. But whether he originates the idea or not, he handles the problem first, and he can come pretty near telling what the solution will be.

The general question is: how to make fair interest out of a safe investment in an office building? So thoroughly has this problem been worked out that the expert real estate man can state with reasonable certainty the following known quantities: the rent per annum per square foot, the cost of the building per cubic foot, the value of the ground per square foot, and the cost of maintenance per square foot. The figures vary, of course, according to the city, the neighborhood, the exact location, and the markets for materials, rents, etc. In New York last spring the figures for the Wall Street neighborhood were $3.50 a square foot for rentable space, which should be about 66 to 70 per cent, of the whole floor room, and 40 cents a cubic foot for building. There were few sales of lots, and the prices paid were very high. One was next to the highest ever known, $228.57 a square foot. But the cost of the ground and the location are variables that are subjects of discussion in the light of the determinants, and the expert has to adjust the venture on them as a basis before the business begins.

He may know, for instance, that while one piece of property under consideration is costly, it is better for the whole scheme, either because there is a demand near it for office space, or because that particular neighborhood is not likely to be overbuilt. If a cheaper lot is thought of, he has to advise whether the class of tenants who will occupy it is good; whether a better class of tenants can be drawn so far (it may be only a hundred yards) from the places where they are now; whether the growth of the kind of business they think to build for is in their direction. In short, knowledge and foresight and judgment have to be exercised in settling these preliminaries, which differ in each case from every other the real estate expert has ever had, and he knows that the success of the enterprise depends upon his first decision, the location of his building.

When that is determined, he has one absolute figure for his exact estimates, and he goes over his variables again, square foot and cubic foot, with fresh interest. The shape of the lots may cut off or add to his guess as to the amount of rentable space, which depends on height and air and the class of his probable tenants. If his client has taken a corner, he has increased the first item, the cost of the ground, which is the greatest, but he has gained in spacing and attractiveness. On the other hand, again, he has made it necessary to count on a greater charge per cubic foot for construction, since two fronts demand more for decoration and finish. These readjustments were all considered, however, before the price was paid, and the next question is taken up, also not altogether fresh.

The location decided in a general way what the character of the building must be, but before any plans are ordered that matter has to be considered in detail. The architect needs to know whether there is to be a big bank or a number of small businesses on the ground floor, and whether above there are to be many offices to the story or spacious lofts for storage and factories. The real estate agent, or, if he has been chosen, the owner's own renting agent, sounds for tenants, sometimes getting his principal tenants engaged, always finding out whether he is to have lawyers or merchants. Corporations and large businesses have these first questions off their hands, since they are to be their own principal tenants, but even they have to have an expert pronounce after inquiry upon the possibilities of their building for other uses.

If the architect has not been called in before this point is reached, he is now, for without him no further progress can be made. He may have been consulted first, but his work would not have begun any sooner; he would have engaged some real estate man to do all this preliminary study of the business anyway. When it is done, the architect goes over the financial estimates, taking the dimensions and form of the lot, looking up on his map the character of the subsoil to obtain an idea of the sort of foundation he has to build on, and making observations of the surrounding buildings. He draws roughly the plan of the new building to see what rentable space he can count on for each floor, and then he and the real estate expert compare notes and reckon out the height of the structure.

Assuming a certain number of stories, they multiply the rentable space on the ground plan by it, and that result by the market rate per square foot of rents in the neighborhood. From this they subtract the cost of maintenance, getting the income, which they compare with the interest at the desired rate on the cost of the ground and the estimated cost of the building. If the two figures do not balance in the investor's favor, a story or two is added. Increasing the height, however, may complicate the problem by the considerations of good service and foundation costs. Up to a certain height four elevators may be sufficient, but the car space has to bear a definite ratio to the rentable area, and one added story may just pass the limit of capacity of the assumed number of cars, so that more have to be allowed for. This means more room for shafts and a corresponding loss of rentable space. Again, a building of from eight to twelve stories will stand safely on a shallow, inexpensive foundation, while fourteen stories would have to be settled on the bedrock, seventy-two feet down at Broadway and Pine Street, New York, or have an elaborate and costly bed made for it, as in Chicago. Thus the rising calculations reach a point where the owner must change his scheme radically. Unless he is willing to venture a much greater amount of capital for a very high building, he has either to relinquish a little income or cut something, the quality of the material or the elaboration of finish; and if he chooses to reach high for the coveted income, he increases the risk of having vacant rooms, since he may exceed the space needs of the neighborhood. For a structure that is built in twelve months, the consideration of these preliminary matters often lasts two or three years..

When they are decided, the architect begins drawing his plans, and continues to draw them till the building is completed. There are some forty sets necessary for a high building. The details are innumerable, and each one has to be fully conceived in imagination before it can be executed in steel or stone. All the possible uses of the building have to be foreseen; every pound of dead and live weight has to be calculated and prepared for; each particular beam, girder, pillar, and arch must be located and marked with its dimensions, material, and the load and lateral pressure it has to bear; the paths of a network of pipes and wires have to be traced through all their ramifications. But even to sketch the architect's work would be a long story in itself. It will have to suffice to indicate some of the features of it that bear obviously on the success or failure of the building as a business enterprise.

There are buildings close together that seem to the layman to be equally attractive for their purposes, but one of them will be filled with tenants, while others will always have vacant rooms and many removal signs outside. In one case of two such contrasting buildings, everybody who knew anything about it—clients, manager, and disinterested architects—said the failure of the building was the fault of the man who drew the plans. One architect will distribute his rentable space in stores or offices nicely adapted to the business of the neighborhood, another will have them too large or too small; one will grasp too much rentable space, another will be extravagant with halls and lobbies. Errors can be made either way on almost any point, and not be the fault of a careless study. The conflict of requirements calls for sacrifices of one set of considerations for some other. The elevators, with their first floor vestibule, should not take up valuable front space that is light, but they should be conspicuously in sight the moment the entrance is passed. The corridors may be inside, away from the daylight, but to leave them dark or dim is fatal. So insistent are tenants of the best class on convenience and approachableness of their offices that they prefer to be in a "tower" building at any height than in a large building with intricate, half-lighted hallways, and this observation weighs in the balance for upward instead of surface expansion. The architect has to conjure up every conceivable need and whim of the tenant, and then, after providing for them, he has to arrange for changes after all. He plans large rooms, not too large, and small rooms, not too small; then specifies partitions that may be changed. He may have one front exposed to the light, or he may have two or three, but in any case, no matter what the depth of the lot, he is expected to have height and good ventilation for every room. When all else is done he may strive for beauty, or the owner's substitute.

Beauty absolute is believed by some critics to be incompatible with remunerative height. Most architects of enlightenment admit that the beautiful "skyscraper" has not yet been designed, but their striving for it proves that they do not despair, and an acknowledged achievement would pay, for advertisement is the mercantile equivalent of applause. Conspicuousness helps rent a building. Men like to be in one so well known that the name of it is address enough without the street number, which is easily forgotten; and a corporation that erects a home for itself striking enough to be talked about, and pictured throughout the country, finds by actual experience that the investment, though a failure as a renting enterprise, pays astonishingly. Hideousness, if recognized as such generally, is harmful, for the notoriety frightens off the best class of tenants, leaving the building to those who do not know or care and do not pay regularly and well.

The fundamental aesthetic problem talked of in the great architects' offices is to design the exterior to express in some way the character of the construction. To have a light, airy, all-supporting steel cage veneered with a stone that suggests enormous weight and massive walls, is an ugly lie. The conventional notions of the owner may be an explanation of the architect's appointment of such monstrous atlantes as those on page 46 that are pretending to carry a thirty-story building. But the economy of simplicity would excuse saving this expense, and clear the facades for the study of the real question, which the serious architect is trying to answer, to wit: how to make his building look as high as it is, and light and graceful besides. The necessity of a fireproof wrapping for the metal frame is one obstacle; the other is the centuries-old preconception of beauty of proportion. Business interest makes for the destruction of the latter; the former is falling before tireless ingenuity.

While the architect is wrestling with light and space, the contractor begins his race against time. He joins the building committee, and either undertakes for a fee the execution of the plans or offers to do it for a lump sum, taking all risks and making such profits as he can. If he is to finance the construction, he competes for the contract by bidding on the architect's specifications, which are a big book of particulars, prescribing the materials to be used, the amount and quality, the date of completion, and a clause exempting the owner from responsibility for damages by accidents to life or property and the builder from the loss of time in strikes. On some of the specifications the builder estimates for himself, taking the masonry if he is a mason-builder, the woodwork if he is a carpentry-builder, but most of them he has to sublet to specialists: the manufacturer of steel, the plumber, the tile-maker, and the roofer. When all the estimates are in, the builder adds to the sum his profits, and submits the total with a stipulation for periodical payments, one when so many beams are set, another when the iron work is in, another when so many floors are down, and so on to the end, when the balance, including fifteen per cent, withheld from each part payment, is paid. Thus the builder, who is rarely a capitalist, is enabled to arrange for the payment of his labor and the contractors under him. Sometimes a contract on a set of specifications is sublet several times; the hardware contractor, for example, giving out the locks and door-springs to patentees. But the owner knows only the builder, who conducts the whole and has all the responsibility.

    If the builder is engaged for a fee, the architect, or, now and then, the owner, lets the contracts and manages the finances of the operation. The builder furnishes his trained office force, his staff of experts, his plant, and his own executive ability, and distributes the payments of labor and contractors on the order of the financing agent. His duties are the same; he is the captain of industry. He orders the movements of thousands of men and thousands of tons of material, according to a plan of campaign that he lays out carefully in advance. With a small space of ground to work on, and a limited time, he has to foresee precisely when each beam and each man shall come and go. The sixth-story piers must be delivered when those of the fifth are in place, and they must not be a day late, for the girders of the seventh come then, and there is no room to store anything, since the masons are there at work on the lower walls, and the ground is occupied by their materials. Each squad of workmen follows another, and if one is late, all that come after are delayed, and the completion of the building is not on time.

That means a loss to the owner, and disarranges the whole scheme, for, from the time the old building is torn down to the day the new one is opened, a large amount of capital is earning nothing. The period of construction when no interest is coming in is reckoned in the cost of the building, and, counting on its coming to an end at a certain date, the rooms are rented from that time long ahead. Even the tenants are inconvenienced and may be lost by any failure of the builder's plans.

To hurry at first is the rule now. The builder has to know how long it takes to manufacture the materials, and he gets out the orders for the difficult work first, and all as soon as possible. With the acceptance of each contract there is a clause binding the contractor to deliver at the date fixed by the builder, no sooner and no later; but the builder informs himself from time to time whether the promise is to be kept, whether the cornice-maker, for instance, who is to be ready a month hence, has begun the work that will take a month to do. That is to say, the builder watches the progress of his building, not at the scene of construction alone, but in the shops and factories also. While the borings are making for the foundation he sends one of his staff up to the quarry to see if the stone is being taken out of the ground, and to report whether the vein is of the quality that was shown when the surface inspection was made. A year is the time allowed to erect the highest buildings, and the foundation and labor difficulties

The Modern Business Building   23

are the only elements of doubt provided for in the contract. Dividing the year into twelve periods, the builder reduces it to days, and appoints a clerk of the work and a timekeeper to enforce the schedule. Each load of cement, iron, piping, or brick is examined as it arrives, and if it is "up to specifications" is receipted for and turned over to the workmen who put it in place. As the construction proceeds, reports are made to the masterbuilder, who sometimes has photographs taken to save himself a personal inspection. If the masons are lagging, the mason contractor is called upon to put more men on his job, and some other contractor, the tile man perhaps, is asked to begin a day or two earlier to make up the loss.

The architect also keeps tally on the work, for the builder's reports of progress have to be countersigned by the designer before any payments are sanctioned by the owner. These architect's certificates play another part in the financial scheme if the owner is building on credit. In that case he has negotiated for a loan which, when the building is done, becomes a mortgage on the whole property, but interest is saved to the borrower by receiving the money only as it is needed to pay the contractor's bills, in parts timed according to the advancement of the work. The whole loan may be of an amount for which the ground would not be a sufficient security, so, as the improvements increase the value of it, the lender, assured by the certificates of builder and architect, advances the sums that carry on the scheme till, at the end, there is a general settlement by which the owner gets his building, the capitalist the mortgage, if there is one, the architect and the builder their fees or profits, and the manufacturers and labor the capital invested.

But that does not end the business. The completion of the building is the materialization of the architect's plans, but those of the financier culminate in the management, which begins now to realize the expectations of the enterprise as a whole. In the days of the old buildings, this was easy. An agent sat with his feet up on a desk, scrutinizing loftily or lazily the applicants who approached him, credentials in hand, with a request for a place on the waiting list for the offices that might fall vacant from time to time. He accepted those who seemed to his fancy to be up to the mark, rejecting the others in the line with slight courtesy. He rarely went to the building. A tyrant ruled there, some pensioner of the owner, whom all the tenants addressed respectfully as "Mr. Janitor." Sometimes he was a good-natured ignoramus who became a "character;" oftener he was a peevish, useless hanger-on, whose sole purpose was to grind as much as he could out of his natural prey, the creatures given him with the building by his patron, the owner. All the tenant's lease included was the office, the daylight the carpenter failed to exclude, the right to pass up and down the stairs and halls, and, in the finer offices, a gas-jet or two and a fireplace. There was water on the lower floors. Fuel the janitor provided, for an extra fee and a share. Gas or lamp light the tenant arranged for himself. The cleaning was done by some woman hired through the janitor.

Competition and the high buildings changed all that. It is the tenant's turn now to scrutinize and reject the offers of the line of agents, who have taken down their feet to run about, "hustling" to fill their gaping space. The janitor was hard to subjugate, but he is passing away. The cross old autocrats had to be discharged; the young men who harbored the traditions of their office had their salaries cut in half, and, if that did not reduce their insolence, were put in livery and called head-porters. The owner had set a new example, and he had to choose between the janitor and the spoiled tenant.

Now the lawyer or business man who has been induced to come into a modem skyscraper has the cab-door opened by a uniformed giant, who escorts him (under an umbrella, if it is raining) across a clean sidewalk to the revolving storm-door. Inside the janitor's ghost salutes him, a detective sees that no thief slips in to pick his pocket, or peddler or beggar to annoy him, while the hall-man indicates the one of several elevators that is waiting to shoot him to his floor so swiftly that it can make no appreciable difference in time whether he is on the third or the twentieth story. But, lest a second may be missed, there is an express elevator that does not stop at any floor below the fifteenth. His room has been swept, dusted, and put in order by a staff of servants he never sees. He touches a button to fix the temperature of his room; another to turn on the electric light, if the day is dull or the hour is late, otherwise the daylight will stream in gloriously, for there are "no dark rooms." The dust of the street he may rinse from his hands with hot or cold water, and on his rack are fresh towels, which come he knows not whence. Telephone, messenger calls, and mail-chutes are conveniently near. In the latest of the new buildings there is an internal telephone system that connects through the first floor switch with any other room in the building or with the city service. They furnish also a bathroom on each floor, and a private bath if desired. One of the latest conveniences is a bicycle storage-room in the basement of a building not finished at this writing. Libraries for the use of tenants are not so new, but running ice water and bachelor apartments are.

This last feature makes it possible for a business man to live in a building day in and day out. The manager arranges to have a restaurant somewhere within his walls, on or near the roof, if possible, and some large buildings run their own kitchen, to be sure of first-class service. In the corridor are cigar, news, and boot-blacking stands. Elevators do not stop, as they used to, at six o'clock, but take turns running all night. For society, the tenant has the club, which is coming to be a feature of the high building. The bedroom was all that was lacking, when a New York business man recently called the attention of a manager to the omission, and suggested one for himself. He thought of the fine view of cities and rivers and harbors from his office-window near the roof, imagined the cool, fresh air of that altitude, and recalled the hot and lonely summer months when his family was out of town, and he asked why he should go five miles to an abandoned home every night. The manager said he need not. A bedroom was drawn in the plans, and finding other tenants charmed by the idea of chambers, he adopted them as a novelty for his building. And to complete the scheme, he is talking of having a roof garden, with a variety stage, to while away the evenings of tenants and to catch the pleasure-seekers who now pass through the lower part of the city to go to the theatres uptown.

To make changes suggested by a tenant in this way it is necessary that the manager should have consulted with him before the building was completed, and should have power to carry out his ideas. In a properly conducted enterprise, the manager joins the council of builders before anything is done. He begins his work with the real estate man, sometimes in his stead, and is as busy as the builder throughout the period of construction; for the future of the building is in his charge, and he represents the tenants who are to use it. The time has passed when the capitalist can put so much money into brick and stone regardless of any fact except the insatiable demand for office room in crowded neighborhoods. All the fads and prejudices of a fastidious tenantry have to be anticipated now, and new luxuries may have to be suggested and provided to draw men from buildings equipped only with all the necessaries of business life. The manager, who has to rent the building, knows these things, and he is supreme from the start in all matters of internal arrangement. The only excuse for not heeding his directions is the plea that they are structurally or financially impossible. It is he who decides whether the first floor is to be planned for a bank or a number of stores, and divides the upper floors into small offices or large suites, according to his judgment or knowledge of the needs of the neighborhood.

Usually it is knowledge. The manager keeps himself posted on the movements of business firms, getting in the form of gossip the names of those who are dissatisfied with their quarters, and of owners of old buildings who are preparing to tear down and rebuild, thus threatening the tenure of their tenants. To these people the manager of a proposed new building goes with his offer to let them space with the privilege of subdividing it to suit their requirements. Getting them pledged, he hastens to others, and though he may not secure many tenants so soon, he learns exactly what is wanted on the spot where his building is to be. There may be conflicting demands; he may be on the boundary between importers who require lofts or storerooms, and lawyers who wish offices, and it is often a difficult and delicate task to arrange with the architect for a compromise plan that will satisfy both clients. But the man for such a place has to be able to solve many nice problems, as many as any of the other experts engaged in building operations.

When the manager has determined the character of the building, the contracts are drawn, and the date of completion is set. That limits and drives him just as it does the builder and the contractors, for when the building is delivered he is expected to have ready the occupants, who are counted on to make the capital invested begin again to pay interest, and any failure on his part disturbs the calculations of the financier in the same way that the builder's delay does. And there is another factor that whips on the manager. In every city there are what are called "moving days," when old leases expire and new ones begin. May 1st, for example, is the date when "downtown" New York makes its general shift. Above Chambers Street, and as far north as Fourteenth, the change is made on February 1st, chosen, doubtless, because the old stock of merchandise is low at that time, and the new goods are not yet in. The residence districts of the city move on October 1st, which is about the time when the people who have been out of town for the summer are returning. Why the extreme southern end of Manhattan Island picked out May 1st, no one has been able to explain, but settled it is unalterably, and the new buildings erected there are hurried through so as to be ready for occupancy by that day; and the manager who rushes around seeking tenants knows that he will have in his building all the first year only as many as he has secured on Mayday. He may add a few firms who happen to open business in the interval, and chance may throw in his way two or three tenants who are so dissatisfied with some other building that they move out at a sacrifice of rent paid; but, as a rule, the space vacant on the moving day remains a losing investment for a year.

    Hence, besides the advantage of offering the tenant a voice in the planning of his space, the manager is urged to commence early the canvass for occupants by the time limitation and the serious consequences of exceeding it. While the architect is drawing the projected floor plans, the manager takes them, and makes up his schedule of rents. He has already told the committee what he can get for the space per square foot, and the financier has calculated on that figure for a certain income, which has now to be arranged for in detail. It has to be divided among the floors, and then among the rooms. If he has set $3.50 a square foot as the average, the manager now starts with, say, $8 as the rate on the ground floor, $5 on the second, and $2.50 on the others up to the top stories, where he can charge $3 or $3.50. Then, as he puts in the partitions asked for by his first clients, he raises or lowers the rates for the other rooms according to minute considerations of light, convenience, and conspicuousness, taking care, however, to make the sum of his various prices produce the total expected of that floor, and yet have each charge fall within the general market rates.

When this is done he prepares his prospectus, a handsomely printed paper book with diagrams of each floor, a description of the building, with the names of the specialists engaged on it—the architect, the builder, the elevator maker, the electrician, the plumber, the mason, the carpentry-men. There are pictures of the front and sides of the proposed building, of the main hall and the machinery room, views from the windows, sketches of the interior decoration, and little essays on the novelties and special features. The pamphlet is sent out to possible tenants and to the newspapers for "written notices" which are free advertisements, but the most effective use of it is in the hands of the staff of renting agents.

Personal solicitation of the cleverest and most alluring kind is necessary to fill in a year one of these great buildings that will house from one to four thousand people. There are ten or twelve other buildings to be ready, and for them also an active canvass is being made. The competition is almost desperate in some cities where there has been overbuilding in hard times. In New York the stress is such that it is said the only sure source of tenants is in the continuance of the process, as the tearing down of more old buildings for the next year's crop of new buildings supplies the tenants for this May's openings.

Despite the scramble, however, the best manager is the one who knows when to reject an application and stand a loss in vacant space; for a building, like a neighborhood, has character, and if it is a new structure he has to create that essential to permanent success. The reputation of the building affects the trade, custom, and clientele of its inhabitants, injuring those who are above it, and injured in turn by those who are below it. Anyone can call to mind well-known buildings that would be creditable as business addresses; they might help to sell a bill of goods. And there are others, equally familiar, that would cause a doubt as to a man's credit, unless his "line" were as low as the reputation of his building. The experienced manager is well aware of this, and, eager as he is for tenants, hard as he labors and plots for good men to come into his space, he resists the temptation to take everybody who applies.

The method some managers follow to give their place a fine start toward respectability is to get an old firm of national renown to head their rent roll. There are many such that have stuck to the ramshackle, antiquated building where they began their careers fifty years ago. Again and again they have been urged to move into the pretentious new buildings. The darkness of their rooms, the inconvenience of the arrangements, bad plumbing, bad air, slow elevator service, all these and other disagreeable conditions of their environment have been pointed out by the eloquent man with the beautiful little pamphlet; in vain. The old firm has always been there; their clients know the familiar place; they are making a couple of hundred thousand dollars a year as it is; their books and papers could not be moved. It is hard to persuade the head of the profession to the top of the town. But one by one they are pulled up, almost by the roots. Perhaps the most obdurate member of the firm dies or his energetic son joins the office. The sharp-witted manager, who knows everything that touches his business, hears of the change, and he reopens his case for a last trial.

Sometimes the case is won by making sacrifices. In New York, a year ago, the manager of a new building, desperate for a brilliant opening, went to a grand old firm of lawyers, offered them his best floor, ripped out and rearranged to suit, at a lower rate than they paid in the old building, and undertook to move them free of charge in one day and night—furniture, papers, books, documents, pictures, all to be taken up as they were, and set down in relatively the same positions in the new quarters.

This was an extreme case, but it paid. The name of that firm was used as a charm to draw other firms of equal stability though of less fame, and many more that were seeking in obscurity a similar practice. And the manager foresees that when so immovable a firm is once established in his building it will take root for another half century, while the branches it shoots forth, younger men reared in the office, will seek growing space near the old trunk. The character of his building is assured.

An example on the other side, of a building that made a bad beginning, was furnished by an expert manager who tried to reclaim it. At the time of its completion it was the tallest structure in New York. The man who erected it was a man of low tastes, but of great ability as a sensational business manager. His creation was like him, and it soon expressed his character as well as his mind. He let the first comers settle about him, and did not see he had made a mistake till he discovered that his low class of tenants were not good pay. Then, after himself trying to mend the case, he asked the trained specialist to see what he could do. It was a novel experiment at that time, and the manager entered upon it with energy and ideas. He turned out the worst tenants, and induced respectable people to take their places at very low rents. That was as far as he got. He says with a laugh that he might have succeeded if his exemplary tenants had stayed, but they could not stand it; they told him they would not have minded for themselves two or three months of being crowded and jostled about in the elevators by their neighbors—the trouble was that their clients did not like to see and smell the obnoxious clients of the neighbors, and, besides, thought it disreputable to be seen going into the building. The manager had to give up the task, convinced of the futility of reformation of buildings in general, and more impressed than ever with the necessity of starting aright.

As the opening day approaches, the manager has to organize his system and staff for the conduct, the maintenance, and the cleaning of his building. Everything must be in perfect order on the first day when the tenants arrive, so the staff often enters the building while the last workmen are there, and follows them up with the cleaning, room by room. From twenty to a hundred men and women are employed, according to the size of the building and the manager's notion of economy, and since these people are to furnish the permanent service for possibly six thousand tenants, and their twenty thousand (in one building the estimate on an elevator count of one day was forty-five thousand) clients, each employee, from the machinist down to the scrubwoman, is chosen with the scrupulousness of a civil service examination. The "pull" that used to decide in this business, as it still does in politics, has been abolished by the competition for efficient service.

The methods of running the business of a modern high building are so various that it is impossible to determine either a typical case or the drift of practice under experience. Some owners have a superintendent of the building, an expert machinist and electrician, who attends to the maintenance and reports to the manager, whose functions are renting and financing. Other buildings are in the control of the manager, who lets out the cleaning and heavy repairing by contract, and has in his janitor and chief engineer executive heads of staffs for routine work. One corporation that has fourteen buildings distributed over the United States, Europe, Australia, and South America has in New York a financial manager for all, with local managers in each building to rent, supply, and keep them in good condition. The central office receives the rent and authorizes extraordinary expenditures, requires regular reports in detail of all changes and expenses, and supervises all the business of each building through a travelling inspector.

These are corporation methods. Individuals who own modern buildings usually abandon the management of them after they have tried it long enough to learn that it is a distinct business, requiring expert direction. They turn it over to some real estate firm that has a staff of men who do nothing else. There is the manager or superintendent of buildings, who is an able organizer of men and a keen executive. Under him is a corps of renting agents and collectors, bookkeepers who carry the general account of expenses for all the buildings and separate individual and proportionate accounts of each owner. Outside this office staff there are an inspector, who visits each building every day, and a machinist, an electrician, a carpenter, a plumber, and a painter, whose duty it is to direct repairs. Then, each building has its own janitor, with his squad of hall and elevator men, scrubwomen, sweepers, moppers, dusters, and outside window cleaners; and the engineer, with his assistants, electrician, and firemen. The janitor makes weekly reports in writing to the central office of repairs, of changes, complaints, and requests of tenants, while the engineer accounts for the coal and other supplies used by him in amounts and in the power expended in heat, light, and elevators.

The cost of maintenance for a year, including taxes, insurance, supplies, repairs, and service, is from two to three percent of the capital invested, and increases with the age of the building. One manager, who had eleven years' experience in a building about fifteen years old, said he spent an average of $5.50 a day to repair pipes and plumbing; $4 a day for bricking and tiling; he replaced 2,000 of his 11,000 lights a year; bought sixteen tons of coal a day. But the new methods of construction of everything that goes into the later buildings are expected, and indeed promise, to reduce these items to absurdities. The latter-day managers are setting the builders, contractors, and manufacturers who supply the plant fresh problems of economy by their close figuring on expenses. A boiler that needs more than so much per pound of power for repairs is not satisfactory. Masonry must wear only so much a cubic foot a year to be within the specifications. Lights and plumbing and wiring and tubing that have to be renewed at a cost of more than so many cents per thousand feet are charged up against the supplier of them; and the manager is equally exacting with himself. He doles out coal at so many tons the week per thousand cubic feet of rentable space, and hires scrubwomen on the basis of 32,000 square feet of floor a day for each mop.

Despite all his precise reckoning, however, and his reduction of the problem to an accuracy of calculation that is almost scientific, the inexorable laws of the market gradually cut down his income. The building earns less year by year. The manager's own requirements of economy and ingenuity of construction involve the solution of fresh problems, lowering the cost of building, which entails the increase of new and higher structures; and that carries with it higher values of the ground

The Modern Business Building   33

built on, and correspondingly lower rents. But it is capital that loses by the inevitable process, capital and labor. Competition and progress reduce the one to two or three percent a year, the other to $1.50 a day. But the same forces stir up brains and strengthen character; they develop a skyscraping builder, earning $50,000 a year, whose name is an advertisement for the buildings he puts up, out of a master mason who began life as a bricklayer. And the end is not yet; our cities, as their ragged skylines show, will be rebuilding for many years to come. The grind between capital and labor will go on, while the financier, the architect, the builder, the manager—the brains of business enterprise—will grow and profit mightily.

McClure's Magazine
September, 1897

Life in the Klondike Gold Fields

Personal Observations of the Founder of Dawson

JOE LADUE had run away from San Francisco to escape the people who wished to hear about the Klondike and his luck there; he had fallen in with a carload of Christian Endeavor tourists who were as eager as the Californians to know how gold was picked up; in Chicago he stepped off the train into a circle of questioners; hurrying on to his native Plattsburg in the Adirondacks, he met the same inquiries. Here, however, the curious were his friends; so he talked a day and a night more; then he drove out to the farmhouse that to him is home, and for a short time he felt safe. Saturday morning some of the neighbors came across the fields to see his nuggets and photographs, and to hear his good-luck story. Surely that was the end! Sunday morning he came downstairs in his slippers to have a day of rest. He had just finished breakfast and was standing idly in the farmyard with his friends of the house, when I came down upon him with my request for an account, the longest and most complete he had told yet.

"You must be tired telling about it all," I began.

He smiled faintly. "Yes, I am," he said.

He was the weariest-looking man I ever saw. I have known bankers and business men, editors and soldiers and literary men, who had the same look out of the eyes that this pioneer of the Northwest country has; they were men who had made money or a name, earned by hard labor that which others envied them. They were tired, too. Their true stories were "hard-luck" stories. The disappointments that ran before the final triumph limped in had spoiled the taste for it. None of them showed the truth so plainly as the founder of Dawson, the city of the Klondike. Joe Ladue is a sad-eyed man with a tale of years which no one thinks of, which no one wants to hear about. That is all his own. He is willing to begin where you wish him to, on the day when he "struck it rich." But when his friends and neighbors trooped in as I was leaving him that Sunday, he dropped the bagful of nuggets for them to pass around, finger, and stare at. He went off down to the barn and hid.

He is about forty-five years old. Twenty-five years ago he started away from the woods of Lake Champlain, going to Colorado, Wyoming, Dakota, chasing each rumor of gold, and working—for nothing. His old friend, Mr. Lobdell, "staked him" when he failed, and, at last, some fifteen years ago, he went into Alaska, trading with the Indians, prospecting, milling, building, moving on, working hard all the time. The gold was there. Everybody knew it was somewhere near, that they were walking over it, and some men were finding it. I was in Alaska myself in 1888, and I met miners who were bringing out gold year after year. But Joe Ladue had to stay there till he could dig it out, risking what others met—failure and death. Now he has the gold. What of it? Everybody wished to know how much he got.

"Enough," he told them, dryly. And he sighed as he saw the listeners' eyes sparkle with sordid imaginings. He seemed to covet, as they did the gold, their desire for it.

Why was he going back in the spring, then?

"I have to," he answered. "I've got so many interests to look after. There's the sawmill and the logging and Dawson and a couple of claims staked out that have to be worked. You've got to attend to things, you know." So it was not a mere matter of picking up a fortune and coming back to spend and enjoy it.

The whole interview was in the tone of this answer, simple, plain, colorless, almost lifeless. His description of an outfit, his guide to the route, a remark about the shooting of Miles Canon, the proper way to stake out and work a claim, his view of miners' meetings—all were given in even mood. Yet it was not indifference or bored patience. He was painstaking in his offerings of facts not asked for, which he thought should be included in an account of the Klondike. His interest was altogether in the men who might be going there, and what he put into the article was framed for actual use. The information which would help no one directly he gave because it was asked for, but briefly, and with a side glance at the trail of the gold-seekers.

Some of the crossings of our purposes were worthwhile. Once, for instance, when he was making his list of the equipment of a Yukon mine on the way in, I pointed out to him that he had forgotten his "gun," and I meant that he had omitted to mention the revolver which plays such a conspicuous part in the life of most mining camps.

"You don't need a gun," he answered. "There's no game to speak of."

"But you surely take a revolver."

"No use; it only adds weight to the pack."

"What do you have, then — knives ?"

"Yes, you must have knives and forks and spoons, of course."

When I made my meaning clear, Mr. Ladue gave an interesting glimpse of the order maintained by the miners of the Yukon in their lawless communities, but he was unable to explain it. Most of the men were good fellows, he said. Were there no thieves? Not one. No cutthroats? None. Gamblers?

"Plenty. Everybody gambles, especially in the long winter nights."

"Don't they cheat?"

"No."

"Why not?"

"The saloon-keepers won't have it."

"How can they prevent it? Are there no professional gamblers in the camps?"

"Yes, but they put up a straight game. And there are men, too, who have been pretty bad before; I have heard that some of them were ex-convicts and fellows who had run away to escape prison and hanging. But none of them try anything on in there."

"But why don't they?"

"I don't know; but they don't."

"What are they afraid of? Has any one ever been punished?"

"Not that I remember."

"Well, why don't thieves steal on the Klondike?"

"I guess it's because they dasent."

Though quietly spoken, this vague answer came with an expression of face — just a quick flash of light and a slight shifting of the body, which suggested the complete explanation. And there was a hint, too, of the man who was resting under the calm surface I was prospecting; so I kept digging.

The first sentence of Mr. Ladue's story, as he gave it, was a warning to the men who were rushing into the Northwest. He foresaw starvation ahead not only for them, but for those who were already on the ground. Some would have provided themselves with a supply of food sufficient to last them, but others would not. All would suffer in consequence.

"Not the men who have taken enough," I protested.

"Yes, they all will. Won't the food have to be divided up even all around?"

This is Joe Ladue.

LADUE'S STORY

"I am willing to tell all I can think of about the Klondike and the great Northwest country so long as it is understood that I am not advising anybody to go there. That I will not do. It goes pretty hard with some of the men who go in. Lots of them never come out, and not half of those who do make a stake. The country is rich, richer than anyone has ever said, and the finds you have heard about are only the beginnings, just the surface pickings, for the country has not been prospected except in spots. But there are a great many hardships to go through, and to succeed, a man has to have most of the virtues that are needed in other places not so far away and some others besides. This winter I expect to hear that there is starvation on the Klondike on account of the numbers that have rushed in without sufficient supplies, for I know that the stores there have not enough to go around, while the men who laid in provisions have only enough for themselves. They will divide up, as they always do, but that will simply spread the trouble and make things worse. Next spring, from the fifteenth of March on, is the time to go.

"What you call the Klondike we speak of as the Throndike. I don't know exactly why. The Klondike Creek, which names the district where the richest streaks have been struck, was the Throchec to the Indians, which means salmon, not reindeer, as I have read since I came out in the spring. There is sense in that name, because the stream, which is about the size of the Saranac River up here in the Adirondacks, is chock-full of salmon, and you never see a reindeer there, not even a moose. In fact, game is very scarce on the Klondike, as it is all along the Yukon.

"No guns or pistols or anything of that kind are needed. Here is what ought to be put in an outfit: A camp-stove, frying-pan, kettle, coffee-pot, knives and forks and spoons, and a drill or canvas tent; an ax, a hatchet, a whipsaw, a handsaw, a two-inch auger, a pick and shovel, and ten pounds of nails. For wear, heavy woolen clothes are best — not furs — and the stoutest overshoes you can get, with arctic socks. Then, there is a "sleigh," as we call it, really a sled, six or eight feet long and sixteen inches in the run. It is safest to buy this in Juneau, for those you pick up in other places won't track. I don't take a canoe unless I am late going in, but they make the lightest and strongest in Victoria, at about 160 to 200 pounds weight. The simplest thing to go down the river on is a raft, but to make that or a boat, you need, besides the nails and tools I named, two pounds of oakum and five pounds of pitch. A year's supply of grub, which can be bought as cheaply in Juneau as anywhere, I think, is: 10 sacks of flour, 150 pounds of sugar, 100 pounds of bacon, thirty pounds of coffee; ten pounds of tea, 100 pounds of beans, fifty pounds of oatmeal, 100 pounds of mixed fruits, twenty-five pounds of salt, about ten dollars' worth of spices and knickknacks, and some quinine to break up colds. The total cost of this outfit is about $200, but no man should start with less than $500, and twice that is ten times as good.

"The easiest way to get there is by boat, which will take you around by St. Michael's at the mouth of the Yukon, and transferring you there to the side-wheeler, carry you seventeen hundred miles up the river to Dawson. But that isn't independent.

"If a man wants to go in with his own provisions, free

of connections with the transportation companies, which will sell but will not let anybody take along his own supplies, then the Chilkoot Pass route is the best. And that isn't so bad. You start from Juneau and go by steamer to Chilkat, then to Dyea, eight miles, where you hire Indians to help you to the summit of this pass. From Dyea you walk ten miles through snow to Sheep Camp, which is the last timber. From there it is a climb of six miles to the summit, 4,100 feet high, and very often you or the Indians have to make two or three trips up and down to bring up the outfit. Leaving the Indians there, you go down, coasting part way, fourteen miles to Lake Linderman. That is five miles long, with a bad piece of rapids at the lower end. But if it is early in the season, you sled it on the lake and take the mile of rapids in a portage to Lake Bennett, which is a twenty-eight-mile tramp. It is four miles' walk to Caribou Crossing, then a short ride or tramp to Takoon Lake, where, if the ice is breaking, you can go by boat or raft, or if it is still hard, you must sled it twenty-one miles, to the Tagish River and Lake, four miles long. Take the left bank of the river again, and you walk four miles to Marsh Lake, where you may have to build a raft or boat to cover its twenty-four miles of length. If not, then you must at the bottom, for there begins the Lynx River, which is usually the head of navigation, for unless the season is very late or the start very early, the rest of the way is almost all by water.

"Thirty miles down the Lynx River you come suddenly upon Miles Caflon, which is considered the worst place on the trip. I don't think it is dangerous, but no man ought to shoot the rapids there without taking a look at them from the shore. The miners have put up a sign on a rock to the left just before you get to it, so you have warning and can go ashore walk along the edge on the ice. It is sixty feet wide and seven-eighths of a mile long, and the water humps up in the middle, it goes so fast. But very few have been caught there, though they were killed, of course. Below the canyon there are three miles of bad river to White Horse Rapids, which are rocky and swift, with falls, but taking chances is unnecessary, and I consider it pretty good dropping. After the rapids it is thirty miles down to Lake Labarge, the last of the lakes, which is thirty-one miles to row, sail, or tramp, according to the condition of the water. From there a short portage brings you to the head of the Lewis River, really the Yukon, though we do not call it that till, after drifting, poling, or rowing two hundred miles, the Pelly River flows in and makes one big, wide stream. I must warn men who are going in to watch out for Five Fingers Rapids, about 141 miles down the Lewis, where they must take the right-hand channel. That practically ends the journey, for, though it is 180 miles from the junction of the Pelly and Lewis, it is simply a matter of drifting. And I want to say for the hardness of this whole trip, that I have brought horses in that way, using a raft. And it is curious to see how soon they learn to stand still while you are going, and to walk on and off the raft mornings and evenings at camping-places.

"When I left Dawson in the spring there were some two thousand white men, forty families, and two hundred Indians in the Klondike district, most of them living in cabins or tents on claims. The town, which I named after the man who fixed the boundary between American and Canadian possessions, is new, having only a few houses in it, and is chiefly a source of supplies and a place of meeting. The Alaska Commercial Company has the store there, and the Canadian government has a reservation with a squad of sixty mounted police and a civil officer or two. The site is on the east bank of the Yukon and on the north bank of the Klondike River, which comes into the Yukon at that point. The boundary line is seventy miles southwest.

"The gold has been found in the small creeks that flow into the Klondike. First comes Bonanza Creek, a mile and a half back of Dawson. It is thirty miles long and very rich, but its tributaries are still better. Ten miles up it the Eldorado, for example, is the most productive stream that has been turned up; it is only six miles long, and is all staked out in claims, but $250 has been taken out in a pan there, and I estimate that the yield will be $20,000,000, Seven miles above Bonanza the Klondike receives the waters of Bear Creek, which is also good, but its six miles of length is claimed by this time. Hunker Creek is fifteen miles up the Klondike, and up that is a little stream, about the size of a brook, which is called Gold Bottom. All these streams flow from the south, and they come from hills that must have lots of gold in them, for other creeks that run out of them into Indian River show yellow, too. Indian River is about thirty miles south or up the Yukon from Dawson. Stewart River and Sixty Mile Creek with their tributaries, all south, and Forty Mile Creek with its branches, off to the northwest — all have gold, and though they have been prospected some, they have not been claimed like the Klondike. Claims have to be staked out, of course, according to the Canadian laws, which I think are clear and fair. The only fault I find with them is that they recognize no agreements that are not in writing, and they do not give a man who "stakes" a prospector any share in a claim. But I suppose these difficulties can be got around all right by being more careful about having things in writing hereafter.

"Another point that is hard to get over is that you have to swear that no man before you took gold off that claim, which you can't do, not knowing whether there was anybody ahead of you or not. The rest of the requirements are sensible. All you have to do is to find gold, to which you must swear, then you mark off about five hundred feet along the bed of the creek where no one has laid a claim, and stick up four stakes with your name on them, one at each corner of your land. Across the ends you blaze the trees. This done, you go to the register of claims, pay fifteen dollars, and, after a while, the surveyor will come along and make it exact. Claims run about ten to the mile, and are limited practically only by the width of the ground between the two "benches," or sides of the hills, that close in the stream. The middle line of a series of claims follows the "pay streak," which is usually the old bed of the creek, and it runs across the present course of the water several times, sometimes, in a short distance.

WORKING A CLAIM

"Working a claim can go on at all seasons of the year, and part of the process is best in winter, but prospecting is good only in summer, when the water is flowing and the ground loose. That is another reason why it is useless for new hands to go in now. They cannot do anything except work for others till spring. Then they can prospect with water flowing and the ground soft. If they strike it they can stake out their claim, clear a patch of trees, underbrush, and stones, and work the surface tilt winter sets in. We quit the "pan" or "hand" method then. The "rocker" is almost never used except in "sniping," which is a light surface search on unclaimed land or on a claim that is not being worked for enough to pay expenses or to raise a "grub-stake." As soon as the water freezes so that it won't flow in on a man, we begin to dig to the bedrock, sometimes forty feet down. The ground is frozen, too, in winter, of course, but by "burning" it, as we say, we can soften it enough to let pick and shovel in. All the dirt is piled on one side, and when spring opens again, releasing the water, we put up our sluices and wash it all summer or till we have enough. There has not been any quartz mining yet on the Yukon, but back of the placers, in the hills which have not been prospected, the original ledges must be holding good things for the capitalist.

LOCAL GOVERNMENT ON THE KLONDIKE

"Life on the Klondike is pretty quiet. Most of the men there are hard workers; but the climate, with the long winter nights, forces us to be idle a great deal, and miners are miners, of course. And there is very little government. The point is, however, that such government as there is, is good. I like the Canadian officers, the Canadian laws, and the Canucks themselves. The police are strict and efficient. The captain was a fine man, but he had more than he could do this last season, when the rush for the Klondike came. That began in August a year ago, and as the rumor spread up and down the Yukon, the towns and mining camps were deserted by everybody who could get away. Men left the women to come on after them, and hurried off to the Klondike to lay out claims. Circle City was cleaned out. There wasn't room enough on the steamer to take all who wanted to get away to the new diggings, and many a good-paying claim was abandoned for the still better ones on the creeks that make the Klondike. The captain of the police had only a few men without horses to detail around over the claims, and, besides his regular duties, he had to act as register of claims and settle disputes that were brought to him. And there were a good many of these. The need of civil officers is very great, especially of a surveyor.

"The miners on the Yukon are shrewd, experienced men, and sometimes they are tricky. I do not like the kind of government they set up for themselves, except in the very first stages. It is all by miners' meetings. They begin by being fair, but after a while cliques are formed, which run things to suit the men who are in them, or, which is just as bad, they turn the sessions into fun. Nobody can get justice from a miners' meeting when women are on one side.

"When Bonanza Creek was opened up some of the claims got mixed up in the rush, and the measurements were all wrong. Notices were posted on the store doors and on the houses, calling a miners' meeting to settle the boundaries of claims. As was usual in such meetings, a committee was selected to mark off the claims all the way up the creek with a fifty-foot rope. Somehow a rope only forty feet long sneaked in, and that made all the claims short. The space that was left over was grabbed by the fellows who were in the game.

"Sometimes in winter, when there is plenty of time, a dispute that is left to the miners' meeting grows into a regular trial with lawyers (there are several among the miners) engaged for a fee, a committee in place of the judge, and a regular jury. Witnesses are examined, the lawyers make speeches, and the trial lasts till nobody who listens to it all knows what to think. I never liked it. The best way, according to my experience, for two men who can't agree to have a settlement is to choose their own committee, each side picking a representative and both selecting a third. Then the committee is fair, and generally the decision is satisfactory.

"Most of the time when the men cannot work is spent in gambling. The saloons are kept up in style, with mirrors, decorations, and fine, polished, hardwood bars. No cheating is allowed, and none is tried. The saloon-keepers won't have it in their places. Nobody goes armed, for it is no use. Some of the men are the kind that would take naturally to shooting, but they don't try it on the Yukon. The only case that I know of was when James Cronister shot Washburn, and that didn't amount to anything, because Washburn was a bad man. There was a jury trial, but the verdict was that Cronister was justified.

"The only society or organization for any purpose besides business in there is the Yukon Pioneers. I don't belong to that, so I don't know much about it. It is something like the California Pioneers of '49. They have a gold badge in the shape of a triangle with Y. P. on it and the date '89. To be a member you must have come into the country before 1889. But the time limit used to be earlier, and it may be later now, for they have shoved it on up several times since I have noticed. The society does some good. When a man gets sick and caves in it raises money to send him out. Now and then it gives a ball, and there are plans on foot to have more pleasure of that sort next winter and after that. But we need a hotel or some other big building before much of that can be done.

"In fact, we need a great many things besides gold. We have no coin. Gold dust and nuggets pass current by weight at about fifteen dollars and fifty cents to the ounce. It is pretty rough reckoning, as, for instance, when a man brings in a nugget mixed with quartz. Then we take it altogether, gravel and gold, for pure gold, and make it up on the goods. Carpenters, blacksmiths—all the trades—are wanted, and men who can work at them can make much more than the average miner. They can't make what a lucky miner can, but if they are enterprising they can make a good stake. Wages are fifteen dollars a day, and a man who works for himself can earn much more than that. I have gone into the logging business with a mill in Dawson. The spruce trees are thirty inches through and, after rafting them down from Ogilvie and Forth Mile, you get $130 a thousand foot for them sawed into boards. Then there is butchering for the man who will drive sheep over in the summer. It has been done, and is to be done again. But it is useless for me to go on telling all the occupations that would pay high profits. The future of the Northwest country is not so long as that of a country that can look forward to other industries than mining and the business that depends on mining, but it is longer than the lifetime of any of us. The surface has been pricked in a few places, but I do not know that the best has been found, and I am quite sure no one has any idea of the tremendous extent of the placer diggings, to say nothing of the quartz that is sure to follow. Then, all the other metals, silver and copper and iron, have been turned up, while coal is plentiful. I believe thoroughly in the country. All I have doubt about is the character of some of the men who are rushing in to get rich by just picking up the gold."

Scribner's Magazine
October, 1897

The Conduct of Great Businesses

The Business of a Newspaper

THE executive heads of some two-score of the great newspapers in America, "talking shop" on a railway train last spring, spoke of their properties as factories, and when the editorial department was mentioned discussed "their traffic in news," and likened the management of it to that of a department store. White paper was the raw material which was bought in bulk by the ton to be sold at a profit retail, and the price and quality of the several brands was the favorite topic of conversation. The machinery by which it was prepared for the market was interesting; circulation and advertising were fascinating subjects, too delicate and dangerous, however, for easy chat. Public questions were not once raised, and editorial policies might never have existed. These men were the publishers and business managers and proprietors of newspapers, not editors and writers, but they "ran" their papers; they represented "the press." Journalism today is a business. To write of it as such is to write of it as it is.

This may seem to the " constant reader" a rather brutal conception of the fourth estate, but it is the inside view, and Mr. Leigh, who has taken it for his illustrations, partly accounts for, if he does not wholly justify, it. His pictures of the press, composing, and stereotyping rooms, with their immense, complicated, delicate machinery, look like glimpses of a factory plant. The paper on which the news is printed is the heaviest single item of expense; the manager of a New York newspaper who used 337,558 miles of it last year said his bill was $617,000. The mechanical apparatus and processes have been as potent a factor in the growth of the newspaper as the enterprise of men or the price of white paper. And in the editorial rooms the comparison with the department store is borne out in principle and method. The managing editor aims to supply all the wants of all sorts of people, and the variety of interests handled there is divided into departments, each with a subeditor: the foreign news, with a cable editor; the national and state news with a telegraph editor; the local news, with a city editor; and so on through the dramatic, the financial, the society, the exchange, the art, the literary, the sporting departments, with their expert managers and corps of assistants.

The man who paid the paper bill of $617,000 expended altogether that year more than two millions of dollars. He has a morning and an evening paper, and he employs 1,300 men and women every day in the year, besides twice that number who serve him at occasional critical moments. His stock in trade, the news, is collected from all over the world. The course of his business affects and is affected by every interest in the civilized world, and he has connections in two or three, often conflicting, capacities with all the businesses in the community where his paper is published. To conduct such a business requires expert skill. The methodical expenditure of so much money is difficult enough, while to do it and make a profit is a financial operation of the first magnitude. It means that a multitude of complex problems have been solved, that all sorts of intricate, delicate transactions have been carried through in accordance with a well-studied plan and carefully defined principles. It means brains and character, such as were found in all the other businesses described in this series of articles.

Now this whole article might be written to show this in detail. But the truth of the proposition is quite obvious in this case, and in the course of my preparation of material I came upon something better. I talked with the editors, proprietors, and managers of nearly a hundred newspapers, representative journals of New York, Chicago, Boston, Philadelphia, St. Louis, San Francisco, Richmond, Baltimore, Washington, and of many cities, towns, and villages in between, and while they related their experiences, described their methods, and showed their plants, they disclosed, often unconsciously (which was best), their point of view and the direction they are taking. These bear on the future of journalism.

The magnitude of the financial operations of the newspaper is turning journalism upside down. There are still great editors whose personalities make the success of their organs, but, always few, the number of them has not increased with the multiplication of newspapers, and even where they dominate they have to leave to others the mass of detail that has accumulated under and about the editorial chair. If the editor is the owner and has business capacities, he is attracted downstairs to the counting rooms. If he is deficient in executive ability he has to engage a man who has it, and the requirements are such that the business manager is likely to have a personality of his own so strong, indeed, that he will demand a share in the property and the profits and the policy. Then, too, the old editors die. Their heirs, seldom inheriting the brains with the business, turn it over to a financial manager to maintain it for the income he can produce. If there is no heir and the property is sold, the price is so high that business men who have become capitalists in other businesses, not writers, are best able to acquire control. The most common mode of transition heretofore, however, has been through the news department. The expansion there has been the characteristic development of modern journalism, till now the news service is a tremendous piece of machinery. The managing editor, who engineers it, is a man who seldom puts pen to paper. He may have been a writer; he is always a trained journalist; but he has risen to his place because of his executive ability, not because his style was good. Having to do so much that was business, having cultivated the news instinct, which is merely a sense of a market, it was natural that he should reach out from the principal to the dependent branches of the organization.

Newspaper men see the drift of their profession into commercial hands. I found editors everywhere who deplored it as a fact, and business managers who rejoiced at it as a hope yet to be fully realized. The question that rises in the layman's mind was in theirs: What is the business man going to do with the newspaper?

When a commercial journalist sets out to build up a newspaper, he does not have an ideal before him. He does not say to himself that modern journalism is bad, that there is no paper in the world that is perfect, and that the way it ought to be is thus and so. I met a dozen men who had begun with their papers during the last fifteen years, some who had succeeded within five years, and their stories were all alike in essentials. They had picked up the business in the news or business departments. While they were doing that they were studying the field. Just as a thrifty grocer's clerk goes around, not with ideas of the sweetest butter and the purest sugar in his head, but with savings in his pocket, and a clear notion of the peculiarities of neighborhoods, and picks out a vacant corner in a residence district, so the would-be newspaper publisher seeks a place. If there is a chance to open a store in Fifth Avenue, the young grocer may undertake to stock up with fine goods, otherwise he will be content to supply the Third Avenue trade.

One of the most recent journalistic successes I inquired about closely was a one-cent evening newspaper in Philadelphia which was established by a man who had gone to that city as the head of a subordinate department on a high-priced paper. He spent two or three years surveying the field. There were high-class morning and evening papers, more than enough morning papers to satisfy all tastes, but among all the evening papers there was only one for a penny and that had no news. It had absolutely no telegraph service, and the local matter was cheap gossip. There was a vacant corner, he thought. He analyzed the demand he believed existed, talking with people he met wherever he went and reading the penny papers that were succeeding in other large cities. Then he bought a moribund two-cent evening paper. Feeling his way cautiously, he altered the sheet to conform to his empirical ideas and reduced the price to one cent. From 6,000 a day the circulation increased in a month to 28,000, in a year to over 50,000. In three years his paper was a paying property.

Every city of the first rank has some such example of quick success, and the most recent are evening papers, showing that there has been a movement in that direction. The field has been neglected till the rise of the commercial spirit and the fall of the price of white paper opened it. The old journalist, though he valued his dividend, aimed primarily at power. He strove to make a great organ, so he preferred the daily which has all day and half the night to grow big and complete in, and plenty of time (on comparatively slow presses) to be printed. The old evening paper was high in price, small in size and circulation, and its influence, often very powerful, was not popular. It had no attractions for editors with an ambition for democratic power. It was the commercial journalist who saw the possibility of a popular evening paper. That it had to be cheap meant, as he saw it first, that he could not afford able writers, nor could he print very much news, but both these drawbacks were economies to him. The readers existed. More people have time to read in the evening than in the morning, and, what was still more vital, papers bought on the way home were carried into the family. That insured him advertisers, business. It is not to be wondered at that the evening newspaper field has been oversown with penny papers, or that they are, when successful, the most profitable ventures in journalism.

All the "extras" are not successful, however. To pick an opening is not all that has to be done. The publisher must satisfy the demand he has perceived, which requires that his perceptions shall be definite and numerous, or some more thorough man without his initiative will surpass him in imitation. The executive and organizing faculties must second the powers of observation. The only sound sources of income for a newspaper are from the sales of it and from the letting of space to advertisers. Journals that have special features in the way of news or of judgment (like an expert financial column) sometimes have a revenue from the sale of them to papers in other cities. But this is comparatively small. The circulation is the measure of the earning power ordinarily, for that brings in the wholesale price and is the basis both of the amount and the charge for advertisements. The publisher's most constant care, therefore, is the circulation. The ideal would be universality within the limits of daily delivery. Since no paper in a place of any size has ever approached it, however, the first thing to be defined is the character of the circulation to be sought. If the publisher has an established paper with a field that he proposes merely to extend, the lines along which he can work are laid out for him, and he studies the class of readers he has in order to reach out for more of the same general kind without losing those that he has. This is a very delicate undertaking. For our purpose, however, it will be more satisfactory to follow the man who is founding a paper or turning an old one into a new sphere, his problem being more difficult and more typical.

It is pretty generally recognized now that a newspaper has to print the news. The commercial journalists may not have an editorial page. I have heard them complain of the cost of very cheap ones, and they select reporters with more care than they do editorial writers. But even the old organs of class and political prejudices, which rely for their standing upon their editorial and literary articles, find it necessary to keep up a news service. They did not always do so. Papers with a small clientele could not afford to spend what it cost to get much news till the development of the wholesale news collecting business made a good service comparatively inexpensive. Now the poorest country paper can have all the important news of the world every day in as little or as much space as it cares to order and pay for.

The organization that makes this possible is so commercial in form that it is often called "the newspaper trust." It is the Associated Press, which, to use its own description of itself, "is a mutual organization of newspapers having for its object the collection and distribution of the important news of the world." The origin of this great machine was the combination in the forties of two keen New York newspaper proprietors for the purpose of extending their news service in directions that were very expensive. They could hire one boat instead of two to go out to sea to meet the ships from foreign ports, and sift the news and prepare it for the press by the time they got ashore. But from that it grew along the line of routine news, the papers in the agreement supporting one reporter at a point where intelligence that was best when colorless was constantly forthcoming and where competition was costly and not at all showy. Commercial, law, and shipping news were of this class, and while these arrangements were never altogether satisfactory and were constantly supplemented, as they are even to this day, by individual effort, the combination grew, taking in other papers, breaking up frequently in quarrels, but spreading till now nearly all the newspapers in the country are included in the Associated Press, which, by the failure of a rival, the United Press, is at its strongest.

At the last annual meeting in Chicago, April 21, 1897, there were 684 members, and the number of papers served was about 2,400. Each of these papers is a source of news for all the others, and covering as they do nearly every place that is large enough to support a newspaper, the country is pretty carefully watched and very little that happens escapes the press. To handle this system the central body, an executive committee of five, elected by the members, has divided the United States into four parts, the Eastern, the Central, the Western and the Southern divisions, each with a central office and a division superintendent. When there is an event of more than local interest in a town, the newspaper there notifies the division superintendent, who, after considering the probable value of it for the other members, and the time of day or night, telegraphs back the amount he wants and the moment when the wire will be free for it. As it comes in the superintendent transmits it over all the circuits in his territory and to the other division superintendents, who in turn send it out through their parts of the country. If it was late at night when the news started the first agent will ask for a condensed account so as to get the essential facts into the eastern division before the papers there go to press, and after that is on the wire he will ask for more for the nearer and the western papers. News that is worth a column in the West may be of less value elsewhere, and the superintendent of each division has a staff of condensers who judge of the amount to be forwarded, so that as a piece of news travels it is reduced to a half column in the central division, a paragraph in the east and a line in the south. Similarly the papers that cannot take the "full service" are put in a less expensive class, and have the news condensed for them. All the papers of a class in a division are on what is called a circuit, a wire that is connected with their offices and from which as the news passes they take it off on a typewriter. The whole system has 6,869 miles of leased wire by day and 16,365 miles by night.

Besides this mutual service, the Associated Press has correspondents to send out to any point where there is news but no newspaper, and agents all over the world. It is connected with the European news associations, has agreements for the news of certain foreign newspapers, like the Times in London, and has a division office in London with a large staff of correspondents. In such out-of-the-way places as Adelaide, N. S. W., Fez, Morocco, Teheran, Persia, there are agents. And recently, by an arrangement with the Navy Department, some officer on every United States war vessel is a correspondent for the Associated Press. Though this system is mutual, and brings the news by free exchange, the newspapers are assessed at regular intervals, the total last year being $1,700,000.

Serving as it does newspapers of all classes, creeds, and political and sectional opinions and prejudices, it is absolutely necessary that the news sent out by the Associated Press shall be colorless statements of facts, and for that reason the existence of such an organization is a public good. That it furnishes almost all the news that most newspapers print, and is the foundation of the service of nearly every paper in the country, compensates somewhat for the tremendous influence the organization wields against the establishment of any more papers. It is the beginning of a monopoly; under the circumstances, a beneficial rather than a harmful one, for it tends to restrict the "individuality" and the bias of opinion and taste to other than the news pages. And if there were space to go into the organizations that supply in bulk "special" reading matter, anecdotes, descriptive articles, stories and serials, the sameness of third and fourth rate papers everywhere would be accounted for, but the improvement with financial success of the matter distributed would show commercialism bearing another boon to the commonplace man.

That, however, is not the view of the enterprising individual publisher. To him the improving quality of the output of the "literary syndicates" is no inducement to depend upon them, for the equality with other papers is deadly to competition, and the matter-of-fact monotony of the "A. P.," as he calls the Associated Press reports, though indispensable, are only the basis of his news service. His object is not to inform the world. Neither is that what his readers expect of him. The theory which underlies the methods of conducting the business (especially, though not exclusively, at the beginning of an enterprise) is that most people buy a newspaper for a sensation, and the reward for gratifying this demand is advertisement which increases circulation. When a man opens his paper on his way downtown after breakfast, or on his way home after a day's work, he wants a surprise—shocks, laughter, tears. If it were something to think about that he wanted, the best commodity to offer for sale might be editorials, essays, and important facts. But the commercial journalist, after studying and testing his market, is convinced that his customers prefer something to talk about. There are some who do not, but they are quickly disposed of.

"What good does it do me," said a successful manager, "to send a man off in a day dream? I might as well put him to sleep. What I want is the reader who likes to talk, and then I want to set him talking; to make him turn to the next man and ask him if he has read something in my paper. That advertises the paper and sells it, which is the thing I am after. I have no mission, you know."

So the expenditure of a newspaper that is operated on a large scale, was as follows last year: editorial and literary matter, $220,000; local news, $290,000; illustrations, $180,000; correspondents, $125,060; telegraph, $65,000; cable, $27,000; mechanical department, $410,500; paper, $617,000; business office, ink, rent, light, etc., $219,000. This paper has a very expensive staff of editorial writers, but the $220,000 is largely for special articles of a very miscellaneous character. Most papers of the same class—the cheap "great daily"—put about two percent of their total expenditure on this item.

And this apportionment and the paper that results from it are not to be attributed to the intellectual makeup of the publisher. In this very case, he intended, when he was looking about for an opening in New York, to establish the highest class newspaper that the city ever had. It was only when he found that field closed to him that he turned, like the Philadelphia man, to the cheap journal. The commercial journalist's newspaper is very seldom to his taste. He usually reads and would prefer to conduct some other paper than his own. He might not be able to. That the finished product of his efforts is not utterly unsatisfactory to him shows limitations of mind. But the day of the personal organ is waning, and the new journalism is the result of a strictly commercial exploitation of a market.

"Why do you go into crime in this city?" "Because," answered the Boston newspaper manager, to whom the question was put, "the Boston people like it as well as New Yorkers do."

"But you seem to avoid scandal?"

"We have to be pretty careful about that, for while it would increase the circulation it would lose me a small class of readers who are worth a good deal to some of our advertisers."

The only instance encountered (out of Chicago) of moral restraint in a typical newspaper business man, except where the talk was obviously for publication, was in a New York circulation manager. He was lauding sensationalism to an extreme when a protest checked him.

"Of course," said he, "when I speak of sensationalism I don't mean extra sensationalism."

"Extra sensationalism? What do you mean by that?"

"I'll give you an example. One day as I was looking over the 'cases' I saw an article that told how to crack a safe. I kicked to the proprietor about it, and he killed it. That article would have a tendency to teach something immoral, and I call that extra sensationalism."

From the point of view of science the neglect of the ethics and aesthetics of the business is offset in a measure by the keen regard for psychology. The more intelligent publishers had the relation of effect and means down almost to formal statement, but the plainest and truest expression came from those who acted by intuition; they were never secretive or apologetic when their first suspicions were lulled. They liked the tricks of the trade.

One of the commonest and most offensive of these tricks is the use of the "scare head," large, heavily inked headlines, that set forth as in bulletins the salient facts of a news article. A business manager who was enlightened enough to admit that this device was in bad taste found psychological justification for it in the profound sensation produced by the simultaneous impression upon the mind of all the striking features. There was art in that, he said. It told the news, moreover, as an excited messenger would who came running breathlessly from the scene; and that was the way news was brought in ancient times. A franker man in the same town said:

"The beauty of the scare head is that it scares. And, besides, it catches the eye on a newsstand or over the shoulder of the man who has bought the paper."

It is the managing editor who wields this instrument of the trade, and in his hands it is one of the means by which the paper is colored to reach and hold the kind of readers the publisher conceives to be of his field. If he aims at political partisans the manager sees that the colorless reports of political news that come into the office from the Associated Press are interpreted in the headings. Thus an anti-administration paper in New York printed over a brief, plain statement that a congress under President Cleveland convened that day the sarcastic phrase, "Congress on His Hands," which determined, no doubt, the mood of the reader throughout the article. If the publisher is planning simply for the largest possible number of customers, sensationalism is the motive of the headings. Another means of attaining either end is to "edit" the Press dispatches, and the managing editor of a metropolitan journal has a staff of "copy readers" and telegraph editors who do this work, along with the correcting of bad English and the condensing which are absolutely necessary. These skilful men also "cut down" or "spread" a piece of news according to its value for the particular purposes of the paper. A suicide which in a staid paper would be worth no more than three lines on an inside page might occupy a column on the front page of a strictly commercial sheet, while a bit of political news that is unpleasant reading for a Democrat would be short in the paper made up to catch his custom, and for the opposite reason expanded by the Republican organ. The facts are rarely twisted. That is utterly unnecessary, and when it is done it is due rather to lack of skill than to dishonesty. The business manager will not readily risk being discredited by his rivals, for that loses him circulation. He has tried it and has found that a "fake" does not pay.

The most approved method of getting news suited to the assumed predilection of the readers is to have it collected by the paper's own correspondents and reporters, of whom the enterprising publishers have large and expensive staffs. They are men trained in the methods, and sometimes filled with the spirit of their chief, the managing editor, who selects and directs them. They know what facts to take and what to leave or subordinate, so that the accounts of the same event by writers for different papers may both be correct while not at all alike. The managing editor, or, if the subject is local, his lieutenant, the city editor, studies his staff, developing the peculiar faculties — for description, perception, speed, accuracy, shrewd understanding, imagination, humor—of each man, and then, adding men from elsewhere who possess abilities lacking in those at hand, he is in a position to assign without very obvious instruction just the right man to any given piece of work. They do independently many of the subjects "covered" by the "flimsy," as the press reports are called. Through them also the managing editor reaches out for news that no other paper has, for "beats," which are believed to be one of the most effective expedients for increasing the circulation and prestige of a newspaper. An exclusive story is supposed to cause talk, to suggest purchasing to the man who has it not, to mix up generally in discussion the paper and its "beat," and, best of all, perhaps, to instill in the reader interest and pride in "his paper's" triumph. It is to the new journalism what common opinion was to the old, a good shared by the reader and his paper. A business manager told me that the publication every day of the circulation had the same effect, and he went on to explain that this was natural because it played on the gambling passion, which was stronger than love.

 Another device of the managing editor for the advertisement of his paper is "featuring," which is to distend and print conspicuously under scare heads accounts of any subject that is supposed to be interesting. In a city like New York, for instance, where crimes are committed every day, a managing editor can make an "epidemic of crime" at almost any time by ordering the thefts, burglaries, highway robberies, and murders which would be reported ordinarily in small paragraphs and distributed about in the corners of the paper, to be spread out at length in the writing and then grouped with pictures on one page. Care must be exercised not to overdo one subject, for the theory of sensationalism includes the belief that the average newspaper reader's mind is as fickle as it is shallow, so the managing editor has to be always on the lookout for fresh material or novel ideas. This is the most difficult duty he has, and the few fertile journalistic minds are very highly prized. An editorial writer in Chicago said that a New York newspaper proprietor had offered him $10,000 a year to submit each day an "original idea." But originality is not indispensable. Old schemes that have not been used for a long time are revived. Trust agitation is always effective, but charity is the best; the newspaper finds and describes distress, then tells how it brought relief to the suffering. The "constant reader" can have a share in this "featuring," for subscription lists are opened to all, full acknowledgment being made in print. It does not matter much what the paper uses in this way, and sometimes the agitation takes the form of an exposure of some political or other public corruption, when the community is served and the newspaper advertised as well. One business manager said a campaign against such an evil paid best in the end, because it was a practical demonstration of the power of the press.

 Not one managing editor in a hundred directs his department to his taste. Besides the limitations set by his own conception of the market, he has to regard the notions others have of it and of the best means of supplying it, for he is a subordinate. He is the agent of some mastermind that may be in any person, on or off the paper. There is one case of a managing editor, acting as the representative of an absentee proprietor, but even this fortunate man is said to hold his position by his delicate sense of the desires of the owner, who keeps him under constant secret supervision by telegraph. Other owners let their business managers represent them to the heads of the other departments, sometimes to the subordinates as well. But there has to be a publisher who is legally responsible, for libel, for instance, and though he may be the editor-in-chief, the business manager, or the managing editor, I have used that title to designate the central power which carries out in all branches of the business of newspaper-making the general policy that gives unity to them all and individuality to their printed product.

While the managing editor, thus controlled, is organizing his various departments, the publisher goes to work upon the business office, beginning by selecting a chief who is to superintend downstairs, just as the managing editor does above. He appoints a business manager, whose duties are not only, as in the old days of journalism, to reap what the editorial staffs have sown, but to push the business of the paper in all directions. The work is divided into departments here also: the composing, press, and stereotyping rooms, with foremen in charge; the delivery department, with a superintendent of delivery and his lieutenant, the superintendent of the mailing room; the counting-room; the advertising department; and the circulation manager. All of these are important and interesting, for they show how necessary is perfect cooperation. The superintendant of delivery has to know exactly when he must have the first papers in order to catch the first mail; the foreman of the pressroom must say how little time he needs to run off the first thousand copies; the foreman of the stereotyping room times his process to a second; and so on back to the news department, which has to be ready for the night editor's "makeup" in season to "go to press" at the moment determined by the closest reckoning of each chief of staff. And once set, the man who delays is held responsible if a driver misses a train and starts the distant subscribers writing complaints. To go into these departments one by one is impossible in my space, and it will be sufficient, I think, to take up the two, circulation and advertising, which affect more than the others the news and editorial policy of the paper.

  The circulation manager of today is so new that not much is known about him, and on some papers he is not distinctly differentiated from the superintendent of delivery, out of whom he evolves. He embodies that phase of the spirit of commercialism that is called "push," for he came into journalism as the solicitor or drummer did into other businesses. As the manager of a high office building goes forth in search of tenants, and as the bank president, in more dignified mien, invites depositors to patronize his institution, so the circulation man in the newspaper business sends out his agents to "drum up" readers. It is slow business to let the worth of the paper win readers on its merits. The managing editor might put out a sensation a day without many people being aware of it. A modern circulation has to be worked up by artificial means, and so important is this function that the man who does it is paid the salary of an editor, and one such manager I met had been promoted to his position from the managing editorship. He said his "advancement, though unusual, was natural, for," he explained, "first, you've got to make a paper that will sell, then you've got to sell it, and, to do that, you have to let people know you're alive." In short, he advertises his paper.

    When the paper is a new one, his work is general. He placards the town with posters, runs out his brightly painted delivery wagons, and offers premiums to the news dealers to dispose of the paper, even if it has to be given away. Copies are sent free to any address the manager can procure, and sometimes he is able to buy the subscription lists of his rivals. It is not enough, however, to drop free papers at a man's front door. The householder's attention should first be called to it, so a small army of solicitors is dispatched to a neighborhood to go from house to house telling people about the features of the paper, which any shrewd man or woman can see will be attractive to the individual addressed. Then when a promise has been exacted to try the paper, it is delivered by the news dealer at the manager's expense for a week. The results of this method are always satisfactory. Circulars sent by mail are not so good, but they are less expensive, and are by no means useless, especially when they are supported by guessing, luck and lottery schemes, mystery stories, chromos and other such devices, described in the announcements distributed and carried on in the columns of the paper. More enterprising are offerings of trips around the world, and a very telling advertisement is a bicycle parade with prizes for the "best lady's costume," the most comical, the best riders of each sex, etc. It is necessary, as in the news department, that new schemes shall be planned, for the old ones lose their effect by repetition. The "chromo with every number" is one that a circulation manager said had been done till people seemed to have lost the taste for such pictures. The mystery story had failed because it required a discrimination in favor of the intelligent few, to guess how the plot would turn out. The art poster was merely a fad, a manager said who stopped using it as an advertisement, and he preferred something more striking and insistent, like the circus bill. But all these methods are crude, and are resorted to chiefly to start the paper.

The finer work comes with the increase of circulation, when a fair sale is assured and the manager is endeavoring to attract the readers he has missed in the first rush of business. He studies his subscription lists, talks to the delivery superintendent and canvasses among the news-dealers, to find out where his sales are small. If one suburb or neighborhood is behind the others, he reports to the managing editor, who sends there a correspondent to write it up. When a sensational story is secured in the place the circulation manager is notified, and he arranges with the delivery department to have a score of boys go there with great bundles of the paper and cry it about the street, calling especially the "scare heads" of the local piece of news. Before them, if there is time, the solicitors have spread the reports of the "great story," and after them subscriptions are drummed up or the news dealers are induced to make extraordinary efforts to continue the sales. In much the same way the population of a town is analyzed in comparison with the subscription list, to ascertain what classes have been untouched by the general canvass. If the sporting men have not been buying the paper, the sporting department is improved, perhaps reorganized with a new sporting editor taken from the paper that has the most readers of that class, and the circulation manager has to find a way to let the change be known on the racetrack.

The limit to all these expedients of the circulation manager is in the advertising department. A business manager whose circulation man set out to secure for him the readers of sporting news in New York City, gave a page to the subject which had formerly had only half a page. He succeeded. But when he reckoned the gains he found that he had added not more than 10,000 to his circulation, which was not enough to pay for the increase of space. It was out of proportion to the space allotted to "Woman's Realm," for example, and brought in very little revenue from advertisers. The merchants who deal in sporting goods are one in fifty of those who trade with women, and the latter are the most lavish of advertisers. This manager let the sporting men go and cut their department down to the original size. The advertising manager objects also to the use of many of the circulation manager's schemes as bad examples to his clients, who say that if billposters and circulars are good for a newspaper they should be good for soap. The two departments clash sharply on the Sunday paper, which has been a strong factor in increasing the circulation. It became possible to publish an edition of great bulk when the price of white paper declined under improved processes of manufacture and the Sunday paper was developed as a means of advertising the business. The managing editor was able to concentrate upon one day's issue the numerous and various features that he had not time for during the week, and the circulating manager saw in it an opportunity to make an entering wedge for increasing the total number of readers. To him it was a medium of advertisement for the daily. The manager of the advertising department rejoiced at first with the rest, for his clients, the advertising shopkeepers and professions, saw quickly the value of the Sunday paper with its leisurely readers, and their patronage was tremendously profitable. But the circulation grew so far beyond that of the daily, and was so much more effective for business announcements, that the revenue of the daily fell off more in many cases than the Sunday paper had gained. The advertisers concentrated their resources, in disastrous imitation of the news, circulation, and business managers of the papers, and the curtailment of the Sunday edition is a step very seriously considered in all advertising departments. Competition may preserve it from violent, sudden attack, but if the advertising manager makes up his mind that the Sunday paper is a bad thing it will have to go, since his department is the final court for the settlement of all business questions.

  No newspaper can survive without the revenue from advertisements. A circulation of 100,000, which in a one cent paper that is sold to dealers at fifty or sixty cents a hundred, brings in $500 or $600 a day, pays only for the white paper, the press and composing room expenses, and part of the cost of delivery. All the other charges and the profits have to be earned by space-letting to other businesses. Anything that touches this spot, therefore, reaches the quick. And everything touches it. In commercial journalism it is the very soul of the concern. So well understood is this by laymen and journalists that the degeneration of the profession is ascribed to it, and it is believed to be an insurmountable obstacle to future improvement. I did not find any reason to despair. On the contrary it was when my inquiry took me into this department that I came first upon business considerations that are bound in time to check the excesses of sensationalism. The character of the circulation begins to be looked to there. The space let to advertisers is charged for on the basis of so much a line for a thousand readers. But the papers with the largest circulation do not receive the highest rate per line, because the merchant knows that the readers of sensationalism are not the best class of customers; that is to say, they are not the people who are able to pay the best prices for goods, or to buy the best and most profitable qualities of his stock. The paper with a small circulation may be the most remunerative to the advertising trades. The manager of the advertising department of a newspaper opposes any features that are likely to keep the paper out of homes, unless he has turned deliberately, as some of them do, to a class of advertising as low as the worst journalism.

More significant for the future, however, are the principles that govern advertising in its relation to news space and editorial independence. The advertiser is a shrewd, selfish man, who realizes his power over the press, and he is insatiable in his demands for concessions. When he comes into a newspaper office he wants to stick the name of his bicycle or his patent medicine into the middle of some important news. If he is not permitted to do that, he would like to have it next to reading matter or at the head of a column. That granted, he asks for the most conspicuous place on the first page, covering preferably two or three columns across the top. Then he wishes to insert a "reading notice," an article printed without any mark to distinguish it from news. When he runs for office he expects to be "puffed." If he were allowed to have his way he would deflect the editorial page and make the news pages of all papers like those of Boston, which are the worst in appearance in the country. They let out half the first page to the highest bidder, keeping for their own scare heads only the part that lies uppermost on the news-stand; they break the news articles for advertisements and make the reader follow a story through three and four disorderly pages over shoes and under toothpowder; they print "reading notices," give "puffs," and permit a firm to make up a page recommending its wares in typographical imitation of the editorial page. It is a curious fact that the other extreme, good taste and high business principles in dealing with advertisers, is in the business offices of the Chicago newspapers.

  The temptation to let the advertisers have their way is hard for a business manager to resist, as they are always willing to pay well for an unusual concession. But he does resist it, and the tendency to restrict them is growing with every year of the experience of the business man in journalism, and with every step he takes toward complete control. The progress is more marked in this department than in the others, perhaps because here his experience as the master has been long. He has had time to move past the crudely experimental period in which the circulation manager is struggling. The good has been separated from the bad by the test of profits, and it is acknowledged that the best paying papers are those that are the strictest with their advertisers. The fact that the basis of his right ethical conclusions is commercial is all the better as an assurance of permanency and of their value for the other departments which he will take more and more actively in hand. I met a few business men who were guided in part by other considerations than moneymaking, and I heard of two or three more I did not have a chance to interview. Vanity, love of power, social ambition, religious prejudices often crossed mercenary motives and, at some risk of error, I should say in general that the weaker of these entered more powerfully into the management of the rich purchasers of newspapers than high principles did or do into the policies of most of the great editors who seem to disregard business considerations altogether. Men reared in the business department, recalling times I could not know, and incidents I could not possibly verify, declared that the editors often fell, that their position proved a pose which broke down when confronted with hard facts. And the facts were such that a business man, accustomed to their threatening aspect, was better able to dare and beat them down. It is perfectly true that some business men have risked and stood tremendous losses for principles that to them were purely moral. There is a man in Chicago who has bought, and is conducting personally, an influential newspaper, and he is known to have rejected a sum much greater than his valuation of his organ because he knew the purpose of the bidders was to reverse his editorial policy. Another business man refused, at considerable cost, to make to one of the principal advertising agencies in the country a concession that was technical (in his opinion), harmless to the paper, and of no consequence to its readers, and his reply to an inquiry for his reason indicated that it was pride in business principles and a willful spirit. But the comment with which his contemporaries dismissed my citation of the Chicago man as an example was that his paper did not pay. It is important to know that there are such men and such motives in the business of newspaper-making, but since they are not typical and their example is not influential, except where, as in the case of the man who defied the big advertiser, it happened to pay, I need not say much more about them than I do about the few editors who conduct newspapers for the ideal satisfaction of seeing them powerful forces for the right. It is a surer ground for optimism regarding the future of journalism that the worst examples of the "new journalism" today are not so fundamentally bad as were the beginnings of some of the papers that are respectable in their later prosperity. The growth of commercialism pure and simple has been toward improvement, and the betterment, though attributed by a most estimable publisher to skill—to the knowledge and use of a greater variety of methods—is instructive to the more unscrupulous and less expert managers or publishers. Success along lines chosen for business reasons appeals to business men. A hustling proprietor who said he had tried all the "Boston methods," and failed because another fellow came along and started a decent paper which got all the readers away from him, held the attention of his fellow publishers for an hour one night, and when he finished talking they said that he was right, "only just a little ahead of the procession." This man was understood. His motives are common; his ideas will be pondered, and whatever he does will be watched, with a chance of imitation. Should he succeed, his influence would affect newspapers all over the country.

He maintained that it paid in the long run to conduct every part of the paper for the readers. The advertising columns must be a directory. No announcement should have a "preferred position" of any sort. The dry-goods advertisements should be together by themselves; the boots and shoes should be grouped; and so on with each trade and want. This classified arrangement was right not because it was orderly and a protection of the reading matter from distasteful foreign subjects, but, as this manager said, to make his paper an effective advertising medium, a paper in which a man who sought something could find the address of the shop that sold it. That this was good business he illustrated by recounting how he inserted for a dealer one day a special sale of a particular kind of chair and then on his way home stopped himself to buy one. They were sold out. The announcement had been put simply and briefly in its class, yet 1,700 of the chairs had been bought by readers who had seen that one notice. If he had allowed his advertisers to break up his pages in their eagerness for conspicuousness, more unwilling eyes would have caught sight of the advertisement, but not so many readers would run over his business directory every day. The same principle has been followed by a small one-cent evening newspaper in Chicago which makes a profit of half a million dollars a year, and, though the plant of this paper cost half a million, it was all paid for out of profits; the original investment was only a few hundred dollars. The most profitable newspaper in the country is a three-cent daily that has made itself so effective as an advertising medium that thousands of people who do not read it use no other paper for that purpose.

When a newspaper has reached this point it is past the stage where it is a mere business. It is spoken of as a property by the rivals who are striving to establish themselves on a similarly firm footing, and the word is full of meaning to them and to everybody interested in journalism. It contains the commercial ideal of a newspaper.

The basis of this ideal is, strange to say, the old newspapers built up by the editors of earlier days, who, by their forceful personalities, gained a hold on their readers that death cannot shake off. The children of the readers cling to the paper of the children of the founder. This makes the old organ a property. Its earning power may be comparatively small, but it is sure, the expenses are low, and the "good name" can be sold at a moment's notice. Many men would bid for the honor of owning it, whereas very few would seek the proprietorship of a sensational newspaper. Few businesses are quite so precarious as journalism, for there is nothing tangible about it. The plant of a newspaper that is earning a good dividend on ten million dollars, is actually worth not half a million, and its value may be reduced to this by the competition of a younger, more energetic rival.

But what the new journalist covets in this old property is its field, the foundation of an intelligent class of readers upon which to build a still greater newspaper. The old editors neglected the news and the business departments. Their footing was in opinion and prejudice, which, though solid, is not broad enough. The new journalist has no prejudices that interfere with his business ends. The founder of his school was the first man to make an absolutely nonpartisan paper, and the successful men I talked with declared that the best way commercially to make an editorial page was to turn it over to some man with mind and character who would direct its policy independently and in good faith in the interests of the community as a whole, regardless of parties, cliques, advertisers, or any other interests, however powerful. But while this is being done the business man who proposes to conduct the enterprise would have an equally independent news department and, having the most intelligent readers to begin with, he would broaden the news policy from their point of view, spending as much as sensationalism costs for more important, better written news. In short, the commercial ideal contains distinct appreciation of the power of opinion, but it prizes just as highly the value of the authoritative statement of all the news.

"There's not room for many such newspapers, but that's the kind that would live and pay forever," said my new, commercial journalist.

McClure's Magazine
May, 1899

Theodore Roosevelt, Governor

WHEN Colonel Theodore Roosevelt disembarked at Montauk Point from the transport which brought him and his Rough Riders from Santiago, he was full of the fight that was over. A score of his friends who had hurried down eager to see him were pressing against the line of bayonets at the end of the pier; they were full of something else. One by one they seized him, and one by one they whispered to him:

"You are the next governor of New York."

"Good," he said, half hearing; but he turned to wave at the yellow fellows just tumbling out of the boat. "What do you think of the regiment?" he asked.

"Campaign buttons are out with your picture already."

"Yes? Bully! Look at them. Aren't they crack-a-jacks?"

"But how do you feel? Do you think you can stand the strain of a political campaign?"

"I feel like a bull moose. I'm ashamed of myself to be so sound and well. See, that's K Troop."

And he pointed out men who had distinguished themselves. It was impossible to get his attention.

"Colonel, Croker said a few weeks ago that the man who would be the next governor mast have been wounded in battle."

"Did he? Well, I have a wound. See here on my wrist, a piece of shrapnel—see?" There was no trace left. "Well, it was there, anyhow."

He laughed with the crowd, but again he turned to the column of khaki, and was soon off with his men in Cuba again, when a sober-faced man with a steady, quiet voice said:

"Platt wants you to run for governor, Colonel."

The soldier turned sharply, looked at the man a moment, then said:

"I'll see you again about this matter."

It began then. Senator Thomas C. Platt, the boss of the Republican party, and President Roosevelt of the Police Board had not been friends, for the police commissioner had refused to serve any of the purposes of the boss in New York City. The Assistant Secretary of the Navy and Mrs. Roosevelt had called, in Washington, upon the United States senator from New York state and Mrs. Platt; but that was official courtesy, a social duty, and a personal and private pleasure. Politically the two men were out. The one was a reformer, the other was the head and front of the machine; but both were politicians, different, yet practical politicians.

Mr. Platt realized the truth of what the Tammany boss had said, that only a soldier could carry the state. That was not all, however. Mr. Platt had blundered the year before. He and his party had established the Greater New York, and then had lost it to Tammany by fighting obstinately for a machine candidate for mayor against Seth Low, an independent Republican. The whole of the reform element in the party had been alienated, and had turned up with more votes than the machine could show. Theodore Roosevelt represented that body of voters. The reformer as much as the soldier, therefore, was needed to unite the party and play good politics.

But would a man like Mr. Roosevelt be useful to the machine? And could a man like Mr. Roosevelt afford to strengthen the machine?

The boss sent emissaries to Montauk, and so did the independent Republicans. While the machine men talked to the Rough Rider in his tent, the independents lay waiting on the grass under the regimental colors, watching the cowboys ride their bucking broncos.

"Mr. Platt does not expect much of you," was the gist of the party's message. "The party needs a leader who can carry the state. After that, the candidate for governor shall be governor."

That was fair.

Then the reformers spoke: "We want to smash Platt. He's down now. One more blow will end him. Take an independent nomination, and the machine will have to support you. You must do so. You are of us, you belong to us. If you don't, you are a ruined man."

This sounded rather like the threatening language of boss-ship.

One day the Colonel walked slowly down over the plain, kicking little stones across the sand and thinking. He had fought hard for reform; he always would. He had stood for it in the city of New York, and the city had turned to Tammany. He owed the city allegiance, but it could not command him to disregard everything else. And since he had served it he had served the nation, which had its claims and its attractions. But to do large things in the nation the individual must act through, for, and with his party.

Was he thinking of the Presidency?

He stopped short. "No, no. Don't ever say that again. I never sought an office. I always wanted a job, for I like work. Do you know, I have been thinking lately that I should like to have a professorship of history in some good college? I'd enjoy that sort of work. Still there is one big public job I'd like to do, a bully big job, and I hope to get it some day, but it is under, much under, that of governing the United States."

Then he walked on, and told what his ambition was, and how he would go about accomplishing the task of its achievement. But long before he approached it there were other things; and these, like that, required organization, party.

Why not be a boss, then, and do something fine in bossship?

Again he stopped. "There is a chance for big things there, but they are not for me. I know what I can do, and I know what I can't do. And my limitations end at that. It is impossible, it is unattractive. The cavalry for me, not the engineers."

The Republican party in New York state should stand for the higher interests of the state. It must, for Tammany can win at the Tammany game. All the "cranks," "theorists," "reformers," "kickers," all the "fools" are naturally of the Republican party. It is the problem of the Republican leader to lead all, not some, of these elements, and leadership there must be, since "bossing" will not do. Croker has another problem. He has none of the cranks, etc. He has the ignorant, the selfish, the naturally subordinate minds which need, love, caress a master. Republican politicians in New York state have learned too much politics from the Democrats, and their mistake always has been the application of Tammany methods to a party these do not fit.

Colonel Roosevelt saw not any one great specialized service that he could do to the state by governing it, only the general one of governing well. There was the canal scandal; the Republican superintendence of the Department of Public Works had been extravagant, incompetent, and notoriously corrupt, and the great Erie Canal, which is in this department, was not effectively improved, though nine millions was set aside and spent on it for that purpose.

"I'll stick the knife way into that," the Rough Rider said, "and I'll turn it clear around."

A few other things required vigorous treatment, but nothing lay waiting in the state to compare with the reform of the police department—nothing that was worth risking everything in the world for.

The big thing would be to lead the party to victory; then, as governor, carry out a policy which would be a party policy and would be so plainly, constantly, and bravely for the good of the state that the party would be set solidly down on public confidence. That meant to hold all the elements of the party together: the good—all except the useless asses; the "bad"—all except the incorrigible rascals. The utmost hope would be by thus strengthening the party, with the restoration to it of all the best and most difficult independents, to prove that, at least for the Republican party of the state of New York, good public service was good practical politics—a policy on which the machine could win.

Colonel Roosevelt decided to accept the party nomination, if it came properly to him, and to decline the independent nomination anyway.

Oh, what a howl there was then! The independents would not, they declared they could not, believe Mr. Roosevelt would "betray them," put his "neck into Platt's collar," resuscitate the "dead boss," etc., etc. The outcry could be heard at Camp Wikoff; but the Colonel was dictating his report on deficiencies of the Santiago campaign, disbanding his regiment, and writing the story of the Rough Riders. He paused as he was about to mount his horse for a ride down to the surf for a bath, to say that his friends the enemy forgot that he always had been a party man; that he stuck to the party when he fought hardest for decency in the legislature; that he voted for Blaine after leading the opposition to him in convention. And when he rode off with his cowboy troopers, he led the laughter.

Then the city wished to know how the nomination would be arranged. Would the boss go to the candidate, or would the candidate go to the boss? Both sides were anxious about this. The Independents said that would be the final humiliation, and the machine men shook their heads solemnly over it. They picked out a tactful man to approach the candidate, who alone thought nothing of this terrible question of etiquette. This man called on Mr. Roosevelt, and, announcing that the nomination was practically decided upon, asked whether he would call on Mr. Platt in town.

"Of course I will. But why doesn't the senator come down here and see our camp? He may not have a chance to see such a sight for a generation."

It appeared then that the senator was a little particular about the etiquette of the matter.

"Oh, well, I'm not. I'll be in New York any time he says after I'm through here."

"What's the difference?" he said afterward. "Can you see how it matters whether I call on Platt or Platt calls on me ? I can't. Since I have decided to accept the party nomination and to work with the party and for it, I have to see the leaders. I want to, anyway. For I am acting in good faith. I mean to go as far as I can with them. Of course I may have to break away and fight, and in that case I will fight hard, as they know. But I wish to start fair, give the leaders of the party every possible chance, and see. And mark this now: I'll do much more for Mr. Platt than I'll promise to do. I won't promise anything, but all that I possibly can do for the machine I will. It seems to me that that is no more than honest; it certainly is necessary to the achievement of my hope to strengthen the party by bettering it. See Platt ? Yes, I'll see him now, and I'll see him after election; I'll see him when I'm governor."

So when all was arranged, Colonel Roosevelt called publicly on the boss. He went to the Fifth Avenue Hotel, and his cab stopped at the main entrance. Some machine men seized him as he stepped out on the curb, and led him surreptitiously off to a by-entrance and up a side stairway. They wished to spare him the publicity, perhaps, of an entrance among the reporters in the main hall; but when he left Mr. Platt, he came down the main stairway and talked with the reporters, greeted some of his Rough Riders, and drove away from the front door.

That first interview with the boss was characteristic of both men. When Mr. Roosevelt entered the room and shook hands with the senator, he said at once: "Before you say anything, Mr. Platt, let me say this: that if I accept the nomination of the Republican organization I will stand with the ticket. Any support that is not for the rest of the ticket I will not seek, and an independent nomination of myself without my colleagues I will refuse. Now I am ready to listen."

Mr. Platt paused. But he said the thing that was uppermost in his mind; something of the old enmity.

He wanted Mr. Roosevelt to be the candidate of the party for governor, because he thought Mr. Roosevelt could win. If he thought any other man would run better, he'd take that other man. But he believed Mr. Roosevelt was the leader who could carry the ticket to victory, and he did want this year to win.

Then they talked. Benjamin B. Odell, the Chairman of the state Committee, was there, and Lemuel Ely Quigg, the chairman of the New York County Committee. They had reports from the districts everywhere showing the conditions which indicated that the party could carry the state, but only by a fight, a hard fight. Most of the returning soldiers were not fit for much more fighting, but a look at Mr. Roosevelt was enough. They laughed. He was ready for another campaign.

The conference was going off smoothly. But the conditions! Mr. Platt asked that the governor would give him an opportunity to express his views on any important matter that came up before deciding upon it.

Mr. Roosevelt said certainly he would; he would always listen to anything Mr. Platt had to say about any act of his. He would give a hearing to any party leader. But, if he was elected governor, he would be governor.

The senator said of course. He would have no respect for Mr. Roosevelt if he were not the governor.

That was all.

Then happened one of those surprising disappointments of politics which make skeptics of good men and try the courage of the strong. When Mr. Roosevelt came out of that conference and walked down into the crowd in the hotel lobby, he was elated that his old party opponents had accepted him on the strength of his character. They had exacted no pledges; they had suggested none. Nothing had been breathed or hinted to make either him or his friends regret that he had gone there. He meant to act fairly by these politicians whom he had antagonized in the past; but he could not, would not, tell them this. That they did not ask him to say so, but took him on faith, was a gratifying compliment to his self-respect. It showed that they believed they knew him well enough to foresee what he would do and what he would not do, without saying a word about it.

There was no reason why they should not. His life had been a public career from the year he left college. But if his enemies trusted him, why should not his friends? The independents, the reformers, the "better element" had a personal acquaintance with him, the intimacy of which should have made them surer than this boss of his sense of dignity and decency. Indeed, if the boss had expressed a distrust and asked a pledge, though Mr. Roosevelt would have left the room and quit the business altogether, he would have been able to understand the psychology of the insult. He might even have called it natural.

It was not the boss, however, who offered the insult, but those others. When he walked out into the street rejoicing over the outcome of his visit, he heard the uproar of reproach, and he saw that it came from his old political allies. They wanted to know what had been said, they wanted to know how he could have brought himself to "see Platt." They drew back from him and asked what kind of a man Croker would offer them. Of course Croker's man would be Croker's man, and Croker named his candidate, a Van Wyck, who, though a judge, was taken by the boss because, being a brother of Mayor Van Wyck and like him in character, he would probably prove as satisfactory to a boss. And many of the independents said "a Van Wyck" was good.

It is true most of these political friends of Mr. Roosevelt did in the end vote the Republican ticket, but they did not help his canvass. It was to be a hard campaign, and they started it off with their backs for a damper. Those who supported him did so in a way that hurt more than it helped him. "We'll have to vote for him," they said. "There's nothing else for us to do. But it is hard, and we cannot advise others to follow our example."

So the campaign began coldly, with the candidate standing alone among the strangers of yesterday, the politicians of his party and their leaders. It looked as though defeat were ahead of Mr. Roosevelt, and he was bitterly disappointed. But the Rough Rider soon remembered that, if defeat had to come, it was distant a month or more and that in the meantime there was a chance for a fight. That cheered him up. He went to Benjamin B. Odell, the chairman of the Republican state Committee, and asked to be allowed to stump the state. Mr. Odell did not like the idea. A candidate who goes about making speeches is apt to say something which will hurt somebody's feelings and give the other party a chance to make points. The district leaders throughout the state, however, began to send in reports which changed Mr. Odell's view. There was apathy everywhere, and it appeared that, if victory was possible at all, the Rough Rider personally would have to win it, for he alone would be able to warm the rank and file to enthusiasm. So Mr. Roosevelt was allowed to go his way.

He stumped the state up and down and across and zigzag, speaking by day from the end of his special train and at night at mass meetings, in the towns and cities. A promise of good government was his principal theme. Most of his speeches were pleas for the public confidence which had always been his. Twenty times a day he referred to the canal scandal, and he said that he would punish the corruptionists of the Public Works Department. But he had to depend for the most part on his appeal to the people to trust him to be what he had been before.

The only special incident of his campaign which helped him was the nomination of Judge Joseph F. Daly to be reelected judge of the Supreme Court—and this had a sequel. Daly was a Democrat, and had long been on the bench. The New York bar petitioned both parties to nominate him, but his own party refused because Daly had declined to remove, at the request of Richard Croker, a clerk of good service and abilities, to make way for a friend of the boss. Mr. Roosevelt made very effective use of this as an instance of the encroachment of the boss power upon the courts, which last of all should be touched by any influence that would diminish public faith in ultimate justice. Even this, however, was more forcible in the city, where Judge Daly sat and was known, and Tammany had the city sure. In the country, where Mr. Roosevelt made his fight, it was his personality that counted; and it did count. The campaign which began so gloomily brightened up as the Rough Rider went on, and toward the end there was genuine enthusiasm. The bets that had been at odds against him changed, till a few days before election (November 8th) they were ten to seven in his favor, and then most of the Democrats' stakes were put up to affect public opinion and influence doubtful voters.

The whole Republican ticket was elected, but Mr. Roosevelt ran ahead of the other candidates. He had 661,707 against 643,921 for Van Wyck, a plurality of 17,786. The next highest plurality was 15,839, the lowest 8,664.

Mr. Platt said: "I feel that Colonel Roosevelt deserves all honor and credit for the victory in the state, for I am certain that he is the only man who could have carried our standard to victory this year. The Republicans of New York state are indebted to Colonel Roosevelt in no small degree for our splendid triumph today, and he has my heartiest congratulations and best wishes."

The moment the result was known, the interest in the relations of Mr. Roosevelt and Mr. Platt intensified. Governor Frank S. Black had begun his term by consulting the boss and obeying him, and now at the end he and Mr. Platt were strangers, political foes. Mr. Black's friends, Mr. Platt's, and Mr. Roosevelt's almost all agreed that the new governor would succeed no better than the old in keeping peace with the boss. Mr. Roosevelt himself was not very hopeful, but he was cheerful; for, as he said in the first postelection days, he was trying, in good faith, to serve both the state and the party, and, as he had declared at Montauk, he believed sincerely that these were not only compatible, but identical. At any rate, he would stand for the state, so that whatever happened that should not suffer; and if the party did not prosper, it should not be for lack of a good administration.

Part of this universal skepticism about the durability of such an alliance was due to the supposed character of the new governor. People who do not know him personally think he is quarrelsome, egoistic, headstrong, self-sufficient, and unthinking. He is a fighter, but he is more wary of entrance to a quarrel than any self-respecting man I know; it is only when "being in" that he bears it as Polonius advises. One of his faults is his openness to the counsel of others. But here again, and in the matter of thinking, he is two personalities in one—the first slow, reflective, open-minded; the other quick, reckless, and set. He gives time to making a decision; after he has settled upon a course, he ceases to be a man of thought and becomes altogether the man of action, the character, naturally enough, in which he is most widely known.

So far, as governor he has appeared in the other character. He himself says the deliberate side predominates now, and I infer from some of his remarks about his experiences in the war, that he thinks fighting under arms altered him in some essential way. Once in arguing with him about a certain public measure he had determined upon, I exclaimed:

"That's right, governor."

"It is not only right," he answered quickly, "it is wise. I'm a changed man."

But I will leave it to Mr. Platt whether the change isn't only one of proportion, not of fundamentals. The senator knows that the fighting man in Colonel Roosevelt was not fought out on San Juan Hill. He and the governor have not "split" yet (March 18th), despite some of the interesting reports that they had; but they have seen fight in each other's eyes. However, this is a story of peace.

The governor-elect began at once to do what he said privately at Montauk that he would do—more for Mr. Platt than he would promise him. He recognized in the senator the head of the regular party organization, and, after his Cuban experience and his campaign for governor, Mr. Roosevelt acknowledged respectfully the first-rate fighting qualities of the regulars. But the volunteers also had their good points, so the governor-elect asked Seth Low as well as Senator Platt to advise him. Others also were invited to the first council—Benjamin B. Odell, who is the executive head of the state machine; Elihu Root, an able lawyer; Joseph H. Choate, and some more. This was good politics, for it brought together all wings of the party, and the governor-elect, being for the first time a straight-out party man, sought the unification of all the elements in it.

Right at the start Mr. Roosevelt declared the first principle of his dealings with these party leaders. Governor Black not only refused to make some of the appointments the boss asked; he chose men with a following, to the end that they would in their grateful allegiance to him be Black men. That is to say, he undertook to build up a machine of his own. His success was not great. His party group was not strong enough to renominate him, but it was distinct enough to vote for him in the convention with uncompromising loyalty.

Mr. Roosevelt was the leader of no wing of the party, and when he said at Montauk that he could not be a boss, he meant also that he would not try to be. This was not because he was not ambitious.

"I should like at the end of my first term," he said one day, "to be renominated and reelected; but it must be on my own terms. If the machine shall wish to defeat me, however, it will be able to do so, and I shall not grieve or regret it. I shall have no rival machine to oppose it. It cannot have all its men appointed. But whenever I reject its nominations and take other men, they will not be mine. They will simply be better men than the leaders found, and, if they have any party services to render, I do and shall refer them to the organization that represents the party. I am the governor of the state of New York, and all I care for is to have an administration that will be an honor to my name, a service to the state, and a credit to the party."

Another principle which the governor laid down for his own guidance in machine politics was to stand, not for the appointment of men of his own selection, but simply for good men, better than those he removed. The only exceptions he made to this rule were in the departments or places where, either because very bad work had been done in them or extraordinary duties remained in them to be done, exceptional qualifications were needed. In such cases the governor has not allowed the machine to have a voice in appointments, and he has sought out his own men. But as an offset he has given over to the machine all the unimportant minor positions and, under some restrictions, many of the secondary departments.

The Department of Public Works, which had been conducted to the disgrace of the party, was one of the places he kept for himself. That was to be cleaned out; and since party politicians were pretty sure to be injured by exposures and possibly prosecutions, a courageous man was needed for superintendent; and since this necessary reorganization was a tremendous work, the superintendent had to be able. Mr. Platt had a candidate for the place, but the governor would not consider him. He went about among the greatest engineers in the state trying to induce them to give up private enterprises worth twenty thousand and fifty thousand dollars a year to take the state's seven thousand. They refused; but the governor finally induced Colonel J. M. Partridge, a man of great executive ability, to undertake the job. Likewise the post of adjutant-general was important. General Tillinghast, who held it during the war, had blundered so badly that the state militia was disorganized. The governor took this matter into his own hands by appointing Major-General Roe to the command, Avery D. Andrews to be Adjutant General. Mr. Andrews is a Democrat, but he is a graduate of West Point; and as for his personal and political character, the governor had learned all about that in the New York City police board, where they had served together as commissioners. Again, in the appointment of a surrogate of New York County the governor went beyond the machine. Edward J. Fallows, a young assemblyman who had practiced in the court, knew that one of the branches was corrupted, and he headed a legislative committee which proved his allegations publicly. The Tammany surrogate resigned, and the governor, who had himself as a young assemblyman exposed the same court, backed up Mr. Fallows by insisting upon appointing to the bench a man of his own choosing. The machine had its man, and the machine "demanded" his appointment; but the governor quietly nominated James M. Varnum, and the Senate as quietly approved.

The machine accepted all these independent acts of the governor, and in at least two cases, those of Colonel Partridge and Surrogate Varnum, Mr. Platt said the men chosen against his wishes were his men. And in a way he spoke truly, for they certainly were no other man's men, and the governor advised all his appointees to adopt his rule of relationship with the machine. He consulted Mr. Platt, and so might they. He disregarded the boss, if necessary, when anything large was at stake, and rendered unto Caesar the things that were Caesar's. The point was to do the utmost for the state and the party, and to that end the whole administration had to work together—governor, heads of departments, and the legislature, which, being regular Republican, was the machine's.

The only time the boss and the governor disagreed hopelessly over an appointment was when a Democratic justice of the Supreme Court, Judge Morgan J. O'Brien, talked of resigning. Mr. Roosevelt thought at once of Judge Daly, the Democrat whom the Republican party had renominated for the bench at the request of the New York bar. Daly had been defeated, and here was an opportunity to appoint him and show that the party was sincere in its declaration for a free bench. But the bar had urged also the nomination on both tickets of Justice Cohen; the Democrats had rejected him, and the Republicans had accepted him. Judge Cohen likewise had been defeated, and Mr. Platt urged him for Judge O'Brien's place. When two candidates were equally worthy, surely the Republican should be preferred, he argued, and the governor personally rather preferred Cohen. But the principle of nonpartisanship on the bench would be more emphatically illustrated by the choice of Daly, and the governor decided to appoint him.

This decision the governor conveyed to Mr. Platt one evening in December. They were to meet the next morning, and, in order to keep the Daly-Cohen controversy off the table, the governor sent word that he had made up his mind about it. Just what was done that night I do not assume to know, but Mr. Platt and some of his friends were up quite late, and before the meeting next day it became known that Mr. Croker, who hated Daly and was interested, for the sake of discipline, in the punishment of a judge who disobeyed him, had persuaded Judge O'Brien to withdraw his resignation. Of course the inference was that Mr. Platt had passed on to Mr. Croker the governor-elect's decision, and that the Tammany boss took the hint and kept his judge on the bench. There is nothing a politician enjoys more than a "move" of this sort, and when Mr. Platt was asked if he had inspired it he winked wickedly and smiled.

And Mr. Roosevelt—he laughed outright when he was told. He knew how the politician loved the sensation of driving a knife into a man's back, and he said: "They can beat me at that game every time. I never look under the table when I play, and I never shall. Face to face I can defend myself and make a pretty good fight, but any weakling can murder me. Remember this, however, that if I am hit that way very often I will take to the open, and the blows from the dark will only help me in an out-and-out battle." The Daly controversy was ended, of course; but it served a good end. It put the Rough Rider on his guard. He dropped it out of sight, however, and went on telling his political allies all that was in his mind, what he would and what he would not do, giving his confidence in perfect good faith and assuming honesty and fair play. But he foresaw that, if the fight should come, the first blow would come unawares, and would catch him in the space between his shoulder-blades.

It was thought and said that this thrust was delivered in the legislature. In the period between November 8, 1898, and January 1, 1899, the policy of the party as to legislation was, of course, frequently discussed at the meetings of the governor and Messrs. Platt, Odell, and Seth Low. At first the governor and the machine leaders were far apart. For instance, Mr. Roosevelt wished to have passed a civil-service bill which should "put back the starch" that Governor Black had had taken out of the law on this subject. Mr. Platt opposed any change in the Black or "starchless" law. On the other hand, Mr. Platt was set on a police bill which should loosen Tammany's grip upon the New York City police department. Mr. Roosevelt was opposed to any interference by the state in the purely local affairs of the city.

Now Mr. Roosevelt had a peculiar interest in police affairs. His administration of the police department had brought up out of the vileness of it a set of men who had caught some of his spirit. There were honest, enthusiastically loyal patrolmen, and among the officers a few had either "reformed" or pretended to; they at least were doing what the governor used to call "straight police duty." The moment Tammany recovered control, these officers were sent off to the country precincts, while the rascals who had been dismissed from the force and barely escaped prison were promoted to the highest places. The men in the lower grades were "pounded"—that is to say, they were shifted about from Coney Island to Kingsbridge, as far as possible from their homes, and, when they moved their families to Kingsbridge, they were "fired back to Coney" or staten Island. Good police service was punished. This is no exaggeration. Tammany requires good political service, and the discipline of gross injustice and petty abuse was applied to teach the police force that "reform" does not pay, whereas corruption and blackmail bring the highest rewards.

Mr. Roosevelt knew all about this. The men who suffered told their stories, and other witnesses whom he had trusted at the police headquarters reported it to him. His old friends of police days begged him to lay an iron hand on the department, but he would not. The city had chosen the Tammany rule--let the city abide by its choice. He was concerned about the men on the force who were known as "Roosevelt men," and if he had been anything of the boss he would have cared, for political reasons, to foster his party or following on the force. But he never seemed to think of this. He ground his teeth over the persecutions of the honest fellows, and he laid away a hope that later on he would have the right to help them. Tammany, if left free to do its worst, might make the city turn to him, and always he said the city was a part of the state. "Home rule" was no fetish for him. Now, however, his demesne was the state at large, and the city should work out its own salvation. He would not investigate, he would not consent to a reorganization law, nothing to check police excesses.

Mr. Platt urged and the other machine leaders grumbled, but none of their schemes found favor with the governor till Elihu Root stepped in and drew a bill to abolish the bipartisan board of police and turn over all the power of four commissioners to one single head, who was to be appointed by the mayor, but was to be removable by the governor if the police were allowed to interfere in elections. This attracted the governor. The mayor was a Tammany man. He would name a police commissioner who would give Tammany absolute control, and leave it free to do its very worst. At the same time it would give the governor the right to prevent the abuse of police power for political purposes, which affected the state and the nation. This bill, moreover, would make it certain that, if the city of New York should elect a good Republican mayor, he could appoint to the police department a man who would have sufficient power to clean it out from top to bottom, without having to fight or compromise with three other commissioners of various degrees of ability and morality.

Mr. Platt accepted this bill. Mr. Roosevelt liked it immensely. It was introduced, and with it went a civil-service bill, both of which were to be party measures. The Republicans had a large majority in the Assembly, but the Senate was theirs by only two votes, and it soon developed that four Republican senators were opposed to the police bill. A caucus was held, and these men bolted. It was time for the party whip, but none was applied. The police bill was "dead," the civil-service bill was "asleep in committee," and, when Congress adjourned, Senator Platt went to Florida to rest.

"Ha, ha," said the Black men. "What did we tell you? If Platt wanted those bills to pass, they would pass."

There is an alternative. Senator Platt has tried in the past to beat two of the objecting senators in their home districts; but they have won out over him, and they are really independent. They trade their votes freely, and they work with the Democrats, who, unfortunately, in New York state, are almost always able to buy up as many Republicans as they want in an emergency. So it may be that Mr. Platt is boss only when it is easy to boss (he has called himself the "easy boss"), and that he is "pulling straight" as hard as he can. He came back from the South in time to try pressure at Albany, and he said he meant to apply it.

So far as the governor is concerned, the situation is clear, a little amusing, but quite simple. Mr. Platt wanted the police bill, agreed to the construction of it step by step, and says he still is for it. Mr. Odell says that it is a party measure, and that he is working for it. No one knows to the contrary. It is all very well for irresponsible persons to see the knife in the gloved hand, but the governor has started out to give and take confidence, and in good faith he must act till the blood flows. The experiment-making is too interesting and too important to shy off from at the first whisper of suspicion, and no one wound of this sort can kill.

McClure's Magazine
June, 1900

Governor Roosevelt—As An Experiment

THEODORE ROOSEVELT'S career is a practical experiment in politics. He is aiming at success. If he were content to be good, he would not stand out as he does among the honest men who are known in political life, but who for the most part maintain their personal purity by holding aloof and exerting only so much influence as is possible by arousing or directing public opinion. Mr. Roosevelt always has recognized that he had not only to keep clean himself, but to get things done.

He hesitated once when he was an assemblyman. He became a leader in the House during his first term, and he put through several reform laws by forcing or persuading the party to take them up. In a subsequent term he was so influenced by his many Mugwump friends that he stood out alone, with a few followers to fight; just to fight. This lasted only a few weeks, however. He saw that he could accomplish nothing by personifying a universal protest; so in he went again to get things done, to put through all that it was possible to force upon his party, and his record in this legislature was a good one.

When he returned from Cuba, the old question arose in no very new form. Should he stand out with the comparatively few so-called independents and fight everything, or should he join with the machine and as governor do things? I told that story in the May, 1899, number of this magazine; and the decision to accept the regular Republican nomination and make his fight within the party was recounted there with some of the differences which were bound to come between such a man and an organization. The question raised then was, "Would Mr. Roosevelt succeed in doing the right thing always and carrying the organization with him?" The experiment was going on. It is still going on. The first term of his governorship is about over. What is the result? To tell what laws were passed would not signify, from my point of view; that is a matter of mere local interest. It is the success or failure of the man that is significant, because, not alone that he is honest and practical, but because people believe he is honest; and especially the politicians know this. The only man I ever heard question it was a notorious Tammany legislator; this is the way he put it:

"Say, do you know the governor's got the best lay I ever seen in politics? I don't see why nobody thought of it before. It's dead easy. He just plays the honesty game, and see how it works!"

Thus even he did not really doubt Mr. Roosevelt's honesty. He simply could not rise to a point where he could grasp the idea of sincerity. Life was a game, and honesty was a pretty good trick to play; that was all.

The two years at Albany have been a severe trial. There were no great pieces of legislation up to attract popular enthusiasm and help the governor carry his will over the machine's. Neither was there any important executive act to give his position the force of public feeling. It was a commonplace term, and the fights were all quiet contests. All the better for the present purpose. They were within the organization, practical politics.

For there were fights. The governor and the organization clashed with dangerous frequency; and two or three times Mr. Roosevelt and the leaders looked red into one another's faces, lips tight and jaws set, separating as if for good and all. But each time the governor won, the party leaders submitted, and cooperation was resumed without any unpleasant recollections. Two of these disagreements, or "splits," as they were called, will do here to tell the whole story.

Louis F. Payn was superintendent of insurance when Mr. Roosevelt was elected. He was a Republican grown old in the party; a friend of Senator Platt, the state leader, from the days when the senator was a novice in politics; and he had been appointed by Governor Black, Mr. Roosevelt's Republican predecessor. Mr. Payn had been a lobbyist who did business on a grand scale, but his friends said for him (he never speaks for himself) that no matter what his past had been, his administration

Governor Roosevelt—As An Experiment

of the Department of Insurance was above reproach. He wanted to stay. His term in office expired on January 1, 1900, and he was glad the end came in the middle of Mr. Roosevelt's term, because he would like to have had the stamp of approval which an honest man could put upon the honest end of his life. The man with a past seemed to be really proud of his virtuous present.

    The governor laughed in a merry way he has, and said that Mr. Payn would have to go. Mr. Payn declared he meant to stay. He didn't laugh, and the governor didn't laugh so much after that. It is known that Roosevelt is a fighter. So is Lou Payn. He is a surly, vindictive man who knows no limitations. There is a story that Senator Platt tried once to persuade Payn to "let up" on an enemy of theirs. Mr. Platt showed that it was good politics in this case to forgive; the enemy was a man of power in his district. "No, sir," said Payn, "I won't quit on that cuss while he stands above ground." The senator looked in the angry face, and saw that this was true. "That," he said, "is the reason you are the leader of only a small section of the country, Lou."

    Payn fought at first very fairly. A flood of petitions from the insurance companies poured in asking the governor to retain the superintendent. They all endorsed his official conduct. This did no good. The governor began to ask men to take Payn's place. Payn saw the leaders. The leaders remonstrated with the governor, who answered simply that Payn had to go. The Senate would not confirm any successor, was the answer. Payn had the Tammany senators, and he had had personal relations with enough Republican senators to make them stand by him. Very well. The governor answered that he would name a man whom the Senate could not fail to confirm, an ex-senator or some good party man. This would have been hard on the Senate, but he was told to go ahead. He asked an ex-senator, and the Payn men hustled around for a day; they laughed in their sleeves. The ex-senator declined the nomination. The party was squarely with Payn, who felt safe enough, to say to the governor that, if he would renominate him, "old Lou Payn" would stand by the governor when, when—well, when Tom Platt had thrown Teddy Roosevelt over into the ditch.

The governor sounded the Senate. The Senate was sound for Payn. He spoke plainly to the leaders. They were plainly for Payn. It was a solid front the enemy was showing, but there was one weak place.

All right. The governor said that if the Senate wouldn't confirm a man in Payn's place, he would wait till the Senate adjourned; then he would bring charges against Payn, and put him on trial. What could he charge? What did he know—"know" meaning prove?

Well, for example—about that time two big Wall Street men were quarreling, and one of them in a huff got some information about a trust company his rival had a remote interest in. The facts had been laid before the governor. Among the items was a very large loan to Lou Payn by a prominent corporation officer. It appeared that if charges were made against Lou Payn quite a large lot of miscellaneous trouble would be kicked up for many more beside the Superintendent of Insurance.

That was enough. The leaders asked for that list of names the governor had. He brought it out again, unchanged, and the first man on it was chosen, nominated, confirmed, installed. Mr. Payn said things privately about interminable war, but this fight was won.

The next was less personal and far more important. It brought the governor into conflict with the corporations, and only very wise men can foresee the end; some of them say it is the end of Roosevelt.

The governor has a notion that the way to deal with "capital" is to be fair. That was the way also to deal with "labor." That was the best policy with all the big things, as it was with the little things.

"If there should be disaster at the Croton Dam strike," he said one day, when that difficulty was beginning to disturb New York, "I'd order out the militia in a minute. But I'd sign an employer's liability law, too."

Half an hour later Major General Roe telegraphed for troops, and he got leave instantly to call out all he needed.

There is in the man contempt for the demagogic cry against capital, and there is in him also a fierce contempt for the

Governor Roosevelt—As An Experiment 89

dishonesty and grasping selfishness of capitalists. So with labor. He would shoot into a murderous mob with grim satisfaction, just as he stood up for fair play for strikers in New York when he was a police commissioner.

When he was elected governor, he said privately that no corporation should get a privilege without paying the state for it, and pretty soon he went on to the logical conclusion that all corporations should pay for the privileges they already had. They were not paying their share of the taxes. They paid on their buildings, real estate, cars, trackage, etc., but not for their franchises. Mr. Roosevelt broached the subject of a franchise tax. Objections were raised, but not much was said till the idea appeared in the first draft of the message to the legislature of 1899. Then the organization opposed it strenuously.

Most of the corporations contribute largely to the campaign funds of both political parties in New York. Republicans never offer any anti-capital legislation; the Democrats offer a great deal, and intend none. The Democratic position in the state is well understood. Most of the big Tammany men are interested heavily in the local corporations, and their private secretaries sometimes write the antitrust, anti-capital planks. This is all part of what our Tammany legislator above quoted would call "the game."

The Republican organization presented some good arguments against the franchise tax paragraph in the governor's message: the difficulty of finding honest, expert assessors; the lack of standards by which to determine the value of such intangible property; the danger in the future of hateful taxation which would be confiscation. The governor said these were all matters of skill. He meant to be only just, and he would consult with the corporations about drawing up the bill. But the leaders urged that there was no public demand for such a tax; and that the party had promised nothing of the kind in the platform. To these the governor replied that it would be all the wiser to legislate in these matters quietly, without arousing any popular excitement like that which had been turning the West upside down, and he thought that a piece of legislation against the abuses of corporations, put through decently in a "capitalist state" of New York's wealth by the Republican party, would be a good example to set to the "crank" states, which, like Tammany, shouted mightily and did nothing, or wanted to hit "money" out of spite, envy, and ignorance.

The difference of opinion grew to a "split." The period of reason was past, and the state of war was declared. For a while it looked as if all legislation and all appointments would be involved. But the organization chose another course. The governor might present his message if he would, but the legislature should not heed that part of it which advised a franchise tax law. The message was sent in, and the corporations began to move. They were told by Mr. Roosevelt that they might have a voice, if they wished, in the drawing of the bill. This invitation was public, and it was perfectly understood.

"Yes, I saw it in the paper," said one corporation officer, "but I guess we won't have to see the governor."

They saw the organization. They had a man at Albany, the regular man, to watch the bill, and it was said that he had a quarter of a million dollars to beat it with. He saw it introduced, referred, "put to sleep." He reported it dead, killed by the organization, so that he did not have to spend a cent.

"I haven't drawn a contract on it," he said, meaning that he had not even promised to pay anything to legislators to vote against it. "It's a dead duck. I listened to the heart of it, and there wasn't a flutter."

The governor worried a little. He talked a great deal to legislators one by one, two by two. Pretty soon he was cheerful. He talked to the organization about it. Then he was angry. He saw the leaders of the party in the House and Senate. "Orders were orders," they said, and they could do nothing.

One day, toward the end of the session, soon after the watchman in the lobby had given his expert opinion on the state of the bill, the governor, finding he could not get it out of committee otherwise, sent in a special message. The "steering committee" would have to report it out if that was read. The word flew about from man to man, the message was there at the Speaker's desk; there, too, were the orders. What could be done? Somebody seemed to recall the exact phrasing of the orders.

Governor Roosevelt—As An Experiment

This somebody tore the message up—an unprecedented piece of audacity; it was worse: it was a political mistake. The cool heads were shocked. Suppose the governor should appeal to public opinion with his torn message in his hand! The Speaker became ill, and went home for a day. The watchman out in the lobby was in a fine frenzy. Perhaps he was sorry then that he had no contracts drawn. He ran to telephone to New York; he flew back, and began sending page boys to legislators. The sweat rolled off his face and head.

The governor drew down his upper lip to bite at his mustache, as he does when he is in a rage. Then he saw, as the Assembly leaders had seen, and he laughed. He dictated another message, and had that delivered at the Speaker's desk. The Speaker received it; it was read; it was heeded. The steering committee reported the bill, and both houses passed it; the sweating watchman with his contracts had come to the rescue too late.

This woke up the corporations, and they began to respond to the governor's invitation to see him. They had suggestions to offer, amendments, but it was too late. The bill was before the governor, and the legislature had adjourned. It was a ridiculous situation. The usual hearing was given. Some of the corporations had their lawyers on hand to argue their side. Even this was not in vain. They did succeed in persuading the governor that the bill was imperfect, and should not be signed as it stood. Would he let it drop and have another bill introduced next year? No, he said, with some humor; he could not very well do that. Would he call an extra session? He would consider that. He decided that it would be fair and worth while. Then he need not sign this bill? Well, he thought that, all things considered, he had better sign this bill, so that he would be sure of having something to show when all was over. Moreover, with a franchise law on the books, the amendments to be suggested would probably be more acceptable to him. The extra session was called, a few amendments were adopted, but these changes were so unsatisfactory to the corporations that they are going to fight the law in the highest courts.

What is the result? The organization doesn't like Mr. Roosevelt as governor, neither does "Lou" Payn, neither do the corporations. The corporations cannot come out openly to fight him; they have simply served notice on the organization that if he is renominated they will not contribute to campaign funds. But the organization cannot refuse to renominate him, for he has said openly that he wants to finish up his work: levy the franchise tax, see to the amendment, keep in a fair board of assessors, etc. And besides, he has marked the administration as his, so that for the party to fail to honor him again would be to repudiate its own work.

For the politicians the obvious solution of the problem would be to promote him to a place where there would be nothing for him to do but be good. The vice presidency is just the thing. But Mr. Roosevelt wants work, not a soft place; and he would refuse the nomination. But inasmuch as the organizations of all the states are equally interested in getting rid of such a man, the policy would be to work up a wave of popular enthusiasm which should roll up from the West and Southwest a nomination by acclamation in the convention of his party. This he could not refuse, and thus it might seem that the people had shelved the colonel of the Rough Riders in the most dignified and harmless position in the gift of his country. Then everybody could say, "We told you so," for both the theorists and the politicians have said that it is impossible in practical politics to be honest and successful too.

McClure's Magazine
April, 1902

The Overworked President

THERE is in America a concern much greater than the United States Steel Corporation or any other commercial company, railway, industrial, or financial. It has the equivalent of a capital, not of a hundred millions, but of a hundred billions; an income of a hundred millions, and an annual expenditure sometimes as great as the income, sometimes greater. The stockholders number 76,000,000, and the conduct of the business affects their welfare more directly, immediately, and seriously than the management of any other company does its small partners, for the affairs of this concern are extraordinarily various and general. The greatest business organization on this side of the Atlantic Ocean, it is the foundation of all other enterprise.

Now the president of this concern has powers commensurate with the magnitude of its interests. So, too, his responsibility is great, his duties manifold, and his labor onerous. He has directors to advise, and executive officers to do for him; the organization is complete, well-tried, and sound, but all this machinery is subsidiary. The president himself is held accountable by the stockholders for everything. If he had none but the most important functions to fulfill, his time would be crowded.

Besides these essential duties, however, the president of this organization is expected, and does try, to perform a great many services that are utterly trivial. He is called upon to settle not alone the rows among his important agents, but also the petty squabbles of employees no better than gang foremen and section bosses; he himself appoints all sorts of menials, investigating and choosing between the claims of applicants for places relatively about as important as those of janitors and mule-drivers. He receives and distributes much of the mail of his subordinates, handling some of it with his own hands, and acting upon no little of it. Moreover, this man thus burdened is required by custom to keep open house for all comers. He has to allow his idlest stockholders to enter his own residence, walk curiously about his parlor; and those who are not satisfied may go into the room where he is talking to his business advisers, speak to him, shake him by the hand, while he is bound to listen to their troubles and congratulations and express sympathy or pleasure with them.

Absurd, is it not? No president of a purely business concern would or could do it. It could be true only of a government, of a democratic state, of the United States of America. Well, the point is that it is both true and absurd.

The president of the United States is the most powerful constitutional ruler on earth, and the most responsible. He is king and prime minister; as commander-in-chief of the army and navy, he really commands—directing and approving operations in the field during a war, and signing all commissions in time of peace—he is the head of all the departments, the adviser of the legislature, the responsible chief of the treasury, the controller of our international relations, and the active director of public improvements.

But the president is the head of the people also, and it is in this role and in that of party leader that we find him doing as outlined above. It is as the first citizen of the republic that he has to throw open part of his house "daily, Sundays excepted, for the inspection of visitors between the hours of 10 A.M. and 2 P.M.," as the White House rules put it. No other citizen's home has to be open for inspection; no other government office is subjected to this visitation. Here are the other White House rules:

"The Cabinet will meet on Tuesdays and Fridays from 11 A.M. until 1 P.M."

"Senators and Representatives will be received from 10 A.M. to 12 M., excepting on Cabinet days."

"Visitors having business with the president will be admitted from 12 to 1 o'clock daily, excepting Cabinet days, so far as public business will permit."

By this arrangement the president should have for public business two whole days, Tuesdays and Fridays, when the Cabinet meets; all but three hours of every other day; and of these three, two hours for senators and representatives, who are supposed to call on matters of state. As a matter of fact, those rules are broken all to pieces. Visitors call on all days; they arrive before 10 o'clock, and the senators and representatives who call commonly bring with them constituents, so that the congressmen's two hours are spoiled for them and for business by being made a time for public reception. The hour for citizens from 12 to 1 is no different from the two earlier hours, and there is usually such a crowd that the president is kept busy handshaking till 1.30 o'clock. Then he is likely to have at luncheon visitors whom he really wishes to see, but who could not reach him at the proper time. After luncheon, there are a few men with special appointments, and it is not till 3.30 o'clock or 4 that President Roosevelt, by an innovation which other presidents have tried and failed to introduce, gets away for a walk or a horseback ride. The evening is for public functions, or if they are private, the president has guests, often statesmen or politicians, almost always men of affairs, who keep the talk on "shop." They stay after dinner, and others come in during the evening. This is, of course, all further testimony to the great power of the president; indeed, the position is magnificent. But it is ridiculous also, as anyone must see who spends a day with him.

    Mr. Roosevelt is a man of uncommon vigor. All his life he has sought work for the work's sake. Position, like salary, he has not needed, and his strenuous spirit has put him in this category because he needed always to be doing. Neither did it matter much what the work was—assemblyman and rancher: civil service commissioner and historian; police commissioner and essayist; secretary of the navy and biographer; cavalry colonel, historian of his regiment, and candidate for governor; governor and hunter; vice president and then president—he has piled on the work, dropping the job done for the next with an avidity for the doing of things which has made him hardier and more eager than ever, president at the earliest age recorded in the place. Surely he is the man who of all others could carry the people's burden and laugh at the toil. And he does laugh. But those nearest him say that the strain is beginning to be felt, and that he, even Theodore Roosevelt, is often weary.

An early riser and up betimes, he darts into the breakfast room with a cheerful hail to those already there, some of his family and a visitor or two. The visitors are confidential friends, and their interests are his. But his are government and politics. In other words, the day's work is begun. By nine he is in his office, where he and Mr. George B. Cortelyou, the secretary to the president, are to have a quiet hour forecasting and planning the business before them. Mr. Cortelyou shows him the list of his appointments; the notes of bills, orders, and reports to come up, and such mail as he has to see. The president has to hurry because, as an exception (which occurs nearly every day), an appointment has been made before 10 o'clock, at 9.45; and it is 9.30 now.

Just then the President's usher looks in. The president is indicating—not dictating, mind you (there is no time for that), but flashing hints of the replies he would make to the cream of his mail; and the secretary is making shorthand signs to recall them.

"Senator —," says the usher; "important."

The president waves to let Senator — come in, pelts some more hints at Mr. Cortelyou, and turns just in time to welcome his visitor. Before their hands have relaxed the grasp, the president and the senator are at it. It is important; and they go over it all, but at high speed. Before they are through another senator joins them, and by 9.45 the man with the special appointment is there. He hears the news; perhaps the others discuss it with him, and then go out leaving him to his special business. Before 10 o'clock other men with important and immediate business are there, and they drive one another on, while outside the crowd gathers.

On the White House door hangs a sign "Closed," and two men in simple blue uniform guard the entrance. You go up to the door. "I wish to see the president," you say.

The door is opened, and you pass up, following others, and followed by many more. Servants still are busy in the East Room; upstairs belated doorkeepers and clerks are hanging up their hats and overcoats. There are twenty people waiting in the hall; for if you are the public, you cannot go beyond, unless you have a special appointment; that is the rule. But you see many men and women filing in through the door to the office of the secretary to the president, and you send in your card. The doorkeeper nods an invitation to enter.

There is no chair unoccupied. The room is a large one, and chairs and sofas are set all about it; but they are filled, and many persons are standing. There are senators and representatives. They were admitted at once because it was their hour; but who are the other people—all these well-dressed men and shabby women? They are the constituents of the congressmen, who are breaking the rules established for their own convenience. They stand about in groups, some talking aloud and laughing, others whispering. Except for the dignified secretary standing at his desk, the scene is one of picturesque self-assurance, of a democratic holiday.

Time passes and more people come in. Ten o'clock comes and goes, and the secretary steps into the Cabinet room. You can see the president talking there with a new set of "important" visitors. You look about you and count again the relatively important visitors, fifty-three in all: seven senators, seventeen Representatives, two politicians and two police officers from New York, three women, two officers, and—the rest unclassified.

"I have here a constituent," says a Representative to a senator, "who wants to see a live president," and a good-natured hand claps the shoulder of a countryman abashed at the loudness of the introduction.

"Well," the senator says from his armchair, "he'll see the livest president we ever had."

The Cabinet door opens and the president in a long frockcoat springs up the steps into the room. He looks about and halts. "I can't see all these people, Mr. Cortelyou. I won't. I cannot do it." But his eye has been flashing about him, and in the window-seat spies a man he knows.

"Senator, I am glad to see you," he says, and he seizes the senator's hand. "I want to talk to you about—"

The senator turns to a man and a woman with him.

"Mr. President, I wish to present to you Mr. and Mrs. —— They have come all the way —"

"I am glad to meet you. I am glad to meet you," the

president says to each of his new acquaintances, and his mind springs back to the business suggested by the sight of the senator. "Senator," he says, "come in here with me. I want to see you about—"

He dives back into the Cabinet room, and the senator follows. The door slams shut and the crowd, which has been silent to gaze, rallies and takes up the conversation again by groups. More visitors file in, more Congressmen, more constituents. Then comes Admiral Evans, whom all know to have been summoned to talk over with the president the plans for the reception of Prince Henry of Prussia. When the president reappears, he comes as before with a leap and a pause, then steps out a few paces, and swings all the way around. He sees the Admiral, and seems about to hail him as he used to do before he was president, but he checks his arm and points it straight at Evans, who rises, and the arm points off to the Cabinet-room door. Admiral Evans disappears within, and the president goes up briskly to the first group. A senator is the center of it, and you expect to hear business; but no, it is constituents—a lot of them. The president shakes each by the hand, and to each says, "I am glad to see you," "I am very glad to see you," "I am very glad indeed to see you," "It is a pleasure to meet you," and so on, each greeting varying a little by word or accent. But the president is intent on something he has to say to that senator, and he pushes through up to him and carries him over to the fireplace, where they talk for a moment. Then the host fends away to some one else, striking out first for the faces he recognizes, usually those of Congressmen or officers of some department or branch of the service. Usually, too, the president has something serious to say, but rarely can he say it till he has "met" somebody. I wished the day I was there that not less but more Americans could have been there to see what the busiest man of us all was busied with.

It is some consolation to see that Mr. Roosevelt saves as many seconds as he can. He is very energetic, very brief with the people who "just want to see" him, and as soon as he has got at it he keeps the out-flowing stream ahead of that which is flowing in.

"Mr. President, I want you to meet Mr. ---, a constituent of mine who only wants to see a live president." It was the good-natured Representative with his farmer friend.

"I am very glad to meet you," the president says, and he says it with a grasp of the hand and a cordiality that flashes conviction from his face, but it is only a flash. He drops the hand, his face sobers, and he moves off with the old senator who has called him "the livest president." It is business again, and evidently it is important. They differ; there is a quick word from Mr. Roosevelt, and a slow shake of the older head, a ripping sentence, and a quiet answer; then:

"Think of it. senator, think it over, and we'll talk about it another time."

And that is done with; and yet this senator had business, real business with the president; you could tell by the way the president answered. When he speaks in a low, inaudible tone, you may be pretty sure that they are concerned with some matter of state; when, on the other hand, he has to meet requests that are matters not of state, but of politics, or worse, Mr. Roosevelt often speaks right out so that everybody hears. Petitioners whisper in vain; the answer is clear and distinct, and sometimes these answers are amusing to hear, seriously significant to reflect about afterwards.

They tell how one of the most eminent dignitaries of the government was among the callers one day. The president gave him precedence, expecting that his business was important, and the visitor did lean over and whisper most seriously. To the amazement and amusement of the knowing onlookers, the president's reply aloud was:

"Mr. ---, in the army, promotions go by seniority and merit alone."

The dignitary whispered even more softly than before; but again the reply was:

"Mr. ---, promotions in the army go by seniority and merit. It is a good practice, and I shall not interfere with it."

Mr. --- retreated, and the people who had heard told one another that he had in the army a son, who was very dear to him.

Another time it is related that a committee of New Englanders called to make some sort of a universal peace address. They presented their paper. Then they talked a bit. Finally one of them expressed a hope that the president's known impetuosity would not lead him to make war unnecessarily. The president answered, with some impetuosity and some irony:

"You don't suppose I'd want a war while I'm cooped up here in the White House, do you?"

The personal rebuke to General Miles occurred in just this way. The General was among the many visitors of a busy day, and, since it was delicate business, the president invited him to go into the Cabinet room. When General Miles insisted on an answer in the large room, he got it.

The day I was there such diversions were few. One Representative, however, drew the president into a corner and began to whisper.

"I told you," said the president, interrupting aloud, "that you should take those claims to the Postmaster General."

The flustered Congressman laid his hand on the president's shoulder; but the answer was sharper than before. "Now, Congressman, you are only hurting your brother's case. He will have his chance for the place when the present incumbent's term is out. I have said I would not remove postmasters except for a cause and after a fair hearing; and I won't."

When the Representative spoke again he talked to the air, for the president was saying he was "very glad to meet you" to some one else.

The two police officers were next. They also whispered—at least one of them did, and he was pointing at the other, who looked meek. The president heard enough, and said very distinctly:

"I shall not interfere in the New York police force."

Both officers drew up closer to him and buzzed very earnestly a second; but he cut them off, saying more loudly than before :

"You must see Mayor Low about that."

They would have said more, but the president seized upon a senator, and with him retreated into the Cabinet room. He was gone for fully twenty minutes. When he returned the crowd seemed to be greater than ever, but the sight of it did not faze him this time. Pretty soon he came upon a man who had just "one word " to say in favor of one candidate for an appointive office, as against all the rest of a large number of politicians involved in a small party squabble out in a western state. The office at stake was a petty one, but as "the future of the Republican party in that commonwealth depended upon the outcome of it," the president was being appealed to decide among the factions. I knew personally of seven such disagreements in six different states that had been appealed to Mr. Roosevelt at about that time. Probably there were twice as many more before him which I knew nothing of. The politicians concerned could not understand why, in view of the importance of their own control, Mr. Roosevelt did not give them more time and attention. He did decide afterwards in three cases, and in these three left hard feelings among those against whom his decision fell; he refused to act in two, and caused hard feelings on both sides.

 The president was now shaking hands so fast that he was rapidly reducing the crowd. Two persons he evidently wished to talk to he asked to precede him into the Cabinet room, and at 1.30 he joined them there, leaving in the secretary's room about a score of people who were invited to call the next day. Out in the anteroom was another crowd, and these also were bidden to call again.

 The worst of the day's work was over. If he had followed the day's programme, he would have looked over the telegrams and important mail that had come in during the day, but there were his two remaining visitors to see, and after that he hurried off to luncheon with two other guests invited to that meal with him. After luncheon an unexpected visitor arrived, and not till this man was gone did the president and the secretary get down to some business that could not be postponed. It was three o'clock when the president retired for his daily exercise, a horseback ride. They say in Washington the president found he could not take walks without meeting some one who would stop him to shake hands, or join him to talk about business or politics, and that to get away from all this he has to go mounted. Yet his companion usually is some senator or government officer. In the interval between his return and dinner he goes over some more mail with his secretary, signs commissions, and, on my day, he received a report of the Isthmian Canal Commission.

The evening was spent talking politics and state policies with an editor, two senators, and a well-known public man, all interested with him in politics. Toward the end of the session the late evening will probably be devoted to signing or vetoing bills. That was the time President Cleveland and President McKinley gave to such work, and Mr. Cleveland often stole time for strictly governmental business in the early mornings.

It is preposterous. Ex-Senator W. E. Chandler, who uttered a protest in a Washington newspaper, said: "The evil is a serious one, and cannot much longer be endured. It is injuring the public service by preventing the president from giving enough attention to large public questions. It is shortening the lives of the presidents. Unless a remedy is applied, few presidents will go through one term, and come out with health sufficient to allow the remainder of life to be enjoyable; no one will thus go through two terms."

And Senator Chandler reviews the effect of this evil as he personally has observed it on other presidents. Lincoln was weakening under it when he was assassinated; President Hayes left the Presidency in poor health; Garfield "held office only four months, but long enough to lessen his vitality"; Arthur " suffered unusually, left Washington in 1885 with low vitality, did not rally, and died in 1886"; "President Cleveland has seemed an exception—but four years of leisure intervened between his two terms; he has a strong constitution, is an imperturbable person, yet Mrs. Cleveland is now appealing to the public against a renewal of applications for all sorts of things which can hardly be considered even by a man in robust health"; President Harrison "had a good physique—he would have been spared longer if he had not undergone the inevitable strain of four years of the Presidency."

Mr. Chandler described the change in President McKinley from the "elasticity and joyousness of the first term" to the "sadness and mere endurance" of the second term, and attributes his death indirectly to his bodily condition as the result of his long service in the White House.

The origin of this abuse was natural enough. George Washington had a sense not only of the dignity of the presidency, but of the use which a sentiment of deference toward the Chief

Magistrate might have in a democracy; he received only people who had business with him or were his social or personal friends, and at public functions he stood with one hand on his sword-hilt, the other behind his back. A very intimate friend of his who dared, on a wager, to lay a hand on his shoulder was severely snubbed. After Washington, many of the forms which he established were observed, though with ever-lessening rigidity, until Andrew Jackson swept them all away and opened his house to everybody. There was some excuse for Jackson. In those days there was a strong tendency in some parts of the country toward aristocracy. Moreover, transportation was difficult, slow, and expensive then, and even to Jackson's open house no great crowds came. Those who traveled to the Capitol to see the president usually had some motive stronger than curiosity. They may have come on politics; indeed, we know that much of it was low and trivial politics; but none came "just to see a live president," or "just to shake hands." So it was down to the Civil War. With that crisis, business of all kinds increased at the White House; the president had a great war and most difficult foreign relations to handle; he had politics and war politics, besides all the intense legislative activity consequent upon war. After that the business did not lessen; it increased, and the open-house policy of Jackson went on becoming more and more ridiculous, while the new railroads poured in such crowds as "Old Hickory" never dreamed of. General Grant's hand was shaken till it swelled. "He did not know how to shake hands," a senator explained to me. "A president must learn to rush up, seize and grasp the other man's hand; he should never let the other man get the first grip and squeeze him." What an art for a president to have to learn!

But it is not alone the president that suffers. Public business, the interests of the people, lose more by it than the man who happens to be at the head of the nation. Perhaps Mr. Roosevelt can stand it; he can if anybody can. But as things are going now, one-third of his working day of ten hours is given mainly to business worse than trivial. It is an abuse of democratic privilege. Moreover, this third of all his time is the best part of it, the morning stretch from 10 till 2; the rest is broken up by luncheon, dinner, and recreation.

There must be some remedy for the evil, and Washington is beginning to take the matter up seriously. A bill was introduced this session to provide a separate building for the executive officers and the president and his staff, which has increased from one secretary, two doormen, two furnace-keepers, and a watchman, to one secretary, two assistant secretaries, nine clerks, six messengers, five ushers regularly employed, and eleven clerks and six messengers loaned to the White House by departments. It keeps one man and four clerks busy handling social invitations. The mail amounts to 1,000 or 1,200 letters a day. The executive building would relieve the president and his family of the inconvenience and the indignity of living "over the shop"; it might spare them the visits of sightseers; there would be more room for home and social functions and for business, too; and the president could get some fresh air and exercise passing between his house and office. The separation of the president's home from his office seems to be inevitable, but it will not entirely solve the problem. Much more remains to be done.

Senator Chandler suggests an assistant president, but that is coming gradually in the growing functions of the Secretary to the president. Formerly called the private secretary, this official has always had much of the president's work to do, and some of his power; but the personalities of some of the recent secretaries, especially John Hay and Daniel S. Lament, have enlarged the scope and importance of the position, till now under Mr. Cortelyou we hear it spoken of as "tantamount to a seat in the Cabinet." Mr. Cortelyou certainly performs a vast amount of important and delicate service, so that he is more truly assistant to the president than a mere secretary. He has attacked the problem of an impossible amount of business for one man, and has reduced the mail that goes to Mr. Roosevelt personally to about one one-hundredth of the whole. A large part of it is forwarded to departments without executive acknowledgment or even a record being taken of its receipt. The secretary himself conducts most of the correspondence, and the older Congressmen will tell you that they would rather put their business into the hands of the deliberate, painstaking, tactful secretary than in those of the overworked and hurried president. The Congressmen who take their constituents or their cases to the president personally either are green, or they wish to shift the responsibility from their own upon broader shoulders. And it is the Congressmen's abuse of their privileged two hours a day that is the most hopeless feature of the situation. No secretary can shut them out. But they can be reduced to reason, and the way suggested is to forbid them to introduce constituents, except with consent; to require them when they call to approach the president only on political or state business, and then through the head of a department, and the meeting with the president shall be by special appointment on the day when all the papers of the case shall have been prepared and summarized by the secretary. As to citizens, no citizen should be admitted, except by appointment previously made by correspondence with the secretary. This would shift to the secretary a large part of the labor of the Presidency, and to heads of departments most of the small politics. It is this urgent and necessary reform to which Secretary Cortelyou is now giving his best endeavors.

    The man to solve the whole problem, however, is the president; not any president, but President Roosevelt. The reform must be established by the will of a strong man who is truly democratic and not afraid of a fight. A president who was physically weak might be excused for closing his doors, but he could not thus set a binding precedent. The rule must be laid down by a man who may back it up by saying, "I can, but I won't stand it." And when the politicians cry out against him, and the statesmen slip out of the way of the blame; when the sightseers and bridal couples complain and the committees of merchants denounce, he must appeal to the many people with the great common interest against the vain and curious few. There is no doubt about the democracy of President Roosevelt; it lies as deep as his courage, and rises as high as his ambition; none would accuse him of exclusiveness or aristocratic leanings. If he should say that he needed time to study, think, and deliberately decide on public measures; that a week divided into two days for affairs of state, and four for politics and handshaking was not fair to him or to the people; if he should prefer the precedent of Washington over that of Jackson, it is likely that he would receive the popular support of American common sense.

McClure's Magazine
August, 1902

A Labor Leader of Today

John Mitchell and What He Stands For

IT is convenient to group all labor leaders under one head and call them demagogues; it is convenient and stupid. In the beginning they all were orators. Now there are businessmen among them. When labor knew only its emotions, when the workingmen only felt that something—they knew not what—was wrong, the expression of that feeling carried the natural reward of leadership. Eloquence, in competition with eloquence, aroused passions which begot violence. The orators could not control the force they set in motion. Hence public opinion, which decides strikes, was outraged by riots and bloodshed; capital would not treat seriously with men who had no knowledge, power, or tact; labor itself became disgusted with leaders who could not win. Thus it came about that the workingmen turned from the orators to men who talked little and worked hard; who commanded them, and knew how to compromise with their employers.

Such a leader John Mitchell, the young president of the United Mine Workers, is trying to prove himself. He is a small, spare man, with black eyes steady in a white, smooth face, which, with his habitual clerical garb and sober mien, gives him the appearance of a priest. The breaker boys find him kind; their elders approach him easily, but only on business, which they talk while he listens coldly, giving answers that are soft but short, cast in the form of advice or a direction, with the reason for it. He is never dictatorial, only patient and reasonable. He has no vanity, no fear for his dignity. It is said he is brave. Once during a strike in Pana, Illinois, his men set out to attack some nonunion men at work behind a stockade with guards who shot to kill. The strikers seized two of their employers, and putting them in front, made them lead the attack. Mitchell heard of it, and running to the scene, rescued the "bosses." His men turned on him in wrath, but he explained, and led off the captives from the furious crowd.

But it is no one trait, however conspicuous, that will win success for Mitchell, if he wins (and that is a question which may be answered before this article is printed). At present he stands not quite midway between Wall Street and the mines. He has the personal respect of both. When President McKinley was shot, and the news spread to the coal region, the workmen gathered into a mob, crying, "Who shot our president?" They dispersed when they learned that it wasn't President Mitchell who was shot. When Mitchell went to New York in 1900 to see J. P. Morgan, the financial head of the coal business, he was not received. This year an associate of Mr. Morgan happened to meet him socially; and when he reported what manner of labor leader Mitchell was, Mr. Morgan received him at his downtown office.

For Mitchell knows his business; he handles it like a business; and businessmen and miners alike respect in him the conservative manager of large affairs. Best of all, however, he stands for something definite and intelligent. Where the old-fashioned leader had theories to dazzle ignorance and disgust common sense, this small man in black and white has a policy, which the employers understand much better than their employees.

Labor is a commodity. It can be traded in like gold, or wheat, or coal. The success of the labor union, like that of the trust, depends largely upon the completeness of its control of the output. Unlike a trust, however, a labor organization is not incorporated and has no property. Its promises to deliver cannot be enforced. Contracts with labor organizations rest upon honor; they have no demonstrated legal validity.

Right or wrong, win or lose, the policy which Mitchell represents is so to conduct the business of organized labor that its leaders will have credit with any businessman and their contracts a certain value. In other words, he would put himself in a position to sell mining labor just as Mr. Rockefeller would sell oil, Mr. Havemeyer sugar, or a political boss public franchises or legislative privileges.

Now capital, which has found it advantageous to buy everything else wholesale, fights for the retail trade in labor. Mitchell, however, in something less than six years, has won over the bituminous coal mine owners to his system; they meet with him and his committee each year, fix rates and conditions of labor, and sign contracts. The soft coal operators express themselves well satisfied so far with the results. But they trust John Mitchell, not the union. The hard coal operators are skeptical and shy. Mitchell entered that field only a year and a half ago. The hard-coalers also are respectful of Mitchell, but they distrust the scheme, and they doubt his control. They did "confer" with him in 1900, and settled with him the strike of that year. They refused to meet him this year to renew the agreement. All things considered, however, for the time he has been at them, his progress with the operators has been great.

With the workers his achievement is not so clear. The hardest fight of a conservative labor leader is always within the union, and Mitchell's finest work has been done there. The passions and the ignorance of the men, who are mostly foreigners from the backlands of Europe; the vanity and the envy of the orators, and the cunning politics of his associates in the councils of the organization—all working for immediate results, higher pay, shorter hours, and their leader's place—these try the soul of the leader. But Mitchell keeps still, meets plot with openness, passion with reason, eloquence with dry statements of hard facts, and against impulse he plants a patience which is wonderful to see. "A little at a time," he says. "Anything is better than nothing. And the big thing is the main thing—honor. That is all a union has."

For that he has made many a secret stand, both within and without his organization. When the great steel strike was on, and the issue seemed to depend upon the decision of the men of the South Chicago mills to join the strike or stand to their machines, Mitchell went to Theo. J. Shaffer, an old-fashioned leader, ex-clergyman, and orator, who had called out some steel workers who were under contract.

"Put them back, Shaffer," said Mitchell. "Your organization can't afford to violate its contracts. If you break your agreement, the cause of organized labor will be put back farther than any victory you may gain will advance it."

Shaffer would not listen to Mitchell. He kept out the contract breakers, and tried to force out the South Chicago men, who had learned the idea of the honor involved in a labor contract, and had refused to obey Shaffer's call. They were jeered at and threatened; their women wept with shame for them; their children hung their heads, and they themselves groaned under the taunts flung at them by the strikers. But they gritted their teeth and worked. The steel strike was lost, but men like Mitchell count it a victory. And it was. At this writing (June 21st) Mitchell is fighting the same battle himself. The anthracite coal strike is at its height. The beginning of it was a defeat for the leader. He did not want a strike then. His reasoning was that the hard coal miners' organization was new, and that it was composed largely of men who were foreigners and had not yet learned their lesson of self-restraint and sound principles. They had, indeed, won the strike of 1900, but only under exceptional circumstances (the intercession of a political influence to save the election of a President). This was luck, and the men had profited in wages, and the union (though unrecognized) in prestige. To ask more so soon was to teach the mine owners that concessions would cause only endless discontent among their employees and extravagant demands. But the men did not heed him; they listened to the orators and went out. Mitchell, the leader, had to lead them or give way to the politicians, eager for his place.

Beaten at the beginning, he was beaten at the middle, too. The strike was slow. The operators were firm, and the workers impatient. The organization had in reserve a force which the strikers clamored to have it apply—a general strike. The United Mine Workers is made up of two great divisions, the hard-coalers and the soft. It was the hard-coalers who had struck; the soft-coalers were contented, and remained at work. Mitchell, the leader of all, had in his pocket a call for a convention to consider the question of making common cause of the anthracite demands. That surely would settle the difficulty one way or another. Business could go on without hard coal; the railroads and factories unable to get anthracite could use bituminous. If all the mines were closed, industry would stop.

But most of the soft coal workers were under contract. Therefore Mitchell, who had told Shaffer it was better to lose a strike than to break a business contract, kept that convention call six weeks in his pocket. The constitution of the organization, however, required him to issue it upon the demand of six district unions. These came, and Mitchell had to yield. But he fixed the date of the convention one month ahead, on July 17th.

His hope, of course, was that a settlement could be negotiated in the interval. If that failed, then—well, then the great question of the inviolability of a union contract for the labor of coal miners could be answered in the open with all the world to see. Mitchell says it all is a matter of honor. Wall Street says it is a matter of his control over his organization. If Mitchell, appealing, as I think he will, privately or publicly, to the men's sense of honor, can keep them from voting to repudiate the soft coal unions' contracts, then he will have triumphed the greater for his defeats and his patience, and organized labor the world over will have scored a most conspicuous victory. This whether the coal strike of 1902 is won or lost. Or, should the men leave it all to Mitchell, as they well may, and he can resist the temptation to play the demagogue in order to keep his place and his power, then he will have proved that he is what he has seemed, a sound, conservative manager of labor. The temptation to surrender his principles will be almost irresistible. But whether he wins or loses this victory over himself he already has pointed the way for unionism and union leadership.

McClure's Magazine
October, 1902

Tweed Days in St. Louis

Joseph W. Folk's Single-handed Exposure of Corruption, High and Low

St. Louis, the fourth city in size in the United States, is making two announcements to the world: one that it is the worst-governed city in the land; the other that it wishes all men to come and see it. It isn't our worst-governed city; Philadelphia is that. But St. Louis is worth examining while we have it inside out.

There is a man at work there, one man, working all alone, but he is the circuit (district or state) attorney, and he is "doing his duty." That is what thousands of district attorneys and other public officials have promised to do and boasted of doing. This man has a literal sort of mind. He is a thin-lipped, firm-mouthed, dark little man, who never raises his voice, but goes ahead doing, with a smiling eye and a set jaw, the simple thing he said he would do. The politicians and reputable citizens who asked him to run urged him when he declined. When he said that if elected he would have to do his duty, they said, "Of course." So he ran, they supported him, and he was elected. Now some of these politicians are sentenced to the penitentiary, some are in Mexico. The circuit attorney, finding that his "duty" was to catch and convict criminals, and that the biggest criminals were some of these same politicians and leading citizens, went after them. It is magnificent, but the politicians declare it isn't politics.

The corruption of St. Louis came from the top. The best citizens—the merchants and big financiers—used to rule the town, and they ruled it well. They set out to outstrip Chicago. The commercial and industrial war between these two cities was at one time a picturesque and dramatic spectacle such as is witnessed only in our country. Businessmen were not mere merchants and the politicians were not mere grafters; the two kinds of citizens got together and wielded the power of banks, railroads, factories, the prestige of the city, and the spirit of its citizens to gain business and population. And it was a close race. Chicago, having the start, always led, but St. Louis had pluck, intelligence, and tremendous energy. It pressed Chicago hard. It excelled in a sense of civic beauty and good government; and there are those who think yet it might have won. But a change occurred. Public spirit became private spirit, public enterprise became private greed.

Along about 1890, public franchises and privileges were sought not only for legitimate profit and common convenience, but for loot. Taking but slight and always selfish interest in the public councils, the big men misused politics. The riff-raff, catching the smell of corruption, rushed into the Municipal Assembly, drove out the remaining respectable men, and sold the city—its streets, its wharves, its markets, and all that it had—to the now greedy business men and bribers. In other words, when the leading men began to devour their own city, the herd rushed into the trough and fed also.

So gradually has this occurred that these same citizens hardly realize it. Go to St. Louis and you will find the habit of civic pride in them; they still boast. The visitor is told of the wealth of the residents, of the financial strength of the banks, and of the growing importance of the industries, yet he sees poorly paved, refuse-burdened streets, and dusty or mud-covered alleys; he passes a ramshackle fire-trap crowded with the sick, and learns that it is the City Hospital; he enters the "Four Courts," and his nostrils are greeted by the odor of formaldehyde used as a disinfectant, and insect powder spread to destroy vermin; he calls at the new City Hall, and finds half the entrance boarded with pine planks to cover up the unfinished interior. Finally, he turns a tap in the hotel, to see liquid mud flow into wash-basin or bathtub.

The St. Louis charter vests legislative power of great scope in a Municipal Assembly, which is composed of a council and a House of Delegates. Here is a description of the latter by one of Mr. Folk's grand juries:

"We have had before us many of those who have been, and most of those who are now, members of the House of Delegates. We found a number of these utterly illiterate and lacking in ordinary intelligence, unable to give a better reason for favoring or opposing a measure than a desire to act with the majority. In some, no trace of mentality or morality could be found; in others, a low order of training appeared, united with base cunning, groveling instincts, and sordid desires. Unqualified to respond to the ordinary requirements of life, they are utterly incapable of comprehending the significance of an ordinance, and are incapacitated, both by nature and training, to be the makers of laws. The choosing of such men to be legislators makes a travesty of justice, sets a premium on incompetency, and deliberately poisons the very source of the law."

These creatures were well organized. They had a "combine"—a legislative institution—which the grand jury described as follows:

"Our investigation, covering more or less fully a period of ten years, shows that, with few exceptions, no ordinance has been passed wherein valuable privileges or franchises are granted until those interested have paid the legislators the money demanded for action in the particular case. Combines in both branches of the Municipal Assembly are formed by members sufficient in number to control legislation. To one member of this combine is delegated the authority to act for the combine, and to receive and to distribute to each member the money agreed upon as the price of his vote in support of, or opposition to, a pending measure. So long has this practice existed that such members have come to regard the receipt of money for action on pending measures as a legitimate perquisite of a legislator."

One legislator consulted a lawyer with the intention of suing a firm to recover an unpaid balance on a fee for the grant of a switch-way. Such difficulties rarely occurred, however. In order to insure a regular and indisputable revenue, the combine of each house drew up a schedule of bribery prices for all possible sorts of grants, just such a list as a commercial traveler takes out on the road with him. There was a price for a grain elevator, a price for a short switch; side tracks were charged for by the linear foot, but at rates which varied according to the nature of the ground taken; a street improvement cost so much; wharf space was classified and precisely rated. As there was a scale for favorable legislation, so there was one for defeating bills. It made a difference in the price if there was opposition, and it made a difference whether the privilege asked was legitimate or not. But nothing was passed free of charge. Many of the legislators were saloon-keepers—it was in St. Louis that a practical joker nearly emptied the House of Delegates by tipping a boy to rush into a session and call out, "Mister, your saloon is on fire,"—but even the saloon-keepers of a neighborhood had to pay to keep in their inconvenient locality a market which public interest would have moved.

From the Assembly, bribery spread into other departments. Men empowered to issue peddlers' licenses and permits to citizens who wished to erect awnings or use a portion of the sidewalk for storage purposes charged an amount in excess of the prices stipulated by law, and pocketed the difference. The city's money was loaned at interest, and the interest was converted into private bank accounts. City carriages were used by the wives and children of city officials. Supplies for public institutions found their way to private tables; one itemized account of food furnished the poorhouse included California jellies, imported cheeses, and French wines! A member of the Assembly caused the incorporation of a grocery company, with his sons and daughters the ostensible stockholders, and succeeded in having his bid for city supplies accepted although the figures were in excess of his competitors'. In return for the favor thus shown, he endorsed a measure to award the contract for city printing to another member, and these two voted aye on a bill granting to a third the exclusive right to furnish city dispensaries with drugs.

Men ran into debt to the extent of thousands of dollars for the sake of election to either branch of the Assembly. One night, on a street car going to the City Hall, a new member remarked that the nickel he handed the conductor was his last. The next day he deposited $5,000 in a savings bank. A member of the House of Delegates admitted to the grand jury that his dividends from the combine netted $25,000 in one year; a Councilman stated that he was paid $50,000 for his vote on a single measure.

Bribery was a joke. A newspaper reporter overheard this conversation one evening in the corridor of the City Hall:

"Ah there, my boodler!" said Mr. Delegate.

"Ah there, my boodler!" said Mr. Delegate.

"Stay there, my grafter!" replied Mr. Councilman. "Can you lend me a hundred for a day or two?"

"Not at present. But I can spare it if the Z——- bill goes through to-night. Meet me at F——'s later."

"All right, my jailbird; I'll be there."

The blackest years were 1898, 1899, and 1900. Foreign corporations came into the city to share in its despoilation, and home industries were driven out by blackmail. Franchises worth millions were granted without one cent of cash to the city, and with provision for only the smallest future payment; several companies which refused to pay blackmail had to leave; citizens were robbed more and more boldly; payrolls were padded with the names of non-existent persons; work on public improvements was neglected, while money for them went to the boodlers.

Some of the newspapers protested, disinterested citizens were alarmed, and the shrewder men gave warnings, but none dared make an effective stand. Behind the corruptionists were men of wealth and social standing, who, because of special privileges granted them, felt bound to support and defend the looters. Independent victims of the far-reaching conspiracy submitted in silence, through fear of injury to their business. Men whose integrity was never questioned, who held high positions of trust, who were church members and teachers of Bible classes, contributed to the support of the dynasty—became blackmailers, in fact—and their excuse was that others did the same, and that if they proved the exception it would work their ruin. The system became loose through license and plenty till it was as wild and weak as that of Tweed in New York.

Then the unexpected happened—an accident. There was no uprising of the people, but they were restive; and the Democratic party leaders, thinking to gain some independent votes, decided to raise the cry "reform" and put up a ticket of candidates different enough from the usual offerings of political parties to give color to their platform. These leaders were not in earnest. There was little difference between the two parties in the city; but the rascals that were in had been getting the greater share of the spoils, and the "outs" wanted more than was given to them. "Boodle" was not the issue, no exposures were made or threatened, and the bosses expected to control their men if elected. Simply as part of the game, the Democrats raised the slogan, "reform" and "no more Ziegenheinism."

Mayor Ziegenhein, called "Uncle Henry," was a "good fellow," "one of the boys," and though it was during his administration that the city grew ripe and went to rot, his opponents talked only of incompetence and neglect, and repeated such stories as that of his famous reply to some citizens who complained because certain street lights were put out: "You have the moon yet—ain't it?"

When somebody mentioned Joseph W. Folk for circuit attorney the leaders were ready to accept him. They didn't know much about him. He was a young man from Tennessee; had been president of the Jefferson Club, and arbitrated the railroad strike of 1898. But Folk did not want the place. He was a civil lawyer, had had no practice at the criminal bar, cared little about it, and a lucrative business as counsel for corporations was interesting him. He rejected the invitation. The committee called again and again, urging his duty to his party, and the city, etc.

"Very well," he said, at last, "I will accept the nomination, but if elected I will do my duty. There must be no attempt to influence my actions when I am called upon to punish lawbreakers."

The committeemen took such statements as the conventional platitudes of candidates. They nominated him, the Democratic ticket was elected, and Folk became circuit attorney for the Eighth Missouri District.

Three weeks after taking the oath of office his campaign pledges were put to the test. A number of arrests had been made in connection with the recent election, and charges of illegal registration were preferred against men of both parties. Mr.

Folk took them up like routine cases of ordinary crime. Political bosses rushed to the rescue, Mr. Folk was reminded of his duty to his party, and told that he was expected to construe the law in such a manner that repeaters and other election criminals who had hoisted Democracy's flag and helped elect him might be either discharged or receive the minimum punishment. The nature of the young lawyer's reply can best be inferred from the words of that veteran political leader, Colonel Ed Butler, who, after a visit to Mr. Folk, wrathfully exclaimed, "D—n Joel, he thinks he's the whole thing as circuit attorney."

The election cases were passed through the courts with astonishing rapidity; no more mercy was shown Democrats than Republicans, and before winter came a number of ward heelers and old-time party workers were behind the bars in Jefferson City. He next turned his attention to grafters and straw bondsmen with whom the courts were infested, and several of these leeches are in the penitentiary today. The business was broken up because of his activity. But Mr. Folk had made little more than the beginning.

One afternoon, late in January, 1903, a newspaper reporter, known as "Red" Galvin, called Mr. Folk's attention to a ten-line newspaper item to the effect that a large sum of money had been placed in a bank for the purpose of bribing certain assemblymen to secure the passage of a street railroad ordinance. No names were mentioned, but Mr. Galvin surmised that the bill referred to was one introduced on behalf of the Suburban Railway Company. An hour later Mr. Folk sent the names of nearly one hundred persons to the sheriff, with instructions to subpoena them before the grand jury at once. The list included councilmen, members of the House of Delegates, officers and directors of the Suburban Railway, bank presidents and cashiers. In three days the investigation was being pushed with vigor, but St. Louis was laughing at the "huge joke." Such things had been attempted before. The men who had been ordered to appear before the grand jury jested as they chatted in the anterooms, and newspaper accounts of these preliminary examinations were written in the spirit of burlesque.

It has developed since that Circuit Attorney Folk knew nothing, and was not able to learn much more during the first days; but he says he saw here and there puffs of smoke and he determined to find the fire. It was not an easy job. The first break into such a system is always difficult. Mr. Folk began with nothing but courage and a strong personal conviction. He caused peremptory summons to be issued, for the immediate attendance in the grand jury room of Charles H. Turner, president of the Suburban Railway, and Philip Stock, a representative of brewers' interests, who, he had reason to believe, was the legislative agent in this deal.

"Gentlemen," said Mr. Folk, "I have secured sufficient evidence to warrant the return of indictments against you for bribery, and I shall prosecute you to the full extent of the law and send you to the penitentiary unless you tell to this grand jury the complete history of the corruptionist methods employed by you to secure the passage of Ordinance No. 44. I shall give you three days to consider the matter. At the end of that time, if you have not returned here and given us the information demanded, warrants will be issued for your arrest."

They looked at the audacious young prosecutor and left the Four Courts building without uttering a word. He waited. Two days later, ex-Lieutenant Governor Charles P. Johnson, the veteran criminal lawyer, called, and said that his client, Mr. Stock, was in such poor health that he would be unable to appear before the grand jury.

"I am truly sorry that Mr. Stock is ill," replied Mr. Folk, "for his presence here is imperative, and if he fails to appear he will be arrested before sundown." That evening a conference was held in Governor Johnson's office, and the next day this story was told in the grand jury room by Charles H. Turner, millionaire president of the Suburban Railway, and corroborated by Philip Stock, man-about-town and a good fellow: The Suburban, anxious to sell out at a large profit to its only competitor, the St. Louis Transit Co., caused to be drafted the measure known as House Bill No. 44. So sweeping were its grants that Mr. Turner, who planned and executed the document, told the directors in his confidence that its enactment into law would enhance the value of the property from three to six million dollars. The bill introduced, Mr. Turner visited Colonel Butler, who had long been known as a legislative agent, and asked his price for securing the passage of the measure. "One hundred and forty-five thousand dollars will be my fee," was the reply. The railway president demurred. He would think the matter over, he said, and he hired a cheaper man, Mr. Stock. Stock conferred with the representative of the combine in the House of Delegates and reported that $75,000 would be necessary in this branch of the Assembly. Mr. Turner presented a note endorsed by two of the directors whom he could trust, and secured a loan from the German American Savings Bank.

Bribe funds in pocket, the legislative agent telephoned John Murrell, at that time a representative of the House combine, to meet him in the office of the Lincoln Trust Company. There the two rented a safe-deposit box. Mr. Stock placed in the drawer the roll of $75,000, and each subscribed to an agreement that the box should not be opened unless both were present. Of course the conditions spread upon the bank's daybook made no reference to the purpose for which this fund had been deposited, but an agreement entered into by Messrs. Stock and Murrell was to the effect that the $75,000 should be given Mr. Murrell as soon as the bill became an ordinance, and by him distributed to the members of the combine. Stock turned to the council, and upon his report a further sum of $60,000 was secured. These bills were placed in a safe deposit box of the Mississippi Valley Trust Co., and the man who held the key as representative of the council combine was Charles H. Kratz.

All seemed well, but a few weeks after placing these funds in escrow, Mr. Stock reported to his employer that there was an unexpected hitch due to the action of Emil Meysenburg, who, as a member of the Council Committee on Railroads, was holding up the report on the bill. Mr. Stock said that Mr. Meysenburg held some worthless shares in a defunct corporation and wanted Mr. Stock to purchase this paper at its par value of $9,000. Mr. Turner gave Mr. Stock the money with which to buy the shares.

Thus the passage of House Bill 44 promised to cost the Suburban Railway Co. $144,000, only one thousand dollars less than that originally named by the political boss to whom Mr. Turner had first applied. The bill, however, passed both houses of the Assembly. The sworn servants of the city had done their work and held out their hands for the bribe money.

Then came a court mandate which prevented the Suburban Railway Co. from reaping the benefit of the vote-buying, and Charles H. Turner, angered at the check, issued orders that the money in safe-deposit boxes should not be touched. War was declared between bribe-givers and bribe-takers, and the latter resorted to tactics which they hoped would frighten the Suburban people into submission—such as making enough of the story public to cause rumors of impending prosecution. It was that first item which Mr. Folk saw and acted upon.

When Messrs. Turner and Stock unfolded in the grand jury room the details of their bribery plot, Circuit Attorney Folk found himself in possession of verbal evidence of a great crime; he needed as material exhibits the two large sums of money in safe-deposit vaults of two of the largest banking institutions of the West. Had this money been withdrawn? Could he get it if it was there? Lockboxes had always been considered sacred and beyond the power of the law to open. "I've always held," said Mr. Folk, "that the fact that a thing never had been done was no reason for thinking it couldn't be done." He decided in this case that the magnitude of the interests involved warranted unusual action, so he selected a committee of grand jurors and visited one of the banks. He told the president, a personal friend, the facts that had come into his possession, and asked permission to search for the fund.

"Impossible," was the reply. "Our rules deny anyone the right."

"Mr. —," said Mr. Folk, "a crime has been committed, and you hold concealed the principal evidence thereto. In the name of the state of Missouri I demand that you cause the box to be opened. If you refuse, I shall cause a warrant to be issued, charging you as an accessory."

For a minute not a word was spoken by anyone in the room; then the banker said in almost inaudible tones:

"Give me a little time, gentlemen. I must consult with our legal adviser before taking such a step."

"We will wait ten minutes," said the circuit attorney. "By that time we must have access to the vault or a warrant will be applied for."

At the expiration of that time a solemn procession wended its way from the president's office to the vaults in the sub-cellar—the president, the cashier, and the corporation's lawyer, the grand jurors, and the Circuit Attorney. All bent eagerly forward as the key was inserted in the lock. The iron drawer yielded, and a roll of something wrapped in brown paper was brought to light. The circuit attorney removed the rubber bands, and national bank notes of large denomination spread out flat before them. The money was counted, and the sum was $75,000!

The boodle fund was returned to its repository, officers of the bank were told they would be held responsible for it until the courts could act. The investigators visited the other financial institution. They met with more resistance there. The threat to procure a warrant had no effect until Mr. Folk left the building and set off in the direction of the Four Courts. Then a messenger called him back, and the second box was opened. In this was found $60,000. The chain of evidence was complete.

From that moment events moved rapidly. Charles Kratz and John K. Murrell, alleged representatives of Council and House combines, were arrested on bench warrants and placed under heavy bonds. Kratz was brought into court from a meeting at which plans were being formed for his election to the national Congress. Murrell was taken from his undertaking establishment. Emil Meysenburg, millionaire broker, was seated in his office when a sheriff's deputy entered and read a document that charged him with bribery. The summons reached Henry Nicolaus while he was seated at his desk, and the wealthy brewer was compelled to send for a bondsman to avoid passing a night in jail. The cable flashed the news to Cairo, Egypt, that Ellis Wainwright, many times a millionaire, proprietor of the St. Louis brewery that bears this name, had been indicted. Julius Lehmann, one of the members of the House of Delegates, who had joked while waiting in the grand jury's anteroom, had his laughter cut short by the hand of a deputy sheriff on his shoulder and the words, "You are charged with perjury." He was joined at the bar of the criminal court by Harry Faulkner, another jolly good fellow.

Consternation spread among the boodle gang. Some of the men took night trains for other states and foreign countries; the majority remained and counseled together. Within twenty-four hours after the first indictments were returned, a meeting of bribe-givers and bribe-takers was held in South St. Louis. The total wealth of those in attendance was $30,000,000, and their combined political influence sufficient to carry any municipal election under normal conditions.

This great power was aligned in opposition to one man, who still was alone. It was not until many indictments had been returned that a citizens' committee was formed to furnish funds, and even then most of the contributors concealed their identity. Mr. James L. Blair, the treasurer, testified in court that they were afraid to be known lest "it ruin their business."

At the meeting of corruptionists three courses were decided upon. Political leaders were to work on the Circuit Attorney by promise of future reward, or by threats. Detectives were to ferret out of the young lawyer's past anything that could be used against him. Witnesses would be sent out of town and provided with money to remain away until the adjournment of the grand jury.

Mr. Folk at once felt the pressure, and it was of a character to startle one. statesmen, lawyers, merchants, clubmen, churchmen—in fact, men prominent in all walks of life—visited him at his office and at his home, and urged that he cease such activity against his fellow townspeople. Political preferment was promised if he would yield; a political grave if he persisted. Threatening letters came, warning him of plots to murder, to disfigure, and to blackguard. Word came from Tennessee that detectives were investigating every act of his life. Mr. Folk told the politicians that he was not seeking political favors, and not looking forward to another office; the others he defied. Meantime he probed the deeper into the municipal sore. With his first successes for prestige and aided by the panic among the boodlers, he soon had them suspicious of one another, exchanging charges of betrayal, and ready to "squeal" or run at the slightest sign of danger. One member of the House of Delegates became so frightened while under the inquisitorial cross-fire that he was seized with a nervous chill; his false teeth fell to the floor, and the rattle so increased his alarm that he rushed from the room without stopping to pick up his teeth, and boarded the next train.

It was not long before Mr. Folk had dug up the intimate history of ten years of corruption, especially of the business of the North and South and the Central Traction franchise grants, the last-named being even more iniquitous than the Suburban.

Early in 1898 a "promoter" rented a bridal suite at the Planters' Hotel, and having stocked the rooms with wines, liquors, and cigars until they resembled a candidate's headquarters during a convention, sought introduction to members of the Assembly and to such political bosses as had influence with the city fathers. Two weeks after his arrival the Central Traction bill was introduced "by request" in the council. The measure was a blanket franchise, granting rights of way which had not been given to old-established companies, and permitting, the beneficiaries to parallel any track in the city. It passed both houses despite the protests of every newspaper in the city, save one, and was vetoed by the mayor. The cost to the promoter was $145,000.

Preparations were made to pass the bill over the executive's veto. The bridal suite was restocked, larger sums of money were placed on deposit in the banks, and the services of three legislative agents were engaged. Evidence now in the possession of the St. Louis courts tells in detail the disposition of $250,000 of bribe money. Sworn statements prove that $75,000 was spent in the House of Delegates. The remainder of the $250,000 was distributed in the Council, whose members, though few in number, appraised their honor at a higher figure on account of their higher positions in the business and social world. Finally, but one vote was needed to complete the necessary two-thirds in the upper chamber. To secure this a councilman of reputed integrity was paid $50,000 in consideration that he vote aye when the ordinance should come up for final passage. But the promoter did not dare risk all upon the vote of one man, and he made this novel proposition to another honored member, who accepted it:

"You will vote on roll call after Mr.—. I will place $45,000 in the hands of your son, which amount will become yours, if you have to vote for the measure because of Mr.—'s not keeping his promise. But if he stands out for it you can vote against it, and the money shall revert to me."

On the evening when the bill was read for final passage the City Hall was crowded with ward heelers and lesser politicians. The men had been engaged by the promoter, at five and ten dollars a head, to cheer on the boodling Assemblymen. The bill passed the House with a rush, and all crowded into the Council Chamber. While the roll was being called the silence was profound, for all knew that some men in the Chamber whose reputations had been free from blemish were under promise and pay to part with honor that night. When the clerk was two-thirds down the list those who kept count knew that but one vote was needed. One more name was called. The man addressed turned red, then white, and after fully a minute's hesitation he whispered "aye"! The silence was so death-like that his vote was heard throughout the room, and those near enough heard also the sigh of relief that escaped from the member who could now vote "no" and save his reputation.

The Central Franchise bill was a law, passed over the mayor's veto. The promoter had expended nearly $300,000 in securing the legislation, but within a week he sold his rights of way to "Eastern capitalists" for $1,250,000. The United Railways Company was formed, and without owning an inch of steel rail, or a plank in a car, was able to compel every street railroad in St. Louis, with the exception of the Suburban, to part with stock and right of way and agree to a merger. Out of this grew the St. Louis Transit Company of today.

Several incidents followed this legislative session. After the Assembly had adjourned, a promoter entertained the $50,000 councilman at a downtown restaurant. During the supper the host remarked to his guest, "I wish you would lend me that $50,000 until tomorrow. There are some of the boys outside whom I haven't paid." The money changed hands. The next day, having waited in vain for the promoter, Mr. Councilman armed himself with a revolver and began a search of the hotels. The hunt in St. Louis proved fruitless, but the irate legislator kept on the trail until he came face to face with the lobbyist in the corridor of the Waldorf-Astoria. The New Yorker, seeing the danger, seized the St. Louisan by the arm and said soothingly, "There, there, don't take on so. I was called away suddenly. Come to supper with me; I will give you the money."

The invitation was accepted, and an hour later champagne was flowing. When the man from the West had become sufficiently maudlin the promoter passed over to him a letter, which he had dictated to a typewriter while away from the table for a few minutes. The statement denied all knowledge of bribery.

"You sign that and I will pay you $5,000. Refuse and you don't get a cent," said the promoter. The St. Louisan returned home carrying the $5,000, and that was all.

Meanwhile the promoter had not fared so well with other spoilsmen. By the terms of the ante-legislation agreement referred to above, the son of a councilman was pledged to return $45,000 if his father was saved the necessity of voting for the bill. The next day the New Yorker sought out this young man and asked for the money.

"I am not going to give it to you," was the cool rejoinder. "My mamma says that it is bribe money and that it would be wrong to give it to either you or father, so I shall keep it myself." And he did. When summoned before the grand jury this young man appealed to one of the circuit judges to relieve him from answering questions. "I am afraid I might commit perjury," he said. The jurist, concealing a smile behind a pocket handkerchief, replied, "Tell the truth and there will be no risk."

"It would be all right," said the son," if Mr. Folk would tell me what the other fellows have testified to. Please have him do that."

Two indictments were found as the result of this Central Traction bill, and bench warrants were served on Robert M. Snyder and George J. Kiobusch. The state charges the former with being one of the promoters of the bill, the definite allegation being bribery. Mr. Kiobusch, who is president of the American Car Wheel Company, is charged with perjury.

The first case tried was that of Emil Meysenburg, the millionaire who compelled the Suburban people to purchase his worthless stock. He was defended by three attorneys of high repute in criminal jurisprudence, but the young circuit attorney proved equal to the emergency, and a conviction was secured. Three years in the penitentiary was the sentence. Charles Kratz, the congressional candidate, forfeited $40,000 by flight, and John K. Murrell also disappeared. Mr. Folk traced Kratz to Mexico, caused his arrest in Guadalajara, negotiated with the authorities for his surrender, and when this failed arranged for his return home to confess, as he did three weeks ago, and so brought about the indictment, on September 8, of eighteen members of the municipal legislature. The second case was that of Julius Lehmann. Two years at hard labor was the sentence, and the man who had led the jokers in the grand jury anteroom would have fallen when he heard it, had not a friend been standing near.

Besides the convictions of these and other men of good standing in the community, and the flight of many more, partnerships were dissolved, companies had to be reorganized to rid themselves of men disgraced and save their credit, business houses were closed because their proprietors were absent, clubs expelled prominent members, and families were broken up. Mr. Folk, deterred as little by success as by failure, moved right on; he was not elated; he was not sorrowful. The man proceeded with his work quickly, surely, smiling, but without fear or pity. The terror spread, and the rout was complete.

When another grand jury was sworn and proceeded to take testimony there were scores of men who threw up their hands and crying "Mea culpa!" begged to be permitted to tell all they knew and not be prosecuted. The inquiry broadened. The son of a former mayor was indicted for misconduct in office while serving as his father's private secretary, and the grand jury recommended that the ex-mayor be sued in the civil courts, to recover interests on public money which he had placed in his own pocket. A true bill fell on a former city register, and more assemblymen were arrested, charged with making illegal contracts with the city. At last the ax struck upon the trunk of the greatest oak of the forest. Col. Edward R. Butler, the man who has controlled elections in St. Louis for many years, the multi-millionaire who has risen from bellows' boy in a blacksmith's shop to be the maker and guide of the governors of Missouri, one of the men who helped nominate and elect Folk—he also was indicted on two counts charging attempted bribery. That Butler has controlled legislation in St. Louis has long been known. Few believe that he ever offered a bribe. It was generally understood that he owned Assemblymen before they ever took the oath of office, but that he did not have to pay for votes. And yet open bribery is the allegation. Two members of the Board of Health stand ready to swear that he offered them $2,500 for their approval of a garbage contract.

Pitiful? Yes, but typical. Other cities are today in the same condition as St. Louis before Mr. Folk was invited in to see its rottenness. Chicago is cleaning itself up just now, so is Minneapolis, and Pittsburgh recently had a bribery scandal; New York is contented with a respectable outside, Boston is at peace, Cincinnati and St. Paul are satisfied, while Philadelphia is happy in the worst government in the world. As for the small towns and the villages, many of these are as busy as bees at the loot.

St. Louis, indeed, in its disgrace, has a great advantage. It was exposed late; it has not been reformed and caught again and again, until its citizens are reconciled to corruption. But, best of all, the man who has turned St. Louis inside up, turned it, as it were, upside down, too. In all cities, the better classes—the business men—are the sources of corruption; but they are so rarely pursued and caught that we do not fully realize whence the trouble comes. And so most cities blame the politicians and the ignorant and vicious poor. Mr. Folk has shown St. Louis that its bankers, brokers, corporation officers, its business men are the sources of evil, so that from the start it will know the municipal problem in its true light. With a tradition for public spirit, it may drop Butler and its runaway bankers, brokers, and brewers, and pushing aside the scruples of the hundreds of men down in blue book, and red book, and church register, who are lying hidden behind the statutes of limitations, the city may restore good government. Otherwise the exposures by Mr. Folk will result only in the perfection of the corrupt system. For the corrupt can learn a lesson when the good citizens cannot. The regime in New York taught Tammany to organize its boodle business; the police exposure taught it to improve its method of collecting blackmail. And both now are almost perfect and safe. The rascals of St. Louis will learn in like manner; they will concentrate the control of their bribery system, excluding from the profit-sharing the great mass of weak rascals, and carrying on the business as a business in the interest of a trustworthy few. District Attorney Jerome cannot catch the Tammany men, and Circuit Attorney Folk will not be able another time to break the St. Louis ring. This is St. Louis' one great chance.

But, for the rest of us, it does not matter about St. Louis any more than it matters about Colonel Butler et al. The point is, that what went on in St. Louis in going on in most of our cities, towns, and villages. The problem of municipal government in America has not been solved. The people may be tired of it, but they cannot give it up—not yet.

McClure's Magazine
December, 1902

The American Man on Horseback

The Bronco-Busting Contest at Denver for the Championship of the World

"THAD SOWDER can't ride; never could. He's worked for me, and I know. He is a gentleman, and I was glad to see him get the belt last year, but there are boys here this year he can't pack a saddle for — not on a bucker."

So said a judge, one of the five who were to decide, again, the world's championship of rough riding, contested for at Denver in the fall of every year. A group of other ranchers stood about, with foremen, cowboys, and strangers, listening, in the lobby of the Brown Palace Hotel, at Denver, and it did not seem to them strange that a judge should have and express a personal opinion on the event before it happened; on the contrary, they seemed, most of them, to agree.

"Well," said a cow puncher, "he done and he won, and I hear he's learned a lot about ridin' 'em since he's been with the show."

"Huh! That ain't ridin'," another puncher said, "hangin' on to leather on the side of a horse. There's a certain yaller dog come down from Idaho, a mean cuss, but a horseman—oh, but he can ride! I've seen him take off his saddle with the horse a-jumpin'—"

"Tom Minor, you mean," said the judge. "Let me tell you right here, that man's a rider. He is a boaster. I've heard that he told up in Idaho what he was going to do with the money he won down here. He may boast, but I bet we give him the belt."

"He says pretty plain how he can ride," said another rancher. "That isn't usual; but the curious part of it is, he can do it. Says he will tie Sowder up in his blankets and put him to bed."

The anger that flashed around the group looked ominous. All were silent for a moment. Then the rancher added:

"And I'll bet he will."

"Oh, Sowder — yes. But how about Harry Brennen and Lee Van Houten, and that boy Thompson, over there on the step?"

"That kid!" exclaimed the cow puncher.

"Who is he? Why, he's bleached with town. He ain't off the range."

"No; but you watch the kid ride to win."

"Won't last the first day," said the cow puncher. "Funning aside, Brennen's the man. He rides with both feet free, a-scratchin', and his hand in the air, givin' 'em the quirt every time they go up."

Most of the ranchers, from whom the judges were drawn, favored Van Honten, the only rancher to ride; the rest backed Harry Brennen or Minor. And they were riding their opinions hard when Sowder came in, a tall, slender young man, clear eyed, healthy skinned, and shy to the point of mental mystification. He was warmly greeted. Everybody liked the man. But Sowder had something on his mind, and he drew aside Mr. John M. Kuykendall, the director in charge of the busting. Sowder put his question slow and direct. He had heard things.

"Will the Judge turn me?" he said.

"Go on and say your say," said Mr. Kuykendall, his genial face as hard as stone.

Sowder was as hard. "You know what they are saying. You know what the Judge says himself. And I have had a round-up with him since last year."

"Sowder," said Kuykendall, "the Judge is a gentleman."

They studied each other a moment, till Sowder's face cleared.

"All you got to do is ride," said Mr. Kuykendall.

"I'll ride," Sowder said.

The worst horses and the best riders of all the West — the big West — are brought together for the Mountain and Plain Festival, and they wrangle there for three or four days till the judges, a committee of five knowing ranchers, can pick the best horseman and the worst horse. The rider is proclaimed the champion of the world; and that he is without a doubt, though these Westerners will never be satisfied till their world-challenge is accepted, and the horsemen and the horses of Italy, Australia, and Russia have been pitted against their own. There is faith in the result. There is fretting only for the proof and the sight thereof; and this is so because, unconscious, but plain, the Western man has a sense of manhood that is secure — no fear, no weakness, no pretentiousness. Each man knows the other, and the other knows he is known, so takes himself the place that is his, by force, if need be; but he will get and take no more than his own. His fellows won't let him. His world is only fair; rough to brutality, kind to sentimentality, it settles finally at justice. It is seeing this that warms the soul at Denver.

  The festival is rich in excitement and the picturesque. The arena is on a plain beside one of those flat-bottomed creeks that have either no water, or so much that the stream spreads over its course like a herd of cattle over a trail. Behind are the yellow prairies, in front the Rockies, blue and white, near at eighty miles distance. All this is filled with sunshine which beats through your clothes into your heart, sunning without heating it. Perhaps this explains why the Westerner is so full of fun; why cowboys will rope and ride from four o'clock in the morning till dark, do their chores, eat dinner, then, instead of rolling up to sleep, play for an hour, roping and riding one another, in wild imitation of the day's work; why nearly every city or town or county from Missouri to the Pacific has its festival of flowers or fruit, Indians or maskers; why, when the season of range riding is over, the rancher and his cow punchers ride off to Cheyenne or Denver and ride. Some day the West will be the gayest part of this land. Gay and clean. It is character that counts every time.

  When, the day before the busting, the ninety head of horses were collected in the corrals back of the arena, Mr. Kuykendall walked in among them with some cowboys and ranchers to "cut out" the "good ones." Now the "good ones" are "bad ones," and very few were known to the choosers; but they ran them, one or two at a time, pitching and kicking, into a small pen to "look 'em over." The good, that is to say, the bad, were turned into a corral on the right, the "unknown" and the "saddle horses" (a comparative term) to the left. Mr. Kuykendall, whip in hand, stood in the pen, dodging some, climbing the fence for others, turning back those he dared face, deciding by the look of the animal or the reputation of its shipper, whether it was a "fighter" or "gentle."

"Who knows that circle-dot mare?" he cried, pointing to a small goat-like bay that was trying to crawl under the fence.

"Ain't that the little mare that threw the kid at Cheyenne?" asked a rancher.

"No; that was a white-stockinged, lazy D horse. This is one of the four that Perry Williams sent down."

"That's right," said Kuykendall. "Open the gate and put her in the bad bunch. Perry said all his would deliver the goods."

"If Perry Williams said she'd buck," a cowboy drawled, "I wouldn't want to buy her for my wife to ride Sundays."

"Now the circle P. Oh, that's 'Deadeasy,'" said Kuykendall. "To the right."

"What's the story?" asked the cowboy on the fence.

The man at the gate opened, and fell back to wave the horse to the right, but the animal rose at him, and he ran. Pitched him back scrambling on the ground.

"You from Wall Street?" asked a rancher, and they all jumped down as the horse leaped into a wire fence. Sprung back by the fence, Deadeasy leaped into the boxes on one of the spectators' stands, and ran through the rails as if they were matches.

"What's the price of them seats?" some one inquired, as all the men scattered out into the arena to head off Deadeasy, who quit the boxes like a winged beast, and broke for the gate, which was swinging shut. He went through it, and out where he belonged — in the bad bunch. Back on the fence, the cow puncher repeated his question, "How about Deadeasy?"

"More horses," called Kuykendall. A horse came in on his hindlegs, pawing at the director, who met him with a crack of the whip which turned him.

"I know this one. To the left. Samuels sent him. Said he'd buck. But he's just a fighter." Out the horse ran, the man at the gate dodging.

"What's that you got at the gate?" a rancher asked, nodding contemptuously at a man who was afraid of a horse shipped by Samuels.

"Rum soaked," said Kuykendall. " 'Nother horse," he called, and the man who admitted a big roan ran for the fence, and the director dodged, as his "rum soaked" helper at the outer gate had. But there was no similar comment. They recognized another horse from another kind of a man.

"That's one John Coble sent down off his ranch. A circle 2, isn't he? Yes; let him out to the right. Coble says—"

The horse turned to hit at the gate-keeper, but the man was up on the fence.

"The story," said Kuykendall, "is that a tenderfoot got on the horse; the horse loped off nice and gentle a few. 'Oh, he's dead easy,' said the tenderfoot. Then — 'Nother horse," Mr. Kuykendall called, and he added, "So they called him Deadeasy, that horse, and we'll keep him for the finish."

A big, clumsy looking black horse came in, and everybody cheered. The horse had all the marks of a plug, and he trotted in like a work horse. "Steamboat" they called him, in the tone of a man speaking the name of some delicious food.

"To the right," said Mr. Kuykendall. "He is to be kept for Sowder on the last day."

And it was explained that this horse was a gentle horse to saddle, let his man on, then bucked, twisting, "sun fishing," and pounding the earth, or jumping round and round. He had won the prize for the best, i.e., the worst, horse on Frontier Day at Cheyenne.

"Ought to let Minor from Idaho have him," said a cowboy. "We want sure to find out about him."

"But the champion ought to have the best horse; he only rides once, and ought to have every chance to win. Besides, you want to know about him too, don't you? You don't think he will get it, do you?"

Then the riders were discussed all over again, while the horses were sorted or "worked" till Mr. Kuykendall feared he would tire them out with the "milling" and "ginning" that resulted from the efforts to ride into the bunch and cut out individual horses. They had the very worst out, and the men sat on the fence and discussed them, as they had the riders, with a brutal sentiment warmest for the hardest fighter, man or beast. To an outsider, the one striking point about these bad horses was that they were of all colors, sizes, and shapes. There is no type of the bucker, and no breed predominates. Those collected at Denver were cayuses, mustangs, and crosses in all degrees with both standard and thoroughbred stock; and though they did not all buck, the seventy-odd that did, bucked each in his own way, so that, except for the hard pounding of the big horse and the snaky wriggle of the small horse, there was no picking them for excellence except by experience with the horse, or knowledge of the kind of man who recommended him for a "hard one."

The horses disposed of, Mr. Kuykendall rode down town to see the riders at their headquarters, where the sixty-seven entered were gathered. It was a bare room, and the men "sat on their spurs" or saddles, or stooped and kneeled silent, with their heads pointed in, for all the world like a lot of street arabs "shooting craps." They squatted thus all the while the director talked.

"Boys," he said, "I want you to be clear about what we expect of you. You are to ride with the hackamore and a clean saddle. No bridles, no bits, no bucking straps or rolls. And the man that is seen to pull leather or choke his horn is out of it. Also, I want you not to cut your horses up to make them buck. If they won't buck, we will give you another horse; but I don't want you to force them with the quirt or spur. Do what you want when they are up in the air, but when they're down—you understand. And remember, the hackamore, a clean saddle, no grabbing for leather, and no riding on your spurs."

That was all. There was no comment for half a minute; then a voice from the depths of the bunch said:

"Gotasaw?"

"A saw!" the speaker exclaimed. No. Why?"

"Want to saw off my pommel so's I can't find it."

The laugh that went up broke up the "powwow." The next morning they had a street parade of Indians and two hundred or more horsemen, not all cowboys, and very few on cow horses. Generally speaking, the men were mounted and placed by the committee, according to the degree of respect for their ability to stick to the saddle. At the end of the line, on a little old mare with a bell, and a colt, rode "Rick Thompson," the kid we were advised to watch. Everybody laughed as he went by, but the boy was serious to sadness. "I sure got to ride," he said at the grounds that afternoon, and the other boys laughed. "I've been working in town lately, but I've ridden the range." Another laugh. "I have, for two years." Now they roared.

"Two years!" they jeered; "and a palefaced city kid at that."

The bunch drew their numbers, then squatted again close up to the wire outside the arena, their backs to the crowd gathering in the stands, their eyes turned on the judges and ropers out in the center. "Thad" Sowder sat on his show horse apart, as he was told to do. Tom Minor leaned, also apart, against the fence, waving now and then to the stand, where his Idaho friends were seated. The other cowboys viewed them, as they did the horses, as the enemy; they had to "make good."

"Can't tell," said Harry Brennen to some one near him. "The best man goes up in the air sometimes, and I hear they've got some horses here."

Sowder wet his lips.

"I'll ride anything they got," said Minor, "and I'll drink out of a bottle while he is a-jumpin'."

The bunch became dead still. The band struck up a march. There was a sound of horses kicking in the pen, boards creaking, and out leaped a wild red horse on the end of a rope. He fought, and the ropers galloped up and caught him by the forefeet and threw him. The rider was called. He and some friends from the silent bunch ran out, put on the hackamore, kicked up the horse, and, holding him by the ears, saddled him. Another horse and another rider came out; then another couple. The first man was fighting to mount, and his horse threw himself. The second rider mounted first, but his horse did not buck, and the first rider, up at last, soon had his tired horse quiet and "done."

"All in," called the judges to the two disappointed riders. "Get off."

"Give 'em another horse," cried the crowd.

Other horses came, and other riders, all in rapid succession. Most of the animals fought from the pen to the "squeezer," and from the squeezer to the arena, where they fought the hardest. Some got away, and the ropers, the two "Clark boys," LeRoy Van Houten and Charlie Irwin, all horsemen famous in the West, had their hands full catching and holding them. It was a wild scene, with horses bucking across the arena among the loose horses, driving judges before them and stopping only at the fence. Two riders were thrown at the fence, the wire of which gave to the rush of the horse, and pitched him back scrambling on the ground. One man, Ed Thorpe, had his leg broken in this way. In the confusion, individual riders were lost except to the judges, until in a pause the name of R. R. Thompson was called, and the Kid ran out with his saddle on his back. The crowd fixed on him; the people and the judges saw how young he was.

"Who let that boy in here?" one of the committee asked. But the boy's horse stood for the saddle, and before any answer came Thompson was up, and he was riding. His horse went up in the air and reached ahead for space. The boy smiled. The horse landed with a squeal, "side bucked," "back bucked," then flashed ahead straightaway in long pitches.

"He's a rider," said a judge.

"A rider!" yelled the crowd.

"He sure can ride," said one of the cowboys; and they rose and cheered, while, hat off, Thompson rode through the air, jolted, but happy—so happy you could see his face shine.

"All in," said a roper, catching up his horse. "Say, you're all right, Kid. Get down. You're sure a rider."

The man who said that was a famous horseman. The Kid, already elated, looked up and drank in the praise. It made him drunk. He reeled in his saddle, flopped off, and staggered about. The band crashed into the cheers, and Kid Thompson, blind with the joy of it all, snatched off his hat and reeled off to the bunch.

"Did I make good?" he was muttering. "Did I make good?"

One of the older riders—one of the scoffers—called just then, got up, and, understanding Thompson's state of mind, handed his saddle to the Kid.

"Here," he said harshly, "help me saddle, will you, Thompson?"

That sobered the boy. It was another triumph to be so recognized, but the request was in the hard tone of the plains. Thompson caught himself and the saddle at the same time, and went to work as if he had forgotten himself and the crowd and the band—everything but the fighting horse his friend was to ride. And when the day was done, and the judges announced that out of the seventeen who had been tested, but two had survived —Thompson and one other—Thompson took it pretty well. He did not seem to hear that he was one of the ten to ride for the privilege of meeting the champion.

The rejected men were not all thrown; they "pulled leather," or "rode on a cinch," or "did stunts" instead of "straight riding." Not five men in all the four days were "thrown," and two of these fell at the fence. The horsemanship was superb, but the riders were not the greatest spectacle; the display of manhood was greater. It was exhilarating to see these outspoken Western judges swallow their own words to pass Thompson, just as it was worthwhile to see them rejoice openly when their friend, the rancher, Le Roy Van Houten, on the second day, threw, saddled, and mounted a fighting black, and rode off with him fighting still; and also it was good to hear the cowboys cheer the rancher, giving that approval, "He's a rider," which the Westerners keep back until it is earned. Van Houten was put into the ten, and some of the judges and many of the cowboys said he would ride it off with Sowder. Then Stone, a "bad man" with a good smile, leaped upon a mad horse and, like a wolf, grinning and waving, rode rejoicing till the animal was "broke." Luther Dennison, a gentle, bashful fellow in ordinary clothes and his shirt sleeves, unknown to judges and cowboys alike (he had been range riding only four years), rode attentively, without a flourish, but perfectly, a horse that twisted, pitched, then ran bucking and shaking clear across the arena. Dennison let him buck, giving him a dangling rein while he swung the quirt at each jump. In his fury the horse pitched forward so hard that he went over on his head, poised there a moment, then turned a complete somersault. When he came up out of the tangle, Dennison was in the saddle. He took a place at once. So did Jack McGuire, who said nothing and did nothing but ride a hard bucker to a finish. But the popular triumph of the second day was Harry Brennen, a sunny, blond young man, who was forever playing pranks. He is the reckless type of Western rider. When he was called he got a horse that rose straight into the air, squealed, landed with a grunt, rose again, going ahead, pounding with all his weight, and bucking from side to side. Brennen kicked away his stirrups, gave his horse his head, and with legs swinging, arms in air, this natural horseman crossed the arena, hit the fence, went down with his horse, came up with him, and rode back. It was a sight, and you heard then that Brennen was the man to meet Sowder, who, ever watchful, serious, silent, thought so, too.

Minor was called. "And give him a horse," said the judges.

"Now we'll see," the cowboys whispered. They brought out a cat-like little beast, which three men held blindfolded for the saddling. "Turn him loose," said Minor, settling into place, and the horse sprang to his feet, darted here, there; side-buck, crow hop, rear, and jolt, he went across the arena. Minor was drinking from a bottle of soda water. When it was empty, he tossed away the bottle and bowed. The horse bucked on, and the rider slipped behind the saddle. But it wasn't the "stunts" that held everybody spellbound; it was the consummate grace of the man and his complete identity with the horse.

"He's a rider," said the cowboys grimly.

"He's the man," said the judge, bitterly, yet with involuntary admiration. "Sowder can never equal that; none of them can."

Others rode, and ten were selected for the finals, but it was plain already that, partly because it was hateful to them, these judges believed they had in Minor the champion horseman of the world. The bottle of soda water, and the other tricks, pricked like spurs. "Let some friend tell him to quit his monkey business," they said, and someone conveyed the warning. The feeling was intense.

For relief the riders and ropers started up some cowboy fun. The biggest and strongest got down on their hands and knees, and boys and lighter men tried to ride them. The imitation bucking broke the spell, and Minor was accepted as inevitable—as inevitable as Western justice.

On the third day the ten were cut to five. "Rick" Thompson fell out among the first. He had a good bucker, and he rode him with ease, but the boy could not help showing just a little. He twisted in his saddle, threw his right hand around back, down to the horse's left flank; the animal swerved from the touch, and out went "the Kid"; he tried to get back without touching the leather, but he couldn't—his hand clutched the horn, and the judges smiled. "Another time," they said. And they turned to see their favorite, Van Houten, ride a running bucker. He might beat Minor. The man sat his horse beautifully, crashed with him into the fence, and turned, unmoved, to ride on. The crowd, though its sympathy was with the cowboys, stood up to cheer the rancher, and all voices were for one to save the day from Minor the boaster.

"But he's riding on his spurs," said a judge.

"No—yes," said another.

"I don't believe it," said a third, as the rider dismounted. He hunched his hack, bucked high, and landed hard.

"Give him another horse and watch him."

Now, many good riders hold on with the spurs caught in the cinch, and usually it is called fair riding, but it was counted against men at Denver, where the contest soon came down to a fine point, and when Van Houten, all unconscious, got on his new horse, he stuck in the rowels and the judges, his friends, threw him out without debate. He said not a word; so far as I could learn, he never asked why. When some of the cowboys were sulking under their disappointment, the rancher, game to the end, said, "I'll ride again next year."

The five men who were in the final list were: Thomas F. Minor, of Shoshone, Idaho; B. F. Stone, of Rosier, Wyoming; Harry Brennen, of Sheridan, Wyoming; Jack McGuire, of Schley, Colorado; Luther Dennison, of Caddoa, Colorado. It was announced that these men should ride against the champion; but the rules provide that the judges shall first pick one man from the five, then calling for the champion, bid these two ride it out. They believed in their hearts, these judges, that Minor was the best rider, not only of the five, but of the world; and some of them said, as they all seemed to think, that Sowder couldn't ride. It was a "bitter pill," as one of them said, but it was plain they were prepared to swallow it.

"Say, Minor says he'll ride any horse you got and take the saddle off while he's bucking." This message was like a challenge, and an offer to bet five hundred dollars went back. "Mark the spot where I am to leave the saddle," was the reply; but there was no acceptance of the wager.

"Let Sowder ride," the judges ordered, "and give him a horse that will kill him if he doesn't."

"It's Minor," they said to their friends. "He rides with Sowder, and that means that he wins." But this was not generally known. The four other cowboys thought they were all to compete for the first place, and among themselves they decided that Brennen was the best man. They collected in a bunch, squatted, and three of them said so. Brennen objected, and pointed to Stone the Wolf. "I can ride any horse Brennen can," said the Wolf, "but I can't ride him the way Brennen can."

"Bring out Steamboat," called Mr. Kuykendall. "Sowder is to ride him."

The four cowboys looked up as Sowder rode in on his show horse. The horse pranced to the music, but the rider was modest and flushed. There was no swagger about him; only earnest preoccupation.

"Maybe he can ride," they said. "If he can, let him win. He's the best man of the two, anyway."

Brennen got up, went over to Sowder, and when the champion dismounted and had his saddle off, ready for the bucker, Brennen said to him:

"Sowder, I hear you drew Steamboat. I saw him back at Cheyenne, and he can sure buck. But I tell you this, he bucks high and he lands hard, but he goes mostly ahead. When he turns, he turns mostly to the left. Anyhow, I never saw him turn no other way."

"I'll remember," said Sowder, and as Brennen slouched off to the bunch, the champion looked after him with as much gratitude in his face as a man can express in a look.

Steamboat trotted in, took the saddle quietly, and when ready, Sowder turned for the word. The judges waved to mount, and the clean limbed fellow rose slowly, cautiously, into the saddle, his eyes on the horse's head. Steamboat hesitated a moment, then went right up into the air; he hunched his back, bucked high, and landed hard. Then he pitched, "mostly ahead." The rider sat easily, leaning a little to the left, and when the big black "turned, he turned to the left," Sowder going with him. It was as if every move of the horse were anticipated by the man. There had been nothing like this. The crowd arose to cheer as the horse straightened out for more pitching, and the judges yelled like cowboys when, the horse wheeling again, with high bucks to the left, found the rider before him.

The cowboys joined the yelling.

"He can ride; he can ride; he's a rider. Hi, yi!"

There was no mistaking the joy of this faith; it was universal.

"Minor's beaten!" they shouted; but Minor was to have every chance. They brought him horses, eight in a string, and he rode them; but only two bucked.

"He's a horseman, and can prevent his horses from bucking," they said in the arena.

"These are dead ones," Minor said each time as he rode past. "Got any horses that can buck?"

"Bring out that A. E. horse, Deadeasy," was the reply; and the Deadeasy horse was brought.

He bucked. Even Minor admitted that he was not an "easy horse," and as the snaky little beast crept along, wiggling and twisting, he showed daylight under his rider three times.

"But he rode him," the judges said, and the decision, thus predisposed, went over to another day.

"Steamboat for Minor, Deadeasy for Sowder," was the order then, and Minor rode first. "He cinched him in two, and held up his head," said the judge. "The man's a horseman. He's so clever they can't buck hard with him. I guess he's got it all right."

But he hadn't it yet. Sowder mounted A. E. with his characteristic care and watchfulness. Once up, he gave the horse his head, and the little bay flew, zig-zag, across the arena. The rider did not move. He kept just a point ahead of his horse. There was absolute silence, for with that animal turning the unexpected way every other second, no one could see the end. Besides, the situation was not spectacular— only very nervous and intense. Points or an accident would decide. The horse was headed for it, with his head down as if he did not see it. But his head went up suddenly, ten feet away, and from full speed he stopped short, throwing himself about, end to end. Sowder went up in the air. "Oh!" cried the crowd, rising to see. Sowder came down off his balance, and he bent to save himself, his right hand reaching down.

"Pulled leather!" someone shouted. But he didn't. His free hand went down the side of the horse's neck and caught the hackamore rope. That righted him. The discussion ran high, both on the stands and in the arena, and the judges talked long. When they decided, at last, their secretary walked over to Sowder.

"Give me the belt," he said.

Sowder unbuckled it, staring at the man.

"Who won it?" he asked quietly.

"M. T. Sowder," said the secretary, and he buckled it on again.

"Sowder! Sowder! Sowder!" The cry went bucking into the air like a bronco, and the cowboys caught up the winner.

Then they gave Minor a boost, but Minor was sullen. He sought out Sowder. "Sowder," he said, "you're no rider; not with me. I challenge you to ride me again."

Sowder looked down, then up, flushed. "Minor," he said very slowly, very steadily, "if you'd a won, I'd a said you were the champion of the world. But you didn't. I did. And since you're talking this way, I'll say right now that there's two men better than you."

"You and who?" "Frank Stone and Harry Brennen."

"And you?"

"I'll meet you here again next year."

McClure's Magazine
January, 1903

The Shame of Minneapolis

The Rescue and Redemption of a City That Was Sold Out

Whenever anything extraordinary is done in American municipal politics, whether for good or for evil, you can trace it almost invariably to one man. The people do not do it. Neither do the "gangs," "combines," or political parties. These are but instruments by which bosses (not leaders; we Americans are not led, but driven) rule the people, and commonly sell them out. But there are at least two forms of the autocracy which has supplanted the democracy here as it has everywhere democracy has been tried. One is that of the organized majority by which, as with the Republican machine in Philadelphia, the boss has normal control of more than half the voters. The other is that of the adroitly managed minority. The "good people" are herded into parties and stupefied with convictions and a name, Republican or Democrat, while the "bad people" are so organized or interested by the boss that he can wield their votes to enforce terms with party managers and decide elections. St. Louis is a conspicuous example of this form. Minneapolis is another. Colonel Ed Butler is the unscrupulous opportunist who handled the non-partisan minority which turned St. Louis into a "boodle town." In Minneapolis "Doc" Ames was the man.

Minneapolis is a New England town on the upper Mississippi. The metropolis of the Northwest, it is the metropolis also of Norway and Sweden in America. Indeed, it is the second largest Scandinavian city in the world. But Yankees, straight from Down East, settled the town, and their New England spirit predominates. They had Bayard Taylor lecture there in the early days of the settlement; they made it the seat of the University of Minnesota. Yet even now, when the town has grown to a population of more than 200,000, you feel that there is something Western about it too—a Yankee with a round Puritan head, an open prairie heart, and a great, big Scandinavian body. The "Roundhead" takes the "Squarehead" out into the woods, and they cut lumber by forests, or they go out on the prairies and raise wheat and mill it into fleet-cargoes of flour. They work hard, they make money, they are sober, satisfied, busy with their own affairs. There isn't much time for public business. Taken together, Miles, Hans, and Ole are very American. Miles insists upon strict laws, Ole and Hans want one or two Scandinavians on their ticket. These things granted, they go off on raft or reaper, leaving whoso will to enforce the laws and run the city.

  The people who were left to govern the city hated above all things strict laws. They were the loafers, saloon keepers, gamblers, criminals, and the thriftless poor of all nationalities. Resenting the sobriety of a staid, industrious community, and having no Irish to boss them, they delighted to follow the jovial pioneer doctor, Albert Alonzo Ames. He was the "good fellow"—a genial, generous reprobate. Devery, Tweed, and many more have exposed in vain this amiable type. "Doc" Ames, tall, straight, and cheerful, attracted men, and they gave him votes for his smiles. He stood for license. There was nothing of the Puritan about him. His father, the sturdy old pioneer, Dr. Alfred Elisha Ames, had a strong strain of it in him, but he moved on with his family of six sons from Garden Prairie, Ill., to Fort Snelling reservation, in 1851, before Minneapolis was founded, and young Albert Alonzo, who then was ten years old, grew up free, easy, and tolerant. He was sent to school, then to college in Chicago, and he returned home a doctor of medicine before he was twenty-one. As the town waxed soberer and richer, "Doc" grew gayer and more and more generous. Skillful as a surgeon, devoted as a physician, and as a man kindly, he increased his practice till he was the best-loved man in the community. He was especially good to the poor. Anybody could summon "Doc" Ames at any hour to any distance. He went, and he gave not only his professional service, but sympathy, and often charity. "Richer men than you will pay your bill," he told the destitute. So there was a basis for his "good-fellowship." There always is; these good fellows are not frauds—not in the beginning.

  But there is another side to them sometimes. Ames was

sunshine not to the sick and destitute only. To the vicious and the depraved also he was a comfort. If a man was a hard drinker, the good doctor cheered him with another drink; if he had stolen something, the doctor helped to get him off. He was naturally vain; popularity developed his love of approbation. His loose life brought disapproval only from the good people, so gradually the doctor came to enjoy best the society of the barroom and the streets. This society, flattered in turn, worshiped the good doctor, and, active in politics always, put its physician into the arena.

Had he been wise or even shrewd, he might have made himself a real power. But he wasn't calculating, only light and frivolous, so he did not organize his forces and run men for office. He sought office himself from the start, and he got most of the small places he wanted by changing his party to seize the opportunity. His floating minority, added to the regular partisan vote, was sufficient ordinarily for his useless victories. As time went on he rose from smaller offices to be a Republican mayor, then twice at intervals to be a Democratic mayor. He was a candidate once for Congress; he stood for governor once on a sort of Populist-Democrat ticket. Ames could not get anything outside of his own town, however, and after his third term as mayor it was thought he was out of politics altogether. He was getting old, and he was getting worse.

Like many a "good fellow" with hosts of miscellaneous friends downtown to whom he was devoted, the good doctor neglected his own family. From neglect he went on openly to separation from his wife and a second establishment. The climax came not long before the election of 1900. His wife died. The family would not have the father at the funeral, but he appeared—not at the house, but in a carriage on the street. He sat across the way, with his feet up and a cigar in his mouth, till the funeral moved; then he circled around, crossing it and meeting it, and making altogether a scene which might well close any man's career.

It didn't end his. The people had just secured the passage of a new primary law to establish direct popular government. There were to be no more nominations by convention. The voters were to ballot for their party candidates. By a slip of some sort, the laws did not specify that Republicans only should vote for Republican candidates, and only Democrats for Democratic candidates. Any voter could vote at either primary. Ames, in disrepute with his own party, the Democratic, bade his followers vote for his nomination for mayor on the Republican ticket. They all voted; not all the Republicans did. He was nominated. Nomination is far from election, and you would say that the trick would not help him. But that was a presidential year, so the people of Minneapolis had to vote for Ames, the Republican candidate for mayor. Besides, Ames said he was going to reform; that he was getting old, and wanted to close his career with a good administration. The effective argument, however, was that, since McKinley had to be elected to save the country, Ames must be supported for mayor of Minneapolis. Why? The great American people cannot be trusted to scratch a ticket.

Well, Minneapolis got its old mayor back, and he was indeed "reformed." Up to this time Ames had not been very venal personally. He was a "spender," not a "grafter," and he was guilty of corruption chiefly by proxy; he took the honors and left the spoils to his followers. His administrations were no worse than the worst. Now, however, he set out upon a career of corruption which for deliberateness, invention, and avarice has never been equaled. It was as if he had made up his mind that he had been careless long enough, and meant to enrich his last years. He began promptly.

Immediately upon his election, before he took office (on January 7, 1901), he organized a cabinet and laid plans to turn the city over to outlaws who were to work under police direction for the profit of his administration. He chose for chief his brother, Colonel Fred W. Ames, who had recently returned under a cloud from service in the Philippines. But he was a weak vessel for chief of police, and the mayor picked for chief of detectives an abler man, who was to direct the more difficult operations. This was Norman W. King, a former gambler, who knew the criminals needed in the business ahead. King was to invite to Minneapolis thieves, confidence men, pickpockets and gamblers, and release some that were in the local jail. They were to be organized into groups, according to their profession, and detectives were assigned to assist and direct them. The head of the gambling syndicate was to have charge of the gambling, making the terms and collecting the "graft," just as King and a Captain Hill were to collect from the thieves. The collector for women of the town was to be Irwin A. Gardner, a medical student in the doctor's office, who was made a special policeman for the purpose. These men looked over the force, selected those men who could be trusted, charged them a price for their retention, and marked for dismissal 107 men out of 225, the 107 being the best policemen in the department from the point of view of the citizens who afterward reorganized the force. John Fitchette, better known as "Coffee John," a Virginian (who served on the Jefferson Davis jury), the keeper of a notorious coffee-house, was to be a captain of police, with no duties except to sell places on the police force.

And they did these things that they planned—all and more. The administration opened with the revolution on the police force. The thieves in the local jail were liberated, and it was made known to the underworld generally that "things were doing" in Minneapolis. The incoming swindlers reported to King or his staff for instructions, and went to work, turning the "swag" over to the detectives in charge. Gambling went on openly, and disorderly houses multiplied under the fostering care of Gardner, the medical student. But all this was not enough. Ames dared to break openly into the municipal system of vice protection.

There was such a thing. Minneapolis, strict in its laws, forbade vices which are inevitable, then regularly permitted them under certain conditions. Legal limits, called "patrol lines," were prescribed, within which saloons might be opened. These ran along the river front, out through part of the business section, with long arms reaching into the Scandinavian quarters, north and south. Gambling also was confined, but more narrowly. And there were limits, also arbitrary, but not always identical with those for gambling, within which the social evil was allowed. But the novel feature of this scheme was that disorderly houses were practically licensed by the city, the women appearing before the clerk of the Municipal Court each month to pay a "fine" of $100. Unable at first to get this "graft," Ames's man Gardner persuaded women to start houses, apartments, and, of all things, candy stores, which sold sweets to children and tobacco to the "lumberjacks" in front, while a nefarious traffic was carried on in the rear. But they paid Ames, not the city, and that was all this "reform" administration cared about.

The revenue from all these sources must have been large. It only whetted the avarice of the mayor and his Cabinet. They let gambling privileges without restriction as to location or "squareness"; the syndicate could cheat and rob as it would. Peddlers and pawnbrokers, formerly licensed by the city, bought permits now instead from the mayor's agent in this field. Some two hundred slot machines were installed in various parts of the town, with owner's agent and mayor's agent watching and collecting from them enough to pay the mayor $15,000 a year as his share. Auction frauds were instituted. Opium joints and unlicensed saloons, called "blind pigs," were protected. Gardner even had a police baseball team, for whose games tickets were sold to people who had to buy them. But the women were the easiest "graft." They were compelled to buy illustrated biographies of the city officials; they had to give presents of money, jewelry, and gold stars to police officers. But the money they still paid direct to the city in fines, some $35,000 a year, fretted the mayor, and at last he reached for it. He came out with a declaration, in his old character as friend of the oppressed, that $100 a month was too much for these women to pay. They should be required to pay the city fine only once in two months. This puzzled the town till it became generally known that Gardner collected the other month for the mayor. The final outrage in this department, however, was an order of the mayor for the periodic visits to disorderly houses, by the city's physicians, at from $5 to $20 per visit. The two physicians he appointed called when they willed, and more and more frequently, till toward the end the calls became a pure formality, with the collections as the one and only object.

In a general way all this business was known. It did not arouse the citizens, but it did attract criminals, and more and more thieves and swindlers came hurrying to Minneapolis. Some of them saw the police, and made terms. Some were seen by the police and invited to go to work. There was room for all. This astonishing fact that the government of a city asked criminals to rob the people is fully established. The police and the criminals confessed it separately. Their statements agree in detail. Detective Norbeck made the arrangements, and introduced the swindlers to Gardner, who, over King's head, took the money from them. Here is the story "Billy" Edwards, a "big mitt" man, told under oath of his reception in Minneapolis:

"I had been out to the Coast, and hadn't seen Norbeck for some time. After I returned I boarded a Minneapolis car one evening to go down to South Minneapolis to visit a friend. Norbeck and Detective DeLaittre were on the car. When Norbeck saw me he came up and shook hands, and said, 'Hullo, Billy, how goes it?' I said, 'Not very well.' Then he says, 'Things have changed since you went away. Me and Gardner are the whole thing now. Before you left they thought I didn't know anything, but I turned a few tricks, and now I'm It.' 'I'm glad of that, Chris,' I said. He says, 'I've got great things for you. I'm going to fix up a joint for you.' 'That's good,' I said, 'but I don't believe you can do it.' 'Oh, yes, I can,' he replied. 'I'm It now—Gardner and me.' 'Well, if you can do it,' says I, 'there's money in it.' 'How much can you pay?' he asked. 'Oh, $150 or $200 a week,' says I. 'That settles it,' he said; 'I'll take you down to see Gardner, and we'll fix it up.' Then he made an appointment to meet me the next night, and we went down to Gardner's house together."

There Gardner talked business in general, showed his drawer full of bills, and jokingly asked how Edwards would like to have them. Edwards says:

"I said, 'That looks pretty good to me,' and Gardner told us that he had 'collected' the money from the women he had on his staff, and that he was going to pay it over to the 'old man' when he got back from his hunting trip next morning. Afterward he told me that the mayor had been much pleased with our $500, and that he said everything was all right, and for us to go ahead."

"Link" Crossman, another confidence man who was with Edwards, said that Gardner demanded $1,000 at first, but compromised on $500 for the mayor, $50 for Gardner, and $50 for Norbeck. To the chief, Fred Ames, they gave tips now and then of $25 or $50. "The first week we ran," said Crossman, "I gave Fred $15. Norbeck took me down there. We shook hands, and I handed him an envelope with $15. He pulled out a list of steerers we had sent him, and said he wanted to go over them with me. He asked where the joint was located. At another time I slipped $25 into his hand as he was standing in the hallway of City Hall." But these smaller payments, after the first "opening, $500," are all down on the pages of the "big mitt" ledger, photographs of which illuminate this article. This notorious book, which was kept by Charlie Howard, one of the "big mitt" men, was much talked of at the subsequent trials, but was kept hidden to await the trial of the mayor himself.

    The "big mitt" game was swindling by means of a stacked hand at stud poker. "Steerers" and "boosters" met "suckers" on the street, at hotels, and railway stations, won their confidence, and led them to the "joint." Usually the "sucker" was called, by the amount of his loss, "the $102-man" or "the $35-man." Roman Meix alone had the distinction among all the Minneapolis victims of going by his own name. Having lost $775, he became known for his persistent complainings. But they all "kicked" some. To Detective Norbeck at the street door was assigned the duty of hearing their complaints, and "throwing a scare into them." "Oh, so you've been gambling," he would say. "Have you got a license? Well, then, you better get right out of this town." Sometimes he accompanied them to the station and saw them off. If they were not to be put off thus, he directed them to the chief of police. Fred Ames tried to wear them out by keeping them waiting in the anteroom. If they outlasted him, he saw them and frightened them with threats of all sorts of trouble for gambling without a license. Meix wanted to have payment on his check stopped. Ames, who had been a bank clerk, told him of his banking experience, and then had the effrontery to say that payment on such a check could not be stopped.

    Burglaries were common. How many the police planned may never be known. Charles F. Brackett and Fred Malone, police captains and detectives, were active, and one well-established crime of theirs is the robbery of the Pabst Brewing Company office. They persuaded two men, one an employee, to learn the combination of the safe, open and clean it out one night, while the two officers stood guard outside.

The excesses of the municipal administration became so notorious that some of the members of it remonstrated with the others, and certain county officers were genuinely alarmed. No restraint followed their warnings. Sheriff Megaarden, no Puritan himself, felt constrained to interfere, and he made some arrests of gamblers. The Ames people turned upon him in a fury; they accused him of making overcharges in his accounts with the county for fees, and, laying the evidence before Governor Van Sant, they had Megaarden removed from office. Ames offered bribes to two county commissioners to appoint Gardner sheriff, so as to be sure of no more trouble in that quarter. This move failed, but the lesson taught Megaarden served to clear the atmosphere, and the spoliation went on as recklessly as ever. It became impossible.

Even lawlessness must be regulated. Dr. Ames, never an organizer, attempted no control, and his followers began to quarrel among themselves. They deceived one another; they robbed the thieves; they robbed Ames himself. His brother became dissatisfied with his share of the spoils, and formed cabals with captains who plotted against the administration and set up disorderly houses, "panel games," and all sorts of "grafts" of their own.

The one man loyal to the mayor was Gardner; and Fred Ames, Captain King, and their pals plotted the fall of the favorite. Now anybody could get anything from the doctor, if he could have him alone. The Fred Ames clique chose a time when the mayor was at West Baden; they filled him with suspicion of Gardner and the fear of exposure, and induced him to let a creature named "Reddy" Cohen, instead of Gardner, do the collecting, and pay over all the moneys, not directly, but through Fred. Gardner made a touching appeal. "I have been honest. I have paid you all," he said to the mayor. "Fred and the rest will rob you." This was true, but it was of no avail.

Fred Ames was in charge at last, and he himself went about giving notice of the change. Three detectives were with him when he visited the women, and here is the women's story, in the words of one, as it was told again and again in court: "Colonel Ames came in with the detectives. He stepped into a side room and asked me if I had been paying Gardner. I told him I had, and he told me not to pay no more, but to come to his office later, and he would let me know what to do. I went to the City Hall in about three weeks, after Cohen had called and said he was 'the party.' I asked the chief if it was all right to pay Cohen, and he said it was."

The new arrangement did not work so smoothly as the old. Cohen was an oppressive collector, and Fred Ames, appealed to, was weak and lenient. He had no sure hold on the force. His captains, free of Gardner, were undermining the chief. They increased their private operations. Some of the detectives began to drink hard and neglect their work. Norbeck so worried the "big mitt" men by staying away from the joint, that they complained to Fred about him. The chief rebuked Norbeck, and he promised to "do better," but thereafter he was paid, not by the week, but by piece work—so much for each "trimmed sucker" that he ran out of town. Protected swindlers were arrested for operating in the street by "Coffee John's" new policemen, who took the places of the negligent detectives. Fred let the indignant prisoners go when they were brought before him, but the arrests were annoying, inconvenient, and disturbed business. The whole system became so demoralized that every man was for himself. There was not left even the traditional honor among thieves.

It was at this juncture, in April, 1902, that the grand jury for the summer term was drawn. An ordinary body of unselected citizens, it received no special instructions from the bench; the county prosecutor offered it only routine work to do. But there was a man among them who was a fighter—the foreman, Hovey C. Clarke. He was of an old New England family. Coming to Minneapolis when a young man, seventeen years before, he had fought for employment, fought with his employers for position, fought with his employees, the lumber jacks, for command, fought for his company against competitors; and he had won always, till now he had the habit of command, the impatient, imperious manner of the master, and the assurance of success which begets it. He did not want to be a grand juryman, he did not want to be a foreman; but since he was both, he wanted to accomplish something.

Why not rip up the Ames gang? Heads shook, hands went up; it was useless to try. The discouragement fired Clarke. That was just what he would do, he said, and he took stock of his jury. Two or three were men with backbone; that he knew, and he quickly had them with him. The rest were all sorts of men. Mr. Clarke won over each man to himself, and interested them all. Then he called for the county prosecutor. The prosecutor was a politician; he knew the Ames crowd; they were too powerful to attack.

"You are excused," said the foreman.

There was a scene; the prosecutor knew his rights. "Do you think, Mr. Clarke," he cried, "that you can run the grand jury and my office, too?"

"Yes," said Clarke, "I will run your office if I want to; and I want to. You're excused."

Mr. Clarke does not talk much about his doings that summer; he isn't the talking sort. But he does say that all he did was to apply simple business methods to his problem. In action, however, these turned out to be the most approved police methods. He hired a lot of local detectives who, he knew, would talk about what they were doing, and thus would be watched by the police. Having thus thrown a false scent, he hired some other detectives whom nobody knew about. This was expensive; so were many of the other things he did; but he was bound to win, so he paid the price, drawing freely on his own and his colleagues' pockets. (The total cost to the county for a long summer's work by this grand jury was $259.) With his detectives out, he himself went to the jail to get tips from the inside, from criminals who, being there, must have grievances. He made the acquaintance of the jailer, Captain Alexander, and Alexander was a friend of Sheriff Megaarden. Yes, he had some men there who were "sore" and might want to get even.

Now two of these were "big mitt" men who had worked for Gardner. One was "Billy" Edwards, the other "Cheerful Charlie" Howard. I heard too many explanations of their plight to choose any one; this general account will cover the ground: In the Ames melee, either by mistake, neglect, or for spite growing out of the network of conflicting interests and gangs, they were arrested and arraigned, not before Fred Ames, but before a judge, and held in bail too high for them to furnish. They had paid for an unexpired period of protection, yet could get neither protection nor bail. They were forgotten. "We got the double cross all right," they said, and they bled with their grievance; but squeal, no, sir!—that was "another deal. "

But Mr. Clarke had their story, and he was bound to force them to tell it under oath on the stand. If they did, Gardner and Norbeck would be indicted, tried, and probably convicted. In themselves, these men were of no great importance; but they were the key to the situation, and a way up to the mayor. It was worth trying. Mr. Clarke went into the jail with Messrs. Lester Elwood and Willard J. Hield, grand jurors on whom he relied most for delicate work. They stood by while the foreman talked. And the foreman's way of talking was to smile, swear, threaten, and cajole. "Billy" Edwards told me afterwards that he and Howard were finally persuaded to turn state's evidence, because they believed that Mr. Clarke was the kind of a man to keep his promises and fulfill his threats. "We," he said, meaning criminals generally, "are always stacking up against juries and lawyers who want us to holler. We don't, because we see they ain't wise, and won't get there. They're quitters; they can be pulled off. Clarke has a hard eye. I know men. It's my business to size 'em up, and I took him for a winner, and I played in with him against that whole big bunch of easy things that was running things on the burn." The grand jury was ready at the end of three weeks of hard work to find bills. A prosecutor was needed. The public prosecutor was being ignored, but his first assistant and friend, Al J. Smith, was taken in hand by Mr. Clarke. Smith hesitated; he knew better even than the foreman the power and resources of the Ames gang. But he came to believe in Mr. Clarke, just as Edwards had; he was sure the foreman would win; so he went over to his side, and, having once decided, he led the open fighting, and, alone in court, won cases against men who had the best lawyers in the state to defend them. His court record is extraordinary. Moreover, he took over the negotiations with criminals for evidence, Messrs. Clarke, Hield, Elwood, and the other jurors providing means and moral support. These were needed. Bribes were offered to Smith; he was threatened; he was called a fool. But so was Clarke, to whom $28,000 was offered to quit, and for whose slaughter a slugger was hired to come from Chicago. What startled the jury most, however, was the character of the citizens who were sent to them to dissuade them from their course. No reform I ever studied has failed to bring out this phenomenon of virtuous cowardice, the baseness of the decent citizen.

Nothing stopped this jury, however. They had courage. They indicted Gardner, Norbeck, Fred Ames, and many lesser persons. But the gang had courage, too, and raised a defense fund to fight Clarke. Mayor Ames was defiant. Once, when Mr. Clarke called at the City Hall, the mayor met and challenged him. The mayor's heelers were all about him, but Clarke faced him.

"Yes, Doc Ames, I'm after you," he said. "I've been in this town for seventeen years, and all that time you've been a moral leper. I hear you were rotten during the ten years before that. Now I'm going to put you where all contagious things are put—where you cannot contaminate anybody else."

The trial of Gardner came on. Efforts had been made to persuade him to surrender the mayor, but the young man was paid $15,000 "to stand pat," and he went to trial and conviction silent. Other trials followed fast—Norbeck's, Fred Ames's, Chief of Detectives King's. Witnesses who were out of the state were needed, and true testimony from women. There was no county money for extradition, so the grand jurors paid these costs also. They had Meix followed from Michigan down to Mexico and back to Idaho, where they got him, and he was presented in court one day at the trial of Norbeck, who had "steered" him out of town. Norbeck thought Meix was a thousand miles away, and had been bold before. At the sight of him in court he started to his feet, and that night ran away. The jury spent more money in his pursuit, and they caught him. He confessed, but his evidence was not accepted. He was sentenced to three years in state's prison. Men caved all around, but the women were firm, and the first trial of Fred Ames failed. To break the women's faith in the ring, Mayor Ames was indicted for offering the bribe to have Gardner made sheriff—a genuine, but not the best case against him. It brought the women down to the truth, and Fred Ames, retried, was convicted and sentenced to six and a half years in state's prison. King was tried for accessory to felony (helping in the theft of a diamond, which he afterward stole from the thieves), and sentenced to three and a half years in prison. And still the indictments came, with trials following fast. Al Smith resigned with the consent and thanks of the grand jury; his chief, who was to run for the same office again, wanted to try the rest of the cases, and he did very well.

All men were now on the side of law and order. The panic among the "grafters" was laughable, in spite of its hideous significance. Two heads of departments against whom nothing had been shown suddenly ran away, and thus suggested to the grand jury an inquiry which revealed another source of "graft," in the sale of supplies to public institutions and the diversion of great quantities of provisions to the private residences of the mayor and other officials. Mayor Ames, under indictment and heavy bonds for extortion, conspiracy, and bribe-offering, left the state on a night train; a gentleman who knew him by sight saw him sitting up at eleven o'clock in the smoking room of the sleeping-car, an unlighted cigar in his mouth, his face ashen and drawn, and at six o'clock the next morning he still was sitting there, his cigar still unlighted. He went to West Baden, a health resort in Indiana, a sick and broken man, aging years in a month. The city was without a mayor, the ring was without a leader; cliques ruled, and they pictured one another hanging about the grand-jury room begging leave to turn state's evidence. Tom Brown, the mayor's secretary, was in the mayor's chair; across the hall sat Fred Ames, the chief of police, balancing Brown's light weight. Both were busy forming cliques within the ring. Brown had on his side Coffee John and Police Captain Hill. Ames had Captain "Norm" King (though he had been convicted and had resigned), Captain Krumweide, and Ernest Wheelock, the chief's secretary. Alderman D. Percy Jones, the president of the council, an honorable man, should have taken the chair, but he was in the East; so this unstable equilibrium was all the city had by way of a government.

Then Fred Ames disappeared. The Tom Brown clique had full sway, and took over the police department. This was a shock to everybody, to none more than to the King clique, which joined in the search for Ames. An alderman, Fred M. Powers, who was to run for mayor on the Republican ticket, took charge of the mayor's office, but he was not sure of his authority or clear as to his policy. The grand jury was the real power behind him, and the foreman was telegraphing for Alderman Jones. Meanwhile the cliques were making appeals to Mayor Ames, in West Baden, and each side that saw him received authority to do its will. The Coffee John clique, denied admission to the grand-jury room, turned to Alderman Powers, and were beginning to feel secure, when they heard that Fred Ames was coming back. They rushed around, and obtained an assurance from the exiled mayor that Fred was returning only to resign. Fred—now under conviction—returned, but he did not resign; supported by his friends, he took charge again of the police force. Coffee John besought Alderman Powers to remove the chief, and when the acting mayor proved himself too timid, Coffee John, Tom Brown, and Captain Hill laid a deep plot. They would ask Mayor Ames to remove his brother. This they felt sure they could persuade the "old man" to do. The difficulty was to keep him from changing his mind when the other side should reach his ear. They hit upon a bold expedient. They would urge the "old man" to remove Fred, and then resign himself, so that he could not undo the deed that they wanted done. Coffee John and Captain Hill slipped out of town one night; they reached West Baden on one train and they left for home on the next, with a demand for Fred's resignation in one hand and the mayor's own in the other. Fred Ames did resign, and though the mayor's resignation was laid aside for a while, to avoid the expense of a special election, all looked well for Coffee John and his clique. They had Fred out, and Alderman Powers was to make them great. But Mr. Powers wobbled. No doubt the grand jury spoke to him. At any rate he turned most unexpectedly on both cliques together. He turned out Tom Brown, but he turned out also Coffee John, and he did not make their man chief of police, but another of someone else's selection. A number of resignations was the result, and these the acting mayor accepted, making a clearing of astonished rascals which was very gratifying to the grand jury and to the nervous citizens of Minneapolis.

But the town was not yet easy. The grand jury, which was the actual head of the government, was about to be discharged, and, besides, their work was destructive. A constructive force was now needed, and Alderman Jones was pelted with telegrams from home bidding him hurry back. He did hurry, and when he arrived, the situation was instantly in control. The grand jury prepared to report, for the city had a mind and a will of its own once more. The criminals found it out last.

Percy Jones, as his friends call him, is of the second generation of his family in Minneapolis. His father started him well-to-do, and he went on from where he was started. College graduate and business man, he has a conscience which, however, he has brains enough to question. He is not the fighter, but the slow, sure executive. As an alderman he is the result of a movement begun several years ago by some young men who were convinced by an exposure of a corrupt municipal council that they should go into politics. A few did go in; Jones was one of these few.

The acting mayor was confronted at once with all the hardest problems of municipal government. Vice rose right up to tempt or to fight him. He studied the situation deliberately, and by and by began to settle it point by point, slowly but finally, against all sorts of opposition. One of his first acts was to remove all the proved rascals on the force, putting in their places men who had been removed by Mayor Ames. Another important step was the appointment of a church deacon and personal friend to be chief of police, this on the theory that he wanted at the head of his police a man who could have no sympathy with crime, a man whom he could implicitly trust. Disorderly houses, forbidden by law, were permitted, but only within certain patrol lines, and they were to pay nothing, in either blackmail or "fines." The number and the standing and the point of view of the "good people" who opposed this order was a lesson to Mr. Jones in practical government. One very prominent citizen and church member threatened him for driving women out of two flats owned by him; the rent was the surest means of "support for his wife and children." Mr. Jones enforced his order.

Other interests—saloon-keepers, brewers, etc.—gave him trouble enough, but all these were trifles in comparison with his experience with the gamblers. They represented organized crime, and they asked for a hearing. Mr. Jones gave them some six weeks for negotiations. They proposed a solution. They said that if he would let them (a syndicate) open four gambling places downtown, they would see that no others ran in any part of the city. Mr. Jones pondered and shook his head, drawing them on. They went away, and came back with a better promise. Though they were not the associates of criminals, they knew that class and their plans. No honest police force, unaided, could deal with crime. Thieves would soon be at work again, and what could Mr. Jones do against them with a police force headed by a church deacon? The gamblers offered to control the criminals for the city.

Mr. Jones, deeply interested, declared he did not believe there was any danger of fresh crimes. The gamblers smiled and went away. By an odd coincidence there happened just after that what the papers called "an epidemic of crime." They were petty thefts, but they occupied the mind of the acting mayor. He wondered at their opportuneness. He wondered how the news of them got out.

The gamblers soon reappeared. Hadn't they told Mr. Jones crime would soon be prevalent in town again? They had, indeed, but the mayor was unmoved; "porch climbers" could not frighten him. But this was only the beginning, the gamblers said: the larger crimes would come next. And they went away again. Sure enough, the large crimes came. One, two, three burglaries of jewelry in the houses of well-known people occurred; then there was a fourth, and the fourth was in the house of a relative of the acting mayor. He was seriously amused. The papers had the news promptly, and not from the police.

The gamblers called again. If they could have the exclusive control of gambling in Minneapolis, they would do all that they had promised before, and, if any large burglaries occurred, they would undertake to recover the "swag," and sometimes catch the thief. Mr. Jones was skeptical of their ability to do all this. The gamblers offered to prove it. How? They would get back for Mr. Jones the jewelry recently reported stolen from four houses in town. Mr. Jones expressed a curiosity to see this done, and the gamblers went away. After a few days the stolen jewelry, parcel by parcel, began to return; with all due police-criminal mystery it was delivered to the chief of police.

When the gamblers called again, they found the acting mayor ready to give his decision on their propositions. It was this: There should be no gambling, with police connivance, in the city of Minneapolis during his term of office.

Mr. Jones told me that if he had before him a long term, he certainly would reconsider this answer. He believed he would decide again as he had already, but he would at least give studious reflection to the question: Can a city be governed without any alliance with crime?

It was an open question. He had closed it only for the four months of his emergency administration. Minneapolis should be clean and sweet for a little while at least, and the new administration should begin with a clear deck.

McClure's Magazine
May, 1903

Pittsburgh: A City Ashamed

The Story of a Citizen's Party That Broke Through One Ring into Another

Minneapolis was an example of police corruption; St. Louis of financial corruption. Pittsburgh is an example of both police and financial corruption. The two other cities have found each an official who has exposed them. Pittsburgh has had no such man and no exposure. The city has been described physically as "Hell with the lid off"; politically it is that same with the lid on. I am not going to lift the lid. The exposition of what the people know and stand is the purpose of these articles, not the exposure of corruption, and the exposure of Pittsburgh is not necessary. There are earnest men in the town who declare it must blow up of itself soon. I doubt that; but even if it does burst, the people of Pittsburgh will learn little more than they know now. It is not ignorance that keeps American citizens subservient; neither is it indifference. The Pittsburghers know, and a strong minority of them care; they have risen against their ring and beaten it, only to look about and find another ring around them. Angry and ashamed, Pittsburgh is a type of the city that has tried to be free and failed.

The Iron City and Its Men of Steel

A sturdy city it is, too, the second in Pennsylvania. Two rivers flow past it to make a third, the Ohio, in front, and all around and beneath it are natural gas and coal which feed a thousand furnaces that smoke all day and flame all night to make Pittsburgh the Birmingham of America. Rich in natural resources, it is richest in the quality of its population. Six days and six nights these people labor, moulding iron and forging steel, and they are not tired; on the seventh day they rest, because that is the Sabbath. They are Scotch Presbyterians and Protestant Irish. This stock had an actual majority not many years ago, and now, though the population has grown to 354,000 in Pittsburgh proper (counting Allegheny across the river, 130,000, and other communities, politically separate, but essentially integral parts of the proposed greater Pittsburgh, the total is 750,000), the Scotch and Scotch-Irish still predominate, and their clean, strong faces characterize the crowds in the streets. Canny, busy, and brave, they built up their city almost in secret, making millions and hardly mentioning it. Not till outsiders came in to buy some of them out did the world (and Pittsburgh and some of the millionaires in it) discover that the Iron City had been making not only steel and glass, but multi-millionaires. A banker told a business man as a secret one day about three years ago that within six months a "bunch of about a hundred new millionaires would be born in Pittsburgh," and the births happened on time. And more beside. But even the bloom of millions did not hurt the city. Pittsburgh is an unpretentious, prosperous city of tremendous industry and healthy, steady men.

Superior as it is in some respects, however, Scotch-Irish Pittsburgh, politically, is no better than Irish New York or Scandinavian Minneapolis, and little better than German St. Louis. These people, like any other strain of the free American, have despoiled the government—despoiled it, let it be despoiled, and bowed to the despoiling boss. There is nothing in the un-American excuse that this or that foreign nationality has prostituted "our great and glorious institutions." We all do it, all breeds alike. And there is nothing in the complaint, that the lower elements of our city populations are the source of our disgrace. In St. Louis corruption comes from the top, in Minneapolis from the bottom. In Pittsburgh it comes from both extremities, but it began above.

Corruption from On High

The railroads began the corruption of this city. There "always was some dishonesty," as the oldest public men I talked with said, but it was occasional and criminal till the first great corporation made it business-like and respectable. The municipality issued bonds to help the infant railroads to develop the city, and, as in so many American cities, the roads repudiated the debt and interest, and went into politics. The Pennsylvania Railroad was in the system from the start, and, as the other roads came in and found the city government bought up by those before them, they purchased their rights of way by out-bribing the older roads, then joined the ring to acquire more rights for themselves and to keep belated rivals out. As corporations multiplied and capital branched out, corruption increased naturally, but the notable characteristic of the "Pittsburgh plan" of misgovernment was that it was not a haphazard growth, but a deliberate, intelligent organization. It was conceived in one mind, built up by one will, and this master spirit ruled not like Croker in New York, a solid majority; nor like Butler in St. Louis, a bi-partisan minority; but the whole town—financial, commercial, and political. The boss of Pittsburgh was Christopher L. Magee, a great man, and when he died he was regarded by many of the strongest men in Pittsburgh as their leading citizen.

"Chris," as he was called, was a charming character. I have seen Pittsburghers grow black in the face denouncing the ring, but when I asked, "What kind of a man was Magee?" they would cool and say, "Chris? Chris was one of the best men God ever made." If I smiled, they would say, "That is all right. You smile, and you can go ahead and show up the ring. You may describe this town as the worst in the country. But you get Magee wrong and you'll have all Pittsburgh up in arms." Then they would tell me that "Magee robbed the town," or, perhaps, they would speak of the fund-raising to erect a monument to the dead boss.

So I must be careful. And, to begin with, Magee did not, technically speaking, rob the town. That was not his way, and it would be a carelessly unnecessary way in Pennsylvania. But surely he does not deserve a monument.

The Dynasty of Pittsburgh

Magee was an American. His paternal great-grandfather served in the Revolution, and settled in Pittsburgh at the close of the war. Christopher was born on Good Friday, April 14, 1848. He was sent to school till he was fifteen years old. Then his father died, and "Squire" or "Tommy" Steele, his uncle, a boss of that day, gave him his start in life with a place in the City Treasury. When just twenty-one, he made him cashier, and two years later Chris had himself elected City Treasurer by a majority of 1,100 on a ticket the head of which was beaten by 1,500 votes.

Such was his popularity; and though he systematized and capitalized it, it lasted to the end, for the foundation thereof was goodness of heart and personal attractiveness. Magee was tall, strong, and gracefully built. His hair was dark till it turned gray, and then his short mustache and his eyebrows held black, so that his face expressed easily sure power and genial, hearty kindness. But he was ambitious for power, and all his goodness of heart was directed by a shrewd mind.

When Chris saw the natural following gathering about him he realized, young as he was, the use of it, and he retired from office (holding only a fire commissionership) with the avowed purpose of becoming a boss. Determined to make his ring perfect, he went to Philadelphia to study the plan in operation there. Later, when the Tweed ring was broken, he spent months in New York looking into Tammany's machine methods and the mistakes which had led to its exposure and disruption. With that cheerful candor which softens indignation he told a fellow townsman (who told me) what he was doing in New York; and when Magee returned he reported that a ring could be made as safe as a bank. He had, to start with, a growing town too busy for self-government; two not very unequal parties; neither of them well organized; a clear field in his own, the majority party in the city, county, and state. There was boodle, but it was loosely shared by too many persons. The governing instrument was the old charter of 1816, which lodged all the powers—legislative, administrative, and executive—in the councils, common and select. The mayor was a peace officer, with no responsible power. Indeed, there was no responsibility anywhere. There were no departments. Committees of councils did the work usually done by departments, and the councilmen, unsalaried and unanswerable individually, were organized into what might have become a combine had not Magee set about establishing the one-man power there.

Enter William Flinn

To control councils, Magee had to organize the wards, and he was managing this successfully at the primaries when a new and an important figure appeared on the scene--William Flinn. (Flinn was Irish, a Protestant of Catholic stock, a boss contractor, and a natural politician.) He beat one of Magee's brothers in his ward; Magee laughed, inquired, and finding him a man of opposite or complementary disposition and talents, took him into the partnership. A happy, profitable combination, it lasted for life. Magee wanted power, Flinn wealth. Each got both these things; but Magee spent his wealth for more power, and Flinn spent his power for more wealth. Magee was the sower, Flinn the reaper. In dealing with men they came to be necessary to each other, these two. Magee attracted followers, Flinn employed them. The men Magee won Flinn compelled to obey, and those he lost Magee won back. When the councils were first under his control Magee stood in the lobby to direct them, always by suggestions and requests, which sometimes a mean and ungrateful fellow would say he could not heed. Magee told him it was all right, which saved the man, but lost the vote. So Flinn took the lobby post, and he said: "Here, you go and vote aye." If they disobeyed the plain order Flinn punished them, and so harshly that they would run to Magee to complain. He comforted them. "Never mind Flinn," he would say, sympathetically, "he gives me no end of trouble, too. But I'd like to have you do what he asked. Go and do it for me, and let me attend to Flinn. I'll fix him."

Magee could command, too, and fight and punish. If he had been alone he probably would have hardened with years.

And so Flinn, after Magee died, softened with time, but too late. He was useful to Magee, Magee was indispensable to him. Molasses and vinegar, diplomacy and force, mind and will, they were well mated. But Magee was the genius. It was Magee that laid the plans they worked out together.

Boss Magee's idea was not to corrupt the city government, but to be it; not to hire votes in councils, but to own councilmen; and so, having seized control of his organization, he nominated cheap or dependent men for the select and common councils. Relatives and friends were his first recourse, then came bartenders, saloon-keepers, liquor dealers, and others allied to the vices, who were subject to police regulation and dependent in a business way upon the maladministration of law. For the rest he preferred men who had no visible means of support, and to maintain them he used the usual means—patronage. And to make his dependents secure he took over the county government. Pittsburgh is in Allegheny County, which has always been more strongly Republican than the city. No matter what happened in the city, the county payroll was always Magee's, and he made the county part of the city government.

Corrupting the Minority

With all this city and county patronage at his command, Magee went deliberately about undermining the Democratic party. The minority organization is useful to a majority leader; it saves him trouble and worry in ordinary times; in party crises he can use it to whip his own followers into line; and when the people of a city rise in revolt it is essential for absolute rule that you have the power not only to prevent the minority leaders from combining with good citizens, but to unite the two organizations to whip the community into shape. Moreover, the existence of a supposed opposition party splits the independent vote and helps to keep alive that sentiment, "loyalty to the party," which is one of the best holds the boss has on his unruly subjects.

All bosses, as we have seen in Minneapolis and St. Louis, rise above partisan bias. Magee, the wisest of them, was also the most generous, and he liked to win over opponents who were useful to him. Whenever he heard of an able Democratic worker in a ward, he sent for his own Republican leader. "So-and-so is a good man, isn't he?" he would ask. "Going to give you a run, isn't he? Find out what he wants and we'll see what we can do. We must have him." Thus the able Democrat achieved office for himself or his friend, and the city or the county paid. At one time, I was told, nearly one-quarter of the places on the payroll were held by Democrats, who were, of course, grateful to Chris Magee, and enabled him in emergencies to wield their influence against revolting Republicans. Many a time a subservient Democrat got Republican votes to beat a "dangerous" Republican, and when Magee, toward the end of his career, wished to go to the state Senate, both parties united in his nomination and elected him unanimously.

Corrupting Business

Business men came almost as cheap as politicians, and they came also at the city's expense. Magee had control of public funds and the choice of depositories. That is enough for the average banker—not only for him that is chosen, but for him also that may some day hope to be chosen--and Magee dealt with the best of those in Pittsburgh. This service, moreover, not only kept them docile, but gave him and Flinn credit at their banks. Then, too, Flinn and Magee's operations soon developed on a scale which made their business attractive to the largest financial institutions for the profits on their loans, and thus enabled them to distribute and share in the golden opportunities of big deals.

There are ring banks in Pittsburgh, ring trust companies, and ring brokers. The manufacturers and the merchants were kept well in hand by many little municipal grants and privileges, such as switches, wharf rights, and street and alley vacations. These street vacations are a tremendous power in most cities. A foundry occupies a block, spreads to the next block, and wants the street between. In St. Louis the business man boodled for his street. In Pittsburgh he went to Magee, and I have heard such a man praise Chis, "because when I called on him his outer office was filled with waiting politicians, but he knew I was a business man and in a hurry; he called me in first, and he gave me the street without any fuss. I tell you it was a sad day for Pittsburgh when Chris Magee died." This business man, the typical American merchant, everywhere, cares no more for his city's interest than the politician does, and there is more light on American political corruption in such a speech than in the most sensational exposure of details. The businessmen of Pittsburgh paid for their little favors in "contributions to the campaign fund," plus the loss of their self-respect, the liberty of the citizens generally, and (this may appeal to their mean souls) in higher taxes.

As for the railroads, they did not have to be bought or driven in; they came, and promptly too. The Pennsylvania appeared early, just behind Magee, who handled their passes and looked out for their interest in councils and afterwards at the state legislature. The Pennsylvania passes, especially those to Atlantic City and Harrisburg, have always been a "great graft" in Pittsburgh. For the sort of men Magee had to control a pass had a value above the price of a ticket; to "flash" one is to show a badge of power and membership in the ring. The big ringsters, of course, got from the railroads financial help when cornered in business deals—stock tips, shares in speculative and other financial turns, and political support. The Pennsylvania Railroad is a power in Pennsylvania politics, it is part of the state ring, and part also of the Pittsburgh ring. The city paid in all sorts of rights and privileges, streets, bridges, etc., and in certain periods the business interests of the city were sacrificed to leave the Pennsylvania Road in exclusive control of a freight traffic it could not handle alone.

The Deal for the state

With the city, the county, the Republican and Democratic organizations, the railroads and other corporations, the financiers and the business men, all well under control, Magee needed only the state to make his rule absolute. And he was entitled to it. In a state like New York, where one party controls the legislature and another the city, the people in the cities may expect some protection from party opposition. In Pennsylvania, where the Republicans have an overwhelming majority, the legislature at Harrisburg is an essential part of the government of Pennsylvania cities, and that is ruled by a state ring. Magee's ring was a link in the state ring, and it was no more than right that the state ring should become a link in his ring.

The arrangement was easily made. One man, Matthew S. Quay, had received from the people all the power in the state, and Magee saw Quay. They came to an understanding without the least trouble. Flinn was to be in the Senate, Magee in the lobby, and they were to give unto Quay political support for his business in the state in return for his surrender to them of the state's functions of legislation for the city of Pittsburgh.

Now such understandings are common in our politics, but they are verbal usually and pretty well kept and this of Magee and Quay was also founded in secret good faith. But Quay, in crises, has a way of straining points to win, and there were no limits to Magee's ambition for power. Quay and Magee quarreled constantly over the division of powers and spoils, so after a few years of squabbling they reduced their agreement to writing. This precious instrument has never been published. But the agreement was broken in a great row once, and when William Flinn and J. O. Brown undertook to settle the differences and renew the bond, Flinn wrote out in pencil in his own hand an amended duplicate which he submitted to Quay, whose son subsequently gave it out for publication. A facsimile of one page is reproduced in this article. Here is the whole contract with all the unconscious humor of the "party of the first part" and "said party of the second part," a political-legal-commercial insult to a people boastful of self-government:

"Memorandum and agreement between M. S. Quay of the first part and J. O. Brown and William Flinn of the second part. The consideration of this agreement being the mutual political and business advantage which may result therefrom.

"First—The said M. S. Quay is to have the benefit of the influence in all matters in state and national politics of the said parties of the second part, the said parties agreeing that they

will secure the election of delegates to the state and national convention who will be guided in all matters by the wishes of the said party of the first part, and who will also secure the election of members of the state senate from the Forty-third, Forty-fourth, and Forty-fifth senatorial districts, and also secure the election of members of the house of representatives south of the Monongahela and Ohio rivers in the county of Allegheny, who will be guided by the wishes and request of the said party of the first part during the continuance of this agreement upon all political matters. The different candidates for the various positions mentioned shall be selected by the parties of the second part, and all the positions of state and national appointments made in this territory mentioned shall be satisfactory to and secure the endorsement of the party of the second part, when the appointment is made either by or through the party of the first part, or his friends or political associates. All legislation affecting the parties of the second part, affecting cities of the second class, shall receive the hearty co-operation and assistance of the party of the second part, and legislation which may affect their business shall likewise receive the hearty co-operation and help of the party of the first part. It being distinctly understood that at the approaching national convention, to be held at St. Louis, the delegates from the Twenty-second congressional district shall neither by voice nor vote do other than what is satisfactory to the party of the first part. The party of the first part agrees to use his influence and secure the support of his friends and political associates to support the Republican county and city ticket, when nominated, both in the city of Pittsburgh and Allegheny and the county of Allegheny, and that he will discountenance the factional fighting by his friends and associates for county offices during the continuation of this agreement. This agreement is not to be binding upon the parties of the second part when a candidate for any office who [sic] shall reside in Allegheny county, and shall only be binding if the party of the first part is a candidate for United States senator, to succeed himself so far as this office is concerned. In the Forty-third senatorial district a new senator shall be elected to succeed Senator Upperman. In the Forty-fifth senatorial district the party of the first part shall secure the withdrawal of Dr. A. J. Barchfeld and the parties of the second part shall withdraw as a candidate Senator Steel, and the parties of the second part shall secure the election of some party satisfactory to themselves. In the twenty-second congressional district the candidates for congress shall be selected by the party of the second part. The term of this agreement to be for —— years from the signing thereof, and shall be binding upon all parties when signed by C. L. Magee."

Delivery of a City

Thus was the city of Pittsburgh turned over by the state to an individual to do with as he pleased. Magee's ring was complete. He was the city, Flinn was the councils, the county was theirs, and now they had the state legislature so far as Pittsburgh was concerned. Magee and Flinn were the government and the law. How could they commit a crime? If they wanted something from the city they passed an ordinance granting it and if some other ordinance was in conflict that was repealed or amended. If the laws in the state stood in the way, so much the worse for the laws of the state; they were amended. If the constitution of the state proved a barrier, as it did to all special legislation, the legislature enacted a law for cities of the second class (which was Pittsburgh alone) and the courts upheld the legislature. If there were opposition on the side of public opinion, there was a use for that also.

The new charter which David D. Bruce fought through councils in 1886-7 was an example of the way Magee and after him, Quay and other Pennsylvania bosses employed popular movements. As his machine grew Magee found council committees unwieldy in some respects, and he wanted a change. He took up Bruce's charter, which centered all executive and administrative power and responsibility in the mayor and heads of departments, passed it through the legislature, but so amended that the heads of departments were not to be appointed by the mayor, but elected by councils. These elections were by expiring councils, so that the department chiefs held over, and with their patronage insured the re-election of the councilmen who elected them. The Magee-Flinn machine, perfect before, was made self-perpetuating. I know of nothing like it in any other city. Tammany in comparison is a plaything, and in the management of a city Croker was a child beside Chris Magee.

Pittsburgh, a Private Business

Magee and Flinn, owners of Pittsburgh, made Pittsburgh their business and, monopolists in the technical economic sense of the word, they prepared to exploit it as if it were their private property. For convenience they divided it between them. Magee took the financial and corporate branch, turning the streets to his uses, delivering to himself franchises, and building and running railways. Flinn went in for public contracts for his firm, Booth & Flinn, Limited, and his branch boomed. Old streets were repaired, new ones laid out; whole districts were improved, parks made, and buildings erected. The improvement of their city went on at a great rate for years, with only one period of cessation, and the period of economy was when Magee was building so many traction lines that Booth & Flinn, Ltd., had all they could do with this work. It was said that no other contractors had an adequate "plant" to supplement properly the work of Booth & Flinn, Ltd. Perhaps that was why this firm had to do such a large proportion of the public work always. Flinn's Director of Public Works was E. M. Bigelow, a cousin of Chris Magee and another nephew of old Squire Steele. Bigelow, called the Extravagant, drew the specifications; he made the awards to the lowest responsible bidders, and he inspected and approved the work while in progress and when done.

Flinn had a quarry, the stone of which was specified for public buildings; he obtained the monopoly of a certain kind of asphalt, and that kind was specified. Nor was this all. If the official contractor had done his work well and at reasonable prices the city would not have suffered directly; but his methods were so oppressive upon property holders that they caused a scandal. No action was taken, however, till Oliver McClintock, a merchant, in rare civic wrath, contested the contracts and fought them through the courts. This single citizen's long, brave fight is one of the finest stories in the history of municipal government. The frowns and warnings of cowardly fellow-citizens did not move him, nor the boycott of other business men, the threats of the ring, and the ridicule of ring organs. George W. Guthrie joined him later, and though they fought on undaunted, they were beaten again and again.

The Director of Public Works controlled the initiative in court proceedings; he chose the judge who appointed the Viewers, with the result Mr. McClintock reported, that the Department prepared the Viewers' reports. Knowing no defeat, Mr. McClintock photographed Flinn's pavements at places where they were torn up to show that "large stones, as they were excavated from sewer trenches, brick bats, and the debris of old coal tar sidewalks were promiscuously dumped in to make foundations, with the result of an uneven settling of the foundation, and the sunken and worn places so conspicuous everywhere in the pavements of the East End." One outside asphalt company tried to break the monopoly; but was easily beaten in 1889, withdrew, and after that, as one of them said, "We all gave Pittsburgh a wide berth, recognizing the uselessness of offering competition so long as the door of the Department of Public Works is locked against us, and Booth & Flinn are permitted to carry the key."

The monopoly enabled not only high prices on short guarantee, but carried with it all the contingent work. Curbing and grading might have been let separately, but they were not. In one contract Mr. McClintock cites, Booth & Flinn bid 50 cents for 44,000 yards of grading. E. H. Bochman offered a bid of 15 cents for the grading as a separate contract, and his bid was rejected. A property owner on Shady Lane, who was assessed for curbing at 80 cents a foot, contracted privately at the same time for 800 feet of the same standard curbing from the same quarry, and set in place in the same manner, at 40 cents a foot!

"During the nine years succeeding the adoption of the charter of 1887," says Mr. Oliver McClintock in a report to the National Municipal League,"one firm (Flinn's) received practically all the asphalt paving contracts at prices ranging from $1 to $1.80 per square yard higher than the average price paid in neighboring cities. Out of the entire amount of asphalt pavements laid during these nine years, represented by 193 contracts and costing $3,551,131, only nine street blocks paved in 1896, and costing $33,400, were not laid by this firm."

[Note]
The graft of Pittsburgh falls conveniently into four classes: Franchises, public contracts, vice, and public funds. There was, besides these, a lot of miscellaneous loot—public supplies, public lighting, and the water supply. You hear of second-class fire engines taken at first-class prices, water rents from the public works kept up because a private concern that supplied the South Side could charge no more than the city, a gas contract to supply the city lightly availed of. But I cannot go into these. Neither can I stop for the details of the system by which the public funds were left at no interest with favored depositories from which the city borrowed at a high rate, or the removal of funds to a bank in which the ringsters were shareholders. All these things were managed well within the law, and that was the great principle underlying the Pittsburgh plan.

The vice graft, for example, was not blackmail as it is in New York and most other cities. It is a legitimate business, conducted, not by the police, but in an orderly fashion by syndicates and the chairman of one of the parties at the last election said it was worth $250,000 a year. I saw a man who was laughed at for offering $17,500 for the slot machine concession; he was told that it was let for much more. "Speak-easies" (unlicensed drinking places) pay so well that when they earn $500 or more in twenty-four hours their proprietors often make a bare living. Disorderly houses are managed by ward syndicates. Permission is had from the syndicate real estate agent, who alone can rent them. The syndicate hires the houses from the owners at, say [$35] a month, and he lets it to a woman at from $35 to $50 a week. For furniture the tenant must go to the "official furniture man," who delivers $1,000 worth of "fixings" for a note for $3,000, on which high interest must be paid. For beer the tenant must go to the "official bottler," and pay [$2] for a one-dollar case of beer; for wines and liquors to the "official liquor commissioner," which charges $10 for five dollars' worth; for clothes to the "official wrapper maker." These women may not buy shoes, hats, jewelry, or any other luxury or necessity except from the official concessionaires, and then only at the official, monopoly prices. If the victims have anything left, a police or some other city official is said to call and get it (there are rich ex-police officials in Pittsburgh). But this is blackmail and outside the system, which is well understood in the community. Many men, in various walks of life, told me separately the names of the official bottlers, jewelers, and furnishers; they are notorious, but they are safe. They do nothing illegal. Oppressive, wretched, what you please, the Pittsburgh system is safe.

That was the key-note of the Finn-Magee plan, but this vice graft was not their business. They are credited with the suppression of disorder and decent superficial regulations of vice, which is characteristic of Pittsburgh. I know it is said that under the Philadelphia and Pittsburgh plans, which are much alike, "all graft and all patronage go across one table," but if any "dirty money" reached the Pittsburgh bosses it was in the form of contributions to the party fund, and came from the vice dealers only as it did from other business men.

[End Note]

Flinn's Methods Exposed

The building of bridges in this city of bridges, the repairing of pavements, park-making, and real estate deals in anticipation of city improvements were all causes of scandal to some citizens, sources of profit to others who were "let in on the ground floor." There is no space for these here. Another exposure came in 1897 over the contracts for a new Public Safety Building. J. O. Brown was Director of Public Safety. A newspaper, The Leader, called attention to a deal for this work, and George W. Guthrie and William B. Rogers, leading members of the Pittsburgh bar, who followed up the subject, discovered as queer a set of specifications for the building itself as any city has on record. Favored contractors were named or their wares described all through, and a letter to the architect from J. O. Brown contained specifications for such favoritism, as for example: "Specify the Westinghouse electric light plant and engines straight. Describe the Van Horn Iron Co.'s cells as close as possible."

The stone clause was Flinn's, and that is the one that raised the rumpus. Flinn's quarry produced Ligonier block, and Ligonier block was specified. There was a letter from Booth & Flinn, Ltd., telling the architect that the price was to be specified at $31,500. A local contractor offered to provide Tennessee granite set up, a more expensive material, on which the freight is higher, at $19,880; but that did not matter. When another local contracting firm, however, offered to furnish Ligonier block set up at $18,000, a change was necessary, and J. O. Brown directed the architect to "specify that the Ligonier block shall be of a bluish tint rather than a gray variety." Flinn's quarry had the bluish tint, the other people's "the gray variety."

It was shown also that Flinn wrote to the architect on June 24, 1895, saying: "I have seen Director Brown and Comptroller Gourley to-day, and they have agreed to let us start on the working plans and get some stone out for the new building. Please arrange that we may get the tracings by Wednesday...." The tracings were furnished him, and thus before the advertisements for bids were out he began preparing the bluish tint stone. The charges were heard by a packed committee of councils, and nothing came of them; and, besides, they were directed against the Director of Public Works, not William Flinn.

The boss was not an official, and not responsible. The only time Flinn was in danger was on a suit that grew out of the conviction of the City Attorney, W. C. Moreland, and L. H. House, his assistant, for the embezzlement of public funds. These officials were found to be short about $300,000. One of them pleaded guilty, and both went to prison without telling where the money went, and that information did not develop till later. J. B. Connelly, of The Leader, discovered in the City Attorney's office stubs of checks indicating that some $118,000 of it had gone to Flinn or to Booth & Flinn, Ltd. When Flinn was first asked about it by a reporter he said that the items were correct, that he got them, but that he had explained it all to the Comptroller and had satisfied him.

This answer indicated a belief that the money belonged to the city. When he was sued by the city he said that he did not know it was city money. He thought it was personal loans from House. Now House was not a well-to-do man, and his city salary was but $2,500 a year. Moreover, the checks, two of which are reproduced here, are signed by the City Attorney, W. C. Moreland, and are for amounts ranging from five to fifteen thousand dollars. But where was the money? Flinn testified that he had paid it back to House. Then where were the receipts? Flinn said they had been burned in a fire that had occurred in Booth & Flinn's office. The judge found for Flinn, holding that it had not been proven that Flinn knew the checks were for public money, nor that he had not repaid the amount.

Chris Magee's Business

As I have said before, however, unlawful acts were exceptional and unnecessary in Pittsburgh. Magee did not steal franchises and sell them. His councils gave them to him. He and the busy Flinn took them, built railways, which Magee sold and bought and financed and conducted, like any other man whose successful career is held up as an example for young men. His railways combined into the Consolidated Traction Company were capitalized at $30,000,000. The public debt of Pittsburgh is about $18,000,000, and the profit on the railway building of Chris Magee would have wiped out the debt. "But you must remember," they say in the Pittsburgh banks, "that Magee took risks, and his profits are the just reward of enterprise." This is business. But politically speaking it was an abuse of the powers of a popular ruler for Boss Magee to give to Promoter Magee all the streets he wanted in Pittsburgh at his own terms: forever, and nothing to pay. There was scandal in Chicago over the granting of charters for twenty-eight and fifty years. Magee's read: "for 950 years," "for 999 years," "said Charter is to exist a thousand years," "said Charter is to exist perpetually," and the councils gave franchises for the "life of the Charter."

There is a legend that Fred Magee, a waggish brother of Chris, put these phrases into these grants for fun, and no doubt the genial Chris saw the fun of it. I asked if the same joker put in the car tax, which is the only compensation the city gets for the use forever of its streets; but it was explained that that was an oversight. The car tax was put upon the old horse-cars, and came down upon the trolley because, having been left unpaid, it was forgotten. This car tax on $30,000,000 of property amounts to less than $15,000 a year, and the companies have until lately been slow about paying it. During the twelve years succeeding 1885 all the traction companies together paid the city $60,000. While the horse vehicles in 1897 paid $47,000, and bicycles $7,000, the Consolidated Traction Company (C. L. Magee, president) paid $9,600. The speed of bicycles and horse vehicles is limited by law, that of the trolley is unregulated. The only requirement of the law upon them is that the traction company shall keep in repair the pavement between and a foot outside the tracks. This they don't do. On the contrary, the city furnishes twenty policeman as guards for crossings of their lines at a cost of $20,000 a year in wages.

City Mulcted for Bridges

Not content with the gift of the streets, the ring made the city work for the railways. The building of bridges is one function of the municipality as a servant of the traction company. Pittsburgh is a city of many bridges, and many of them were built for ordinary traffic. When the Magee railways went over them some of them had to be rebuilt. The company asked the city to do it, and despite the protests of citizens and newspapers, the city rebuilt iron bridges in good condition and of recent construction to accommodate the tracks. Once some citizens applied for a franchise to build a connecting line along what is now part of the Bloomfield route, and by way of compensation offered to build a bridge across the Pennsylvania tracks for free city use, they only to have the right to run their cars on it. They did not get their franchise. Not long after Chris Magee (and Flinn) got it, and they got it for nothing; and the city built this bridge, rebuilt three other bridges over the Pennsylvania tracks, and one over the Junction Railroad--five bridges in all, at a cost of $160,000!

[Note]
All the street railways terminating in the city of Pittsburgh were in 1901 consolidated into the Pittsburgh Railways Company, operating 404 miles of track, under an approximate capitalization of $84,000,000. In their statement, issued July 1, [1902], they report gross earnings for 1901 as $7,081,452.82. Out of this they paid a car tax for 1902 to the city of Pittsburgh of $20,099.94. At the ordinary rate of 5 per cent on gross earning the tax would have been $354,072.60.
[End Note]

What the People Did About It

Canny Scots as they were, the Pittsburghers submitted to all this for a quarter of a century, and some $34,000 has been subscribed toward the monument to Chris Magee. This sounds like any other well-broken American city; but to the credit of Pittsburgh be it said that there never was a time when some few individuals were not fighting the ring. David D. Bruce was standing for good government way back in the fifties. Oliver McClintock and George W. Guthrie we have had glimpses of, struggling, like John Hampden, against their tyrants; but always for mere justice and in the courts, and all in vain, till in 1895 their exposures began to bring forth signs of public feeling, and they ventured to appeal to the voters, the sources of the bosses' power. They enlisted the venerable Mr. Bruce and a few other brave men, and together called a mass-meeting. A crowd gathered. There were not many prominent men there, but evidently the people were with them, and they then and there formed the Municipal League, and launched it upon a campaign to beat the ring at the February election, 1896.

A committee of five was put in charge--Bruce McClintock, George K. Stevenson, Dr. Pollock and Otto Heeren—who combined with Mr. Guthrie's sterling remnant of the Democratic party on an independent ticket, with Mr. Guthrie at the head for mayor. It was a daring thing to do, and they discovered then what we have discovered in St. Louis and Minneapolis. Mr. Bruce told me that, after their mass-meeting, men who should have come out openly for the movement approached him by stealth and whispered that he could count on them for money if he would keep secret their names. "Outside of those at the meeting," he said, "but one man of all those that subscribed would let his name appear. And men who gave me information to use against the ring spoke themselves for the ring on the platform."

Mr. McClintock in a paper read before a committee of the National Municipal League says: "By far the most disheartening discovery, however, was that of the apathetic indifference of many representative citizens—men who from every other point of view are deservedly looked upon as model members of society. We found that prominent merchants and contractors who were 'on the inside,' manufacturers enjoying special municipal privileges, wealthy capitalists, brokers and others who were holders of the securities of traction and other corporations, had their mouths stopped, their convictions of duty strangled, and their influence before and votes on election day preempted against us. In still another direction we found that the financial and political support of the great steam railroads and largest manufacturing corporations, controlling as far as they were able the suffrages of their thousands of employees, were thrown against us, for the simple reason, as was frankly explained by one of them, that it was much easier to deal with a boss in promoting their corporate interests than to deal directly with the people's representatives in the municipal legislature. We even found the directors of many banks in an attitude of cold neutrality, if not of active hostility, toward any movement for municipal reform. As one of them put it, 'if you want to be anybody, or make money in Pittsburgh, it is necessary to be in the political swim and on the side of the city ring.'"

This is corruption, but it is called "good business," and it is worse than politics.

The Break Between Quay and Magee

It was a quarrel among the grafters of Minneapolis that gave the grand jury a chance there. It was a low row among the grafters of St. Louis that gave Joseph W. Folk his opening. And so in Pittsburgh it was in a fight between Quay and Magee that the Municipal League saw its opportunity.

To Quay it was the other way around. The rising of the people of Pittsburgh was an opportunity for him. He and Magee had never got along well together, and they were falling out and having their differences adjusted by Flinn and others every few years. The "mutual business advantage" agreement was to have closed one of these rows. The fight of 1895-96 was an especially bitter one, and it did not close with the "harmony" that was patched up. Magee and Flinn and Boss Martin of Philadelphia set out to kill Quay politically, and he, driven thus into one of those "fights for his life" which make his career so interesting, hearing the grumbling in Philadelphia and seeing the revolt of the citizens of Pittsburgh, stepped boldly forth upon a platform of reform, especially to stop the "use of money for the corruption of our cities." From Quay this was comical, but the Pittsburghers were too serious to laugh. They were fighting for their life, too, so to speak, and the sight of a boss on their side must have encouraged those business men who "found it easier to deal with a boss than with the people's representatives." However that may be, a majority of the ballots cast in February, 1896, were against the ring.

Counted Out by the Ring

This isn't history. According to the records the reform ticket was defeated by about 1,000 votes. The returns up to one o'clock on the morning after election showed George W. Guthrie far ahead for mayor; then all returns ceased suddenly, and when the count came in officially a few days later the ring had won. But besides the prima facie evidence of fraud, the ringsters afterward told in confidence not only that Mr. Guthrie was counted out, but how it was done. Mr. Guthrie's appeal to the courts, however, for a recount was denied. The courts held that the secret ballot law forbade the opening of the ballot boxes.

Thus the ring held Pittsburgh—but not the Pittsburghers. They saw Quay in control of the legislature, Quay, the reformer, who would help them. So they drew a charter for Pittsburgh which would restore the city to the people. Quay saw the instrument, and he approved it; he promised to have it passed. The League, the Chamber of Commerce, and other representative bodies, all encouraged by the outlook for victory, sent to Harrisburg committees to urge their charter, and their orators poured forth upon the Magee-Flinn ring a flood of, not invective, but facts, specifications of outrage, and the abuse of absolute power. Their charter went booming along through its first and second readings, Quay and the Magee-Flinn crowd fighting inch by inch. All looked well, when suddenly there was silence. Quay was dealing with his enemies and the charter was his club. He wanted to go back to the Senate, and he went. The Pittsburghers saw him elected, saw him go, but their charter they saw no more. And such is the state of Pennsylvania that this man who did this thing to Pittsburgh, and has done the like again and again to all cities and all interests—even politicians—he is the boss of Pennsylvania today!

The good men of Pittsburgh gave up, and for four years the essential story of the government of the city is a mere thread in the personal quarrels of the bosses in state politics. Magee wanted to go to the United States Senate, and he had with him Boss Martin and John Wanamaker of Philadelphia, as well as his own Flinn. Quay turned on the city bosses and, undermining their power, soon had Martin beaten in Philadelphia. To overthrow Magee was a harder task and Quay might never have accomplished it had not Magee's health failed, causing him to be much away. Pittsburgh was left to Flinn, and his masterfulness, unmitigated by Magee, made trouble. The crisis came out of a row Flinn had with his Director of Public Works, E. M. Bigelow, a man as dictatorial as Flinn himself. Bigelow threw open to competition certain contracts. Flinn, in exasperation, had the councils throw out the director and put in his place a man who restored the old specifications.

Enter Tom Bigelow

This enraged Thomas Steele Bigelow, E. M. Bigelow's brother, and another nephew of old Squire Steele. Tom had an old grudge against Magee, dating from the early days of traction deals. He was rich, he knew something of politics, and he believed in the power of money in the game. Going straight to Harrisburg, he took charge of Quay's fight for senator, spent his own money and won; and he beat Magee, which was his first purpose.

But he was not satisfied yet. The Pittsburghers, aroused to fresh hope by the fight of the bosses, were encouraged also by the news that the census of 1900 put a second city, Scranton, into "cities of the second class." New laws had to be drawn for both. Pittsburgh saw a chance for a good charter. Tom Bigelow saw a chance to finish the Magee-Flinn ring, and he had William B. Rogers, a man whom the city trusted, draw the famous "Ripper Bill." This was a good charter, concentrating power in the mayor, but changes were introduced into it to enable the governor to remove and appoint mayors, or recorders, as they were to be called, at will until April, 1903, when the first elected Recorder was to take office. This was Bigelow's device to rid Pittsburgh of the ring office holders. But Magee was not dead yet. He and Flinn saw Governor Stone, and when the governor ripped out the ring mayor, he appointed as recorder, Major A. M. Brown, a lawyer well thought of in Pittsburgh.

Major Brown, however, kept all but one of the ring heads of the departments. This disappointed the people; it was a defeat for Bigelow; for the ring it was a triumph. Without Magee, however, Flinn could not hold his fellows in their joy, and they went to excesses which exasperated Major Brown and gave Bigelow an excuse for urging him to action. Major Brown suddenly removed the heads of the ring and began a thorough reorganization of the government. This reversed emotions, but not for long. The ring leaders saw Governor Stone again; he ripped out Bigelow's Brown and appointed in his place a ring Brown. Thus the ring was restored to full control under a charter which increased their power.

Second Rise of Pittsburgh

But the outrageous abuse of the governor's unusual power over the city incensed the people of Pittsburgh. A postscript which Governor Stone added to his announcement of the recorder did not help matters; it was a denial that he had been bribed. The Pittsburghers had not heard of any bribery, but the postscript gave currency to a definite report that the ring--its banks, its corporations, and its bosses—had raised an enormous fund to pay the governor for his interference in the city, and this pointed the intense feelings of the citizens. They prepared to beat the ring at an election to be held in February, 1902, for comptroller and half of the councils. A Citizens' Party was organized. The campaign was an excited one; both sides did their best, and the vote polled was the largest ever known in Pittsburgh. Even the ring made a record. The citizens won, however, and by a majority of 8,000.

This showed the people what they could do when they tried, and they were so elated that they went into the next election and carried the county—the stronghold of the ring. But they now had a party to look out for, and they did not look out for it. They neglected it just as they had the city. Tom Bigelow knew the value of a majority party: he had appreciated the Citizens' from the start. Indeed he may have started it. All the reformers know is that the committee which called the Citizens' Party into existence was made up of twenty-five men—five old Municipal Leaguers, the rest a "miscellaneous lot." They did not bother then about that. They knew Tom Bigelow, but he did not show himself, and the new party went on confidently with its passionate work.

When the time came for the great election, that for recorder this year, the citizens woke up one day and found Tom Bigelow the boss of their party. How he came there they did not exactly know; but there he was in full possession, and there with him was the "miscellaneous lot" on the committee. Moreover, Bigelow was applying with vigor regular machine methods. It was all very astonishing but very significant. Magee was dead;

Flinn's end was in sight; but there was the Boss, the everlasting American Boss, as large as life. The good citizens were shocked; their dilemma was ridiculous, but it was serious too. Helpless, they watched. Bigelow nominated for recorder a man they never would have chosen. Flinn put up a better man, hoping to catch the citizens, and when these said they could see Flinn behind his candidate, he said. "No; I am out of politics. When Magee died I died politically, too."

Nobody would believe him. The decent Democrats hoped to retrieve their party and offer a way out, but Bigelow went into their convention with his money and the wretched old organization sold out. The smell of money on the Citizens' side attracted to it the grafters, the rats from Flinn's sinking ship; many of the corporations went over, and pretty soon it was understood that the railroads had come to a settlement among themselves and with the new boss, on the basis of an agreement said to contain five specifications of grants from the city. The temptation to vote for Flinn's man was strong, but the old reformers seemed to feel that the only thing to do was to finish Flinn now and take care of Tom Bigelow later. This view prevailed and Tom Bigelow won. This is the way the best men in Pittsburgh put it: "We have smashed a ring and we have wound another around us. Now we have got to smash that."

There is the spirit of this city as I understand it. Craven as it was for years, corrupted high and low, Pittsburgh did rise; it shook off the superstition of partisanship in municipal politics; beaten, it rose again, and now, when it might have boasted of a triumph, it saw straight: a defeat. The old fighters, undeceived and undeceiving, humiliated but undaunted, said simply: "All we have got to do is to begin all over again." Meanwhile, however, Pittsburgh has developed some young men, and with an inheritance of this same spirit, they are going to try out in their own way. The older men undertook to save the city with a majority party and they lost the party. The younger men have formed a Voters' Civic League, which proposes to swing from one party to another that minority of disinterested citizens which is always willing to be led, and thus raise the standard of candidates and improve the character of regular party government.

Tom Bigelow intended to capture the old Flinn organization, combine it with his Citizens' Party, and rule as Magee did with one party, a union of all parties. If he should do this, the young reformers would have no two parties to choose between; but there stand the old fighters ready to rebuild a Citizens' Party under that or any other name. Whatever course is taken, however, something will be done in Pittsburgh, or tried, at least, for good government, and after the cowardice and corruption shamelessly displayed in other cities, the effort of Pittsburgh is a spectacle good for American self-respect, and its sturdiness a promise for poor old Pennsylvania.

McClure's Magazine
July, 1903

Philadelphia Corrupt and Contented

Other American cities, no matter how bad their own condition may be, all point with scorn to Philadelphia as worse—"the worst-governed city in the country." St. Louis, Minneapolis, Pittsburgh submit with some patience to the jibes of any other community; the most friendly suggestion from Philadelphia is rejected with contempt. The Philadelphians are "supine," "asleep"; hopelessly ring-ruled, they are "complacent." "Politically benighted," Philadelphia is supposed to have no light to throw upon a state of things that is almost universal.

This is not fair. Philadelphia is, indeed, corrupt; but it is not without significance. Every city and town in the country can learn something from the typical political experience of this great representative city. New York is excused for many of its ills because it is the metropolis, Chicago because of its forced development; Philadelphia is our "third largest" city and its growth has been gradual and natural. Immigration has been blamed for our municipal conditions; Philadelphia, with 47 per cent of its population native-born of native-born parents, is the most American of our greater cities. It is "good," too, and intelligent. I don't know just how to measure the intelligence of a community, but a Pennsylvania college professor who declared to me his belief in education for the masses as a way out of political corruption, himself justified the "rake-off" of preferred contractors on public works on the ground of a "fair business profit." Another plea we have made is that we are too busy to attend to public business, and we have promised, when we come to wealth and leisure, to do better. Philadelphia has long enjoyed great and widely distributed prosperity; it is the city of homes (there is a dwelling house for every five persons—men, women, and children—of the population; and the people give one a sense of more leisure and repose than any community I ever dwelt in). Some Philadelphians account for their political state on the ground of their ease and comfort. There is another class of optimists whose hope is in an "aristocracy" that is to come by and by; Philadelphia is surer that it has a "real aristocracy" than any other place in the world, but its aristocrats, with few exceptions, are in the ring, with it, or of no political use. Then we hear that we are a young people and that when we are older and "have traditions," like some of the old countries, we also will be honest. Philadelphia is one of the oldest of our cities and treasures for us scenes and relics of some of the noblest traditions of "our fair land." Yet I was told how once, "for a joke," a party of boodlers counted out the "divvy" of their graft in unison with the ancient chime of Independence Hall.

Philadelphia is representative. This very "joke," told, as it was, with a laugh, is typical. All our municipal governments are more or less bad, and all our people are optimists. Philadelphia is simply the most corrupt and the most contented. Minneapolis has cleaned up, Pittsburgh has tried to, New York fights every other election, Chicago fights all the time. Even St. Louis has begun to stir (since the elections are over), and at the worst was only shameless. Philadelphia is proud; good people there defend corruption and boast of their machine. My college professor, with his philosophic view of "rake-offs," is one Philadelphia type. Another is the man, who, driven to bay with his local pride, says: "At least you must admit that our machine is the best you have ever seen."

All Through With Reform

Disgraceful? Other cities say so. But I say that if Philadelphia is a disgrace, it is a disgrace not to itself alone, nor to Pennsylvania, but to the United States and to American character. For this great city, so highly representative in other respects, is not behind in political experience, but ahead, with New York. Philadelphia is a city that has had its reforms. Having passed through all the typical stages of corruption, Philadelphia reached the period of miscellaneous loot with a boss for chief thief, under James McManes and the Gas Ring way back in the late sixties and seventies. This is the Tweed stage of corruption from which St. Louis, for example, is just emerging. Philadelphia, in two inspiring popular revolts, attacked the Gas Ring, broke it, and in 1885 achieved that dream of American cities—a good charter. The present condition of Philadelphia, therefore, is not that which precedes, but that which follows reform, and in this distinction lies its startling general significance. What has happened since the Bullitt Law or charter went into effect in Philadelphia may happen in any American city "after reform is over."

For reform with us is usually revolt, not government, and is soon over. Our people do not seek, they avoid self-rule, and "reforms" are spasmodic efforts to punish bad rulers and get somebody that will give us good government or something that will make it. A self-acting form of government is an ancient superstition. We are an inventive people, and we all think that we shall devise some day a legal machine that will turn out good government automatically. The Philadelphians have treasured this belief longer than the rest of us and have tried it more often. Throughout their history they have sought this wonderful charter and they thought they had it when they got the Bullitt Law, which concentrates in the mayor ample power, executive and political, and complete responsibility. Moreover, it calls for very little thought and action on the part of the people. All they expected to have to do when the Bullitt Law went into effect was to elect as mayor a good business man, who, with his probity and common sense, would give them that good business administration which is the ideal of many reformers.

Business Men as Mayors

The Bullitt Law went into effect in 1887. A committee of twelve—four men from the Union League, four from business organizations, and four from the bosses—picked out the first man to run under it on the Republican ticket, Edwin H. Fitler, an able, upright business man, and he was elected. Strange to say, his administration was satisfactory to the citizens, who speak well of it to this day, and to the politicians also; Boss

McManes (the ring was broken, not the boss) took to the next national convention from Philadelphia a delegation solid for Fitler for president of the United States. It was a farce, but it pleased Mr. Fitler, so Matthew S. Quay, the state boss, let him have a complimentary vote on the first ballot. The politicians "fooled" Mr. Fitler, and they "fooled" also the next business mayor, Edwin S. Stuart, likewise a most estimable gentleman. Under these two administrations the foundation was laid for the present government of Philadelphia, the corruption to which Philadelphians seem so reconciled, and the machine which is "at least the best you have ever seen."

Philadelphians Disfranchised Like Negroes

The Philadelphia machine isn't the best. It isn't sound and I doubt if it would stand in New York or Chicago. The enduring strength of the typical American political machine is that it is a natural growth—a sucker, but deep rooted in the people. The New Yorkers vote for Tammany Hall. The Philadelphians do not vote; they are disfranchised, and their disfranchisement is one anchor of the foundation of the Philadelphia organization.

This is no figure of speech. The honest citizens of Philadelphia have no more rights at the polls than the negroes down South. Nor do they fight very hard for this basic right. You can arouse their Republican ire by talking about the black Republican votes lost in the southern states by white Democratic intimidation, but if you remind the average Philadelphian that he is in the same position, he will look startled, then say, "that's so, that's literally true, only I never thought of it in just that way." And it is literally true.

The machine controls the whole process of voting, and practices fraud at every stage. The assessor's list is the voting list, and the assessor is the machine's man. "The assessor of a division kept a disorderly house; he padded his lists with fraudulent names registered from his house; two of these names were used by election officers . . . The constable of the division kept a disreputable house; a policeman was assessed

Philadelphia: Corrupt and Contented 191

as living there. . . . The election was held in the disorderly house maintained by the assessor . . . The man named as judge had a criminal charge for a life offense pending against him . . . Two hundred and fifty-two votes were returned in a division that had less than one hundred legal votes within its boundaries." These extracts from a report of the Municipal League suggest the election methods. The assessor pads the list with the names of dead dogs, children, and non-existent persons. One newspaper printed the picture of a dog, another that of a little four-year-old negro boy, down on such a list. A ring orator in a speech resenting sneers at his ward as "low down" reminded his hearers that that was the ward of Independence Hall, and, naming over signers of the Declaration of Independence, he closed his highest flight of eloquence with the statement that "these men, the fathers of American liberty, voted down here once. And," he added, with a catching grin, "they vote here yet." Rudolph Blankenburg, a persistent fighter for the right and the use of the right to vote, sent out just before one election a registered letter to each voter on the rolls of a certain selected division. Sixty-three per cent were returned marked "not at," "removed," "deceased," etc. From one four-story house where forty-four voters were addressed, eighteen letters came back undelivered; from another of forty-eight voters, came back forty-one letters; from another sixty-one out of sixty-two; from another forty-four out of forty-seven. Six houses in one division were assessed at one hundred and seventy-two voters, more than the votes cast in the previous election in any one of two hundred entire divisions.

    The repeating is done boldly, for the machine controls the election officers, often choosing them from among the fraudulent names; and when no one appears to serve, assigning the heeler ready for the expected vacancy. The police are forbidden by law to stand within thirty feet of the polls, but they are at the box and they are there to see that the machine's orders are obeyed and that repeaters whom they help to furnish are permitted to vote without "intimidation" on the names they, the police, have supplied. The editor of an anti-machine paper who was looking about for himself once told me that a ward leader who knew him well asked him into a polling place. "I'll show you how it's done," he said, and he had the repeaters go round and round voting again and again on the names handed them on slips. "But," as the editor said, "that isn't the way it's done." The repeaters go from one polling place to another, voting on slips, and on their return rounds change coats, hats, etc. The business proceeds with very few hitches; there is more jesting than fighting. Violence in the past has had its effect; and is not often necessary nowadays, but if it is needed the police are there to apply it. Several citizens told me that they had seen the police help to beat citizens or elections officers who were trying to do their duty, then arrest the victim; and Mr. Clinton Rogers Woodruff, the executive counsel of the Municipal League, has published a booklet of such cases. But an official statement of the case is at hand in an announcement by John Weaver, the new machine mayor of Philadelphia, that he is going to keep the police out of politics and away from the polls. "I shall see," he added, "that every voter enjoys the full right of suffrage and that ballots may be placed in the ballot box without fear of intimidation."

But many Philadelphians do not try to vote. They leave everything to the machine, and the machine casts their ballots for them. It is estimated that 150,000 voters did not go to the polls at the last election. Yet the machine rolled up a majority of 130,000 for Weaver, with a fraudulent vote estimated all the way from forty to eighty thousand, and this in a campaign so machine-made that it was called "no contest." Francis Fisher Kane, the Democrat, got 32,000 votes out of some 204,000. "What is the use of voting?" these stay-at-homes ask. A friend of mine told me he was on the lists in the three wards in which he had successively dwelt. He votes personally in none, but the leader of his present ward tells him how he has been voted. Mr. J. C. Reynolds, the proprietor of the St. James Hotel, went to the polls at eleven o'clock last election day, only to be told that he had been voted. He asked how many others from his house had voted. An election officer took up a list, checked off twelve names, two down twice, and handed it to him. When Mr. Reynolds got home he learned that one of these had voted, the others had been voted. Another man said he rarely attempted to vote, but when he did, the officers let him, even though his name had already been voted on; and then the negro repeaters would ask if his "brother was coming 'round to-day." They were going to vote him, as they vote all good-natured citizens who stay away. "When this kind of man turns out," said a leader to me, "we simply have two repeaters extra—one to balance him and one more to the good." If necessary, after all this, the machine counts the vote "right," and there is little use appealing to the courts, since they have held, except in one case, that the ballot box is secret and cannot be opened. The only legal remedy lies in the purging of the assessor's lists, and when the Municipal League had this done in 1899, they reported that there was "wholesale voting on the very names stricken off."

Deprived of self-government, the Philadelphians haven't even self-governing machine government. They have their own boss, but he and his machine are subject to the state ring, and take their orders from the state boss, Matthew S. Quay, who is the proprietor of Pennsylvania and the real ruler of Philadelphia, just as William Penn, the Great Proprietor, was. Philadelphians, especially the local bosses, dislike this description of their government, and they point for refutation to their charter. But this very Bullitt Law was passed by Quay, and he put it through the legislature, not for reform reasons, but at the instance of David H. Lane, his Philadelphia lieutenant, as a check upon the power of Boss McManes. Later, when McManes proved hopelessly insubordinate, Quay decided to have done with him forever. He chose David Martin for boss, and from his seat in the United States Senate, Penn's successor raised up his man and set him over the people. Croker, who rose by his own strength to the head of Tammany Hall, has tried twice to appoint a successor; no one else could, and he failed. The boss of Tammany Hall is a growth. So Croker has attempted to appoint district leaders and failed; a Tammany district leader is a growth. Boss Martin, picked up and set down from above, was accepted by Philadelphia and the Philadelphia machine, and he removed old ward leaders and appointed new ones. Some leaders in Philadelphia own their wards, of course, but Martin and, after him, Durham have sent men into a ward to lead it, and they have led it.

Philadelphia Machine Upside Down

The Philadelphia organization is upside down. It has its root in the air, or, rather, like the banyan tree, it sends its roots from the center out both up and down and all around, and there lies its peculiar strength. For when I said it was dependent and not sound, I did not mean that it was weak. It is dependent as a municipal machine, but the organization that rules Philadelphia is, as we have seen, not a mere municipal machine, but a city, state, and national organization. The people of Philadelphia are Republicans in a Republican city in a Republican state in a Republican nation, and they are bound ring on ring on ring. The president of the United States and his patronage; the national cabinet and their patronage; the Congress and the patronage of the senators and the congressmen from Pennsylvania; the governor of the state and the state legislature with their powers and patronage; and all that the mayor and city councils have of power and patronage—all these bear down upon Philadelphia to keep it in the control of Quay's boss and his little ring. (This is the ideal of party organization, and, possibly, is the end toward which our democratic republic is tending.) If it is, the end is absolutism. Nothing but a revolution could overthrow this oligarchy, and there is its danger. With no outlet at the polls for public feeling, the machine cannot be taught anything it does not know except at the cost of annihilation.

No Choice of Parties

But the Philadelphia machine-leaders know their business. As I said in a previous article ("Tweed Days in St. Louis"), the politicians will learn, if the people won't, from exposure and reform. The Pennsylvania bosses learned the "uses of reform"; we have seen Quay applying it to discipline McManes, and he since has turned reformer himself, to punish local bosses. The bosses have learned also the danger of combination between citizens and the Democrats. To prevent this, Quay and his friends have spread sedulously the doctrine of "reform within the party," and, from the Committee of One

Hundred on, the reformers have stuck pretty faithfully to this principle. But lest the citizens should commit such a sin against their party, Martin formed a permanent combination of the Democratic with the Republican organization, using to that end a goodly share of the federal and county patronage. Thus the people of Philadelphia were "fixed" so that they couldn't vote if they wanted to, and if they should want to, they couldn't vote for a Democrat, except of Republican or independent choosing. In other words, having taken away their ballot, the bosses took away also the choice of parties.

Making Graft Safe

But the greatest lesson learned and applied was that of conciliation and "good government." The people must not want to vote or rebel against the ring. This ring, like any other, was formed for the exploitation of the city for private profit, and the cementing force is the "cohesive power of public plunder." But McManes and Tweed had proved that miscellaneous larceny was dangerous, and why should a lot of cheap politicians get so much and the people nothing at all? The people had been taught to expect but little from their rulers: good water, good light, clean streets well paved, fair transportation, the decent repression of vice, public order and public safety, and no scandalous or open corruption. It would be good business and good politics to give them these things. Like Chris Magee, who studied out the problem with him, Martin took away from the rank and file of the party and from the ward leaders and office holders the privilege of theft, and he formed companies and groups to handle the legitimate public business of the city. It was all graft, but it was to be all lawful, and, in the main, it was. Public franchises, public works, and public contracts were the principal branches of the business, and Martin adopted the dual boss idea, which we have seen worked out by Magee and Flinn in Pittsburgh. In Philadelphia it was Martin and Porter, and just as Flinn had a firm, Booth & Flinn, Ltd., so Porter was Filbert and Porter.

Filbert and Porter got all the public contracts they

could handle, and the rest went to other contractors friendly to them and to the ring. Sometimes the preferred contractor was the lowest bidder, but he did not have to be. The law allowed awards to be the "lowest and best," and the courts held that this gave the officials discretion. But since public criticism was to be considered, the ring, to keep up appearances, resorted to many tricks. One was to have fake bids made above the favorite. Another was to have the favorite bid high, but set an impossible time limit; the department of the city councils could extend the time afterwards. Still another was to arrange for specifications which would make outsiders bid high, then either openly alter the plans or let the ring firm perform work not up to requirements.

Many of Martin's deals and jobs were scandals, but they were safe; they were in the direction of public service; and the great mass of the business was done quietly. Moreover, the public was getting something for its money—not full value, but a good percentage. In other words, there was a limit to the "rake-off," and some insiders have told me that it had been laid down as a principle with the ring that the people should have in value (that is, in work or benefit, including a fair profit) ninety-five cents out of every dollar. In some of the deals I have investigated, the "rake-off" over and above profit was as high as twenty-five per cent. Still, even at this, there was "a limit," and the public was getting, as one of the leaders told me, "a run for its money." Cynical as it all sounds, this view is taken by many Philadelphians almost if not quite as intelligent as my college professor.

Philadelphia Corrupted

But there was another element in the policy of conciliation which is a potent factor in the contentment of Philadelphia, and I regard it as the key to that "apathy" which has made the community notorious. We have seen how Quay had with him the federal resources and those of the state, and the state ring, and we have seen how Martin, having the city, mayor, and councils, won over the Democratic city leaders.

Here they had under pay in office at least 15,000 men and women. But each of these 15,000 persons was selected for office because he could deliver votes, either by organizations, by parties, or by families. These must represent pretty near a majority of the city's voters. But this is by no means the end of the ring's reach. In the state ring are the great corporations, the Standard Oil Company, Cramp's Shipyard, and the steel companies, with the Pennsylvania Railroad at their head, and all the local transportation and other public utility companies following after. They get franchises, privileges, exemptions, etc.; they have helped finance Quay through deals: the Pennsylvania paid Martin, Quay said once, a large yearly salary; the Cramps get contracts to build United States ships, and for years have been begging for a subsidy on home-made ships. The officers, directors, and stockholders of these companies, with their friends, their bankers, and their employees, are of the organization. Better still, one of the local bosses of Philadelphia told me he could always give a worker a job with these companies, just as he could in a city department, or in the mint, or post-office. Then there are the bankers who enjoy, or may some day enjoy, public deposits; those that profit on loans to finance political financial deals; the promoting capitalists who share with the bosses on franchises; and the brokers who deal in ring securities and speculation on ring tips. Through the exchange the ring financiers reach the investing public, which is a large and influential body. The traction companies, which bought their way from beginning to end by corruption, which have always been in the ring, and whose financiers have usually shared in other big ring deals, adopted early the policy of bribing the people with "small blocks of stock." Dr. Frederick Speirs, in his "The Street Railway System of Philadelphia," came upon transactions which "indicate clearly that it is the policy of the Union Company to get the securities into the hands of a large number of small holders, the plain inference being that a wide distribution of securities will fortify the company against possible attacks by the public." In 1895 he found a director saying: "Our critics have engaged the Academy of Music, and are to call an assemblage of people opposed to the street railways as now managed. It would take eight Academies of Music to hold the stockholders of the Union Traction Company."

But we are not yet through. Quay has made a specialty all his life of reformers, and he and his local bosses have won over so many that the list of former reformers is very, very long. Martin drove down his roots through race and religion, too. Philadelphia was one of the hot-beds of "know-nothingism." Martin recognized the Catholic, and the Irish-Irish, and so drew off into the Republican party the great natural supply of the Democrats; and his successors have given high places to representative Jews. "Surely this isn't corruption!" No, and neither is that corruption which makes the heads of great educational and charity institutions "go along," as they say in Pennsylvania, in order to get appropriations for their institutions from the state and land from the city. They know what is going on, but they do not join reform movements. The provost of the University of Pennsylvania declined to join in a revolt because, he said, it might impair his usefulness to the university. And so it is with others, and with clergymen who have favorite charities; with sabbath associations and City Beautiful clubs; with lawyers who want briefs; with real estate dealers who like to know in advance about public improvements, and real estate owners who appreciate light assessments; with shopkeepers who don't want to be bothered with strict inspections.

If there is no other hold for the ring on a man there always is the protective tariff. "I don't care," said a manufacturer. "What if they do plunder and rob us, it can't hurt me unless they raise the tax rates, and even that won't ruin me. Our party keeps up the tariff. If they should reduce that, my business would be ruined."

The Dollar Mark on Martin

Such, then, are the ramifications of this machine, such is its strength. No wonder Martin could break his own rules, as he did, and commit excesses. Martin's doom was proclaimed not in Philadelphia, but in the United States Senate, and his offense was none of this business of his, but his failure to nominate as successor to Mayor Stuart the man, Boise Penrose, whom Matt Quay chose for that place. Martin had consented, but at the last moment he ordered the nomination of Charles F. Warwick instead. The day that happened Mr. Quay arose on the floor of the Senate and, in a speech so irrelevant to the measure under consideration that nobody out of Pennsylvania understood it, said that there was in his town a man who had given as his reason for not doing what he had promised to do, the excuse that he was "under a heavy salary from a great corporation (the Pennsylvania Railroad) and was compelled to do what the corporation wished him to do. And," added Senator Quay, "men in such a position with high power for good or evil ought . . . to go about . . . with the dollar mark of the corporation on their foreheads." Quay named as the new boss Israel W. Durham, a ward leader under Martin.

Martin having the city through Mayor Warwick fought Quay in the state, with Chris Magee for an ally, but Quay beat them both there, and then prepared to beat them in their own cities. His cry was Reform, and he soon had the people shouting for it.

"Shaking the Plum Tree"

Quay responded with a legislative committee to investigate abuses in the cities, but this so-called "Lexow" was called off before it amounted to much more than a momentary embarrassment to Martin. Martin's friends, on the other hand, caught Quay and nearly sent him to prison. The People's Bank, James McManes, president, failed. The cashier, John S. Hopkins, had been speculating and letting Quay and other politicians have bank funds without collateral for stock gambling. In return Quay and the state treasurer left heavy state deposits with the bank. Hopkins lost his nerve and shot himself. McManes happened to call in friends of Martin to advise him, and these suggested a Martin man for receiver. They found among the items money lent to Quay without security, except the state funds, and telegrams asking Hopkins to buy "1,000 Met" (Metropolitan) and promising in return to "shake the plum tree." Quay, his son,

Richard R., and Benjamin J. Haywood, the state treasurer, were indicted for conspiracy, and every effort was made to have the trial precede the next election for the legislature which was to elect a successor to Quay in the United States Senate; but Quay got stays and postponements in the hopes that a more friendly district attorney could be put in that office. Martin secured the election of Peter F. Rothermel, who was eager to try the case, and Quay had to depend on other resources. The trial came in due course, and failed; Judge Biddle ruled out the essential evidence on the ground that it was excluded by the statute of limitation. Rothermel went on with the trial, but it was hopeless; Quay was acquitted and the other cases were abandoned.

Popular feeling was excited by this exposure of Quay, but there was no action till the factional fighting suggested a use for it. Quay had refused the second United States senatorship to John Wanamaker, and Wanamaker led through the state and in Philadelphia a fight against the boss, which has never ceased. It took the form of a reform campaign, and Quay's methods were made plain, but the boss beat Wanamaker at every point, had Penrose made senator, and through Penrose and Durham was gradually getting possession of Philadelphia. The final triumph came with the election of Samuel H. Ashbridge as mayor.

Martin Out – "Is" Durham Boss

"Stars-and-Stripes Sam," as Ashbridge is sometimes called, was a speech-maker and a "joiner." That is to say, he made a practice of going to lodges, associations, brotherhoods, Sunday-schools, and all sorts of public and private meetings, joining some, but making at all speeches patriotic and sentimental. He was very popular. Under the Bullitt Law, as I have said, all that is necessary to a good administration and complete though temporary reform is a good mayor. The politicians feel that they must nominate a man in whom the people as well as themselves have faith. They had faith in Warwick, both the ring and the people, and Warwick had found it impossible to satisfy two such masters. Now they put their faith in Ashbridge, and so did Durham, and so did Martin. All interests accepted him, therefore, and all watched him with hope and more or less assurance; none more than the good people. And, indeed, no man could have promised more or better public service than Ashbridge. The result, however, was distracting.

Mr. Ashbridge "threw down" Martin, and he recognized Quay's man, "Is" Durham, as the political boss. Durham is a high type of boss, candid, but of few words; generous, but businesslike; complete master of himself, and a genius at organization. For Pennsylvania politics he is a conservative leader, and there would have been no excesses under him, as there have been few "rows." But Mr. Durham has not been the master of the Philadelphia situation. He bowed to Quay, and he could not hold Ashbridge. Philadelphians say that if it should come to a fight, Durham could beat Quay in Philadelphia, but it doesn't come to a fight. Another thing Philadelphians say is that he "keeps his word," yet he broke it (with notice) when Quay asked him to stand for Pennypacker for governor. As I said before, however, Philadelphia is so constituted that it apparently cannot have self-government, not even its own boss, so that the allegiance paid to Quay is comprehensible. But the submission of the boss to the mayor was extraordinary, and it seemed to some sagacious politicians dangerous.

For Mr. Ashbridge broke through all, the principles of moderate grafting developed by Martin. Durham formed his ring—taking in James P. McNichol as co-ruler and preferred contractor; John M. Mack as promoter and financier; and he widened the inside circle to include more individuals. But while he was more liberal toward his leaders, and not inclined "to grab off everything for himself," as one leader told me, he maintained the principle of concentration and strict control as good politics and good business. So, too, he adopted Martin's programme of public improvements, the filtration, boulevards, etc., and he added to it. When Ashbridge was well settled in office, these schemes were all started, and the mayor pushed them with a will. According to the "Philadelphia Plan," the mayor should not be in the ring. He should be an ambitious man, and his reward promotion, not riches. If he is "out for the stuff," he is likely to be hurried by the fretful thought that his term is limited to four years, and since he cannot succeed himself as mayor, his interest in the future of the machine is less than that of a boss, who goes on forever.

"All There Is In It For Ashbridge"

When he was nominated, Ashbridge had debts of record amounting to some $40,000. Before he was elected these were satisfied. Soon after he took office he declared himself to former Postmaster Thomas L. Hicks. Here is Mr. Hicks's account of the incident:

"At one of the early interviews I had with the mayor in his office, he said to me: 'Tom, I have been elected mayor of Philadelphia. I have four years to serve. I have no further ambitions. I want no other office when I am out of this one, and I shall get out of this office all there is in it for Samuel H. Ashbridge.'

"I remarked that this was a very foolish thing to say. 'Think how that could be construed,' I said.

" 'I don't care anything about that,' he declared. 'I mean to get out of this office everything there is in it for Samuel H. Ashbridge.' "

When he retired from office last April, he became the president of a bank, and was reputed to be rich. Here is the summary published by the Municipal League at the close of his labors:

"The four years of the Ashbridge administration have passed into history, leaving behind them a scar on the fame and reputation of our city which will be a long time healing. Never before, and let us hope never again, will there be such brazen defiance of public opinion, such flagrant disregard of public interest, such abuse of powers and responsibilities for private ends. These are not generalizations, but each statement can be abundantly proved by numerous instances."

Blackmailing the Press

These "numerous instances" are notorious in Philadelphia; some of them were reported all over the country. One of them was the attempted intimidation of John Wanamaker. Thomas B. Wanamaker, John Wanamaker's son, bought the *North American*, a newspaper which had been, and still is, exposing the abuses and corruption of the political ring. Abraham L. English, Mr. Ashbridge's Director of the Department of Public Safety, called on Mr. John Wanamaker, said he had been having him watched, and was finally in a position to demand that the newspaper stop the attacks. The merchant exposed the whole thing, and a committee appointed to investigate reported that: "Mr. English has practically admitted that he attempted to intimidate a reputable citizen and unlawfully threatened him in an effort to silence criticism of a public newspaper; that from the mayor's refusal to order an investigation of the conduct of Mr. English on the request of a town meeting of representative citizens, the community is justified in regarding him as aiding and abetting Mr. English in the corrupt act committed, and that the mayor is therefore to be equally censured by the community."

Vice Cultivated and Protected

The other "instances of brazen abuse of power" were the increase of protected vice—the importation from New York of the "white slavery system of prostitution," the growth of speakeasies, and the spread of gambling and of policy-playing until it took in the school children. This last the *North American* exposed, but in vain till it named police officers who had refused when asked to interfere. Then a judge summoned the editors and reporters of the paper, the mayor, Director English, school children, and police officers to appear before him. The mayor's personal attorney spoke for the police during the inquiry, and it looked black for the newspaper till the children began to tell their stories. When the hearing was over the judge said:

"The evidence shows conclusively that our public school system in this city is in danger of being corrupted at its fountain; that in one of the schools over a hundred and fifty children were buyers of policy, as were also a large number of scholars in other schools. It was first discovered about eighteen months ago, and for about one year has been in full operation." The police officers were not punished, however.

Public Schools a Graft

That corruption had reached the public schools, and was spreading rapidly through the system, was discovered by the exposure and conviction of three school directors of the twenty-eighth ward. It was known before that teachers and principals, like any other office holders, had to have "pull" and pay assessments for election expenses. "Voluntary contributions" was the term used, but over the notices in blue pencil was written "2 percent," and teachers who asked directors and ward bosses what to do were advised that they had "better pay." Those that sent less than the amount suggested, got receipts: "Check received; shall we hold for balance or enter on account?" But the exposure in the twenty-eighth ward brought it home to the parents of the children that the teachers were not chosen for fitness, but for political reasons, and that the political reasons had become cash.

Miss Rena A. Haydock testified as follows: "I went to see Mr. Travis, who was a friend of mine, in reference to getting a teacher's certificate. He advised me to see all of the directors, especially Mr. Brown. They told me that it would be necessary for me to pay $120 to get the place. They told me of one girl who had offered $250, and her application had been rejected. That was before they broached the subject of money to me. I said that I didn't have $120 to pay, and they replied that it was customary for teachers to pay $40 a month out of their first three months' salary. The salary was $47. They told me they didn't want the money for themselves, but that it was necessary to buy the other faction. Finally I agreed to the proposition, and they told me that I must be careful not to mention it to anybody or it would injure my reputation. I went with my brother to pay the money to Mr.

Johnson. He held out a hat, and when my brother handed the money to him he took it behind the hat."

"Macing" Corporations

The regular business of the ring was like that of Pittsburgh, but more extensive. I have space only for one incident of one phase of it: Widener and Elkins, the national franchise buyers, are Philadelphians, and they were in the old Martin ring. They had combined all the street railways of the city before 1900, and they were withdrawing from politics, with their traction system. But the Pennsylvania rings will not let corporations that have risen in corruption reform and retire, and, besides, it was charged that in the Martin-Quay fight, the street railways had put up money to beat Quay for the United States Senate. At any rate, plans were laid to "mace" the street railways.

"Macing" is a form of high blackmail. When they have sold out all they have, the politicians form a competing company and compel the old concern to buy out or sell out. While Widener and Elkins were at sea, bound for Europe, in 1901, the Philadelphia ring went to the legislature and had introduced there two bills, granting a charter to practically all the streets and alleys not covered by tracks in Philadelphia, and to run short stretches of the old companies' tracks to make connections. Clinton Rogers Woodruff, who was an assemblyman, has told the story. Without notice the bills were introduced at 3 P.M. on Monday, May 29; they were reported from committee in five minutes; by 8.50 P.M. they were printed and on the members' desks, and by 9 P.M. were passed on first reading. The bills passed second reading the next day, Memorial Day, and on the third day were passed from the Senate to the House, where they were "jammed through" with similar haste and worse trickery. In six legislative days the measures were before Governor Stone, who signed them June 7, at midnight, in the presence of Quay, Penrose, Congressman Foerderer, Mayor Ashbridge's banker, James P. McNichol, John M. Mack and other capitalists and politicians. Under the law, one hundred charters were applied for the next morning—thirteen for Philadelphia. The charters were granted on June 5, and that same day a special meeting of the Philadelphia Select Council was called for Monday. There the citizens of Philadelphia met the oncoming charters, but their hearing was brief. The charters went through without a hitch, and were sent to Mayor Ashbridge on June 13.

$2,500,000 Declined for a Franchise

The mayor's secretary stated authoritatively in the morning that the mayor would not sign that day. But he did. An unexpected incident forced his hand. John Wanamaker sent him an offer of $2,500,000 for the franchises about to be given away. Ashbridge threw the letter into the street unread. Mr. Wanamaker had deposited $250,000 as a guarantee of good faith and his action was becoming known. The ordinances were signed by midnight, and the city lost at least two and one-half millions of dollars; but the ring made it and much more. When Mr. Wanamaker's letter was published, Congressman Foerderer, an incorporator of the company, answered for the machine. He said the offer was an advertisement; that it was late, and that they were sorry they hadn't had a chance to "call the bluff." Mr. Wanamaker responded with a renewal of the offer of $2,500,000 to the city, and, he said, "I will add $500,000 as a bonus to yourself and your associates personally for the conveyance of the grants and corporate privileges you now possess." That ended the controversy.

But the deal went on. Two more bills, called "Trolley Chasers," were put through, to finish off the legislation, too hurriedly done to be perfect. One was to give the company the right to build either elevated or underground, or both; the second to forbid all further such grants without a hearing before a board consisting of the governor, the Secretary of the Commonwealth, and the attorney-general. With all these franchises and exclusive privileges, the new company made the old one lease their plant in operation to the company which had nothing but "rights," or, in Pennsylvania slang, a "good, husky mace."

Ashbridgeism put Philadelphia and the Philadelphia machine to a test which candid ring leaders did not think it would stand. What did the Philadelphians do? Nothing. They have their reformers: they have men like Francis B. Reeves, who fought with every straight reform movement from the days of the Committee of One Hundred; they have men like Rudolph Blankenburg, who have fought with every reform that promised any kind of relief; there are the Municipal League, with an organization by wards, the Citizens' Municipal League, the Allied Reform League, and the Law and Order Society; there are young men and veterans; there are disappointed politicians and ambitious men who are not advanced fast enough by the machine. There is discontent in a good many hearts, and some men are ashamed. But "the people" won't follow. One would think the Philadelphians would follow any leader; what should they care whether he is pure white or only gray? But they do care. "The people" seem to-prefer to be ruled by a known thief than an ambitious reformer. They will make you convict their Tweeds, McManeses, Butlers, and Shepherds, and even then they may forgive them and talk of monuments to their precious memory, but they take delight in the defeat of John Wanamaker because they suspect that he is a hypocrite and wants to go to the United States Senate.

All the stout-hearted reformers had made a campaign to re-elect Rothermel, the district attorney who had dared to try Quay. Surely there was an official to support! But no, Quay was against him. The reformers used money, some $250,000, I believe—fighting the devil with fire—but the machine used more money, $700,000 from the teachers, "speak-easies," office holders, bankers, and corporations. The machine handled the ballots. Rothermel was beaten by John Weaver. There have been other campaigns, before and since, led by the Municipal League, which is managed with political sense, but each successive defeat was by a larger majority for the machine, and against good government.

There is no check upon this machine excepting the chance of a mistake, the imminent fear of treachery, and the remote danger of revolt. To meet this last, the machine, as a state organization, has set about throttling public criticism. Ashbridge found that blackmail was ineffective. Durham, Quay, and Governor Pennypacker have passed a libel law which meant to muzzle the press. The governor was actuated apparently only by his sufferings from cartoons and comments during his campaign; the Philadelphia ring has boodling plans ahead which exposure might make exasperating to the people. The *Philadelphia Press*, the leading Republican organ in the state, puts it right: "The governor wanted it [the law] in the hope of escaping from the unescapable cartoon. The gang wanted it in hope of muzzling the opposition to jobs. . . . The act is distinctly designed to gag the press in the interest of the plunderers and against the interest of the people."

Disfranchised, without a choice of parties; denied, so the Municipal League declares, the ancient right of petition; and now to lose "free speech"—is there no hope for Philadelphia? Yes, the Philadelphians have a very present hope. It is in their new mayor, John Weaver. There is nothing in his record to inspire faith in an outsider. He speaks himself of two notorious "miscarriages of justice" during his term as district attorney; he was the nominee of the ring; and the ring men have confidence in him. But so have the people, and Mr. Weaver makes fair promises. So did Ashbridge. There is this difference, however: Mr. Weaver has made a good start. He compromised with the machine on his appointments, but he declared against the protection of vice, for free voting, and he stopped some "wholesale grabs" or "maces" that appeared in the legislature, just before he took office.

Scheme to Sell Out the Water Works

One was a bill to enable (ring) companies to "appropriate, take, and use all water within this commonwealth and belonging either to public or to private persons as it may require for its private purposes." This was a scheme to sell out the water-works of Philadelphia, and all other such plants in the state. Another bill was to open the way to a seizure of the light and power of the city and of the state. Martin and Warwick "leased" the city gas works. Durham and his crowd wanted a whack at it. "It shall be lawful," the bill read, "for any city, town, or borough owning any gas works or electric light plant for supplying light, heat, and power, to sell, lease, or otherwise dispose of the same to individuals or corporations, and in order to obtain the best possible returns therefor, such municipal body may . . . vest in the lessees or purchasers the exclusive right, both as against such municipal corporations and against any and all other persons and corporations, to supply gas or electricity." As in St. Louis, the public property of the city is to be sold off. These schemes are to go through later, I am told, but on Mr. Weaver's declarations that he would not "stand for them," they were laid over.

It looks as if the Philadelphians were right about Mr. Weaver, but what if they are? Think of a city putting its whole faith in one man, in the hope that John Weaver, an Englishman by birth, will give them good government! And why should he do that? Why should he serve the people and not the ring? The ring can make or break him; the people of Philadelphia can neither reward nor punish him. For even if he restores to them their ballots and proves himself a good mayor, he cannot succeed himself; the good charter forbids.

McClure's Magazine
August, 1903

Jacob A. Riis

Reporter, Reformer, American Citizen

IF any rich man could mark a city with as many good works as Jacob A. Riis has thrust upon New York, his name would be called good and himself great; no matter how he made his money, the man would be a philanthropist. Riis is a reporter. The evils he exposed he discovered as a reporter; as a reporter he wrung men's hearts with them; and the reporter with his "roasts" compelled indifferent city officials to concede the reforms he suggested or approved. Consider these reforms: It was Riis who exposed the contaminated state of the city's water supply, and thus brought about the purchase of the whole Croton watershed. It was Riis who forced the destruction of rear tenements, and thus relieved the hideous darkness and density of life among the poor. It was the reporter with his nagging that wiped out Mulberry Bend, the worst tenement block in the city, and had the space turned into a park. Riis spoke the word that incited Commissioner Roosevelt to abolish police station lodging-houses. Riis fought for and secured a truant school, where boys who play hooky are punished—they used to be imprisoned with juvenile criminals. Riis did the work that won small parks for bad spots in the city; he labored years for enough schools; he drove bake shops with their fatal fires out of tenement basements; he demanded light for dark tenement hallways, got it, and thus opened one hiding place of vice, crime, and filth. He worked for the abolition of child labor, and, when a law was enacted, compelled its enforcement. Playgrounds for schools and the opening of schoolrooms to boys' and girls' clubs were of his work. And he raised the cry for flowers for the healthy as well as the sick poor.

Theodore Roosevelt once said that Riis was "the most useful citizen of New York." A Harvard professor who heard the remark spoke of it as a "generous exaggeration" characteristic of Mr. Roosevelt. The man who is president never chose words more nicely. People don't realize it, but no citizen of New York ever devoted himself so completely to the welfare of the city as Riis, and truly no one has accomplished so much—so many specific, tangible reforms.

Of course he did not do all these things singlehanded, and he did not pay for them out of his own pocket. Riis was poor in pocket, but he was rich in sentiment and strength and courage. He gave facts and made the city pay. The man has cost New York City millions of dollars. According to the latest principle of public benefaction, however, this makes him all the more a philanthropist, for such men as Rockefeller and Carnegie have been giving money only on condition that the city or institution receiving the gifts should raise as much more, and Mr. Carnegie told me once that he was prouder of what he had made cities do for themselves than of all that he himself had given. So Riis, who has made his city foot the whole bill, is the greatest philanthropist of them all.

Now Riis does not care for fame; that is one secret of his success, and he used to say the elevation of his name with an account of his methods would hinder him. But his work is about done and he has told his own story in "The Making of an American." Besides, he told me not long ago to "go ahead and expose him," so that, though I know he will denounce some of the things I am going to say, I should like to help urge the claim he has made to the titles "reporter, reformer, American citizen." Then, too, he is such a good man to know.

Riis is a lusty Danish emigrant, with a vigorous body, an undisciplined mind that grasps facts as he himself sees them, an imagination to reconstruct, emotion to suffer, and a kind, fighting spirit, to weep, whoop, laugh, and demand. As a reporter he saw straight, told about it in words hot with emotion, and, because his feeling was genuine, he was not content with the pleasant sensation of horror he gave his readers, neither could he be ordered off on some other assignment; he turned reformer, and while the man continued to pity, the reporter continued to report, and the reformer worked through despair to set the wrong right.

As a citizen, public business came first in his interest, his own second. His love for his wife is such that his story of it is one of the most amazing and beautiful love stories in the world. But having given her this love of faith, passion, and imagination, he gave the rest "to God and New York."

Oh, he is a fanatic, this Riis. But he has such a laugh, and such luck. I used to remonstrate with him for neglecting his family. He had bought a home, with a mortgage all over it, and instead of hastening to pay it off, he was giving lectures free, or for ten, twenty-five, or fifty dollars, writing articles for about the same prices, and laboring for small parks or school playgrounds, or to tear down rear tenements. His lectures and his articles, he said, helped along the cause, and, besides, it was not worth more than ten dollars to stand up and talk about what he loved to tell. Thus he reasons: As for the family, "God will provide."

When I reminded him one morning that he might die and that the friends of a reformer, unlike those of the rascal, forget, he told me to get out and picked up his mail.

"I know what I'm talking about," he said. "I've been in all sorts of trouble and He always has provided. Right now, for instance, I'm broke. My oldest boy needs an overcoat and the winter is coming. How I'm going to get the money for that overcoat I don't know, but it will come because I must have—"

He stopped, intent on a letter. "What's this!" he exclaimed. Then he jumped up, and waving a check, roared the jolly laugh which all Mulberry Street knows well. "Hi, yi," he bawled, and as I quit him in disgust he yelled at my back the explanation that some man down South had paid at last a bill for an advertisement Riis wrote for him years before. Riis swore he had forgotten all about it, and I believed him. I gave him up. I scoffed at his "luck," and he jeered at me for calling it that. And I really came to believe in whatever it was myself. Besides, he has since raised his rates, wiped out the mortgage, and gone to work for his family, and, though I'd like to reform almost every other reformer I ever knew, I shouldn't change Riis, even if I could, in any particular, least of all in his roaring follies.

One winter day he asked me to go with him to a case of distress on the East Side; two lone women, mother and daughter, were starving in a rotten tenement. We found them on the top floor, where the stench was shocking. At his knock the door reluctantly opened, and from a closet-sized room, with no window, the pent-up reek burst forth like a backdraft. Riis recoiled and I halted on the top stair. A white old head stuck out, the daughter's, and said she and her mother were in dire need; they had no food, and were staying in bed to keep warm.

"But haven't I seen you before?" Riis asked after a while.

"Are you Mr. Riis? Oh!" and she was about to close the door.

"Hold on," said he; "didn't I put you and your mother on a nice farm over in Jersey a year ago, with nothing to do but enjoy the flowers and the cows—why didn't you stay there?"

"Because—well, because—because there was nothing to do; nobody to see or nothing."

"So you'd rather starve in filth in this beastly place than do—"

"What you'd like best of all to do," I interrupted.

"Come on," said Riis, disgusted, and he called back that he would "see."

I don't know what he finally "saw" in this case; it was pretty surely a "fairly worthy case," but he never could see how it was that city poor preferred city poverty to the green fields, etc., which he loved and recommended and often had thrown back at him. He was easily imposed upon because he believed so thoroughly in human nature and loved it, but he knew that he could be deceived, and that, I think, is why he tolerated organized charity. I have heard him denounce it in private many a time, then go right off to support it publicly with an eloquence that must have derived some of its force from the passion of his rage at it.

His worship of women is one of the most beautiful of his traits. He knew all the good women in New York, and they loved Riis as he adored them. Since they were in organized charity, organized charity must be right. I may be wrong about this, but unless I can trace a trait of Riis to his heart, I don't feel that I have reached bottom, and I know positively that he couldn't tell a bad woman from a good one; they were all just women to him.

"There," he said one afternoon, as he pointed across Mulberry Street to a bleached blonde in Cat Alley. "There you have the basis of my faith in the slums. See that face!"

It was a young face, and though hard lines were coming, the general aspect still was soft and tired and very white. I had the advantage of knowing who and what the girl was, but I nodded.

"Well, as long as there are women like that in the slums," he declared, in his vigorous, positive way, "there is hope for the slums and a rock to build on."

"Go speak to her, Riis," I suggested.

"I will," he said, and he walked casually into the alley, looked around, and then remarked that he intended some day to bring his camera and take pictures of "all you people."

The girl looked at him a moment, and her face hardened. "Ye will, will ye?" she said. "Ye will, eh? Well, say, ye —— —— bring your — machine in here and we'll break every bone in your body, and the thing besides. Go chase yerself."

Riis staggered back, and neither of us enjoyed "the joke." It was too practical, and I was sorry for my part in it. But it did not shake his faith even in that woman, one of the worst white women in Chinatown. He charged her up to the slums.

For is it not a wonderful thing that this man who has worked all the best part of his mature life as a police reporter, "covering" murders, suicides, burglaries, crimes, and vices of all sorts, from body snatchers down to "mixed ale" rows in brothels, should come out as sweet and clean and as full of faith and follies as his old Danish village made him? Priests and nurses have done it, but Riis was tried far more than they. He did not go about merely to see and help, he went back and reported it. When he had done that he struggled with corrupt city officials for relief. Their chicaneries he saw; he caught them red-handed at their sordid tricks. Then, too, he was fighting other reporters who had combined to "beat the Dutchman" and who were willing "to fake to do him." Severest test of all, he was wading up to his neck in police corruption, knowing well men who lived by blackmail and profits shared with thieves, gamblers, and prostitutes. None of this soiled this man outside or in, neither himself nor his ideals nor his belief in his fellow men.

Riis was never really "wise." When I first met him we all were busy exposing further the Tammany police system of corruption from which Dr. Parkhurst first lifted the veil. We had just written one day something about the divulgences of the Lexow Committee, and Riis's article was as vigorous as anybody's. Yet when he had written it he came into my office and closed the door.

"Do you know," he said, "I don't believe it."

"What?"

"Why, what we've been writing."

"You know it's true," I said, astonished.

"I suppose I do; I suppose I ought to," he said thoughtfully. Then he broke out with force. " But I don't believe it. I can't. I don't believe, for instance, that Captain —"

At that name I sprang up. The man he was about to cite was a sanctimonious rascal, "smooth," but one of the very worst offenders; Tammany had trusted him; Roosevelt trusted him then; Devery has trusted him since; Commissioner Partridge trusted him. But everybody who knew anything about police affairs knew that Captain — was the brains of the whole police syndicate, the most hypocritical, the most intelligent, and the most grasping of corrupt police officials. Riis found him out later, five or six years later, but at that time Riis had known this man for fifteen years, and was discrediting his own ears and eyes.

The power to conceive evil in its vicious form failed Riis always. He has a brilliant imagination. He has gathered with the cleverest reporters in New York the facts of a news story, and, by grasping them with his sympathy and his imagination, has so written them that his paper appeared to have a "beat." His imagination was that of a child or a genius. If this hadn't been so he never would have done his great work, which, indeed, all came out of his imagination and feeling. The evils of the slums lay before the other reporters' eyes; they too had to pass and repass the Bowery; they too had to dive into Mulberry Bend night and day. They got the murders, as Riis did, but he got something else, which finally blew the Bend off the face of the city. Riis realized and visualized where ordinary men "faked."

Far deeper than any intellectual faculty lay his sympathy. His life, as you can see in "The Making of an American," has been one long stretch of emotional excitement. The world has played upon his sensibilities as it does upon the soul of a musician, and since his feelings found no expression in art, they went off, not as with most men of his temperament in weird dissipations or lay sermons, but in action. A natural shrewdness guided his conduct and directed his impulses. Loose and careless as I have shown him in his personal afairs, when it came to his work for others, whether for his newspaper or his town, he could wait, plot, pull wires!—yes, he could even play tricks; and a successful trick gave him the most robust enjoyment.

A story he used to tell with great gusto was of the defeat of a sanitary expert who had written a report of an especially important investigation. All the reporters wanted that report; none could get it from the expert, least of all Riis, his friend. The commissioner had forbidden its publication. There was no other reason than the form of the thing for withholding it, and Riis made up his mind to get it. He worked long in vain till one day a committee of women from a charity organization called on Riis for an address.

"Very well," he said. "But no, I won't. You ask Dr. — to talk to you about overcrowding in the tenements; he's full of it and will talk well."

They did, the doctor was glad to overflow, and Riis, who was a member of the women's organization, sat in the committee room off the main room and wrote down the gist of that report, and to hear Riis tell about it, especially if the defeated official were by, was to get as much fun out of Riis's "deviltry" as he got out of the "beat."

Indeed it was this roaring humor as much as his shrewdness that kept his sentimentality within bounds, and turned into a working force his human sympathies. The evils he suffered and the evils he saw moved his pity, but, his emotions stirred, turned him not to tears, but to imprecations and strife. Christian though he was, he was a heathenish Viking, first and last, and his life has been one long fight. He wanted always to be a soldier, and three times he tried hard to enlist for the wars.

Human misery, however, was his born enemy, and the struggle with that began in his childhood. That's the spirit of the man. Things never were matters of course with him, and he "never could mind his own business." Willful and combative, he has been a bother to many a man. His father, a teacher, wanted him to be a scholar; he became a carpenter. He loved a girl who didn't love him, quarreled with her father, came to America, continued to love the girl, starved, peddled flatirons, starved again, fought with a French consul who wouldn't send him to France to enlist against Denmark's ancient enemy — Germany; slept in police station lodging-houses; quarreled with a German bum because he was for Germany against France, with the police sergeant who killed his dog; edited a paper and turned its editorials against the owners who were in politics; won his girl; got a job as a reporter and was promoted for knocking down the city editor; was sent to police headquarters because all the reporters there had combined against his paper, which needed a fighter. Well, he fought. A foreigner, he didn't write very good English; it was vigorous, but not always correct. (He learned to write and to speak with eloquence, not by study, but by sheer force of the necessity to express his ideas and his feelings.) Mixed with his facts were his opinions on them, and these editorial expressions were often in conflict with his editors', who interdicted them, but Riis kept on writing them, and at last the editors either cut them out or let them go. "They gave me up as a bad job," Riis says. And beaten at first, Riis soon was beating his rival reporters. They went to work at noon, he came down at eleven; they came at eleven, he at eight; they came at eight, Riis was soon covering the town from the time the morning papers went to press at 2.30 o'clock in the morning, and to that "crazy" extreme the others would not follow.

"I was in a fight not of my own choosing," he says in his book, "and . . . I hit as hard as I knew how, and so did they." And I know that he enjoyed it.

One of his great public benefactions, the most costly to New York, was a newspaper "beat," and typical of the shrewdness and intelligence of the man. Riis picked up in the Health Department one day the weekly analysis of the Croton water, and read "a trace of nitrites." "What are nitrites?" he asked. Getting an evasive answer, he went off and found out what nitrites were, published the news, explaining that they meant sewage contamination, and advising people to boil the water. Then, while the other papers were pooh-poohing the news, he went up through the Croton watershed with a camera and took pictures of towns sewering into the streams, public dumps on their banks, people and animals washing in the water. He made good his case. The other papers belittled the conditions, saying running water purifies itself; but Riis inquired how long it took the water to come down from the worst town, sixty miles away. The answer was, four days. He asked the experts how long a cholera germ might live in running water; "seven days" was the answer. New York had to buy up that watershed, and the cost ran into the millions; but Riis had his "beat" and New York has pure water.

"Beat" though it was, however, and insist as I do and as Riis himself does always that he accomplished all his best work as a reporter, the rivalry of journalism was not the source of his power, nor its triumphs his leading motive. Keen, fresh-minded observation discovered for him the facts of abuses, and the reporter gloried in the discovery, but it was the man that raised the reporter to a reformer. There was nothing professional in his observation that truant boys sent among criminal children in the reform schools soon began to turn up as criminals. Any of the men who crossed on his ferry with him might have brought flowers gathered by their children to throw to the children of the poor, and, discovering that they loved them, any man might have appealed to the public for flowers for the slums; any of the reporters might have seen any of the evils Riis saw as they went for crime and accident stories among the tenements. Riis saw and reported; then Riis, after many years, obtained a separate school for truants. When the flowers poured into Mulberry Street by the wagon load, so that he, with the help of all the other reporters, a special detail of police, and volunteers, couldn't distribute them, Riis founded a society of women to attend to this pleasant business, and that society, with Riis as vice-president, does this work to this day. The tenements were a larger task, but he went at them in the same way, hand and head and heart. With all his newspaper work and its fights on his mind, he studied and counseled and made notes, then wrote "How the Other Half Lives," which created a sensation. Investigating committees were appointed, and "The Children of the Poor" came out to show that Riis was still at work, and would let the awakened public conscience have no rest. Ten years followed of fighting, of despair, but of no relaxation for Riis, till in the end he won his victories and wrote "The Ten Years' War."

Now how did Riis win these victories? An effective reformer is so rare that he should be accounted for; a bold exposition of the methods by which an obscure reporter wrought so many reforms might make useful some of the well-meaning meddlers who never get anywhere. I fear not, however. Riis was simply a good citizen; the big, jolly, sentimental Dane took his adopted citizenship literally, and literally "worked for the public good"—"worked" like a political rascal.

His methods were much like those of a boss. In the first place he kept himself in the background, sought no office, indulged no vanity and no self-glorification. In the second place he worked all the time. "The churches may close, the saloons and the slums are open all day and all night, all week and the year round," he said once to me. In the third place he played upon men, used them, and women too, and while he preached he pulled wires. In the fourth place he bided his time, to strike when the right iron turned up hot.

Once, as he has told, when he was out of work and starving, he sat in the cold rain beside the river, contemplating a dive out of it all, when a little cur he had befriended crept up under his arm. That saved him and he moped off to a station lodging-house. There it was he got into his row with a German tramp over the Franco-Prussian war, and the next morning a German sergeant wouldn't heed Riis's complaint that a locket his mother had given him was stolen from his neck. Riis "kicked" and they put him out. As he appeared his little dog jumped toward him, a police boot kicked it, and, when Riis remonstrated, a police brute caught the dog, swung it up in the air, and down on the stone step, crushing its head.

Police station lodging-houses had to go; but Riis waited years and years till Roosevelt came. One night he took the commissioner up to the old station house, showed him the filthy place, unchanged, and told him his dog story. The next day the lodging-houses were condemned.

Not all reform officials were "right irons," however, and few were ever "hot" long enough to hit. Riis wrung many changes out of the Strong Administration, but only by dint of much scheming and wire pulling, and by those means he won reforms out of Tammany as well. He worked when his side was out of power just as he did when it was in, and there was nothing partisan about his associations. His method was in general the same in all cases. When he knew all about an evil—like the Bend, for instance—he would get some prominent men or women to form a committee. Having described the inhuman conditions of the place, with photographs, he furnished the material to his committee, who signed an address Riis wrote, gave it to Riis to publish, and went off with it to the mayor or legislature. Riis was there to take down and print the "promises." Every time a murder occurred in the Bend, Riis recalled the promises, and after a while he sent his committee off to make more urgent demands, while he happened along to collect more emphatic promises. Meanwhile, he would start other organizations—the Academy of Medicine, the Chamber of Commerce, etc.—to resolution-making. With these he would go, as a reporter, to "hold up" the mayor for an interview. "Done anything?" "Why not?" "Then you still intend to?" "Well, when?" "All right." So he bored and bothered until he got a commission appointed to condemn property. This commission he pursued in the same way. The property condemned, Riis went after the Public Works Commissioner. Riis saw that the officials did not forget, and he saw that it didn't matter if his reform committee forgot or went away. If the members were at the seashore, Riis was capable of getting out a protest in their names, or of uttering an interview for some good citizen, who had to "stand for" Riis's ideas, feelings, and hot wrath.

"Everything takes ten years," said ex-Mayor Hewitt, who was one of Riis's most active fellow-conspirators. The Bend, the small parks, the rear tenements, each took ten years, and though many men and women did excellent service in those causes at one time or another, Riis alone worked on them from beginning to end; he alone never despaired or got tired or rested. Riis was the backbone of these reforms and many others with which his name was hardly ever connected.

I shall never forget the day Mulberry Bend Park was opened. There was to be a formal dedication with speeches that evening, and Riis and I walked together down there in the afternoon to see it. Where the old criminal block with its squalor and death had stood, were free air and sunshine; where later the wreck had lain, while Riis fought for its removal, were smooth sodded soil and curving walks. While we stood there Riis related again the story of his ten years' fight with the Bend, and he told it with humor, sentiment, even pathos; then some of his old rage at it came back, and he cursed some of the traits of his species. To distract him I said:

"I'm coming down to hear what'll say tonight, Riis."

"But I'm not going to speak."

"Why not?"

"Not invited."

"So they forgot you?"

"Ye—es," he said, and it was plain he was hurt; but he added vigorously, "and that's the greatest success of all. Nobody would help me if I were 'It'; if I were the chairman of this, and the chief speaker of that. As it is, so long as I let others have the glory, I can get these things done, things like this, like tearing down that beastly old Bend and having a park made where the children can step on the earth; dirt, dirt, like this, the children and I too."

And he stamped out upon the sward, sinking his feet deep into the tender sod, rejoicing. A policeman came running up shouting, "Keep off'n th' grass, ye bum." He seized Riis by the coat and gave him a resounding whack across his seat. Riis said never a word, and we walked on through the park, keeping "off the grass," Riis to his office, I to the City Hall to find out who were going to dedicate Mulberry Bend Park. They were all prominent men and women, most of them excellent folk, "reformers," too. But reformers are not so thoughtful as the professional politicians, not so kind; they forget.

McClure's Magazine
October, 1903

Chicago: Half Free and Fighting On

Ever since these articles on municipal corruption have been appearing, readers of them have been asking what they were to do about it all. As if I knew, as if "we" knew; as if there were any one way to deal with this problem in all places under any circumstances. There isn't, and if I had gone around with a ready-made reform scheme in the back of my head, it would have served only to keep me from seeing straight the facts that would not support my theory. The only editorial scheme we had was to study a few choice examples of bad city government and tell how the bad was accomplished, then seek out, here and abroad, some typical good governments and explain how the good was done—not how to do it, mind you, but how it had been done. The bad government series is not yet complete, but since so many good men apparently want to go to work right off, it was decided to pause for an instance on the reform side. I have chosen the best I have found. Political grafters have been cheerful enough to tell me they have "got a lot of pointers" from the corruption articles. I trust the reformers will pick up some "pointers" from—Chicago.

Yes, Chicago. First in violence, deepest in dirt; loud, lawless, unlovely, ill-smelling, irreverent, new; an overgrown gawk of a village, the "tough" among cities, a spectacle for the nations—I give Chicago no quarter, and Chicago asks for none. "Good," they cheer, when you find fault; "give us the gaff. We deserve it and it does us good." They do deserve it. Lying low beside a great lake of pure, cold water, the city has neither enough nor good enough water. With the ingenuity and will to turn their sewer, the Chicago River, and make it run backwards and upwards out of the lake, the city cannot solve the smoke nuisance. With resources for a magnificent system of public parking, it is too poor to pave and clean the streets. They can balance high buildings on rafts floating in mud, but they can't

Chicago: Half Free and Fighting On   223

quench the stench of the stockyards. The enterprise which carried through a World's Fair to a world's triumph is satisfied with two thousand five hundred policemen for two million inhabitants and one hundred and ninety-six square miles of territory, a force so insufficient (and inefficient) that it cannot protect itself, to say nothing of handling mobs, riotous strikers, and the rest of that lawlessness which disgraces Chicago. Though the city has an extra-legal system of controlling vice and crime, which is so effective that the mayor has been able to stop any practices against which he has turned his face—the "panel game," the "hat game," "wine rooms," "safe blowing"—though gambling is limited, regulated, and fair, and prostitution orderly; though, in short—through the power of certain political and criminal leaders—the mayor has been able to make Chicago, criminally speaking, "honest"—burglary and cruel hold-ups are tolerated. As government, all this is preposterous.

But I do not cite Chicago as an example of good municipal government, nor yet of good American municipal government; New York has, for the moment, a much better administration. But neither is Chicago a good example of bad government. There is grafting there, but after St. Louis it seems petty and after Philadelphia most unprofessional. Chicago is interesting for the things it has "fixed." What is wrong there is ridiculous. Politically and morally speaking. Chicago should be celebrated among American cities for reform, real reform, not moral fits and political uprisings, not reform waves that wash the "best people" into office to make fools of themselves and subside leaving the machine stronger than ever—none of these aristocratic disappointments of popular government—but reform that reforms, slow, sure, political, democratic reform, by the people, for the people. That is what Chicago has. It has found a way. All that I am sure of is that Chicago has something to teach every city and town in the country—including Chicago.

For Chicago is reformed only in spots. A political map of the city would show a central circle of white with a few white dots and dashes on a background of black, gray, and yellow. But the city once was pretty solid black. Criminally it was wide open; commercially it was brazen; socially it was thoughtless and raw;

it was a settlement of individuals and groups and interests with no common city sense and no political conscience. Everybody was for himself, none was for Chicago. There were political parties, but the organizations were controlled by rings, which in turn were parts of state rings, which in turn were backed and used by leading business interests through which this corrupt and corrupting system reached with its ramifications far and high and low into the social organization. The grafting was miscellaneous and very general; but the most open corruption was that which centered in the city council. It never was well organized and orderly. The aldermen had "combines," leaders, and prices, but, a lot of good-natured honest thieves, they were independent of party bosses and "the organizations," which were busy at their own graft. They were so unbusiness-like that business men went into the city council to reduce the festival of blackmail to decent and systematic bribery. These men helped matters some, but the happy-go-lucky spirit persisted until the advent of Charles T. Yerkes from Philadelphia, who, with his large experience of Pennsylvania methods, first made boodling a serious business. He had to go right into politics himself to get anything done. But he did get things done. The aldermanic combine was fast selling out the city to its "best citizens," when some decent men spoke up and called upon the people to stop it, the people who alone can stop such things.

And the people of Chicago stopped it; they have beaten boodling. That is about all they have done so far, but that is about all they have tried deliberately and systematically to do, and the way they have done that proves that they can do anything they set out to do. They worry about the rest; half free, they are not half satisfied and not half done. But boodling, with its backing of "big men" and "big interests," is the hardest evil a democracy has to fight, and a people who can beat it can beat anything.

Every community, city, town, village, state—the United States itself—has a certain number of men who are willing, if it doesn't cost anything, to vote right. They don't want to "hurt their business"; they "can't afford the time to go to the primaries"; they don't care to think much. But they will vote. This may not be much, but it is enough. All that this independent, non-partisan vote wants is leadership, and that is what Chicago reformers furnished.

Chicago: Half Free and Fighting On

They had no such definite idea when they began. They had no theory at all—nothing but wrath, experience, common Chicago sense, and newspapers ready to back reform, not for the news, but for the common good. Theories they had tried; and exposures, celebrated trials, even some convictions of boodlers. They had gone in for a civil service reform law, and, by the way, they got a good one. probably the best in any city in the country. But exposés are good only for one election; court trials may punish individuals, but even convictions do not break up a corrupt system; and a "reform law" without reform citizenship is like a ship without a crew. With all their "reforms," bad government persisted. There was that bear garden—the city council; something ought to be done to that. Men like William Kent, John H. Hamline, W. R. Manierre, A. W. Maltby. and James R. Mann had gone in there from their "respectable" wards and their presence proved that they could get there; their speeches were public protests, and their votes, "no," "no," "no" were plain indicators of wrong. But all this was not enough. The Civic Federation, a respectable but inefficient universal reforming association, met without plans in 1895. It called together two hundred representative men, with Lyman J. Gage at their head, "to do something." The two hundred appointed a committee of fifteen to "find something to do." One of the fifteen drew forth a fully drawn plan for a new municipal party, the old, old scheme. "That won't do," said Edwin Burritt Smith to Mr. Gage, who sat beside him. "No, that won't do," said Gage. But they didn't know what to do. To gain time Mr. Smith moved a sub-committee. The sub-committee reported back to the fifteen, the fifteen to the two hundred. And so, as Mr. Smith said, they "fumbled."

But notice what they didn't do. Fumblers as they were, they didn't talk of more exposures. "Heavens, we know enough," said one. They didn't go to the legislature for a new charter. They needed one, they need one today, and badly, too, but the men who didn't know what, but did know what not to do, wouldn't let them commit the folly of asking one corrupt legislature another corrupt legislature out of existence. And they didn't wait till the next mayoralty election to elect a "business mayor" who should give them good government.

They were bound to accept the situation just as it was—the laws, the conditions, the political circumstances, all exactly as they were—and, just as a politician would, go into the next fight, whatever it was, and fight. All they needed was a fighter. So it was moved to find a man, one man, and let this man find eight other men, who should organize the "Municipal Voters League." There were no instructions; the very name was chosen because it meant nothing and might mean anything.

But the man! That was the problem. There were men, a few, but the one man is always hard to find. There was William Kent, rich, young, afraid of nothing and always ready, but he was an alderman, and the wise ones declared that the Nine must not only be disinterested, but must appear so. William Kent wouldn't do. Others were suggested; none that would do. "How about George H. Cole?" "Just the man," said Mr. Gage, and all knew the thought was an inspiration.

George H. Cole described himself to me as a "second-class business man." Standing about five feet high, he knows he is no taller; but he knows that that is tall enough. Cole is a fighter. Nobody discovered it, perhaps, till he was past his fiftieth year. Then one Martin B. Madden found it out. Madden, a prominent citizen, president of the Western Stone Company, and a man of tremendous political power, was one of the business men who went into the council to bring order out of the chaos of corruption. He was a Yerkcs leader. Madden lived in Cole's ward. His house was in sight of Cole's house. "The sight of it made me hot," said Cole, " for I knew what it represented." Cole had set out to defeat Madden, and he made a campaign which attracted the attention of the whole town. Madden was reelected, but Cole had proved himself, and that was what made Lyman J. Gage say that Cole was "just the man."

"You come to me as a Hobson's choice," said Mr. Cole to the committee, "as a sort of forlorn hope. All right," he added, "as a last chance. I'll take it."

Cole went out to make up the Nine. He chose William H. Colvin. a wealthy business man. retired; Edwin Burritt Smith, publicist and lawyer; M. J. Carroll, ex-labor leader, ex-typesetter, an editorial writer on a trade journal; Frank Wells, a well-known real estate man; R. R. Donnelly, the head of one of the greatest printing establishments in the city; and Hoyt King, a young lawyer who turned out to be a natural investigator. These made, with Cole himself, only seven, but he had the help and counsel of Kent, Allen B. Pond, the architect. Judge Murray F. Tuley, Francis Lackner, and Graham Taylor. "We were just a few commonplace, ordinary men," said one of them to me, "and there is your encouragement for other commonplace, ordinary men." These men were selected for what they could do, however, not for what they "represented." The One Hundred, which the Nine were to complete, was to do the representing. But the One Hundred never was completed, and the ward committee, a feature of the first campaign, was abandoned later on. "The boss and the ring" was the model of the Nine, only they did not know it. They were not thinking of principles and methods. Work was their instinct and the fighting has always been thick. The next election was to be held in April, and by the time they were ready February was half over. Since it was to be an election of aldermen, they went right out after the aldermen. There were sixty-eight in all—fifty-seven of them "thieves," as the League reported promptly and plainly. Of the sixty-eight, the terms of thirty-four were expiring, and these all were likely to come up for reelection.

The thing to do was to beat the rascals. But how? Mr. Cole and his committee were pioneers; they had to blaze the way and, without plans, they set about it directly. Seeking votes, and honest votes, with no organization to depend upon, they had to have publicity. "We had first to let people know we were there," said Cole, so he stepped "out into the limelight" and, with his short legs apart, his weak eyes blinking, he talked. The League was out to beat the boodlers up for reelection, he said with much picturesque English. Now Chicago is willing to have anybody try to do anything worthwhile in Chicago; no matter who you are or where you come from Chicago will give you a cheer and a first boost. When, therefore, George B. Cole stood up and said he and a quiet little committee were going to beat some politicians at the game of politics, the good-natured town said: "All right, go ahead and beat 'em; but how?" Cole was ready with his answer. "We're going to publish the records of the thieves who want to get back at the trough." Alderman Kent and his decent colleagues produced the records of their indecent colleagues, and the league announced that of the thirty-four retiring aldermen, twenty-six were rogues. Hoyt King and a staff of briefless young lawyers looked up ward records, and "these also we will publish," said Cole. And they did; the Chicago newspapers, long on the right side and ever ready, printed them, and they were "mighty interesting reading." Edwin Burritt Smith stated the facts; Cole added "ginger" and Kent "pepper and salt and vinegar." They soon had publicity. Some of the committee shrank from the worst of it but Cole stood out and took it. He became a character in the town. He was photographed and caricatured; he was "Boss Cole" and "Old King-Cole," but all was grist to this reform mill. Some of the retiring aldermen retired at once. Others were retired. If information turned up by Hoyt King was too private for publication, the committee was, and is today, capable of sending for the candidate and advising him to get off the ticket. This was called "blackmail," and I will call it that, if the word will help anybody to appreciate how hard these reform politicians played and play the game.

While they were talking, however, they were working, and their work was done in the wards. Each ward was separately studied, the politics of each was separately understood, and separately each ward was fought. Declaring only for "aggressive honesty" at first, not competence, they did not stick even to that. They wanted to beat the rascals that were in, and, if necessary, if they couldn't hope to elect an honest man, they helped a likely rascal to beat the rascal that was in and known. They drew up a pledge of loyalty to public interest, but they didn't insist on it in some cases. Like the politicians, they were opportunists. Like the politicians, too, they were non-partisans. They played off one party against another, or, if the two organizations hung together, they put up an independent. They broke many a cherished reform principle, but few rules of practical politics. Thus, while they had some of their own sort of men nominated, they did not attempt, they did not think of running "respectable" or "business" candidates as such. Neither were they afraid to dicker with ward leaders and "corrupt politicians." They went down into the ward, urged the minority organization leader to name a "good man" on promise of independent support, then campaigned against the majority nominee with circulars, house-to-house canvassers, mass-meetings, bands, speakers, and parades. I should say that the basic, unstated principle of this reform movement, struck out early in the practice of the Nine, was to let the politicians rule, but through better and better men whom the Nine forced upon them with public opinion. But again I want to emphasize the fact that they had no fine-spun theories and no definite principles beyond that of being always for the best available man. They were with the Democrats in one ward, with the Republicans in another, but in none were they respecters of persons.

Right here appeared that insidious influence which we have seen defeating or opposing reform in other cities—the interference of respectable men to save their friends. In the Twenty-second Ward the Democrats nominated a director (now deceased) of the First National Bank and a prominent man socially and financially. John Colvin, one of the "Big Four," a politician who had gone away rich to Europe and was returning to go back into politics, also was running. The League preferred John Maynard Harlan, a son of Justice Harlan, and they elected him. The bank of which this candidate was a director was the bank of which Lyman J. Gage, of the League, was president. All that the League had against this man was that he was the proprietor of a house leased for questionable purposes, and his friends, including Mr. Gage, were highly indignant. Mr. Gage pleaded and protested. The committee was "sick of pulls" and they made short work of this most "respectable" pull. They had "turned down" politicians on no better excuse, and they declared they were not going to overlook in the friend of their friends what they condemned in some poor devil who had no friends.

There were many such cases, then and later; this sort of thing has never ceased and it never will cease; reform must always "go too far," if it is to go at all, for it is up there in the "too far" that corruption has its source. The League, by meeting it early, and "spotting it," as Mr. Cole said, not only discouraged such interference, but fixed its own character and won public confidence. For everything in those days was open. The League works more quietly now, but then Cole was talking it all out, plain to the verge of brutality, forcible to the limit of language, and honest to utter ruthlessness. He blundered and they all made mistakes, but their blundering only helped them, for while the errors were plain errors, the fairness of mind that rejected an Edward M. Stanwood, for example, was plain too. Stanwood, a respectable business man, had served as alderman, but his reelection was advised against by the League because he had "voted with the gang." A high public official, three judges, and several other prominent men interceded on the ground that "in every instance where he is charged with having voted for a so-called boodle ordinance, it was not done corruptly, but that he might secure votes for some meritorious measure." The League answered in this style: "We regard this defense, which is put forward with confidence by men of your standing, as painful evidence of the low standard by which the public conduct of city officials has come to be measured by good citizens. Do you not know that this is one of the most insidious and common forms of legislative corruption?" Mr. Stanwood was defeated.

The League "made good." Of the twenty-six outgoing aldermen with bad records, sixteen were not renominated. Of the ten who were, four were beaten at the polls. The League's recommendations were followed in twenty-five wards; they were disregarded in five; in some wards no fight was made.

A victory so extraordinary would have satisfied some reformers. Others would have been inflated by it and ruined. These men became canny. They chose this propitious moment to get rid of the committee of One Hundred respectables. Such a body is all very well to launch a reform, when no one knows that it is going to do serious work; but, as the Cole committee had learned, representative men with many interests can be reached. The little committee incorporated the League, then called together the big committee, congratulated it, and proposed a constitution and by-laws which would throw all the work— and all the power—to the little committee. The little committee was to call on the big committee only as money or some "really important" help was needed. The big committee approved, swelled up, adjourned, and that is the last time it has ever met.

Thus free of "pulls," gentlemanly pulls, but pulls just the same, the "nine" became nine by adding two—Allen B. Pond and Francis Lackner—and prepared for the next campaign. Their aldermen, the "reform crowd" in the city council were too few to do anything alone, but they could protest, and they did. They adopted the system of William Kent, which was to find out what was going on and tell it in council meetings.

"If you go on giving away the people's franchises like this," Alderman Harlan would say, "you may wake up some morning to find street lamps are useful for other purposes than lighting the streets." Or, "Some night the citizens, who are watching you, may come down here from the galleries with pieces of hemp in their hands." Then he would picture an imagined scene of the galleries rising and coming down upon the floor. He made his descriptions so vivid and creepy that they made some aldermen fidget. "I don't like dis business all about street lamps and hemp—vot dot is?" said a German boodler one night. "We don't come here for no such a business."

"We meant only to make headlines for the papers," said one of the reform aldermen. "If we could keep the attention of the public upon the council we could make clear what was going on there, and that would put meaning into our next campaign. And we certainly did fill the galleries and the newspapers."

As a matter of fact, however, they did much more. They developed in that year the issue which has dominated Chicago local politics ever since—the proper compensation to the city for public franchises. These valuable rights should not be given away, they declared, and they repeated it for good measures as well as bad. Not only must the city be paid, but public convenience and interest must be safeguarded. The boodlers boodled and the franchises went off; the protestation hurried the rotten business; but even that haste helped the cause. For the sight, week after week, of the boodle raids by rapacious capital fixed public opinion, and if the cry raised then for municipal ownership ever becomes a fact in Chicago, capital can go back to those days and blame itself.

Most of the early Chicago street railway franchises were limited, carelessly, to twenty-five years—the first one in 1858. In

1883, when the earliest franchises might have been terminated, the council ventured to pass only a blanket extension for twenty years—till July 30, 1903. This was well enough for Chicago financiers, but in 1886-7, when Yerkes appeared, with Widener and Elkins behind him, and bought up the West and North side companies, he applied Pennsylvania methods. He pushed bills through the legislature, saw them vetoed by Governor Altgeld, set about having his own governor next time, and in 1897 got, not all that he wanted (for the people of Illinois are not like the people of Pennsylvania), but the Allen bill which would do—if the Chicago City Council of 1897 would give it force.

The Municipal Voters' League had begun its second campaign in December, 1856, with the publication of the records of the retiring aldermen, the second half of the old body, and, though this was before the Allen bill was passed, Yerkes was active, and his men were particularized. As the campaign progressed the legislation at Springfield gave it point and local developments gave it breadth. It was a mayoralty year, and Alderman John Maynard Harlan had himself nominated on an independent, non-partisan ticket. "Bobbie" Burke, the Democratic boss, brought forward Carter H. Harrison, and the Republicans nominated Judge Nathaniel C. Sears. Harrison at that time was known only as the son of his father. Scars was a fine man; but neither of these had seized the street railway issue. Mr. Harlan stood on that, and he made a campaign which is talked about to this day in Chicago. It was brilliant. He had had the ear of the town through the newspaper reports of his tirades in the council, and the people went to hear him now as night after night he arraigned, not the bribed legislators, but the rich bribers. Once he called the roll of street railway directors and asked each what he was doing while his business was being boodled through the state legislature. Earnest, eloquent, honest, he was witty too. Yerkes called him an ass. "If Yerkes will consult his Bible," said Harlan, "he will learn that great things have been done with the jaw-bone of an ass." This young man had no organization (the League confined itself to the aldermen); it was a speaking campaign; but he caught the spirit of Chicago, and in the last week men say you could feel the drift of sentiment to him. Though he was defeated, he got 70,000 votes, 10,000 more than the regular Republican candidate, and elected Harrison. And his campaign not only phrased the traction issue in men's minds; it is said it taught young Mayor Harrison the use of it. At any rate, Harrison and Chicago have been safe on the city's side of it ever since.

The League also won on it. They gave bad records to twenty-seven of the thirty-four outgoing aldermen. Fifteen were not renominated. Of the twelve who ran again, nine were beaten. This victory gave them a solid third of the council. The reform crowd combined with Mayor Harrison, the president of the council, and his followers and defeated ordinances introduced to give effect to Yerkes's odious Allen law.

Here again the League might have retired in glory, but these "commonplace, ordinary men" proposed instead that they go ahead and get a majority, organize the council on a nonpartisan basis, and pass from a negative, anti-boodling policy to one of positive, constructive legislation. This meant also to advance from "beating bad men" to the "election of good men," and as for the good men, the standard was to be raised from mere honesty to honesty and efficiency too. With such high purposes in view, the Nine went into their third campaign. They had to condemn men they had recommended in their first year, but "we are always ready to eat dirt," they say. They pointed to the franchise issue, called for men capable of coping with the railways, and with bands playing, orators shouting, and Cole roaring like a sea-captain, they made the campaign of 1898 the hottest in their history. It nearly killed some of them, but they "won out"; the League had a nominal majority of the city council.

Then came their first bitter disappointment. They failed to organize the aldermen. They tried, and were on the verge of success, when defeat came, a most significant defeat. The League had brought into political life some new men, shopkeepers and small business men, all with perfect records, or none. They were men who meant well, but business is no training for politics; the shop-keepers who knew how to resist the temptations of trade, were untried in those of politics, and the boodle gang "bowled them over like little tin soldiers." They were persuaded that it was no more than right to "let the dominant party make up committees and run the Council"; that was "usage," and, what with bribery, sophistry, and flattery, the League was beaten by its weak friends. The real crisis in the League had come.

Mr. Cole resigned. He took the view that the League work was done; it could do no more; his health was suffering and his business was going to the dogs. The big corporations, the railroads, great business houses and their friends, had taken their business away from him. But this boycott had begun in the first campaign and Cole had met it with the declaration that he didn't "care a d—n." "I have a wife and a boy," he said. "I want their respect. The rest can all go to h—l." Cole has organized since a league to reform the legislature, but after the 1898 campaign the Nine were tired, disappointed, and Cole was temporarily used up.

The Nine had to let Cole and Hoyt King go. But they wouldn't let the League go. They had no successor for Cole. None on the committee would take his place; they all declined it in turn. They looked outside for a man, finding nobody. The prospect was dark. Then William Kent spoke up. Kent had time and money, but he wouldn't do anything anyone else could be persuaded to do. He was not strong physically, and his physicians had warned him that to live he must work little and play much. At that moment he was under orders to go west and shoot. But when he saw what was happening, he said:

"I'm not the man for this job; I'm no organizer. I can smash more things in a minute than I can build up in a hundred years. But the League has got to go on, so I'll take Cole's place if you'll give me a hard-working, able man for secretary, an organizer and a master of detail."

Such a secretary was hard to find, but Allen B. Pond, the architect, a man made for fine work, took this rough and tumble task. And these two, with the committee strengthened and active, not only held their own, they not only met the receding wave of reactionary sentiment against reform, but they made progress. In 1899 they won a clear majority of the council, pledged their men before election to a non-partisan organization of the council, and were in shape for constructive legislation. In 1900 they increased their majority, but they did not think it necessary to bind candidates

Chicago: Half Free and Fighting On   235

before the election to the non-partisan committee's plan, and the Republicans organized the house. This party maintained the standard of the committees; there was no falling off there, but that was not the point. Parties were recognized in the council, and the League had hoped for only one line of demarcation: special interests versus the interests of the city. During the time of Kent and Pond, however, the power for good of the League was established, the question of its permanency settled, and the use of able conscientious aldermen recognized. The public opinion it developed and pointed held the council so steady that, with Mayor Harrison and his personal following among the Democrats on that side, the aldermen refused to do anything for the street railway companies until the Allen bill was repealed. And, all ready to pass anything at Springfield, Yerkes had to permit the repeal, and he soon after closed up his business in Chicago and went away to London, where he is said to be happy and prosperous.

  The first time I went to Chicago, to see what form of corruption they had, I found there was something the matter with the political machinery. There was the normal plan of government for a city, rings with bosses, and a grafting business interest behind. Philadelphia, Pittsburgh, St. Louis, are all governed on such a plan. But in Chicago it didn't work. "Business" was at a standstill and business was suffering. What was the matter? I beleaguered the political leaders with questions: "Why didn't the politicians control? What was wrong with the machines?" The "boss" defended the organizations, blaming the people. "But the people could be fooled by any capable politician," I demurred. The boss blamed the reformers. "Reformers!" I exclaimed. "I've seen some of your reformers. They aren't different from reformers elsewhere, are they?" "No," he said, well pleased. But when I concluded that it must then be the weakness of the Chicago bosses, his pride cried out. "Say," he said, "have you seen that blankety-blank Fisher?"

  I hadn't, I said. "Well, you want to," he said, and I went straightway and saw Fisher—Mr. Walter L. Fisher, secretary of the Municipal Voters' League. Then it was that I began to understand the Chicago political situation. Fisher was a reformer: an able young lawyer of independent means, a mind ripe with high purposes and ideals, self-confident, high-minded, conclusive. He showed me an orderly bureau of indexed information, such as I had seen before. He outlined the scheme of the Municipal Voters' League, all in a bored, polite, familiar way. There was no light in him nor anything new or vital in his reform as he described it. It was all incomprehensible till I asked him how he carried the Seventeenth Ward, a mixed and normally Democratic ward, in one year for a Republican by some 1,300 plurality, the next year for a Democrat by some 1,800, the third for a Republican again. His face lighted up, a keen, shrewd look came into his eyes, and he said: "I did not carry that ward; its own people did it, but I'll tell you how it was managed." And he told me a story that was politics. I asked about another ward, and he told me the story of that. It was entirely different, but it, too, was politics. Fisher is a politician—with the education, associations, and the idealism of the reformers who fail, this man has cunning, courage, tact, and, rarer still, faith in the people. In short, reform in Chicago has such a leader as corruption alone usually has; a first-class executive mind and a natural manager of men.

When, after the aldermanic campaign of 1900, Messrs. Kent and Pond resigned as president and secretary of the League's executive committee, Charles R. Crane and Mr. Fisher succeeded in their places. Mr. Crane is a man with an international business, which takes him often to Russia, but he comes back for the Chicago aldermanic campaigns. He leaves the game to Mr. Fisher, and says Fisher is the man, but Crane is a backer of great force and of persistent though quiet activity. These two, with a picked committee of experienced and sensible men—Pond, Kent Smith, Frank H. Scott, Graham Taylor, Sigmund Zeisler, and Lessing Rosenthal—took the League as an established institution, perfected its system, opened a headquarters for work the year around; and this force, Mr. Fisher with his political genius has made a factor of the first rank in practical politics. Fisher made fights in the "hopeless" wards, and won them. He has raised the reform majority in the city council to two-thirds; he has lifted the standard of aldermen from honesty to a gradually rising scale of ability, and in his first year the council was organized on a non-partisan basis. This feature of municipal reform is established now, by the satisfaction of the aldermen themselves with the way it works. And a most important feature it is, too. "We have four shots at every man headed for the Council," said one of the League—"one with his record when his term expires; another when he is up for the nomination; a third when he is running as a candidate; the fourth when the committees are formed. If he is bad he is put on a minority in a strong committee; if he is doubtful, with a weak or doubtful majority in an important committee with a strong minority—a minority so strong that they can let him show his hand, then beat him with a minority report." Careful not to interfere in legislation, the League keeps a watch on every move in the council. Cole started this. He used to sit in the gallery every meeting night, but under Crane and Fisher, an assistant secretary—first Henry B. Chamberlain, now George C. Sikes—has followed the daily routine of committee work as well as the final meetings.

Fisher has carried the early practice of meeting politicians on their own ground to a very practical extreme. When tact and good humor failed, he applied force. Thus, when he set about preparing a year ahead for his fights in unpromising wards, he sent to the ward leaders on both sides for their lists of captains, lieutenants, and heelers. They refused, with expressions of astonishment at his "gall." Mr. Chamberlain directed a most searching investigation of the wards, precinct by precinct, block by block, and not only gathered a rich fund of information, but so frightened the politicians who heard of the inquiries that many of them came around and gave up their lists. Whether these helped or not, however, the wards were studied, and it was by such information and undermining political work, combined with skill and a fearless appeal to the people of the ward, that Fisher beat out with Hubert W. Butler the notorious Henry Wulff, an ex-state treasurer, in the ward convention of Wulff's own party, and then defeated Wulff, who ran as an independent, at the polls.

Such experience won the respect of the politicians, as well as their fear, and in 1902 and 1903 the worst ot them, or the best, came personally to Fisher to see what they could do. He was their equal in "the game of talk," they found, and their superior in tactics, for when he could not persuade them to put up good men and "play fair," he measured himself with them in strategy. Thus one day "Billy" Loeffler, the Democratic leader in the Democratic Ninth Ward, asked Mr. Fisher if the League did not want to name the Democratic candidate for alderman in his ward. Loeffler's business partner, "Hot Stove" Brenner, was running on the Republican ticket and Fisher knew that the Democratic organization would pull for Brenner. But Fisher accepted what was a challenge to political play and suggested Michael J. Preib. Loeffler was dazed at the name; it was new to him, but he accepted the man and nominated him. The Ninth is a strong Hebrew ward. To draw off the Republican and Jewish vote from Brenner, Fisher procured the nomination as an independent of Jacob Diamond, a popular young Hebrew, and he backed him too, intending, as he told both Preib and Diamond, to prefer in the end the one that should develop the greater strength. Meanwhile the League watched Loeffler. He was quietly throwing his support from Preib to Brenner. Five days before election it was clear that, though Diamond had developed unexpected strength, Preib was stronger. Fisher went to Loeffler and accused him of not doing all he could for Preib. Loeffler declared he was. Fisher proposed a letter from Loeffler to his personal friends asking them to vote for Preib. Loeffler hesitated, but he signed one that Fisher dictated. Loeffler advised the publication of the statement in the Jewish papers, and, though he consented to have it mailed to voters, he thought it "an unnecessary expense." When Fisher got back to the League headquarters, he rushed off copies of the letter through the mails to all the voters in the ward. By the time Loeffler heard of this it was too late to do anything; he tried, but he never caught up with those letters. His partner, Brenner, was defeated.

  A politician? A boss. Chicago has in Walter L. Fisher a reform boss, and in the Nine of the Municipal Voters' League, with their associated editors and able finance and advisory committees, a reform ring. They have no machine, no patronage, no power that they can abuse. They haven't even a list of their voters. All they have is the confidence of the anonymous honest men of Chicago who care more for Chicago than for

Chicago: Half Free and Fighting On

anything else. This they have won by a long record of good judgments, honest, obvious devotion to the public good, and a disinterestedness which has avoided even individual credit; not a hundred men in the city could name the Committee of Nine.

Working wide open at first, when it was necessary, they have withdrawn more and more ever since, and their policy now is one of dignified silence except when a plain statement of facts is required; then they speak as the League, simply, directly, but with human feeling, and leave their following of voters to act with or against them as they please. I have laid great stress on the technical, political skill of Fisher and the Nine, not because that is their chief reliance; it isn't: the study and the enlightenment of public opinion is their great function and force. But other reform organizations have tried this way. These reformers have, with the newspapers and the aldermen, not only done it thoroughly and persistently; they have not only developed an educated citizenship; they have made it an effective force, effective in legislation and in practical politics. In short: political reform, politically conducted, has produced reform politicians working for the reform of the city with the methods of politics. They do everything that a politician does, except buy votes and sell them. They play politics in the interest of the city.

And what has the city got out of it? Many things, but at least one great spectacle to show the world, the political spectacle of the year, and it is still going on. The properly accredited representatives of two American city railway companies are meeting in the open with a regular committee of an American board of aldermen, and they are negotiating for the continuance of certain street railway franchises on terms fair both to the city and to the corporations without a whisper of bribery, with composure, reasonableness, knowledge (on the aldermen's part, long-studied information and almost expert knowledge); with an eye to the future, to the just profit of the railways, and the convenience of the people to the city. This in an American city—in Chicago.

Those franchises which Yerkes tried to "fix" expired on July 30. There was a dispute about that, and the railways were prepared to fight. One is a Chicago corporation held by Chicago capital, and the men in it knew the conditions. The other belongs to New York and Philadelphia capitalists, whom Yerkes got to hold it when he gave up and went away; they couldn't understand. This "foreign" capital sent picked men out to Chicago to "fight." One of the items said to have been put in their bill of appropriation was "For use in Chicago—$1,000,000." Their local officers and directors and friends warned them to "go slow."

"Do you mean to tell us," said the Easterners, "that we can't do in Chicago what we have done in Philadelphia, New York, and—?"

Incredulous, they did do some such "work." They had the broken rings with them, and the "busted bosses," and they had the city on the hip in one particular. Though the franchises expired, the city had no authority in law to take over the railways and had to get it from Springfield. The Republican ring, with some Democratic following, had organized the legislature on an explicit arrangement that "no traction legislation should pass in 1903." The railways knew they couldn't get any; all they asked was that the city shouldn't have any either. It was a political game, but Chicago was sure that two could play at it. Harrison was up for reelection; he was right on traction. The Republicans nominated a business man, Graeme Stewart, who also pledged himself. Then they all went to Springfield, and, with the whole city and state looking on, the city's reform politicians beat the regulars. The city's bill was buried in committee, but to make a showing for Stewart the Republican ring had to pass some sort of a bill. They offered a poor substitute. With the city against it, the Speaker "gavelled it through" amid a scene of the wildest excitement. He passed the bill, but he was driven from his chair, and the scandal compelled him and the ring to reconsider that bill and pass the city's own enabling act.

Both the traction companies had been interested in this Springfield fiasco; they had been working together, but the local capitalists did not like the business. They soon offered to settle separately, and went into session with the city's lawyers, Edwin Burritt Smith, of the League, and John C. Mathis. The Easterners' representatives, headed by a "brilliant" New York lawyer, had to negotiate too. Their brilliant lawyer undertook to "talk sense" into the aldermanic committee. This committee had been out visiting all the large Eastern cities, studying the traction situations everywhere; on their own account they had drawn for them one of the most complete reports ever made for a city by an expert. Moreover, they knew the law and the finances of the traction companies, better far than the New York lawyers. When, therefore, the brilliant legal light had made one of his smooth, elaborate speeches, some hard-headed alderman would get up and say that he "gathered and gleaned" thus and so from the last speaker; he wasn't quite sure, but if thus and so was what the gentleman from New York had said, then it looked to him like tommy rot. Then the lawyer would spin another web, only to have some other commonplace looking alderman tear it to pieces. Those lawyers were dumbfounded. They were advised to see Fisher. They saw Fisher.

"You are welcome, if you wish," he is said to have said, "to talk foolishness, but I advise you to stop it. I do not speak for the council, but I think I know what it will say when it speaks for itself. Those aldermen know their business. They know sense and they know nonsense. They can't be fooled. If you go at them with reason they will go a long way toward helping you. However, you shall do as you please about this. But let me burn this one thing in upon your consciousness: Don't try money on them or anybody else. They will listen to your nonsense with patience, but if we hear of you trying to bribe anybody—an alderman or a politician or a newspaper or a reporter—all negotiations will cease instantly. And nobody will attempt to blackmail you, no one."

This seems to me to be the highest peak of reform. Here is a gentleman, speaking with the authority of absolute faith and knowledge, assuring the representatives of a corporation that it can have all that is due it from a body of aldermen by the expenditure of nothing more than reason. I have heard many a business man say such a condition of things would be hailed by his kind with rejoicing. How do they like it in Chicago? They don't like it at all. I spent one whole forenoon calling on the presidents of banks, great business men, and financiers interested in public utility companies. With all the evidence I had had in other places that these men are the chief source of corruption, I was unprepared for the sensation of that day. Those financial leaders of Chicago were "mad." All but one of them became so enraged as they talked that they could not behave decently. They rose up, purple in the face, and cursed reform. They said it had hurt business; it had hurt the town. "Anarchy," they called it; "socialism." They named corporations that had left the city; they named others that had planned to come there and had gone elsewhere. They offered me facts and figures to prove that the city was damaged.

"But isn't the reform Council honest?" I asked.

"Honest! Yes, but—oh, h—l!"

"And do you realize that all you say means that you regret the passing of boodle and would prefer to have back the old corrupt council?"

That brought a curse or a shrewd smile or a cynical laugh, but that they regretted the passing of the boodle regime is the fact, bitter, astonishing—but natural enough. We have seen those interests at their bribery in Philadelphia and St. Louis; we have seen them opposing reforms in every city. Here in Chicago we have them cursing reform triumphant, for, though reform may have been a benefit to the city as a community of freemen, it is really bad; it has hurt their business!

Chicago has paid dearly for its reform, and reformers elsewhere might as well realize that if they succeed, their city will pay too, at first. Capital will boycott it and capital will give it a bad name. The bankers who offered me proof of their losses were offering me material to write down the city. And has Chicago had conspicuous credit for reform ? No, it is in ill-repute, "anarchistic," "socialistic" (a commercial term for municipal ownership); it is "unfriendly to capital." But Chicago knows what it is after and it knows the cost. There are business men there who are willing to pay; they told me so. There are business men on the executive and finance committees of the League and others helping outside who are among the leaders of Chicago's business and its bar. Moreover, there are promoters who expect to like an honest council. One such told me that he meant to apply for franchises shortly, and he believed that, though it would take longer than bribery to negotiate fair terms with aldermen who were keen to safeguard the city's interests, yet business could be done on that basis. "Those reform aldermen are slow, but they are fair," he said.

The aldermen are fair. Exasperated as they have been by the trifling, the trickery, and past boodling of the street railways, inconvenienced by bad service, beset by corporation temptations, they are fairer today than the corporations. They have the street railways now in a corner. The negotiations are on, and they could squeeze them with a vengeance. What is the spirit of those aldermen? "Well," said one to me; "I'll tell you how we feel. We've got to get the city's interests well protected. That's first. But we've got more to do than that. They're shy of us; these capitalists don't know how to handle us. They are not up to the new reform, on-the-level way of doing business. We've got to show capital that we will give them all that is coming to them, and just a little more—a little more, just to get them used to being honest." This was said without a bit of humor, with some anxiety, but no bitterness, and not a word about socialism or "confiscating municipal ownership"; that's a "capitalistic" bugaboo. Again, one Saturday night a personal friend of mine who had lost a half-holiday at a conference with some of the leading aldermen, complained of their "preciseness." "First," he said, "they had to have every trivial interest of the city protected, then, when we seemed to be done, they turned around and argued like corporation lawyers for the protection of the corporation."

Those Chicago aldermen are an honor to the country! Men like Jackson and Mavor, Herrmann and Werno, would be a credit to any legislative body in the land, but there is no such body in the land where they could do more good or win more honor. I believe capital will some day prefer to do business with them than with blackmailers and boodlers anywhere.

When that day comes the aldermen will share the credit with the Municipal Voters' League, but all the character and all the ability of both council and League will not explain the reform of Chicago. The citizens of that city will take most of the glory. They will have done it, as they have done it so far. Some of my critics have declared they could not believe there was so much difference in the character of communities as I have described. How can they account then for Chicago? The people there have political parties, they are partisans. But they know how to vote. Before the League was started, the records show them shifting their vote to the confusion of well-laid political plans. So they have always had bosses, and they have them now, but these bosses admit that they "can't boss Chicago." I think this is partly their fault. William Lorimer, the dominant Republican boss, with whom I talked for an hour one day, certainly does not make the impression, either as a man or as a politician, that Croker makes, or Durham of Philadelphia. But an outsider may easily go wrong on a point like this, and we may leave the credit where they lay it, with the people of Chicago. Fisher is a more forceful man than any of the regulars, and, as a politician, compares with well-known leaders in any city; but Fisher's power is the people's. His leadership may have done much, but there is something else deeper and bigger behind him. At the last aldermanic election, when he discovered on the Saturday before election that the League was recommending, against a bad Democrat, a worse Republican, he advised the people of that ward to vote for the Socialist; and the people did vote for the Socialist and they elected him! Again, there is the press, the best in any of our large cities. There are several newspapers in Chicago which have served always the public interest, and their advice is taken by their readers. These editors wield, as they wielded before the League came, that old-fashioned power of the press which is supposed to have passed away. Indeed, one of the finest exhibitions of disinterestedness in this whole reform story was that of these newspapers giving up the individual power and credit which their influence on public opinion gave them, to the League, behind which they stepped to get together and gain for the city what they lost themselves. But this paid them. They did not do it with that motive; they did it for the city, but the city has recognized the service, as another fact shows: There are bad papers in Chicago—papers that serve special interests—and these don't pay.

  The agents of reform have been many and efficient, but back of them all was an intelligent, determined people, and they have decided. The city of Chicago is ruled by the citizens of Chicago. Then why are the citizens of Chicago satisfied with half-reform? Why have they reformed the council and left the administrative side of government so far behind? "One thing at a time," they will tell you out there, and it is wonderful to see them patient after seven years of steadfast fighting reform.

But that is not the reason. The administration has been improved. It is absurdly backward and uneven; the fire department is excellent, the police are a disgrace, the law department is expert, the health bureau is corrupt, and the street cleaning is hardly worth mention. All this is Carter H. Harrison. He is an honest man personally, but indolent; a shrewd politician, and a character with reserve power, but he has no initial energy. Without ideals he does only what is demanded of him. He does not seem to know wrong is wrong, till he is taught; nor to care, till criticism arouses his political sense of popular requirement. That sense is keen, but think of it: Every time Chicago wants to go ahead a foot, it has first to push its mayor up inch by inch. In brief, Chicago is a city that wants to be led, and Carter Harrison, with all his political ambition, honest willingness, and obstinate independence, simply follows it. The League leads, and its leaders understand their people. Then why does the League submit to Harrison ? Why doesn't the League recommend mayors as well as aldermen? It may some day; but, setting out by accident to clean the council, stop the boodling, and settle the city railway troubles, they have been content with mayor Harrison because he had learned his lesson on that. And, I think, as they say the mayor thinks, that when the people of Chicago get the city railways running with enough cars and power; when they have put a stop to boodling forever; they will take up the administrative side of the government. A people who can support for seven years one movement toward reform, should be able to go on forever. With the big boodle beaten, petty political grafting can easily be stopped. All that will be needed then will be a mayor who understands and represents the city; he will be able to make Chicago as rare an example of good government as it is now of reform; which will be an advertisement; good business; it will pay.

The Bookman
October, 1903

The New School of Journalism

IF our colleges were what they should be and if our newspapers were what they should be, there might be then no need of a School of Journalism. As things are, there is a place for the Joseph Pulitzer Foundation at Columbia University, and the best evidence thereof is the attitude of the educator on the one hand and the journalist on the other toward this enterprise. The newspapers have been on the whole very courteous in comment on Mr. Pulitzer's gift, but also very empty of suggestions for its application. They do not see what a college can teach journalism. The professors and presidents have been very polite also, and also very barren of ideas. They can't see what further their colleges can do.

If the Pulitzer School shall instil a little more humility into both these professions, it will have been worth the million dollars Mr. Pulitzer has laid down in cash. And if in its operation it substitutes for this self-satisfaction some dynamic unhappiness it will have justified the second million which the editor of the *New York World* promises. His spirit is the right spirit. Mr. Pulitzer is a self-made journalist, and he founded his newspaper fortune in yellow journalism, the yellowest known in his day. But he has grown and he has learned. He has improved the *New York World* till now it is almost as accurate and more truthful than many a "better paper," and, in editorial expression, free, sane, simple, forcible, and earnest. But Mr. Pulitzer knows he never succeeded in making "the" paper for the masses; he knows his yellow journalists never knew what yellow journalism might be; and he knows that nobody he can get knows how to make the newspaper he can now imagine. He must know this since he has run a life career throughout the business, has "succeeded" so far that he can give away two millions of dollars and yet, standing, many of his contemporaries say, at the head of his profession, he gives this money into the hands of others, men with the learning he did hot have, men of the kind that have found fault with his journalism and then he asks to do what he could not do: teach journalism and, perhaps, make journalists. "Make journalism a profession" is his phrase.

A business it is, and business it must always be. All this talk we hear of a subsidized newspaper is essentially wrong. The idealists, even more than the moneymakers, should insist that the good newspaper be so made that it will pay; since it is not the paper but the readers they are after and the profits are the proof of the reading. But a business man cannot make a great newspaper. That takes an editor, a man, a personality; all the best paying papers have either been produced by an editor or have produced one. Journalism, a business, is a profession too, like law and medicine, and just as the best lawyer or the best physician, in the long run, makes the best collections, so the best journalist gets in the end the best "ads." The "newspaper man" with one eye on the circulation and the other on the ads, does not see how his trade can be elevated into a profession, and he scoffs and sneers, like the business man at the college graduate, like the old doctors at all the first schools. And they challenge, these apprentices, this veteran, who does not see how himself. His correspondence contains no plan for his school. He knows only that he does not know; but, bowed by the failure perceived from the vantage point of success, he thinks others may know. The veteran is a humble journalist.

And he may well be humble. The commodity of journalism is all knowledge and all wisdom and the market is all ignorance and all folly. The world is full of these things, full of knowledge and full of ignorance too, and ignorance is curious. The business of journalism is to sell in the form of books, periodicals or newspapers, all the world's knowledge to all the world's ignorance. "All," I say, and this is no "literary" statement of an "academic" idea. It is a "journalistic" observation made in the day's work at the news desk of a daily newspaper. There is no knowledge that is not general which cannot be printed as news if it can be put into "news form." And this phrase is only a technical expression of the requirement that the information be offered in a shape comprehensible to "all the world's ignorance." In other words, the news editor has to have the new facts presented in their relation to the old facts, the news in its bearing on what his readers already know. He can sell a scientific fact just as well as he can a fact of local politics, but he usually will give politics "preferred position" because both his reporters and his readers will be more interested in it; and they are more interested because they have the history of politics in mind and will see just how the new alters the old. The reporter will write it intelligently and the reader will read it intelligently. If the news editor could have a scientific discovery stated as well, then, if it is really as significant, he can "hit it up" as just as "big news." The scientific report of Darwin's theory of acquired variations was news only to the scientific world; the statement that man may have been evolved from the ape was news to the great world.

The lack of journalism is the lack of understanding. The editors cannot know all things, nor the reporter, nor the scientist. None of these is seeking knowledge. All alike are "after the news," and the keenest on the scent is the ordinary scientist. He is the most absorbed and of the least understanding. He does not pursue his researches with a sense of the bearing of his hypothesis on our knowledge or even upon his own philosophy of life. He is doing the world's work like all the rest of us, each in his separate sphere, and is elated at the discovery of a new variety of his particular plant. That is news in his world. To the world where the stars shine, it may be no more news than the discovery that the Bowery lodging houses are filling up with bums. If the bums turn a Republican majority into a Democratic majority and if this may carry New York and decide a presidential election, it is news that may interest the botanist. And if the botanist's new variety should complete a chain and show the genesis of animal life from plant life, then his discovery, if reported as intelligently as the reporter would report the discovery of the bums, would be offered as news in the lodging houses and it might interest the bums.

One great difficulty in journalism, one reason why it is thrown back upon crime, scandal, and gossip, is that the scientist cannot report his own results. Sought in the abstract, they are seized in the abstract and the abstraction is passed on in the dead slang of science. Now and then a mind comes along, takes the materials piled up by the day laborers of science, perceives the possibilities in them, prosecutes an intelligent search for the missing links, then conceives the whole and "builds him a structure brave." Since he is an intelligent being, he probably speaks a living language and tells the world what has been going on in the laboratories. This is understanding. Also it is journalism. The news may go out in book form, but bookmaking today is largely journalism, and books are a rich source of newspaper news. Think of the "news" in the books, old and new, which the newspapers could get out if their reviewers had understanding!

For the understanding I am talking about is that which understands not only what is known but what is not known. The editor cannot, he does not have to know everything. He needs only to understand, and to know what he and we do not know. That is part of what used to be called culture till the uncultivated got hold of the word and emptied it of its contents. The editor, whether of a book publishing house, a magazine, or a newspaper, should be in touch with the men who know, but he must not, like them, draw back from those who do not know. He has to have human sympathy. The pupil of the learned, he is the teacher of the ignorant.

The objection to the school of journalism that it will have to prepare such men, not specialists, but men of broad culture, and that that is what the universities are supposed to do, is sound enough as far as it goes. But that is my point. Perhaps the Pulitzer School will do what the universities are supposed to do. Having a special purpose, and that purpose as broad as life, maybe it will teach what it teaches in its relation to life. Maybe it will teach what it teaches, and teach men to tell it. There is the niche for the School of Journalism: knowledge so understood by men so intelligent that they can tell it so that all men may read as they run. Let the students of journalism learn—what you please; there is a choice, but no matter. The point is, having learned, let them write it, write it, write it. They cannot write without understanding it, so writing is not the one thing to learn. That will come, or not, with the trying. But having the habit of seeing and learning, they can go, such students, where they will—to the North Pole, into business, into politics, into literature, into journalism; they will be journalists all. They will be able to tell what they know.

Teach Latin and Greek in the School of Journalism. Teach them for the great "stories" in those languages, but also to teach the future reporter to tell these great stories and deliver these great orations in good English. They can't do that without conning correctly and feeling truly the classics, and that will teach them, as it teaches the educated Englishman, English.

Teach philosophy. Teach it for its own sake, for the sake of the great news assignments its ultimate queries contain for man, for the relationship which it develops of knowledge to knowledge and of knowledge to life. But tell the student how the best paid editorial writer in New York is selling his penny paper to thousands on thousands of men, some with brokers' orders in their pockets, some with dinner pails in their hands, by simply writing simply the ideas of the metaphysicians. Journalism has run mad (like science and like art) after facts, and my penny journalist almost alone is selling ideas. The college-bred editor has so far lost his humanity that he forgets the intellectual pleasure he had when as a junior he saw the whole world as Hegel saw it. Schopenhauer speaks bitterly of the unsatisfied "metaphysicial needs of the human mind." Christian Scientists are building marble churches and Dowie is founding a city upon the recognition and satisfaction of this demand of the ignorant. The supply is bad and my metaphysician journalist may offer bad philosophy, but he can write it and why should not some other think sound thought and write that as simply for the journals, yellow and pink. The world wonders, like a child, at the world and the sophisticated keep back its secrets. By all means teach metaphysics and philosophy in the School of Journalism, but teach it so that Hegel will not have become old before he was news.

Teach literature; not only for the English of it, but also that the journalist may be able to see that a murder is not merely a sensation but a tragedy; so that the yellow journalist who means well will not begin his crime news with the announcement that "Patrick Healey shot and killed Mary Healey, his wife, in their apartment on the fifth floor of the tenement at No. 7032 Ridge Street, today," but at the beginning of their story, "how Patrick Healey met Mary McCormick on the emigrant ship seven years ago." If we can't have science and must have crime, let us have the human story, not as Shakespeare gave Othello's, but with some sense of the growth of love through jealousy into hate and despair. There is some mighty good reporting in literature, and that I would see taught as reporting, not literature. Let us have more of the mere telling, less of the literature; if the young writers would learn to report, the literature might be left to the Lord. My experience of the college graduates on newspapers was that they were so full of inspiration from literature that they had no eye left for the inspiration of life, and thus, bent on the literary career, they missed both that and the news.

Teach English, of course, the spelling of it, the punctuation, the grammar, rhetoric, and etymology. But teach it, somehow, as it is not often taught in colleges now. Why not begin with the use of it? The fact first, cold and hard, but the student's very own, and simply stated in the student's own way; then the humor or the pity of it genuinely felt and imagined; then the idea, perceived and put true. Never mind the style. Like murder, that will out, if it is in the man. Hammer out of the student only clearness; the rest leave to him and the facts, and—to the brutal copy desk where "fine writers" are killed and only fine men who write escape.

Teach ethics, not alone the ethics of journalism. Teach ethics and teach it so that it will stick. The School of Journalism cannot make good men any more than it can make good journalists. You cannot teach sincerity and humor, but you can teach the poverty of cynicism and the meanness of lying and "faking," and you can make men who cannot be bad and be happy. Now we have editors who "roast" with a serene conscience public men who submit to "pulls," the while they and their own newspapers are "pulled" all to pieces. Tell the future journalist what his special temptations are going to be, how the advertiser, as well as the party leader, asks to have reading notices inserted and proper news suppressed—and tell him this so that, though he may surrender, his surrender will be with all the discomfort of guilty knowledge. In brief teach him special ethics with the special morals of his craft. This for himself. For his newspaper he will need, moreover, ethics, plain everyday ethics, and this also should be backed with morals; and so also he has need of the ethics of other professions and businesses, and their morals, which differ most surprisingly, those of the merchant from those of the politician, those of the promoter from those of the banker and the lawyer and the physician. The journalist has to understand other men, how they differ and how very like they are, and often he has to judge them. He could judge the harder for a sympathetic knowledge of their customs, temptations, and the atmosphere in which they live. The way to reach a politician is to reach his politics—the sins of his craft which he knows are sins.

Teach the sciences. Here is a great unexploited field for journalism and there is room in it (as the Sunday newspapers show) for specialization almost as various as science itself. Suppose a man should study botany with the purpose of reporting it all his life. He would ground himself in this science as thoroughly as the man bent on original research; he would learn the "lingo," the methods, master the "literature," and open his mind to its lesser and greater queries. But if he were a student in the School of Journalism, he should be translating all he learned into English through a mind kept open to the interests of other men. Adding to accuracy imagination, he would spend a useful life (and make money) telling us plant "stories," their lives and habits; the pursuits and triumphs of the botanist and the philosophy of botany. If we had had such a man in chemistry, we should not have had to wait so long to find out what Professor and Madame Curie know about radium. Oh, I know I am asking for John Burroughs. But that is not asking too much. Why should not more of the half-educated, wholly wholesome and beautiful men we all know, be such as he? Not so wonderful, yet true, gentle, understanding reporters.

Teach law, but teach it for a man's use, not a lawyer's, so that the reporter can report trials and interpret opinions correctly and intelligently, and so that editors, secure in the ethics of the profession and in the principles and traditions of the law, may feel safe in holding the bench and bar up to their duty. We need right now a man who can call the courts back to their duty, but who but a lawyer can do it with authority? and how many lawyers can do it with plain, human force?

Teach history, but teach it with an eye on today, and teach the history of today with an eye on the history of the past. Give special courses on the history of the East and the Far East for correspondents and editorial writers. And why should not students ambitious to become correspondents have the rudiments of war; the history of diplomacy; international law, etc., etc.? I remember well the time when I wished that my college course had included finance in its relation to Wall Street and the Treasury Department, to railroads in operation, and trusts in their up-building. But I can remember many courses which I wish I had known when I took them were good not in themselves alone.

Any university has the beginnings of a School of Journalism. A professor of journalism who was man enough to judge by the instructor as well as the subject could probably designate several courses fit for the future journalist to take. So he might find others which, unintelligently taught, but necessary, might be supplemented by the professor of journalism himself; he to point out the human significance of the subject matter of the course. Add to these courses in subjects like geography, practical politics, the ethics of journalism, modern industrial problems (like labor studied by a man in the field and taught for field work)—these, if all made writing courses, would come pretty near rounding out the school for general purposes. But this scheme would not furnish what is very much needed, courses, possibly postgraduate, for what is sure to come, the specialist in journalism of whom I have spoken. The business in nearly all its branches, books, magazines, and journals is in need of trained historians, geographers, economists, experts in finance, and politics—and government—who can write. And there is dire need of writers who know the arts, music, painting, and literature; and can interpret the works thereof. The United States with all its book reviewers, has not one such critic of literature as Russia has two or three of, a guide to both writer and reader.

Something has been said about teaching the business and mechanism of newspapers. This is not very important. It is not true that we all learn it all in the course of business. The newspaper man in a small place may "pick up" knowledge of all branches of the business, but he does not do it in the great cities. It might be worth while to run a newspaper in connection with the school, and it might be well worthwhile if it printed, besides the gossip of the campus, the news of the colleges; if it reported the laboratories as well as the training table. But one very serious service of the School of Journalism might be rendered by a study of journalism. A self-made business journalist is full of crass theories and blind cocksureness. One man who is a successful manager will tell you that the thing to do to succeed is to print local news—detailed; petty neighborhood news; and he can point to examples to prove his theories. Another will say you have to have but very little news, only interesting reading, and he can point to examples of success along those lines. None of them knows the whole business, nor just why he succeeds or why he fails. Each knows something well, and they all know a great deal. If a trained man could go to all of them, get from each his best knowledge of experience, and were big enough to apply it all or the substance of it all, he certainly could teach them all something, and he might make a great newspaper. Someone should gather the experimental knowledge, analyze it and sum it up. Then there are the foreign journalists; we Americans despise them, but they know something. Let the College of Journalism find out what it is and teach it to us. In a word, teach journalism, yes, but learn it first, somebody.

McClure's Magazine
November, 1903

New York: Good Government to the Test

Just about the time this article will appear, Greater New York will be holding a local election on what has come to be a national question—good government. No doubt there will be other "issues." At this writing (September 15) the candidates were not named nor the platforms written, but the regular politicians hate the main issue, and they have a pretty trick of confusing the honest mind and splitting the honest vote by raising "local issues" which would settle themselves under prolonged honest government. So, too, there will probably be some talk about the effect this election might have upon the next presidential election; another clever fraud which seldom fails to work to the advantage of rings and grafters, and to the humiliation and despair of good citizenship. We have nothing to do with these deceptions. They may count in New York, they may determine the result, but let them. They are common moves in the corruptionist's game, and, therefore, fair tests of citizenship, for honesty is not the sole qualification for an honest voter; intelligence has to play a part, too, and a little intelligence would defeat all such tricks. Anyhow, they cannot disturb us. I am writing too far ahead, and my readers, for the most part, will be reading too far away to know or care anything about them. We can grasp firmly the essential issues involved and then watch with equanimity the returns for the answer, plain yes or no, which New York will give to the only questions that concern us all:

Do we Americans really want good government? Do we know it when we see it? Are we capable of that sustained good citizenship which alone can make democracy a success? Or, to save our pride, one other: Is the New York way the right road to permanent reform?

For New York has good government, or, to be more precise, it has a good administration. It is not a question there of turning the rascals out and putting the honest men into their places. The honest men are in, and this election is to decide whether they are to be kept in, which is a very different matter. Any people is capable of rising in wrath to overthrow bad rulers. Philadelphia has done that in its day. New York has done it several times. With fresh and present outrages to avenge, particular villains to punish, and the mob sense of common anger to excite, it is an emotional gratification to go out with the crowd and "smash something." This is nothing but revolt, and even monarchies have uprisings, to the credit of their subjects. But revolt is not reform, and one revolutionary administration is not good government. That we free Americans are capable of such assertions of our sovereign power, we have proven; our lynchers are demonstrating it every day. That we can go forth singly also, and, without passion, with nothing but mild approval and dull duty to impel us, vote intelligently to sustain a fairly good municipal government, remains to be shown. And that is what New York has the chance to show; New York, the leading exponent of the great American anti-bad government movement for good government.

According to this, the standard course of municipal reform, the politicians are permitted to organize a party on national lines, take over the government, corrupt and deceive the people, and run things for the private profit of the boss and his ring, till the corruption becomes rampant and a scandal. Then the reformers combine the opposition: the corrupt and unsatisfied minority, the disgruntled groups of the majority, the reform organizations; they nominate a mixed ticket, headed by a "good business man" for mayor, make a "hot campaign" against the government with "Stop, thief!" for the cry, and make a "clean sweep." Usually, this effects only the disciplining of the reckless grafters and the improvement of the graft system of corrupt government. The good mayor turns out to be weak or foolish or "not so good." The politicians "come it over him," as they did over the business mayors who followed the "Gas Ring" revolt in Philadelphia, or the people become disgusted as they did with Mayor Strong, who was carried into office by the anti-Tammany rebellion in New York after the Lexow exposures.

New York: Good Government to the Test 257

Philadelphia gave up after its disappointment, and that is what most cities do. The repeated failures of revolutionary reform to accomplish more than the strengthening of the machine have so discredited this method that wide-awake reformers in several cities—Pittsburgh, Cincinnati, Cleveland, Detroit, Minneapolis, and others—are following the lead of Chicago.

The Chicago plan does not depend for success upon any one man or any one year's work, nor upon excitement or any sort of bad government. The reformers there have no ward organizations, no machine at all; their appeal is solely to the intelligence of the voter and their power rests upon that. This is democratic and political, not bourgeois and business reform, and it is interesting to note that whereas reformers elsewhere are forever seeking to concentrate all the powers in the mayor, those of Chicago talk of stripping the mayor to a figurehead and giving his powers to the aldermen who directly represent the people, and who change year by year.

The Chicago way is but one way, however, and a new one, and it must be remembered that this plan has not yet produced a good administration. New York has that. Chicago, after seven years' steady work, has a body of aldermen honest enough and competent to defend the city's interests against boodle capital, but that is about all; it has a wretched administration. New York has stuck to the old way. Provincial and self-centered, it hardly knows there is any other. Chicago laughs and other cities wonder, but never mind. New York, by persistence, has at last achieved a good administration. Will the New Yorkers continue it? That is the question. What Chicago has, it has secure. Its independent citizenship is trained to vote every time and to vote for uninteresting, good aldermen. New York has an independent vote of 100,000, a decisive minority, but the voters have been taught to vote only once in a long while, only when excited by picturesque leadership and sensational exposures, only against. New York has been so far an anti-bad government, anti-Tammany, not a good-government town. Can it vote, without Tammany in to incite it, for a good mayor? I think this election, which will answer this question, should decide other cities how to go about reform.

The administration of Mayor Seth Low may not have been perfect, not in the best European sense: not expert, not co-ordinated, certainly not wise. Nevertheless, for an American city, it has been not only honest, but able, undeniably one of the best in the whole country. Some of the departments have been dishonest; others have been so inefficient that they made the whole administration ridiculous. But what of that? Corruption also is clumsy and makes absurd mistakes when it is new and untrained. The "oaths" and ceremonies and much of the boodling of the St. Louis ring seemed laughable to my corrupt friends in Philadelphia and Tammany Hall, and New York's own Tweed regime was "no joke," only because it was so general, and so expensive—to New York. It took time to perfect the "Philadelphia plan" of misgovernment, and it took time to educate Croker and develop his Tammany Hall. It will take time to evolve masters of the (in America) unstudied art of municipal government—time and demand. So far there has been no market for municipal experts in this country. All we are clamoring for today in our meek, weak-hearted way, is that mean, rudimentary virtue miscalled "common honesty." Do we really want it?

Certainly Mayor Low is pecuniarily honest. He is more; he is conscientious and experienced and personally efficient. Bred to business, he rose above it, adding to the training he acquired in the conduct of an international commercial house, two terms as mayor of Brooklyn, and to that again a very effective administration, as president, of the business of Columbia University. He began his mayoralty with a study of the affairs of New York; he has said himself that he devoted eight months to its finances: and he mastered this department and is admitted to be the master in detail of every department which has engaged his attention. In other words, Mr. Low has learned the business of New York; he is just about competent now to become the mayor of a great city. Is there a demand for Mr. Low?

No. When I made my inquiries—before the lying had begun—the Fusion leaders of the anti-Tammany forces, who nominated Mr. Low, said they might renominate him. "Who else was there?" they asked. And they thought he "might" be re-elected. The alternative was Richard Croker or Charles F.

New York: Good Government to the Test

Murphy, his man, for no matter who Tammany's candidate for mayor was, if Tammany won, Tammany's boss would rule. The personal issue was plain enough. Yet there was no assurance for Mr. Low.

Why? There are many forms of the answer given, but they nearly all reduce themselves to one—the man's personality. It is not very engaging. Mr. Low has many respectable qualities, but these never are amiable. "Did you ever see his smile?" said a politician who was trying to account for his instinctive dislike for the mayor. I had; there is no laughter back of it, no humor, and no sense thereof. The appealing human element is lacking all through. His good abilities are self-sufficient; his dignity is smug; his courtesy seems not kind; his self-reliance is called obstinacy because, though he listens, he seems not to care; though he understands, he shows no sympathy, and when he decides, his reasoning is private. His most useful virtues—probity, intelligence, and conscientiousness—in action are often an irritation; they are so contented. Mr. Low is the bourgeois reformer type. Even where he compromises he gets no credit; his concessions make the impression of surrenders. A politician can say "no" and make a friend, where Mr. Low will lose one by saying "yes." Cold and impersonal, he cools even his heads of departments. Loyal public service they give, because his taste is for men who would do their duty for their own sake, not for his, and that excellent service the city has had. But members of Mr. Low's administration helped me to characterize him; they could not help it. Mr. Low's is not a lovable character.

But what of that? Why should his colleagues love him? Why should anybody like him? Why should he seek to charm, win affection, and make friends? He was elected to attend to the business of his office and to appoint subordinates who should attend to the business of their offices, not to make "political strength" and win elections. William Travers Jerome, the picturesque district attorney, whose sincerity and intellectual honesty made sure the election of Mr. Low two years ago, detests him as a bourgeois, but the mayoralty is held in New York to be a bourgeois office. Mr. Low is the ideal product of the New York theory that municipal government is business, not politics, and that a business man who would manage the city as he would a business corporation would solve for us all our troubles. Chicago reformers think we have got to solve our own problems; that government is political business; that men brought up in politics and experienced in public office will make the best administrators. They have refused to turn from their politician mayor, Carter H. Harrison, for the most ideal business candidate, and I have heard them say that when Chicago was ripe for a better mayor they would prefer a candidate chosen from among their well-tried aldermen. Again, I say, however, that this is only one way, and New York has another, and this other is the standard American way.

But again I say, also, that the New York way is on trial, for New York has what the whole country has been looking for in all municipal crises—the non-political ruler. Mr. Low's very faults, which I have emphasized for the purpose, emphasize the point. They make it impossible for him to be a politician even if he should wish to be. As for his selfishness, his lack of tact, his coldness—these are of no consequence. He has done his duty all the better for them. Admit that he is uninteresting; what does that matter? He has served the city. Will the city not vote for him because it does not like the way he smiles? Absurd as it sounds, that is what all I have heard against Low amounts to. But to reduce the situation to a further absurdity, let us eliminate altogether the personality of Mr. Low. Let us suppose he has no smile, no courtesy, no dignity, no efficiency, no personality at all; suppose he were an It and had not given New York a good administration, but had only honestly tried. What then?

Tammany Hall? That is the alternative. The Tammany politicians see it just as clear as that, and they are not in the habit of deceiving themselves. They say "it is a Tammany year," "Tammany's turn." They say it and they believe it. They study the people, and they know it is all a matter of citizenship; they admit that they cannot win unless a goodly part of the independent vote goes to them; and still they say they can beat Mr. Low or any other man the anti-Tammany forces may nominate. So we are safe in eliminating Mr. Low and reducing the issue to plain Tammany.

New York: Good Government to the Test

Tammany is bad government; not inefficient, but dishonest; not a party, not a delusion and a snare, hardly known by its party name—Democracy; having little standing in the national councils of the party and caring little for influence outside of the city. Tammany is Tammany, the embodiment of corruption. All the world knows and all the world may know what it is and what it is after. For hypocrisy is not a Tammany vice. Tammany is for Tammany, and the Tammany men say so. Other rings proclaim lies and make pretensions; other rogues talk about the tariff and imperialism. Tammany is honestly dishonest. Time and time again, in private and in public, the leaders, big and little, have said they are out for themselves and their own; not for the public, but for "me and my friends"; not for New York, but for Tammany. Richard Croker said under oath once that he worked for his own pockets all the time, and Tom Grady, the Tammany orator, has brought his crowds to their feet cheering sentiments as primitive, stated with candor as brutal.

The man from Mars would say that such an organization, so self-confessed, could not be very dangerous to an intelligent people. Foreigners marvel at it and at us, and even Americans—Pennsylvanians, for example—cannot understand why we New Yorkers regard Tammany as so formidable. I think I can explain it. Tammany is corruption with consent; it is bad government founded on the suffrages of the people. The Philadelphia machine is more powerful. It rules Philadelphia by fraud and force and does not require the votes of the people. The Philadelphians do not vote for their machine; their machine votes for them. Tammany used to stuff the ballot boxes and intimidate voters; today there is practically none of that. Tammany rules, when it rules, by right of the votes of the people of New York.

Tammany corruption is democratic corruption. That of the Philadelphia ring is rooted in special interests. Tammany, too, is allied with "vested interests"—but Tammany labors under disadvantages not known in Philadelphia. The Philadelphia ring is of the same party that rules the state and the nation, and the local ring forms a living chain with the state and national rings. Tammany is a purely local concern. With a majority only in old New York, it has not only to buy what it wants from the

Republican majority in the state, but must trade to get the whole city. Big business everywhere is the chief source of political corruption, and it is one source in New York; but most of the big businesses represented in New York have no plants there. Offices there are, and head offices of many trusts and railways, for example, but that is all. There are but two railway terminals in the city, and but three railways use them. These have to do more with Albany than New York. So with Wall Street. Philadelphia's stock exchange deals largely in Pennsylvania securities, New York's in those of the whole United States. There is a small Wall Street group that specializes in local corporations, and they are active and give Tammany a Wall Street connection, but the biggest and the majority of our financial leaders, bribers though they may be in other cities and even in New York state, are independent of Tammany Hall, and can be honest citizens at home. From this class, indeed, New York can, and often does, draw some of its reformers. Not so Philadelphia. That bourgeois opposition which has persisted for thirty years in the fight against Tammany corruption was squelched in Philadelphia after its first great uprising. Matt Quay, through the banks, railways, and other business interests, was able to reach it. A large part of his power is negative; there is no opposition. Tammany's power is positive. Tammany cannot reach all the largest interests and its hold is upon the people.

Tammany's democratic corruption rests upon the corruption of the people, the plain people, and there lies its great significance; its grafting system is one in which more individuals share than any I have studied. The people themselves get very little; they come cheap, but they are interested. Divided into districts, the organization subdivides them into precincts or neighborhoods, and their sovereign power, in the form of votes, is bought up by kindness and petty privileges. They are forced to a surrender, when necessary, by intimidation, but the leader and his captains have their hold because they take care of their own. They speak pleasant words, smile friendly smiles, notice the baby, give picnics up the River or the Sound, or a slap on the back; find jobs, most of them at the city's expense, but they have also newsstands, peddling privileges, railroad and other business

New York: Good Government to the Test 263

places to dispense; they permit violations of the law, and, if a man has broken the law without permission, see him through the court. Though a blow in the face is as readily given as a shake of the hand, Tammany kindness is real kindness, and will go far, remember long, and take infinite trouble for a friend.

The power that is gathered up thus cheaply, like garbage, in the districts is concentrated in the district leader, who in turn passes it on through a general committee to the boss. This is a form of living government, extra-legal, but very actual, and, though the beginnings of it are purely democratic, it develops at each stage into an autocracy. In Philadelphia the boss appoints a district leader and gives him power. Tammany has done that in two or three notable instances, but never without causing a bitter fight which lasts often for years. In Philadelphia the state boss designates the city boss. In New York, Croker has failed signally to maintain vice-bosses whom he appointed. The boss of Tammany Hall is a growth, and just as Croker grew, so has Charles F. Murphy grown up to Croker's place. Again, whereas in Philadelphia the boss and his ring handle and keep almost all of the graft, leaving little to the district leaders, in New York the district leaders share handsomely in the spoils.

There is more to share in New York. It is impossible to estimate the amount of it, not only for me, but for anybody. No Tammany man knows it all. Police friends of mine say that the Tammany leaders never knew how rich police corruption was till the Lexow committee exposed it, and that the politicians who had been content with small presents, contributions, and influence, "did not butt in" for their share till they saw by the testimony of frightened police grafters that the department was worth from four to five millions a year. The items are so incredible that I hesitate to print them. Devery told a friend once that in one year the police graft was "something over $3,000,000." Afterward the syndicate which divided the graft under Devery took in for thirty-six months $400,000 a month from gambling and poolrooms alone. Saloon bribers, disorderly house blackmail, policy, etc., etc., bring this total up to amazing proportions.

Yet this was but one department, and a department that was overlooked by Tammany for years. The annual budget of the city is about $100,000,000, and though the power that comes of the expenditure of that amount is enormous and the opportunities for rake-offs infinite, this sum is not one-half of the resources of Tammany when it is in power. Her resources are the resources of the city as a business, as a political, as a social power. If Tammany could be incorporated, and all its earnings, both legitimate and illegitimate, gathered up and paid over in dividends, the stockholders would get more than the New York Central bond- and stockholders, more than the Standard Oil stockholders, and the controlling clique would wield a power equal to that of the United States Steel Company. Tammany, when in control of New York, takes out of the city unbelievable millions of dollars a year.

No wonder the leaders are all rich; no wonder so many more Tammany men are rich than are the leaders in any other town; no wonder Tammany is liberal in its division of the graft. Croker took the best and the safest of it, and he accepted shares in others. He was "in on the Wall Street end," and the Tammany clique of financiers have knocked down and bought up at low prices Manhattan Railway stock by threats of the city's power over the road; they have been let in on Metropolitan deals and on the Third Avenue Railroad grab; the ice trust is a Tammany trust; they have banks and trust companies, and through the New York Realty Company are forcing alliances with such financial groups as that of the Standard Oil Company. Croker shared in these deals and businesses. He sold judgeships, taking his pay in the form of contributions to the Tammany campaign fund, of which he was treasurer, and he had the judges take from the regular real estate exchange all the enormous real estate business that passed through the courts, and give it to an exchange connected with the real estate business of his firm, Peter F. Meyer & Co. This alone would maintain a ducal estate in England. But his real estate business was greater than that. It had extraordinary legal facilities, the free advertising of abuse, the prestige of political privilege, all of which brought in trade; and it had advance information and followed, with profitable deals, great public improvements.

Though Croker said he worked for his own pockets all the time, and did take the best of the graft, he was not "hoggish."

Some of the richest graft in the city is in the Department of Buildings: $100,000,000 a year goes into building operations in New York. All of this, from outhouses to sky-scrapers, is subject to very precise laws and regulations, most of them wise, some impossible. The Building Department has the enforcement of these; it passes upon all construction, private and public, at all stages, from plan-making to actual completion; and can cause not only "unavoidable delay," but can wink at most profitable violations. Architects and builders had to stand in with the department. They called on the right man and they settled on a scale which was not fixed, but which generally was on the basis of the department's estimate of a fair half of the value of the saving in time or bad material. This brought in at least a banker's percentage on one hundred millions a year. Croker, so far as I can make out, took none of this; it was let out to other leaders and was their own graft.

District Attorney William Travers Jerome has looked into the Dock Department, and he knows things which he yet may prove. This is an important investigation for two reasons. It is very large graft, and the new Tammany leader, Charlie Murphy, had it. New York wants to know more about Murphy, and it should want to know about the management of its docks, since, just as other cities have their corrupt dealings with railways and their terminals, so New York's great terminal business is with steamships and docks. These docks should pay the city handsomely. Mr. Murphy says they shouldn't; he is wise, as Croker was before he became old and garrulous, and, as Tammany men put it, "keeps his mouth shut," but he did say that the docks should not be run for revenue to the city, but for their own improvement. The Dock Board has exclusive and private and secret control of the expenditure of $10,000,000 a year. No wonder Murphy chose it.

It is impossible to follow all New York graft from its source to its final destination. It is impossible to follow here the course of that which is well known to New Yorkers. There are public works for Tammany contractors. There are private works for Tammany contractors, and corporations and individuals find it expedient to let it go to Tammany contractors. Tammany has a very good system of grafting on public works; I mean that it is "good" from the criminal point of view—and so it has for the furnishing of supplies. Low bids and short deliveries, generally speaking (and that is the only way I can speak here), is the method. But the Tammany system, as a whole, is weak.

Tammany men as grafters have a confidence in their methods and system which, in the light of such perfection as that of Philadelphia, is amusing, and the average New Yorker takes in "the organization" a queer sort of pride, which is ignorant and provincial. Tammany is way behind the times. It is growing; it has improved. In Tweed's day the politicians stole from the city treasury, divided the money on the steps of the City Hall, and, not only the leaders, big and little, but heelers and outsiders; not only Tweed, but ward carpenters robbed the city; not only politicians, but newspapers and citizens were "in on the divvy." New York, not Tammany alone, was corrupt. When the exposure came, and Tweed asked his famous question, "What are you going to do about it?" the ring mayor, A. Oakey Hall, asked another as significant. It was reported that suit was to be brought against the ring to recover stolen funds. "Who is going to sue?" said Mayor Hall, who could not think of anybody of importance sufficiently without sin to throw the first stone. Stealing was stopped and grafting was made more businesslike, but still it was too general, and the boodling for the Broadway street railway franchise prompted a still closer grip on the business. The organization since then has been gradually concentrating the control of graft. Croker did not proceed so far along the line as the Philadelphia ring has, as the police scandals showed. After the Lexow exposures, Tammany took over that graft, but still let it go practically by districts, and the police captains still got a third. After the Mazet exposures, Devery became chief, and the police graft was so concentrated that the division was reduced to fourteen parts. Again, later, it was reduced to a syndicate of four or five men, with a dribble of miscellaneous graft for the police. In Philadelphia the police have nothing to do with the police graft; a policeman may collect it, but he acts for a politician, who in turn passes it up to a small ring. That is the drift in New York. Under Devery the police officers got comparatively little, and the rank and file themselves were blackmailed for transfers and promotions, for remittances of fines, and in a dozen other petty ways.

New York: Good Government to the Test

Philadelphia is the end toward which New York under Tammany is driving as fast as the lower intelligence and higher conceit of its leaders will let it. In Philadelphia one very small ring gets everything, dividing the whole as it pleases, and not all those in the inner ring are politicians. Trusting few individuals, they are safe from exposure, more powerful, more deliberate, and they are wise as politicians. When, as in New York, the number of grafters is large, this delicate business is in some hands that are rapacious. The police grafters, for example, in Devery's day, were not content with the amounts collected from the big vices. They cultivated minor vices, like policy, to such an extent that the Policy King was caught and sent to prison, and Devery's wardman, Glennon, was pushed into so tight a hole that there was danger that District Attorney Jerome would get past Glennon to Devery and the syndicate. The murder of a witness the night he was in the Tenderloin police station served to save the day. But, worst of all, Tammany, the "friend of the people," permitted the organization of a band of so-called Cadets, who made a business, under the protection of the police, of ruining the daughters of the tenements and even of catching and imprisoning in disorderly houses the wives of poor men. This horrid traffic never was exposed; it could not and cannot be. Vicious women were "planted" in tenement houses and (I know this personally) the children of decent parents counted the customers, witnessed their transactions with these creatures, and, as a father told with shame and tears, reported totals at the family table.

Tammany leaders are usually the natural leaders of the people in these districts, and they are originally goodnatured, kindly men. No one has a more sincere liking than I for some of those common but generous fellows; their charity is real, at first. But they sell out their own people. They do give them coal and help them in their private troubles, but, as they grow rich and powerful, the kindness goes out of the charity and they not only collect at their saloons or in rents cash for their "goodness"; they not only ruin fathers and sons and cause the troubles they relieve; they sacrifice the children in the schools; let the Health Department neglect the tenements, and, worst of all, plant vice in the neighborhood and in the homes of the poor.

This is not only bad; it is bad politics; it has defeated Tammany. Woe to New York when Tammany learns better. Honest fools talk of the reform of Tammany Hall. It is an old hope, this, and twice it has been disappointed, but it is not vain. That is the real danger ahead. The reform of a corrupt ring means, as I have said before, the reform of its system of grafting and a wise consideration of certain features of good government. Croker turned his "best chief of police," William S. Devery, out of Tammany Hall, and, slow and old as he was, Croker learned what clean streets were from Colonel Waring, and gave them. Now there is a new boss, a young man, Charles F. Murphy, and unknown to New Yorkers. He looks dense, but he acts with force, decision, and skill. The new mayor will be his man. He may divide with Croker and leave to the "old man" all his accustomed graft, but Charlie Murphy will rule Tammany and, if Tammany is elected, New York also. Lewis Nixon is urging Murphy publicly, as I write, to declare against the police scandals and all the worst practices of Tammany. Lewis Nixon is an honest man, but he was one of the men Croker tried to appoint leader of Tammany Hall. And when he resigned Mr. Nixon said that he found that a man could not keep that leadership and his self-respect. Yet Mr. Nixon is a type of the man who thinks Tammany would be fit to rule New York if the organization would "reform."

As a New Yorker, I fear Murphy will prove sagacious enough to do just that: stop the scandal, put all the graft in the hands of a few tried and true men, and give the city what it would call good government. Murphy says he will nominate for mayor a man so "good" that his goodness will astonish New York. I don't fear a bad Tammany mayor; I dread the election of a good one. For I have been to Philadelphia.

Philadelphia had a bad ring mayor, a man who promoted the graft and caused scandal after scandal. The leaders there, the wisest political grafters in this country, learned a great lesson from that. As one of them said to me:

"The American people don't mind grafting, but they hate scandals. They don't kick so much on a jiggered public contract for a boulevard, but they want the boulevard and no fuss and no dust. We want to give them that. We want to give them what

New York: Good Government to the Test

they really want, a quiet Sabbath, safe streets, orderly nights, and homes secure. They let us have the police graft. But this mayor was a hog. You see, he had but one term and he could get his share only on what was made in his term. He not only took a hog's share off what was coming, but he wanted everything to come in his term. So I'm down on grafting mayors and grafting office holders. I tell you it's good politics to have honest men in office. I mean men that are personally honest."

So they got John Weaver for mayor, and honest John Weaver is checking corruption, restoring order, and doing a great many good things, which it is "good politics" to do. For he is satisfying the people, soothing their ruffled pride, and reconciling them to machine rule. I have letters from friends of mine there, honest men, who wish me to bear witness to the goodness of Mayor Weaver. I do. And I believe that if the Philadelphia machine leaders are as careful with Mayor Weaver as they have been and let him continue to give to the end as good government as he has given so far, the "Philadelphia plan" of graft will last and Philadelphia will never again be a free American city.

Philadelphia and New York began about the same time, some thirty years ago, to reform their city governments. Philadelphia got "good government"—what the Philadelphians call good—from a corrupt ring and quit, satisfied to be a scandal to the nation and a disgrace to democracy. New York has gone on fighting, advancing and retreating, for thirty years, till now it has achieved the beginnings, under Mayor Low, of a government for the people. Do the New Yorkers know it? Do they care? They are Americans, mixed and typical; do we Americans really want good government? Or, as I said at starting, have they worked for thirty years along the wrong road—crowded with unhappy American cities—the road to Philadelphia and despair?

McClure's Magazine
April, 1904

Enemies of the Republic

The Political Leaders Who are Selling Out the State of Missouri, and the Leading Businessman Who are Buying It

Business as Treason --- Corruption as Revolution

EVERY time I attempted to trace to its sources the political corruption of a city ring, the stream of pollution branched off in the most unexpected directions and spread out in a network of veins and arteries so complex that hardly any part of the body politic seemed clear of it. It flowed out of the majority party into the minority; out of politics into vice and crime; out of business into politics, and back into business; from the boss, down through the police to the prostitute, and up through the practice of law into the courts; and big throbbing arteries ran out through the country over the state to the nation —and back. No wonder cities can't get municipal reform! No wonder Minneapolis, having cleaned out its police ring of vice grafters, discovered boodle in the council! No wonder Chicago, with council-reform and boodle beaten, found itself a Minneapolis of police and administrative graft! No wonder Pittsburgh, when it broke out of its local ring, fell, amazed, into a state ring! No wonder New York, with good government under Mayor Seth Low, voted itself back into Tammany Hall!

They are on the wrong track; we are, all of us, on the wrong track. You can't reform a city by reforming part of it. You can't reform a city alone. You can't reform politics alone. And as for corruption and the understanding thereof, we cannot run round and round in municipal rings and understand ring corruption; it isn't a ring thing. We cannot remain in one city, or ten, and comprehend municipal corruption; it isn't a local thing. We cannot "stick to a party," and follow party corruption;

it isn't a partisan thing. And I have found that I cannot confine myself to politics and grasp all the ramifications of political corruption. It isn't political corruption. It's corruption. The corruption of our American politics is our American corruption, political, but financial and industrial, too. Miss Tarbell has shown it in the trust, Mr. Baker in the labor union, and my gropings into the misgovernment of cities have drawn me everywhere, but, always, always out of politics into business, and out of the cities into the state. Business started the corruption of politics in Pittsburgh; upheld it in Philadelphia; boomed with it in Chicago and withered with its reform; and in New York, business financed the return of Tammany Hall. Here, then, is our guide out of the labyrinth. Not the political ring, but big business—that is the crux of the situation. Our political corruption is a system, a regularly established custom of the country, by which our political leaders are hired, by bribery, by the license to loot, and by quiet moral support, to conduct the government of city, state and nation, not for the common good, but for the special interests of private business. Not the politician, then, not the bribe-taker, but the bribe-giver, the man we are so proud of, our successful business man—he is the source and sustenance of our bad government. The captain of industry is the man to catch. His is the trail to follow.

    We have struck that trail before. Whenever we followed the successful politician, his tracks led us into it, but also they led us out of the cities—from Pittsburgh to the state legislature at Harrisburg; from Philadelphia, through Pennsylvania, to the national legislature at Washington. To go on was to go into state and national politics, and I was after the political corruption of the city ring then. Now I know that these are all one. The trail of the political leader and the trail of the commercial leader are parallels which mark the plain, main road that leads off the dead level of the cities, up through the states into the United States, out of the political ring into the System, the living System of our actual government. The highway of corruption is the "road to success."

    Almost any state would start us right, but Missouri is the most promising. Joseph W. Folk, the circuit attorney of St.

Louis, has not only laid wide open the road out there; he knows it is the way of a system. He didn't at first. He, too, thought he was fighting political corruption, and that the whole of it was the St. Louis ring. But he got the ring. Mr. Folk convicted the boss and nearly all the members of the "boodle combine" that was selling out his city; yet the ring does not break. Why? Because back of the boodlers stand the big business men who are buying the city up. But Folk got the business men, too; Charles H. Turner, president of the Suburban Railway Company, president of the Commonwealth Trust Company; Philip Stock, secretary of the St. Louis Brewery Association; Ellis Wainwright, the millionaire brewer; George J. Kobusch, president of the St. Louis Car Company; Robert N. Snyder, banker and promoter, of Kansas City and New York; John Scullen, ex-president of street railways, a director then and now of steam railways, a director then and to the end of the Louisiana Purchase Exposition. These are not "low-down politicians"; they are "respectable business men." Having discovered early that boodlers flew in pairs; that wherever there was a bribe-taker there also was a bribe-giver. Folk hunted them in pairs. And in pairs he brought them down. And still the ring does not break. What is the matter?

That's what's the matter. "That man Folk" is attacking the System. If he had confined his chase to that unprotected bird, the petty boodler, all might have been well. Indeed, there was a time, just before the first trial of the boss, Colonel Ed Butler, when the ring was in a panic and everybody ran. If he had stayed his hand then. Folk could have been governor of Missouri with the consent of "his party," and a very rich man besides. But he would not stop. These were not the things he was after. At that moment he was after Boss Butler; and he got him.

"And the conviction of Butler was the point," he said, "where we passed out of the ring into the System."

Butler was not only the boss of the ring; he was the tool of the System. He was the man through whom the St. Louis business man did business with the combine, and Folk hadn't caught all the business men involved. The first time I met him, early in his work, he was puzzled by the opposition or silence of officials and citizens, who, he thought, should have been on his side. The next time I saw him this mystery was clearing. One by one those people were turning up in this deal or way back of that one. He could not reach them; he can never reach them all; but there they were, they, their relatives, their friends, their lawyers, their business and social associates —"nobody can realize," said Mr. Folk, "the infinite ramifications of this thing." "They," "this thing," the "vested interests" of St. Louis, are the St. Louis System.

Corruption was saved, not ended, by the very thoroughness of Mr. Folk. The ring was rallied, not smashed, by his conviction of its boss. The boodlers who had wanted to turn state's evidence "stood pat." Why? They had an assurance, they said, that "not one of them would go to the pen." Who made this promise? Butler. Ed Butler, himself sentenced to three years in the penitentiary, gave this explicit assurance, and he added (this was last summer) that "the courts will reverse all Folk's cases, and, when Folk's term expires, we will all get off, and the fellows that have peached will go to jail." Maybe Butler lied; some of the politicians said that it would be "bad politics" to reverse "all Folk's cases," and that some, possibly Butler's own, would have to be affirmed. Butler, however, was not afraid, and, sure enough, in December his case was reversed. All the boodle cases so far have been reversed. Not a boodler is in jail today (January 22, 1904), and the same court gave a ruling which made it necessary for Folk to reindict and retry half a dozen of his cases. The boodlers are a power in politics. Butler sits in the councils of the Democratic party. He sat there with the business men and with the new, young leaders who drew up the last platform, which made no mention of boodle, and he assisted in the naming of the tickets. After the last election, Butler was able to reorganize the new House of Delegates, with his man for Speaker, and the superintendent of his garbage plant (in the interest of which he offered the bribe for which he was convicted) for chairman of the Sanitary Committee. But the nominations he had helped to make were not only those of aldermen, but of the candidates for the vacancies on the bench which was to try boodle cases, and also for that court which was to hear these cases, and his own, on appeal! And the presiding justice of this, the criminal branch of the Supreme Court of Missouri, went upon the stump last fall and declared that a man who thought as Mr. Folk thought, and did as Mr. Folk did, had better leave the state!

Appalling? It did not appall Mr. Folk. He realized then that it was a System, not the ring, that he was fighting, and he went after that. There was another way into it. One Charles Kratz, the head of the council combine, did business, like Butler, with and for business men. Kratz fled to Mexico with means supplied by his business backers, but Mr. Folk used the good offices of the president and the secretary of state to get the man back. And he succeeded; he had Kratz brought back. The hope was that Kratz would confess and deliver up his principals. The other boodlers, however, received Kratz with a champagne dinner, and he also stood pat. But even if Kratz should surrender, and even if Folk thus were to smash the Butler ring and catch not five or six, but fifty, of the captains of industry behind it—still, I believe, the System would stand. Why? Because "this thing" is more than men, and bigger than St. Louis.

All the while Mr. Folk was probing the city he kept an eye on the state. It was out of his jurisdiction, but it affected his work. Some of the silent opposition he encountered came from state officials, and the court which was inspiring so much faith in boodlers was a state court. These officials were not implicated in his exposures, and these judges were honest men, but the state legislature, at Jefferson City, sent forth significant rumors, and about these Folk gossiped with the St. Louis boodlers, who explained that corruption was an ancient custom of the state. Helpless but informed, Folk watched and waited, till at last his chance came.

One day in February, 1903, when a bill in which the Speaker of the House was interested failed of passage, that officer left his chair in anger, saying, "There is boodle in this." The House was disturbed. Folk's work had opened the public mind to suspicion, and the newspapers were alert. Investigations were ordered, one by the House committee, which found nothing; another by a Jefferson City grand jury, which resulted in a statement by Circuit Attorney R. P. Stone that it was all "hot air" and that, anyhow, he had no ambition "to become a second Folk." (Stone was indicted himself afterward.) Then the governor directed Attorney-General E. C. Crow to take charge, and Crow took charge. Picking Lieutenant-Governor Lee for a weakling, he concentrated on him. Lee was telling things, bit by bit, but he kept denying them, and the jury was uneasy and reluctant. The outcome of the inquiry was in doubt in Jefferson City, when Mr. Folk heard that "floating all around town "were a lot of thousand-dollar bribe bills which were distributed at the Laclede Hotel. The Laclede Hotel is in St. Louis, and St. Louis is Folk's bailiwick. Folk jumped in. He traced the bills, and, in a jiffy, he had the whole inside story. He gave out an interview directed at Lieutenant-Governor Lee, who saw it; saw, he said, that Folk had him, and ran to Attorney General Crow to confess. Changing his mind, he fled the state, but Folk gave out another interview that brought him back. Meeting and agreeing on a course, Folk and Crow worked together. They got Lee's confession in full, and his resignation of the lieutenant-governorship; and with all this for a lever, they opened the mouths of other legislators. Indictments followed, and trials; Crow took all the evidence and carried on the dull, slow trials, which we need not follow.

    The lid was off Missouri. The stone Mr. Folk had had so long to leave unturned was lifted. What was under it? Squirming in the light and writhing off into their dark holes were state senators and state officers, state committee-men and party leaders, but also there were the Western Union Telegraph Company, the Missouri Pacific Railroad, the St. Louis and San Francisco, the Iron Mountain and Southern, the Wabash; Mr. Folk's old friend, the St. Louis Transit Company; the breweries, the stock yards, the telephone companies; business men of St. Louis, St. Joseph, and Kansas City—the big business of the whole state. There they were, the "contemptible" bribe-taker and the very "respectable" bribe-giver, all doing business together. So they still traveled in pairs; and the highway still lay between the deadly parallels—business and politics. The System was indeed bigger than St. Louis; it was the System of Missouri.

    What, then, is the System of Missouri? The outlines of it can be traced through the "confessions of state senators which,"

Folk's grand jury said, "appall and astound us as citizens of this state. Our investigations," they added, "have gone back twelve years, and during that time the evidence shows that corruption has been the usual and accepted thing in state legislation, and that, too, without interference or hindrance... We have beheld with shame and humiliation the violation of the sacred trust reposed by the people in their public servants."

Just as in the city, the System in the state was corruption settled into a "custom of the country"; betrayal of trust established as the form of government. The people elect, to govern for them, representatives who are to care for the common interest of all. But the confessing senators confessed that they were paid by a lobby to serve special interests. Naturally enough, the jurors, good citizens, were incensed especially at the public servants "who sold them out." But who did the buying? Who are the lobby? The confessions name Colonel William H. Phelps, John J. Carroll and others, lawyers and citizens of standing at the bar and in the state, and they were the agents of the commanding business enterprises of the state. Moreover, they were aggressive corruptionists. You hear business men say that they are blackmailed, that the politicians are corrupt, and that the "better people" have to pay.

Colonel Phelps, an officer of the Missouri Pacific, and the lobbyist of the Gould interests, has said that he had to exercise great cunning to keep the legislature corrupt. New legislators often bothered him, especially "honest men," Senators who would not take money. Sometimes he got them with passes, which was cheap, but not sure, so he had been compelled sometimes actually to "rape " some men, as he did Senator Fred Busche, of St. Louis.

Busche is himself a business man, a well-to-do pie-baker, and he went to Jefferson City full of high purpose and patriotic sentiment, he said. Among the measures up for passage was a bill to require all railways to keep a flagman at all crossings. It was a "strike" bill. Phelps himself had had it introduced, to prove his usefulness in killing it, perhaps, or to raise money for himself and his pals. (The corrupt corporations are often cheated by their corrupt agents.) At any rate, Phelps asked Busche to vote against the bill, and Busche did so. A day or two later Phelps came up to Busche, thrust a hundred-dollar bill into his pocket, then hurried away and remained out of sight till Busche had become reconciled to the money. "After that," Busche added, "Phelps had me." Busche accepted a regular salary of $500 a session from the railroad lobbyist, and other bribes: $500 on the St. Louis transit bill, $500 on an excise bill, etc. He estimated that he had made corruptly some $15,000 during his twelve years.

Phelps put Busche into the "Senate Combine," which is just such a non-partisan group of a controlling majority as that which Colonel Butler wielded in the municipal legislature councils of St. Louis. Butler, however, was a boss; Phelps is not. There is no boss of Missouri as there is of New York, Pennsylvania, and other more advanced states. Phelps is the king of the lobby, and the lobby rules by force of corruption. The lobbyists, representing different special business interests, bought among them a majority of the legislators, organized the Senate, ran dominant committees, and thus controlled legislation. You could do business with any lobbyist, and have the service, usually, of all, or you could deal with a member of the combine. Indeed, the "combine" was free to drum up trade when times were dull, and Mr. Folk quotes a telegram from a member sent on such a mission to St. Louis: "River rising fast," it said. "Driftwood coming down. Be there tomorrow."

"Driftwood" was boodle bills for business men, and some of it was blackmail, but it was all irregular. The regular business was more businesslike. The "combine" was only the chief instrument of the lobby and was made up of dishonest legislators. The lobby controlled also the honest men. For these belonged to their party. The corporations and big businesses contribute to all campaign funds, and this is the first step toward corruption everywhere. It is wholesale bribery, and it buys the honest legislator. He may want to vote against the "combine," but the lobby serves the party as well as business, and the "state Committee" has to "stand in." That is the way the Democratic party got control of the police and election machinery of Missouri cities and forced those normally

Republican communities into the Democratic line. The lobby delivers the dishonest votes. In return for such services and for the campaign contributions, the state committee of the dominant Democratic party has to deliver the honest votes, and often, too, the governor of the state. As for the minority party, the Republicans in Missouri are like the minority everywhere: just as corrupt and more hungry than the majority. Disrupted by quarrels over the federal patronage, the Republican legislators follow the Democrats for more, for dribblets of graft, and the first senator convicted by Crow was a Republican.

There is nothing partisan about graft. Only the people are loyal to party. The "hated" trusts, all big grafters, go with the majority. In Democratic Missouri, the Democracy is the party of "capital." The Democratic political leaders, crying "down with trusts," corner the voters like wheat, form a political trust, and sell out the sovereignty of the people to the corporation lobby. And the lobby runs the state, not only in the interest of its principals, but against the interest of the people. Once, when an election bill was up—the bill to turn over the cities to the Democrats—citizens of Kansas City, Democrats among them, had to hire a lobbyist to fight it, and when this lobbyist found that the interest of his corporations required the passage of the bill, he sent back his fee with an explanation. And this story was told me as an example of the honesty of that lobbyist! Lieutenant-Governor Lee in his confession gave another such example. Public opinion forced out of committee, and was driving through the Senate, a bill to put a just tax on the franchises of public service corporations. The lobby dared not stop it. But Colonel Phelps took one day "his accustomed place" behind a curtain back of the Lieutenant-governor's chair, and he wrote out amendment after amendment, passed them to Senator Frank Farris, who introduced them, and the lobby put them through, so that the bill passed, "smothered to death."

When Lieutenant-Governor Lee drew aside that curtain he revealed the real head of the government of Missouri. I mean this literally. I mean that this system I have been describing is a form of government; it is the government. We must not be confused by constitutions and charters. The constitution of

Missouri describes a governor and his duties, a legislature and the powers lodged in a Senate and a House of Representatives, etc., etc. This is the paper government. In Missouri this paper government has been superseded by an actual government, and this government is:—a lobby, with a combine of legislators, the Democratic state Committee, and state leaders and city bosses for agents. One bribe, two bribes, a hundred bribes might not be so bad, but what we have seen here is a System of bribery, corruption installed as the motive, the purpose, the spirit of a state government. A revolution had happened. Bribes, not bullets, were spent in it, and the fighting was slow and quiet, but victory seemed sure; the bribe-takers were betraying the government of the people to an oligarchy of bribe-givers, when Joseph Folk realized the truth.

"Bribery," he declared, "is treason, and a boodler is a traitor."

"Bosh!" cried the lawyers. "Poppy-cock," the cynics sneered, and the courts ruled out the cases. "Bribery," said Judge Priest, at the trial of the banker, Snyder, "is, at the most, a conventional crime." "Corruption is an occasional offense," the ring orators proclaim, but they answer themselves, for they say also, "corruption is not a vice only of Missouri, it is everywhere."

"It is everywhere," Folk answers, and because he has realized that, because he realized that boodling is the custom and that the "occasional" boodler who sells his vote is selling the state and altering the very form of our government, he has declared boodle to be a political issue. And because the people do not see it so, and because he saw that no matter how many individual boodlers he might catch, he, the circuit attorney of St. Louis, could not stop boodling even in St. Louis. Mr. Folk announced himself a candidate for governor, and is now appealing his case to the people, who alone can stop it. His party shrieked and raged, but because it is his party, because he thinks his party is the party of the people, and because his party is the responsible, the boodle party in his state, he made the issue first in his own party. He has asked his people to take back the control of it and clean it up.

Thus, at last, is raised in St. Louis and Missouri the plain, great question: Do the people rule? Will they, can they, rule? And the answer of Missouri will be national in importance. Both the Democracy and democracy are being put to the test out there.

But Missouri cannot decide alone. "Corruption is everywhere." The highway of corruption which Folk has taken as the road to political reform goes far beyond Missouri. When he and Attorney-General Crow lifted the lid off Missouri, they disturbed the lid over the United States, and they saw wiggling among their domestic industries and state officials, three "foreign trusts"—the American Sugar Refining Company, the American Book Company, and the Royal Baking Powder Company. These are national concerns; they operate all over the United States; and they are purely commercial enterprises with probably purely commercial methods. What they do, therefore, is business pure and simple; their way will be the way of business. But off behind them slunk a United States senator, the Honorable William J. Stone. He was on the same road. So they still run in pairs, and the road to success still lies between the two parallels, and it leads straight to Washington, where, in political infinity, as it were, in that chamber of the bosses, the United States Senate, the parallels seem to meet. Are the corrupt customs of Missouri the custom of the country? Are the methods of its politics the methods of business? Isn't the System of that state the System of the United States? Let us see.

Among the letters of the confessed boodler, Lieutenant-Governor Lee, to his friend Daniel J. Kelly, are many references to his ambition to be governor of the state. When Folk decided to run for that office the politicians were shocked at his "ambition"; he had not served the party, only the people. But Lee, whom they knew to be a boodler, was not regarded as presumptuous. He was a "possibility." And, in his first letter on the subject to Kelly, he asks how he can sell himself out in advance to two trusts. "Of course you can help me get a campaign fund together," he says, "and I will be grateful to you. . . . How would you tackle Sugar-Tobacco if you were me in the campaign-fund matter?" Kelly must have advised Lee to write direct, for the next letter is from H. O. Havemeyer, expressing "my hopes that your political aspirations will be realized," and adding, suggestively, "If I can be of any service I presume your representative will appear. (Signed) H. O. Havemeyer." Lee wanted Kelly to "appear," and there was some correspondence over a proposition to have the contribution made in the form of advertisements in Lee's two trade journals. But Lee "needed help badly, as the country papers must be taken care of," so he asks Kelly "to so present the case to Mr. H. that he will do some business with the papers and help me out personally besides. Do your best, old man," he pleads, "and ask Mr. H. to do his best. A lift in time is always the best." And Mr. H. did his best. Lee had arranged that Kelly was to see Havemeyer on both personal and business accounts, but the "personal" came by mail, and Lee wires Kelly to "drop personal matter and confine to advertising. Personal arranged by mail." And then we have this note of explanation to "Friend Kelly":

"The party sent me $1,000 personally by mail. If you do anything now it will be on the advertising basis. Truly and heartily, Lee."

Here we have a captain of industry taking a "little flyer" in a prospective governor of a state. Mr. Havemeyer probably despises Lee, but Mr. Havemeyer himself is not ashamed. Business men will understand that this is business. It may be bad in politics, but such an investment is "good business." And there is my point ready made: This "bad" politics of ours is "good" business.

A longer trail is that of William Ziegler; his business, the Royal Baking Powder Company; and the company's agent, Daniel J. Kelly. In Missouri they said Crow was "after" United States Senator Stone, but "they travel in pairs," so he had to begin with the business men, as Folk did. He indicted first Kelly, then Ziegler, for bribery. Lee, whose confession caused the indictment of Kelly, wired this warning: "D. J. Kelly: Your health being poor, brief recreation trip if taken would be greatly beneficial. James Sargent." Kelly took the recreation trip to Canada, and Ziegler, in New York, resisted extradition to Missouri for trial. The prospect was of a long lawyers' fight, the result of which need not be anticipated here. Our interest is in the business methods of this great commercial concern, the Royal Baking Powder "trust," and the secrets of the success of this captain of the baking-powder industry. And this, mind you, as a key to the understanding of "politics."

We have been getting into business by following politics. Now, for a change, we will follow a strictly business career and see that the accepted methods of business are the despised methods of politics, and that just as the trail of the successful politician leads us into business, so the trail of the successful business man leads us into politics.

Ziegler's "success story" is that of the typical poor boy who began with nothing, and carved out a fortune of many, many millions. He was not handicapped with a college education and ethical theories. He went straight into business, as a drug-clerk, and he learned his morals from business. And he is a "good business man." This is no sneer. He told me the story of his life one night, not all, of course, for he knew what the purpose of my article was to be; but he told me enough so that I could see that if the story were set down—the daring enterprise, the patient study of details, and the work, the work, the terrible, killing work—if this all were related, as well as "the things a business man has to do," then, I say, the story of William Ziegler might do him, on the whole, honor as well as dishonor. But this, the inspiring side, of such stories, has been told again and again, and it does not give "our boys" all the secrets of success, and it does not explain the state either of our business or of our politics. I have no malice against Mr. Ziegler; I have a kind of liking for him, but so have I a liking for a lot of those kind, good fellows, the low-down politicians who sell us out to the Zieglers. They, too, are human, much more human than many a "better man." How often they have helped me to get the truth! But they do sell us out, and the "good business men" do buy us out. So William Ziegler, who also helped me, he, to me here, is only a type.

Ziegler went into the baking-powder business way back in 1868 with the Hoaglands, a firm of druggists at Fort Wayne, Indiana. The young man mastered the business, technically as a pharmacist, commercially as a salesman. He fought for his share in the profit; he left them and established a competitive business to force his point, and in 1873 they let him in. So you see, Young Man, it isn't alone sobriety, industry, and honesty that make success, but battle, too. Ziegler organized the Royal Baking Powder Company in 1873, with himself as treasurer.

The business grew for three or four years, when it was discovered that alum and soda made a stronger leaven, and cheaper. Worse still, alum was plentiful. Anybody could go into its manufacture, and many did. The Royal, to control the cream of tartar industry, had contracted to take from European countries immense quantities of argol, the wine-lees from which cream of tartar is made. They had to go on making the more expensive baking-powder or break a contract. That would be "bad business."

So Ziegler was for war. His plan was to "fight alum." His associates, less daring than he, objected, but Ziegler won them over, and thus was begun the "Alum War," famous in chemistry, journalism, and legislation. Outsiders knew little about it, but they can find the spoils of Ziegler's battle in the bosom of their own family. Let any man in the North, East, and West, ask himself if he does not think "alum in food is bad"; if he can't answer, let him ask his wife. She will not know exactly why, but she is pretty sure to have a "general impression" that it is injurious in some way and that "the Royal is pure," "the best." This general impression was capitalized by Ziegler in 1898, at a valuation of many millions of dollars. He combined, in a trust, the Cleveland, Price, and Royal cream of tartar companies; their separate capitalization amounted to something over one million. The trust was capitalized at $20,000,000.

Now, how did Ziegler plant this general impression which was sold as so much preferred and common stock? He began the war by hiring chemists to give "expert opinions" against alum and for cream of tartar. The alum people, in alarm, had to hire chemists to give opposite opinions for alum and against cream of tartar. What the merits of the chemical controversy are, no man can decide now. Hundreds of "eminent scientific men," chemists, physiologists, and doctors of medicine, have taken part in it, and there are respectable authorities on both sides. The Royal's array of experts, who say "alum is bad," is the greater, and they are right as to "alum in food." But that is a trick phrase. The alum people say, and truly, that the alum in baking-powder disappears in the bread, just as cream of tartar does, and that the whole question resolves itself into the effects on the human system of what is left. In the case of the alum, the residuum is hydrate of aluminum, of which Dr. Austin Flint, who experimented with Professor Peter F. Austin and Dr. E. E. Smith, says that it "is inert; has no effect upon the secretion of gastric juice, nor does it interfere with digestion; and it has no medicinal effects." On the other hand, the alum party say that the residuum of cream of tartar powder is "Rochelle salts, an irritant drug with purgative qualities." This the Royal overwhelmed with testimony, but Ziegler does not believe much in defense. He attacks. His was a war on "impure food," and his slogan was short and sharp: "alum, a poison." That was all.

And that is enough for us. Our war is on "impure business," and, whatever the truth is about alum and cream of tartar, the truth about Ziegler and the Royal Baking Powder is this: they were making alum baking-powders themselves. All the while Ziegler was buying those expert testimonials against it, he was manufacturing and selling alum baking-powder.

This, on his own testimony. He brought a suit once against the Hoaglands, his associates, and he wanted to show that he, not they, had made the business what it was; so he went upon the stand and swore that he started the alum war; he hired Dr. Mott, the first chemist, etc., etc. Listen, then, to this captain of industry confessing himself:

"I have heard the testimony about what is called the alum war," he says. "I instituted it upon the part of the company. I employed Dr. Mott personally—it is possible that Mr. Hoagland may have made the money arrangement with him; I also visited other chemists and got certificates; I did all that business connected with the chemical part of the investigation, preparing the matter; I originated that matter; Mr. Joseph C. Hoagland bitterly opposed it; he said war on alum would injure the sale of all baking-powders; that it would bring all baking-powders into disrepute, and it was difficult for the public to tell an alum baking-powder from a cream of tartar powder.

"We had also as a company been manufacturing alum baking-powder, which was in the market, not under our brand Royal but another brand. The theory was that our competitors might get hold of some of that, analyze it, and show that we also manufactured alum baking-powder"

Nor is that all. Ziegler says he "got" the chemists. How he "got" them I don't know, but the company had at one time an ammonia skirmish. They were making ammonia baking-powder, and the alum people "showed them up," so Ziegler had to have ammonia testimonials from leading chemists, and he sent out for them.

"I got some myself," he testifies. "I went over and saw Professor Norton, who had given an adverse opinion. I got him to change his mind. He did not deny what he had said before, but he gave us something that answered our purpose."

"Answered our purpose!" There you have the equivalent in business of the political platform. The purpose answered in the alum war was advertisement. Having "got" the chemists' opinion, he had to turn that into public opinion, so he had to "get" the press. And he got the press, and his method of advertising fixed public opinion. How?

The Chamber of Commerce of Richmond, Va., recently "in seeking the source of a prejudice which once existed in the state [against alum baking-powder, which is a staple in the South] believes," it says, "that it is to be found in a comprehensive system of what may be called 'blind advertising' or 'reading notices' inaugurated years ago in the newspapers of the country by the Royal." The Chamber printed a sample contract:

Please publish articles as below, each one time, in Daily and Weekly, as pure, straight reading, on top half of fifth page, set in the same size and style of type, and with the same style of heading as the pure reading adjoining, leaded or solid to correspond with such pure reading, to be surrounded by pure reading, and without date, mark or anything to designate them as paid matter; and with the express understanding that they are not at date of publication or afterward to be designated or classed by any article or advertisement in your paper as advertisements, or as paid for, or as emanating from us. Start with top one on list and publish, in same order, daily two days apart and weekly one week apart.

ROYAL BAKING POWDER CO.

This step paved the way to the publication of anything the Royal might want to say as news or as the disinterested opinion of the paper. They would get a case of poisoning, for example, have it investigated and reported in one newspaper, then they would send the clipping for publication to their other newspapers. Here is one from the *Commercial-Appeal*, Memphis, Tenn., Jan. 9, 1900.

SAID TO BE ALUM POISONING—SERIOUS CASE OF ILLNESS REPORTED FROM THE USE OF IMPURE BAKING POWDER.

Johnstown (Pa.) Tribune.

The poisoning of the Thomas family, of Thomas Mill, Somerset County, four members of which were reported to have been made dangerously ill by impure baking powder used in making buckwheat cakes, has been further investigated.

The original can, with the remainder of the baking powder left over after mixing the cakes, was secured by Dr. Critchfield. The powder had been bought at a neighboring country store and was one of the low-priced brands.

Dr. Critchfield said that the patients had the symptoms of alum poisoning. As the same kind of baking powder is sold in many city groceries as well as country stores, Dr. Critchfield thought it important that a chemical examination should be made to determine its ingredients. He therefore transferred the package of powder to Dr. Schill, of this city, for analysis. Dr. Schill's report is as follows:

"I certify that I have examined chemically the sample of . . . baking powder forwarded to me by Dr. Critchfield. The specimen contained alum."

DR. FRANCIS SCHILL, JR., *Analyst.*

Alum is used in the manufacture of the lower-priced baking powders. It is a mineral poison, and for this reason the sale of baking powders containing it is in many cities prohibited.

The Thomas family tried to answer this "news item." Six of them signed a statement that they were sickened not by alum baking-powder, but by arsenical poisoning from a newly-painted sausage machine; that "the doctors did not tell us that the symptoms was alum poisoning, but arsenical poisoning"; that they were "using alum baking-powder then and are yet, as Dr. Schill and Dr. Critchfield said it was all right." And the physicians made affidavits to the same effect, one of which, Dr. Critchfield's, covers both:

Personally appeared before me J. B. Critchfield, who deposes and says as follows: That I am the doctor who attended the Thomas family who were poisoned some time ago. The statements and advertisements of the Royal Baking Powder Company that I stated that they (the Thomas family) were poisoned by alum in baking powder is false. I never made any such statement. Mr. La Fetra, the agent of the Royal Baking Powder Company, called on me and asked me if I would state that the poisoning was alum poisoning, and I told him I would not. They have in their advertisements misquoted me and have made false statements in regard to the matter, as the symptoms were arsenical poisoning and not alum.

J. B. CRITCHFIELD
April 20, 1900.

Such lying was not so common as a more subtle deception. A typical form of "reading notice" was to speak of alum as a poison, and then add suggestively: "Recently in New York two deaths occurred from poisoning by the use of powders sent to victims in samples." This does not say that the powders were alum, and, so far as I can learn, the only two deaths that occurred in this way at about that time were those of Bamett and Mrs. Adams, for whose murder Molineux was tried and acquitted; and Kutnow and bromo-seltzer were the powders alleged to have been used on them.

Such methods are corruption: not in law, not in business; "seeing" a chemist and getting him "to change his mind" and give "something that will answer a purpose," would be "fraud" and "pull" in politics; in business it is only a "trick of the trade." Printing lies is "faking," when the newspaper itself does it; but to do it for a big advertiser is a common practice of every-day business. It pays, and what pays is right. In the years preceding the formation of the trust, the Royal company, capitalized at $160,000, made profits which rose from $17,647, in 1876, to $725,162, in 1887. In other words, the income in 1887 was more than four times the capital, and the largest item of expense was for advertising, which ran up from $17,647, in 1876, to $291,084, in 1887. As the Hoaglands swore: "The great value of the property, estimated at millions of dollars, consists not in goods, nor in factories, nor in substantial assets, but in the goodwill and popularity of its name and trademark." In short, as I said before, in a capitalization of twenty millions, eighteen represented a "general impression" that "alum was bad" and that cream of tartar was "the best."

But this was not enough. One year's profits of a million and a half were made on only twenty percent of the baking-powder business. If they could get the other eighty percent, they could make six and one-half millions a year. And why not? Alum had not been driven out of the trade; it made gains steadily. The Royal had to keep up its fight. As Mr. Hoagland said: "A subtle tenure hangs upon its continued success which can be maintained only by the most unique and peculiar abilities, by the most cunning tact and long experience." Since, then, they had to fight for life, why not fight for a monopoly? Ziegler was for entirely driving alum out of use.

How? By legislation. But success would cost the consumer thirty millions a year. The consumer is the people, and legislators are representatives of the people. No matter. The representatives of the people must use the power of the people to build up a trust by compelling the people to use only trust baking-powder. Impossible? Not at all. Legislation favorable to the Royal has been enacted or offered in twenty-four states of the Union! How the trust worked in all these states I do not know. Ziegler charged the Hoaglands with having "paid money to influence legislators in the legislature of the state (of New York) and paid the same out of the funds of the company." I don't know about New York. I must go by the experience of Missouri, and, while Attorney-General Crow charges Ziegler with bribery out there, all I can prove is that bribes were paid in the interest of the Royal. Besides, direct bribery by a captain of industry himself is not typical, and it is the typical that we want to understand. This commercial concern went into politics, and it applied to the politics of Missouri those "peculiar abilities" and the "cunning tact" which we know and which we see have met the supreme test of business—success. Now we can see what business methods look like in politics.

Ziegler becomes a mere shadow. Corrupt Royal agents do the work. One of these was Daniel J. Kelly, publisher of the *American Queen*. Kelly organized, in 1890, the National Health Society, a "fake" as to national membership; just like fake political organizations. "Pure food" is the Royal's platform, and Kelly made pure food his hobby. "I have made a study of the subject," he said in an affidavit submitted to the United States Industrial Commission. "Such time as I have had free from the demands of my publishing business I have largely devoted . . . to furthering the passage of pure-food bills in the various states. For the past two or three years my attacks . . . have been largely directed against alum baking-powder, and I have been interested in the movement that has spread through nearly all the states of the Union in favor of pure-food laws, prohibiting the use of alum baking-powders on the ground that they are poisonous."

To follow Kelly through "nearly all the states of the Union" would be interesting, but Missouri's experience was probably typical. In 1899 a bill was introduced into the legislature of that state, prohibiting the use of poisons in food, "arsenic, calomel, bismuth, ammonia or alum." "Or alum" was the point. Missouri is an alum state; $15,000,000 was invested there in the alum baking-powder industry, which was one of the largest in the state and represented all the capital and all the enterprise of many of its citizens. "Or alum" would drive them out of business and leave a foreign trust a monopoly. But those legislators, in this Democratic state, advanced that bill out of turn and passed it, without a hearing, without notice, in secret. And the alum men did not learn till August 14, that after August 17 they could not continue in business, and then they heard of the law by accident.

This outrage aroused public opinion, and the alum men prepared a repeal bill for the next session, two years later. Meanwhile, however, Kelly and the National Health Society extended their organization. The Health Society of Missouri was formed and the founder thereof was that "friend of the people," the Hon. William J. Stone, ex-governor of Missouri, and then a candidate for United States senator. Now, Stone is no boodler. He and Colonel Phelps, after a long political friendship, quarreled once, and Stone called Phelps a lobbyist. "Oh," said Phelps, "'we both suck eggs, Stone and I, but Stone, he hides the shells." But I do not believe that Stone handles bribes. He is that other type, the orator of the people whose stock in trade is his influence; "an embezzler of power" Folk called him once. This anti-trust orator was hired by the trust to bring action under the trust's "or alum" law against his fellow citizens and thus install the foreign trust in the field of a general local industry. "Ah, but he acted as a lawyer." Do you know who said that? None other than William J. Bryan, arch-Democrat, arch-friend of the people, arch-foe of the trust, and that does excuse this political treason—in law and in business. I asked one of Folk's confessed boodlers, once, whether, if he had it all to do over again, he would boodle again. "Yes," he said thoughtfully, "but I would study law." "Why?" I asked. "So as I could take fees instead of bribes," he said, without humor. In other words, he saw, as Bryan saw, and Stone and the commercial world see, that what is boodling in politics is business in the practice of the law. And the practice of law is business.

When the alum men's repeal bill was introduced in the session of 1901, Kelly's plan to beat it was laid. Lieutenant-Governor Lee, who has told the story, referred the measure to a picked committee which was to have a hearing. The Hon. William J. Stone was to appear on the trust side, but not for the trust. There was no hearing, but Stone's speech, full of the Royal expert's chemical facts, in the Royal's phraseology, was laid on the desks of the members, and this is the way it begins:

"I appear before you on the request of the Health Society of Missouri. This association is composed of a number of people—good people, both men and women— living in different parts of the state, with headquarters in St. Louis." There was no such society. The "number" was three. They were not "good people," not "both men and women"; they were Stone, his son, and one other man. And the headquarters in St. Louis was in the safe of Stone's law office.

And this is a United States senator! The Democrats of Missouri have sent him to Washington to do battle there for the "good people, both men and women," against the Republican representatives of the Octopus. Well, we also are bound for Washington and we'll be interested chiefly in the Republican senatorial traitors, but we shall meet Stone there, too, and an introduction to a Democrat or two may help us. Let us turn now to an honest boodler, the Hon. John A. Lee, and hear how the "little alum fellows' " repeal bill was killed in 1901, and how again, in 1903, in the session which elected Stone United States senator, it was beaten.

"When I was elected Lieutenant-governor in 1900," Lee says, "I was entirely unfamiliar with the ways of legislation. The Royal Baking Powder Company had been doing extensive advertising in the paper with which I was connected. I have known Daniel J. Kelly for some years and he has been ostensibly my friend. In the beginning of the session of 1901, I made no secret of the fact that it was my desire to defeat the repeal of the (anti-) alum law.

"One day Senator Farris came to me and said that it ought to be worth a good deal to the Royal Baking Powder Company to keep the anti-alum law on the statute books; and that the boys on the committee did not think that they ought to prevent its repeal without some compensation. I asked him what the boys wanted. He said they wanted $1,000 apiece for six of the committee, which was all of the committee except Senator Dowdall, and $1,000 for the senator who introduced the bill. Unfortunately for me, Kelly called me up over the long-distance telephone from New York that same day, and I communicated to him the proposition made to me by Farris. He said he would see his principal and wire me the next day whether or not the proposition would be accepted. I received a telegram the next day from Kelly stating that the proposition was agreeable. This telegram I gave to Farris in Senator Morton's room, who was ill at the time. The agreement was that the bill, in return for the money to be paid each senator, would be killed in committee—that is, never reported from the committee. The committee did keep the bill, and though there were various protests all over the state demanding a report from the committee, none was made.

"I have since learned that the chairman of the committee, in order to escape the pressure being brought upon the committee, left Jefferson City with the bill in his pocket, not returning until the closing day of the session, and that the report of the committee on the bill was filed by the chairman after the session adjourned, and the journal falsified, so as to have it appear that the report over to Farris, and this report was made a report of the committee, I believe, without any change.

"On February 28, 1901, I received a check from Kelly for $8,500, being the $7,000 for the seven senators mentioned and $1,500 for myself. On March 19, 1901, the day after the adjournment of the legislature, I met Farris by appointment at the Laclede Hotel and settled with him and his associates in accordance with his proposition. I went to the bank and drew $7,000, leaving $1,500 for my share, went to Farris's room, and there handed the money to Senator Farris. He divided the $7,000 into seven different packages or envelopes. While I was in the room Senator Mathews and Senator Smith came in, and to each of these Senator Farris gave one of the packages. The $1,500 was to go to me, and was used by me in a trade paper.

"Just prior to the last session (1903) Kelly sent for me to come to the Planters' Hotel. I went to his room, found Senator Farris there, and Kelly told me in the presence of Farris that he had $15,000 for the senators to defeat the repeal of the alum law of this session, and that $1,000 was for me. I told him I could not take it. He communicated with me at various other times, that he had $1,000 for me in return for what I should do for him, etc., but I was determined to take no more money in that way, and refused. Finally, it seems he sent for my brother and gave him a check for $1,000, telling him to give it to me, tendering it as payment to me for my official influence."

Poor Lee! The miserable bribe-taker is disgraced and abandoned. He might have been governor. The alum people were for him in the last session; he had promised them a fair committee, and he hoped not to have to vote himself. But Senator Farris was against him, and Farris arranged it so that, when the measure came up, there was a tie in the Senate. At the close of the roll, when the clerk turned to the chair for the deciding vote, Farris rose in his place. The chamber was still; everybody was aware that a weak boodler "wanted to reform," and that the "game was to show him up." Lee hesitated.

"Mr. President," said Farris, pointing his finger at Lee, "we are waiting for you."

"Nay," Lee voted, in a whisper, and the trust was left in control for two years more.

Even then Lee's hopes were not dead, nor his chances. But he "peached" and that ended Lee. He is a traitor—to the System.

But what of the captain of industry? What of the Royal Baking Powder Company, what of the Gould railroads, what of the breweries? What of Ellis Wainwright and George J. Kobusch and John Scullen? What of all the rest of the big business men? They are the sources of our political corruption. What of the System back of the corrupt rings? That is the sustenance of our political degradation. Ellis Wainwright, a fugitive from justice, dines in Paris with the American ambassador, who is negotiating a treaty for the extradition of bribers. A group of the ablest criminal lawyers in New York, at a hearing before Governor Odell at Albany, could not speak of John A. Lee without twisting their faces into ludicrous scorn; but they were defending William Ziegler from extradition to Missouri. And John Scullen!—I cited once, as an example of the shamelessness of St. Louis, the fact that Turner, the state's witness in the boodle cases, was still president of his trust company. When I returned to the city, some honest business men told me triumphantly that Turner had had to resign.

"Is John Scullen still a director of the World's Fair?" I asked. He was, they said. "Then why has Turner been punished?" I inquired. "Was it because he boodled, or because he was a traitor to the System and peached?"

"Because he peached, I guess," was the answer, and there lies the bitter truth. There is no public opinion to punish the business boodler, and that is why Joseph W. Folk had to go into politics and run for governor out in the state with "boodle" for the sole issue. He is laying down as a political platform the doctrine of the new patriotism: that corruption is treason; that the man who, elected to maintain the institutions of a government by the people, sells them out, is a traitor; whether he be a constable, a legislator, a judge, or a boss, his act is not alone bribery, but treason. Folk's appeal is to the politician, the people, and the business man, all three, and there is hope in all three. The politician is not without patriotic sentiment: Ed Butler does not mean harm to his country; he is only trying to make money at his business. And as for the business man—

One night, at a banquet of politicians, I was seated beside a man who had grown rich by unswerving loyalty to a corrupt ring—"the party organization," he would have called it—which had done more permanent harm to his country than a European army could do in two wars. He was not a politician, but a business man; not a boodler, but the backer of boodlers, and his conversation was a defense of "poor human nature," till the orchestra struck up a patriotic air. That moved him deeply.

"Isn't it beautiful!" he exclaimed; and when the boodlers joined in the chorus, he murmured, "Beautiful, beautiful," then leaned over and with tears in his eyes he said:

"Ah, but the tune for me, the song I love, is 'My Country, 'tis of Thee.' "

I believe this man thinks he is patriotic. I believe H. O. Havemeyer thinks his success is success, not one kind of success, but success, not alone his, but public "prosperity." And William Ziegler, who is spending millions to plant the American flag first at the North Pole, I am sure regards himself as a peculiarly patriotic American—and he is. They all are, according to their light, honorable men and patriotic citizens. They simply do not know what patriotism is. They know what treason is in war; it is going over to the enemy, like Benedict Arnold, and fighting in the open against your country. In peace and in secret to seize, not forts but cities and states, and destroy, not buildings and men, but the fundamental institutions of your country and the saving character of American manhood—that is not treason, that is politics, and politics is business, and business, you know, is business.

"Do you really call it wrong to buy a switch?" asked a St. Louis business man. "Even if it is necessary to your business?"

"Say," said a politician, "if a rich mogul comes along and shakes his swag in your face and asks for a switch that he has a right to get, because he needs it in his business, wouldn't you grab off a piece? On the level, now, wouldn't you?"

They answer each other, these two, and each can judge the other, but neither can see himself as he is or the enormity of his crime. And "that man Folk," rising out of the wrecked machinery of justice in Missouri, may lead his people to see that the corruption of their government is not merely corruption, but a revolutionary process making for a new form of government; and the people of Missouri, rising out of the wrecked machinery of the government of Missouri, may teach their politicians a lesson in liberty and honor. But that is not enough. That will reach neither the source nor the head of the evil. Some power greater than Folk, greater than that of the people of Missouri, must rise to bring home to the captain of industry the truth: That business, important as it is, is not sacred; that not everything that pays is right; that, if bribery is treason, if the corrupt politician is a traitor, then the corrupting business man is an enemy of the republic. No matter how many bonds he may float in war, or how much he may give for charity and education, if he corrupts the sources of law and of justice, his business is not success, but—treason, and his own and a people's failure.

McClure's Magazine
August, 1904

Enemies of the Republic

Illinois: A Triumph of Public Opinion – After an Eight Year's Political War, The Republican Party is Brought to Represent the People – A Missouri Parallel

ILLINOIS is a Republican state. Missouri, which we studied last, is Democratic. "Graft" knows no politics, but the "good citizen" does. To the grafter a party is but a tool of his trade, and the party to which a majority of the citizens "belong" is his party. He does not belong to it; it belongs to him. The result is that neither of our great parties truly represents us; both stand today for graft. They differ upon other, unessential things; they are alike in this, that whichever is in power is the grafter's party. Now, wherever we have gone, we have found that the biggest grafter is Big Business, and Big Business kept changing its party to be of the majority. After Missouri I visited three Republican states—Ohio, New York, and Illinois. The railroad that took me into Illinois turned Republican at the state line. The Royal Baking Powder Company, which had dealt with the Democrats in Missouri, appeared in New York with the Republicans. So with the American Book Company—in Missouri a Democrat, at home in Ohio it is a Republican. And so it goes in national politics. Wall Street, and all that "Wall Street" connotes, was Republican till President Roosevelt, refusing to acknowledge the privilege of capital, enforced the law against a combination of railroads. Then Wall Street began plotting with the Republican leaders for the nomination of a "safe man" for president, and, when that "safe man" died, looked to the Democrats—looked with its great campaign contribution for a bribe—and corrupt Democratic leaders, itching for the great financial graft, began its search for a "safe man."

How Parties Deliver Good Citizens

If the good citizen would do as the corrupt politician and the corrupting business man do, shift freely from one party to the other as the change served his interest, then both parties would represent good citizenship. They would differ—more than they do now—on broad questions of public policy, but they would both stand, as they do not now, for the public interest. But the good citizen is "loyal to party." Half the loyalty that is betrayed by parties would, if devoted to the state and the nation, save the country and the parties, too! Such independence, however, would mean non-partisanship in state and national politics, and the good citizen is only just learning, with many a qualm of conscience, to vote independently in municipal elections. In state and national politics he votes too constantly, not for his state and the United States, but for "his party." Hence his party can deliver his vote. Hence his party does deliver his vote in Ohio, New York, and Illinois, as in Missouri—to all comers with "pulls" and bribes.

What Corruption Really Is

This is serious, since we realized, in Missouri, that "bribery and corruption" are not accidental and occasional, but general and deliberate. I quoted the declaration made in open court by Judge Priest, one of the leaders of the Missouri bar, that bribery, at the most, is a "conventional crime." And he was right. Bribery out there was "a custom of the country," and political corruption was a system. And this system, laid wide open by Joseph W. Folk, proved to be, not an evil of government, but the government itself. Corruption had worked a revolution there. The representative democracy described in the state constitution of Missouri was a thing of paper. Drawn by dead men, it was dead. In its stead stood a reorganization of society, a commercial oligarchy, a government of special, not of common, interests; and this, the actual, government of this great state, was not a creation of paper and ink; you could not study it in the state library. We traced its superstructure in the crimes, the indictments, and the confessions of living men, and we saw that its foundation was laid, true and nice, upon the exact adjustment of the sordid ambitions of the political leaders of Missouri to the financial lusts of her captains of industry.

Political corruption, then, is a force by which a representative democracy is transformed into an oligarchy representative of special interests, and the medium of the revolution is the party.

So we must recognize parties and take up next a Republican state—Illinois. Illinois is not so demonstrably corrupt as Missouri. Other Republican states are worse, but these two offer just now a remarkable parallel, superficially in this, that at the same time Joseph W. Folk, the Democratic circuit attorney who had "done his duty" in St. Louis, was running for the Democratic nomination for governor of Democratic Missouri, Charles S. Deneen, the Republican state's attorney (the same office), who had "done his duty" in Chicago, was running for the Republican nomination for governor of Republican Illinois. There are many unessential differences, and we shall note them as we go along, but fundamentally the parallel is still more striking and significant in this, that while the Democrats of Missouri were being asked to take back from Democratic boodlers the control of their party, the Republicans of Illinois were being asked to take back from Republican boodlers the control of their party. Boodle was the issue in both campaigns; boodle is the underlying issue in most American political campaigns, but here it was a party issue. Politicians, anxious to preserve their parties, have always pleaded for "reform within the party." Well, here we have it. Here we have the fighting done within the party, and that is right. For parties do rule us, and if American citizens will "stick to party," then it is important for all of us to know what each party decides within itself to represent: all of us or a few of us, the common interests which ask for nothing but law, order, and fair play, and pay for these in taxes that sustain the state; or those special interests which seek special favors and pay for them in bribes which corrupt the state.

Municipal Reform Impossible By Itself

Folk began the movement which his candidacy is bringing to a logical conclusion. Deneen did not. This does not matter. We are interested not in the men, but in the issue for which they stand, and the issue arose in both states in the same way—in a fight for municipal reform and the failure to get it. Fortunate failure! "Municipal reform" is a mean ideal. We have talked about it for years now, till it has come to be the highest aim of American citizenship. But think of it for a moment: It is not the cities alone that are corrupt, but the states also and the United States, and we all know that this is so. Yet we of the cities say, "Give us good government in the cities where we live, and the states and the United States may go to the deuce." It is a mistake. It is more than a mistake. Municipal reform, all by itself, is impossible. City government and state government are of one sovereignty, and, as for corruption, the city and the state are in one system, and the city man and the "up-state" man have to work together to get what each needs.

The big grafter knows this; there is nothing narrow and "provincial" about him, and Folk and the Chicago reformers got over their municipal narrowness by following the big grafter. They started right. They did not begin their reform by passing and enforcing laws to make other people good. They saw early that the "best citizens" were the worst grafters, and they went after them and the municipal legislators who were selling out to them. Folk's method was that of the criminal prosecutor, and he put the municipal bribe-givers and bribe-takers on trial, and when they appealed to the state courts, the pursuit into the state taught the circuit attorney of St. Louis that boodling was not a crime of city individuals, but the established method of conducting public business in both city and state. Boodle was a question of government, and Mr. Folk, in order to finish his job, had to go into politics, and he went into politics. Declaring boodle to be the issue in both city and state, he appealed to the people.

The Corrupt System of Chicago

The Chicago reformers went into politics at the first plunge. The system that confronted them was like that of St. Louis; it was the typical form of municipal government in all unreformed American cities. The citizens were divided between two parties. These parties were organized by two groups of "leaders": Robert E. Burke, John Powers, Mayor John P. Hopkins, and Roger C. Sullivan, "Democrats"; and William Lorimer, "Doc" T. N. Jamieson, James Pease, et al., "Republicans." (Others there were, but those named are active today.) They had a rough working agreement by which the Democrats took the city, the Republicans Cook County, and these governments they ran "for the good of the party." That was their highest spoken sentiment—not the good of the community, but of the party, and the good of the party came to mean the good of the leaders and their friends. They and their friends were in politics for "what there was in it for them." Thus the government of Chicago and Cook County was not a government in the interest of the people.

The followers of the two groups of leaders, operating like bandits, held up citizens and robbed them, just as train robbers and brigands do. Everybody had to pay for everything, lawful and unlawful; taxpayers had to help the tax-collector defraud the city, and shared with him the "reduction"; merchants paid to violate ordinances; contractors to be freed from inspections; health board supervision was largely blackmail; and the police operated a system such as that which we found exposed in Minneapolis. The police of Chicago did not protect life and property; they protected the criminals; they licensed burglars and hold-up men by districts, guarded them while at work, and shared in their booty.

How Corruption Produces an Oligarchy

Now this is preposterous, but this is not the worst. This is crime, and if, when they had committed their crimes, the criminals had run away, all might have been well. But these were not private robbers, they were public plunderers; they not only robbed the citizens, they plundered the city. And they not only plundered the city and county once or twice, they operated methodically and systematically. And they not only stayed by the loot, they stayed as judges, legislators, and executives. They were the government, and they sold the law, they rotted the sources of the law, they gave away public property, and they carried off the self-respect of the citizens of Chicago. For hold-up men and vulgar criminals were not the only "friends" of the leaders. Their circle included some of the leading citizens of the city. All men who were against the law were with the party rings; all men whose interests ran counter to the public interests were satisfied customers of this traffic in a people. Thus, though boodle was all that the politicians were after, their business was the sale of privileges; and the effect of the establishment of that business as the actual government was to transform the representative democracy of Chicago into an oligarchy—representative of privileged classes.

Our Privileged Classes

Nor is this all. The classes favored were: first, those who—like pickpockets, hold-up men, gamblers, and keepers of saloons and bawdy houses—wanted to break the law; second, those who—like tax-dodgers, railroads, and established big businesses—wanted to evade the law; and third, those who—like traction, gas, and other public utility companies—wanted to abuse general and procure and misuse special laws. In other words, boodle and graft, the "evils" happy pessimists speak of so lightly, had turned the city government of Chicago into an oligarchy of the worst citizens, of the enemies of the city.

Two Kinds of Municipal Reform

The Chicago reformers attacked the third form of corruption, that of active boodling for franchises and other special ordinances. As I have pointed out in "The Shame of the

Cities," there are two main roads to reform. One goes down among the vulgar criminal classes to the correction of obvious police scandals, and leads to what we call "good government." This is easily achieved. Minneapolis got it in a summer. New York has fought longer for it, but has it at last—from Tammany Hall! The other road takes the reformer higher up among his own friends through high finance to higher politics, and leads, when successful, to an awakened public opinion against corrupt misrepresentation in government—to what I call self-government. Chicago's Municipal Voters' League had every incentive to fight for "good government." The city had police graft and administrative abuses as bad as any Minneapolis or New York ever had. But John H. Hamline, William Kent, and other young men who were serving as aldermen, and the best of the newspapers, advised the League to strike at the council, and George E. Cole and his associates struck at the council. And when they struck there they struck the trail we traveled with Folk from St. Louis, the trail that runs between the two great parallels, business and politics, out of the city, up through the state to the United States.

Council Reform and the Political Rings

The council was the heart of the corrupt system of Chicago. The aldermen, supposedly elected to represent the city, but really chosen by the leaders of the two parties, were selling out the city. Peter Dunne ("Mr. Dooley"), a reporter in those days, described many of the members as criminals marked by nature as such. Two-thirds of them were organized into a bipartisan "combine," which operated under the direction of a "good business man," Martin B. Madden, president of the Western Stone Company. "I rounded up the boys," said Johnnie Powers (Democrat), "and Madden (Republican) told 'em what for." There we have the linking of the two rings, political and financial. Back of the Democrats in the "combine" were the party bosses—"Bobbie" Burke, Mayor Hopkins, and Roger Sullivan, and back of the Republicans were the Republican bosses—Billy Lorimer, "Doc" Jamieson, Pease, and others. Lorimer,

Jamieson and Company did not direct or share in the bribery of Republican aldermen. The city council was not a Republican graft; the Republicans, as I explained, had the county. But just as the Republican sheriff, in return for noninterference by the Democratic police in his horse-racing graft, let the police alone in vice graft, so for general immunity from all hindrances in their county contracts, the Republican leaders delivered over to the Democrats the Republican aldermen to vote with the "combine" that sold out municipal legislation. This was the bipartisan political system back of the corrupt council.

In front of the council were two financial rings. One of these was intact when I began my study of Illinois; this is the ring which centers in the Chicago National Bank— John R. Walsh, president. Walsh is a Democrat. He is the owner of the Democratic party organ, *The Chronicle*, and the power behind the throne of the Democratic bosses. The power behind the throne of the Republican bosses is John M. Smyth, the head of one of Chicago's "big stores." Smyth (Republican) is a director of the bank of Walsh (Democrat), and its former cashier, now vice-president, is Fred M. Blount, an active Republican politician.

The great graft of the Chicago Republicans is public contracts, and they control the sources of contracts—state and county boards and, through judges like Hanecy, and the governor, park boards. Lorimer was a street-car driver, but in politics he became a contractor and a friend of Walsh. Walsh is treasurer of the South Park Board; William Best, a director of the Chicago National Bank, is a member of the board, and so is Lyman A. Walton, vice-president of (Walsh's) Equitable Trust Company. Blount has been treasurer of the West Park Board and of the Sanitary Board. The latter is the board which has spent millions to reverse the Chicago River, and make it, the city's sewer, run out of, instead of into, the Lake. This developed a water power which the board once proposed to sell to a private corporation. Thomas M. Smyth, a relative of John M. Smyth, is an ex-president of the board. Contracts from all these boards have gone sometimes to a Democratic firm like Lyden & Drews (Lyden is a nephew of ex-Mayor Hopkins), more often to a

Lorimer firm. Walsh's institutions bond public officials and public officials deposit funds in his institutions. So do many of the politicians and sporting people. Other banks share in all this "legitimate graft," of course; the Chicago National group does not get it all. Here, briefly outlined, is one great business ring which profits by, is satisfied with, and gives financial aid and moral support to the debased political system of the city, county, and state.

The other ring, now broken, was that of which the world-famous promoter, Charles T. Yerkes, was the center. He went to Chicago as a representative of Widener & Elkins, the street railway "financiers" of Philadelphia. He bought *The Inter Ocean*, the newspaper organ of the "stalwart" Republicans, and became a financial leader. He banked at the Illinois Trust and Savings Bank, John J. Mitchell, president. Now Mitchell is to Chicago what J. P. Morgan is to New York. But when Yerkes, recognized and beaten by Chicago, organized his street railway properties to leave them, the financial scheme involved a capitalization which could only be floated upon the theory that a new franchise was obtainable, and upon terms which it is incredible would be granted by an honest city council; yet Mitchell in Chicago and Morgan in New York helped float this plan for the Union Traction Company. Such financial cooperation is moral support, and Yerkes had that from Mitchell and from other banks; he had it from the financial world generally. And when you consider the ramifications of influence from such banks in both rings, their directors, stockholders, customers, and friends, and from associated institutions, companies, and businesses, you can begin to understand what upheld the Hopkins-Sullivan Democrats, the Lorimer-Jamieson Republicans, the corrupt city council, and the whole rotten system of Chicago graft. What I have given is but a superficial sketch of the two main groups of those respectable powers which the Chicago reformers attacked when they attacked the Chicago City Council.

In 1895, when the Municipal Voters' League began its work, these financial powers had big plans before them. We shall follow two of them. The People's Gas and Coke Company wanted to combine all the Chicago gas companies and make a monopoly. The Hopkins-Sullivan Democrats, knowing this, had put through the council, when Hopkins was mayor, a franchise for the Ogden Gas Company. The organizers boast that they paid no bribes, but why should they? In the deal were Martin B. Madden, Johnnie Powers, Thomas Gahan, Roger Sullivan, and others. Chicago believes Mayor Hopkins had a two-elevenths interest, but I was most urgently persuaded to think that he had not. Say he wasn't in the deal. His crowd was, and among them were the politicians who sold franchises to business men; why shouldn't they give one to themselves? The scheme had all the marks of what, in Pennsylvania, would be called a "mace"—a company organized to sell out at blackmail prices to a "trust"; and, as a matter of fact, some fellows in the deal did come pretty near blackmail in their efforts to make the People's Company buy them out. Moreover, the two companies are working amicably together now under a financial settlement that made fortunes for the political promoters. But I must not get ahead of my story. In 1895 the gas deal had been passed through the "Democratic" Chicago council and was ready for the Republican state legislature.

The other big plan was Yerkes's own. Many Chicago traction franchises were expiring, and the companies wanted to have them extended. The corrupt municipal system being in good order, the companies could have had from the city council anything bribery could buy, but the council was unable under the law to grant an extension of franchises for more than twenty years, and that was not enough for Yerkes. Some of his bonds ran longer than that, and besides, he had learned his financial politics in Pennsylvania, where they give franchises for 999 years and "in perpetuity." Yerkes wanted a franchise for at least 50 years.

Yerkes Goes to the state System

And he tried to get it. Where? From the Illinois state legislature. Yerkes was a Big Business man, and, like the gas men, he understood the whole machinery of government as it is. He did not try first for home rule in Chicago; his plans took him out into the state. He was not dependent upon the boodlers of Chicago. Yerkes knew that corruption was a state as well as a municipal system in Pennsylvania, and when, in 1895, he went to Springfield, the capital of Illinois, he went confident that he would find the system there. And it was there.

The Old state System

It had been there for at least twenty years and closely resembled that of Missouri. The railroads and other great corporations of the state had built it up, and it was theirs. They hadn't much use for it in Yerkes's day; they had long before got about all they required. They were vulnerable to taxation, but they controlled the state Board of Equalization (of taxes). About the only other use they had for the system was to prevent adverse legislation, and since, as the railroad men say, Illinois is "fair" and harbors no anti-railroad sentiment, they were, and they are, in very little danger. Nevertheless, with a few notable exceptions, the roads have always kept in touch with politics all along their lines, and maintained the system which still is the actual government of Illinois. The head of it is, not the railroad lobby, as in Missouri, but the bipartisan group of senators, called the "Senate combine," which is an old institution now reduced to refined blackmail and the orderly protection, for lump fees, of special interests. The House, more unwieldy and changeable, has to be moved by individual bribes of various amounts, and there is often scandal and quarreling over the division of the spoils; but the "regular business" in the House is done by committees which the Speaker appoints. To complete the legislative system, the governor should be either a figurehead or the boss.

There are railroad officials and corporation managers in Illinois of sufficient moral development to denounce corruption and oppose it, and they think well of themselves, because they never boodle. But the corrupt system which their roads established remains standing ready for the service of all who seek to plunder the people. And when Yerkes arrived, it was at his service. The system put through his 50 years' act for him. There was much talk of money paid; when, after the session, Speaker Meyer died, a large sum in new thousand-dollar bills was found in his safe deposit box. But Governor Altgeld, a Democrat, and neither a figurehead nor the boss of the system, vetoed the bill. The old system was not in good working order.

Yerkes, a great man in his class, set about making it go. In a quiet, "business-like" way, he "favored" John R. Tanner for governor on the Republican ticket for the election of 1896. Tanner was chairman of the Republican Central Committee. As we noted in Missouri, the chairman of a state committee is a powerful factor in a corrupt state system. Tanner came as near being a state boss as any man in Illinois politics, and he was "safe." He was nominated, and in that presidential year "good old Republican" Illinois elected him with a "solid Republican" legislature. Thus was the Republican state system repaired.

All clear before him, Yerkes found trouble brewing in his rear. The Democratic city system was getting out of order. The Chicago reformers were making progress. They were cutting down the corrupt majority of the council and organizing the public opinion which the great Chicago newspapers had developed against franchise stealing. Better men were chosen aldermen, and the League and the newspapers watched them and made the public watch and understand. By the spring of 1897 traction and Yerkes had become an issue in the city, and Carter H. Harrison was elected mayor on it. Yerkes was not afraid of Harrison. "Bobbie" Burke, the Democratic boss, had nominated the young man, and, though Harrison talked inimically, Burke would probably control him; and, anyhow, Yerkes used to say, "every man has his price."

Yerkes Relies Upon the state System

To make sure of his plans, however, Yerkes determined to make the perfected state system do the whole job for him. Instead of having it grant the city council power to extend traction franchises, he would have the state legislature pass bills granting the extension outright. And a set of measures, called the Humphrey Bills, which gave the companies fifty years more of life, were introduced in the Senate. This was an outrage, but it rendered a great service to Chicago. The Humphrey Bills began for the city one of the greatest lessons a city can learn—that the state is a part of the municipal government and that municipal reform must include state reform. The mayoralty campaign was going on when these bills appeared, and the candidates, their orators, and the newspapers lashed themselves and the voters into a white heat over them. These bills violated the principle of "Home Rule," and mass-meetings denounced them in burning resolutions which spoke of "financial anarchists," "bribe-givers and bribetakers," and ordered posted on billboards as political traitors all Cook County senators who voted for the Humphrey Bills. The city recognized the real enemies of the city. John Maynard Harlan, a candidate for mayor, and the city's most effective orator, called a roll of directors and stockholders of the Chicago City Railway Company; these were the most self-respecting men in Chicago—Erskine M. Phelps, George H. Wheeler, Samuel W. Allerton, Marshall Field—but their company was interested with Yerkes; their counsel was with him at Springfield; and the town believed that their company's money was being paid out with his in bribes. This is the way Mr. Harlan called the roll:

"And now we have got to talk plain language. We have got to hold the right people responsible. We have got to name the directors of these companies; call them up. Erskine M. Phelps, I put you on the stand; take your seat; take your oath before the people of Chicago; place your hand upon the Bible of the people; take your oath, and let me question you, a director of the city railway. Erskine M. Phelps, do you know that your general counsel, do you know that the president of your company is down at Springfield—or if not there in person, by his attorney and representative—for the purpose of taking part in a grand larceny of the people of Chicago? There for the purpose of burglarizing the City of Chicago? If you don't know that we tell it to you now. Your agent, your president, your general counsel, formerly an honored member of the bar, that has done great service to this community, your general counsel is there engaged in this vile conspiracy. Now you know it, you know it well, Erskine M. Phelps, and you—should stop it.

"Marshall Field, merchant prince, the founder of a great museum, a museum that shall be the home of art, literature, and science; Marshall Field, whose voice is heard, when he chooses to make it heard, in the councils of the nation; Marshall Field, to whom there has been no such word as failure in all his private undertakings; Marshall Field, stockholder, influential citizen; Marshall Field, bring your influence to bear as a stockholder and stop this robbery."

The People of the state Aroused

Thus Mr. Harlan went through the list. It hurt, and it helped, too, for it aroused public opinion all over the state, and state opinion was needed, for when the reformers and Mayor Harrison, elected, went down to Springfield to protest, they found the state system at work for Yerkes, and it was at work for the gas companies also. It was one of the worst sessions in the history of the state. Everybody—captains of industry and bosses, bootblacks, hack-drivers, and chambermaids—talked graft; all men seemed to have money, and the bars and poker games were awash with it. It was a system in joyous operation, and anybody—the reformers, Chicago, the whole state—could see just what it was and whose it was and who were directing it.

The State System at Work

Yerkes sat in a chair at the head of the stairs in the rotunda of the capitol; he represented the American business man. In the executive chamber was Governor Tanner; he represented the state machine. William Lorimer occupied a chair in the Senate chamber; he represented the Republican party organization of Cook County. In the lobby moved "Doc" Jamieson (Republican) and Roger Sullivan (Democrat). The Democrats of Cook County turn over to the Republicans the legislators they elect just as the Republicans of Chicago deliver Republican aldermen to the Democrats. But Roger Sullivan and his followers represented the Hopkins-Sullivan-Gahan Democrats at Springfield, and the two groups of "leaders" labored together. One day when Mayor Harrison, there to speak for his city, came up the stairs, Yerkes laughed at him, and well he might; for with both party leaders, the governor, and the state delivering over the city to him, what could the mayor of the city do? It was absurd. The mayor protested and the citizens met in mass, but their state government did not represent them; it represented "Business"; special, not common, interests. And the gas and the traction bills were advanced.

The Gas Deal Through the System

There was a hitch over the gas bills. They went to committee with the understanding that everything was "arranged," and gas stock rose. The bills did not come out and the stock dropped. Then "all was settled" and the stock revived. Again the bill hung, and all was unsettled, especially the stock. This happened time and time again, till the impression was spread abroad that the People's and the Ogden were fighting. Then the bills came out and were passed. It developed afterward that while petty legislators may have received cash bribes for gas legislation, the "Senate combine" and the bosses were taking their pay out of the stock market, and the succession of favorable reports and apparent failures were only for stock-jobbing purposes. After the session Lorimer, Jamieson, and others had plenty of money, and people were asking them "where they got it." The answer in the public mind was that they "got it" for putting the gas bills through with the traction deal, and they were silent for two years. Then they suddenly explained. Their belated explanation differed somewhat from that just given, but it admits that they received gas stock and is full of incidental interest.

In 1899 these Republican bosses were accused of a wish to make John W. Gates a United States senator. When such politicians choose such a "business man" for such high office, it is a safe working hypothesis to assume that the man himself or the business he represents has been at least a steady contributor to campaign funds. The Chicago newspapers had to account for the sudden rise of this great financial "sport" to such "bad eminence," and they recalled that in the rush of business men to the scandalous legislature of 1897 Gates was there with two bills for his Illinois Steel and Wire Company, and that Lorimer and

Jamieson helped him to pass them. Now Lorimer and Jamieson were for Gates for United States senator. Why? Report had it that Gates had purchased for them, at 82, two thousand shares apiece of gas stock; and that when the gas bills passed Lorimer sold his at 93, while Jamieson held on till he got 103 and cleared $40,000. The bosses liked this story, for the Gates bills were "honest bills." Here is Jamieson's statement as printed in the *Chicago Evening Journal* and never publicly denied:

The Bosses' Explanation

"As far as the stock story goes, it is correct. It is also true that the start of it was the four thousand shares of gas stock which Mr. Gates margined for us. It was in return for our looking out for Bills 90 and 108 (Gates's), which were liable to be overlooked in the rush of the closing day of the legislature. They were perfectly honest bills, there was no opposition to them, and our influence simply went to the extent of having them called up for discussion and passage. There were no views or votes against them, and naturally they passed. Mr. Gates in return gave us the gas stock and we carried it through the big rise. With the money made we have made other deals. We have speculated freely and I may say with some success, and I do not care who knows it. There is nothing about the entire transaction to conceal, and perhaps it will answer the question some of our enemies have asked, 'Where did you get it?' Since it is out, I have no desire to deny or conceal it.

"As for Mr. Gates' candidacy, that is another matter. I do not know what his ambitions are. But I will say this, that he can have anything I can give him or help him to get. He has been a heavy contributor to the Republican campaign funds for many years, and has taken a big interest in state politics. He is a big man in this state, brainy, influential, and a leading manufacturer. He would make a good senator and he can have my support whenever he wants it. I am making no announcement of his candidacy, neither do I deny it. He could have a very large portion of Cook County back of him."

Lorimer, congressman and boss, said: "I have no desire to conceal anything. What Dr. Jamieson has said I indorse, and

I am inclined to think Mr. Gates would get a good chance of winning if he entered the race as a candidate for senator."

Gates did not go to the Senate, so we may pass this sidelight on the way "the System" produces United States senators. Pass also, but note well, the exposure this "explanation" makes of the character of the Cook County leaders of the Republican party of Illinois. The fact of immediate interest is that the gas bills went through the legislature and were signed by the governor, and that Chicago did not care. The city had been torn up again and again for the mains of companies that promised competition to the trust, and always the competitors sold out to the trust. They were at least relieved of that condition, for the purpose of the bills was to create a monopoly.

Illinois to Chicago's Rescue

Chicago concentrated all its attention upon the Humphrey bills, and that attention began to take effect. These bills had come down from the "Senate combine " to the House, and were in a fair way of being. passed there, when the agitation in Chicago and the fight of the Chicago newspapers, which circulate throughout the state, aroused the country people, who began to speak to their representatives in the lower house. There was no direct appeal from Chicago to the country. I have never yet come upon an instance where a state, having been made intelligent concerning any sound, essential demand of a city, has failed to respond, but few cities have learned to confide in the "farmers," as they call them, and Chicagc had not. Chicago's case was presented only indirectly to Illinois, but the state acted. Illinois killed the Humphrey bills in the House.

That did not beat the bosses. Chicago's chief stated objection to the Humphrey bills was that they violated the home-rule principle, so Yerkes substituted another, called the Allen Bill, which did not grant outright the fifty-year extension of franchises, but permitted the Chicago council to do so. From the point of view of the country this was fair, since it left the problem to Chicago, but as Chicago saw it, the move was an appeal from the state system back to the city system, and, with the implication of threatened bribery of the council, the Allen Bill threw the city into a fresh tempest of passion. The swing of public opinion was so swift that even the Allen Bill seemed in danger. The country members had "lost their nerve," and the bosses saw that the measure must be advanced under the gavel. Speaker Curtis was afraid to use force, and he suddenly developed a "gum boil," and was sent off in a special car to Mammoth Cave. The speaker pro tem hammered the bill through to the third reading, then it was passed by both houses and Governor Tanner signed it.

Traction Fight Back in Chicago

The next step for Yerkes now was to get a Chicago council that would pass an ordinance to carry the Allen Law into effect. The outlook was discouraging, for the town was ringing with wrath, but Yerkes and his friends in both parties went quietly to work. The honest newspapers and the League also went to work, however, and loudly, and their appeal was to the people to send up aldermen that Yerkes couldn't buy. How the people responded, I have told in an article on Chicago in "The Shame of the Cities." But there is a part of the story I did not tell, Mayor Harrison's part. The League had tried to get enough honest aldermen to organize the council, but failed. Johnnie Powers beat them and the combine controlled the committees and had a majority for Yerkes's Lyman ordinance, which was to put the Allen Law into effect. But the mayor presides in the Chicago council, and he has a veto which it takes a two-thirds vote to override. Carter H. Harrison was the key to the situation.

Yerkes "Sees" Mayor Harrison

The time was come for Yerkes to "see" Mayor Harrison. The promoter had called often on the young man in the city hall, but always the mayor's secretary or someone else was by. Yerkes asked the mayor to dismiss the witness or go into a separate room, but the mayor never would. Now, with the council organized and ready, Yerkes had to "see" Harrison, and alone, and he saw him alone, as Yerkes thought; but there was a witness, so I know that Yerkes said that he could not understand why the young mayor was against traction. "Many of my friends in the deal are your friends," he said. "Some of your friends are in it. Why are you against it? " And the mayor answered that. Then Yerkes put to the mayor the great question:

"Mr. Mayor, what is it that you want?"

When the mayor answered that, Mr. Yerkes saw the beginning of the end of his Chicago career. He did not give up at once. The fight proceeded in the council, and it was a fight indeed. Reform aldermen were bought over and Harrison Democrats weakened, but the reformers put spies on their men and Harrison put the whip on his. And the System had its troubles, too. Aldermen in the boodle combine were asked by their children if what the other "scholars said at school was true, that their papa was a boodler." Willing boodlers coming home at night found a mass committee from the ward waiting to ask them if they were going to "sell us out to Yerkes." One alderman, finding his house closed against him one night, knocked for admittance, and, when his wife answered, she asked through the closed door if he was "for Chicago or for Yerkes." Some of these men declared they would have to "go back on the party," and many more had to "turn honest," for a mob, organized by Harrison Democrats, stood ready with ropes at the crisis to hang all "traitors." The council did not make the Allen Law effective; it did not grant a fifty-year extension of franchise for "nothing but boodle." Mayor Harrison defeated the treason of his own party.

National Democrats Speak for Yerkes

Chicago is thinking seriously now of throwing aside Mr. Harrison for a mayor who will give the city administrative reform, and anyone who will talk with this remarkable man must feel that a change is necessary. He has made many improvements. He has abolished some intolerable abuses. With all that he has accomplished, however, graft and inefficiency

Illinois: A Triumph of Public Opinion   315

persist, and I could not find in his own mind any hope of such thorough-going administrative reform as that which Chicago now seems bent upon. No, that will not come from Mr. Harrison; he does not, in his heart, care enough about good government to give it. But Harrison does care about self-government; he really has a sense of government for a people. I don't know how he came by it, whether it was born in him or was acquired from his political experience, nor does that matter. Harrison is not merely a Democrat; he is a democrat with a small d. For the democracy he withstood Yerkes and all Yerkes's money. And he withstood also Richard Croker. The Tammany boss called on the ambitious young mayor just before a national Democratic convention. He spoke for himself, William C. Whitney, and other National Democrats, and his subject was the future of the party and Mr. Harrison. As the mayor once put it with a laugh: "Croker took me up on the mountain and showed me the cities of the earth." And while Harrison contemplated the view, Croker said that he had a friend, Mr. Yerkes, and that anything Mayor Harrison could do for that friend would be appreciated by Mr. Croker and by Croker's and Whitney's Wall Street friends, whom Yerkes had loaded up with Chicago traction stock. The Chicago Democratic mayor put aside the temptation of the national Democrats, and he cut loose from some of the same sort of "Democrats" at home. He did not recognize John R. Walsh. He fought Johnnie Powers and his Democratic combine. He finally dropped "Bobbie" Burke, his own Democratic boss. And when leaders of the Hopkins-Sullivan-Gahan wing of the Cook County Democracy came to him to sign an ordinance to permit them to sell out their Ogden Gas Company and complete the deal with the People's Gas and Coke Company, he refused them also. The two companies have finally come to an understanding with John R. Walsh, Roger Sullivan, etc., on the Ogden board; and C. K. G. Billings, chairman of the People's board, on the board of Walsh's bank. But they could not combine legally, and it was Harrison who foiled them. Harrison has lost all these leaders of the "business end" of his own party, and he had beaten them year by year till this spring. William R. Hearst came along with his anti-trust boom for the Presidency and combined with those fellows who have sold out the democracy to trusts. With such help the Hopkins-Sullivan-Burke-Powers democracy rose and defeated the Harrison democracy. Let Chicago put Harrison aside and go on its way, as it must, but the city should acknowledge that this man has served well the City of Chicago and American democracy.

Fighting Back in the state Again

But this is a Republican article. Yerkes, beaten in Chicago, was looking back to the state again. And Chicago, victorious in Chicago, was also looking back to the state. Yerkes asked only time and no legislation. Chicago demanded the repeal of the Allen Law in the session of 1899. Yerkes's hope was in the state system; Chicago's was in the people of Illinois, and this time the appeal was direct; not sympathetic, but emotional and intimate, and the country papers took it up. Chicago asked the state to keep out of the legislature every man who had voted for the Allen Law, and—I'd like to have every city in every state grasp the significance of the result of this cry of Chicago to Illinois—of sixteen retiring senators who voted for the act, but two were reelected; and of the eighty-two representatives who voted for it, but fourteen were reelected.

By this verdict the state system was thrown out of order once more, and it had to be rebuilt. The "senate combine" was reorganized, but it was timid, and Lawrence Y. Sherman, one of the fourteen representatives reelected over their Allen vote, was elected Speaker of the House. But Sherman, a lean, long, fighting countryman, "deceived," he said, "by Lorimer," was swearing angry at the Cook County ring, and when he organized the House he knew what he was about. It was his House, not Yerkes's, not Lorimer's, and it was going to repeal the Allen Law "first off." No Lorimer-Jamieson leader dared approach Sherman, so Yerkes himself sent for him and wanted the Speaker to "gavel" the repeal down.

"Will the Allen Law be repealed?" he asked Sherman.

"I don't know," said Sherman, "but there will be a roll-call."

"If there's a roll-call the bill will be repealed," said the captain of industry.

"Do you think I would stand up there and suspend a roll-call on a measure so important as that? " Sherman asked. Then Yerkes became angry. "You don't dare let the Allen Law be repealed. No man can turn tail on our interests and live politically."

There was the voice of the system, the sentiment of Big Business. Sherman dared, and Sherman has had to fight for his political life; but he lives politically by fighting. And he lives in Illinois, too. Yerkes lived in New York and London. There was a roll-call on the Allen repeal, and it was carried, with only one or two votes against it. The Senate passed it on up to Governor Tanner, and the governor signed it. That ended traction legislation in the interest of the franchise boodlers; and it ended the use of the state government as a system for turning out laws for special interests. But it did not destroy the System itself.

Chicago Takes the Aggressive

Mayor Harrison and the Chicago reformers, strengthened in the city council, took the aggressive now. They could refuse to extend franchises to the street railways, but they would have to let the companies run over the time, since the city had no power to take the property. They did not all want "municipal ownership," but the city had to obtain from the state legislature power to receive back the property in order to carry on negotiations to compel fair terms. They might not want to exercise that power, but they had to have it. They asked the legislature of 1899 for it. The legislators, afraid of the whole subject, would not touch any phase of it, and nothing was done. Negotiations with the companies proceeded, and the disposition of the city council, mayor, and reformers was to be fair, but the traction people would not give up their faith in corrupt force. They would not settle. In 1901 the city returned to the Springfield legislature with a comprehensive bill for a general street railway law, but the state system was being reorganized, and it was strong enough to strangle the city's bill in committee.

Chicago Takes Up Legislative Reform

That brought home to some of the Chicago reformers with full force the truth that the state legislature, being a part of their municipal government, was as much in need of systematic study and improvement as the council. That was as far as they saw. They did not yet realize that the legislative system is but a part of the whole state system, that this system is rooted in the corruption of the lesser cities, the towns, and country districts, and that general state reform is as necessary as municipal reform in Chicago. But Chicago reformers make their observations, not in a study, but on the firing line, and they see only what is right before them. They shoot at what they see, however, and in 1901 they organized a Legislative Voters' League for Cook County, with George E. Cole as president and Hoyt King as secretary. This League applies to the nomination and election of senators and representatives from Chicago the same methods that proved so effective for aldermanic reform, viz.: it keeps records of legislators' votes and conduct, publishes them, and advises upon their nomination and election. Reform in Chicago always organizes, informs and helps direct the public opinion aroused, and its leaders wield that tremendous power with tact, political skill, and common sense, and with effect—as they proved so dramatically at the next session of the legislature, the session of 1903.

Chicago was bound to have its enabling legislation. Yerkes was gone, but his representatives and successors and the Lorimer-Jamieson Republican ring were bound to have no legislation. There was a new governor, Richard Yates, but Lorimer had led a convention stampede to nominate him, and he was "with the party." The legislature was Republican, as usual. Lawrence Y. Sherman and a group of independent Republicans, called the "Fighting Forty," were preparing to represent Chicago, but the Chicago bosses organized the house with John H. Miller for Speaker. There were rumors that the newspapers and the Legislative Voters' League had warned and won over the "Senate combine," but it was the same old bipartisan combine, and the bosses trusted it. The situation seemed to be in Lorimer's hands when the representatives of the Municipal and Legislative Voters' Leagues, of the city council, and of all the candidates that were running for mayor in the pending Chicago campaign, looked it over at Springfield. Mr. Edwin Burritt Smith, who was there as special counsel to the city council's Traction Committee, sums it up thus in his article in the *Atlantic Monthly* for January, 1904: "It was understood that, as a condition of his election, the Speaker was required to promise to cany out Hinman's (the editor of Yerkes's "Republican" Inter Ocean) orders on all street railway measures, and to use the gavel when necessary to defeat objectionable legislation. Mr. Gus Nohe—Lorimer's member from his own legislative district—when asked whether there was to be any traction legislation, replied: 'I don't know. I do whatever the old man (Lorimer) tells me; and he tells me to do about traction as Hinman says.' Hinman himself announced that there would be no traction legislation at that session."

Chicago Bosses Against Chicago

Congressman Lorimer, the boss, did not want to appear at Springfield, because he was running a "good business man" for mayor on the Republican ticket in Chicago, and his candidate was for traction legislation. But one of the city's bills, drawn by Walter L. Fisher, of the Municipal Voters' League, was going through the Senate. This was the Mueller Bill, and the "combine," under the whip of the League, the Chicago newspapers, and public opinion generally, sent the measure down to the House. Lorimer had to go to Springfield, and he took personal charge in the House. It was indeed an emergency. The Mueller Bill was safely buried in the Municipal Committee, but clearly, with the lobby full of Chicago reformers and committees from citizens' associations, to say nothing of his own "business man for mayor"—all demanding legislation—some bill had to pass. Lorimer gave one day the word for action, and both parties in the House held caucuses that evening. The result was bad—"for the organization." Lorimer sent for the legislators one by one, and late at night called a conference in his own room in the Leland Hotel, of certain ring-leaders, the Chicago Aldermanic Committee, Graeme Stuart, his business candidate for mayor; Frank O. Lowden (a candidate this year for governor), Edwin Burritt Smith, and others. Mr. Smith says Lorimer—a congressman, mind you, not a state legislator—opened the discussion by asking, "What do you want?" Lorimer declared that the Mueller Bill was dead, and he offered as a substitute a bill to be called the Lindley Bill. That the official representatives of Chicago rejected; "it bore unmistakable signs," Mr. Smith says, "of tender regard for traction interests." Lorimer accepted some amendments, proposed others himself, and when these failed to satisfy the friends of the city, the boss, a leader of the Republican party in Illinois, said the Lindley Bill was all Chicago would get. "You must accept it with these amendments, pull down all opposition in the House and from the Chicago press, and actively support the bill. It is the Lindley Bill or nothing."

The Defeat of the Republican Bosses

The Chicago press had been telling the city and state all about the situation, and, with the Allen Bill episode in mind, the organization legislators were anxious and weak. Chicago decided to reject the Lindley substitute and to fight its own boss on the floor of the House. With Sherman's "Fighting Forty" and the Democrats who were willing to help they had the votes, and all that they needed was a roll-call. But the Speaker, asked if he would allow one, refused to say. For two days there were skirmishes, and the voting showed that the "organization" was in a precarious condition, but at last the Speaker rose, pale, but with gavel in hand, to force the amendments to the Lindley Bill. Back of him were some women; beside and before him stood a score of strong men ready to defend him. The bill was called up, and Mr. Lindley offered Lorimer's Amendment Number One. The law required a roll-call upon a demand of five members. Ninety-six rose and shouted "Roll-call!" The Speaker would not hear; he put the amendment and, amid confusion and outcries, swung down his gavel and declared the amendment carried.

Amid great excitement Amendment Number Two was offered; members cried "Roll-call! Roll-call!" But again the gavel fell and the second amendment was "carried," and so, with the storm waxing, Numbers Three, Four, Five, and Six were hammered through. But at the sixth the House broke, and there was a rush for the Speaker's chair. If it hadn't been for the women back of him, missiles would have been showered upon him; as it was, the wave of angry members rose up to the chair, and the Speaker fled through a back door.

Balked, the House paused a moment; then Representative Sherman whispered something to a friendly representative, who called the House to order. The House reorganized with Representative Charles A. Allen as temporary Speaker, a roll-call showed a quorum present, and the Lindley Bill was moved for reconsideration. One by one, on roll-call, the amendments, Numbers Six, Five, Four, etc., were rejected in reverse order, the bill was laid on the table, and the Mueller Bill was substituted for it. Then a scathing resolution of censure was passed upon the fugitive Speaker and the House adjourned. He was in conference with Governor Yates, Lorimer, and Hinman, and when he returned to his seat that afternoon he took his censure and excused himself by making charges of attempts to bribe him, which were investigated and found to be unfounded. After the investigation the Mueller traction bill was finally passed and Governor Yates signed it. He wrote a memorandum giving reasons why the bill should not become a law, but he made it a law.

Boodle a Democratic Issue in Missouri

Now for the Missouri-Illinois parallel. When Mr. Folk realized that the political corruption of St. Louis was but a part of the financial-political state system, which has supplanted a representative democracy with an oligarchy of criminals, he started what he called a counter-revolution. He saw, moreover, that his party, controlled by boodlers, was the organization of this treason. The Democratic party represented not democracy, but the enemies of democracy. What did he do? Because he was a Democrat, he appealed first to the Democrats of Missouri, because they were Democrats, to clear out first of all the Democratic boodlers because they were Democrats. That was putting party loyalty to a pretty severe test. What happened? Such a splendid exhibition of genuine patriotism as this country seldom has a chance to display. The Democrats of Missouri rose up and they smashed that rotten old machine all to pieces; they took back the control of their party and they are making it fit for any American citizen to support. And the good citizens of Missouri will be asked to support it, for, incidentally, the Democrats insured the nomination of Mr. Folk for governor. He will make his campaign on the same issue, "boodle," and since the Republican party also boodled, he will ask all men of all parties to let him organize an administration that will represent, not bribery, but all the men of Missouri.

Boodle a Republican Issue in Illinois

The issue was not made so clear, nor so personal, nor so exciting in Illinois, but Illinois seems to be more intelligent politically than Missouri, less partisan, and boodle was the issue there this summer. Chicago realized after its eight years of war that the existing political system misrepresented the people in both city and state government, and that the Republican party, the dominant one, was the party to try first to clean up. In it the worst traitors to the people were the Lorimer-Jamieson group. The Chicago reformers asked the Republicans of Cook County and of Illinois to take away from them the control of the party and restore it to Republicans who would represent the common interest of all the people of the state. The Chicago *Daily News*, the *Tribune* and the *Record-Herald*, the trusted newspapers that express public opinion in Chicago, and (therefore, I think) wield that "power of the press" which so many journals elsewhere are bemoaning the loss of, voiced a demand to have Charles S. Deneen nominated for governor.

Deneen the Folk of Chicago

Deneen is a Cook County Republican leader, a politician, who associated for years with Lorimer and Jamieson. Chicago is not afraid of politicians. All the city's best reform efforts have been directed, not to put reformers in office, but rather to force the politicians to represent the people, and the "newspaper trust" and the voters' leagues are developing a class of politicians, not always sincere, who recognize that public opinion is a constant force in politics. Deneen is an honest man; I never heard his integrity questioned. He has been state's attorney since 1896, and his record is one of orderly, efficient, fearless, and aggressively honest service. He did not go forth, like Folk, seeking out corruption in all places, but he performed the duties that came to him with tireless, masterful energy, and there is a line of cells in one state prison so full of business men whom Deneen convicted that it is called Bankers' Row. Deneen is a remarkable man. But, for the sake of simplification, let us say only that he is a politician who believes that it is good politics to serve the public.

That is all Chicago requires, and that made the issue in the Republican party of Illinois in the summer of 1904; the fight was over the nomination for governor, but the question raised was: What shall the Republican party represent? Deneen said: "The public interest." He wanted to be governor, but he understood that the men who supported him were seeking to beat the Lorimer-Jamieson ring, which believes that the Republican party exists to serve special interests. Lorimer and Jamieson understood this, too. There were other candidates. Governor Yates, a shallow, pompous person, sought a second term, but he thought Yates was the issue. Then there was an eloquent young lawyer, Frank O. Lowden, son-in-law of George M. Pullman, who wants to be something prominent in politics, United States senator or governor. He is a "fine fellow" and he has more personal friends among the reformers and best citizens of Chicago than Deneen, but when he appeared as a candidate for the nomination the old ring backed him, not all his friends. Mr.

Lowden is a "safe man"; he is the type that "fools" most good citizens. Having a "laudable ambition," he seeks an office, not an issue, and he cannot understand why he should not "welcome the support of his party"; and when he achieves office he cannot understand why he should not support his party. The Lowdens are the kind of men political bosses put up when the ring is on the verge of a defeat, and, being "good men," they cloud issues and save the rings. They do not mislead Chicago. The city saw through Lowden to the ring behind him, and the Republicans of Cook County sent to the convention a large majority of delegates instructed for Deneen. Many of the delegates, and some of the ward leaders, were reluctant and hankered for their old boss, but public opinion held them to their instructions.

If Deneen, or, better still, if Chicago had made as careful a canvass of the country as Folk did of Missouri, I believe Illinois would have responded like Missouri. As it was, the Republicans of Illinois did not decide. The country districts followed their leaders and the nomination was left to the convention. There were six or seven candidates. Yates, with his patronage-built state organization; Lowden, with the old bosses, the special interests, and his money; and Deneen, with Cook County, the Chicago newspapers, and the best public opinion—these three led in strength, and a deadlock ensued which, for duration, was unprecedented in the state.

Federal Branch of the System

The efforts to break it developed the apex of the System. I said a while ago that the United States government was a part of the state and municipal systems of Illinois and Chicago. Speaker Cannon, of the national House of Representatives, was chairman of the convention, and United States senators Cullum and Hopkins were present also. These men—the whole "Federal Bunch," as they are called—"worked" for Lowden. Not that they cared especially for him, though one of them remarked that it was well to have "a governor with a barrel." But their influence was for "harmony," the "good of the party," not of the state, nor even of the Republican citizens of the state—but of the old party leaders and "the thing as it was." Well, they did help to break the deadlock. Chicago and Illinois resent federal interference. When this spring the Municipal League made its successful fight to beat "Doc" Jamieson in that boss's own ward, Congressman Lorimer and Senators Cullom and Hopkins persuaded President Roosevelt to appoint Jamieson Naval Officer of the Port. Upon their advice, confirmed, as he said, by such "respectable business men as John M. Smyth," etc., the president gave the discredited boss the office and the moral and political support that went with it. William Kent says that that helped to defeat Jamieson in his ward. So, at the convention, the Chicago newspapers, talking always of the old ring, were able to point out that the national government was back of Lowden and his backers. This crystallized public opinion. The convention took a recess for ten days. When it reconvened, though the deadlock held for two days more, the current of sentiment was toward Deneen; and Yates, to get even with the ring that had used, then dropped him, directed his delegates to vote for Deneen.

What the Republicans Decided to Represent

There was a "deal" between Yates and Deneen. But the terms were honorable, and besides, "political deals" are, like politicians, not bad in themselves. They are bad when they trade the public interest off for special and personal interests, and the deal which carried out the wishes of the best public opinion in Illinois and made Charles S. Deneen the Republican candidate for governor (and Lawrence Y. Sherman the candidate for lieutenant governor), did for the Republican party of Illinois what the Democratic voters of Missouri did for the Democratic party, when they sent up delegates instructed for Folk—restored the control to the people of the party. That deal completed the political ruin of the Lorimer-Jamieson ring, and, I verily believe, begins a movement to carry on out into the state the reform which was begun eight years ago in Chicago—a reform which aims to make the government, municipal and state, represent, not bribers, not corrupt politicians, not corrupting business men, but the common interests of the state—the citizens and friends, not the enemies, of the republic.

McClure's Magazine
October, 1904

Enemies of the Republic

Wisconsin: Representative Government Restored—
The Story of Governor LaFollette

THE story of the state of Wisconsin is the story of Governor LaFollette. He is the head of the state. Not many governors are that. In all the time I spent studying the government of Missouri I never once had to see or name the governor of Missouri, and I doubt if many of my readers know who he was. They need not. He was only the head of the paper government described in the Constitution, and most governors are simply "safe men" set up as figureheads by the System, which is the actual government that is growing up in the United States in place of the "government of the people, by the people, and for the people, which shall not perish from the earth." The System, as we have found it, is a reorganization of the political and financial powers of the state by which, for boodle of one sort or another, the leading politicians of both parties conduct the government in the interest of those leading businesses which seek special privileges and pay for them with bribes and the "moral" support of graft. And a "safe man" is a man who takes his ease, honors, and orders, lets the boss reign, and makes no trouble for the System.

There is trouble in Wisconsin. Bounded on the east by Lake Michigan, on the north by Lake Superior, on the west by the Mississippi River, Wisconsin is a convenient, rich, and beautiful state. New England lumbermen stripped fortunes of forest off it, and, uncovering a fat soil watered by a thousand lakes and streams, settlers poured in from northwestern Europe and made this new Northwest ripen into dairy farms and counties of golden wheat. From the beginning Wisconsin has paid, nor is there now any material depression or financial distress in the state. Yet there is trouble in Wisconsin. What is the matter? I asked a few hundred people out there to explain it, and though some of them smiled and others frowned, all gave substantially one answer: "LaFolletteism." They blame one man.

The Story of "Bob" La Follette

Robert Marion LaFollette was born on a farm in Dane County, Wisconsin, June 14, 1855. His father was a Kentucky-bred French Huguenot; his mother was Scotch-Irish. When the boy was eight months old the father died, leaving the mother and four children, and, at the age of fourteen, "Little Bob," as his followers still call him, became the head of the family. He worked the farm till he was nineteen years old, then sold it and moved the family to Madison, the county seat and capital of the state. If, with this humble start, LaFollette had gone into business, his talents might have made him a captain of industry; and then, no matter how he won it, his success would have made him an inspiration for youth. But he made a mistake. He entered the state university with the class of '79. Even so, he might have got over his college education, but his father's French blood (perhaps) stirred to sentiment and the boy thrilled for glory. He had a bent for oratory. In those days debates ranked in the Western colleges where football does now, and "Bob" LaFollette won, in his senior year, all the oratorical contests, home. state, and interstate. His interstate oration was on Iago, and his round actor's head was turned to the stage, till John McCullough advised him that his short stature was against that career. Also, he says, his debts chained him to the earth. He had to go to work, and he went to work in a law office. In five months he was admitted to the bar, and in February, 1880, he opened an office and began to practice. A year or so later the young lawyer was running for an office.

"They" say in Wisconsin that LaFollette is ambitious; that he cannot be happy in private life; that, an actor bom, he has to be on a stage. I should say that a man who can move men, as LaFollette can, would seek a career where he could enjoy the visible effect of his eloquence. But suppose "they" are right and the man is vain—I don't care. Do you? I have noticed that a public official who steals, or, like Lieutenant-governor Lee, of Missouri, betrays his constituents, may propose to be governor, without being accused of ambition. "They" seem to think a boodler's aspirations are natural. He may have a hundred notorious vices; they do not matter. But a "reformer," a man who wants to serve his people, he must be a white-robed, spotless angel, or "they" will whisper that he is—what? A thief? Oh, no; that is nothing; but that he is ambitious. This is the system at work. It was the System in Missouri that, after spending in vain thousands of dollars to "get something on Folk," passed about the damning rumor that he was ambitious. And so in Wisconsin, "they" will take you into a back room and warn you that LaFollette is ambitious. I asked if he was dishonest. Oh dear, no. Not that. Not a man in the state, not the bitterest foe of his that I saw, questioned LaFollette's personal integrity. So I answered that we wanted men of ambition; that if we could get men to serve us in public life, not for graft, not for money, but for ambition's sake, we should make a great step forward.

Mr. LaFollette has ambition. He confessed as much to me, but he is after a job, not an office; Governor LaFollette's ambition is higher and harder to achieve than any office in the land.

A Politician and His First Office

The first office he sought was that of district attorney of Dane County, and, though his enemies declare that the man is a radical and was from the start a radical, I gathered from the same source that his only idea at this time was to "pose" before juries "and win cases." Mr. LaFollette married in this year (a classmate), and he says he thought of the small but regular salary of the district attorney. However this may be, he won the office and he won his cases, so he earned his salary. District Attorney LaFollette made an excellent record. That is freely admitted, but my attention was called to the manner of his entrance into politics, as proof of another charge that is made against him in Wisconsin. "They" say LaFollette is a politician.

"They" say in Missouri that Folk is a politician. "They" say in Illinois that Deneen is a politician. "They" say in the United States that President Roosevelt is a politician." "They" are right. These men are politicians. But what of it? We have blamed our politicians so long for the corruption of our politics that they themselves seem to have been convinced that a politician is necessarily and inherently bad. He isn't, of course. Only a bad politician is bad, and we have been discovering in our studies of graft that a bad business man is worse. To succeed in reform, a man has to understand politics and play the game, or the bad business man will catch him, and then—what will he be? He will be an "impracticable reformer," and that, we all know, is awful.

Running Around the Ring

"Bob" LaFollette is a politician. Irish, as well as French, he was born a master of the game, and he did indeed prove his genius in that first campaign. Single-handed he beat the System. Not that he realized then that there was such a thing. All the young candidate knew when he began was that E. W. Keyes, the postmaster at Madison, was the Republican state boss, and, of course, absolute master of Dane County, where he lived. LaFollette was a Republican, but he had no claim of machine service to the office he wanted, and he felt that Boss Keyes and Philip L. Spooner, the local leader, would be against him, so he went to work quietly. He made an issue; LaFollette always has an issue. It had been the practice of district attorneys to have assistants at the county's expense, and LaFollette promised, if elected, to do all his own work. With this promise he and his friends canvassed the county, house by house, farm by farm, and, partly because they were busy by day, partly because they had to proceed secretly, much of this politics was done at night. The scandal of such "underhand methods" is an offense to this day to the men who were beaten by them. Mr. "Phil" Spooner (the senator's brother) speaks with contempt of LaFollette's "night riders." He says the LaFollette workers went about on horseback after dark and that he used to hear them gallop up to their leader's house late at night. Of course he knows now that they were coming to report and plot, but he didn't know it then. And Boss Keyes, who is still postmaster at Madison, told me he had no inkling of the conspiracy till the convention turned up with the delegates nearly all instructed for LaFollette for district attorney. Then it was too late to do anything.

Boss Keyes thought this showed another defect in the character of LaFollette. "They" say in Wisconsin that the governor is "selfish, dictatorial, and will not consult." "They" said that about Folk in Missouri, when he refused to appoint assistants dictated by Boss Butler. Wall Street said it about Roosevelt when he refused to counsel with Morgan upon the advisability of bringing the Northern Securities case, but the West liked that in Roosevelt. The West said it about Parker when he sent his gold telegram to the Democratic National Convention, but the East liked that in Parker. There must be something back of this charge, and a boss should be able to explain it. Boss Keyes cleared it up for me. He said that at the time "Bob" was running for district attorney, "a few of us here were—well, we were managing the party and we were usually consulted about—about things generally. But LaFollette, he went ahead on his own hook, and never said a word to—well, to me or any of us." So it's not a matter of dictation, but of who dictates, and what. In the case of LaFollette, his dictatorial selfishness consisted in this, that he "saw" the people of the county and the delegates, not "us," not the System. No wonder he was elected. What is more, he was reelected; he kept his promises, and, the second time he ran, LaFollette was the only Republican elected on the county ticket.

During the two terms of District Attorney LaFollette, important changes were occurring in the Wisconsin state system beyond his ken. Boss Keyes was deposed and Philetus Sawyer became the head of the state. This does not mean that Sawyer was elected governor; we have nothing to do with governors yet. Sawyer was a United States senator. While Keyes was boss, the head of the state was in the post-office at Madison, and it represented, not the people, but the big business interests of the state, principally lumber and the railways, which worked well together and with Keyes. There were several scandals during this "good fellow's" long reign, but big business had no complaint to make against him. The big graft in this Northwestern state, however, was lumber, and the typical way of getting hold of it wholesale, was for the United States to make to the state grants which the state passed on to railway companies to help "develop the resources of the state." Railroad men were in lumber companies, just as lumbermen were in the railway companies, so railway companies sold cheap to the lumber companies, which cleared the land—for the settlers. This was business, and while it was necessary to "take care" of the legislature, the original source of business was the Congress, and that was the place for the head of the System. Keyes had wished to go to the Senate, but Sawyer thought he might as well go himself. He had gone, and now, when Keyes was willing to take the second seat, the business men decided that, since it was all a matter of business, they might as well take it out of politics. Thus Senator Sawyer became boss, and, since he was a lumberman, it was no more than fair that the other seat should go to the railroads. So the big business men got together and they bought the junior United States senatorship for the Honorable John C. Spooner.

Spooner's Senatorship Bought for Him

At Marinette, Wisconsin, lives today a rich old lumberman, Isaac Stephenson. He was associated for years with Senator Sawyer and the other enemies of the republic in Wisconsin, and he left them because they balked an ambition of his. Having gone over, however, he began to see things as they are, and not many men today are more concerned over the dangers to business of the commercial corruption of government than this veteran who confesses that he spent a quarter of a million in politics.

Once he and Senator Sawyer were comparing notes on the cost to them of United States senatorships.

"Isaac," said Sawyer, "how much did you put in to get the legislature for Spooner that time?"

"It cost me about twenty-two thousand, Philetus. How much did you put in?"

"Why," said Sawyer, surprised, "it cost me thirty thousand. I thought it cost you thirty."

"No, it cost me thirty to get it for you when you ran."

Friends of mine, who are friends of Senator Spooner in Washington, besought me, when they heard I was going to Wisconsin, to "remember that Spooner is a most useful man in the Senate," and I know and shall not forget that. Able, deliberate, resourceful, wise, I believe Senator Spooner comes about as near as any man we have in that august chamber today to statesmanship, and I understand he loathes many of the practices of politics. But the question to ask about a representative is, what does he represent?

Senator Spooner, at home, represented the railroads of his state. He served a term in the Wisconsin assembly, and he served the railroads there. After that he served them as a lobbyist. I do not mean that he went to Madison now and then to make arguments for his client. Mr. Spooner spent the session there. Nor do I mean to say that he paid bribes to legislators; there are honest lobbyists. But I do say that Mr. Spooner peddled passes, and any railroad man or any grafter will tell you that this is a cheap but most effective form of legislative corruption. United States Senator Spooner, then, is a product, a flower, perhaps, but none the less he is a growth out of the System, the System which is fighting Governor LaFollette.

The System was fighting LaFollette way back in those days, but the young orator did not know it. He was running for Congress. So far as I can make out, he was seeking only more glory for his French blood and a wider field to shine in, but he went after his French satisfaction in a Scotch-Irish fashion. Boss Keyes told me about it. Keyes had been reduced to the control only of his Congressional district, and, as he said, "We had it arranged to nominate another man. The place did not belong to Dane County. It was another county's turn, but Bob didn't consult us." Bob was consulting his constituents again, and his night riders were out. The System heard of it earlier than in the district attorney campaign, and Keyes and Phil Spooner and the other leaders were angry. Keyes did want to rule that congressional district; it was all he had, and Phil Spooner (who

Wisconsin: Representative Government Restored

now is the head of the street railway system of Madison) sensed the danger in this self-reliant young candidate.

"What's this I hear about you being a candidate for Congress?" he said to LaFollette one day. "Don't you know nobody can go to Congress without our approval? You're a fool."

But LaFollette's men were working, and they carried all except three caucuses (primaries that are something like town meetings) against the ring. The ring bolted, but the people elected him; the people sent LaFollette to Congress at the same time they elected the legislators that sent John C. Spooner to the United States Senate.

The System at Washington

When LaFollette had been in Washington a few weeks, Senator Sawyer found him out and became "like a father" to him. "Our boy" he called him, for LaFollette was the "youngest member." The genial old lumberman took him about and introduced him to the heads of departments and finally, one day, asked him what committee he would like to go on. LaFollette said he would prefer some committee where his practice in the law might make him useful, and Sawyer thought "Public Lands" would about do. He would "fix it." Thus the System was coming after him, but it held back; there must have been a second thought. For the Speaker put LaFollette not on "Public Lands," but on "Indian Affairs."

The governor today will tell you with a relish that he was so green then that he began to "read up on Indians"; he read especially Boston literature on that subject, and he thought of the speeches he could make on Indian wrongs and rights. But there was no chance for an orator. The committee worked and "our boy" read bills. Most of these bills were hard reading and didn't mean much when read. But by and by one came along that was "so full of holes that," as the governor says, "even I could see through it." It provided for a sale of pine on the Menominee reservation in Wisconsin. Mr. LaFollette took it to the (Cleveland's) Commissioner of Indian Affairs, and this official said he thought it "a little the worst bill of the kind that I have ever seen. Where did it come from?" They looked and they saw that it had been introduced by the member from Oshkosh (Sawyer's home district). None the less, Mr. LaFollette wanted a report, and the commissioner said he could have one if he would sit down and write for it. The report so riddled the bill that it lay dead in the committee. One day the congressman who introduced it asked about it.

"Bob, why don't you report my bill?" he said.

"Bill," said Bob, "did you write that bill?"

"Why?"

"It's a steal."

"Let it die then. Don't report it. I introduced it because Sawyer asked me to. He introduced it in the Senate and it is through their committee."

Sawyer never mentioned the bill, and the incident was dropped with the bill. Some time after, however, a similar incident occurred, and this time Sawyer did mention it. The Indian Affairs Committee was having read, at the rate of two hours a day, a long bill to open the big Sioux Indian reservation in Dakota, by selling some eleven million acres right through the center. It was said to be a measure most important to South Dakota, and no one objected to anything till the clerk droned out a provision to ratify an agreement between the Indians and certain railroads about a right of way and some most liberal grants of land for terminal town sites. LaFollette interrupted and he began to talk about United States statutes which provided not so generously, yet amply, for land grants to railways, when a congressman from a neighboring state leaned over and said:

"Bob, don't you see that those are your home corporations?"

Bob said he saw, and he was willing to grant all the land needed for railway purposes, but none for town site schemes. When the committee rose, and LaFollette returned to his seat in the House, a page told him Senator Sawyer wanted to see him. He went out and the senator talked to him for an hour in a most fatherly way, with not a word concerning the Sioux bill till they were about to separate. Then, quite by the way, he said:

"Oh, say, when that Sioux Injun bill comes up there's a

little provision in it for our folks which I wish you to look after."

LaFollette said the bill was up then, that they had just reached the "little provision for our folks," and that he was opposing it.

"Why, is that so?" said Sawyer. "Let's sit down and . . ." So they had another hour, on town sites. It was no use, however. LaFollette "wouldn't consult." Sawyer gave up reasoning with him, but he didn't give up "the little provision." Political force was applied, but not by the senior senator. The System had other agents for such work.

Henry C. Payne's Part in the System

Henry C. Payne arrived on the scene. Payne was chairman of the Republican state Central Committee of Wisconsin, and we have seen in other states what the legislative functions of that office are. Payne reached Washington forty-eight hours after LaFollette's balk, and he went at him hard. All sorts of influence was brought to bear, and when LaFollette held out, Payne became so angry that he expressed himself—and the spirit of the System—in public. To a group in the Ebbitt House he said:

"LaFollette is a damned fool. If he thinks he can buck a railroad with five thousand miles of continuous line, he'll find he's mistaken. We'll take care of him when the time comes."

The state machine fought the congressman in his own district, and so did Keyes and the "old regency" at Madison, but LaFollette, the politician, had insisted upon a congressman's patronage, all of it, and he had used it to strengthen himself at home. LaFollette served three terms in Congress, and when he was defeated in 1890, for the fourth, he went down with the whole party in Wisconsin. This complete overthrow of the Republicans was due to two causes, the McKinley tariff (which LaFollette on the Ways and Means Committee helped to frame) and a piece of state school legislation which angered the foreign and Catholic voters. We need not go into this, and the Democratic administration which resulted bears only indirectly on our story.

One of the great grafts of Wisconsin (and of many another state) was the public funds in the keeping of the state treasurer. The Republicans, for years, had deposited these moneys in banks that stood in with the System, and the treasurer shared with these institutions the interest and profits. He, in turn, "divided up" with the campaign fund and the party leaders. The Democrats were pledged to break up this practice and sue the ex-treasurers. Now these treasurers were not all "good" for the money, and when the suits were brought, as they were in earnest, the treasurers' bondsmen were the real defendants. Chief among these was Senator Sawyer, the boss who had chosen the treasurers and backed them and the practice for years. Sawyer was alarmed. It was estimated that there had been $30,000 a year in the graft; the attorney-general was going back twenty years, and his suits were for the recovery of all the back interest. Several hundred thousand dollars was at stake. And the judge before whom the cases were to be tried was Robert J. Siebecker, brother-in-law and former law partner of Robert M. LaFollette.

One day in September, 1891, LaFollette received from Sawyer a letter asking for a meeting in the Plankington Hotel, Milwaukee. The letter had been folded first with the letter head on, then this was cut off and the sheet refolded; and, as if secrecy was important, the answer suggested by Sawyer was to be the one word "yes " by wire. LaFollette wired "yes," and the two men met. There are two accounts of what occurred. LaFollette said Sawyer began the interview with the remark that "nobody knows that I'm to meet you to-day"; he spoke of the treasury cases and pulled out and held before the young lawyer a thick roll of bills. Sawyer's subsequent explanation was that he proposed only to retain LaFollette, who, however, insists that Sawyer offered him a cash bribe for his influence with Judge Siebecker.

Since Sawyer is dead now, we would better not try to decide between the two men on this particular case, but there is no doubt of one general truth: that Philetus Sawyer was the typical captain of industry in politics; he debauched the politics of his state with money. Old Boss Keyes was bad enough, but his methods were political—patronage, deals, etc., and he made the

Wisconsin: Representative Government Restored

government represent special interests. But when the millionaire lumberman took charge, he came with money; with money he beat Keyes; and money, his and his friends', was the power in the politics of his regime.

His known methods caused no great scandal so long as they were confined to conventions and the legislature, but the courts of Wisconsin had the confidence of the state, and the approach of money to them made people angry. And the story was out. LaFollette, after consultation with his friends, told Judge Siebecker what had happened, and the Judge declined to hear the case. His withdrawal aroused curiosity and rather sensational conjectures. Sawyer denied one of these, and his account seeming to call for a statement from LaFollette, the young lawyer told his story. Sawyer denied it and everybody took sides. The cases were tried, the state won, but the Republican legislature, pledged though it was to recover in full, compromised. So the System saved its boss.

But the System had raised up an enemy worthy of all its power. LaFollette was against it. "They" say in Wisconsin that he is against the railroads, that he "hates " corporate wealth. It is true the bitterest fights he has led have been for so-called anti-railroad laws, but "they" forget that his original quarrel was with Sawyer, and that, if hatred was his impulse, it probably grew out of the treasury case "insult." My understanding of the state of his mind is that before that incident, LaFollette thought only of continuing his congressional career. After it, he was for anything to break up the old Sawyer machine. Anyhow, he told me that, after the Sawyer meeting, he made up his mind to stay home and break up the System in Wisconsin. And, LaFollette did not originate all that legislation. Wisconsin was one of the four original Granger states. There seems to have been always some discontent with the abuse of the power of the railways, their corrupting influence, and their escape from just taxation. So far as I can make out, however, some of the modern measures labeled LaFolletteism, sprang from the head of a certain lean, clean Vermont farmer, who came to the legislature from Knapp, Wisconsin. I went to Knapp. It was a long way around for me, but it paid, for now I can say that I knew A. R. Hall. He is a man. I have seen in my day some seventeen men, real men, and none of them is simpler, truer, braver than this ex-leader of the Wisconsin assembly; none thinks he is more of a failure and none is more of a success.

A.R. Hall's a Man

Hall knows that there is a System in control of the land. Sometimes I doubt my own eyes, but Hall knows it in his heart, which is sore and tired from the struggle. He went to the legislature in 1891. He had lived in Minnesota and had served as an assemblyman there. When he went to the legislature in Wisconsin, one of the first demands upon him was from a constituent who wanted not a pass, but several passes for himself and others. Hall laughed at the extravagance of the request, but when he showed it to a colleague, the older assemblyman took it as a matter of course and told him he could get all the passes he cared to ask for from the railroad lobbyists. "I had taken passes myself in Minnesota," Hall told me, "but I was a legislator; it was the custom, and I thought nothing of it." A little inquiry showed him that the custom in Wisconsin was an abuse of tremendous dimensions. Legislators took "mileage" for themselves, their families, and for their constituents till it appeared that no man in the state was compelled to pay his fare. Hall had not come there as a reformer; like the best reformers I have known, experience of the facts started him going, and his reforms developed as if by accident along empirical lines. Hall says he realized that the legislators had to deliver votes—legislation—for these pass privileges, and he drew an anti-pass resolution which was offered as an amendment to the Constitution. It was beaten. Not only the politicians, the railroads also fought it, and together they won in that session. But Hall, mild-spoken and gentle, was a fighter, so the anti-pass measure became an issue.

One day Assemblyman Hall happened to see the statement of earnings of a railroad to its stockholders. Railroads in Wisconsin paid by way of taxes a percentage on their gross receipts, and, as Hall looked idly over the report, he wondered how the gross receipts item would compare with that in the statement to the state treasurer. He went quietly about his investigation, and he came to the conclusion that, counting illegal rebates, the state reports were from two to five millions short. So he asked for a committee to investigate, and he introduced also a bill for a state railroad commission to regulate railroad rates. This was beaten, and a committee which was sent to Chicago to look up earnings reported for the railways. But this was not enough. Hall was "unsafe" and he must be kept out of the legislature. So, in 1894, "they" sent down into Dunn County men and money to beat Hall for the renomination. They got the shippers out against him (the very men who were at the mercy of the roads), and one of these business men handled the "barrel" which, as he said himself, he "opened at both ends." Hall had no money and no organization, but he knew a way to fight. The caucuses were held in different places at different times, and Hall went about posting bills asking the voters to assemble one hour before time and listen to him. At these preliminary meetings he explained just what was being done and why; he said that he might not be right, but he had some facts, which he gave, and then he declared he was not against the railroads, that he only wished to make sure that they were fulfilling their obligations and not abusing their power. "I had only been trying to serve honorably the people I represented, and it was hard to be made to fight for your political life, just for doing that. But we won out. Those voters went into those caucuses and Dunn County beat the bribery. They then tried to buy my delegates."

Mr. Hall was leaning against the railroad station as he said this. We had gone over the night before, his twelve years' fight, up to his retirement the year before, and we were repeating now. He was looking back over it all, and a hint of moisture in his eyes and the deep lines in his good face made me ask:

"Does it pay, Mr. Hall?"

"Sometimes I think it does, sometimes I think it doesn't. Yes, it does. Dunn County—" He stopped. "Yes, it does," he added. "They used to cartoon me. They lampooned and they ridiculed, they abused and they vilified. They called me a demagogue; said I was ambitious; asked what I was after, just as they do LaFollette. But he is a fighter. He will never stop fighting. And if I had served them, I could have had anything, just as he could now. It is hard and it hurts, when you're only trying to do your duty and be fair. But it does pay. They don't question my motives now, any more."

And they don't question Hall's motives any more. When "they" became most heated in their denunciations of the governor and all his followers, I would ask them, the worst haters, "What about A. R. Hall?" and the change was instantaneous.

"Now, there's a man," they would say; not one, but everybody to whom I mentioned A. R. Hall.

When LaFollette began his open fight against the System in 1894, he took up the issues of inequalities in taxation, machine politics, and primary elections. Hall and LaFollette were friends and they had talked over these issues together in LaFollette's law office in Madison, during the sessions. "They" say in Wisconsin that LaFollette is an opportunist. They say true. But so is Folk an opportunist, and so are the Chicago reformers—as to specific issues. So are the regular politicians who, in Wisconsin, for example, adopted later these same issues in the platform. The difference is this: the regulars wanted only to keep in power so as to continue the profitable business of representing the railroads and other special interests; Hall and LaFollette really wanted certain abuses corrected, and LaFollette was, and is, for any sound issue that will arouse the people of Wisconsin to restore representative government.

In 1894 LaFollette carried his issues to the state convention with a candidate for governor, Nils P. Haugen, a Norse-American who had served in Congress and as a state railroad commissioner. LaFollette and his followers turned up with one-third of the delegates. The regulars, or "Stalwarts," as they afterward were called, were divided, but Sawyer, declaring it was anybody to beat LaFollette, managed a combination on W. H. Upham, a lumberman, and Haugen was beaten. Hall was there, by the way, with an anti-pass plank, and Hall also was beaten.

Appealing to the Voters Direct

Wisconsin: Representative Government Restored

The contest served only to draw a line between the LaFollette "Halfbreeds" and the "Stalwarts," and both factions went to work on their organizations. Upham was elected, and the Stalwarts, who had been living on federal patronage, now had the state. They rebuilt their state machine. LaFollette, with no patronage, continued to organize, and his method was that which he had applied so successfully in his early independent fights for district attorney and congressman. He went straight to the voters.

"They" say in Wisconsin that LaFollette is a demagogue, and if it is demagogy to go thus straight to the voters, then "they" are right. But then Folk also is a demagogue, and so are all thorough-going reformers. LaFollette from the beginning has asked, not the bosses, but the people for what he wanted, and after 1894 he simply broadened his field and redoubled his efforts. He circularized the state, he made speeches every chance he got, and if the test of demagogy is the tone and style of a man's speeches, LaFollette is the opposite of a demagogue. Capable of fierce invective, his oratory is impersonal; passionate and emotional himself, his speeches are temperate. Some of them are so loaded with facts and such closely knit arguments, that they demand careful reading, and their effect is traced to his delivery, which is forceful, emphatic, and fascinating. His earnestness carries the conviction of sincerity, and the conviction of his honesty of purpose he has planted all over the state by his Halfbreed methods.

What were the methods of the Sawyer-Payne-Spooner Republicans? In 1896 the next governor of Wisconsin had to be chosen. The Stalwarts could not run Governor Upham again. As often happens to "safe men," the System had used him up; his appointments had built up the machine, his approval had sealed the compromise of the treasury cases. Someone else must run. To pick out his successor, the Stalwart leaders held a meeting at St. Louis, where they were attending a national convention, and they chose for governor Edward W. Scofield. There was no demagogy about that.

LaFollette Beaten with Mercy

LaFollette wished to run himself; he hoped to run and win while Sawyer lived, and he was holding meetings, too. But his meetings were all over the state, with voters and delegates, and he was making headway. Lest he might fall short, however, LaFollette made a political bargain. He confesses it, and calls it a political sin, but he thinks the retribution which came swift and hard was expiation. He made a deal with Emil Baensch, by which both should canvass the state for delegates, with the understanding that whichever of the two should develop the greater strength was to have both delegations. LaFollette says he came into the convention with enough delegates of his own to nominate him, and Boensch had 75 or so besides. The convention adjourned overnight without nominating and the next morning LaFollette was beaten. He had lost some of his own delegates, and Baensch's went to Scofield.

LaFollette's lost delegates were bought. How the Baensch delegates were secured, I don't know, but Baensch was not a man to sell for money. It was reported to LaFollette during the night that Baensch was going over, and LaFollette wrestled with and thought he had won him back, till the morning balloting showed. As for the rest, the facts are ample to make plain the methods of the old ring. Sawyer was there; and there was a "barrel." I saw men who saw money on a table in the room in the Pfister Hotel, where delegates went in and out, and newspaper men present at the time told me the story in great detail. But there is better evidence than this. Men to whom bribes were offered reported to their leader that night. The first warning came from Captain John T. Rice, of Racine, who (as Governor LaFollette recalls) said: "I have been with the old crowd all my life and I thought I knew the worst, but they have no right to ask me to do what they did tonight. I won't tell you who, but the head of the whole business asked me to name my price for turning over the Union Grove delegation from you to Scofield." There are many such personal statements, some of them giving prices—cash, and federal and state offices—and some giving the names of the bribery agents. The Halfbreed leaders tried to catch the bribers with witnesses, but failed, and at midnight Charles F. Pfister, a Milwaukee Stalwart leader, called on LaFollette, who repeated to me what he said:

"LaFollette, we've got you beaten. We've got your delegates. It won't do you any good to squeal, and if you'll behave yourself we'll take care of you."

So LaFollette had to go on with his fight. He would not "behave." His followers wanted him to lead an independent movement for governor; he wouldn't do that, but he made up his mind to lead a movement for reform within the party, and his experience with corrupt delegates set him to thinking about methods of nomination. The System loomed large with the growth of corporate wealth, the power of huge consolidations over the individual, and the unscrupulous use of both money and power. Democracy was passing, and yet the people were sound. Their delegates at home were representatives, but shipped on passes to Milwaukee, treated, "entertained," and bribed, they ceased to represent. The most important reform was to get the nomination back among the voters themselves. Thus LaFollette, out of his own experience, took up this issue—direct primary nominations by the Australian ballot.

Stalwarts Take LaFollette's Platform

During the next two years LaFollette made a propaganda with this issue and railroad taxation, the taxation of other corporations—express and sleeping car companies which paid nothing—and the evils of a corrupt machine that stood for corrupting capital. He sent out circulars and literature, some of it the careful writings of scientific authors, but, most effective of all, were the speeches he made at the county fairs. When the time for the next Republican state convention came around in 1898, he held a conference with some thirty of his leaders in Milwaukee, and he urged a campaign for their platform alone, with no candidate. The others insisted that LaFollette run, and they were right in principle. As the event proved, the Stalwarts were not afraid of a platform, if they could be in office to make and carry out the laws. LaFollette ran for the nomination and was beaten—by the same methods that were employed against him in '96; cost (insider's estimate), $8,000. Scofield was renominated.

But the LaFollette-Hall platform was adopted—anti-pass, corporation taxation, primary election reform, and all. "They" say now in Wisconsin that LaFollette is too practical; that he has adopted machine methods, etc. During 1896, 1897, and 1898 they were saying he was an impracticable reformer, and yet here they were adopting his impracticable theories. And they enacted some of these reforms. The agitation (for LaFollette is indeed an "agitator") made necessary some compliance with public demand and platform promises, so Hall got his anti-pass law at last; a commission to investigate taxation was appointed, and there was some other good legislation. Yet, as Mr. Hall said, "In effect, that platform was repudiated." The railway commission reported that the larger companies, the Chicago, Milwaukee & St. Paul and the Northwestern, respectively, did not pay their proportionate share of the taxes, and a bill was introduced by Hall to raise their assessments. It passed the House, but the Senate had and has a "combine" like the senates of Missouri and Illinois, and the combine beat the bill.

The failures of the legislature left all questions open, and LaFollette and his followers continued their agitation. Meanwhile Senator Sawyer died, and when the next gubernatorial election (1900) approached, all hope of beating LaFollette was gone. The Stalwarts began to come to him with offers of support. One of the first to surrender was J. W. Babcock, congressman and national politician. Others followed, but not John C. Spooner, Payne, and Pfister, not yet. They brought out for the nomination John M. Whitehead, a state senator with a clean reputation and a good record. But in May (1900) LaFollette announced his candidacy on a ringing platform, and he went campaigning down into the strongest Stalwart counties. He carried enough of them to take the heart out of the old ring. All other candidates withdrew, and Senator Spooner, who is a timid man, wrote a letter which, in view of his subsequent stand for reelection, is a remarkable document; it declared that he was unalterably determined not to run again

Wisconsin: Representative Government Restored

for the Senate. LaFollette was nominated unanimously, and his own platform was adopted. The victory was complete. Though the implacable Stalwarts supported the Democratic candidate, LaFollette was elected by a 102,000 plurality.

Victory, the Beginning of War

Victory for reform is often defeat, and this triumph of LaFollette, apparently so complete, was but the beginning of the greatest fight of all in Wisconsin, the fight that is being waged out there now. Governor LaFollette was inaugurated January 7, 1901. The legislature was overwhelmingly Republican and apparently there was perfect harmony in the party. The governor believed there was. The Stalwart-Halfbreed lines were not sharply drawn. The Halfbreeds counted a majority, especially in the House, and A. R. Hall was the "logical" candidate for speaker. It was understood that he coveted the honor, but he proposed and it was decided that, in the interest of peace and fair play, a Stalwart should take the chair. The governor says that the first sign he had of trouble was in the newspapers which, the day after the organization of the legislature, reported that the Stalwarts controlled and that there would be no primary election or tax legislation. The governor, undaunted, sent in a firm message calling for the performance of all platform promises, and bills to carry out these pledges were introduced under the direction of the LaFollette leaders, Hall and Judge E. Ray Stevens, the authority of the primary election bill. These developed the opposition. There were two (alternative) railway tax bills; others to tax other corporations; and, later, a primary election bill—nothing that was not promised by a harmonious party, yet the outcry was startling and the fight that followed was furious. Why?

LaFollette and the Railroads

I have seen enough of the System to believe that that is the way it works. Just such opposition, with just such cries of "boss," "dictator," etc., will arise against Folk when he is governor, and possibly against Deneen; any governors who try to govern in the interest of the people. And I believe they will find their legislatures organized and corrupted against them. But in the case of LaFollette there was a "misunderstanding." In the year (1900) when everything was LaFollette, Congressman Babcock, Postmaster-General Payne, and others sought to bring together the great ruling special interests and the inevitable governor. Governor LaFollette said, like President Roosevelt, that he would represent the corporations of his state, just as he would represent all other interests and persons; but no more. He would be "fair." Well, that was "all we want," they said, and the way seemed smooth. It was like the incident in St. Louis when Folk told the boodlers he would "do his duty," and the boodlers answered, "Of course, old man." But some railroad men said LaFollette promised in writing to consult with them before bringing in railroad bills; there was a certain famous letter written in the spring of 1900 to Thomas H. Gill, an old friend of the governor, who is counsel to the Wisconsin Central Railroad; this letter put the governor on record. Everywhere I went I heard of this document, and though the noise of it had resounded through the state for four years, it had never been produced. Here it is:

Madison, Wis., May 12th, 1900

> *Dear Tom:*
> *You have been my personal and political friend for twenty years. Should I become a candidate for the nomination for governor, I want your continued support, if you can consistently accord it to me. But you are the attorney for the Wisconsin Central R. R. Co., and I am not willing that you should be placed in any position where you could be subjected to any criticism or embarrassment with your employers upon my account. For this reason, I desire to state to you in so far as I am able my position in relation to the question of railway taxation which has now become one of public interest, and is likely to so continue until rightly settled. This I can do in a very few words.*
> *Railroad corporations should pay neither more nor less than a justly proportionate share of taxes with the other taxable*

property of the state. If I were in a position to pass officially upon a bill to change existing law, it would be my first care to know whether the rate therein proposed was just in proportion to the property of other corporations and individuals as then taxed, or as therein proposed to be taxed. The determination of that question would be controlling. If such rate was less than the justly proportionate share which should be borne by the railroads, then I should favor increasing it to make it justly proportionate. If the proposed rate was more than the justly proportionate share, in comparison with the property of other corporations, and of individuals taxed under the law, then I should favor decreasing to make it justly proportionate.

In other words, I would favor equal and exact justice to each individual and to every interest, yielding neither to clamor on the one hand, nor being swerved from the straight course by any interest upon the other. This position, I am sure, is the only one which could commend itself to you, and cannot be criticised by any legitimate business honestly managed.

Sincerely yours,

The Mr. Gill to whom this letter was addressed is one of the most enlightened and fair-minded corporation lawyers that I ever met, even in the West, where corporation men also are enlightened. He convinced me that he and the other railroad men really did expect more consideration than the governor gave them, and so there may have been a genuine misunderstanding. But after what I have seen in Chicago, St. Louis, and Pittsburgh, and in Missouri and Illinois and the United States, I almost am persuaded that no honest official in power can meet the expectations of great corporations; they have been spoiled, like bad American children, and are ever ready to resort to corruption and force. That was their recourse now.

Governor LaFollette says he learned afterward that during the campaign, the old, corrupt ring went about in the legislative districts, picking and "fixing" legislators, and that the plan was to discredit him with defeat by organizing the legislature against him. However this may be, it is certain that when his bills were under way, there was a rush to the lobby at Madison. The regular lobbyists were reinforced with special agents; local Stalwart leaders were sent for, and federal officeholders; United States senators hurried home, and congressmen; and boodle, federal patronage, force, and vice were employed to defeat bills promised in the platform. Here is a statement by Irvine L. Lenroot, now the Speaker of the Assembly. He says:

Official Description of the Lobby

"From the first day of the session the railroad lobbyists were on the ground in force, offering courtesies and entertainments of various kinds to the members. Bribery is a hard word, a charge which never should be made unless it can be substantiated. The writer has no personal knowledge of money being actually offered or received for votes against the bill. It was, however, generally understood in the Assembly that any member favoring the bill could better his financial condition if he was willing to vote against it. Members were approached by representatives of the companies and offered lucrative positions. This may not have been done with any idea of influencing votes. The reader will draw his own conclusions. It was a matter of common knowledge that railroad mileage could be procured if a member was 'right.' Railroad lands could be purchased very cheaply by members of the legislature. It was said if a member would get into a poker game with a lobbyist, the member was sure to win. Members opposed to Governor LaFollette were urged to vote against the bill, because he wanted it to pass. A prominent member stated that he did not dare to vote for the bill, because he was at the mercy of the railroad companies, and he was afraid they would ruin his business by advancing his rates, if he voted for it."

I went to Superior and saw Mr. Lenroot, and he told me that one of the "members approached by representatives of the companies and offered positions" was himself. He gave his bribery stories in detail, and enabled me to run down and verify others; but the sentence that interested me most in his statement was the last. The member who did not dare vote for the railway

Wisconsin: Representative Government Restored 349

tax bill, lest the railways raise the freight on his goods and ruin his business, confessed to Governor LaFollette and others. Another member stated that in return for his treason to his constituents, a railroad quoted him a rate that would give him an advantage over his competitors.

Well, these methods succeeded. The policy of the administration was not carried out. Some good bills passed, but the session was a failure. Not content with this triumph, however, the System went to work to beat LaFollette, and to accomplish this end, LaFollette's methods were adopted, or, rather, adapted. A systematic appeal was to be made to public opinion. A meeting of the leading Stalwarts was held in the eleventh story of an office building in Milwaukee, and a Permanent Republican League of the state of Wisconsin was organized. This became known as the "Eleventh Story League." A manifesto was put out "viewing with alarm" the encroachments of the executive upon the legislative branch of the government, etc., etc. (The encroachments of boodle business upon all branches of the government is all right.) An army of canvassers was dispatched over the state to interview personally every voter in the state and leave with him books and pamphlets. Now this was democratic and fair, but that League did one thing which is enough alone to condemn the whole movement. It corrupted part of the country press. This is not hearsay. The charge was made at the time these papers swung round suddenly, and the League said it did not bribe the editors; it "paid for space for League editorial matter, and for copies of the paper to be circulated." This is bribery, as any newspaper man knows. But there was also what even the League business man would call bribery; newspaper men all over the state told me about direct purchase—and cheap, too. It is sickening, but, for final evidence, I saw affidavits published in Wisconsin by newspaper men who were approached with offers which they refused, and by others who sold out, then threw up their contracts and returned the bribes, for shame or other reasons.

These "democratic" methods failed. When the time arrived for the next Republican state convention, the Stalwarts found that the people had sent up delegates instructed for

LaFollette, and he was nominated for a second term. What could the Stalwarts do? They weren't even "regular" now. LaFollette had the party, they had only the federal patronage and the big business System. But the System had resources. Wherever a municipal reform movement has hewed to the line, the leaders of it, like Folk and the Chicago reformers, have seen the forces of corruption retire from one party to the other and from the city to the state. This Wisconsin movement for state reform now had a similar experience. The Wisconsin System, driven out of the Republican, went over to the Democratic party; that had not been reformed; beaten out of power in the state, it retreated to the towns; they had not been reformed.

The System in the Towns

The System in many of the Wisconsin municipalities was intact. There had been no serious municipal reform movements anywhere, and the citizens of Milwaukee, Oshkosh, Green Bay, etc., were pretty well satisfied, and they are still, apparently. "We're nothing like Minneapolis, St. Louis, and the rest," they told me with American complacency. Green Bay was exactly like Minneapolis; we know it because the wretched little place has been exposed since. And Marinette and Oshkosh, unexposed, are said by insiders to be "just like Green Bay." As for Milwaukee, that is St. Louis all over again.

District Attorney Bennett has had grand juries at work in Milwaukee since 1901, and he has some 42 persons indicted—12 aldermen, 10 supervisors, 9 other officials, 1 state senator, and 10 citizens; four convictions and three pleas of guilty. The grafting so far exposed is petty, but the evidence in hand indicates a highly perfected boodle system. The Republicans had the county, the Democrats the city, and both the council and the board of supervisors had combines which grafted on contracts, public institutions, franchises, and other business privileges. The corrupt connection of business and politics was shown; the informants were merchants and contractors, mostly small men, who confessed to bribery. The biggest caught so far is Colonel Pabst, the brewer, who paid a check of $1,500 for leave to break

Wisconsin: Representative Government Restored 351

a building law. But all signs point higher than beer, to more "legitimate" political business. As in Chicago, a bank is the center of this graft, and public utility companies are back of it. The politicians in the boards of management, now or formerly, show that. It is a bipartisan system all through. Henry C. Payne, while chairman of the Republican state Central Committee, and E. C. Wall (the man the Wisconsin Democracy offered to the National Democratic Convention for president of the United States), while chairman of the Democratic state Central Committee, engineered a consolidation of Milwaukee street railway and electric lighting companies, and, when the job was done, Payne became manager of the street railway, Wall of the light company. But this was "business." There was no scandal about it.

The great scandal of Milwaukee was the extension of street railway franchises, and the men who put that through were Charles F. Pfister, the Stalwart Republican boss, and David S. Rose, the Stalwart Democratic mayor. Money was paid; the extension was boodled through. The *Milwaukee Sentinel* reprinted a paragraph saying Pfister, among others, did the bribing, and thus it happened that the Stalwarts got that paper. Pfister sued for libel, but when the editors (now on the *Milwaukee Free Press*) made answer that their defense would be proof of the charge, the millionaire traction man bought the paper and its evidence, too. It is no more than fair to add—as Milwaukee newspaper men always do (with delight)—that the paper had very little evidence, not nearly so much as Pfister seemed to think it had. As for Mayor Rose, his friends declare that he has told them, personally and convincingly, that he got not one cent for his service. But that is not the point. Mayor Rose fought to secure for special interests a concession which sacrificed the common interests of his city. I am aware that he defends the terms of the grants as fair, and they would seem so in the East, but the West is intelligent on special privileges, and Mayor Rose lost to Milwaukee the chance Chicago seized to tackle the public utility problem. Moreover, Rose knew that his council was corrupt before it was proven so; he told two business men that they couldn't get a privilege they sought honestly from him without bribing aldermen. Yet he ridiculed as "hot air" an investigation which produced evidence enough to defeat at the polls, in a self-respecting city, the head of an administration so besmirched. Nevertheless, Milwaukee reelected Rose; good citizens say that they gave the man the benefit of the doubt—the man, not the city.

But this is not the only explanation. The System was on trial with Mayor Rose in that election, and the System saved its own. The Republicans, with the Rose administration exposed, had a chance to win, and they nominated a good man, Mr. Guy D. Goff. Pfister, the Stalwart Republican boss, seemed to support Goff; certainly the young candidate had no suspicion to the contrary. He has now, however. When the returns came in showing that he was beaten, Mr. Goff hunted up Mr. Pfister, and he found him. Mr. Goff, the Republican candidate for mayor, found Charles F. Pfister, the Stalwart Republican boss, rejoicing over the drinks with the elected Democratic mayor, David S. Rose!

Both Rings Against LaFollette

I guess Mr. Goff knows that a bipartisan System rules Milwaukee, and, by the same token, Governor LaFollette knows that there is a bipartisan System in Wisconsin. For when Governor LaFollette beat the Stalwarts in the Republican state convention of 1902, those same Stalwarts combined with the Democrats. Democrats told me that the Republican Stalwarts dictated the "Democratic" anti-LaFollette platform, and that Pfister, the "Republican" boss, named the "safe man" chosen for the "Democratic" candidate for governor to run against LaFollette—said David S. Rose.

"They" say in Wisconsin that LaFollette is a Democrat; that "he appeals to Democratic voters." He does. He admits it, but he adds that it is indeed to the Democratic voters that he appeals—not to the Democratic machine. And he gets Democratic votes. "They" complain that he has split the Republican party; he has, and he has split the Democratic party, too. When "they" united the two party rings of the bipartisan

Wisconsin: Representative Government Restored 353

System against LaFollette in 1902, he went out after the voters of both parties, and those voters combined; they beat Rose, the two rings, and the System. The people of Wisconsin reelected LaFollette, the "unsafe," and that is why the trouble is so great in Wisconsin. The System there is down.

There is a machine, but it is LaFollette's. When he was re-elected, the governor organized his party, and I think no other of his offenses is quite so heinous in Stalwart eyes. They wanted me to expose him as a boss who had used state patronage to build up an organization. I reminded "them" that their federal patronage is greater than LaFollette's state patronage, and I explained that my prejudice was not against organization; their kind everywhere had been urging me so long to believe that organization was necessary in politics that I was disposed to denounce only those machines that sold out the party and the people. And as for the "boss"—it is not the boss in an elective office where he is responsible that is so bad, but the irresponsible boss back of a safe figurehead; this is the man that is really dangerous. They declared, however, that Governor LaFollette had sacrificed good service to the upbuilding of his machine. This is a serious charge. I did not go thoroughly into it. Cases which I investigated at Stalwart behest, held, with one exception, very little water, and I put no faith in the rest. But, for the sake of argument, let us admit that the departments are not all that they should be. What then? As in Chicago, the fight in Wisconsin is for self-government, not "good" government; it is a fight to re-establish a government representative of all the people. Given that; remove from control the Big Business and the Bad Politics that corrupt all branches of the government, and "good " government will come easily enough. But Big Business and Bad Politics are hard to beat.

The defeat of Rose did not beat them. The Stalwarts still had the Senate, and they manned the lobby to beat the railroad tax and the primary election bills. But Governor LaFollette outplayed them at the great game. He long had been studying the scheme for a state commission to regulate railway freight rates. It was logical. If their taxes were increased the roads could take the difference out of the people by raising freight rates. Other states had such commissions, and in some of them, notably Iowa and Illinois, the rates were lower than in Wisconsin. Moreover, we all know railroads give secret rebates and otherwise discriminate in favor of individuals and localities.

When then the battle lines were drawn on the old bills in the legislature of 1903, the governor threw into the fight a bristling message calling for a commission to regulate railway rates. The effect was startling. "Populism," "Socialism," "they" cried, and they turned to rend this new bill. They let the tax bill go through to fight this fresh menace to "business." They held out against the primary election bill also, for if that passed they feared the people might keep LaFollette in power forever. Even that, however, they let pass finally, with an amendment for a referendum. Concentrating upon the rate commission bill, Big Business organized business men's mass meetings throughout the state, and with the help of favored or timid shippers, sent committees to Madison to protest to the legislature. Thus this bill in the interests of fair business was beaten by business, and, with the primary electron referendum, is an issue in this year's campaign.

As I have tried to show, however, the fundamental issue lies deeper. The people of Wisconsin understand this. The Stalwarts dread the test at the polls. But what other appeal was there? They knew one. When the Republican state convention met this year, the Stalwarts bolted; whatever the result might have been of a fight in the convention, they avoided it and held a separate convention in another hall, which, by the way, they had hired in advance. The Halfbreeds renominated LaFollette; the Stalwarts put up another ticket. To the Stalwart convention came Postmaster-General Payne, United States senators Spooner and Quarles, Stalwart congressmen and federal officeholders—the Federal System. The broken state System was appealing to the United States System, and the Republican National Convention at Chicago was to decide the case. And it did decide—for the System. I attended that convention, and heard what was said privately and honestly. The Republicans who decided for Payne-Spooner-Pfister-Babcock, et al., said "LaFollette isn't really a Republican anyhow."

Isn't he? That is a most important question. True, he is very democratic essentially. He helped to draw the McKinley tariff law and he is standing now on the national Republican platform; his democracy consists only in the belief that the citizens elected to represent the people should represent the people, not the corrupt special interests. Both parties should be democratic in that sense. But they aren't. Too often we have found both parties representing graft—big business graft. The people, especially in the West, are waking to a realization of this state of things, and (taking a hint from the big grafters) they are following leaders who see that the way to restore government representative of the common interests of the city or state, is to restore to public opinion the control of the dominant party. The Democrats of Missouri have made their party democratic; the Republicans of Illinois have made their party democratic. The next to answer should be the people of Wisconsin. The Stalwarts hope the courts will decide. They hope their courts will uphold the decision of the National Republican Party, that they, who represent all that is big and bad in business and politics, are the regular "Republicans." This isn't right. The people of Wisconsin are not radicals; they are law-abiding, conservative, and fair. They will lay great store by what their courts shall rule, but this is a question that should be left wholly to the people themselves. And they are to be trusted, for no matter how men may differ about Governor LaFollette otherwise, his long, hard fight has developed citizenship in Wisconsin—honest, reasonable, intelligent citizenship. And that is better than "business"; that is what business and government are for—men.

McClure's Magazine
February, 1905

Rhode Island: A State for Sale

What Senator Aldrich Represents—A Business Man's Government Founded Upon the Corruption of the People Themselves

THE political condition of Rhode Island is notorious, acknowledged, and it is shameful. But Rhode Islanders are ashamed of it. There is the shining truth about this state. Not many American communities are so aware of their political degradation, none has a healthier body of conservative discontent; and the common sense of this good-will, unorganized and impotent though it is, makes the Rhode Islander resent the interest of his neighbors. "Our evils are our troubles," he says; "they don't concern the rest of you. Why should we be singled out? We are no worse than others. We are better than some; we want to set things right, but can't. Conditions are peculiar."

This is all wrong. The evils of Rhode Island concern every man, woman, and child in our land. For example:

The United States Senate is coming more and more to be the actual head of the United States government. In the Senate there is a small ring (called the Steering Committee) which is coming more and more to be the head of the United States Senate. The head of this committee is Senator Nelson W. Aldrich, who has been described as "the boss of the United States," "the power behind the power behind the throne," "the general manager of the United States." The fitness of these titles is questioned, but it is a question of national politics, and all I know to the point in that field is what everybody knows: that Senator Aldrich, a very rich man and father-in-law of young Mr. Rockefeller, is supposed to represent "Sugar," "Standard Oil," "New York," and, more broadly, "Wall Street"; our leading legislative authority on protective tariff, he speaks for privileged business; the chairman of the Senate Finance Committee, he stands for high finance. These facts and suppositions, taken together with the praises I have heard of him in Wall Street and the comfortable faith he seems to inspire in business men all over the country, suggest that we have in Senator Aldrich the commercial ideal of political character, and—if not the head—at least the political representative of the head of that System which is coming more and more to take the place of the passing paper government of the United States.

What sort of a man is Senator Aldrich? What school of politics did he attend, what school of business? What kind of a government is it that forms the traditions and perhaps the ideal of the most powerful man in our national legislature? What kind of a government does he give his own people in his own state? In brief, what is the System that he has produced and that has produced him? These are questions of national interest, and Rhode Island can answer them. Mr. Aldrich is the senior senator for Rhode Island and Providence Plantations.

And Rhode Island throws light on another national question, a question that is far more important: Aren't the people themselves dishonest? The "grafters" who batten on us say so. Politicians have excused their own corruption to me time and again by declaring that "we're all corrupt," and promoters and swindlers alike describe their victims as "smart folk who think to beat us at our own game." Without going into the cynic's sweeping summary that "man always was and always will be corrupt," it is but fair while we are following the trail of the grafters to consider their plea that the corrupt political System they are upbuilding is founded on the dishonesty of the American people. Is it?

It is in Rhode Island. The System of Rhode Island which has produced the man who is at the head of the political System of the United States is grounded on the lowest layer of corruption that I have found thus far—the bribery of voters with cash at the polls. Other states know the practice. In Wisconsin, Missouri, Illinois, and Pennsylvania "workers" are paid "to get out the vote," but this is only preliminary; the direct and decisive purchase of power comes later, in conventions and legislatures.

In these states the corruptionists buy the people's representatives. In Rhode Island they buy the people themselves.

The conditions are peculiar. As the Rhode Islanders say, their state is peculiar in many ways. But it is American. The smallest of the states, it is one of the biggest in our history. Poor in soil, it is rich in waterways, and the Rhode Islanders, turning early from agriculture to manufacture, made goods which they sent forth from their magnificent harbor to all the world in ships that brought home cargoes of wealth. One of the New England group of colonies, Rhode Island was founded as a refuge from the Puritan intolerance of Massachusetts. One of the "Original Thirteen states," it was the first (May 4, 1776) to declare its independence of Great Britain, and the last (May 29, 1790) to give allegiance to the United States. So the American spirit of commercial enterprise and political independence has burned high in Rhode Island. There is nothing peculiar about that, and there is nothing peculiar about the general result of the corruption of the state.

Rhode Island is an oligarchy. But so were Wisconsin and Illinois and Missouri, and so are New York, Pennsylvania, and New Jersey. The oligarchy is the typical form of the actual government of our states. There is one peculiarity about the Rhode Island oligarchy, however. It is constitutional. The oligarchies of other states were grafted upon constitutional democracies. Rhode Island never was a democracy, and in that peculiarity lies the peculiar significance of this state to the rest of us.

Rhode Island has a restricted suffrage. Many a good American thinks that if we could "keep the ignorant foreigner from voting," and otherwise limit the suffrage to persons of property who would have a direct, personal, financial interest in government, we then should have good government. Should we? Rhode Island can answer that question. Again, many "thinkers" have thought that it was the wicked cities with their mixed populations which have degraded and disgraced us, and that if we could but devise some scheme of representation by which the balance of power could be given into the honest hands of the good old American stock out upon the healthy countryside we then should be saved. Rhode Island has such a scheme. The significance to the rest of us of the story of Rhode Island lies in the fact that its essentially typical condition was reached under extraordinary circumstances, which some "leading citizens" in other states think would correct their evils.

"Leading citizens" have made Rhode Island what it is. They always have ruled there. I have called the state an oligarchy. It used to be an aristocracy. "Freeholders" and their eldest sons alone participated in the colonial government under the charter of Charles II, and after the Revolution, when all the other states adopted constitutions, Rhode Island went on under its royal charter of 1663 and an "unwritten constitution" till 1842. I cannot stop to describe this "landed aristocracy" in an American state. It is sufficient that it closed with the Dorr Rebellion. The abuses were so intolerable that the people, the patient American people who have submitted to Croker, Quay, Cox, and other despots, rose in open revolt.

The next experiment was a "commercial aristocracy." The constitution of 1842 "extended" the suffrage from holders of real to those also possessed of personal property—if they were native born. The "foreign vote" was restricted as before to real estate holders till 1888, when personal property qualified a foreign-born as well as a native voter. The "mob," which owned nothing and paid no taxes, was allowed to vote, but only upon registering four months before election and then not "upon any proposition to impose a tax or the expenditure of money." These registered voters, for example, cannot vote for members of city councils.

The most effective restriction of the suffrage, however, was established in the constitutional scheme of disproportionate representation. The governor, elected by a majority (now by a plurality) of the voters of all classes, was made a "pure executive"; he had no veto. All legislative powers were lodged in the General Assembly of two houses. The lower branch, the House of Representatives, is limited to seventy-two members, no matter what the population may be, and while each town shall have at least one representative, no city may have more than one-sixth of the membership. This is undemocratic enough, but the

Senate, says the constitution, "shall consist of one senator from each town and city in the state."

Here is the crux of the situation. A town in Rhode Island is what is known to most of us as a township. There are thirty-eight "towns and cities" in the state. Their population in 1900 was 428,551. Of this total, 36,027 lived in twenty towns. Thus less than one-eleventh of the people of the state elect more than five-tenths—a majority—of the Senate. Providence, with 29,030 qualified voters, has one senator; Little Compton elected one, one year, by a unanimous vote of seventy-eight. There are fourteen such "towns" with less than 500 qualified voters; there are twenty with less than 2,000 each. Thus was the sovereignty of the state put into the hands of the " good old American stock, but in the country."

What happened? The "best people" continued to rule. The "best people" of the period after the new constitution were manufacturers, but their fine old houses stand today as witnesses not only to their wealth, but also to a refined taste. There can be no doubt that they came as near forming a real aristocracy as commercialism can produce! They certainly were just the kind of men that many theorists say should have control of government. Well, they got control in Rhode Island. How? With money. Aristocrats though they were, they were business men first, and they went after the key to control in a businesslike way. They bought up the towns. The "best people" sent offers of bribes to the good people of the countryside, and the good people took the bribes and let the best people run the government. It was a commercial aristocracy that corrupted the American stock in Rhode Island and laid the foundation of the present financial and political System of corruption in the state.

This class ruled till well down into the eighties, and its leader, Senator Henry B. Anthony, "discovered" and promoted Nelson W. Aldrich, his successor, who represents the System, and General Charles R. Brayton, the boss who developed and directs it. Since Anthony's time, the latter-day business man— he who makes, not cotton goods, but money—the captain of finance, has succeeded to the control, but he has not disturbed the foundation stone of the System. He also rules with money.

He, too, sends bribes to the towns of Rhode Island, and to him also the good "country" American has surrendered his sovereignty. There is no doubt about this. The corruption of the voters of the towns of Rhode Island is so ancient and so common that Governor Lucius F. C. Garvin addressed in March, 1903, a "Special Message concerning Bribery in Elections to the Honorable, the General Assembly," etc.:

> *Gentlemen: —... That bribery exists to a great extent in the elections of this state is a matter of common knowledge. No general election passes without, in some sections of the state, the purchase of votes by one or both of the great political parties. It is true that the results of the election may not often be changed, so far as the candidates on the state ticket are concerned, but many assemblymen occupy the seats they do by means of purchased votes.*
>
> *In a considerable number of our towns bribery is so common and has existed for so many years that the awful nature of the crime has ceased to impress. In some towns the bribery takes place openly; is not called bribery, nor considered a serious matter. The money paid to the voter, whether two, five, or twenty dollars, is spoken of as "payment for his time." The claim that the money given to the elector is not for the purpose of influencing his vote, but is compensation for time lost in visiting the polls, is the merest sophistry, and should not deceive any adult citizen of ordinary intelligence. It is well known that in such towns, when one political party is supplied with a corruption fund and the other is without, the party so provided invariably elects its Assembly ticket, thus affording positive proof that the votes are bought and the voters bribed....*

This startling official arraignment had no appreciable effect within the state. It was too true. But the message attracted outside attention, and Mr. Edward Lowry, of the *New York Evening Post*, and Mr. Waldo L. Cook, of the Springfield (Mass.) *Republican* made investigations so thorough and reports so complete that, though I went over the same ground with more time and more deliberation, I found nothing to correct and little to add to their facts.

Nine of the towns are absolutely purchasable; that is to say, they "go the way the money goes." Eleven more can be influenced by the use of money. Many of their voters won't go to the polls at all unless "there is something in it." But there need not be much in it. Governor Garvin quoted a political leader in one town who declared that if neither party had money, but one had a box of cigars, "my town would go for that party—if the workers would give up the cigars." In another town one party had but one man in it who did not take money, and he never voted. A campaign marching club organized for a presidential campaign paraded every night with enthusiasm so great that the leaders thought it would be unnecessary to pay for votes in this town; few of the members voted. Another time, when no money turned at a state election, one town, by way of rebuke to the regular party managers, elected a Prohibition candidate to the Assembly.

Both parties buy votes, and though the practice seems to have destroyed completely all loyalty to the state, some loyalty to party remains in most of these towns. But even this sentiment is mercenary. The Democratic leader of a Democratic town told me that he has to pay something always. "For instance," he explained, "my town is all right. The Republicans can come in there with more money than I have, and I still can hold it. Suppose they have enough to pay ten dollars a vote and I can give but three; I tell my fellows to go over and get the ten, then come to me and get my three; that makes thirteen, but I tell them to vote my way. And they do. And the Republicans do the same in their solid towns when we go in to outbid them." Another instance stated to me by a campaign manager was the experience of a "respectable business man" who lived in a town that usually "went wrong." The manager wanted to carry that town, and he asked the business man to do it. "I offered him a few hundred dollars," he said, "and he wouldn't take the money at first; said it would be of no use among the kind of men he could influence. But I got him to try it, and after election when he came to report he had learned something. He had spent most of the money, and he was astonished at the character of the men who took such money. 'Why,' he said, 'they took it as easy as you please.' They asked why we hadn't done that before. They said they were willing to vote our way if only we would make it interesting!"

This "respectable business man" discovered the most depressing development of the Rhode Island practices— the kind of voters that take bribes. They are Americans; others, too, but the worst of these rotten boroughs are the "hill towns," so called because they lie back away from the harbor and river and "big cities," up on the hills. There is the American stock pure; too pure, some apologists say; the hill towns are called degenerate. Maybe they are. The population of many of them has decreased slowly, but pretty steadily, for a hundred years. "The most courageous of the people have gone out," you hear, "and little new blood has gone in." But that only proves the point. These pure Americans are corrupt. Another consideration to be weighed is that the temptation has been severe and long. With so much power to bestow, their votes have been eagerly sought, as very valuable. But this accident only explains, perhaps, why other, more populous districts elsewhere are not corrupt; they have not been tried. It is cheaper in Providence to bribe the opposition leaders, and in Missouri and Wisconsin to wait and buy the select men of the people, not the people. Where the people are tempted, in the country "towns" of Rhode Island, the people sell out. And Rhode Island proves the willingness to buy. The respectable business man, who was astonished at the standing of the men who sold, was ready enough to buy, and he did buy, and he had no astonishment for his own conduct. Bribe-giving is "not so bad." Some men who talked to me of their vote-buying knew and said, and one of them plainly felt, that it was a shameful practice, but they all regarded it as necessary. Governor Garvin referred once publicly to a "district judge" who so regarded it, and so notorious is this case that a dozen men named the judge to me. The Democrats, who, being out of power, stand for reform and a new constitution, do not see how they can get control long enough to make the needed changes without more money than they can raise in the state, and the hope of some of the leaders is that an exigency will arise, say in national politics, which will enable them to collect enough "outside capital" to buy up the state for their party.

Bribery, bribery of the people, is a custom of the country in Rhode Island; it is an institution, and, like the church or property, it is not safe to attack it. This may sound preposterous, and there is a public opinion against the custom, but the country clergy, as Mr. Lowry showed and as Bishop McVickar of the Rhode Island diocese of the Episcopal Church confirmed, do not denounce bribery from their pulpits; they do not dare. The bishop declared that the country clergy could not "speak out without coming to financial grief and ruin," and he proposed "doing something, so that no one will dare threaten local ministers with the loss of their positions." What does the Bishop mean by such language? "It is an outrage on our civilization," he added, "that young men of the church with high ideals should be put under the ban of the power of political immoralities and forced to acquiesce in evil for the sake of their families."

The good bishop was pointing, when he spoke thus, at the System, of which this bribery institution is the cornerstone. Back of the vote-buyers are the most powerful interests of the state, the friends of "all that is," and even Bishop McVickar has been unable to do the "something" to free the clergy. The head men in the churches, the leading citizens in the state, the captains of finance and industry, won't let the clergy "preach politics"; they may preach the Gospel, not morality, not practical morality.

What is this precious System that can compel the respect, of silence at least, even from the Church? It is just such a typical financial political organization as we have seen in other states, only plainer; as General Brayton, the boss, says: "bad, but not a bit worse than in many other states. Because Rhode Island is small, you can see things better; that's what makes the difference." But that is a most encouraging difference to those who want to see things better. Business men are back of the politicians that rule most corrupt states; in Rhode Island they are in plain sight, and everybody knows them and their operations. Here, also, there are politicians to "do the dirty work," but the very politicians in this state are not of the "low-down" sort. They are not "Irish immigrants"; the Irish are in opposition here. Nor are they saloonkeepers and keepers of disorderly houses, gamblers, and the "scum of the earth." So purely a business government is this that the officers and legislators, the bosses and the leaders, are typically native-born citizens of professional and business occupations. General Brayton himself comes of a fine old Rhode Island family, with a revolutionary record and a line of sons reaching from the Supreme Court bench to Congress; the boss went to Brown University and served with credit in the Civil War. Though he had himself admitted to the bar apparently only to enable him, as a St. Louis grafter put it, "to take fees, not bribes," none the less the boss is a lawyer.

And he is a "character." He is old now, blind, and some of his political friends said he was mentally weakened. I think they feared his candor; though, when I called, his relatives, after consulting with him, and reporting that he felt he had better not talk, they put the refusal on other grounds. It is better so, for whereas I make it a rule to treat such interviews as confidential, Mr. Lowry had his for publication, and here it is, a remarkable outline of the Rhode Island government by General Brayton himself:

"There is a lot of talk of bribery here, but . . . I don't think there is much outright vote-buying done; the voters are paid for their time, because they have to leave their work and come down to the polls. Sometimes that takes all day. The Republican party shouldn't be blamed for the present state of affairs. The Democrats are just as bad, or would be if they had the money.

"The manufacturers in the state are really to blame for present conditions. If they would only hang together and wanted to do it, they could clean out the state in no time at all. They give to the Republican campaign fund in presidential years, but usually when you go to them to get money for state elections they say: 'Oh! we'll take care of our town'; so in that way all of the towns in the state are peddled around, each manufacturer caring for his own town. Some of them haven't treated the party just right. The Republicans have never passed any legislation that would bother them, like the ten-hour law and things like that, until there was such a strong demand from the labor people and the citizens that the party had to do it."

"What is your share in the forming of legislation and the passage of bills?"

"I am an attorney for certain clients and look out for their interests before the legislature. I am retained annually by the New York, New Haven and Hartford Railroad Company, and am usually spoken of as 'of counsel' for that road. Of course, I don't have anything to do with damage suits or matters in relation to grade crossing. As everyone knows, I act for the Rhode Island Company (street-railway interests), and I have been retained in certain cases by the Providence Telephone Company. In addition to these I have had connections, not permanent, with various companies desiring franchises, charters, and things of that sort from the legislature. I never solicit any business," added General Brayton, without a smile. "It all comes to me unsought, and if I can handle it I accept the retainer."

"What is your power in the legislature that enables you to serve your clients?"

"Well, you see, in managing the campaign every year I am in a position to be of service to men all over the state. I help them to get elected, and, naturally, many warm friendships result, then when they are in a position to repay me they are glad to do it."

The elected governors of Rhode Island are called "administrative mummies." They have sat for years without power and without homage in the state-house, while across the hall, in the office of the High Sheriff, Boss Brayton was the state. He directed the General Assembly. His word was law. He did not have to "dicker, trade, and buy," there was no "addition, division, and silence" for him. He handled the campaign funds of "the party," and with them the voters were bought at the polls. The legislator returned by the electors came bought. When the time for local caucuses was approaching, the party leaders came down to Providence to get money for expenses from Brayton.

"How much do you think you will need?" he would ask.
"Oh, say $500."
"Five hundred dollars to carry that town! Who's your man for senator?"

The leader would tell him. If the local candidate suited Brayton, a bargain was struck as to the amount; if not, he would say pointedly: "I guess there isn't any money for you this year."

The leader then had to go back and pick out another candidate, or, perhaps, Brayton would give him a suggestion which the "other fellows" would have to "agree upon." At any rate, Brayton had to be satisfied or the party got no money for expenses.

When the General Assembly met he directed its labors, and his masterfulness is unprecedented. A good-natured, generous man, he adopted a cross, surly tone, which, alternating with kindness, made men fear and like him, too. Not at all vindictive, he punished severely as a matter of policy. If a member of the legislature disobeyed him, he would say, "That man sha'n't come back," and that man rarely could be renominated and reelected. He was very open, and hundreds of anecdotes are told to illustrate his methods. The *Springfield Republican* reported two, which are well known. Once, when the House of Representatives was in prolonged session, Brayton became hungry. "D—it!" he exclaimed, "who is that fool talking in the house? It's lunch time and past. Sheriff, go in and see that the house adjourns."

The house adjourned. Another time, this conversation was overheard between the angry boss and a most humble Repoblican floor leader:

"D—it, can't I have a little bill passed when I want it?" said the boss.

"But, General, I didn't know you were interested in that bill."

"Well, I am, and I want it passed right away."

That little bill was passed right away.

"Where's Senator —?" said the boss in his blindness one morning when he arrived in the state-house.

"In the Senate," said someone. "Get him," said Brayton. "Bring him here. I want him to lead me out to (let us say) drink."

Such was the discipline of a coarse man made peevish by too much power. The only wonder is that men put up with it. But Brayton could reward, too. He had "success" as well as "failure" to bestow. The General Assembly "elects" judges, sheriffs, and fills most of the offices in between. It is the road to success, and Brayton has made it a rule to send on to these higher offices, even to the Supreme Court of the state, men who have served him in the General Assembly, thus controlled and thus disciplined. The law allows legislators to serve as district judges while sitting in the legislature, and they do. The effect on the courts of all this is not for me to discuss (it is said to be "not so bad as you would think"). The effect on the legislature is to make it absolutely subservient to the boss, who really appoints to all these offices, and thus controls all the patronage of the state. More than that, he has business to give—business that is not political. It puzzled me at first to find that there was so little bribery in a legislature so corruptly devised. The pay of senators and representatives was small, and some of them served for years without the reward of promotion to the bench or any other office. The chairman of a most important committee explained it all frankly to me. There was some bribery, he said, but it wasn't typical. When he first opened his law office, a small corporation offered him $5,000, besides his fee, if he could put through the legislature an amendment to their charter. William G. Roelker, the senator at the head of the committee that would decide, said it should not pass. The young lawyer did not know Brayton, but he went to him and told him all about his business.

"I told Brayton," he said, "just how it was; that I wanted that $5,000, and after talking a long time to me, the General said he'd see about it; for me to come the next day. I went at the appointed time and Brayton was out. I was 'hot,' till a friend of mine came up and said my bill was through. Brayton had done it before he said he would, and when I offered to divide the five thousand with him, he nearly threw me out of his office. But he threw me into politics all right. He knew he was putting me under obligations forever; oh, he was shrewd all right. But wouldn't you go the limit for a man that gave you your first lift like that?"

I have heard thoughtful Rhode Islanders say that by such methods, by a cynical tone with young men and sneers at their college education and high ideals, by assisting them in "crooked business" and getting his corporations to employ the "good fellows" and ignore the "fools," General Brayton has corrupted more of the youth of the state than any man that ever lived in it—Brayton and his business backers—the men and interests he says he represents.

For Brayton was the front, not the head, of the System. Say what you will about the "boss," no one man can do what any American boss has done without the powerful backing of the "vested interests" of a community. Brayton had great personal power; he "organized" the Republican party; he systematized the corruption of voters; he chose legislators; he organized the General Assembly and ran it; he has gradually altered the government of the state. But he did not do this for his own uses. Brayton is not rich. He says himself that he took "fees" for legislation, but they were fees, not fortunes. The New Haven Railroad's annual retainer was only $10,000. His fee for an ordinary bill was $500. I know of one company that paid him as high as $1,000, but that was for a piece of legislation worth, in Missouri, for instance, at least $55,000. Like the voters of Rhode Island, like the local leaders, like the legislators, the boss of Rhode Island was cheap. "I often told him that," said one of his lieutenants to me when I had expressed this opinion, "and now that he is getting out, we'll raise some prices." Brayton was a bad and an able man, but he was a tool, and he realizes it now: "I have been the scapegoat of the party for twenty years."

Who are "the party" in Rhode Island? As I have said above, they are and they always have been the "leading business men" of the state. First the old aristocracy, then the old manufacturers, and Brayton's growl because they would not let him spend their bribery funds in their own towns is an echo of a past relationship. Then came the railroads, and the annual retainer of $10,000 is what the scientists would call a rudimentary vestige of their interest. After steam comes electricity, and it is the electric railway men who are at the head of the government now. For, as General Brayton explained to Mr. Lowry, he serves others "with the understanding that when their interests conflict with those of the Rhode Island (street-railway) Company, the street-railway people are to have first call." So the Brayton government is a business government. The cost to the character of the people of the state is heavy, but never mind; Rhode Island has what honest business men of this country have long honestly said we ought to have in all states and all cities in the United States, a business government—of the business men, by the business men, and for the business men. What have the Rhode Island business men done with it?

The old aristocracy, we have seen, drove the people to revolt. The old manufacturers sought a high protective tariff, and they got it. The railroads sought rights, privileges, and property, and they got them in the way they preferred, by bribery, not by a fair contract with the state. This is what Rhode Island's older business rulers did with political power. Now for the "trolley crowd"; what have they done with it?

They financed it. They organized it into a company which they are selling to outside capitalists.

"They" are Marsden J. Perry, William G. Roelker, and the Hon. Nelson W. Aldrich. Perry is the business man. He began life a poor boy, had some sort of connection with a theatrical show, till, entering the chattel mortgage business, he made himself a banker, promoter, and finally Rhode Island's first captain of finance. He is really an able man, dangerous, but only because he is spoiled by power. Roelker is the lawyer. Counsel to corporations, he was after money, and when they all got that he retired to play at Newport. Aldrich is the politician of the group. He also began life humbly, as a clerk and bookkeeper, first in a market, then in a wholesale grocery business, and in this he worked up to a partnership. Thus he was a business man originally—he is yet, for that matter—but business men in Rhode Island do not neglect politics, and Aldrich became alderman, legislator, speaker of the house, congressman, and, finally, senator. Having served it step by step, this leader of the United States Senate may truly be said to be a product, as he is now the supreme head, of the Rhode Island System.

There were others concerned with these three men, but they, representing the business, the law, and the politics of the state, conceived and carried to success a scheme to buy up, equip with electricity, and not only run, but finance, the old horse-car lines of Providence, Pawtucket, and, later, of the state. The first steps were taken in secret, but I understand that the plan originated with Perry. He was getting interested in public utilities and had put a lighting deal through the (business men's) city council of Providence. While he was thus in touch both with finance and politics, he had neither the capital, credit, nor political power needed for such a scheme as this. You don't have to have money for big as you do for small business; influence will do, financial and political "pull," Aldrich had both. As the highest representative of political power in the state, its senior senator should have been the man most to be avoided and feared. His duty, if he took any part at all, was to see that the interests of the state were protected. But that is a moral, not a practical view to take of business and politics. Aldrich, as the senator for Rhode Island, had gone to Congress as the representative of protected, that is to say, privileged, business. Indeed, it was as the representative of manufacturers of his state that he felt bound to make himself an authority on tariff legislation. And it was as such that the chairman of the Senate Finance Committee came in touch with Wall Street, the trusts, and the so-called moneyed interests. It was natural for a Rhode Islander to think of him for such business as Perry had before him. And Aldrich joined Perry; he became a partner in his scheme; he delivered Brayton and Brayton's System; and, besides the actual government of his state, Senator Aldrich brought, to back the scheme, capital from out of the state.

One of the explicit charges against Senator Aldrich was offered as an explanation of the scandalous campaign to elect about this time (1892) a legislature to return him to the United States Senate. It was repeatedly made by Colonel A. K. McClure, the editor of the *Philadelphia Times*, and never denied by Mr. Aldrich, who, however, says he never denies such things. Colonel McClure declared that Aldrich, as chairman of the Finance Committee of the Senate, added to the House tariff schedules one mill—worth $3,000,000 a year to the trust—to the duty on Sugar. "When this bill came to the Senate," said Colonel McClure in his Boston speech, "there was no open demand for an increase, but Senator Aldrich had a battle in Rhode Island, and it was a battle royal for cash. He had to be rejected to the Senate, and he gave an additional one-tenth of one percent to the sugar men, and the sugar men fought that battle in Rhode Island and reelected him."

Just as Providence people were wondering where the money for that campaign came from, so they wondered who the men were in the railway deal and where that money came from. The street-car stock was bought up at advancing prices, and Brayton's legislature was turning out bills to enable willing councils to grant franchises. Evidently they were powerful men, but all was a mystery till in 1893 the United Traction and Electric Co. was organized. Then Senator Aldrich appeared as president; John E. Searles (sugar) as vice-president; F. P. Olcott (Central Trust Company), treasurer; and Perry and Roelker as officers, directors, or stockholders in the subordinate companies; and the money proved to have been loaned by what is known in New York as the (Central) "trust company of the sugar crowd." The promoters issued $8,000,000 of bonds to pay for the property they bought and to equip it with electricity, and $8,000,000 of stock, which they divided among themselves, they and their outside backers, eight in all. But they were not yet through. Considering their inexperience in such business, Aldrich, Perry & Co. displayed unusual foresight. The scheme, still to be executed, was to gather practically all the public utility companies in and around Providence into one great parcel, "The Rhode Island Company," and, way back in 1891, their first legislation was a general act providing that any town or city might grant exclusive franchises. In 1892 the General Assembly passed special acts for such exclusive franchises to the street-railway, gas, and electric light companies. These franchises were to be for twenty years; they might just as well have had them for ninety-nine years, but it is amazing to see how often these public utility political business men all over the country have been satisfied with short-term grants. Apparently they thought only of a quick turn for cash. Perry, Aldrich & Co. made this mistake. It is said that they discovered it when they began to approach Philadelphia capital to sell out. Down there the captains of political industry had grants for 999 years, and they pointed out the defect in the Rhode Island charters. By that time it was almost too late.

Opposition was developing to this abuse of the powers of the state for private exploitation. The public, especially in

Rhode Island: A State for Sale   373

Providence, began to ask questions and make demands. These demands were very moderate, and they seem finally to have resolved themselves into one—for a transfer system. Now, any expert street-railway man knows that transfer tickets wisely given increase traffic and profits, but President Aldrich was not such an expert. He was a "power behind a power," and he declared that the company could not pay interest on the bonds and dividends on its (watered) stock if the transfer privilege were granted. The absurd public continued, none the less, to regard this private business as a public convenience, and the cry was still for transfers. The company, which had got so much for little or nothing (a graduated tax of from three to five percent of the gross receipts), seeing that it might have to yield, looked about for something to get out of the public for the transfer privilege. Why not an extension of its twenty-year franchise? A bill was put through the ever-ready Greneral Assembly providing that a new contract, for transfers, etc., might be entered into by the companies and the City of Providence "for a term of not more than twenty-five years from the date of such contracts." Thus was the franchise to be extended. The trick was seen, and the public, having no effective representation in any branch of the government, resorted to mass meetings to prevent the city council from entering into the new agreement. The city council, composed, mind you, of business men, not of typical aldermen, and elected by a restricted suffrage, was a part of the state System; it had been put up to ask for this bill; it had asked for it; and now failed to clinch the bargain only through fear of the extra-legal expression of the public will.

The next scheme appeared in an act (General Assembly, 1896) which provided for transfers at certain valuable central sites, which the city was to give to the company. This was no more preposterous than giving away miles of streets, but the public, again by sheer indignation, beat its own government. The transfer controversy went on for years, till 1902, and then the legislature required the company to give transfers, but only so long as five-cent fares were paid. The agitation for three-cent fares had arisen in other places, and the Rhode Island Company, under the guise of giving "free transfers," fixed the fare at a nickel forever. That was the purpose of the act. And the effect of the "free transfers" was a sudden upward leap of earnings!

Meanwhile the company had been extending its lines, procuring franchises, privileges and unlimited rights in all the cities and towns that it cared to "tap." I know no councils so "respectable" and I know few grants more ridiculous in their terms. That of Bristol, which is typical, gives the company every license, excepting that it is subject to police and health regulations which the town authorities shall prescribe. This sounds almost "socialistic" in Rhode Island, but a characteristic clause is added: "with the consent of the company."

But Aldrich, Perry & Co. were in this business to sell out, and they had to have a perpetual franchise. They got it, and the act by which they got it is the "smartest" piece of legislation that I know of anywhere. "An act to increase the revenues of the state" is the title. The company, having failed to pay to the city of Providence the increased tax due, was being annoyed by public clamor, and irresponsible persons were beginning to take up the franchise tax notion. To head off all such dangerous radicalism once and forever, the company's legislature put a state tax of one percent on the gross earnings of all street-railway companies, this to be "in lieu and satisfaction of all other taxes, excises, burthens, or impositions by or under the authority of the state." As in the Bristol franchises, as in the Providence transfer act, as in practically all such corporation legislation in this state, the law, however, was to become binding only when each company had given its consent.

But all this is by the way. The masterpiece of legislative treason—for it is no less—in this act, is the rest of this consent clause; which says that when the company has agreed, the act "shall be binding and in full force between the state and such assenting company, and shall not be altered or amended without the consent of both parties." Governor Garvin characterized this as an "irrepealable law." It is a contract between United States Senator Aldrich as the state and President Nelson W. Aldrich of the street railway company, by which, without the consent of his company, his state cannot tax his company or alter or take back its franchise. It passed, and is believed by the company to be what Boss Brayton calls it, a "perpetual franchise."

With this legislation, these remarkable men passed for themselves also a charter, a sort of onmibus grant to lease, buy, etc., etc., all gas, electric light, street-railway, etc., etc., corporations in the state. This also was irrepealable, unlimited, etc., etc.; it was for a company to "hold" the public utilities in the state, and the name thereof was, fittingly, the Rhode Island Company. Even Pennsylvania capital could ask no more than the Rhode Island captains of industry, politics, and law had to offer, and the deal was going through when a gross error was made.

There had been some outcry at the doings of the legislature of 1902, and to pacify the workingman a ten-hour law was enacted for street-railway conductors and motor-men. The company consented and notice was posted on the car barns. Suddenly the notice came down, and Aldrich resigned the presidency of the company. It is understood that the "Philadelphia folks kicked; said they'd agreed to buy an eleven-hour road, and they wouldn't take a ten-hour road." The law was mandatory, but that didn't matter to the Rhode Island Company. They refused to obey the law. There was a strike. The men "had recourse to lawlessness," especially in Pawtucket. This was anarchy. The company was breaking a law itself, but that wasn't anarchy. Anarchy arises where other people break laws and injure my property. The company demanded police protection, such police protection as it had in Providence, where the state controlled the city police. Not satisfied with the conduct of the Pawtucket police, they had deputy sheriffs appointed and the militia called out to enforce the law (against the men). Thus the company won the strike, but the law that caused it stood. The courts were asked to declare it unconstitutional, but the courts could not see it so, and the company was in a bad fix. It was not without resources, however. Rhode Island has among its other preposterous institutions a post-election session of the legislature. The General Assembly meets in the winter, and having done all it dares, adjourns till after election day in the fall; then the expiring body, no longer answerable at the polls, does what the "power behind the power" directs. After the election of 1902 the General Assembly which had passed it unanimously killed that ten-hour law and threatened to take from the city and give to the state the control of the Pawtucket police!

Aldrich, Perry & Co. were in a position now to proceed with their business, and they moved fast. We need not follow them. It was all a matter of high finance. By a complicated process of stock transfers, leases (for 999 years), and "sales," all among themselves, but through the medium of several underlying operating and holding companies, they managed to develop a total capitalization of $39,160,200, while they still left the control of the property in the Rhode Island Company, with a capital of $2,000,000. Perry is president of this company, but the famous U. G. I. (the United Gas Improvement Co.) of Philadelphia owns it. What the promoter's profits are I can't reckon, and the brokers to whom I applied in Providence declared they couldn't; they said they didn't understand it all. This much is certain, however: Aldrich, Perry, and Roelker made fortunes out of it.

They made these fortunes out of their political power, but, as one of their defenders said, they did it without breaking a law or committing a crime. But how could they commit a crime? They were above the law. It was their law; they made it. True, they disobeyed the ten-hour law, but that was "necessary," and exceptional. As in Philadelphia and Pittsburgh, the System was so perfect that all they had to do, if they wished to commit a wrong, was to pass a law to make it right. This might take time, but wherever they could afford the time, they were patient. See how they waited, three or four years, for the irrepealable law that gave them their perpetual franchises! Of course, they abused the law; they abused their legislative powers in the General Assembly, but they did this in the interest of business. "This is a business country, and the government is there to help business." Is it? An ex-official of the United state Treasury Department, who now is a prominent banker, said that to me once, and it is a common view taken by business men of the corruption of government in the interest of business. But is that what "the government is there for"? I think not. I think that it is this legitimate, business graft, not police blackmail, which is the chief cause of our political corruption, but this is no place for "academic" reflections. The point is that this must be the view taken of political power by Marsden J. Perry, one of the typical captains of industry of the United States, and by Nelson W. Aldrich, the head of a state and of the United States Senate. Let us say, however, that because the chosen people of Rhode Island sold out at from $5 to $25 a vote the sovereign power of the state, their financial and political representative had a right to sell a part of that power to outside capital for some $40,000,000.

The next question is, what did they do with the rest of their power? They ruled; how did they rule? Suppose that it was right for them to rule and, ruling, to grant themselves extraordinary privileges. We hear that we cannot have the services in politics and government of able business men without paying for it. Let us put this forty millions down as fair pay for the privilege Rhode Island had of being governed by the ablest business men in the state. What have the business rulers of Rhode Island given in return? The old manufacturers, having got what they wanted, a protective tariff, gave loyal allegiance to—what? To the state, to the United States? No, to "the party," to the Republican party. They let Brayton do as he pleased with the state. So with the railroad. The New York, New Haven and Hartford has "about all that it wants," but for "protection" in those bribe-bought rights, for license to break or "beat the law," it supports the System. That is the way it continues to pay the people of the state, by helping to keep the state corrupt.

And as for the Aldrich-Perry trolley crowd—their wants were very large and they were so exacting and so jealous that General Brayton often complained to his lieutenants about them; some people declare that the eleven-hour labor law was due to one of his revolts. And we have seen that he had to condition all his contracts for legislation with the understanding that the street-railway had first call. However, the street-railway did not want everything. What of the rest? Boss Brayton could do what he would with what was left. They didn't care apparently. And that was Brayton's business, to sell the rest. A man could go to Rhode Island and, if he respected the rights of the trolley crowd, he needn't pay any attention to the rights of the people of the state. Rhode Island was, and it is, a state for sale. In other words, these business men's business government was a government of boodle. Having their "legitimate graft," they let the rest be held for sale to other business men who applied with—fees. Incredible? What else did General Brayton mean when he said that in addition to his regular retainment by the steam and electric railways, he had "connections, not permanent, with various companies desiring franchises, charters, and things of that sort from the legislature"?

Senator Aldrich declared to me, in the face of all this, that his government of Rhode Island was "good government." Now, he means what men of his class usually mean by the term: an administration, convenient and liberal to business, but strict with vice and disorder, and free from scandals and petty police graft. The senator does not know whether this is true or not, nor does he care enough to inform himself. He is an inordinately selfish man, so selfish that in all the time I spent in his state I did not find, even among his associates, a single warm personal friend of the man. And as for the government of Rhode Island, General Brayton summed up the senator's attitude toward that when he told Mr. Lowry that Aldrich took no active part until "about a year or two before it comes time for him to be elected again; then he gets active."

It is true that in some of the cities and towns of Rhode Island petty graft has been neglected. At one time or another this evil has appeared among them, but the small business men selected for the council of Providence, for example, by a restricted suffrage, have offended chiefly on the side of supine indulgence toward larger business graft. Just now, however, the trains are laid for the development of this wretched political-vice business there, and a man who has the confidence of Mr. Ferry, and is in the pay of Senator Aldrich, is at the head of it; his patrons may not know it, but I believe they don't care, for the same man is corrupting Democratic leaders and wrecking the opposition organization; getting it to put up tickets so bad that the Republicans can win. The Democratic city of Pawtucket is subject to the corrupt control of the Third Ward Democratic

Rhode Island: A State for Sale 379

gang in combination with one branch of the local Republican organization, and when a Republican leader of another branch pleaded last fall with the state organization to cut loose from this connection, the answer he received was "not this year." "This year" a legislature was to be elected to return Aldrich to the senate. The worst case of "good government," however, is that of Block Island. This ocean community has a population of 1,396, almost all descended from the sixteen original families that settled there. They always have had what they call a "king." The reigning king is Christopher E. Champlin, state senator and a "Democrat." But Champlin "stood in" with Brayton, and this is what Brayton's business system permitted Champlin to do to his own people in his own town: The chief business of the Block Islanders is that of hotel keeping. Champlin owns one of the largest hotels. Most of the traffic and most of the hostelries are at the eastern end of the island; Champlin's hotel is at the other end. Near it is the "Great Salt Pond," which the senator proposed to make a harbor of by opening a breach to the ocean. The United States Government said it was not a feasible scheme; the channel could be made, but the sand drift of the seashore would close it. The state authorized the town to undertake the work, the state to pay part, the town the rest with money loaned by the state from school funds. Year by year, fresh appropriations had to be made to keep open the breach, till the state had spent $129,123.90, the town $62,000. Mr. Edward M. Sullivan, a young lawyer whom Governor Garvin appointed a commissioner to investigate the situation, reported that "the harbor is used exclusively by excursion steamboats and island craft," for which there was already a haven. "Some local interest more influential than the demands of coastwise commerce . . . actuated those appropriations. The opening of Great Salt Pond was manifestly designed by its promoters, who are the principal owners of the land and its vicinity, to transfer the business center . . . to the head of Great Salt Pond. . . . Each of these appropriations was made in the closing hours of the session . . . and were not included in the appropriation bill of the committee of finance of any year. No report of the expenditure was made by the town council or the state committee . . . There has been no public bidding or competition for the work, which has been done throughout by one contractor," etc., etc.

Besides this work, Champlin received state authority to build an electric railway line between the two ends of the island. Champlin made the town borrow at four per cent, the money on which the road was to pay four per cent. The town pays its interest; but the horse-cars, which are all there is of the electric railway company, have never made any accounting. Also, in much the same way, he had the town vote a steamboat, which he ordered of such a draft that it could enter his but not the town harbor. The town passed the legal limit of indebtedness, and the citizens were worried, but Champlin "owns" the council of five members—his brother, his father-in-law, another relative, and two loyal followers of his. The "town" voted his measure, and it might as well, for if it failed to the legislature would. Brayton's General Assembly enacts special legislation so freely that I had almost forgotten to mention this absurdity explicitly. Besides the police of Providence and Newport, the state has taken the election machinery and many other local offices and functions from municipalities that have "gone Democratic," and where it has set up bipartisan boards. Republicans select the Democrats and thus use this power to corrupt the minority organization. The General Assembly, corrupt itself, is a corrupting upper council for every municipality in the state, as Block Island illustrates: A majority of the voters then declared, six years or so ago, under the local option law, for absolute prohibition on the island, but Champlin put through the General Assembly a special act permitting the sale of liquor on Block Island. Again, the Society for the Prevention of Cruelty to Animals arrested a street-car driver for driving the pitiful horses that draw the miserable cars of the Champlin line. The General Assembly passed a special act which prevented such interference by the society in this one town!

They will tell you in Rhode Island that Block Island is an exceptional case. It isn't. It is typical; on a small scale it is like the case of Providence. But suppose we grant that it is extraordinary—it happened, it was possible. Doesn't it show that if you or I should go to a small town of Rhode Island, get political control, and send ourselves to the General Assembly, we could do what we would to our town? If we delivered to Aldrich, Perry, and Brayton the things that are Caesar's, couldn't we have our Salt Pond, our poor little street-car line, and our great public debt? "Ah, but," they told me at first, "Champlin is a Democrat, and the Republican party cannot be blamed for his misdeeds." Champlin, the Democrat, was repudiated by his own party, and the Republican party took him up. He fought for his place in his party, and while he was making the contest for his "good Democratic standing," with a group of his own party for him, this man was the regular Republican leader in the Republican state senate!

    Both parties betray the common interests of this state. Political-financial, the System is bipartisan, too, especially in the Democratic municipalities where, as in Providence, certain Democratic leaders sell outright to the Republicans; or where, as in Pawtucket, the worst elements in both parties combine to graft upon the city; or as in Bristol, where they trade, the Democrats sharing the council and giving the Republicans the legislative delegation. Colonel Colt, the great manufacturer and financier, controls Bristol, and when he ran on the Republican ticket for governor a year ago the Democrats put up no legislative ticket. There are many exceptions among both "organizations" and leaders, but they are indeed exceptions. Generally speaking, the people of Rhode Island are represented only by individuals and they can do nothing but protest. One of these protestants was Dr. Garvin, but he was governor of the state and powerless.

    This country doctor is the most singular figure in American politics. A New Englander reared down South, he attended a Friends' school, and traces of all these influences are marked in his character. A single-taxer, an individualist, an advocate of the "popular intiative for constitutional amendments"—this sweet-tempered radical who has stood for every reform that looked in the direction of democracy, marched, unmoved by ridicule, abuse, or defeat, without a sign of anger or of pain, straight into the confidence of a majority of the voters of this conservative New England community.

When the slowly rising discontent in the state approached the height of a majority, the Democratic party nominated Dr. Garvin, and his party, with help from independent Republicans, Prohibitionists, Socialists—all the opposition to the System that usually scatters, voted for him. He was elected in 1902 and again in 1903. He was elected as a protest, however, and that is all he has been. He could not be governor in fact; Greneral Brayton was that. As we have seen, the gubernatorial chair never had amounted to much more than an empty honor for "safe men." No veto power went with it, and the appointive power was really wielded by Brayton in the interest of the machine of the System. A governor like Dr. Garvin would have made his own appointments, but Brayton and the System had seen Governor Garvin coming. They rifled the office before he got into it. When this Aldrich-Perry-Brayton company foresaw that the people might elect a governor to represent the common interests of the state, they had the appointive power transferred to the Senate. They left it so that a "safe" Republican governor, obedient to them, might seem to appoint, but not a "dangerous" Democrat like Dr. Garvin. The governor's nominations go to the Senate, which may confirm or reject or ignore them; and, if it ignores them for three days, this senate, constituted as we have seen, may proceed to make its own appointments. The United States Senate in its dignity is sensitive about the independence of the (upper) legislative branch of the government, and it is jealous of any encroachment by the executive. Its leader, Mr. Aldrich, comes honestly by his senatorial sensitiveness; where he comes from, the executive, representing a majority of all the voters, is something which the Senate, representing the System, ignores, overrides, and insults, and, as for encroachment, that is a sacred prerogative of the legislative branch.

Such, then, is the government of Rhode Island. Such is the System that has developed with a restricted suffrage, with the balance of power against the cities, with business men conducting both politics and government. What is the matter? What is the cure? The local reformers think that these very features which other reformers yearn for are the cause of the Rhode Island troubles, and that the constitution, "which did it," must be changed. A new constitution is indispensable to Rhode Island. Theoretically it is unjust, in practice it is tyranny, to maintain a government controlled by the purchase of twenty country districts which poll less than one-eleventh of the vote of the state. But the old constitution did not "do it." This instrument facilitated, it did not produce, the System, and a new constitution will not destroy it. Other states, with constitutions as ingenious as the best that the reformers in Rhode Island can hope for, have developed essentially the same System. The Enemies of the Republic will overcome any obstacle that is merely constitutional, legal, or mechanical.

The trouble lies deeper, and the cure must cut deeper. We have blamed our laws and our constitution long enough, and in turn we have charged our disgrace to our foreign population, to the riffraff of the cities, to our politicians, to our business men. And now, in Rhode Island, the American farmer is the guilty fool and his fellow-culprits are American captains of finance, law, and politics. Are they alone at fault? I cannot see it so. It seems to me that, in one way or another, we all are at fault. The provision of the Rhode Island constitution which lodged the dominant power out in the country, simply pointed to the farmer as the first man to corrupt; and he proved corruptible only because the strain came hardest upon him. His power should be spread out over the whole population, but then the pressure will bear hardest upon the political representatives of the people, and we know from other states that the representatives will sell, if there are offers to buy; and we know that the business representatives will offer to buy. And we know that we all will condone or submit, for some consideration—cash or protection, office or friendship, party loyalty or comfort. The best hope of Rhode Island, for example, should be in the leadership of the old manufacturing families, and the best of this aristocratic class have voted for Dr. Garvin. But would they if his office were not powerless? They told me, these gentlemen, that Aldrich did not represent them or their state. "He may represent our corrupt towns and your own New York," they said, "but he doesn't represent Rhode Island!" Yet Governor Garvin was defeated this year (by some

500 votes) because a Republican president had to be elected, and a legislature to return to the United States Senate the arch-representative of protected, privileged business.

Aldrich does represent Rhode Island, and that is what is the matter with Rhode Island, and that is what is the matter with Aldrich. And he represents the rest of us, and that is what is the matter with all of us. Rhode Island will have reform when we all have reform; when we are all willing to make sacrifices for the sake of our country and our self-respect; when the American farmer will give up his two or thirty dollars "pay for time lost in voting"; when the business man will be content to do a little less "business"; when the manufacturer will risk his unnecessary protective tariff (the graft, not the protection); when the captains of finance will be content with honest profit; when the clergy will face "the loss of their position" and "financial grief and ruin," rather than "be put under the ban of political inunorality, and forced to acquiesce in evil." The Republican hope of compelling the other fellow to quit "within the party," is stupid; reform within a party so degraded and so happy as "the party" in Rhode Island is impossible. The Democratic party may prove a good engine for the work ahead, but the notion of those of its leaders who think to restore pure, representative democracy by buying up the people for a year or two, is American corruption carried to the limit of Anglo-Saxon hypocrisy. There is no reform but reform, and reform begins at home—with all of us.

McClure's Magazine
April, 1905

New Jersey: A Traitor State

Every citizen who cares for his country, his state, or his city, should know the facts in this article. When we began to investigate New Jersey we thought we knew something of political and commercial corruption. We had charted some of its submerged depths but here we have found ourselves at times off soundings and the leadsman has reported no bottom. This is the longest of Mr. Steffens' articles and the most important; yes and the most interesting; this unrelenting story of sordid things. And if the reader feels as we do, how old, how intelligent, how sure the corruption of the state has been, let the truth serve to arouse a courage equal to the task ahead. THE EDITOR.

PART I.—THE CONQUEST

EVERY loyal citizen of the United States owes New Jersey a grudge. The state is corrupt; so are certain other states. That the corruption of those other states hurts us all I have tried to indicate by tracing the corrupt origin of the senators they send to Washington to dominate our national legislation; and there is nothing very exceptional about the senators from New Jersey. But this state doubly betrays us. The corrupt government of Illinois sold out its people to its own grafters; the organized grafters of Missouri, Wisconsin, and Rhode Island sold, or are selling, out their states to bigger grafters outside. Jersey has been bought and sold both at home and abroad; the state is owned and governed today by a syndicate representing capitalists of Newark, Philadelphia, New York, London, and Amsterdam. The offense which commands our special attention, however, and lifts this state into national distinction, is this: New Jersey is selling out the rest of us.

New Jersey charters the trusts. Now, I am not "antitrust," and I have no words to waste upon an economic discussion of the charter-granting function of government, state or national. Citizenship is my theme, the character of a "sovereign people" and the effect on the nation as a whole of the failure of any part—ward, town, county, or state—to do its full duty. And the point to fix in mind at present is that when, a few years ago, the American people were disposed to take up deliberately and solve intelligently the common great trust problem, some of the American people seized it and settled it alone; when the states united were considering whether to maintain the system of competition, which was called the "life of trade," some of the states declared for monopolies; when the United States was contriving to curb the growth of overwhelming combinations of capital, New Jersey, for one, sold to the corporations a general law which was a general license to grow, combine, and overwhelm as they would, not in Jersey alone, but anywhere in the United States. Maybe this was wise, but that isn't why Jersey did it. She not only licensed companies to do in other states what those states would not license; she licensed them to do in those other states what she would not let them do in Jersey. No, our sister state was not prompted by any abstract consideration of right and wisdom. New Jersey sold us out for money. She passed her miscellaneous incorporation acts for revenue. And she gets the revenue. Her citizens pay no direct state tax. The corporations pay all the expenses of the state, and more. It was " good business." But it was bribery, the bribery of a whole state; and it was treason. If there is such a thing as treason by a state, then New Jersey is a traitor state.

Disloyalty an Old Charge Against Jersey

Nor is this the first time she has appeared in that character. Way back in the middle of the last century public opinion in the other states was declaring Jersey a "foreign country," "out of the Union." In New York they spoke of "the United States and New Jersey," and Philadelphia sang a street song calling her "Spain." The grudge of those olden days was the grudge of our day: her "liberal policy" toward corporations. She maintained a railroad monopoly which exploited interstate commerce. It exploited her also, as we shall see, but her chief loss was her good name, and she was paid for that. states, like cities, have specialties. When I was studying municipal corruption I found that most of the big cities had near them lesser towns, to which the vicious could retreat when, during "reform" or other emergencies, the cities had to be "good." St. Louis had its East St. Louis; Pittsburgh, its Allegheny; Philadelphia, its Camden; and New York has had Greenwich, Hoboken, Jersey City, and now Brooklyn may play the part. What these retreats are to the vices of their cities, New Jersey is to the vicious business of the states—a resort, a commercial road house, a financial pirate's haven. New Jersey is the business Tenderloin of the United States.

And that is her history. From the moment the family of states was formed, the fathers have gone there to do things they dared not do at home; beginning with Alexander Hamilton. Every American child knows how this great statesman stole off to Jersey Heights to fight his fatal duel with Aaron Burr. He had gone there before. He had gone there on business before. He was the founder of the first great Jersey corporations, and his charters initiated the liberal policy of the state toward corporate business. It was Alexander Hamilton who discovered the uses of New Jersey. Lying undeveloped between two thriving cities, New York and Philadelphia, New Jersey, in the early part of the last century, was a barrier between the East and the South and West. How to get over or around Jersey was a national problem; as it still is. Geographical then, it is political now, and it has come down to us political and unsolved because the old solution was political. The geographical barrier was turned to commercial advantage by political power under the lead of Hamilton. He foresaw that the state was to be a national highway, and that the key to its control was the Hudson shore opposite New York. So he interested the governor, an ex-governor, a future governor, and other leading citizens of New Jersey, and they formed, in 1804, The Associates of the Jersey Company—to protect the public interest? Not at all.

Founded on the Hamilton Theory

Hamilton had a theory. He honestly believed that the people could not govern themselves. Thomas Jefferson believed they could, and he organized the Democratic party, which stood, for a while, for a representative democracy, a government representing the common interests of all the people, with special privileges for none. Hamilton, who led the Federalist party, held that, since there was no king and no nobility, the Republic must be built upon the grateful loyalty of a specially interested business class. Hamilton's theory has prevailed. It is a condition now in every state that I have studied. The Jeffersonian idea still lives here and there, as in President Roosevelt's platform, a "square deal," but wherever it is revived—in Wisconsin, Missouri, Illinois, or in the Congress—there is trouble. There is no trouble in New Jersey. Hamilton himself nursed the infancy of that state.

The great Federalist from New York and the leading citizens of New Jersey combined to have and to hold "the gateway of the continent" as private property, and Hamilton's charter not only gave his company governmental powers and rights and privileges, troublesome to the commonwealth down to today, it taught the "best people" to rule and, ruling, to use the state for private business purposes. The lesson was well learned. In 1830, when a railroad was projected from Camden to Amboy, the promoters, being pioneer railroad men, were doubtful of the success of the scheme; but they were leading citizens of the state, and they went to the state for aid and easy terms. Though the route chosen was the shortest way through Jersey from Philadelphia waters to a water connection with New York, they talked in modern terms of "developing the resources of the state," and the legislature of 1830, to which they applied, met full of popular enthusiasm to grant all that the company might ask. And this is all that it asked: a monopoly forever of the New York-Philadelphia traffic; exemption in perpetuity from taxation; a state subscription to their stock; and plenty of time to build. And they got all this. What return did they make, these leading Jerseymen, for the generosity of their own people and the substantial aid of their own state? Gratitude? Loyalty? Hamilton's theory is a modern theory; this question is a modern question; only the answer is old. These men made the same return to their state that such men so favored have made in our other states: political corruption. So far as I can make out, our privileged classes are not grateful; they are disloyal. The very favors granted them make our leading men enemies of the Republic.

The promoters of the Camden and Amboy foresaw what the people did not, that their monopoly was against public interest; that their exemption would become a public burden; that their success would tempt rivals into the field; and that the development of the resources of the state, which they promised, would make more railways necessary. To protect their precious privileges, therefore, they set deliberately about corrupting the state. And how they did corrupt it! Like the "best people" of Rhode Island, they bought the voters with cash at the polls; they bought the political parties with contributions to the campaign funds; they organized machines and reorganized the government, county by county, town by town, legislature after legislature. They nominated their men for office, petty and important, made themselves and their kind governors and United States senators; they ruled the state. They put the railroad above the state. With the fat profits of their state-granted privileges, they so corrupted the state that the government represented, not the people of New Jersey, but its railroad. It was a national scandal.

New Jersey became known as the state of Camden & Amboy, and that is what she was; and as such she was execrated and ridiculed throughout the Union. The railroad monopoly charged excessive rates, but it was a monopoly; there was no way around it. Canals and waterways were used; the Camden & Amboy fought, then bought them. Other railroads over better land routes were projected, one to Jersey City. When these were forced through, the Camden & Amboy forced leases and combinations, and with one of them acquired the majority stock of Hamilton's old associates of Jersey. Since the associates held the exclusive ferry privilege from all the available shore, the political monopoly was made physical; no other roads could have a New York terminal in Jersey, except by "making land" at inconvenient places.

The period that followed, down to 1873, was one of the most disgraceful in the history of the commercial corruption of American politics. The United States was growing, business was increasing, and the traffic had to pass over "the highway of the continent." Other roads had to come, and they did come. The new companies "made land," dug tunnels, crossed mountains—the physical difficulties were overcome in time; it was the political monopoly, the highwayman state itself, that held up the business enterprise of the whole country. Not that these new promoters were not willing to pay. They, also, were great captains of industry, and they went to Trenton with their pockets full of bribe money. Ask an aged Jersey grafter for the traditions of that time, and a lascivious expression of greedy contemplation will come over his face. "Those were the days!" The new roads paid cheerful blackmail to the Jersey legislature, and the Jersey legislators took money from "the foreigners," but they stood by the Camden & Amboy, which paid more. And the people of the state were with the monopoly. The people of the United States were back of the new roads, and public opinion ran high, but Jersey was grateful and loyal to the railroad that "made the state." Jersey had "state pride." She was a "state's rights" state. She had a few slaves, and leaned to the South; she is the one northern state that refused, during the war, to let her soldiers vote in the field, and so cast her electoral vote against Lincoln. The state that lets trusts do in other states what those states won't permit, and what Jersey won't permit in Jersey, was ever for herself and her own; and in the great "National Railway fight" you find her legislative (Camden & Amboy) orators appealing to the local sentiment against "foreign railroad companies which propose to use the state only as a convenience," and a "corporation chartered by Pennsylvania in which the state of New Jersey has no particular interest."

First Bribery of the State as a State

What "particular interest" had the state in the Camden & Amboy? Indignant public opinion in the nation asked and the newspapers found out. In lieu of all taxes, the Camden & Amboy

Railroad had arranged with the Camden & Amboy legislature in its charters that the state was to collect so much a head on passengers, and so much a ton on freight carried across the state on the road. In other words, besides the onerous charges for transportation, the railroad was to collect what was called a "transit duty" for the state. It was this discovery that finally enraged the national mind and brought down upon Jersey the old charge of treason referred to above. The "transit duty" was called by the press of New York and Philadelphia an "import duty." Jerseymen to this day are sensitive on the point. They declare, as Governor Randolph put it in a special message to the legislature of 1869, that the transit duty system was "either persistently misunderstood or willfully misrepresented by the citizens of other states." The Jersey reasoning is that any tax on a railroad is borne by the traffic, and, of course, this is sound. None the less the "misrepresentation" by the other states was just: the obvious intention of that transit duty, levied only on through freight and through passengers, was to relieve the road of a tax, and let the state take it out of the country at large!

That is New Jersey. That was the spirit of those old transit duties, that is the spirit of her modern corporation policy. Being that, however, being what she was to the Camden & Amboy, Jersey was sure, sooner or later, to let others in unto her. The business which builds a monopoly on political corruption, prepares the way for its own undoing. One by one, the Delaware, Lackawanna & Western, the Erie, the Jersey Central, etc., famous bribers all, bribed their way in, fighting the Camden, fighting one another, till, being in, they joined together to fight with bribery belated newcomers who came with fresh bribes. None of these roads, however, could compete for the New York-Philadelphia traffic. The Camden, reorganized as the United Railroads of New Jersey, held that fast, and a National Railroad Company which proposed to parallel the monopoly was held at bay, session after session, by the state of Camden & Amboy. And to what end?

Sold Out to Pennsylvania Capital

In 1871 the Camden & Amboy was "leased" to the Pennsylvania Railroad. The "leading citizens" of Jersey—a "specially interested business class," if there ever was one—had not only not been made "gratefully loyal," they had developed in the state a loyalty to their company, corrupt and sordid, but none the less grateful, and then they turned their favored Jersey railroad over to a foreign corporation, owned in Philadelphia, New York, London, and Amsterdam. Like the Rhode Island captains of industry and politics, those of New Jersey financed their political power and sold it—sacred charters, rights, privileges, property, exemptions, and all—to Pennsylvania capital, whither, apparently, all our curses flow.

New Jersey, dumbfounded, turned to rend the now "foreign" monopoly. The lease was attacked and a just tax was proposed for the road. The National and other railway promoters who rushed with fresh hope to Trenton, were cheered on by the state, and a general railway law to permit anybody to build a railway anywhere was broached. It looked as though Jersey meant to be free. But the "leading Jerseymen," who had delivered over the great Jersey railroad, threw into the bargain their old Camden & Amboy political organization. In other words, with the monopoly, they sold also their people, their state, or, the political machinery which held the sovereignty of the state! This machinery was somewhat run down and the sale had given it a bad jar, but the buyers were men who knew their business. Heavily owned though it is abroad, the Pennsylvania has always been managed by American captains of industry, and they know how to protect their stockholders against the American people; other American businesses have beaten them at times; the government very seldom. They are, and they always have been, masters of American politics. When the Pennsylvania went into Jersey, it went in with eyes wide open. It knew it had to conquer the state, and it did conquer it. The Pennsylvania Railroad completed the corruption of that state, perfected the present Jersey government, and, as we shall see, adopted for purposes of its own the charter-granting system which has produced, for example, the Shipbuilding Trust.

New Jersey: A Traitor State 393

Conquest of Jersey by the Pennsylvania

The conquest of New Jersey by the Pennsylvania was slow but exciting, and to a people once so swollen with state pride, now so meek under their state's humiliation, the story must be fascinating. Politically speaking, the state was Democratic. Now it is Republican. It was Democratic before and during the war. The soldiers returning home in 1866 made the legislature Republican for two years, but the state was only going back to its own when, in 1869 and 1870, the Democrats carried both houses of the legislature. The preparation for the "lease" was begun in 1870, and the legislature reflected the popular feeling, which was intense, against the "foreign monopoly." There was nothing for it, therefore, but to take control, and that is the settled Pennsylvania policy: not to buy legislators, but to own the legislature; not to corrupt government, but to be the state. So, while the Jerseymen in the proposed National Company were charging up to Trenton to get their charter, the foreign conquerors laid a plan to get New Jersey.

Buying the Crown of New Jersey

The first step toward getting a government to represent you (whether you are a grafter or a good citizen) is to get a party to represent you. The Pennsylvania plan was to buy at the polls the election of a Republican legislature, for 1871, to represent the Pennsylvania. That legislature would have to reapportion the state upon the basis of the census of 1870, and it could gerrymander the districts so as to hold the assembly for years. The Democrats nearly spoiled the scheme. Getting wind of it, they and the national undertook to anticipate the gerrymander with one of their own. This was "unprecedented"; but a bill was drawn and the Pennsylvania had to fight it with fire. The Camden machine owned some Democrats along the line of the road, and they bought enough more to beat that Democratic gerrymander in that Democratic legislature, even though the Democrats knew it might mean the loss of their power for ten years.

The campaign that followed was one of those tests of democratic government which go to show that the cynics may be right when they say the people can't govern themselves. The issue was plain—monopoly vs. competition—and popular sentiment was strong and all one way. Money was spent by both sides in immense sums at the polls, and voters took money from both sides. No one knows, of course, which party put up the greater amount, but here is the result: the anti-monopoly voters threw out the "anti-monopoly party," and elected a Republican majority to both houses.

The monopoly victory was so decisive that the National made no open fight in the next session. The Republicans had little else to do but to reapportion the state; and they did indeed reapportion it! I have come upon some interesting gerrymanders in the course of my investigations, never one like this. It amounted to a reorganization of government. Jersey City was a Democratic stronghold. This Republican legislature drew a district shaped like a horseshoe to contain almost all the Democratic voters, made that one assembly district, and divided up the rest of the city so that the Republican minority could easily elect all the other assemblymen. This is but a sample of what was done all over the state. That gerrymander made Jersey a national scandal again, but it "worked"; the Democrats could roll up a majority of 10,000 for a governor without budging the Republicans from the legislature. Nor is that all that was accomplished. The (Pennsylvania) Republicans legislated Democrats out of office, even down into cities and counties, turned local elective officers into commissions appointed by the legislature, transferred purely municipal functions over to Republican boards and so fastened the hold of rings upon cities, towns, and counties that stealing was overdone. Two cities, Rahway and Elizabeth, were run into bankruptcy. One senator who legislated himself into power robbed himself into prison. The ring treasurer of a third, Jersey City, had to flee with $60,000 to Mexico, where bandits robbed him. The evils were so great, indeed, that the next legislature (1872) had to send a committee to "investigate" Jersey City. The ring wined and dined and otherwise so entertained the committee that their report was a "whitewash," and, meanwhile, the riot of special legislation went on at Trenton. Governor Joel Parker in his message of 1873 said: "The general laws passed at the last session are contained in about one hundred pages of the Session Laws, while the special and private laws occupy over 1,400 pages of the same book." The constitutional amendment, forbidding special and private legislation, which the governor proposed, was finally forced through by public clamor, and a timely church raid (which I cannot stop to describe) upon the public treasury.

The First Pitched Battle

We must not blame the Pennsylvania for all this, nor the Republicans. The Democrats were "just as bad." The governor of New Jersey appoints all but two state officers, all law judges, and all county prosecutors of pleas, so that even when the corrupted people elected corrupted Republicans to the legislature, the corrupt Democratic "state Ring" had the state graft; and that was rich and exhaustive. The Republicans were compelled to resort to the local graft, and the Pennsylvania had to let them have it. As representatives of our ruling special interests have often explained to me, they have no time to rule well; they cannot be bothered giving us good government; it is all they can do to protect themselves. And certainly the Pennsylvania was fully occupied at this period. The National Railway people returned to the charge in 1873, with boodle in their hands, and public opinion at their backs. Both houses were Republican, but the Pennslyvania's system was not perfected and the Republican legislators were untried; corruption was at that low stage where "money talks"— not the campaign fund, but cash bribery. So you find the press of the day asking, "Do the Pennsylvania people own the legislature, or must they buy it?" The answer was that they owned it, but it was so corrupt that they had to buy it over again. They organized the Senate, but the opposition showed strong in the Assembly.

When the Assembly took up and advanced a National Railway bill, the state was in a passion of delight. The promoters had filled up their directorate with well-known Jersey names, and Jersey turned out to help these honest Jerseymen break the corrupt foreign monopoly. The monopoly men had a chance to deliver a crushing blow to this provincialism. Through the legislature of 1872, somebody had "sneaked" an act ostensibly for a small ore railroad up in Morris County. After it was passed somebody else had bought the ore franchise, and had begun to connect a lot of small railroads to make a continuous line from Jersey City to Philadelphia. A section of the act permitted this. The railroad Republicans, "called down" to Philadelphia, declared that that section was inserted after passage. Ordered to prove it, they produced evidence that a certain official had received $162,800 to put through the job, and that the money came from the National. The Pennsylvania cried "fraud," but public opinion would not credit such trickery in honest Jersey directors till the Pennsylvania took the matter to court. Just when everybody was rejoicing over the progress of the National's charter bill, a decision was handed down declaring in effect that there was indeed fraud, and that the National's franchise steal should not succeed.

    The Jersey public was prepared now to turn in disgust from the National, but, after all, as one senator put it, "while some of that crowd should be in state's prison, some of the Pennsylvania men deserve as richly to be there." So the fight went on. The assembly passed the National bill up to the senate. There a Pennsylvania bill, authorizing that company to occupy the disputed territory, was introduced. Thirty days' notice was required for such a bill, but the Pennsylvania appropriated a notice published for another bill. Senator Sewell (Rep.) confessed the trick; Senator McPherson (Dem.), besought his colleagues not to entertain such a suspicion. The Pennsylvania already was getting representatives in the Democratic party as well as in its own, and these two senators were for "the road"; they advanced "the Pennsy's" bill. There was no expectation of passing it; it was meant only to block the game. And it did, for a few days. Then a belief spread that the National's bill could be passed. Between bribery and the pressure of public opinion, certain doubtful members were "fixed to vote right." But where was the bill? The Senate called for it; it was not forthcoming.

The committee was asked to report. But the committeeman who had it was missing, too. There was an uproar, and the Senate demanded a report. Senators Sewell and McPherson, in defense of the committee, besought their colleagues to modify their tone, and "demand" was amended to "request." Then the Secretary of the Senate produced the bill from his pocket, saying the absent committeeman had ordered him "not to let it get out." Why? The Pennsylvania had bought back those doubtful senators, but hoped to save them the exposure of a vote. They did their best, but when the lobbyists saw that the roll must be called they stood behind pillars grinning. They foresaw the howl that would rise from the Jersey crowd, but they did not foresee the full force of the rage. The bill was beaten. There was a pause, then the crowd, yelling "Kill him!" rushed at one senator, and he had to be rescued and escorted to his hotel by a bodyguard of lobbyists.

Thus again the Pennsylvania was victorious, but the triumph this time was short-lived. The public was incensed, and the crowd at Trenton was reckless. The old cry for a general railway law was taken up. The sentiment for such a law had been so strong that the Pennslyvania's orators in the legislature had been using it all through the session, not because "the" road wanted to throw the state open, but to divide the National's forces. Now the National's legislators saw their chance to get even and to win. A general railway bill had been introduced early in the session; it had come from an obscure member and been consigned to obscurity in a "safe" committee. In the heat of defeat, the National legislators called for that bill. "The Pennsylvania want a general railroad bill; here they have one." So, with the sullen citizens looking on, this bill was passed. Some say the Pennsylvania had surrendered in a deal with its rivals; others that the road "couldn't make its legislators stand up." At any rate, it was without any open opposition from this quarter that the present general railway law of New Jersey was enacted—amid cheers, speeches, and the firing of cannon. Jersey was a free state!

How Corruption Wins When Defeated

Was she? Eternal vigilance, they say, is the price of liberty. It is, and the corruptionists pay it. When the good citizens of Jersey went home, the Pennsylvania went to work. Hence, the Pennsylvania came to rule again. When the people separated, having beaten one bribing railroad with another and opened the way to all bribing railroads, all the railroads got together to beat all the people. They had to. They had privileges and exemptions which were valuable, and against the public interest. Hence Jersey became, not free, but common—free only to the railroads, which had to control the government.

The Pennsylvania took the lead. Being a non-resident ruler, the company must depend upon the loyalty (to it) of citizens of the state. The long monopoly fight had served to test men, and the road used all its machinery, political and financial, to reward and advance those who had stayed bought, or, for any reason, had stood by it, and to punish and retire those who, for any reason, had stood up for the public. General William J. Sewell, the Republican state senator whom we have had a glimpse of speaking openly for the monopoly, was made "the" man. He was a "good fellow." An Irishman, unlettered, but able; generous, but firm; unscrupulous, but magnificently candid, he never made any bones about the fact that he represented "the road." He was an officer of the company. The head of a lot of subsidiary Camden & Amboy companies, he was the boss of the old South Jersey Tammany-Republican political machine, and under the eye of the "head offices" of the Pennsylvania Company at Philadelphia he extended his power until he became the recognized Republican boss of the state.

The Pennsylvania's Jersey Viceroy

General Sewell was more than that. As the representative of that railroad which was the chief source of corruption, he was a power in both parties. His policy was broad. He furthered business, especially privileged business; he encouraged all industry and enterprise, but his chief care was for those that wanted things, favors or protection, and were willing to help bear the expense of corrupting the state. All the railroads were in this governing class, and, though some of them were Democrats, they had so much in common that they exercised eternal vigilance together, i.e., let their lobbies and legislators labor together. For example, Miles Ross, the Democratic boss of Middlesex County, who represented the Lehigh Valley Railroad both in his county and in the legislature (till he went to Congress), was practically a lieutenant of Sewell, and politicians and newspaper men told me that most of the time the election of a Democratic governor and a Republican senate was the result of an understanding between the parties. They fought for the assembly, but even that was to be always "railroad." So Sewell became in time a bipartisan boss and the actual head of the state. That is to say, he, with United States Senator John R. McPherson, a Democrat, but also a "Penn. man," ruled New Jersey in the interest of the Pennsylvania and the other railroads and "business."

Under Sewell's guidance all went well in Jersey for a while. There were troubles, but they were purely political troubles, and we have little to do with "pure politics" in this state. Business prospered, and every American knows that business prosperity is all that men and government exist for. The Democratic state house ring was grafting on the state, and the county rings were grafting on their counties. Miles Ross was financiering his Middlesex; David Baird, Sewell's Camden lieutenant, was making his county pay; Garret A. Hobart was getting control of water, both for power and for life, up in Passaic, etc., etc. The railroads were grabbing water fronts down around Jersey City; the Lehigh had bought and was running down its cheap competitor, the Morris Canal, which the road and the politicians were turning, without a license, into a water supply for towns and factories. I cannot go into all the "enterprises" of this kind that show the beneficence of Jersey's business government in that period of prosperity and no trouble. One will have to do, an incident that illustrates the most points and leads us up to the second pitched battle between Jersey and her foreign conquerors.

By 1880, Sewell's government was so entrenched that both parties represented the railroads, to which both looked for campaign funds, patronage, and other favors. Some of the Democratic leaders showed a dangerous leaning to public opinion, however, and it was decided that the time had about come to elect a Republican governor, and make everything "safe and solid." This would take lots of money, so Sewell and his company looked around for a rich candidate. They chose a suburbanite, Frederic A. Potts, a "coal king" of New York City, with many corporation connections, and a director of the Jersey Central. To bring in the rest of the railroads, and to finance the campaign, Hobart was made chairman of the Republican state committee.

This was a combination of sovereigns, and the Democrats in alarm put up to break it a candidate who was expected to draw Pennsylvania railroad support—George C. Ludlow, a state senator who was a local attorney for "the" road. His nomination was forced, the campaign was a scandal, and there was fraud at the polls, but Ludlow was elected. Mr. Potts declared that the Pennsylvania did go back on him, and when Ludlow's majority proved to be only 861, innocent Republican partisans cried "fraud," and demanded an investigation. Their managers suppressed this move. The Republicans were in no position to investigate, and besides, the legislature was Republican, and the governor, though a Democrat, was a Pennsylvania railroad man. "Business" would be "safe."

Jersey Produces a Democrat

Much stress has been laid in these articles upon the number of corporation men who are promoted to high places in our government, and the regularity with which they represent their clients is significant. But the exceptions are also significant, and Governor Ludlow was an exception. When he became governor of New Jersey he represented New Jersey. His Republican legislature, with Hobart president of the senate, represented the railroads and the joint session, with "Gardner of Atlantic" in the chair, sent General Sewell to the United States

New Jersey: A Traitor State 401

Senate to help do to the rest of us what he was doing to Jersey. A flood of railroad and other business bills were passed, and Governor Ludlow could not stop them. He could speak for the common interest of the state, however, and he did, and in 1882 the Assembly turned up Democratic to support him. The Senate, made up, like Rhode Island, of twenty-one senators, one from each county, no matter what the population is, was controlled by eleven "rotten boroughs." So the upper house held Republican, and again the business bills flowed in. Among them were several (introduced by "Gardner of Atlantic") which separately looked innocent enough, but which together carried a deal. One was to enable corporations to increase their capital stock, another was to "file maps," etc. The first was to help one party in the Jersey Central to vote another out of control, and the others secured to the Pennsylvania a right, disputed in the courts at the time, to seize, hold, and exclude Jersey City (and its sewer-pipes) and others from a certain water front. The Standard Oil was in on this. This company had sneaked into the state underground, with her pipe lines, the railroads and the bosses helping her and holding up rivals. That was her way. The Standard Oil hates to go to legislatures herself, so she sends her railroads. She had property on the waterfront. The Pennsylvania had a branch to it. One of the little "niggers" discovered in this group of bills was a provision to exempt from taxation, etc.—this "ten-acre terminal," which included the Standard Oil property.

    These bills crept undebated through the Senate and were well on their way in the House, when their rottenness was discovered and declared. Then the railroads sent counsel to defend them and, with the lobby at work, forced them on up to the governor. Tremendous pressure was brought to bear upon him to sign them; the corporations demanded that he be loyal to them, his professional clients and his political creators, and they threatened to ruin him if he was loyal to the state. Ludlow vetoed those bills in a message that aroused the state. No matter. The Republican Senate passed them over the veto, and the Democratic House was doing likewise, when a member rose in his place and, waving five one-hundred-dollar bills in one hand and an affidavit in the other, announced that this money was half of a bribe of $1,000 promised him for his vote. To "peach" is against the most sacred rules of the game. The House adjourned. A committee was appointed to investigate. That committee heard one assemblyman confess that he had taken a retainer to deliver "three or four speeches" (including his vote, of course) for the bills; another that "Cul" Barcalow, the Pennsylvania's chief lobbyist, had dropped a remark, as he passed him, that it was "worth a thousand" to vote for the bills. So there was money in the business, but the committee reported that the lobbyist's remark was a joke (no lobbyist could mean such a thing seriously); and, as for the cash shown in the House, that could not be traced to a corporation. Nothing was done, therefore. But the "joke" and some sharp maneuvering beat the bills.

Governor Ludlow rendered his state a far greater service than this, however. Whenever a man in public office actually represents the public interest, he revives the Jeffersonian idea, and, as we have noticed before, that makes trouble. Governor Ludlow started the greatest trouble Jersey ever had. He was not a great man and he seems to have had no very definite policy. Like Folk in Missouri, like LaFollette in Wisconsin, and like Theodore Roosevelt now in the United States, whenever he saw an evil head he hit it. That is enough. That brings the special interests out into the light and raises the great question, Who is to govern this country, the people or the few who are corrupting it? It doesn't matter what the particular issue is—a revision of the tariff, a ship subsidy bill, the trial of a boodler, the enforcement of a liquor law, the just taxation of a railroad, or the regulation of railroad rates—let a man press any point that touches the so-called "specially interested business class" and he will arraign against him all the allied forces that are running the government—city, state, and nation—to get privileges from it and to protect those that they already have.

The Perennial Jersey Issue

The particular issue in Jersey is "equal taxation," and Governor Ludlow raised it. It was the underlying issue in the 'sixties, it is the issue over there today, it is the issue for which, principally, the railroads had been preparing all these years. They "had to." Every legislature from the 'thirties on that for any reason, honest or corrupt, admitted to the state a railroad with a charter exempting from taxation "all railroad property used for railroad purposes," made it absolutely necessary, according to business ethics, to help corrupt the government and keep it corrupt. That exemption was a valuable privilege, and it was a burden to the people of the state. As all those many Jersey railroads grew and prospered, the value and the amount of their property increased. They acquired more and more land, more and more buildings, more and more stations, and bigger and bigger terminals. Each purchase, grab, or extension of theirs removed just so much of the most valuable property from local and "equal" taxation. The cost of government increased steadily, of course; the railroads were careful about public improvements, and they permitted very few. But the corruptionists had to let the corrupted local leaders have some money to spend in (and thus appease, satisfy, bribe) their counties. So the expenses went on growing, and, since the railroads could not be taxed, the citizens had to pay; not only, mind you, to meet the normal increase, but the deficiency also, due to the growing railroad exemptions.

Charles L. Corbin, now one of the leading corporation lawyers in the state, summed up the situation at the time. He was explaining how it came about that New Jersey had such a heavy debt and so high a tax rate. It was not due, he said, to stealing. "Although scandalous defalcations have come to light in probably more than half the cities . . . the losses . . . have been made good by bondsmen. No expensive public works have been carried on. No governor of the state has found the cost of the capitol a painful subject to contemplate in his message. There is no state canal, no Brooklyn or St. Louis bridge, no Hoosac tunnel, no Tweed courthouse, to show for all the millions added to the debt of the last decade. I believe there is not in all New Jersey a city park of ten acres extent. . . . The people have been taxed to the limit of their endurance, in some cases beyond it, yet the burden continues to increase. . . . Should another business revulsion take place, the number of bankrupt cities would be greatly increased." After this picture, Mr. Corbin stated the cause: "More than one-fourth the property of the state is exempt from county and local taxation. That exempted property belongs to the railroad companies." Estimating at $250,000,000 the value of this exempt railroad property, Mr. Corbin showed that "the people of New Jersey were paying an annual subsidy of $2,000,000 to the owners of the railroad property in the state!" When Grovernor Ludlow showed himself a free man, this condition was brought to his attention by Mr. Corbin and other men who had been seeking for years to correct it. The governor urged the legislature to take it up, and bills were introduced. The legislature, with "Gardner of Atlantic" presiding over the Senate, killed these bills, and nothing was accomplished in Ludlow's administration. The question was up, however; the railroads had had to show themselves to beat it off, and with the scandal of "Gardner of Atlantic's" little bills, to illustrate the methods of the roads, the American citizen had the sensation needed to excite him to revolt.

Jersey was so excited in 1883 that both parties adopted platforms pledging their candidates to tax reform. We all know what railroad platforms are for; in this railroad state the citizens paid little heed to them; they looked to the candidates. A Jersey governor cannot succeed himself, so Ludlow could not run. The Democrats nominated Leon Abbett, the Republicans a judge on the bench. Now, I make it a rule not to criticise the courts, but some lawyer should—and the place to go first for the facts is New Jersey. The judges over there are not elected; high and low, they all are appointed by the governor. Business men and lawyers tell me that is the way to ensure a strong bench. Rhode Island does not prove this, and taking up one by one the appointments to the bench in Jersey, tracing the past records of the judges, and noting the decisions that bore on my work, I got somehow the impression that those courts were part of the Jersey system. As a layman, I asked corporation lawyers in Wall Street for their opinion, and I heard from them that the Jersey bench ranks among the very best state courts in the land. So I should say that "Jersey justice" offers a fair test. Whatever was found to be true there might be accepted with confidence as more typical than, for instance, the results of an investigation in Missouri.

Whatever may be said of the bench as a bench, however, I feel safe in this generalization: judges make poor leaders of a political campaign. They are not democratic enough. They seem to put too much faith in machinery, legal, political, social, and this judge whom the Republicans nominated in their day of trouble left it to the organization to make him governor, as it had made him judge. As he said, he "waited where he was" in dignified silence for the office and the people to come to him, and, while he waited, Leon Abbett, who went to the people, was elected.

Jersey's Best Man

Abbett had to go to the people. It seems to me that this most interesting man was an instinctive democrat, and would naturally have campaigned the state, county by county, as he did. But no two Jersey witnesses agree about him now any longer, and it is certain that when he ran for governor he was forced by the fury of the attacks on his imperfect record to fight on the stump. Besides the Republican party, some of the state house ring of his own party, and most of the big interests back of both parties, were against him. It is believed that the Pennsylvania's Republican machine secretly supported him, and he was an old Camden & Amboy legislator. But he was called a "politician," a "demagogue," an "anarchist"; and I find that "business" reserves these bad names for men who are brave enough to challenge and able enough to beat bad business; and that was Abbett. There was another charge against the man, however: ambition. His enemies said he cared nothing for the state; which was not true; or for the governorship, which was partly true. They said he wanted to be a United States senator, and believed that by taxing the railroads he could achieve his ambition. Here was the outrageous truth, I guess: Leon Abbett was one of those "unscrupulous politicians" who want, not money, but office, and who think to rise, even to the United States senate, by serving, not the special, but the common interests of the state. This makes the man interesting to all of us; his career was an experiment in democracy.

Abbett did tax the railroads. He did not tax them as they should be taxed, like other property, but there is an excuse for that failure. He represented the people; the legislature did not. The American people too commonly depend upon one man, the executive, to legislate for them; they neglect the legislature, which was meant to be the representative, law-making branch of the government. The result is such typical situations as that of President Roosevelt and the Congress today (1905), and of Governor Abbett in New Jersey In 1884. The president is urging a law granting to the Interstate Commerce Commission power to regulate railroad rates; the Jersey governor was for a law to tax private and railroad property on the same footing; both men were acting for the common against the special interests. Now, note the parallel of their experiences. Abbett had an equal-tax bill introduced in the Assembly, and it was called the "governor's bill"; just as the rate bill introduced in the House of Representatives is known as the "President's bill." Railroad men rushed to Trenton as we have seen them rush to Washington. Abbett had aroused public opinion, however, and the railroads could not make their assemblymen stand up. Like the House of Representatives, the Jersey Assembly passed the "governor's bill" with an overwhelming vote up to the Senate. That is as far as the president's bill has gone up to this writing, but, as it progresses, see if the parallel is not carried out. Public opinion in Jersey was such that even the senators were alarmed. They must do something. When the special interests see that "some legislation" is necessary, they always want to draw the bill themselves. So, the Jersey Senate appointed a committee, with John W. Griggs for chairman; hearings were held; the railroads appeared (United States Senator Sewell for the Pennsylvania), and they pleaded for the sacred rights of (their) property, and the inviolability (by the state) of their contracts with the state. In vain. Some sort of a bill had to be drawn. So the committee drew a bill taxing the railroads, not equally—they were to be put in a class by themselves—still the Griggs bill provided for a tax on railroads. Some of the railroad men objected even to this compromise—"Gardner of Atlantic," for example. But there was the governor's bill to meet, and the Griggs bill was introduced to meet it. There was a deadlock. The railroads used all their power, legitimate and illegitimate; the governor used all his, legitimate and illegitimate—patronage, vetoes, even a threat to veto the appropriation bills. It was no use. The Griggs bill might be passed, not the governor's. As the session drew to a close, the governor was persuaded to take "half a loaf"; the Griggs bill would increase by about $300,000 the revenue of the state. That was something. The governor consented to make terms with the railroads. In the current discussion of the president's rate-regulation bill, I notice that railroad men are saying that they would not mind the regulation so much if only they could have a "better," a "more expert" commission. That was the chief point in the deal between Governor Abbett and the railroads of his state. If the roads must be taxed, then the roads must do the taxing. If laws must be passed against special interests, special interests want not only to draw the laws, but to execute them. Abbett won the present railroad-tax law of New Jersey by making two of the four assessors (Pennsylvania) railroad men.

Some of the roads, left out of the final deal, resisted the law, but Governor Abbett brought them to terms. The Jersey Central appealed to the courts. There was a suspicion abroad that the law had been drawn to be ruled unconstitutional, and, when the Supreme Court so held, the comment through the state was rather excited. This tradition, still believed but unsupported by evidence, goes on to relate that the governor served notice on the roads that if the law was not upheld on appeal he would "equal-tax" them. Anyhow, the Court of Appeals did reverse the lower court and declare the law sound. Even then the Delaware, Lackawanna and Western would not pay; till the governor discovered that this road, so insistent upon its own rights, had not paid even the taxes it admitted it should pay. In a special message, the governor declared that the Delaware, Lackawanna and Western (whose president, by the way, used to put a Bible in each car) had scaled down the value of personal property and equipment, in twenty years, from thirteen to three millions, and that consequently it had cheated the state out of one million dollars. This set the legislature in motion to take away its charter, and the road offered to obey the new law. The governor demanded now, however, those arrears of taxes also, and, upon the decision of umpires that at least $300,000 was due, this "loyally grateful" corporation performed for once its duty to the state.

Wrong Road to the Senate, No. 1

Thus did Leon Abbett seize as governor the powers of the governor, and reassert the sovereignty of his state, even over the railroads. This, to get a United States senatorship. Did he deserve the promotion? He was not a "good man," only a "good politician"; he "dickered" and he "dealt"; to pass that railroad bill he used all the arts of his profession, save only cash bribery, and he showed himself not above that, for, having no money, he paid out public offices; and patronage is simply bribery which the public pays. So Governor Abbett was not the perfect man we are looking for to give us good government. Far from it; personally, Leon Abbett was as bad as William J. Sewell. But Sewell was in the Senate; indeed, it was Sewell's seat that Abbett was after; and Sewell had got it because he was bad. Why, then, shouldn't Abbett have it? What was the difference?

There was a difference, and that difference beat Abbett. What was it? I think it was this: while Sewell was bad in the interest of "business," Abbett was bad in the interest of the state. But let us see: there were other differences between these two men; Sewell was a Republican, Abbett was a Democrat. But Sewell's Jersey colleague in the Senate at that time was John R. McPherson, a Democrat. We have seen him fighting side by side with Sewell for the Pennsylvania in the state Senate; and all Jersey remembers a certain letter which a certain railroad man wrote to Abram S. Hewitt, a director of the Reading (the old National) Railroad, to warn him of a conversation, overheard at the Continental Hotel in Philadelphia, in which Sewell and McPherson were alleged to have agreed, since both represented the Pennsylvania, that neither should fight for his own party when the other was up for reelection to the senate. That is to say, when Sewell (Rep.) was running for his seat, McPherson (Dem.) was to let the Republicans carry certain doubtful districts, so that Sewell (P. R. R.) could go to Washington, and when McPherson (Dem.) was running, Sewell (Rep.) was to let the Democrats carry certain close districts which the "road" could "influence," so that McPherson (P. R. R.) could go back.

So long as the senator represented the Pennsylvania, the party made no difference; was it that? Not exactly. When now (1886) Governor Abbett was running against Sewell, the governor saw to it that the Democrats made a fight. One wing of the party, missing the railroad "backing," wanted to nominate a railroad man for governor, and, since the Jersey Central was angry, not only at the party for taxing it, but at the Pennsylvania for having "grabbed" for itself both "railroad representatives" on the tax board, the railroad Democrats suggested Rufus Blodgett, superintendent of the Long Branch division of the Central. Abbett, by making humiliating concessions to one of the state house ring, beat Blodgett, won the nomination for his man, Robert S. Green, and with "Green for Governor" the Democrats carried the election. They had on a joint ballot in the legislature a majority, narrow, but sufficient to elect a Democrat to the Senate—if the voting was straight. But the voting could not be straight, and Sewell had hopes. The excitement was intense, the scandal was sordid and loud. Some of the Democrats were purchasable, and if Sewell had had the solid support of his party, the "road" could have bought back his seat for him. But, just as the dishonest Democrats made Abbett's election doubtful, so some honest Republicans made Sewell's impossible. They would not vote for him. There was a deadlock. Reluctantly, Sewell had to give up. It was anybody to beat Abbett. The railroad Democrats sent word to the railroad Republicans that they were ready to unite, but only on a Democrat. The railroad Republicans asked for a list of three Democrats to choose from. The railroad Democrats furnished a list, headed by Rufus Blodgett, and the railroad Republicans took him. Thus was Leon Abbett punished by the System which sent Rufus Blodgett to the United States Senate.

Wrong Road to the Senate, No. 2

So any railroad man would do; was that it? Evidently Leon Abbett thought so, for, bitterly disappointed, he set about getting him a railroad. The Baltimore and Ohio, a great corruptionist at home, was coming into Jersey. Under the general railway law, it was free to cross the state. But a bridge over the Kills to staten Island was necessary, and the general law did not provide for bridges. The legislature had to grant a special permission to bridge the Kills, and the Pennsylvania and the other roads objected. The legislature was theirs. Abbett, as governor, had favored this further "development of the resources of the state," so in 1889, when the term of his friend, United States Senator McPherson, expired, the ex-governor went after his seat with Baltimore and Ohio "backing." Abbett's movements were very quiet, and McPherson had no suspicion of his strength till the Democratic caucus was about to meet. Then it appeared that Abbett had a majority. McPherson rushed forth to sound an alarm; the chairman was his, and the meeting was held up while the McPherson and Pennsylvania agents and Miles Ross "argued" with the members. Abbett's Baltimore and Ohio "strength" was soon exhausted, and McPherson (P. R. R. Dem.) was reelected to the Senate.

So a United States senatorship represented not only money, but the most money; and not only a railroad, but the sovereign railroads—the organized power in both parties of established vested interests. Was that the secret? That is the suspicion which I have gathered in other states, where it has seemed that the U. S. Senate must be made up of the representatives from each state, not of the people, not even of the state, but of the corrupt system of each state. This would account for much that happens in the Senate, and it is pretty clear that Leon Abbett saw it so. For this remarkable man, undaunted by two defeats, still pursued his ambition. He fixed his eyes on the seat Rufus Blodgett would vacate four years hence, and to win it the ex-governor proceeded with the organization of his political machine, the establishment of a vested interest, and the creation of a System all his own.

Abbet Gets Him a System

During Abbett's term and that of Governor Green the Jersey Democrats did what the Pennsylvania Republicans had done twenty years before: they gerrymandered the state. The grafters had long ago learned how, by dividing cities and towns into classes, they could evade the constitutional amendment adopted to prevent special legislation, and the Abbett organization now used their legislature to legislate the Republicans out and themselves into control of local governments. This was to strengthen their party, and, for the sake of the "strength," the local leaders had to be allowed to loot their localities, of course; a machine has to be built from the ground up.

But a machine, to become a System, must have a vested interest. The Republicans had made one that just suited the Democrats. It seems that when the Democrats, with their "anti-railroad demagogy," had won the plain people, the Republicans felt the need of "popular support." The Prohibitionists had developed a vote of some 20,000, which was more than the normal difference between the two parties. So the Republicans had drawn a local (county) high-license bill, which, with the Prohibitionists, the clergy, and the "good people" helping, they had passed through the legislature of 1888. The effect of this legislation was startling. It brought about "bad government" in New Jersey.

"Good" laws commonly make for "bad" government, and good people wonder why. They may see now. Before this local-option law was passed the liquor interest had not been very active in politics; and under the law, the people beat them county by county; prohibition was voted for all over the state. This satisfied the good people, and they retired from politics. But, just as governmental grants of privilege force good men into politics to protect their "business," so governmental prohibitions drive vicious business men into politics to save their business. The prohibition law aroused the liquor interest; as the people withdrew, the saloons entered the game; and while the good people were rejoicing over the "good government" victories in the counties, the "bad men" went out for representative government in the state. And they went about it in the right way. They wanted a party to represent them. Since the Republicans represented the "good" people, the "bad people" joined the

Democrats. Leon Abbett was the Democratic leader. They made him attorney for their Liquor Dealers' Association. He wanted to be governor again. He wanted the office, as before, only to get a United States senatorship, but they didn't inquire into his motives. He represented them, and that was all they asked; they backed him and his party. They elected a legislature, which represented them; the party was timid lest the people should resent out-and-out repeal of the prohibition law, so the high-license clause was retained; but local option was "fixed."

Now see how the good citizens played into the hands of the bad. Even after this victory the liquor interest did not go home. It stayed in politics. Leon Abbett had uses for it, and in 1889 it helped elect him governor again, with a legislature solidly Democratic for the first time in ten years. He was a changed man. He was a boss. Having learned (I understand that he said once privately) that by representing the people he could not rise in a government that represented railroad and business corruption, he had accepted the support of "criminal corruption." The cost to Jersey was terrible. With the liquor interest had come all that low following of vice that the saloons collect. These interests, by "work" and by fraud at the polls, practically controlled the legislature, which they turned over to the governor. They delivered into his hands all power: appointments, public institutions, the liquor licensing boards, the state militia, a state police, local and county offices and boards; those legislators even resigned legislation to him, passing his bills and adjourning with them in his hands to sign or veto, as he would. In return, Governor Abbett had to let the government represent crime and vice, and it did. That was the beginning of the race-track scandals of Jersey. There was a race-track at Monmouth, others sprang up, one at Gloucester for Philadelphia, another at Guttenberg for New York, and when the railroads (and the Western Union) saw that the betting vice made traffic, they encouraged the location of tracks in small towns along their lines. With the "sport" came gamblers, prostitution, and all that goes with racing and liquor politics. Jersey became a veritable Tenderloin state.

No matter. Leon Abbett, hardened now, sullen and determined, had a "vested interest" with him. He was pretty sure of election to the United States Senate, but to make doubly sure he reached for another, a more respectable, interest, the railroads. A group of these roads, the Jersey Central, the Lehigh and Susquehanna, the Philadelphia and Reading (and, is was believed, the Delaware and Hudson, and the Delaware, Lackawanna and Western), planned a combination to control the output and price of coal. Seeing that vice, not the Pennsylvania Railroad, was ruling the state, they made overtures to Abbett and his party. And since the Republicans had the Pennsylvania behind them, the Democrats were glad of the chance to get the other roads into their party. The "Coal Combine" bill was passed. The Pennsylvania opposed it, and the newspapers all over the country fought the new monopoly; but Abbett pushed it, and the bill, made a party measure, was put through.

Wrong Road to the Senate, No. 3

And all this also to get a United States senatorship! Did Leon Abbett get it? He did not. Then why not? Because he flinched; when it came to the final test he represented, not the System, not even his System, but the state of New Jersey. When that legislature adjourned, leaving in his hands that "Coal Combine" bill for which he had himself used the whip, public opinion, both in the nation and in the state, continued to clamor against it, and Leon Abbett, the demagogue, hearkened, hesitated, and—he vetoed the bill. This embittered the railroads and the politicians and legislators "in on the deal." They wanted to get even. He had, likewise after adjournment, refused to sign a race-track bill which aroused public opposition. This had embittered the vice interests, and they also wanted to get even. He was too powerful to fight while he was governor, and the Coal Combine which tried it and undertook to complete the deal without his sanction, was held up by his attorney general, taken into court, and, after a famous fight, was forced by a famous decision of Chancellor McGill to disband—till times were better.

But when Abbett, no longer governor, came into the caucus of his party in 1893 to ask for his reward, everybody "got even." All "interests" were against him. Some of them pretended to be for him, and there was money back of him; votes were bought for him; yes, that senatorship was bought as for him. But the money was not Abbett's own, and the men to whom it belonged, the men who owned the votes, cast them for James Smith, Jr., Abbett's right-hand man, and one of the lieutenants who managed his campaign for the senatorship. As for Leon Abbett, he soon died.

I often hear American citizens say that the national government is "all right—if only the cities could be governed as well." How can the national government be good? The System is all one thing. In every state where I have been I have noticed that the men who have tried to serve the state were punished. In New Jersey the pursuit of poor old Governor Ludlow is an oft-told tale; the failure of Leon Abbett is a ringing moral lesson to Jersey politicians. Both were made Supreme Court judges, but late, after their lives had been embittered and their failures plain. And as the System punishes, so does it reward. We have been in at the birth of several United States senators, so we can begin, if we are honest, to realize that that august chamber is the earthly heaven of traitors. But senatorships are not the only federal reward of—the System. We have noted that Hobart became a vice-president, Miles Ross a congressman; but let me give you just as I got it, for once, one of the impressions I am getting all over the country. Several times in the course of this story I have mentioned, without comment or explanation, a certain "Gardner of Atlantic." I did not do this to mystify; that was the way I heard of the man. Time and time again, after listening to some Jerseyman's tale of a bad bill introduced, a good bill held up, a railroad deal put through, or an effort of protesting citizens balked, I would ask, "Who did it?" Time and time again the answer was, "Gardner of Atlantic." The name meant nothing to me; I made no note of it and inquired no further, till one day in exasperation I exclaimed: "Who is this Gardner of Atlantic? And where is he now?"

My Jerseyman was astonished. "Gardner of Atlantic!" he said. "Haven't you come across him before? Why, that is John J. Gardner, the congressman!"

"Oh," I said, and, since I have in mind to study some day the national government, I put Gardner down in my long list of "gone to the House." But while I was writing these pages, the vote on the "president's" rate bill was taken, and I looked for Gardner. That vote was 326 ayes, 17 no's. Among the 17 was "Gardner (Rep. N. J.)."

Some of my critics have found fault with me, mildly, for seeking only the evil in men; others, much more indignantly, have said I looked too eagerly for the good and made heroes of men who palpably have human weaknesses. My criterion and that of my critics are not the same, evidently. I don't know what theirs is, but mine is simple. I ask of a representative, what does he represent? "Gardner of Atlantic" may be an honest man; he certainly has the courage of his conviction; but he is not "Rep. N. J."; he is P. R. R. I prefer Leon Abbett, defeated, to all the Gardners in Congress, because in his practical, compromising crooked Jersey way, he did sometimes represent New Jersey, and because, though dead and buried, he is still the livest Democrat in that state today. For the consequences of his career have lived on; much of both the good and the bad in Jersey can be traced to him, as we shall see, and, as we shall also see, the effects of his influence have spread all over the United States. Leon Abbett adopted the charter-giving policy of New Jersey. That hurts us, but Abbett didn't care about us. He was for Jersey. That was his great limitation. When the national press was imploring him to veto the "coal combine" bill, lest it put up the price of coal for the whole country, Abbett snapped his fingers at that argument. He vetoed the bill, as he said, because while he had made a bargain with the combine to except New Jersey and ensure her cheap coal, there was no way to make that exception binding. So we, the whole people, owe Abbett no tears. He was for Jersey. He was Jersey typified.

The live Jerseymen don't care either how much the Jersey trusts hurt us. They take the same view of them that Abbett did; they are good for Jersey, and they bless him for them. "But," they told me, a hundred of them, "Abbett gave us bad government." He did. He left his party machine so reorganized and so strong that in the next Democratic administration (that of a govenor named Werts), the legislature represented municipal and county rings and the race-tracks. William J. Thompson, owner of the Gloucester track, and better known as the "Duke of Gloucester," was an assemblyman from Camden; Carroll of Hudson was a bookmaker at the Guttenberg track; there were many more such men, but the character of that body may be summed up in this fact: the Speaker of the House was Thomas Flynn, the starter of Thompson's races. The race tracks could have any legislation they wanted, but they didn't want much. Abbett's veto of the bills legalizing all kinds of racing anywhere had proved of advantage. The governments of racing counties represented the tracks, and neither the police nor the local magistrates would enforce the law, which served, therefore, only to keep out more tracks and maintain the vice monopoly. They passed such as they desired, and for the rest they looted the state. These creatures stole the very chairs they sat on. This is "bad government." This is what your average American citizen means by "bad government," and it is disgusting. But it isn't dangerous. It is no more dangerous in a state than in a city, and as I have often remarked before, even Tammany in New York has seen that theft and police blackmail are bad politics.

The government in New Jersey was too bad. It was too bad to last. It became obvious, noisy, a stench, so that even "good citizens" could see and hear and smell it. They protested for a while, which is foolish; the grafters don't mind protests. By and by, when the race-track legislators fell to quarreling over the spoils and passed laws against one another, the scandal was such that the citizens were driven to the polls. They voted in 1893 against the racing rings, and their votes settled the criminal grafters.

Conquest of Jersey Complete

But what did they vote for? What could they vote for? The people of New Jersey had no party that represented them. They had to vote for the Republicans. This party represents the railroads and big graft, but when its leaders saw the people coming they nominated a "good man," John W. Griggs, for governor, on a reform platform, and they "exposed" the Democratic (petty) larceny by way of text for campaign speeches. Thus they "caught the honest vote," and thus, at last, the state of New Jersey was turned over to the Republican party, which delivered it up to the Pennsylvania Railroad. The conquest of New Jersey was complete. Governor Griggs was appointed attorney general in the president's Cabinet. General Sewell perfected his organization, and sent himself back to the U.S. Senate. He treated the other railroads "right";—the coal combine is a fact. The Pennsylvania was fair to all "interests." True, the race tracks were driven out, but the liquor men are quiet, prosperous, and contented. Even the "Democratic Party" is satisfied. There is graft, of course, plenty of it; for the most part, however, the corruption is orderly, respectable, dignified "business." That is bad, but it is not "bad government." The Pennsylvania rules and the government represents "the" road, the other roads, and some other interests; but the syndicate that runs the state for the foreign corporations gives Jerseymen good government, or, at least, what they tell me is "pretty good government."

"Oh," they say, "there are some passing evils in the counties, but in the state we have pretty good government."

"Good government" is the falsest beacon in American politics. I have seen the cities sail by it, and I know. New Jersey has sailed by it since 1895, and I think I can show in the next article that the "passing evils" the Jerseymen speak of in their counties are the vestiges of the wreck of their own citizenship; and that the "good" they point to with pride in their state is their share of the plunder of our business pirates who buy, cheap, her letters of marque, to prey not only on American business, but on American character, and, when caught at their crimes, sail for her ports to purchase cheap, legislative immunity from our laws. Jersey shows, plainer than any other state or city, how we are all betraying one another, and that what we Americans lack is what the poor Russians are asking their czar for—representative government; not good government, not reforms, not privileges, not advantages over one another, but fair play all around and, before the law, equality.

McClure's Magazine
May, 1905

New Jersey: A Traitor State

PART II.—HOW SHE SOLD OUT THE UNITED STATES

A SCHEME "to make New Jersey a Mecca for Corporations" was proposed in these terms to the governor of that state, in the summer of 1890, by a corporation lawyer of New York. There is no doubt about the man: he was James B. Dill, now known as the author of "Dill on Corporations." There is no doubt about the year, and, as for the season, "it must have been in the summertime, because the governor sat in his shirt sleeves." The only question is whether this was the beginning. It was—of the business. Jersey's liberality to corporations is as old as Jersey, and Mr. Dill was not the first New York lawyer to go over there with corporation schemes. Alexander Hamilton (1800) headed a long procession. But Mr. Dill did not know all this. He lived in Jersey, but he was a commuter. He thought he was proposing something new to Jersey, and he was, in a way; his proposition was to put the state regularly into the business of incorporating business companies; it was not merely to let business sneak over there for charters now and then, but to open up the state as a sort of wholesale charter factory and advertise the industry in a business-like way.

It was not a bad scheme, not as he conceived it. Mr. Dill was a young man. His practice was small; large enough to open his eyes to the troubles of corporations, small enough to leave him time to go far afield in his reading. He had been following a series of articles on the rise of business companies in England, and the advantages of the joint-stock arrangement over the old copartnership came to him like a discovery. Mr. Dill believed that what had reached the dimensions of a movement, almost of a fashion, in England, was under way in the United States. Why not promote it? Public opinion here was against "monopolies" and "trusts," but Mr. Dill was no theorist. He was a young American lawyer out for business, and he realized that the lawyer who had a hand in drafting laws favoring corporations could hardly fail to become an authority on corporation law—with a large practice. Just about that time many of our legislatures were passing laws to discourage the growth of corporations. But what did that matter? English legislation encouraged the business. Mr. Dill was a Connecticut Yankee, astute, jolly, energetic, and he set out with his scheme to pass English laws for American corporations and to make himself "Dill on Corporations."

New York Had First Choice

How? By writing articles, making speeches, and appealing to public opinion? No. Mr. Dill was a practical man. He went to the bosses. He put his scheme in shape and offered it first to the rulers of the state of New York. That was where his practice was, and that was where business centered. The New York corporation laws were bad—bad, I mean, for corporations; they were antiquated, complicated, and rather strict. Moreover, operations under them were subject to all sorts of "political grafting." Now, lawyers and business men are not unreasonable about paying for what they want, but they like "fixed charges," and New York had, and has, a most annoying system of variable taxes and miscellaneous feeing. From court stenographers and departmental clerks all along the line, through referees and assessors, up to legislators and bosses, it is tip, tip, tip—all the time. Mr. Thomas C. Piatt, when he was boss, simplified legislative business, but progress elsewhere always had been like a trip abroad; you needed a guide to tell you where to tip and when you were through. For example, a lawyer, lacking experience, was changing the name of a corporation. This was a simple matter, and he thought he had "seen" that all arrangements were made. There was delay, he waited, then inquired. The official said "it was all right, and everything would be ready in a few months." A few months! The lawyer drew the fellow aside. "I want those papers tomorrow morning," he said; "how much will that cost?" That cost only about forty dollars, but think of the bother!

When young Mr. Dill laid his great scheme before his bosses and mine he explained how all this graft would be wiped out. Taxes would be made certain, charges by the state would be fixed, and stated fees would go to named officials. It was beautiful, but it left the bosses cold. They could see the advantage to the state and to business, but they could not see, first, why they should deprive their officeholders of all the good old graft, nor, second, where the bosses "came in." New York has regretted this blindness since and has begun to adopt the scheme, but only recently and—late. New Jersey got it then.

Jersey at that time was opening wide to everything bad. Leon Abbett was governor. He was an ambitious man. He long had wanted to go to the United States Senate, and, to get there, he had, during his first term as governor, listened to a popular demand for a tax on the Pennsylvania and other railroads which ruled the state. The railroads were exempt, by the terms of their charters, from taxation, but when they pleaded the inviolability of those ancient charters as sacred contracts, this man, this politician, said: "All right, then, we'll tax these charters. If they are a contract, and if that contract is irrepealable, it is a pretty valuable piece of property itself; we'll tax that." Leon Abbett was an awfully bad man. The railroads beat him when he ran for the senate at the close of his first term, but he was so unscrupulous that, convinced of the impossibility of reaching the Senate by serving the people of his state, he set about building him a System. He organized the Democratic party into a grafting machine. He accepted the support of the liquor interests, of the race tracks, and even of some of the railroads. He had himself elected governor, and now, in 1890, the first year of his second term, he was making of Jersey a Tenderloin of interstate vice.

How the Scheme Went to Jersey

This, then, was the situation when our young lawyer, rebuffed in New York, looked around for some place to go to do what he was not allowed to do at home. He did not know Abbett; he did not understand the conditions in Jersey. He only lived there. Mr. Dill went to Jersey with his scheme, as Alexander

New Jersey: How She Sold Out the United States

Hamilton did with his, simply because the state was convenient. And Jersey received him, as she receives all, because for a hundred years she has trafficked on her convenience. The state gave the young successor of Hamilton a welcome commensurate with the price he had to offer, and Mr. Dill had a good price to offer. His experience with the New York grafters had matured the young man. He had come to realize that if he hoped to interest men in his scheme he must be able to show them where they "came in." About that time he heard how the secretary of state of West Virginia was in town, at the Fifth Avenue Hotel, where, with the great seal of his state by his side, he was displaying the liberality of his laws and selling charters—for fees. That was the idea. Mr. Dill seized upon it, and when he went to Jersey (in all fairness to the New York bosses this should be noted well) his scheme was immensely improved. It provided now for all; that is to say, for all, excepting only the United States.

But in this exception lay Point One of the scheme: With the United States as a nation of men and women up in arms against trusts, there was need of a state where public opinion was conservative. With "demagogic" legislators in Congress, and in most of the states, passing laws expressive of the public will, there was a demand for a state legislature that would enact the will of the corporations. With business men everywhere forming pools, and trusts, and gentlemen's agreements to break the law or to get around it, and failing because, though there were trustees there was no trust, and while there were agreements, there were so few gentlemen—with all these difficulties abounding in the Union, there was money in it for the state that would throw down her sister states and give a license to business to do business just as business pleased; lawfully, widely, with a legislature to defeat the general public will, and courts to compel private, corporate good faith.

Now, this is my statement of the case, not Jersey's, nor Wall Street's, nor Mr. Dill's. They hold that corporations are inevitable and good, and I don't contradict them. Mr. Dill says that he had in mind many small companies, not the few big trusts; he did not foresee all of the future; and I believe him, for he is openly against some of the recent developments of Jersey's corporation legislation. All that is maintained here is that the men concerned at that time in the adoption of the Dill scheme "didn't care a whoop" what might result, and what the other states might think, or feel, or wish. They were out for themselves and Jersey. Some of them told me so. But let us follow the facts.

How Jersey Received the Scheme

When Mr. Dill, contemplating his descent upon Jersey, inquired who the bosses were over there, he was referred to Governor Abbett. Mr. Dill didn't know enough, then, to be surprised that the head of a state and the governor thereof should be one and the same man. He was much more taken aback to be directed from the capitol at Trenton to the governor's law office in New York, but he went there; and there, to the governor "in his shirt sleeves," he showed how Jersey, by granting licenses to business to do what other states were trying to forbid, might become the Mecca of corporations and make an enormous revenue. Governor Abbett was interested. Leon Abbett was interested in anything that would increase the revenue of his state. That was the backbone of his original policy; that was why he had taxed the railroads and, by the way, the franchises of corporations also. And, as for the cost to the other states, Abbett was not the man to scruple at that. I tried to bring out in the first Jersey article how Abbett, with all his faults, rose head and shoulders above all other Jersey politicians in this, that he did, in his crooked, unscrupulous, Jersey way, sometimes represent his state. And in a nation where the average citizen is out for his own pocket all the time; where the average reformer is for his county or his city; where the noblest cry is for municipal reform; where good citizenship implies a willingness to let the states go to the deuce, if only local government is not too bad—in contrast with this sort of parochial patriotism, the appearance of a man who has a sense of the state, of a whole state, city and county and country, too, is a phenomenon. Leon Abbett was a phenomenon. But, rare as it is in these days, the state-sense is not enough; and Leon Abbett proves that. He was for Jersey; he was Jersey personified. Out of loyalty to Jersey, the selfish, her best man betrayed the United States—to help him get into the United States Senate.

Governor Abbett then, thinking only of Jersey and the Senate, hearkened to the voice of the young corporation lawyer of New York, who was thinking of the corporations and his practice, and there was no one there to think of the rest of us. Abbett saw that the scheme was good, but what more could Jersey do for the corporations? They already were running to Jersey for charters, and they were already getting all that they asked for. Then Mr. Dill displayed Point Two of his scheme; and for those states whose statesmen have asked me covetously how Jersey "got such a lead in this corporation business," let me say that this is the feature of the Jeresy policy to adopt, if they want to out-Jersey Jersey in the betrayal of the rest of us to the trusts. Mr. Dill explained to Governor Abbett that, while his state had liberal laws, other states, like Delaware and West Virginia, were liberalizing their laws, and that while the advantages of Jersey were known to the great captains of industry, the little captains did not know about them. Tobacco was there, and Standard Oil, the Chicago Stock Yards and Cordage, and Thurber-Whyland, and American Gas and Sugar; but where were the little fellows? What was wanted was a state that would not only open up its laws, but would advertise itself; that state would get the business which would go forth with business push, advertising and drumming up trade among the businesses that never had heard of West Virginia, Delaware, and New Jersey as dealers in lawful license. Now a state, as a state, could not afford, even if its officials, like the secretary of state of West Virginia, had the loyal energy to take up the work, to go out on the road showing its goods and advertising itself as the easiest, safest, and best shop for limited-liability charters. The thing to do, therefore, was to make it worthwhile for a private company, incorporated under Jersey laws, to undertake this part of the business. So Mr. Dill proposed to form a company which, for small but numerous fees, should advertise Jersey as a charter-granting state, explain her laws, vouch for her courts, attend to the incorporation of commercial companies, and look out for them at home while they were off doing business in the other states.

Interesting the Ruling Interests

The governor of New Jersey was convinced, but while he was boss of the state and the actual head of the system, he was not "the whole thing." He told Mr. Dill that he must see the secretary of state, Henry C. Kelsey, who was one of the old Democratic state house ring; nothing could be done without that interest. Then he must see Allan L. McDermott, the Abbett lieutenant, who was clerk of the Court of Chancery and chairman of the Democratic state Committee. McDermott handled the legislature, and nothing could be done without legislation, of course. Then he must see some Republican of influence, say, well, say United States District Attorney Henry S. White; for nothing could be done quietly without the minority interest. And last, but not least, Mr. Dill must see some representative of the Pennsylvania Railroad; the road, though not in control, held South Jersey and owned legislators. "You can't do without the Pennsylvania." So Charles B. Thurston, secretary, in Jersey City, of Alexander Hamilton's old Associates of the Jersey Company, which the Pennsylvania controlled, with all the shore front and exclusive ferry privileges, was added to Mr. Dill's visiting list.

The scheme provided for all these men and their interests. To Mr. Kelsey was shown how the secretary of state's office would get fees, fixed, regular, and small, but many and, in the aggregate, large. Also Mr. Kelsey was to come into the company. To Mr. McDermott was shown how the clerk of the Court of Chancery could double his fees and, besides, Mr. McDermott was to have an interest in the company. So, also, with Mr. White. To Mr. Thurston it was shown that the business, by increasing the income of the state and of her officials, would benefit the Pennsylvania and all other railroads. In the first place, the legitimate expenses of the state were growing. When they became a burden to the taxpayer again there would be another howl to tax the railroads. The railroads had just had an experience of that. It probably would not be the last. In the second place, the politicians would be asking for more and more money for political expenses, and, unless the state provided

New Jersey: How She Sold Out the United States 425

graft, the roads would have to meet that demand. The roads were there; they couldn't get away. They would have to go down into their own pocket, unless they could go down into somebody else's pocket. Mr. Dill's scheme provided somebody else's pocket; it would bring all the corporations of the United States into Jersey to pay her expenses, legitimate and political, and save the railroads from that horrid cry, "equal taxation." This line of reasoning won the Pennsylvania, and as for Mr. Thurston, who presented it to his people in Philadelphia, Mr. Thurston himself was to be taken into the company.

Jersey's Drummer for the Trust Trade

Thus was formed the Corporation Trust Company of New Jersey, which in its circulars announced that "we have a Board of Directors which includes Henry C. Kelsey, secretary of state; Charles B. Thurston, of the Pennsylvania Railroad; Allan L. McDermott," etc., etc. Governor Abbett took stock in the company, but, as someone remarked, pointedly, "Abbett paid for his stock, which is more than can be said of some of the others"; and his name was not used. The official, inside character of the company was sufficiently indicated by the other names, and hints like this: "Any forms issued by the secretary of state can be obtained from us without charge"; or this: "Our location, which places us in close touch with the state departments, having charge . . . will be of special benefit to those for whom we may act."

Lest we be unfair, let us proceed now very deliberately. This was a graft. This company was organized to graft upon the incorporating function of the state, and the state officials were in on it. But Jersey is a business man's state; business men and their lawyers have ruled it always, and the laws they have made permit a business man to hold office and engage in private business, almost any office and almost any business. An attorney-general may take a retainer from a railroad; while I was writing these lines the present attorney general, R. M. McCarter, was appearing in court for the Lackawanna Railroad; and so with prosecutors of the pleas (district attorneys); they frequently are of counsel for the public service corporations against whom they have to appear. In other states, as in New York and Pennsylvania, for example, officials in the public contracting business let their friends or their wives appear in their private businesses. In Jersey, the secretary of state could be, as he was, an officer of the Corporation Trust Company of New Jersey.

Moreover, this company, unlike political-business companies in other states, and even in New Jersey, was organized not to rob, but to help the state; it was to make its profits by increasing the profits of the state. As things financial-political go in America, the founders of the Corporation Trust Company of New Jersey were engaging in a singularly patriotic business. True, their prosperity was to be achieved at the expense of the other states, and it might be costly to the United States. But who cares about the United States? That is too big, too great, too grand and glorious to need care. And, as for the other states, Mr. Dill himself, in his recent address at Harvard, said that "the spirit of the charter-granting states is war, interstate war."

Again, we must not charge up to this company all the peculiarities of Jersey corporation laws. That would be not only unjust, but ridiculous. The story of those laws was told me by leaders of the Jersey bar without any mention of Dill or his company. The Jersey policy was a natural growth out of the character of the government and people of the state, as influenced by her neighbors, New York and Philadelphia. From the beginning of the last century, when Alexander Hamilton went over there and drew his two famous charters, for the Associates of the Jersey Company, already mentioned, and for the Society for the Encouragement of Useful Manufactures which preempted the water power of the Passaic River where it falls near what is now the city of Paterson—from that time on Jersey had been a resort for corporation schemes. She was a business man's government by business men, with lawyers and politicians for tools or agents, and the traffic in her special charters went on till in 1875 amendments to the constitution forbade special legislation. After that, when you wanted a special law you procured the passage of a general law, but the foreign railroads and the jealous Jerseymen were so rapacious that in a few years the Jersey legislature had enacted for special purposes enough general corporation laws to permit almost anything—in the way of business. Jersey lawyers go frequently to New York, and in the '80s, when the anti-monopoly agitation arose. New York lawyers and national captains of industry, worried by the law elsewhere, heard of Jersey and went there in such great numbers that, by 1891, a New York newspaper complained that "in the last two years 1,626 (national) corporations with an aggregate capital of over $600,000,000 have been organized imder the New Jersey laws."

Financial Raines Law Hotels

So when in 1890 Governor Abbett and Messrs. Dill, Thurston, McDermott, and their friends sat down together in New York City to perfect the Dill scheme, they were turning a wild growth into a cultivated plant; what had been a natural, subconscious functioning of the state, they raised up into an intelligent, orderly, definite policy. The business was coming of itself to Jersey; all that was necessary was to nurse it along and get possession of it for the state officials in the Corporation Trust Company of New Jersey. This last proved no easy task. At that time the national corporations with Jersey charters were what a New York judge called "tramps"; they had no domicile, no address in the state whence they were launched. They had to hold certain meetings in Jersey, however, so they used to sail now and then by ferry to Jersey City, or Hoboken, where they took rooms for an hour or two in some hotel. Taylor's Hotel, Jersey City, got most of this business. The Corporation Trust Company opened offices nearby. But (so conservative is capital) Sugar, Tobacco, and the others were slow to cross the street. Some of these "hotels" were vice resorts at night, but the trusts didn't care; they continued to use them for financial assignations by day. "We offered them a fine financial Raines law hotel,'" said one of my informants, "with bona fide, lawful sandwiches, but they stuck to their side-doors and the stock, wooden 'meals.' " It was not till the Corporation Trust Company passed laws requiring corporations to have "an office," kept open the year round, with books and an agent, and to hang out a sign, that the corporations were driven out of the hotels. And then the Corporation Trust Company and its branches did not get all the business. The men interested were so careful lest they frighten the corporations away, that, today, under the law, almost anything is "an office," and almost every bank, trust company, and lawyer in the state displays a tablet with the names on it of some corporations doing business out of the state. Most of this trade hangs around the ferries, however, and in Jersey City there is such a clustering of New York business at the Exchange Place landing that this place is called West Wall Street, and the Corporation Trust Company, which has now two or three rooms in a high building on the site of Taylor's Hotel, displays the "signs" of some 1,600 companies—1,600 of the biggest corporations in the world, whose "principal office" is here.

Before legislating for themselves, however, the Corporation Trust group legislated for the state and for the corporations; and the propaganda began at the same time, and very interestingly. Though the first bills were in the direction of sound business, they were passed secretly. The corporation tax had been fixed by Governor Abbett in his first term, and it was low and regular—one-tenth of one percent on the capital stock. Little had to be done to ensure an orderly, simple method of incorporation without any possibility of blackmail, but that little was done. Fees were stated; to be sure they were properly distributed among the inside officials, but the system was to be above board. Thus Dill's idea of giving Jersey an honest advantage over New York and other grafting states was carried out, secretly. Why secretly? Other bills put through were in the interest of corporations, but even these were for all corporations; they were not for some one or two special clients. They were for Jersey, to further the policy that was to enrich her. Yet, I was told: "The legislators did not know what the bills were for. All they knew was that each crowd got orders from its own boss, and, though some of the shrewd fellows remarked that all parties were for these measures, it was assumed that this was some private graft of the leaders; so they voted like blind pigs." Thus, then, the great Jersey policy was initiated, as a policy, by the corrupt Jersey legislature, in cynical ignorance!

New Jersey: How She Sold Out the United States 429

"But why were you so quiet aboat it?" I asked. "You wanted advertisement, and here was something done for Jersey; why not let Jerseymen know?"

"We didn't want Jersey to know till we had had time to prove that the policy was paying the state. Then, when the people felt the effect in their taxes, we knew there would be no kick from Jersey."

How We Helped Jersey Get Business

The other states "kicked," however, and promptly. I have quoted from a New York newspaper of 1891. Other papers took up the discussion, and before long Jersey's liberality to the corporations and her rush of business in charters was the talk from Maine to California. I remember writing myself some newspaper articles on the subject, and you, who read these lines, you may have taken your part in the discussion, too. But here is something neither of us knew at the time: that discussion was inspired in the interest of Jersey. The man who "fed the first facts" to the New York papers told me it was then and thus that the advertisement of Jersey's wide openness to business was begun. Our anti-Jersey anti-trust facts, our figures, and some of our thoughts were passed out to us by men who wanted corporations to come to Jersey for their charters. The System is a wonderful thing; it votes us, it buys and it sells us, and—it does a lot of our thinking for us. It turns our abuses to its uses. Our denunciation of a boss helps to make him a boss, by telling bribers where to go to buy favors. As we shall see, the Jersey drummers for Jersey's trust business have used in their propaganda every offensive act of hers, but, in the beginning, our antitrust passions were aroused against Jersey for the purpose of starting her on the road to become—what she is.

Well, and what is she? I have called her a traitor; let's see if that is too strong a term. Dr. Ernst von Halle, the German economist, says: "By the end of 1894 the federal government, twenty-two states, and one territory, had enacted anti-trust laws." He gives a review of this legislation, state by state, from 1887 to 1894, concluding with the observation that "the United States act was passed in 1891." We need not go into details. This is the point: we, the people of the United States, we're anti-trust. We may have been foolish, we may have been wrong; but in the period from 1887 to 1894 our thinkers were proposing, our legislators were legislating, and our courts were deciding to check the growth of great combinations of capital which threatened competition in trade.

That was the time when New Jersey said to the trusts: "Come to us. We'll let you do anything. You needn't stay here. Pay us for them, and we'll give you letters of marque to sail out into the other states and do business as you please. The other states have made your business a crime; we'll license you to break their laws. We'll sell out the whole United States to you, and cheap; our courts are safe and our legislature is 'liberal,' and our location is convenient."

Jersey's Spirit the Spirit of Treason

Do you think this is putting it too baldly? Listen, then, to a Jerseyman, who, from the politician's standpoint, is thoroughly versed in the Jersey policy from its formal inception. I asked him to sum up for me the spirit of that policy. "When it was being talked over," I said; "when you were considering how corporate legislation would profit you, your friends, your state, just what was your attitude toward the other states and the United States?" "To hell with the rest; what does Jersey care for other states? That was the attitude. Their loss was our gain. As for the trusts, we let them play in everybody's backyard—except ours. And, so far as possible, we fixed it so they couldn't be kicked out." It was in this spirit that, in 1894, when the Great White Spirit Company wanted to run a distillery in Massachusetts, and couldn't do it as a Massachusetts company, because Massachusetts law forbade the organization of domestic companies for distilling purposes, New Jersey provided the charter. Massachusetts had not thought to provide against "foreign corporations," so New Jersey set that distillery right down on the banks of the Charles River, and there it stayed until insolvency closed it.

New Jersey: How She Sold Out the United States 431

This is not war. Mr. Dill's word is too large. This is business. Massachusetts, with her strict law, created a demand for a loose law, and Jersey supplied the demand, cleverly, and for money. Jersey was smart. So we of the United States with our anti-trust laws developed a market for trust laws, and Jersey made them to order. That's business. Jersey sold us out, and that is treason. But what's the difference? There was money in it. Let's follow the growth of a few features of her law, and see how she did it.

How Jersey Made Trusts Lawful

The great companies which we know as trusts are so called because, at first, they were combinations of allied businesses whose management was put into the hands of trustees or pools. state and federal laws forbade such trusts, and business character (or, perhaps, it was human nature), was against them. The several companies broke faith; they gave rates or cut prices, so that between the law and the mutual distrust of trustees, pooling-trusts broke up. Thus, for example, the Standard Oil Company was dissolved by law, and all railroad pools of those days were short-lived. What was needed, therefore, to beat the law and human nature was a perfect, lawful combination. So the corporation lawyers who were steering Jersey legislation devised the "holding company," with power to own absolutely all its subsidiary companies. Starting from a decision of the Jersey court in 1888, that a corporation had no implied power to purchase and hold the shares of another, an act was passed in the next year authorizing directors to purchase the stock of any company "manufacturing and producing materials necessary to its business." This was not enough, and in the course of the next few years the clause was made to read, "manufacturing and producing materials and property necessary," etc. In 1893 this was simplified to let directors "buy stocks of any other company which the directors might deem necessary." And in 1896, when the corporation laws were revised and codified under a Republican administration, this section was broadened like this: "Any corporation may purchase, hold, sell, assign, transfer, mortgage, pledge, or otherwise dispose of the shares . . . or any bonds, securities, or evidences of indebtedness created by any other corporation or corporations of this or any other state, and while owner of such stock, may exercise all the rights, powers, and privileges of ownership, including the right to vote thereon." There we have the holding company, which makes the trust lawful and strong.

Again, the life of charters and the purposes of corporations were limited. The Jersey law specified the things for which a company might be incorporated, and after 1891 the list grew year by year till, in 1896, charters were made perpetual, and instead of a list of permissions, the Revision Act said any "three or more persons may become a corporation for any lawful purpose or purposes whatever," and then followed a list of exceptions. And this list of exceptions was drawn only to protect from the trusts Jersey and Jersey interests—banks, insurance, railroad, telegraph, and telephone companies. As Frank P. McDermott says in his "Pointers on New Jersey Corporations," "Companies for constructing and maintaining railroad, telegraph, and telephone lines outside the state are not within the exceptions."

How Jersey Provided for Exploitation

These and many other such laws were all in the direction of permitting trusts to exist and to stop competition; i.e., to become monopolies. But the captains of industry had other needs. They wanted not only to do business; they wanted also to exploit and finance it, and make money out of the operation. Jersey was willing. The next string of legislation was to enable promoters to buy up competing companies without paying money for them. They were permitted to pay with shares in the trust. In 1891 an act was passed permitting directors to issue additional stock, and another authorizing them to "buy property and pay stock therefor." In 1893, stock issued for property—that is to say, paid out to the owners of the purchased company—might be exempted from calls for cash, but it had to be marked. Later this last requirement, which embarrassed promoters who paid themselves in stock, was abolished. In the famous revision of 1896, all powers necessary to water and pour forth stock were rounded up in the famous dummy-director clause, which declared that "the judgment of directors as to the value of property purchased shall be conclusive." The meaning of this law may be brought out in a story Edwin Lefevre tells. When one of the great steel combinations was forming, a group of financiers, who had been buying companies in one city, got drunk on the train that was taking them home. They talked steel, and somebody suggested buying out a certain mill at a town on the way. They left the train. It was late, but they went to the mill-man's house in a hack and called him to the window. He protested in his night shirt that he did not want to sell.

"How much is your plant worth?" they demanded.
"Two hundred thousand," he said, "but it is not for sale."
"We'll give four hundred thousand."
"Not for sale."
"Five hundred," said the drunken financiers. "Six."

To make a long story short, the man finally came down to the door, went with them to a club, and sold his mill for several times what it was worth. The financiers sold it to their trust for twice what it cost them in watered stock, and then they sold their trust out to the United States Steel Company at so high a price that even Morgan quailed. But Morgan took it, and, as we all know, he sold it to us. All this was possible under the Jersey law permitting trust directors to put their own value on purchased companies.

To Sell a Business and Own It, Too

One more of McDermott's "pointers on Jersey corporations," and we may proceed with our story. Our captains of industry wanted not only to form trusts without the law and to finance them without money; they wanted to control them without owning the majority stock. Jersey let them. In 1891 she passed a law permitting stockholders to vote by proxy; the leaders thus could corner the votes. Another law allowed stockholders to define a quorum. Another gave directors power to decide the amount of dividends. And finally, in the '96 revision, stockholders could be classified, preferred and common, and unequal power given to them. Under this law you and I could organize a company with property worth, say, a million. We could issue bonds for that amount; bonds have no vote. If we then put out one million of preferred stock with no vote, and a million of common stock with no value but a vote, we could sell all the stock that the market would take and yet control the property. In other words, we could eat our cake and have it, too—which is one secret of high finance.

Bad Government in Jersey

The famous revision of 1896, referred to above as the culmination of each line of trust legislation, was a Republican act. The Democrats, the so-called anti-trust Democratic party, initiated the great Jersey policy which gave us the trusts. But that party gave Jersey bad government; the government that sold us out, sold out Jersey as well. Governor Abbett, who, to attain a seat in the United States Senate, let his party represent trusts, railroads, saloons, race-tracks, and local public service "crowds," disappointed the rapacity of these interests. Ambitious as he was, and unscrupulous, this "demagogue" was afraid of public opinion, so when his term expired they beat him, and gave the seat for which he had sacrificed so much to his lieutenant, James Smith, Jr., the boss of Essex County, and the largest contributor in the new public service crowd to the Democratic campaign fund. A representative of corrupt special interests at home, Smith was one of the four "Democratic" senators who helped the Republicans hold up President Cleveland's tariff reform bill till Aldrich got the sugar schedule fixed.

Thus Smith became the boss of the Jersey Democracy, and with Abbett out, Abbett's system went wild. With a weak man for governor and a race-track starter in the speakership (called the startership) the race-tracks and the liquor men, the trolleys and the railroads, got all that they wanted. Legislation was for sale. Cities and towns were thrown open to loot; public property, from franchises down to cheap furniture, was stolen, and vice and crime reigned. This was the era of "bad" government to which Jerseymen look back with horror. As they speak of those days, you would think that only the race-tracks, saloons, and vicious politicians were busy. Jerseymen forget that it was then that the big trusts and the public service corporations put through some of their worst legislation. The stench of the vice graft did not repel, it attracted big business, and such national concerns as the Standard Oil rushed over there, and as for the Jersey public service people, it was in 1893 that they put through as separate, unnoticed bills a lot of legislation which together not only allowed them to merge, consolidate, and finance, but to compel unwilling combinations by threats of parallel lines; and not only to take streets, but to grab turnpikes without county consent. Jersey was made a Tenderloin of vicious finance, at the time she was a Tenderloin of political graft.

Reform in New Jersey

But a change occurred. Jersey rose in revolt. The clergy preached; they threw open the pulpits to lawyers and merchants, and these laymen preached to churches filled with men who went forth and—voted. The Democratic party was thrown out of the legislature in 1894 and 1895, and in 1896 John W. Griggs, the first Republican governor Jersey had had in some thirty years, was elected to make the administration also Republican. Thus ended the Democratic government which gave to Jersey bad government, and to the United States—the trusts. What did the Republicans give us? That was the reform party in New Jersey; what reforms did it bring about? The race-tracks were abolished; the liquor interest was quieted; all criminal vice and crime were driven to cover. The most flagrant of the trolley laws were repealed. But the trolleys went on. They had the roads and streets; they got extensions, but noiselessly. They had their perpetual franchises and their consolidations. They got more, and they combined their consolidations. And, as for the corporation laws, which concerned you and me, they were not repealed. They were "improved." The Revision Commission of 1896 was appointed by Governor Griggs, and it codified, amplified—it perfected in competent, Republican fashion, the charter-granting business policy of Governor Abbett, the Democrat. And this was done with not only the whole country, but with New Jersey also looking on. The policy had begun to pay. In 1890 Jersey had collected only some $292,000 from her miscellaneous corporations; under the stimulus of the corporation-trust legislation and propaganda she gathered in $405,000; and by 1896 her revenue from this source was $707,000. This was good; good business and "good" government.

Good Government in New Jersey

Good government began in New Jersey in 1896—what Jerseymen call "good," and what most of us would call "good" if we lived in New Jersey. General Sewell, the veteran Republican boss, took charge. He was sent back to the United States Senate to represent us. Really he represented the Pennsylvania Railroad, but he was a broad, conservative business man, and he took care of all business interests. He rallied about him all railroads, all protected industries, all the public service groups. Democratic and Republican alike, and he was on friendly terms with the leaders of both political parties. To be sure there was corruption, but it was "good" corruption; quiet, orderly, in the interest of business. The clergy were not scandalized by it and the people heard nothing but rumors which no one could prove. The people were not represented, but the good people do not really want representative government; "good government" is their cry, and the Jerseymen who had that did not "kick."

There was some kicking in the United States. Business was reviving, and the Jersey trusts began to flourish. These caused complaints, but most of us took the advice of the late Governor Flower, who said: "Don't kick at the trusts; get into them." One loud political protest was raised in Governor Flower's state: The Albany legislature appointed a committee to investigate all Jersey trusts that were operating in New York, and that committee came down to New York City after the Sugar Trust. But the Sugar Trust put its books on a boat and rushed them over to Jersey, and Jersey, under the guidance of

New Jersey: How She Sold Out the United States

her New York corporation lawyers, drew up and rushed through the Trenton legislature a bill to protect her own. This so-called protective act is a remarkable measure. It says: "No action or proceeding shall be maintained in any court of this state against any stockholder, officer, or director of any domestic (Jersey) corporation for the purpose of enforcing any statutory personal liability . . . whether . . . penal or contractual, if . . . created . . . by the statutes or laws of any other state."

Here was a defiance to the other states. Put through in eighteen hours, with the whole country watching the "fight for the Sugar Trust's books," Jersey was not ashamed to be seen saving one trust from possibly just punishment for breaking a New York law; on the contrary, she took the occasion to announce to all trusts that she would save them all from all laws "penal or contractual," of all "other states." Her drummers, the corporation trust companies (at least two of them), sent out to their clients, the trusts, an identical circular boasting of the act, as follows:

"May we not refer to this as an instance of the watchful care which the New Jersey Corporation Guarantee and Trust Co. (ditto the Corporation Trust Co. of N. J.) exercises over the corporations located with it when we say that this act, the importance of which cannot be overestimated, was drawn by our counsel, was introduced at 8.30 P.M. of March 29, and by 2.30 P.M. of the following day was signed by the governor and became a law?"

The whole spirit of this "good" Jersey government was toward the indulgence of corporate business, and every step it took in that direction was advertised not only by our clamor, but by circulars sent out by her citizens to attract business to their financial Raines law hotels. I have a lot of these circulars stating the "advantages of corporations organized under the laws of New Jersey." They say: "You are not called upon to disclose the financial standing of your business, nor to make public the details thereof." "We (the financial hotel) attend to every detail, including, if you desire, the organization of your company, notify you of all meetings which you are required to hold and see that they are legally conducted." Again: "It is unnecessary for you to come to New Jersey, as the matter (organization and meetings) can be completed by mail." Again: "We have employees of this office who act as incorporators, who would sign the charter, complete the organization, and return you all the papers ready for the company to do business within three days." But there are some exactions:—"The statute requires one director to be a resident of this state; whom we will furnish if desired without extra charge."

A Resort for Tax Dodgers

No matter how great and good trusts may be, there is something disgusting about this. But these business rulers of this "safe" and businesslike state have gone lower than that. In 1898 they made Jersey a retreat for property that would escape taxes. Take the ease of money. New Jersey does not (in practice) tax deposits in banks and trust companies. New York does, and she requires all foreign corporations to make sworn statements of their balances. So the ferry landings in Jersey are choked with trust companies and banks which are agents of New York companies, and some rich men have little depositories of their own. If you are rich enough to be a tax dodger, you keep an account in a Jersey "bank." You deposit in New York in favor of that bank, and draw your checks on it, but the money comes from the New York bank. This practice is advertised openly in newspapers, and Jersey's "Raines law banks" put out timely hints like this: "The Comptroller of New York has fixed the 31st day of October as the day upon which the report is to be made to him for the purpose of fixing the tax . . . The amount of your bank-balance and the property you have in New York on that day will have a bearing on amount of taxes you must pay." That is all; but before such days you see boys going to Jersey with bags of money and securities.

Jersey is a state in business. The business men who govern her have turned her into a great commercial concern. Does it pay?

Her main line has paid well so far. The miscellaneous corporations, which netted her $707,000 in 1896, paid nearly a million in 1899; nearly a million and a half in 1900, more than a million and a half in 1901; in 1902, nearly two millions, and in 1903, $2,177,297.81. Her debt was wiped out. She is famous for her schools. She has the finest roads in the country; one-third of the macadam roads in the United States are in New Jersey. But listen to her new governor, Edward C. Stokes, summing up. He is a Pennsylvania Railroad man, so he includes the railroad tax receipts in his statement of the case. "At the close of the last fiscal year the balance in the treasury amounted to $2,940,918.98. The ordinary receipts for the year amounted to $4,302,370.61, of which nearly seventy-eight percent, or $3,351,543.69, came from railroads and business companies domiciled in our state. Of the entire income of the government, not a penny was contributed directly by the people.... The state is caring for the blind, the feeble-minded, and the insane, supporting our prisoners and reformatories, educating the younger generations, developing a magnificent road system, maintaining the state government and courts of justice, all of which would be a burden upon the taxpayer except for our present fiscal policy. To have raised last year, by direct taxation, the income of the state, would have imposed upon property a tax rate of nearly one-half of one per cent."

There is no doubt, then, about these profits. But goodwill is the greatest asset of a Jersey corporation. Is her own goodwill all right? Can she hold the business? Jersey is worrying over this question herself. This was what Governor Stokes had in mind when he wrote the passage quoted above. He sees other states getting the business away from Jersey. "The incorporations in one state last year," he says, "show a capital of $111,255,500; in another, $251,971,620; in another, $285,553,700; in New Jersey, $313,569,620." New Jersey still leads, but, says the governor of New Jersey, "our state is by no means attracting all the great moneyed interests seeking articles of incorporation."

Jersey's Business Falling Off

What is the matter? Three things are the matter. In the first place, while Jersey was helping trusts to wipe out competition, she could not create a monopoly in such legislation. Any American state can go into that business, and some have. Jersey is suffering from competition. Her example in betrayal was promptly followed by states that are willing to give lower laws at a lower price, and if the rivalry in lax legislation goes on at the present rate, the trusts will be able to get all they want, and Jersey may have to suffer with the rest of us.

The second thing the matter is that Jersey's trusts have abused Jersey's frailty and discredited her corporation laws. Those trusts which she launched so completely armed with indulgences for every thinkable financial sin, have come sailing back, as we saw Sugar do, for further dispensations and more power. A Jersey charter is a chip off the sovereignty of the state; it is what a constitution is to a state. Under her laws you could draw a charter distributing power and rights at will. You could disfranchise a majority of the stock and let the board of directors declare dividends, earned or unearned, or withhold them. In Jersey, you, not the legislature, made your corporation laws, and Jersey's drummers warned promoters as follows: "You can draw your charter as broad as you please; be sure to use foresight and care." Even after all this the Jersey trusts committed crimes or wanted to, and back they came for amendments to her laws to cover them. In 1901, United States Steel asked that the law which provided for a two-thirds vote be changed to two-thirds of the stock present. In 1902 it was back again for a special act to permit the conversion of stock into bonds which might be sold below par. This operation, Professor William Ripley, in his "Trusts, Pools, and Corporations" says, "betrayed a disregard of the principles of sound finance and even of common honesty and fair dealing with the stockholders." In 1903, Malting, Amalgamated Copper, and other trusts appeared at Trenton for a law to remove the liabilities of directors before the courts for crimes already committed. This was putting the state regularly into the business of selling, not only indulgences, but absolution.

These are but a few instances of what has developed into a large part of Jersey's business, and, taken together with such scandals as the Shipbuilding Trust, which failed, and the Franklin Syndicate of 520-per-cent.-Miller fame, which ended in prison,

New Jersey: How She Sold Out the United States 441

and other unfortunate Jersey companies, a Jersey charter was brought to mean to many men nothing but danger. No wonder, then, that James B. Dill now advocates federal charters, and Governor Stokes, to save the business of his state, recommends a revision of the Jersey laws "to safeguard the public," and "protect the stock-holders of other states."

The third thing the matter is, perhaps, the saddest of all. The betrayer is being betrayed. It was reported in Jersey while I was there that her junior U.S. senator, John F. Dryden, president of the Prudential (life) Insurance Company of America, was in favor of President Roosevelt's recommendation that the federal government take over the charter-granting function of the states. Two states, Wisconsin and Massachusetts, have objected to the Prudential's methods, so Senator Dryden, being a Jerseyman and selfish, might be willing to sacrifice the interest of Jersey if the United States would let him operate in two more states than a Jersey charter can open to him. But Dryden since has introduced a bill to put insurance companies under national control, and that may satisfy him. Her senator still may represent her. But her drummer is lost to her. The Corporation Trust Company, proving a good thing, was bought in 1902 by some New Yorkers belonging to the Equitable Life Lisurance crowd, and those men have broadened the field; they do business not for New Jersey alone, but, as they advertise, in all charter-granting states. Jersey's own original partner is in business for itself.

Abused by her progeny, the trusts; betrayed by the agents of her treason; outdone in self-prostitution by sister states, younger and more reckless in the business, Jersey is finding that her liberal policy was too liberal. Governor Stokes says: "The day of gigantic business combinations is on the wane," and to catch the smaller companies, he is urging legislation to "insure the faithful administration of the affairs" of business companies, to guard the "rights of the owner of a single share of stock," and "to remedy abuses." Coming so late, this sounds pathetic, and when you hear that Governor Stokes thinks that, at best, the business is good for only a few years more, you will see that there is something desperate about it.

But the trusts don't care what becomes of Jersey. They have got what they wanted out of her, and can go elsewhere now. Has her policy paid the trusts? Of course, the promoters have profited by it, but has business? Business men say "No." While I was working on Jersey I had to spend a great deal of time in Wall Street, and I heard this question discussed. The feeling of conservative corporation men can best be indicated by the proposition two of them made to me; one was the president of one of the oldest and cleanest corporations in the country, the other a corporation lawyer of national reputation. They said they would furnish the facts if I would write an article showing the methods by which some typical big corporations were being "wrecked." Why were they willing to tell? Because, they said, the financial licentiousness and the criminal corruption of the financial rings they had in mind were a menace to corporate and all other business. And their examples were all taken from Jersey-made trusts, or from the operations of men interested in the exploitation of that state which protected the wreckers.

Business men stand license no better than politicians. Having no self-restraint, they need the restraint of law, and having been placed by Jersey where they long have wanted to be, above the law, they find that anarchy, financial anarchy, is hurting business. So Jersey's liberal policy does not pay business? Whom does it pay? Not us, not the other states, not the United States. With millions of men holding watered stock in fallen or failing corporations, which have been robbed like cities, and with the President urging national control in the interest of business and fair play, that conclusion needs no enforcement. And, besides, "to hell with the rest." That is Jersey's attitude today; Governor Stokes is advocating other, higher principles; but strong forces are opposing him, and, to carry the state, he is appealing to Jersey motives, to wit: to save the business to the state. And, as for the rest of us, many of us envy Jersey. She is making money at the expense of the rest of us; she is trafficking in treason; but Delaware, Maryland, West Virginia, South Dakota and Maine are seeking by still greater liberality to get the trusts to come to them, and New York, Rhode Island, Massachusetts, and others would like to—because they think it pays. That is the

New Jersey: How She Sold Out the United States 443

American attitude. And the great American question is: Does it pay?

Let us go back to Jersey. Does it really pay her? Has she good government?

How Jersey is Actually Governed

The government of New Jersey is a syndicate. You have noticed, perhaps, that I have had little to say about individual men. The reason is that there aren't any. Since Abbett, the Democratic governor, and Senator Sewell, the Republican boss, died, Jersey hasn't had any conspicuous leading men, good or bad, on the machine side or on the side of reform. There are bosses, like Major Lentz in Essex County and David Baird in Camden, and there are reformers, too, but the bosses are local political agents of the controlling business interests—and the reformers are county reformers. Both parties take contributions from the business interests, organize the voters county by county, appoint candidates, and deliver to the business interests the sovereignty of the citizens in the shape of local and state officers and legislators who take orders like dummy-directors and deliver franchises, charters, and laws to the local, state, and national business interests that pay. The higher officers are representatives, customers, attorneys, or agents of the chief sources of corruption; they typically are business men, sometimes clean-handed, but they represent dirty money washed white in campaign funds and, instinctively, they stand for privileged business. The railroads, with the Pennsylvania at their head, and the so-called "Prudential Insurance—Fidelity Trust-Public Service Corporation" crowd, are the largest political spenders. Therefore they dominate. As between the Pennsylvania and this Public Service group, the Public Service is the stronger. The governor, Mr. Stokes, retired from a Pennsylvania directorate to run for his office, but both the United States senators, John Kean and John F. Dryden, are public utility men. This does not mean that they are against the "roads"; they are showing the Senate that they are "safe" for the railroads in the Senate. All the "rise" of these men means is that the public utilities are the more active corruptionists; the railroads don't want much more now out of Jersey, only to be left alone; they don't care to rule just for the sake of ruling. If some other business, not antagonistic, will attend to the government and put up enough money to keep politics corrupt so that any business man can get what he wants for a fair price, the railroads are glad to neglect politics. Now the trolleys and other public utility businesses are still building up their business In Jersey; they are extending lines, buying and absorbing plants, making contracts all the time, so that they have, anyway, to keep in touch with politics, and at the bottom, too, in the cities and counties. Senator Kean has some independent public utilities down his way, but most of the water, gas, electric light and power, and the trolleys of New Jersey are held by the Public Service Corporation, Thomas N. McCarter, president. This company was financed by the Fidelity Trust Co., Uzal H. McCarter, president. And back of the trust are the men in the Prudential Insurance Company, John F. Dryden, president. Naturally, when General Sewell died Mr. Dryden was elected to the Senate. He had never taken any part in politics before, and his election caused some surprise and some difficulty; his friends had to buy outright several votes for him—unbeknown to him, they say—but that will probably not happen again. Unless there is "reform" in Jersey, the next time he runs for the United States Senate, he will probably go through as the chief visible representative of the System. I say visible, because the Prudential has relations with the Equitable Life in New York City; and since the Pennsylvania resides in Philadelphia, the real seat of the government of New Jersey, the most selfish and provincial of states is outside its borders, and the state government, which so liberally has served national trusts, actually is governed by a syndicate representing national corporate interests. Is this good government?

Present Conditions in Jersey

When I first went to work in Jersey I was made most welcome everywhere, by good citizens who, aware of the corrupt conditions all about them, wanted to help me to expose—what?

New Jersey: How She Sold Out the United States

The charter-granting system by which Jersey was betraying the citizens and the sound business of the whole country? Oh, no, they said. That was all right; that relieved Jerseymen of their state taxes. What, then, the state? The Public Service Corporation and the Lehigh Valley Railroad were preparing at that time to abandon the old Morris Canal, and to divide it up, the railroad to sell off the water and the trolley to have the canal-way for a trolley line. R. H. McCarter, the attorney-general who must pass upon the bill, is a brother of Tom McCarter, president of the Public Service Corporation, and he was counsel for the Lehigh Valley; and the legislature is owned by the Public Service and Railroad lobbies. Did they want me to show up the state government which made them despair of defeating this typical scheme of despoliation? No, they said, the state was in pretty good shape. There might be some evils, but the government was in the hands of good business men, safe and conservative, and they had it in an excellent financial condition. Very well, then, what would they have me "expose"? Why, their county. "Do Passaic county," they said, in Paterson; "we are having an investigation here right now." They were, and the condition was rotten with petty, political graft. In Newark and the Oranges they offered me Essex County. "That is the center of the whole business," they urged. And it is. But Jersey City, bestraddled and hemmed in by railroads which paid her no taxes, and shut her off from the water with their ferries and terminals, which denied the city easement for sewers—Jersey City would have made an interesting article. At the other end of the state, however, there was Camden declaring, "We are the worst. We need exposure the most." Exposure! I have never exposed anybody or anything, and no exposure is needed in any American community. What everybody knows is more than enough material for me, and in Jersey everybody knows everything apparently. The trouble there is that such citizenship as they have is mean, narrow, local. Jersey in the mind of the average Jerseyman is a group of counties, and his concern, if he worries at all, is with the petty evils of his own sordid surroundings. My concern is for the other states that Jersey is selling out, my interest is in the story of the troubles she has caused me and you, not in the troubles of Jerseymen. I didn't know when I set out that they had any. I had heard that Jersey got good government out of her ruling corporations. And when I found that they really had troubles of their own, my first impulse was to rejoice. My first feeling was that I'd like to see the citizens of this selfish state pickle in the corruption of Hudson County and Essex, of Camden, and Passaic, and Middlesex, and Ocean. And when President Roosevelt proposed that the federal government should take over the charter-granting function from the states, I said "Good; it will serve Jersey right. She deserves all the punishment we can give her."

That feeling was wrong. The president's suggestion may be sound, but I notice that many leading corporation men are leaning in that direction, and that makes me pause. Why this bad faith in Washington? Is the national government more corrupt than that of the states? Is it more representative of business than Jersey?

What the Matter Is

But there is another reason why I know my feeling about punishing Jersey is wrong: It is too Jersey-like. That is the spirit which has betrayed Jersey and made her betray the rest of us. It is the spirit of the reformers of the Oranges, of Hudson, and Camden, and they were in a fair way of finding it out when I was there. Camden elected as Mayor Joseph E. Nowrey, a Democrat who represented the city. David Baird, the Republican boss, is chairman of the state board that taxes railroads, and he is in business with the Public Service Corporation in his county. He had the state legislature take away the veto and other powers of the mayor. And thus Camden must see that Camden's issue cannot be fought out in Camden County. Jersey City has for its mayor a Republican, Mark Fagan, who is one of the few real democrats in this state. He has stood for "equal taxation," which is indeed the issue in his city, but he had to go to the legislature. What did he find? He wrote Governor Murphy, a fellow Republican, a letter describing what he found; here is part of it: "The Republican legislature is controlled by the railroad, trolley, and water corporations, and the interests of the people are being betrayed. While I charge no man with personal corruption, I do not hesitate to means that this is a condition of affairs which is essentially corrupt, and which, if unchecked, means the virtual control of our state and our party by corporations. As a citizen I say that this condition is dangerous and demoralizing. As a public official I protest against the injustice done to Jersey City. As a member of the Republican party I deplore its subserviency to corporate greed and injustice. No political party can long receive the support of the people with such a record as this Republican legislature is making." The Orange men are not willing to grant forever and for nothing a trolley extension to the Public Service Corporation. They appeal to their local aldermen, only to find them bought up. By threats they frighten off the company, which proposes a Greater Newark to swallow up Orange in one well-owned municipality. The Orange men go to Trenton with a bill to limit all franchises to twenty-five years, and they find, what Mayor Fagan found, that their legislature does not represent them; not even all the representatives from their own town represent them. Wouldn't you think they would see, Orange and Camden and Hudson, that the trouble is not that their local governments are bad, but that no part of their government represents them? and that the thing to do is to begin in their counties, make their mayors and aldermen, not "good men," but men who will represent them, or be beaten. And that, this done, all the good citizens in all the counties should get together, pledge their own legislators not only to represent their own county, but the wishes of good citizens in all counties, and last, but not least, that all these same citizens should see to it that this legislature should, first, send to the senate senators who would represent you and me, and, second, pass no bills that would betray the will and injure the business of the United States? But, no, the local spirit of Jersey is the spirit of counties, cities, and states all over the country. It is the home-rule sentiment which says: "Give us good government, and to hell with the rest." And that, again, is the American spirit.

If our national government is corrupt, it is because Jersey and other states, being corrupt, send their Keans and Drydens to the Senate, and their Gardners and McDermotts to the House to misrepresent all of us. And if Jersey and the other states are corrupt, it is because their Jersey Cities, and their Hudson and Essex counties, being corrupt, send their graduates in corruption to the state legislature to misrepresent all the counties. Jerseymen can't see it so, but this is the truth: Jersey's policy toward the trusts, which is the cause of so much trouble to all the rest of us, is the cause of the trouble of all the counties of Jersey. The corruption of those counties is the foundation of the "good" state government that sells us out for fees, which, turned back into the counties to relieve them of taxes, act upon the character of Jersey's citizens like bribes: they keep Jerseymen contented with a state government which represents, not you and me and them, but corrupt special business interests, at home and abroad. Not "good government," the cry of Americans in wards, counties, cities, states and the United States should be "representative government."

McClure's Magazine
July, 1905

Ohio: A Tale of Two Cities

THE story of the latter-day politics of Ohio, as I understand the state, can best be told as a tale of two of her cities: Cleveland and Cincinnati; Cleveland, the metropolis of her Northeast, Cincinnati, the metropolis of her Southwest; Cleveland, the best governed city in the United States, Cincinnati, the worst.

Cleveland is, and except during one short period, always has been a business man's government. The *New York Sun* wondered once how it happened so often that in Ohio men who had spent the better part of their lives in business could step into politics up near the top and prove themselves first-rate politicians from the start. The explanation is simple. Those Ohio men came from Cleveland. If I remember aright, the *Sun* had in mind the sudden appearance of the late Mr. Hanna in national politics with the nomination of Mr. McKinley for president. Mr. Hanna had been in politics for years. Mr. Hanna is one type of the business men who have ruled the city of Cleveland. There are other types, as we shall see, but we must begin with Marcus A. Hanna. He is dead. I don't believe in "nothing but good of the dead"; I believe that true obituaries of our great men would do the living good. But I hoped to be able to tell about Ohio without saying much about Mr. Hanna. That is impossible. You can't understand Cleveland, and you can't understand Ohio, without understanding Mark Hanna. And you can't understand the American people and the United States without seeing Hanna as he was—good and bad, a delight and a danger, a business man in politics, a business man who dominated a city, became United States senator and the boss of a state, became national head of the dominant national party and was the choice of big business and bad machine politics for president of the United States.

The Kind of Man Mark Hanna Was

What sort of man was this? He was "our sort." Hanna was American. There are traits American which he lacked, but taken as he stood there was not a fiber of his make-up, not a fault, not a virtue, that is not of us. Of Quaker stock from the Virginias, he was born near Ohio's Western Reserve and the West made him ripe and rich. Hanna described himself once. In the campaign against Mayor Jones, who was running for governor, he got into a hall full of Welshmen. Jones was Welsh, and the crowd jeered at Hanna so that he could not go on with his speech. "There's a lot of American in me," he shouted. "There's some Scotch. Somewheres way back, there is Irish blood. But by —, there's no Welsh. If there was, I'd go down there and lick the whole lot of you." That won the Welshmen. They cheered and they listened while Hanna gave Jones and the Welsh fits.

That was Hanna, mixed, but well mixed, and, as the politicians say, a "good mixer." He was the fighter who can laugh in his wrath, but won't compromise. "Well, what is your bill?" he was heard to demand of two lobbyists in the Marble Room of the U.S. Senate one day. They murmured some reply. "Well, he don't deserve it and he don't get it," said Hanna aloud, and he stumped off to leave them. Then he stopped. "Say, have you two cusses had your lunch? No? Well, I'll give ye a good lunch, but that's all you do get."

Intimate, even familiar, Hanna was always Hanna, in all places, to all men. It is related that at the first inauguration of President McKinley, when he and Hanna rode together from the Capitol to the White House, Mr. McKinley pointed out of the carriage to the Post Office Building and admired it. "Well, that shows how little you know about architecture," said Hanna. And when President Roosevelt spoke to the senator on the funeral train of Mr. McKinley, and said: "Come, old man, be my friend as you were his," Hanna answered out of his grief, "I will, yes, I will, if you will carry out that man's policy, and if, — it, you won't call me 'old man.'"

Such a friendship could not have lasted, however, for the dominant trait of Hanna's character was domination. He was our aggressive type of the egotist. He may not have meant to be selfish. Hanna was our man of brains, not of mind. When he was a boy he showed some inclination to read books, but his father, Dr. Leonard Hanna, a sturdy man, noticed it. "Mark," he would call up the stairs, "what are you doing up there? Reading, eh? Well, you come down here, and saw wood." So the boy was cured of this taste; the man hardly read at all. When he wasn't sawing wood, he was playing cards. He played in the daytime, and in the evening it was his favorite form of amusement to play a game with as many of his friends as he could get around him, and if no friends came, Mr. Hanna played solitaire.

Our Men Spoiled Like Our Children

We admire self-sufficiency, we Americans, and no matter if they do trample upon us, we want to see the strong men win. We are like the American parent, who, because the baby is lusty and big, lets it pull off the table-cloth and break the dishes. Well, our young male was strong, and he began early to grab. When the family moved to Cleveland (in 1852) the father founded the wholesale grocery firm of Hanna, Garretson & Co. Mark went to school for a while, then he worked in the store, then he served as clerk in a Lake Superior carrying vessel. The Superior iron regions were opening and the Hannas saw things. They went into iron and steel and ships, as well as groceries and supplies. Mark married (in 1862) a daughter of D. P. Rhodes, fondly known as "Old Dan Rhodes," a pioneer grown rich in the iron and coal trade. Mark joined the firm of D. P. Rhodes & Co. There were other sons and partners in the business, but by 1885 they all were out or reduced to M. A. Hanna & Co., mines, ships, coal, oil, iron-ore, and pig-iron. Then M. A. Hanna got into a stove company, other mining companies, banks, and shipbuilding, a newspaper, a theater. It's a long story; it's the good old story, oft told and never explained. I heard, from men with feelings sore after all these years, of quick turns, hard fights, and brutal force. But that was Mark having his way, and, I guess, that is the way of success. Certainly Hanna was the true type of our successful men of big business. They are men in whom a want is, not like yours, perhaps, or mine, humble, hopeful, and capable of dismissal unsatisfied; a want with the Hannas is a lust; no matter how big or how little, no matter how vicious or how innocent, it is Hanna's want; it must be sated, and it must be sated now.

One of Hanna's young wants was a street railway. He had largely of the earth, and of the waters under the earth; he had reached out far beyond Cleveland and Ohio for possessions, into Minnesota and New York, Michigan and Pennsylvania; and his hands were full. But he had no street railway. Of course, he got one. He was let into the West Side Company of Cleveland, Elias Sims, president, and two years later (in 1882) Sims resigned and M. A. Hanna became president. And that's how Hanna happened to go into politics.

Mr. Hanna did not want to go into politics. He had to. It was necessary to his business that he should, and it was for the sake of his business that he did; not for the party, not for the city, not to better things, not even for the sport of it. As a young fellow, he had "batted around" some in his ward, for fun; but there was nothing in that for him, so he wasn't regular about it. I inquired closely into this, for I wanted to be sure that I wasn't on another "low down politician's" trail. Mr. Hanna went into politics as a business man, and he always called himself a business man in politics.

And, as a business man in politics he corrupted politics. Mr. Hanna boodled. He degraded the municipal legislature of Cleveland. I don't say he did it alone; I don't say he started it; I don't say he wanted to do that. All Mr. Hanna wanted was that horse-car line, and then some extensions, and then some more franchises. But these he did want, these and other valuable privileges. Since he wanted them he must have them, and since the business way to get a thing is to go and pay for it and get it, Mr. Hanna went and got his privileges. He bought and paid for them. I don't say he paid all this in bribes, nor do I say that he paid bribes with his own hands. That isn't the way a Big Business man does big business. That isn't the System.

Hanna in Cleveland Politics

The System in Cleveland at that time was simple and imperfect. Business men supported it. There was no boss, and such leading politicians as the city boasted were nothing but business men's political agents. They depended largely upon the campaign funds contributed by the business men. In return the business men could get what they wanted out of the city, and they let the politicians do about as they pleased with the rest. The street railways and the other public utility companies which had the most to ask attended to this political business. Not all of them. Cleveland is in many respects an exceptional community. There are, and there seem always to have been, men of business there who disapprove of boodling and corruption, and one of the street-railway presidents, Mr. Horace E. Andrews, has refused always to aid corruption in any disguise. But Hanna and two others have had no such scruples. They kept men to do "dirty business" for them, and these men were the "bosses" for many years. Hanna's man was George Mulhern, an employee of the West Side Company. Hanna sometimes served as treasurer of the campaign fund, and, in hot fights, often directed the politics of the West Side and, indeed, of the whole city.

All he wanted, however, was the right kind of a mayor, and his share of the councilmen. These he secured, he or Mulhern or both, by supervising nominations and paying individual campaign expenses. Other street railways did much the same. Usually they had among them enough councilmen to form a combine which controlled legislation. If they lacked some, if they hadn't bought sufficiently in advance, or if an unexpected emergency arose, they bought more. They didn't always use cash bribery. Mulhern, who picked the president and organized councils, came to control more and more departments, and he had the patronage of these to dispense to the friends and followers of pliable councilmen. But this was making the city pay for its own corruption, and it not only saved Hanna and the company some costs, it strengthened the machine.

Cleveland in Hanna's Day

This was a government by the public utility companies. These councilmen, elected as representatives of the whole community, represented in fact Mr. Hanna and the other holders of public franchises. Of course there was other "business" to be done. Mulhern with the other railway politicians handled it. They let privileges, legitimate and illegitimate, to their friends and Hanna's friends, and after these, to all comers. Citizens have told me how they were referred from the City Hall to the West Side Company offices, when they called on business. There was the head of the government, and it was not a very bad government, not in the Tammany sense. There was not much police blackmail, for example; it was financial, respectable corruption that prevailed, and "good citizens" do not resent that so much. It is quiet, it is convenient; it is theirs; it is the System. Hanna's government of Cleveland was a government of the people by politicians hired to represent the privileged class.

Hanna in National Politics

This is the most dangerous form of our corruption; the most dangerous for this class as well. And yet the political greatness of Mr. Hanna was rooted in such corruption, and his political hopes were the hopes of this class. Hanna may not have thought so. Hanna wasn't a thinker, he was a man of instinct and action, and his unconscious selfishness hurt his effectiveness. The fate of his primitive machine shows that. He did not keep it up regularly. When he wanted something, he worked hard at the organization; when he wanted nothing in particular, he was slack about it. A business man in politics, he ran politics for business, not for political ends. Some political honors came to him. He went to conventions. He saw how governors were made, and presidents. A delegate to the National Republican Convention of 1888, he was for John Sherman, and he missed a hand in the making of President Harrison. Whether that humble failure suggested it or not, I do not know, but all the world knows that Hanna came to have a great ambition that was political. He wanted to have a president. He chose William McKinley, and he planned for years his nomination in 1896. That he succeeded, everybody knows. Hanna often laughed, in his merry way, at the "spontaneous demand" for McKinley, which swept over the country at just the right time. There was such a demand, and much of it was spontaneous, but Hanna organized it. He dotted the country with men primed to shout at a signal, and when he gave the word, the wave rose and rolled in upon the convention where Hanna was dickering for its enthusiastic reception.

And Hanna won with McKinley and money, Hanna and the System—in the United States. What of Ohio? What of Cleveland? When the organizer of the national Republican machine came home, he had no organization. Having wanted very little from the state, he had neglected the state machine, and it was in the control of the Cox-Foraker wing of the party. And he had lost also his own city. A group of common politicians, weary of the selfishness of his street-railway government, had set out the year before (1895) to organize the party along political, not business, lines. They made Hanna and the street railways the issue and, nominating an obscure young lawyer, Robert E. McKisson, for mayor, they beat easily Hanna's lopsided old occasional machine. McKisson, dismissing his creators, built for himself; but he built on politics and political graft, and the McKisson organization was the best machine the Republicans have ever had in Cleveland. But it was an anti-Hanna machine.

Hanna in State Politics

And thus began the making of the Ohio of Hanna, which is the Ohio of today. Whenever the forces of corruption are beaten in a city, they retreat to the state. Hanna had two wants which Cleveland could not or would not satisfy. He wanted to be a United States senator and he wanted an extension of certain of his street-railway franchises. All the traction interests of Cleveland had been combined into two consolidations, the "Big Con," Horace Andrews, president; and the "Little Con," Mark Hanna, president. Both had franchises expiring in the near future, and the state legislature had just enacted the Rogers law, which permitted cities to grant extensions for fifty years. This law was passed by the Cox-Foraker crowd for the Cincinnati traction interest, but it was good in Cleveland while it lasted. There was the rub, however. The people were indignant at this piece of legislation; it might be repealed. Hanna and his associates had to hurry; and that politician, "Bob" McKisson, would not hurry. He would negotiate, however, and there was some dickering. Just what the dealing was I do not know, of course. The McKissonites say a big offer was made to the mayor and that he refused it. The Hanna people say the mayor asked for money and that they refused it. This much is certain: Mr. Andrews was asked to meet Mayor McKisson at the Hollenden Hotel; telling some of his associates about it, he went there; when he returned he reported that he had entered the appointed room, and that there, in the dark, Mr. McKisson began talking about land to be had out near Andrews's country place. Mr. Andrews may have been mistaken, but he understood this to have been an approach, and he left the mayor abruptly. Soon thereafter a definite proposition of corruption was made, not, however, by the mayor, but the railway people certainly believed it was authoritative. The associates of Mr. Andrews wanted to accept it, and the Hanna people were eager for the deal. And when Mr. Andrews refused to countenance it, there was trouble in his board and he resigned. Why the subsequent negotiation fell through, I do not fully understand. James Parmelee, the president, now, of the lighting company, who was to take Mr. Andrews's place, considered making the deal; but, upon the advice of friends that it would be suicidal to put such business through with the whole city looking on and suspecting the purpose of his succession to Mr. Andrews, Mr. Parmelee decided against the job, and Mr. Andrews resumed his office. As for the other company, I was told that the McKissonites would not do business with the "Little Con" alone. However that may be, from that time on the Hanna Republicans cursed for a "Corruptionist" "Bob" McKisson, who prevented Hanna from getting his franchise extensions from his own city.

Meanwhile Mr. Hanna had been making mad rushes for his senatorship. There was no vacancy in the Senate from Ohio,

but that did not matter. One was created. The president took
John Sherman, the senior Ohio senator, into the cabinet. Poor
old John Sherman! He didn't want to be secretary of state; his
mind was failing and he wanted only to be let alone. But there
was Hanna with a Hanna want; it must be satisfied, so Sherman
was moved and the next thing was to get Hanna appointed.

It was rather late to set about arranging this detail, but Hanna
crossed bridges when he came to them. Governor Bushnell
hated Hanna. Bushnell was a friend of the junior Ohio senator,
Joseph B. Foraker, who hated Hanna who hated him. If Hanna
had had control in Cleveland he might have forced terms, but he
was powerful only at Washington. He had to go to Cincinnati,
and Hanna went to Cincinnati. He appealed from Bushnell and
Foraker to the strong man behind both of them; with federal
patronage in his hand, he went to George B. Cox, the laconic
boss of Cincinnati, who, tradition has it, passed to the governor
two words: "Name Hanna." And Hanna was named.

And thus it happened that Hanna first went to Cincinnati;
thus was begun, in an emergency, the alliance of Hanna, the
Cleveland business man, with Cox, the Cincinnati politician—an
alliance full of portent for the state of Ohio. Hanna was building
his system. Not that he knew it. Reputed great as an organizer,
Hanna worked like a bird; all he knew was that he needed a
straw; his genius lay in the sure instinct with which he found
his straw. The nest happened. Cincinnati was a branch to build
on, Cox a straw. So far as I can make out, when Hanna had his
senatorship, he gave Cox some of the president's patronage
and flitted off to Washington satisfied. But he had descended to
Cincinnati and to Cox, and he was to go there again. Let us go
there and see what it means to go to Cox and Cincinnati.

Going to Cincinnati

I shall never forget my first visit. Cities and city bosses
were my subject then, and I thought I knew something about
such things. I didn't know the worst. The train ran through the
early morning sunshine up to a bank of mist and smoke, paused,
as every train since has done, then slowly tunneled its way into

the cul de sac where the Queen City broods in gloom. I wanted to see Cox. The etiquette of my work seems to me to require that I shall call first everywhere on the ruler of the people; if he is the mayor, I call first on him; if the mayor is a figurehead, I call first on the boss. Sometimes one is in doubt. In Cincinnati, immediately after breakfast, I sought out the sign of the "Mecca" saloon, went up one flight to a mean, little front hall-room. A great hulk of a man sat there alone, poring over a newspaper, with his back to the door. He did not look up.

"Mr. Cox?" I said.

There was a grunt; that was all.

"Mr. Cox," I said, "I understand that you are the boss of Cincinnati."

His feet slowly moved his chair about, and a stolid face turned to mine. Two dark, sharp eyes studied me, and while they measured, I explained that I was a student of "politics, corrupt politics, and bosses." I repeated that I had heard he was the boss of Cincinnati. "Are you?" I concluded.

"I am," he grumbled in his hoarse, throaty voice.

"Of course, you have a mayor, and a council, and judges?"

"Yes," he admitted; "but —" he pointed with his thumb back over his shoulder to the desk—"I have a telephone, too."

"And you have citizens, too? American men and women?"

He stared a moment, silent, then turned heavily around back to his paper. Well, I feel the same way now about the citizenship of this city; Cox, their ruler, and I have had several talks since; he doesn't say much, but I am sure he and I agree perfectly about them. But this, also, I never forgot, and let no one else forget it: Cincinnati is an American city, and her citizens are American citizens. Therefore, what has happened In Cincinnati can happen in American cities. What had happened there?

Tweed Days in Cincinnati

We need not go into details. We know Philadelphia, and that is to know most of the truth about Cincinnati. An aristocracy once, the best people were decent about the graft, but selfish, and the criminal classes took over the government. Tom Campbell, a criminal lawyer, led the Republicans, and John R. McLean, the son of "Wash" McLean, also a sort of boss, led the Democrats; but there was no politics. The good people knew parties, not the party politicians. John R. McLean and Tom Campbell were great friends, and they ruled by buying votes and indulging vice and crime. Campbell controlled the criminal bench. He defended criminals, out of the ring and in it; there was brawling, robbery, murder; and, in open court, over evidence which the public was reading in McLean's newspaper, *The Enquirer*—over evidence which convinced all but the corrupt judges and the "fixed" juries, this politician-lawyer got his clients off, till, in 1884, upon the acquittal of two murderers who killed a man for a very small sum of money, the town revolted. A mob burned the criminal courthouse. The McLean-Campbell regime of Cincinnati, which corresponded to the Tweed days of New York and the McManes-Gas-Ring rule of Philadelphia, closed with the famous Cincinnati riots of 1881.

Tom Campbell moved to New York, and McLean soon took up a residence in Washington, D.C., but "better citizens" did not step into their places. The "best citizens" who led the "better citizens" were in gas and other public utilities; they were "apathetic," so other Republican grafters held down the Republican party while McLean, the Democrat, with his "independent" Enquirer and his contributions, kept a paralyzing hand on the Democratic machine. Since McLean was "active" only when he wanted something himself or when he wanted to keep anybody else from getting anything, this dog-in-the-manger weakened the Democracy, even as a graft organization; and gradually the "grand old party" established itself. Among the Republican leaders of this period the only one we need to know is Joseph B. Foraker. He is the senior United States senator from Ohio now, and we are asking what "our" senators represent at home. Mr. Foraker represented the young Republicans of his day. Enthusiastic over his party, passionate in the defense of the Union soldier, eloquent upon the rights of the people, this young orator was dubbed the "Fire Alarm," because of the courage with which he fought corporate greed and corruption. The people of this country need, and they are forever looking for a leader who is not a boss, and Foraker is no boss. He is a politician; he must have been almost a demagogue once; certainly he raised the hopes and won the hearts of a majority of Ohioans, for they elected him governor of their state, twice. What did he do for these, his own people?

Another U.S. Senator Accounted For

Governor Foraker "discovered" Cox. A saloon-keeper and councilman at the time, Cox ruled his own ward and was distinguished in his corrupt city as an honest politician; if there was boodle to divide Cox divided it "on the square," and if he gave his word, he kept it. Wherefore the world of graft trusted Cox. Governor Foraker, needing a boss for Cincinnati, made Cox an oil inspector and the dispensor of patronage in Hamilton County (Cincinnati). An oil inspectorship in Ohio is "good money" and, better still, brings a man into confidential relations with one of the deep sources of corruption in the state, Standard Oil. Foraker and Cox soon got in touch with other such interests. There are several instances to cite; one will do.

A while ago we spoke of the Rogers Law. Cox and Foraker managed that. The Cincinnati traction interests wanted a fifty-year five-cent-fare franchise in Cincinnati. Foraker wanted to go to the U.S. Senate. Public opinion out West is against long franchises, but the "Fire Alarm" expressed public opinion. It was charged in the public prints of Chicago and Ohio that Foraker was paid an enormous "fee" (ranging from $100,000 to $250,000) for his services—as a lawyer. He did not sue for libel, but he denied the charge; he said all he got was a present of $5,000 from an officer of the company. I say it doesn't matter whether Foraker took a bribe, or a fee, or a present, or nothing at all. His firm has been ever since counsel for the Traction Company, and his son became an officer thereof, but that doesn't matter. And it doesn't matter whether the legislature that made Foraker a senator belonged to the company, or whether the legislature that passed the Rogers traction bill belonged to

Foraker. The plain, undeniable, open facts are that the legislature of 1896 which elected Foraker to the U.S. Senate was led by the senator, a popular leader, to pass in the interest of the traction company a bill which granted privileges so unpopular that public opinion required a repeal in the next legislature of 1898. In other words, this man, who by his eloquence won the faith of his people, betrayed them for some reason to those interests which were corrupting the government in order to get privileges from it. That's all any electors need to know about Joseph B. Foraker, that and the report that he hopes some day to be president of the United States.

Let's turn to an honest grafter. Cox made the councils of Cincinnati act for the traction company under the Rogers Law, but he doesn't pretend to represent the people. That isn't his business. Cox's business is to rule the people, and he does it. Cincinnati was enraged, and Cincinnati rose against Cox for this act. Cox was for licking them into obedience, but Hanna was back in Cincinnati again. Hanna had to be elected, in 1898, to the seat he had been appointed to. He wanted "harmony" in Cincinnati. He wanted Cox to hide and let some business men, such as used to rule Cleveland, run the 1897 campaign which was to elect his (Hanna's) legislature. It was selfish of Hanna, but Cox was willing. He told me about it.

"Wanted good men nominated," he said. "Wanted business men. Wanted business men to name the ticket and run the machine. Come to me, a committee of them, bankers and all like that. Said they'd name twelve men, and I was to name twelve. I was to pick six off their list, and they were to pick six off mine. Showed me their twelve and I took 'em all, all twelve, all business men, good people. Called 'em the dozen raw. Let 'em name the ticket and lent 'em the machine to run." He paused. "Who do you think they nominated?" he asked, and he answered: "They nominated fellers they met at lunch."

Cox's scorn of "good business men" reminds me of Croker. Croker has never been able to understand just how "bad" he was; he really was puzzled as to himself. "But," he said one day with assurance, "I know I'm better than them;" and he pointed off downtown toward Wall Street, where his business backers and clients were. And it is so with Cox. He doesn't understand the standards of his critics, but he knows he is better than "them."

"Them," in Cincinnati, were beaten. The "dozen raw" who, largely for Hanna's sake, tried to give "front" to the Republican party, and save it with a respectable business man's ticket, failed. McLean wanted to go to the United States Senate, so he lent the Democratic machine to the Democrats, who combined with the independents, and together they elected an anti-machine ticket. It looked so bad for Cox that he announced his retirement from politics, but the amiable old gentleman who was mayor proved so weak and the "Democrats" and "independents" such poor stuff that Cox recovered his courage. He bought some members of the administration, fooled others, and with the help of these set the rest to fighting among themselves. Cox so disgusted the town with "reform" that it came back to him, laid itself at his feet, and he proceeded at his leisure to, what a judge called, the "Russianization" of Cincinnati.

How Hanna Was Elected U.S. Senator

What that means we shall see when it is done. Hanna waits, his present want, the senatorship, unsatisfied. He thought he had it fixed; though the McKisson anti-Hanna Republicans had elected to the legislature part of the delegation from Cuyahoga County (Cleveland), and the anti-Cox movement had sent up independent Republicans from Hamilton County (Cincinnati). Hanna and his state manager, Major Charles F. Dick, assumed that all "Republicans" would be loyal to "the party." Loyalty to party means, to a boss, loyalty to the boss. Now Hanna wasn't yet the boss of Ohio, but he wanted to be, so he assumed that no one would oppose him. The capital was full of his enemies, Governor Bushnell, Senator Foraker, Mayor McKisson, Charles Kurtz, etc., but Hanna flitted off to Washington, and Major Dick "sat with his feet up on a table cracking jokes."

Secretly, those Republican enemies of Hanna formed a combination with Democrats to beat Hanna. They could do it. They had the votes. This they proved by smashing Hanna's legislative slate, and Ohio and Washington were thrown into a state of excited dismay. Hanna flew to Columbus and took personal charge of his own fight. With him came money, lots of money, and with this money came the influence of the president, of the railroads, the banks, Federal office-holders. Mass meetings were organized at the homes of lost or doubtful legislators, speeches were made, addresses drawn, and committees with petitions were hurled by special trains to the capitol. Columbus was a wonderful scene. The hotels were packed, crowds surged up and down the halls and lobbies. Wine flowed and there were loud rows and fist fights. Legislators were kidnapped, made drunk, and held prisoners. The wife of one member, sent for because of her influence over her husband, was held by one side while the other kept him hidden away in m room. Men carried revolvers and showed them, and witnesses tell me there was really a fear of sudden death. But under all this money was whispering; both sides used it. Hanna always denied that he spent any. The anti-Hanna combine settled finally on McKisson as their candidate, and McKisson says he hadn't any money. But these are technical denials. I don't know who handled the little money the McKissonites had, but after Hanna won (for, of course Hanna won) by one vote, specific charges of bribery were made. A committee took evidence on one case and reported (1) that "on or about Jan. 9, 1898, an attempt was made to bribe John C. Otis, a member of the House . . . to vote for Marcus A. Hanna"; (2) "that Major E. G. Rathbone and Major Charles F. Dick were agents of Marcus A. Hanna, and procured, aided, and abetted the crime."

  The report, sent to the United States Senate, was not credited there, but that means nothing; it means no more than the report of a board of aldermen would mean of an investigation of graft charges against some fellow member. "Senatorial courtesy" seated Mr. Hanna. But if bribery ever was proved, it was on that investigation. The bribe agent, now dead, was followed step by step; he reported by telephone to "Dick," "Major Dick," and to others at Hanna's headquarters everything that he did; and these frequent telephonic communications were overheard by witnesses, with stenographers by to take them down. Hanna's declaration of personal innocence was borne out; the witnesses said the agent said he represented Eastern men and Eastern money; but "Dick" was certainly Hanna's state manager, and Hanna wasn't the sort of man such a lieutenant would be afraid to report to on the use of money. But waive all that.

Hanna rewarded with offices in the state and the United States service the legislators and agents who "stood by him." Hanna said on the stump afterward that he did this. That is enough. As we have noted before, people are often incensed over cash bribery, but bribery with offices is worse; to pay men who betray us by giving them salaries at our cost in our public service is the worst form of bribery; that is systematic corruption; that is the System. For instance, Major E. G. Rathbone, afterward involved in irregularities in the Cuban postal service, was sent down there by Hanna because he had proven his character by helping Hanna in this senatorial fight. And there are others: When Mark Hanna died, the System decreed that Ohio should send his faithful lieutenant, Major Dick, to the Senate, and thus, by the way, another of "our" United States senators is accounted for.

But never mind; Hanna had his senatorship. There remained unsatisfied but one great want of this spoiled child of the American business-political system. That legislature of 1898, which gave Hanna "so much trouble," as he expressed it, repealed the Rogers Law, and he had to begin all over again to get the extensions he wanted for his street-railway franchises. But he began right this time, at home. He went to Cleveland.

McKisson, beaten for the senatorship, was weakened, but he controlled the Republican party, so Hanna did what good people are so reluctant, what the politicians and bosses are so ready to do when the party fails to represent them—Hanna backed the other party. Yes, this same Republican leader who had pleaded so hard for "harmony" in Cincinnati where harmony was in his interest, now supported in Cleveland the Democratic Party. The Democratic Party in Ohio (and in many other states) is cursed by "Democrats" of the John R. McLean type, who believe in "protection," privileges, and big business graft generally just as much as Republicans of the Aldrich stamp do. John Farley is such a "Democrat." I had a talk with him once, and it was like talking to Aldrich; he is candid, able, and a cynic about America and its democratic republic. Farley was nominated by the Democratic Party; he was called a Hanna Democrat—and the Hanna Republicans helped the Democrats elect him. And he was elected to help the street railways get their franchises. Horace Andrews was out of the "Big Con" presidency and Henry Everett of the Everett-Moore Syndicate was in; and the two "Cons" came pretty near getting what they wanted. Farley, the Democrat, stood ready to do his part, the traction people to do theirs; but the business fell through, beaten by—Cleveland, by the citizens of Cleveland.

Finding "Good" in Cleveland

Cheerful idiots who think themselves optimists often ask me why I don't find something good now and then, somebody to praise. I do. I found good in Chicago; I praised Folk and LaFollette, A. R. Hall, and Governor Garvin, and Oliver McClintock; everywhere I have been I have found something good and somebody to praise. I notice, however, that while my evil reports seldom cause resentment, the moment I begin to speak well either of men or of conditions, my mail roars with rage and burns with sarcasm or sorrow. Then I am a fool or a liar. Naturally, therefore, it is with fear and trembling that I approach Cleveland now. There is something good there. The citizens of Cleveland know how to vote; they have a public opinion, and they make it count; they have two truly independent newspapers, and this free press speaks for them, with effect. Nominally Republican, when this city had by sheer force of public opinion stopped the trolley grabs, it turned around and elected to succeed "Democrat" Farley not a "Republican," but Tom Johnson, a Democrat. Now this was the most terrible disappointment in the whole business-political career of Mr. Hanna. And Johnson's administration has hurt "business" generally; it is a sore trial today to a certain kind of business man in Cleveland; and the results of the fight against this—this "socialist-anarchist-nihilist" (as Hanna called Johnson) has upset the charters of all the cities in Ohio and reversed the judicial policy of the state courts. Next to the "wants" of Mr. Hanna, nothing has had such an influence on the politics, government, and "business" interests of Ohio as the policy of the mayor of Cleveland. Yet Cleveland re-elected Mayor Johnson. There is something good in Cleveland and Tom L. Johnson. Good? It seems to me that Tom Johnson is the best mayor of the best-governed city in the United States. This is no snap judgment. The first time I went to Cleveland, on the same trip that took me to Cox and Cincinnati, I knew all about Tom Johnson. He was a dangerous theorist with a dangerous ambition; that was the impression the System had spread of him in New York; and all I had to do was to prove it. Since, though mayor, he was the head of the actual government of the city, I called on him. His office was full, and it was a shock to my prejudice to watch this big jolly man do business—attention, reflection, and a question; a decision, a laugh; next. And so it went. But I wasn't to be fooled. When my turn came, I asked him what his ambition was? He laughed.

"My ambition," he said "is to make Cleveland the first American city to get good government." That was amusing, and he saw my skepticism, and it amused him. "And not only that," he added, with a sober impulse of his tremendous energy. "I'd like to make it not only the first to get good government; I'd like to make it prove things, prove good government possible, prove municipal ownership possible, prove anything is possible that any community of American citizens cares to try to do."

There was something interesting and intelligent about that. I often had wondered why all our leading citizens sought the same thing, money-power; why didn't some of them pursue some other end; why didn't someone seek the everlasting fame that would come to the man who first should achieve good municipal government? But I knew Johnson too well to be taken in by his "ambition." I pried around a little. If a city is corrupt, there are signs of graft about it. The pavements show it and the police on patrol; reporters and certain kinds of businessmen will give you the rumors of it. Cleveland showed none of these signs, so I went away baffled to give Tom Johnson time to show what he was after. And, sure enough, the next time I visited Cleveland the mayor whose ambition it was to give his city good government was running for governor of Ohio! Unfortunately for my prejudice, however, my experience with Folk in St. Louis, with the reformers in Chicago, with reform in all cities, had taught me that no man can finish a municipal reform job without going to the state. Moreover, I had come to regard office-seeking as no worse a crime in a reformer than in a grafter; on the contrary it had occurred to me that one way to beat the grafting system was to promote honest men for giving good government, as the System (Hanna's, for instance) promotes corrupt men for corrupting government. The question still was as to the goodness of Tom Johnson's government. A year ago last winter, after a month of search, I was convinced that there was no graft worth speaking of in Cleveland; certainly if I had tried to make out a case of bad government against Tom Johnson, I should have made myself ridiculous. But how, in a brief space, is one to prove good government?

The best department in this best government is that of the law. Newton D. Baker, the head of it, is clear, able, and, best of all, fair. He has directed all the many obnoxious litigations for the city against "business," and yet "businessmen" sneer at Johnson and all his men, except Baker, because while he fights for the city he "fights fair," they say. But how is this to be shown? All I can say is: Ask any Clevelander about Newton D. Baker.

Mayor Johnson wanted to make his water-works prove that municipal operation was good. It was a political dive when he was elected, and the contractors for a water tunnel to reach far out into the lake had wrecked the job at both ends and given it up as hopeless. The mayor appointed Professor Edward W. Bemis superintendent. There was a howl from the party, for Bemis hailed from another state and had no politics, but Johnson stood his ground while the "foreigner" threw out Republicans and Democrats alike, Protestants and Catholics; put in men without regard to politics; reorganized the department on a business basis; installed meters against another outcry; saved waste; reduced expenses to city and consumer alike, and altogether established a system that did prove things. Furthermore, the city completed that water tunnel. My colleague, Mr. Adams, said Cleveland water was not pure, but that meant either that the tunnel should reach farther out in the lake or that a filtration plant is needed. The Waterworks Department certainly proves that a man like Bemis, backed by a man like Johnson, backed by a citizenship like Cleveland's, can run its waterworks better than a private company. But this is only my assertion; ask any Clevelander if it isn't true.

The Police Department caused trouble at first. Tom Johnson is not interested in the police as a New York reformer would be, but there is but one man in this country who has solved the police problem more satisfactorily. The mayor, after some patient experiments, found on the force a junior officer who struck him as honest, able, and full of nerve. He made him chief of police. That caused more bitter feeling, for Chief Kohler is a Republican. Kohler cared, Johnson didn't. Kohler declared he "wasn't looking for trouble" and didn't want the place. "I wouldn't have given it to you, if you did," said the mayor, and he gave commands. Chief Kohler obeyed the mayor's orders. There is absolutely no graft among the Cleveland police that I could find, and, without any alliance with criminals, this young man handles his criminal problem. Mayor Johnson is a good judge of men, and Cleveland has the best chief of police that I have met so far.

One day a builder stopped me in the street to complain about the Building Department. Certain plans had been held up for three days, he said. That sounded like New York. "What for—graft?" I asked. "Oh, no," he said, "they excused the delay by saying that the head of the department had bought a pair of shoes that hurt his feet. But the man isn't up to his work, and Johnson won't do anything about it." Think of a complaint like that in your city. This builder was perfectly right; but before I left the town he said he and a committee had gone to the mayor, and I happened to hear several cabinet discussions of a rather thorough-going reorganization.

Mr. Adams says the Health Department is weak, and a remark of the mayor to me confirmed this criticism, and, perhaps, explained the condition. Mr. Johnson said he never had been able to understand the workings of the Health Department; he was an ex-officio member of the board, but couldn't get interested in its doings. He has to be interested to do good work, and his interests are pretty wide; but sanitary science marks one of his limitations. Stealing is within his limits. A paving-brick combine that interested him when he came into office was broken up in a clever way, and the Public Works Department was turned over to a Republican, W. J. Springbom, who had proved his honesty and capacity in the city council. The efficiency and correctness of Mr. Springbom I never heard disputed. And the kindness and humanity of Harris R. Cooley, the director of charities and correction, will not be denied. The really remarkable results achieved under this gentle clergyman at the city prison and at Cleveland's Boyville, a farm in the country where "bad boys" are proved to be the best boys in the slums—these works certainly are of good government. So with the parks. The rich men of the city had provided a beautiful, though broken, circle of parks, but they were only decorative till Johnson threw them open to the public. He ordered away the "Keep off the grass" signs, and the Park Department, by games and competitions for prizes, by winter sports and summer music, has taught the people of Cleveland to go out and use their parks. There has been some protest at this policy, but a sight of those parks in use makes the opposition seem mean. Moreover, the city has established playgrounds, and skating-rinks on public ground and in vacant private lots, and the police say these sports lighten police work in their neighborhood.

But this is not a third of the "proof" I gathered of good government in Cleveland, and it isn't the best proof, either. The best evidence of the "goodness" of this government is the spirit of the men in it. They like their work; they like to talk about their work; theirs is a sense of pride and preoccupation such as I have never felt in any other American municipal government. The members of the administration are of all classes, but they get together, they and their wives, and they talk shop, shop, shop. The mayor's levees are the most popular. Everybody goes there, evenings and Sundays, and it is Cleveland, Cleveland,

Cleveland, till an outsider is bored to death. Say what you will, pick flaws as you may and as I could, Tom Johnson has proved what I never heard him say he hoped to prove: He has proved that it can be made a joy to serve one's city.

Isn't this good? Isn't this what we mean by "good government"? There are men in Cleveland, and in Ohio, and in the United States, who say it is not good. They hate and they fear Tom Johnson and all his works. Why? They say he is a politician. I don't think he is, not a good one, but I don't care. And neither do his critics care: Hanna was a politician, and so are Cox and Foraker, and Johnson's critics do not mind that in them. But they say he is not sincere, that he does the good he does to serve his own selfish ends. Hanna did the evil he did for selfish ends, and Tom Johnson's enemies were Mark Hanna's friends. Would they ask if Hanna was sincere, and Cox, and Foraker? But Johnson was a business man, and his old business associates say that while he was in business he was a corrupter of politics. This is true. Mr. Johnson denies it, but let us examine the facts and the denial.

The Truth About Tom Johnson

Tom Johnson was a big business man; there is no denying that; he succeeded; he is rich. And his business was big business, street railways and steel. He was in street railways before he was twenty-one, and he operated in many parts of the country, Indianapolis, Cleveland, Detroit, Brooklyn. In Cleveland he measured himself with Hanna and beat him. I said earlier in this sketch that Hanna was our man of brains, not mind. Johnson has a mind; his brain is no mere muscle; it thinks. He discovered at Indianapolis a principle of street-railway operation. Most street-car lines run from the business center of the city out to the residence districts. They follow the heavy traffic, downtown to work in the morning, uptown home in the evening. Mr. Johnson believed that if he could run a continuous line across town he would catch not only the morning and evening crowds, but the all-day cross-town traffic. He did. This may seem a simple, obvious observation, but as we have noted so often, business men are not so great as they think they are, even at business. They are more often smart and knowing than wise and intelligent, and—well, it was the application of this simple principle that enabled Tom Johnson to come into Cleveland on a little jerk-water horse-car line and go out on the "Big Con," while Mark Hanna was struggling behind with his "Little Con."

But, because Hanna was so simply instinctive, we can excuse many of his evil practices; he didn't know any better. And because Tom Johnson understands things, we can pin him to facts. What are the facts? He says he bought his franchises, not from councils, but from private and corporate owners of them. Yes, but he got extensions and other privileges from cities. How? He declares that he never bribed anybody, directly or indirectly. Very well, but Mr. Johnson says that he contributed to campaign funds, that he contributed to the funds of both parties when he had business to do, and he admits that he did this to influence votes on his business. And he adds, with a candor as honest as Hanna's ever was, "I understand now that that is just as corrupt and dangerous as cash bribery." It is worse. It is systematic. And Mr. Johnson understands what I mean by that. Mr. Johnson understands what perfect honesty is. He says Horace Andrews has it, and to prove it he told me once a story which illustrates perfectly the difference between himself and Hanna and Andrews. Both street-railway combinations wanted something from the city. Hanna went ahead and bought it; the cost was $40,000. Then Hanna thought the "Big Con" ought to pay its share, and the "Big Con" directors, Johnson included, were willing. But Andrews refused absolutely, as his custom was. "Then," said Mr. Johnson, " I discovered that about $20,000 of that $40,000 was for legitimate expenses, so I said to Andrews: 'Here, Horace, is a way out of this. We can pay the honest half of that bill and let Hanna foot the other half.' But Andrews said that that was a flimsy subterfuge, and, of course, he was right." So I concluded that while Mr. Johnson had scruples unknown to the Hannas, he was willing to do things that Horace Andrews wouldn't do. In brief, Tom Johnson, in business, did what was necessary to the furtherance of his business.

But the men who wanted to make Hanna president, and who deal now with Cox and Foraker, Murphy and Platt and

Aldrich—the clients and friends of such as these cannot tell me that they hate Johnson for the evil he may have done as a business man in politics. There is something back of all their charges. What is it? I think we are close now to a truth that we must see plainly if we are to understand why our governments, city, state, and national, are corrupt, and, also, why our reforms fail so regularly.

Tom Johnson is the "business man for mayor" that businessmen have been prophesying so long must come along some day to give us a "good business administration of a city government." Now that he has come, business hates him because he has given Cleveland not only good government, but representative government; not only clean streets, but clean tax lists; he has stopped not only blackmail, but bribery; he tackled not only low-down petty police and political graft, but high-toned, big, respectable, business graft, both legitimate and illegitimate. Tom Johnson is a reformed business man. His reform began at home; he reformed himself first, then he undertook political reform; and his political reform began with the reform of his own class. And that is Tom Johnson's sin.

Tom Johnson's Story

One day, at the height of his money-making career, the newsboy on a train offered him a copy of Henry George's "Social Problems." He was pushing it away, when the conductor, happening to pass, said: "That's a book you ought to read, Mr. Johnson." So he took it, read it; it threw a flood of light, especially upon his business; and he read more of Henry George, met the man, became a disciple, and managed one of the great Single-Taxer's political campaigns. Convinced of the injustice of privileges, Mr. Johnson did not quit turning privileges into money; he was twitted on the point while he was a member of Congress in 1891; and his answer shows how he excused himself. Mr. Johnson moved that the duty on steel rails be removed. Mr. Dalzell, the Republican leader, interrupted Johnson to ask him if he, a manufacturer of steel rails, was not a beneficiary of the duty on them. Johnson said he was;

that he got a higher price for his rails because of that duty; but that, as a member of Congress, he represented not himself, nor his mill, nor his stockholders, but his constituents; and that as a free trader he wished to commence his reforms along the line in which he was interested. So he continued his motion to put steel rails on the free list. In other words his position was that, while as a business man he would take advantage of the favoritism of his government, as a citizen and as a politician he would fight all privileges as economically unjust. Another amusing incident occurred at Detroit. As the manager of the streetcar system, Johnson was seeking from the city a double-track privilege. Mayor Pingree was against the grant, "but," said Mr. Johnson, "Pingree didn't know why; he came to me and said he knew there was something the matter with the ordinance, and wouldn't I tell him what it was that was wrong? I laughed. I said I wouldn't tell him what he wanted to know, but I would tell him this much: 'If,' I said, 'I had the say for the city in this thing, I'd see Tom Johnson in hell before I'd let him have it.'" When the hearing was held, Pingree couldn't make his position very clear; he tried to, hesitated, and then he blurted out that he didn't understand the ordinance, but he pointed at Johnson and he said: "But I can tell you this. Tom Johnson there told me that if he was in our places he'd see Tom Johnson in hell before he'd grant it." Everybody looked at Johnson, who laughed heartily. "Yes, I did say that," he admitted, "but it is a dirty trick to tell it on me."

So he knew what he was about in business, but he kept at it till he had made his money. Then, when some men go in for yachting, or the Senate, and give money to charity and churches, colleges and libraries, Tom Johnson gave himself and his money to politics, to municipal reform as the mayor of Cleveland. And as a mayor he knew what he was about.

His platform as a candidate was equal taxation and "three-cent fares with universal transfers" on the street railways; "good" government was a side issue; he threw that in. His idea was to make that city government represent and serve all its people. That doesn't sound bad, but applied by an expert big business man, who knew just where the System lay and who reached for it with ability and humor, Mayor Johnson's simple idea had mixed and terrible consequences.

His first move was at the inequalities and favoritism of the tax lists. He had Peter Witt organize a Tax School. Peter Witt loved the work. It consisted in finding out the assessments of real estate, block by block, or ward by ward. Great maps were made, and on these each piece of property was plotted, and in each plot Peter Witt wrote the assessment on it. You can imagine the result. But when this was done, Peter Witt asked all the property owners to come together to see that result, and you can imagine the effect of this "first view." There were inequalities, and, with the property owner by to agree, they were straightened out against the next year. Now wasn't that a good thing to do? No. The System got out an injunction and stopped the "unlawful" expenditures on the Tax School.

The next reach, at about the same time, was for the undervaluation of steam railroads. Now the railroads in Ohio had long since got through corrupting the state. As we have seen everywhere, when the railroads have had all they want out of the state in the way of privileges they keep up only enough steam to keep the government corrupt. They are there, though you can't always see them. Mayor Johnson could see them. He, Professor Bemis and, later, Carl Nau, an expert accountant, produced figures showing the gross and ridiculous undervaluation of railroad property as compared with other property in the state and with railroad property in other states. These figures, laid before the auditors by the mayor and his assistant, produced no results. Railroads owned the boards. Detectives who shadowed the auditors found that all the auditors traveled on passes and wined and dined with the railway counsel. Mr. Johnson appealed from the local to the state Board of Equalization, but that board also refused to act. Mayor Johnson appealed next to the Supreme Court to compel the state board to act; the court held that the legislature alone could remedy the evil. Mayor Johnson went to the legislature of 1902, and the legislature adjourned without action. It was not till 1903 that the state tax on railroads was increased from one-half of one to one per cent, on the gross receipts, just about doubling the tax, and then only with railroad consent and in fear of "socialistic" agitation.

Another simultaneous move was "against" the local public utilities companies. The mayor appoints the City Board of Equalization; and Johnson's board added $18,000,000 to the tax valuation of the street-railway and lighting companies. Now it was the System's turn to appeal. They went to the state auditor, and they did not go in vain. The state Board of Tax Remission remitted, without any given reason, the entire increase, and the legislature empowered the Republican county auditor of Cuyahoga County (Cleveland) to destroy the City Board. Johnson appealed to the Common Pleas Court to restore his board's valuation; denied; to the Circuit Court; denied. Meanwhile, however, the citizens were interested, and they elected Robert C. Wright (Dem.) county auditor over Craig (Rep.). Now the biggest item in this fight was a claim by Johnson for $2,000,000 back taxes from the public service corporations, and Wright was to collect it. When he entered his office he found Craig had settled secretly with the companies for $113,000. And when Wright began to investigate the returns the state auditor ordered him off. Wright proceeded, nevertheless; he added back values amounting to $1,858,000; the state board remitted them, and the case was taken into court, where it still is pending. As in the case of the railroads, in spite of this succession of defeats, the public service people have consented to increased assessments from $3,520,245, in 1900, to $7,814,120, in 1904.

Judicial Anarchy of Big Business

All these, however, were mere skirmishes around the great central fight which raged over "three-cent fares and universal transfers." The street railways wouldn't hear of it. Horace Andrews said they couldn't live; Johnson said they could; Hanna, who had been calling Johnson a socialist, now added "anarchist-nihilist." I believe Horace Andrews has proved to Johnson since that universal transfers are not practicable in so large a city, but the mayor still believes in three-cent fares, and when the railways showed no disposition to budge, he and the city council established routes for competing three-cent lines and, advertising for bids, induced street-railway men from out of town to bid. Now, business men apply such methods to one another, and they are all right then; but when this ex-street-railway magnate used them in the interest of a city, Big Business went mad. The first move was made by Johnson on December 9, 1901. Two days later, the state system, through Attorney General Sheets, brought an ouster suit against the City of Cleveland, a suit, that is, to oust the whole administration. This sounds "socialistic-anarchistic-nihilistic," but it wasn't; it was Systematic. There was a run on Hanna's "Savings Bank," as he called his street railway, and something had to be done to save it. And something was done. On June 26 the Supreme Court of the state of Ohio ousted the Board of Control of Cleveland. Why? It had been created by special legislation. But all the charters of all the cities in Ohio were creations of special legislation, and the same court had upheld such special legislation from time immemorial. No matter. That court, to check Tom Johnson and help the Hannas, did declare unconstitutional all the city charters in Ohio. Oh, it was arranged so that the cities could do business, all but one; but that exception points to the whole moral of this supreme act of the corrupt, misrepresentative System that rules the United States today. The exception was Cleveland; Cleveland could not grant, or consider granting, any more franchises.

Going to Cincinnati Again

But "they" were not through, not yet. Having torn down, they—and by "they" I mean the Hannas, the public-service corporations and their political machinery, their banks and their courts—they had to build up something in the place of the ruin. They had to pass a general act giving one and the same city charter to all the cities in Ohio. Where did they go for a model? They went to Cincinnati.

Let's run down there again to see what Cox has done since 1898 to make Cincinnati the model Ohio city. He has "Russianized" it. His voting subjects are all down on a card catalogue, they and their children and all their business, and he lets them know it. The Democratic Party is gone. Cox has all the patronage, city, county, state and federal, so the Democratic grafters are in Cox's Republican Club. That club contains so many former Democrats that "Lewie" Bernard, John R. McLean's political agent, says, happily, that he is waiting for a majority, to turn it into a Democratic club. And "Lewie" Bernard's machine remnant is in touch with Cox when "John," as Cox calls McLean, doesn't want anything, either office or revenge. Conventions are held, and Cox plans them in detail. If he has been hearing mutterings among his people about the boss, he is very ostentatious in dictation; otherwise he sits in his favorite beer hall and sends in to those of his delegates whom he wishes to honor slips containing the motions and nominations each is to make. But there must be no nominating speeches. "Takes time; all foolishness; obey orders and get done." He picks ward leaders, and they deliver the votes. The citizens have no choice of parties, but they must get out and vote. Cox is good to some of them. If they knuckle under, he puts respectable men up for the school board. He has little use for schools; not much graft in them; except to cut down their appropriations in favor of fatter departments, and as a place to try respectable men. If these take orders on the school board, Cox tries them higher up, and he has a-plenty. The press is not free. The *Post* and the *Citizens' Bulletin*, the last a weekly organ of the smallest but one of the most enduring groups of reformers in America—these are the only papers that speak out honestly for the public interest. Official advertising, offices for the editors, public-service stock and political prospects for the owners, hold down the rest. It is terrible. The city is all one great graft; Cox's System is the most perfect thing of the kind in this country, and he is proud of it.

"What you think of it? " he asked, when I had finished and was taking leave.

"Pretty good," I said.

"Pretty —!" He was too disgusted to finish. "Best you ever saw," he retorted, firmly.

"Well, I can't tell," I said. "My criterion for a graft organization is, How few divide the graft? How many divide it here?"

"Ain't no graft," he grumbled.

"Then it's a mighty poor thing."

He pondered a moment. Then, "How many do you say divides up here?"

"Three at least," I said. "You and Garry Herman and Rud Hynicka."

"Ugh!" he grunted, scornfully, and, wagging one finger slowly before my face, he said: "There's only one divides up here."

Of course, that isn't true. He must mean only political graft, the campaign fund, police blackmail, contracts, etc., etc., and even that goes partly to others. Cox admits owning two millions, but some of his followers are very rich also. Cox wouldn't lie about a point like that; but he is growing vain and hates to see other men stand up like men and to hear them admired. They tell how once, in a beer hall, when Herman and Hynicka, his two chief lieutenants, and some others, were talking to some outsiders quite like free, independent men, Cox, who had been poring over his beer, broke in hoarsely, "But when I whistle, you dogs come out of your holes, don't you?" They were still. "Don't you, Garry?" the master repeated. "That's right," said Garry.

But there is lots of graft besides political graft in Cincinnati, bankers' and business men's graft. Cox is reaching for that, too. Some Cleveland and Cincinnati financiers organized a trust company in Cincinnati, and they took Cox in for his pull and the public moneys he could have deposited there. A quarrel arose, and Cox, taking one side, told the others to buy or sell. They sold, of course, and Cox, becoming president, wrote a letter to officeholders, inviting them to use his bank; the letter to school teachers was published. Certain financiers of Cleveland and Cincinnati got up a scheme to take over the Miami and Erie Canal. They gave Cox stock for Cox's pull on the legislature, and his letter to the legislators was published. The bill was beaten; business men all along the canal were grafting the water for power, and they fought for their graft. The company had floated its stock and bonds, and the failure of the legislature threw the "canal scandal" into a receivership. Some of the financiers are in trouble, but Cox is safe, and the scheme was to go through next year. Cox was in the scheme to sell or "lease" the Cincinnati Southern, the only steam railroad under municipal ownership. Leading citizens of Cincinnati concocted this grab, but the Germans beat it; and, though it went through later, the city got much better terms. So, when Cox says only one divides the graft in Cincinnati he probably means that one man can dispose as he will of all of it, police, political, and financial, as the examples cited indicate, but he has to let all sorts of men in on it. And he does. And that is his best hold on the graft. They talk in Cincinnati, as they do in Philadelphia, of apathy. Apathy! Apathy is corruption. Cincinnati and Philadelphia are not asleep; they are awake, alive. The life is like that in a dead horse, but it is busy and it is contented. If the commanding men, of all the natural groupings of society, were not interested in graft, no city would put up with what satisfies Cincinnati. For Cincinnati is not unhappy. Men like Elliot H. Pendleton, Rufus B. Smith, and a dozen others, are eating their hearts out with impotent rage, but as for the rest—

The rest are in it for profit or—fear. The bums get free soup; the petty criminals "get off" in court; the plain people or their relatives get jobs or a picnic or a friendly greeting; the Germans get their beer whenever they want it; the neighborhood and ward leaders get offices and graft; "good" Democrats get their share of both; shopkeepers sell to the city or to politicians or they break petty ordinances; the lawyers get cases, and they tell me that the reputation of the bench is such that clients seek lawyers for their standing, not at the bar, but with the ring; the banks get public deposits and license to do business; the public utility companies get franchises and "no regulation"; financiers get canals, etc. (they "get blackmailed," too, but they can do "business" by "dividing up"); property owners get low assessments, or high; anybody can get anything in reason, by standing in. And anybody who doesn't "stand in," or "stand by," gets "nothing but trouble." And there is the point that pricks deepest in Cincinnati. Cox can punish; he does punish, not with physical cruelty, as a czar may, but by petty annoyances and "trouble," and political and business ostracism. The reign of Cox is a reign of fear. The experience that made my visits there a personal humiliation was the spectacle I saw of men who were being punished; who wanted to cry out; who sent for me to tell me facts that they knew and suffered and hated; and these men, after leading me into their back offices and closing the door, dared not speak. It was rumored that I was shadowed, and that made them afraid. Afraid of what? They were afraid of their government, of their czar, of George Cox, who is not afraid of them, or of you, or of me. Cox is a man, we are American citizens, and Cincinnati has proved to Cox that Americans can be reduced to craven cowards.

Russianization of Ohio

And Ohio proves that the kind of men that rule us would be willing to see us all Russianized like this. When, in the fall of 1902, the legislature of Ohio met in special session to adopt one uniform municipal code for all the cities of the state, the men who dominated that state and its legislature—Hanna, Foraker, Cox, Dick, and the rest—sent to Cincinnati for their bill. Now, I don't believe that charters make governments good or bad; I believe the character of the people of Cincinnati makes Cincinnati what it is; and I believe the citizenship of Cleveland makes Cleveland what it is. But the federal plan of concentrated power and responsibility, on which the charter of Cleveland was drawn, helped her citizens to rule themselves, and the so-called board plan of scattered irresponsibility which has been built up in Cincinnati helped Cox to rule Cincinnati. At any rate, the citizens of each place think so, and so do the grafters, big and little. And, with the citizens of both these cities and of the other cities protesting, the big grafters who ruled Ohio took from Cox's men, who drew it, a code modeled on the Cincinnati board plan; and they made their legislature adopt it for Cleveland and Ohio!

For the Cleveland of Tom Johnson and the Ohio of Hanna, what does it all mean? It means what Hanna means. Hanna is dead, but the spirit of Hanna lives. What does Hanna mean? Unless I have failed to do that man full justice, I have shown that Hanna meant no evil. He was not a bad man. He was the kind of American we all like, the kind that, wanting something, goes after it, fighting, destroying, hurting other men, and, if necessary, corrupting and undermining the government and American institutions, but—winning. They do not mean to do harm. Hanna did not mean to injure the government. When he attended that special session he was there not to make the men of Cleveland what the men of Cincinnati are, not to make the government of Cleveland as bad as the government of Cincinnati. He wanted a street-railway franchise; the Cleveland of Tom Johnson wouldn't give him one. He tried to get one from that special session; his control was so absolute that his friends say they had a hard time making the old man understand why a special legislature, called for another purpose, could not give him a perpetual grant to the streets in Cleveland! No, Hanna saw only that down in Cincinnati a business man who wanted a franchise could have one; he might have to pay Cox, but he would get what he wanted in his business. People called Cox a boss, but what of that? He wasn't a "socialist-anarchist-nihilist" like Tom Johnson. Mark Hanna was a good man spoiled by the privileges our government let him steal; he came to think that, not only his franchises were his very own private property, but our government, also.

Now, is it clear why Mayor Johnson came to run for governor of Ohio? He had to. The System, beaten in Cleveland, had retreated to the state, and there, with its legislature, its courts, and its other cities, it was preparing to crush him and conquer Cleveland. Hanna, Cox, and the Cox-McLean Cincinnati "Democrats " beat Johnson that time. They elected a " good" banker, Myron T. Herrick. Poor Governor Herrick! I saw him soon after he entered office. He is affable, but weak; everybody spoke well of him then, and he would have done very well, but they gave him the veto, and then his boss died. Banker-fashion, he tried to please everybody, made incompatible promises, tried to escape, but was caught naked in his weakness, and now everybody is too hard on him—except the System. The System leaders make a wry face, but they found him "safe." He carried out a bargain Hanna had made with the brewers. Without knowing that there was a System, he signed a bill to transfer city elections from the spring to the fall; after telling me that he believed the Cleveland School System was the best in the country, he signed, against the protest of all the earnest educators in the state, a bill which put upon Cleveland and all the other cities Cincinnati's plan, modified a little, but making possible a big, irresponsible board. Herrick was to be renominated, therefore, and he may be re-elected. The System has a strong hold on Ohio. "We have the fanners always," said one of its leaders. But Ohio will escape.

Cleveland or Cincinnati?

The signs of promise? The boss is dead, the throne is empty, and there is no heir in sight. The people are beginning to see things. Even in Cincinnati (Cox scoffed when I told him so) there is some discontent, and the nucleus of veteran reformers are finding recruits willing to line up against Cox, "just Cox," for a fight, not to throw out the slot machines, not to ameliorate particular evils, but to restore representative government and be free, wholly free. Dayton is bad and glad of it; "we hope to be as 'good' as Cincinnati some day," one of its rulers told me. Southern Ohio is pretty low. But the spirit of the late Mayor Jones lives in Toledo, and though its citizens have to present "petitions in boots" to get it, they do get representative government. And in Cleveland we have, as I write, this spectacle: Two street-railway men. Mayor Johnson, representing the city. President Andrews for his stockholders, negotiating in public for the disposition of the street-railway system. There is no excitement, no bad feeling, no suspicion of boodle or corruption. Some franchises have expired, others are falling in; all must be renewed. Mayor Johnson opposes any renewal except upon terms which will bring to the city two things: First, the removal of the street railways out of politics; second, the benefit, in the form of reduced fares, improved service, or profits, of all that increase of earnings which will come with the natural growth of the city. Mr. Andrews says this is fair, so it is all a question of terms. Mr. Andrews wants par for his stock. Mr. Johnson points to the market price, 78, and offers more—to be fair. But he will not close a deal without a vote of the people.

"And they will be fair," Mayor Johnson told me, and Mr. Andrews said: "Oh, they will be fair."

So the cynics lie who say that capital has to corrupt a democratic government to get a "square deal" from the people. Such men as Horace Andrews, an honest conservative, and Tom Johnson, a patient liberal, could settle Cleveland's street-railway problem, they and the people they both trust. But will they? Their spirit would settle all our political problems. But will it? See now the other side of the picture: Back of Johnson lurk the red radicals, sneering, eager to throw a brick; and back of Andrews sneaks his big stockholder, who also sneers, and, like the anarchist that he is, stands ready to throw—a bribe. And this other spirit, the spirit of the Hannas, who cried "down with the nihilist-anarchist-socialist," and annihilating all city charters, waded through municipal anarchy to the class socialism of Cincinnati, this same spirit was corrupting councilmen in the interest of the lighting company while I was in Cleveland, and it was holding at the state capital a bill to take away from the cities, and give to a state board, the power to deal with all the franchise questions in Ohio, state and country, too.

The forces of evil, beaten in the city, hold the state. The forces of good, winning in Cleveland, fighting in Toledo, hopeful in Cincinnati, to hold their own, must carry Ohio. Ohio—the whole state—has to make the choice, the choice we all have to make: Cleveland or Cincinnati. The Herricks and Dicks and false "Fire Alarms" won't do; we cannot "stand pat." It is the square deal, or bribes and brickbats; Horace Andrews or Mark Hanna; Tom Johnson or Greorge Cox, all over the United States.

McClure's Magazine
January, 1906

A Servant of God and the People

"You saw go up and down Valladolid
A man of mark, to know next time you saw."
                    —ROBERT BROWNING.

THAT Jersey City should have produced Mark Fagan is strange enough. But that Mark Fagan, grave, kind, and very brave, should have been able, as mayor, to make Jersey City what it is: a beginning of better things all over this land of ours, that is stranger still. And no man there pretends to understand it. Yet it is a simple story.

Mark as they call him—the men, the women, and the children—was born September 29, 1869, in the Fifth Ward where he lives now. His parents were poor Irish, very poor. They moved over to New York when Mark was a child, and the father died. Mark sold newspapers. The newsboy dreamed dreams and fought fights. He claimed a corner, Twelfth Street and Avenue A, developed a good trade, and when competition came, appealed to the man in the store to say if he wasn't there first. The man in the store wouldn't decide; he told the boys they must fight it out among themselves, so they laid down their papers and they fought it out. Mark held his corner. "Life is one long fight for right," he says now, this very gentle man, who fights and holds his corner.

The newsboy's dreams, like his fights, were very simple affairs. When I pried into them, I expected to hear of driving a locomotive or the presidency, at least. But no, it seems that some men said roughly that they didn't want to buy a paper, others said it kindly. Mark made up his mind that when he became a man he would be like the kind men. Sometimes the nights were cold and the newsboy felt hungry and lonely; passing houses where the family sat in the basement room, all lighted up and warm,

A Servant of God and the People

with plenty of smoking hot food before them, Mark stopped to look in and he dreamed that when he grew up, he also would have a home. He couldn't go to school; he had only six months of it all told. But he didn't like school; it was indoors, and he has dreamed that he would like to have, in Jersey City, schools on large plots of ground, so that part of the teaching might be done in the open. But this dream came later.

When he was twelve or fourteen Mark became a helper on a wagon. Then he learned the trade of a frame-gilder with William B. Short, a Scotch man who made a deep impression on the boy. Short was a "genuine man." He was a Republican in politics. The boy was a Democrat by birth, breeding, and environment. But the man pointed out to the little Tammany Democrat on election days the Tammany line-up of men from the street into the saloon and out again, with foam on their lips and something in their hands, to the ballot-box. Mark had a painful time, talking to people on both sides, but what he saw with his own staring eyes, with the honest gilder pointing at the living facts, made the Democrat a Republican.

The next period made the boy a man. His uncle, an undertaker in Jersey City, offered Mark a job, and he moved with his mother and sister back there to take it. Now this business often has a demoralizing effect upon men. They see dreadful sights, and they harden or take to drink. Mark saw dreadful sights; you can see that he sees them now when he recalls those days, but they softened, they sweetened Mark Fagan. He saw homes where the dead mother left nothing but a helpless child -- nothing, you understand, but the child. He saw that the poor suffered greatly from the wrongs of others, not alone of those above, but of those also that were about them, and yet, the poor were great in charity for the poor. "I came" he says, in his quiet, level tone, "I came to have pity for the poor and admiration."

You hear that Mark, the undertaker, cared for the living child as well as the dead mother; he stayed with his job after the funeral, and by and by people came to the undertaker with the business of life. His explanation is that he "could write and fix up insurance and things like that." Others could write and fix up insurance; the point was that they trusted Mark to do it, all his neighbors, all nationalities, all ages; and he did it. One of the odd branches of this odd undertaking business was to fix up marriages. It seems that, among the poor also, there comes a time soon after the wedding when husband and wife fall out; love turns to what looks like hate, and sometimes becomes hate. In Jersey City, young married people used, when the crisis arrived, to go to Mark; they'd "tell him on each other"; and he would listen and seem to judge. But what he really did was to get everything said and done with, and then when they were tired and satisfied, and sorry, he "fixed 'em up."

So far there is nothing so very extraordinary about Mark Fagan. He is a type of the men who, winning the faith and affection of their neighbours, become political leaders. "Popularity" makes them "available" as candidates or "ward bosses." Nothing was further from Mark's mind, but it was inevitable that he should go into politics, and the way he went in was natural and commonplace. One Sunday morning as he was leaving church several young fellows stopped him to propose that he run for the board of freeholders. He was "not adapted," he said; why didn't one of them run? They explained that "Bob" Davis, the Democratic boss, wouldn't let them run; wouldn't let anybody run in their party who wouldn't knuckle under to him. But Mark was a Republican. The ward, like the city and county, was heavily Democratic, and since there was so little chance of winning, the Republican ring would let anybody have the nomination. If Mark would let them, they would arrange it, fight with him, and he might be elected. They couldn't persuade Mark himself, but they knew how to get him. They went to his mother. They explained it to her, and she bade Mark run. He asked her if she understood it all, and she said she didn't, except that it seemed to be a chance to do some good in the ward.

Thus Mark Fagan was started in politics. When he took the Republican nomination and his popularity showed, the fellows that got him into the fight got out. They had to; they were called off by the bosses who ran the two parties as one. That made Mark fight the harder. Left high and dry by "the organization," he went to the people of his district.

"I was bound to win," he says, "and I felt that if I was beaten it would be because I wasn't known to enough of the voters. And, anyhow, I wanted to know my people in my ward."

So he started at 5.45 one morning at one corner of his ward, and he went systematically through it, knocking at every door, seeing every man, woman, and child; he climbed 3,700 flights of stairs in seventeen nights; and he promised to "serve the people of his ward faithfully and honestly." Mark was elected, and dirty Jersey City was amazed.

Now comes the first remarkable thing about this remarkable man. The corruption, political and financial, of the United States is built up on the betrayal of the people by the leaders, big and little, whom they trust, and the treason begins in the ward. The ward leader, having the full, fine, personal faith of his neighbours, takes their confidence and their votes, and he delivers these things and his own soul to the party bosses who sell out the interests of the city, state, and nation to the business leaders, who as we know now use the money we entrust to them to rob us and corrupt our political, commercial and our higher life.

When Mark Fagan had taken his oath, the other, older freeholders came to him, and they invited him into "the combine." There was no mystery about it. There was a combine and there was graft; of course a man wants his share of the graft, and though Fagan was a Republican, party made no difference; both parties were in on it, and Fagan had a right to what was coming to him. Something—the man doesn't know exactly what it was—something which he thinks is religious, made him decline to go in. He is a quiet man, and he made no outcry. He didn't perfectly understand anyhow, then, just what it all meant. It simply "didn't look right" to Mark, so he did not sell out the people of his ward who trusted him to serve them. And the worst of it was, he couldn't serve them. If he wouldn't "stand in," the combine wouldn't let him have anything for his ward, not even the needed, rightful improvements. All he got were three political jobs, and they were a gift to him. The combine having distributed all the offices, had three left over. Since these were not enough to go around again, they wrangled till somebody, to save the combine, suggested giving them all to Mark. They "kind of liked" Mark, so this bit of patronage went to him with a whoop. Mark was not re-elected freeholder. He says that his inability to do things for the ward did not hurt him with his people; more of them voted for him than ever before. But the state and city rings had had a gerrymander about that time, and they so arranged the lines of Mark's ward that he was beaten. He served his neighbours privately till the next year the Republicans nominated him for the state senate. Hopeless, anyway, the candidacy fell upon a presidential year, Bryan's first, and the Democratic County of Hudson was wild with party enthusiasm. But the moment Mark was nominated he left the convention and, fifty feet from the door, began his campaign; he met two men; he told them he had just been nominated, that if he was elected he would serve them "honestly and faithfully," and they promised to vote for him. In this fashion, man to man, he canvassed his county and, though it went against him, he ran way ahead of his ticket. And he carried the city.

A Republican who can carry a Democratic city is the "logical" candidate of his party for mayor, and, in 1901, Mark Fagan was nominated. Some of the little bosses warned the big bosses that they couldn't handle him, but the big bosses pooh-poohed the fears of the little bosses. In the first place he wouldn't be elected. The railroads, the public service companies, and some of the greatest corporations in the world have offices and properties in Jersey City, and their agents there had used money so extensively that they ruled absolutely a people supposed to be utterly corrupted. Bribery at the polls, election frauds, ballot-box stuffing, all sorts of gross political crimes had made this home of "common people" and corporations notorious. "Bob" Davis was the Democratic boss, politically speaking; but Mr. E. F. C. Young, banker, leading citizen, public utility magnate, was the business boss who, backing Davis, was the real power. Colonel Sam Dickinson, the Republican boss, was a corporation man, and one might expect that his party, which was in power in the state, would help him. But no. General Sewell, U. S. senator, Pennsylvania railroad official, and Republican state boss, dispensed Republican patronage in Hudson County, through the

Democratic boss, Mr. E. F. C. Young. Sewell was dead now, but the custom survived him, and in 1901 the Democrats nominated against Fagan George T. Smith, Young's son-in-law, an employee of the Pennsylvania. So Fagan had against him the money, the "best citizens," the "solid, conservative business interests" of the state and city, and both rings. Hence, the certainty that Fagan would be defeated. But even if he should win the big bosses believed they could "handle him." They had sized up the man. And if you could size up Mark Fagan—feel his humility and see the pleading, almost dependent look of his honest, trustful eyes—you would understand how ridiculous to the big bosses the worry of the little bosses must have seemed.

An astonished city elected Mark. His quiet campaign from house to house, his earnest, simple promise to "serve you honestly and faithfully," had beaten bribery. His kind of people believed Mark Fagan, and so, though the Republican ticket as a whole was beaten, Mark was mayor. Being mayor, Mark assumed that he was the head of the city government. He didn't understand that his election meant simply that his boss had come into his own. He saw Governor Murphy appoint Colonel Dickinson secretary of state, and he heard that the colonel was to have some of the local patronage of the Republican state government. Mark might have assumed that he had "made" Dickinson. But he was told that it was the other way around. They walked in upon Mark the colonel who "made" him; the editor of the paper that "elected" him; and General Wanser who was ready to help "unmake" him, these and the other big Republican bosses who expected, as a matter of course, to give Jersey City a "good business government," called on the mayor-elect. Mark, who has no humour, tried to tell me how he felt when they came and took charge of him and his office. Putting one fist to his forehead, and pressing the other hand on the back of his head (a characteristic gesture), he said that he looked up to those men; he felt his own deficiencies of education and experience; he had a heavy sense of his tremendous responsibility; and he wanted help and advice, for he wished to do right. But, you see, he was mayor. The people looked to him. He might make mistakes; but since he must answer for them to those people, man to man, you understand, and man by man, when he knocked again at their doors, why, Mark Fagan thought he ought to listen to "his party," yes, and be "true to it," yes; but after all, the whole people would expect him to decide all questions—all.

Mayor Fagan didn't realize, at that time, that our constitutional governments were changed, that this was a business nation and that the government represented not the people, but business; not men, but business men. So he sat silent, apart, and perplexed—not indignant, mind you, not quarreling and arguing; no, the others did that; the mayor only listened perplexed while Colonel Dickinson and General Wanser and the rest discussed "his" policy and "his" appointments; discussed them and disagreed, quarreled, all among themselves, but finally agreed among themselves. And then, when they had settled it all and turned to him, a party in harmony, he "got off something about being mayor and reserving the right to change some items of the slate and policy." It was their turn to be perplexed. Perplexed? They left him in a rage to "go to the devil."

The mayor, abandoned, proceeded with a quiet study he was making all by himself of the city. He went about, visiting the departments, meeting officials, and asking questions. People wrote complaints to him, and some of them were as perplexed as the bosses when Mayor Fagan answered their letters in person, looked into their troubles, and went off to "fix 'em up." There were lots of things for a mayor to do: parents couldn't get their children into school; no room. Families couldn't get water above the second floor; no force. Cellars were flooded; pipes leaked. Jersey City, corrupt, neglected, robbed, needed everything. And Mayor Fagan took its needs seriously. He must have more schools, more and better sewers, more water; and he did want to add a public bath and parks and music in the parks. "I wanted," he says, "to make Jersey City a pleasant place to live in; I'd like to make it pretty." Jersey City pretty! Were you ever in Jersey City? I suppose when your train was coming through Jersey City you were gathering up your things and being brushed by the porter; you probably never looked out of the window. Well, look next time and you will see that what the railroad attorneys say is true:

"It's nothing but a railroad terminal. They talk about the railroads owning it; the railroads ought to own it. It's the terminal of the traffic of a continent."

Nevertheless, Mark Fagan, who lived there and who knew personally so many families that lived and must always live there, he, their mayor, dreamed of making it a pleasant city to live in. How? Money, lots of money, was needed, and how was money to be raised for such a purpose? When he had broached his idea to the bosses it seemed to fill them with disgust, and now that they were gone, he didn't know what to do. He needed help, and help came.

Among the appointments recommended to him by Colonel Dickinson was that of George L. Record, to be corporation counsel. Record, an able lawyer, had been the principal orator in the campaign, and the mayor "took to him." But it was whispered that Record was interested in a contracting company which was building waterworks for the city, and the mayor, suspicious by this time of everybody, hesitated. Record was resentful, but he had had dreams of his own once. He had read Henry George and his dreams were of economic reforms—taxation. But he had fought the bosses in vain, and was about ready to give up when, reflecting upon the rock they all had struck at the bottom of this mild mayor's character, he saw that "by Jove, here was an honest man who could make people believe in his honesty." He went to see him. The water business was explained; Record had been engaged only as a broker, and he was out of it. He was free to take Mark's pledge to be "loyal to the mayor and the people of Jersey City." They had a long, warm talk. The mayor's mind ran to the betterment of the physical conditions of life; Record's to more fundamental reforms, but taxation was the way to raise money to make the city pleasant.

They outlined a policy. They took in others to form a cabinet: Edgar B. Bacon, Frank J. Higgins, Edward Fry, and Robert Carey—all these, and Record and Fagan, are Mark Fagan. They discuss questions as they arise, and the mayor decides; they agree, but Mark is the mayor. Some people say Record is the boss, but he laughs.

"The big grafters know better," he says. "They failed to handle Mark, and when they found that I was 'next' they asked me to sell him out. I didn't tell them that I wouldn't; I told them I couldn't. And I can't, and they know I can't. I can advise, I can instruct, and the man will try, actually try hard to see things as I do. For he trusts me, and he wants to be shown. He wants to know. But he decides; and there's something in him—I don't know what it is—something that tells him what is right. No. I've been a help, a great help, to him, but so have the others of us, and we have helped him to decide to do things no one of us alone would have had the nerve to do. And there's where he is great. It all comes down to this: We all agree on the right thing to do, and we do it; but when the howl goes up and the pull begins to draw, we put it all up to Mark. "Blame him." we say; "we can't help it" and they blame him. But that eases us, and, you see, Mark prefers it that way. He wants to stand for everything; everything. Oh, he should, yes, but you see, he wants to."

The policy the mayor and his corporation counsel outlined was to equalize taxation. They couldn't raise the rates; the city was overburdened with taxes already, but the corporations probably dodged their share. Record didn't know that they did; the mayor was to see, and while he went about with the tax lists and an expert, Record had a talk with the boss, Dickinson. The mayor had consented to let the colonel have most of the patronage if "the party" would let him carry out his policy, and Record argued with Dickinson, that having made all the money he needed, it was time for him to play the big game of straight politics, take his ease and the credit of a good administration. Dickinson liked the idea.

The mayor and his expert reported that the poor paid taxes on about 70 percent of the value of their property; privileged persons on about 50 percent; the corporations on all the way from 30 percent, to nothing. Mark Fagan had a new purpose in life. The others laughed at the old, old story; it was new to Mark, and he raised rates on the tax dodgers. There was an awful clamour, of course, and there were pulls, but all complaints were referred to the little mayor, who, seeing complex business problems in a simple way, was a rock.

Then there were the trolleys. These were valuable privileges. Why shouldn't they pay a fair tax? There was a reason why they shouldn't: Republican, as well as Democratic, bosses were in on them. This didn't deter the mayor, and when Record sounded Colonel Dickinson, the Republican boss winked the other eye. He wasn't in trolleys, and he had had a bit of a row with E. F. C. Young, the Democratic boss who was. As for the other Republican bosses who were in with Young, they might "see the mayor" for themselves. They did. When it was noised about that the sacred private property of the street car company in the middle of the public streets was to be assessed somewhat as ordinary property, General Wanser, for instance, called on the mayor.

"What's this I hear you are going to do with the trolleys, Mark?" he asked.

"Whatever is right," said Mark. "I understand they are undervalued; if they are, we will raise them."

"Well, now, I'm a good friend of yours, Mark, and I don't want you to do anything of that sort."

"If you are a good friend of mine," said Mark, "you shouldn't ask me to do anything wrong."

"Don't you know." said Wanser, "that every dollar I have in the world is in this thing?"

Mark Fagan couldn't see the relevancy of this; he talked about other people having every dollar that they had in houses and lots, and yet paying taxes. As General Wanser remarked when he left in high dudgeon, Mark Fagan had "damn queer ideas about things." He had, and he has. One of his queer ideas is what may be called a sense of public property. All men know that private property is sacred; for centuries that sense has been borne in upon us till even thieves know it is wrong to steal private property. But highly civilized men lack all sense of the sacredness of public property; from timber lands to city streets that is a private graft. And when one day the mayor received an anonymous note advising him to have the underlying franchise of the trolley company looked up, he was interested. He had the note copied in typewriting, then he scrupulously destroyed the original. The copy he gave to Corporation Counsel Record.

Mr. Record discovered to his amazement that the franchise had expired. We need not go into details. The mayor and his cabinet decided to take the matter into the courts; if the court decided that the franchise belonged to the city, the mayor meant to take it. To some of the mayor's advisers this looked like a dreadful step to take; they thought of the "widows and orphans" and other innocent holders of the stock. It didn't look so bad to Colonel Dickinson; he thought only of his rival boss, E. F. C. Young, whom he had seen grabbing up the street railways under his nose. And it didn't look bad to Mayor Fagan; he thought of the "widows and orphans" who held no stock except in Jersey City, which so it seemed to Mark had as much right as an individual or a private corporation to whatever belonged to it.

Unbeknown to the cabinet, however, while they were deliberating on their discovery, the great Public Service Corporation was being formed. The big men in the Prudential Life and its Fidelity Trust Company had gone in with the U. G. I. (United Gas Improvement Co.) of Philadelphia and the Pennsylvania Railroad crowd to buy up practically all the trolleys, electric light, and other available public utility companies of New Jersey. Among these purchases were the Jersey City lines and, also, an electric light company in which Colonel Dickinson was an employee. This was embarrassing to Dickinson; E. F. C. Young was out and Dickinson and his friends were in. Record told Fagan all about it, but, as he says, ''Mark didn't care; he wasn't even interested.'' He made public his plan to test the franchise, the stock fell and there was a great ado. The Public Service Corporation had walked straight into politics. Tom McCarter, the attorney general, was made president of the company and his brother, Robert, was made attorney general of the state. As we all know, the new crowd acquired such a heritage of corrupt power that they were able to send the president of the Prudential, John F. Dryden, to the United States Senate. This power, and the power of the U. G. I. (the same that drove Philadelphia to revolt) came down upon Dickinson and Record. The grafters didn't want to see the mayor, but Dickinson and Record told them they must, so Dryden gave a yachting party up the Hudson. Dryden, Randall Morgan, and

Tom McCarter went and Dickinson, Record, and the mayor's cabinet—all but the mayor. The party was fog-bound off Hoboken, so they had no sail, and, though they talked, they did no business. They had to see Fagan.

They saw Fagan. The U. G. I. has rooms at Sherry's for such business, and there one afternoon was held a conference which has passed into the traditions of New Jersey. The more important persons present were Mayor Fagan, Record, Bacon, Carey, and Dickinson representing Jersey City; Tom McCarter, of the Public Service Corporation; and Randall Morgan of the U. G. I. The rooms were luxurious, the entertainment was good, and the conversation friendly and pleasant. When they got down to business, everybody felt as if they ought to be able to agree—everybody but Mark Fagan. He sat apart, cold and still. He says now that he felt at the time that he shouldn't have gone there at all, but that all the way over on the boat and during the conversation he was conning over just what he would say; that it was "not his business, but the city's, and that the case must go to the courts to decide." Tom McCarter spoke for the trolley, Carey for the city, and they got nowhere. Randall Morgan was talking tactfully to the mayor in a corner, when suddenly McCarter turned upon Mark and said:

"Well, Mr. Mayor, what is your decision?"

The mayor was ready. He had no decision to give, he said. Jersey City was going to take the case into court, and the courts would decide.

McCarter always loses his temper when opposed by an honest government. "You may be an honest man," he shouted at the mayor, "but you act like a blackmailer. And you, George Record, I'll never forgive you for letting me put my good money into this trolley company without telling me what you knew about it." He insulted them all, one by one, in turn, including Sam Dickinson, and then he made a famous threat to the whole party:

"To all of you I say, you can't bring your suit without the consent of the attorney general, and the attorney general is my brother."

No matter what an honest man in office tries to do, if he persists, he comes sooner or later upon the corrupt business back of corrupt politics. And no matter what kind of reform it undertakes, an honest city administration, if it proceeds logically, has to appeal sooner or later to the corrupt state government back of the corrupt city government. Mark Fagan had come, as we have seen, upon the trolley business, and when Tom McCarter pointed to his brother Robert at Trenton, he was showing the mayor of Jersey City where he must go next. And Mayor Fagan went where Tom McCarter pointed, and what Tom McCarter predicted happened. When Jersey City asked attorney general McCarter to take its expired franchise into court, Tom's brother, Robert, refused.

Thus Mark Fagan learned that the trolley was king of his state. And he was to learn that the railroad was queen. During this, his first administration, the mayor had been able, by simply catching tax dodgers and "equalizing" the taxes of privileged individuals and corrupt corporations, to buy a site for a new high school; begin one school, finish another; put up eleven temporary schools, thus providing seats for all the children in the city; and make needed repairs in all the schools. He had built a free bath; established free dispensaries; extended one park, bought another, improved two more, and given free concerts in them all. He improved the fire, street-cleaning, and health departments, and he repaired and extended the sewerage system. But he wanted to do more, and he needed more money. How could he get it?

In the course of his investigations he discovered what well-informed persons long had known, that railroad property was taxed separately in New Jersey. We needn't go into figures. The point was, the railroads were taxed by a state board which they controlled, and which enabled them to fix their own valuation. Not only that, their tax rate, as fixed by law, was lower than the local rate on ordinary property. All localities suffered more or less, but in Jersey City, where the railroads needed much and the most valuable ground (waterfront), every time they bought property for railroad use, they not only paid less taxes on it than the private owner had paid, but they took it off the city list. The obvious effect was that the most valuable taxable property in the city constantly decreased and the tax on the rest has steadily increased and must forever increase.

It was a matter of life and death to Jersey City, to have this system changed, but the city was helpless alone. Mark Fagan, renominated, had to promise to go to Trenton with this business and with the trolley trouble. It was an exciting campaign. The railroads, the public service companies, the taxed corporations—all the corrupt and privileged interests set about beating Mark Fagan, but the mayor, going from house to house, and making, man to man, his simple promise to be "honest and true"—defeated the system.

Elected, he and his cabinet went to the legislature, and they had their bills introduced. Nothing came of a bill against Robert McCarter. A franchise tax measure was still-born. Their equal tax bill was crude, so the Democrats substituted a better one which the Jersey City Republicans accepted and supported. Referred to a committee, there were hearings on the bill, but it was buried there. The silent power of the king and the queen of the state would not let it come out.

Mark Fagan, with his staring eyes, saw that the government of his state, the control of his own party was in the hands of the most favoured men in and out of the state, those that corrupted it to get and keep privileges. And he wanted to say so. As the session drew to a close, he felt he must do something, but what? He must appeal from the state to the people of the state. How? Somebody suggested a letter to Governor Murphy, and they drew up one which described what Mark Fagan saw. The mayor wanted to publish it right away. Record objected that he "couldn't see the end of it." The mayor said it was true; it was his duty to say it; and he wanted to "let the consequences go." Record suggested showing it to Dickinson. The mayor said "no"; it is characteristic of him to avoid consulting those of his advisers who, he thinks, will oppose an act he believes to be right. Record did show it to Dickinson, however, and to his surprise the boss was for it. The Public Service crowd from Essex had beaten some political legislation of his, so the colonel, a vindictive man, was for revenge. Record advised one more appeal to Governor Murphy, and he thought that was agreed upon. And Governor Murphy, understanding that the letter was to be withheld, had a luncheon with the other leaders, who decided to do "anything you want." Meanwhile, however, Fagan and Dickinson had handed to the reporters Fagan's famous letter to the Hon. Franklin Murphy, governor of New Jersey:

March 24, 1904.
"*MY DEAR SIR: As mayor of Jersey City and also a member of the Republican party, I venture to address to you this public communication in the hope of averting a possible calamity to Jersey City and almost certain disaster to the Republican party of New Jersey. The present session of the legislature is drawing to a close. Its record, on the whole, is bad and in some respects is disgraceful. Its control by corporation interests, in the assembly at least, has been absolute. For this condition the Republican party is responsible.*

"*The bills for equal taxation demanded by a practically unanimous public sentiment, in all New Jersey at least, have been buried in committee at the command of the railroad corporations, and every attempt to move them has been resisted by a solid Republican vote upon the test motions. The Republican majority has made no attempt to defend this action, and has thereby admitted that it cannot be defended....*

"*Bills affecting Jersey City, notably several bills to empower the city to sell its surplus water to neighbouring communities, which it has supplied for twenty years, and which desire to renew contracts with us, have been buried in committee.*

"*A bill to ratify a water contract recently made between Jersey City and East Newark was introduced early in the session, and referred to the committee on boroughs, which committee still holds it. The bill was afterward introduced under another number, and re-referred to the committee on municipal corporations, where it still reposes.*

"*A bill to allow Jersey City to test the right to a trolley franchise, which we are advised by counsel has expired, has met a similar fate. Our most determined efforts to get these committees to act have been unavailing, because of the Republican members thereof, but we can get no satisfactory reason for, nor explanation of, this action....*

"What is the meaning of all this? The answer is plain. A Republican legislature is controlled by the railroad, trolley, and water corporations. And the interests of the people are being betrayed.

"While I charge no man with personal corruption, I do not hesitate to say that this is a condition of affairs which is essentially corrupt, and which, if unchecked, means the virtual control of our state and our party by corporations.

"As a citizen I say that this condition is dangerous and demoralizing. As a public official I protest against this injustice done to Jersey City. As a member of the Republican party I deplore its subserviency to corporate greed and injustice. No political party can long receive the support of the people with such a record as this Republican legislature is making. . . ."

Whatever form the issue takes upon which an honest man in politics makes his first fight, if he fights on, he finally will come to the real American issue: representative government. He may start out like Mayor Fagan for good government, or like Folk to prosecute boodlers, or like President Roosevelt to regulate railroad rates; before he gets through, he will have to ask the people to answer the question: "Who is to rule the disinterested majority or the specially interested, corrupt few?" And to make their answer, the people have to beat the boss, who is the agent of the businesses that rule and are destroying representative democracy.

Mayor Fagan's letter to Governor Murphy raised the great question in New Jersey. It took at first the form that the gentle mayor of Jersey City had given it, railroad taxation. The railroads tried to keep it down. Governor Murphy appointed a commission to inquire into the need of a change in railroad tax methods, but the Republicans nominated for governor Edward C. Stokes, who resigned a directorship of a branch of the Pennsylvania Railroad to run, and the issue of the campaign was the Jersey City issue. And Stokes was elected, but he had had to promise, and public opinion and the outrageous facts forced from the commission a report for some change. And "some change" was made; enough to relieve Jersey City, but not enough to hurt the railroads.

The people of Jersey saw that the railroads drew that law, that the railroads dominated still their state government, the railroads and the Public Service Corporation. For, besides the railroad legislation, the Jersey City men continued their franchise tax fight. And, meanwhile, Tom McCarter had aroused the people of Essex County to resist his perpetual franchise "grabs" in the Oranges. Jersey City wanted to tax franchises; Essex reformers were for limiting them. Record saw that they both were fighting one enemy and he advised a union, and, because he was wiser than the Essex leaders, he and Fagan took up their neighbors' less essential issue. Everett Colby, a young Republican assemblyman from Essex, led the fight for limited franchises. He was beaten but the defeat showed what the state government represented.

So they went home to raise the real question. Fagan and Record to Jersey City, Colby and the Orange men to Essex. The Orange men had seen that Carl Lentz, the Republican boss of Essex County, who ruled them at home, was the agent, at Trenton, of the railroads and of the Public Service Corporation. They went after him. Lentz declared that Colby should not go back to the legislature; since he represented the people, not the corporations, he should not be renominated. But Assemblyman Colby said he not only would go back; he would go back as a senator, and he would take his nomination and his election from the people. Fortunately, George L. Record, far-sighted, practical reformer that he is, had engineered through the legislature a primary election law. The people had a chance to control their parties, and the Republicans of Essex went to the primaries, and they turned the party over to Everett Colby. Then the whole people of Essex turned in, and they elected Colby senator and with him, a solid assembly delegation pledged to represent the public interests.

And Jersey City did likewise. After Dickinson and his mayor had given out the Murphy letter, the railroad-trolley rings went after the boss, and they got him. He began to insist in Jersey City upon some sort of compromise with the Public Service Corporation. The company wanted some new grants. The city couldn't get its old case into court; so what was the use of fighting? Why not settle it all out of court? Mayor Fagan hung back, but his cabinet persuaded him to talk it over with Tom McCarter. McCarter called, asking for perpetual franchises. The mayor was willing to negotiate on the basis of a twenty-five-year franchise. McCarter said limited franchises were absurd in Jersey. There they stuck till Record suggested, as a compromise, a perpetual franchise with readjustments of the terms every twenty-five years. McCarter thought this opened a way to a settlement; so did the mayor; and Dickinson, feeling that he had "delivered his man" (the mayor), sailed for Europe. But it wasn't settled. McCarter demanded fifty-year periods, and the mayor, who had had misgivings all along, broke off the negotiations. The Public Service had its way. The Democrats controlled the Street and Water Board, and they passed McCarter's franchise for him.

But it was passed over the mayor's veto, and when Dickinson came home to hear that not his party but the Democrats had sold out to the Public Service, and that he was left, as before, in the ridiculous position of boss who couldn't deliver his mayor, he was angry. And all through the next session he opposed the legislation asked for by his city. He joined the other bosses against the people, and, like Lentz, Dickinson went home to beat "his man" for renomination. Like Everett Colby, Mark Fagan accepted the challenge; he received the nomination for mayor from the Republicans direct and he took the organization besides. Then he turned to the people with this appeal:

"I find myself, at the opening of the campaign, confronted by a threefold opposition. First, that of the Democratic machine and its absolute boss; second, the scarcely concealed and treacherous opposition of a Republican party leader, whose demands in behalf of his corporate clients I have refused to grant; third, the secret but powerful opposition of a combination of public service and railroad corporations, whose unjust corporate privileges are threatened by my reelection. The opposition of the corporations and the reasons therefor, and the close business relations between them and the Democratic boss are well understood by the public. The relations between these corporations, or some of them, and the Republican boss, are not so well known. I explicitly charge that this Republican leader is doing everything in his power to defeat my reelection; that his efforts to that end are jeopardizing the whole Republican ticket; and that this action is in the interest of the public service and railroad corporations. . . .

"These facts, and many others too numerous to mention, have convinced me that it is time to come out in the open and have a square stand-up fight against the Republican boss, the Democratic boss, and the trolley and railroad corporations which control them both. It is impossible for a public official to get along permanently with a boss, except upon terms of abject obedience and the sacrifice of self-respect. Personally I am tired of the experiment. I am sick of talk of party harmony, which means surrender of personal independence and of popular rights. It is time to fight the boss system itself, by which unscrupulous men get between the people and the public officials by control of the party machinery, betray the people, acquire riches for themselves, and attempt to drive out of public life all who will not take orders from the boss, and his real masters, the corporations."

So the fight that fall, in Jersey City, as in Essex County and in New York, as in Toledo and Cincinnati, and Cleveland and Philadelphia, and in Ohio and in Pennsylvania, was a fight against the bosses. And as in those places, so in Jersey City, the people crossed all party lines to follow the leader, and they beat the bosses. Mark Fagan was reelected mayor of Jersey City, and he and Senator Colby and the reformers of Jersey combined against the interests which the bosses represented.

But never mind Jersey! What of Mark Fagan, the man who by following the facts, without a theory of reform, by tackling each obstacle as he approached it, came out upon the truth and gave his state its issues and aroused it finally to take part in the second war for independence that is waging all over this country? I have told simply the simple story of this simple man. The mystery remains. Why did Mark Fagan do it? That is what they ask in Jersey City, and that is what the commercial spirit of this Christian land asks of Folk and La Follette and Tom Johnson. What prompted them to do something for others? What are they after? What is there in it for them? And how and why do they win?

His bitterest foes—the grafters—concede Fagan's honesty. "Bob" Davis was the only one that offered any doubts on that point, and he offered them to me; he had none of his own. Pressed for facts, he admitted that Fagan was "personally on the square." The bigger grafters said Fagan was a demagogue. This is ridiculous. He addresses no prejudices, stirs no passions, makes no appeal to class; he seems to have no sense of class. His talks, like his speeches, are so plain that the wonder is that they count as they do count, winning for him, a Republican, a majority in a Democratic city. I asked the politicians to explain it. Mark has a relative, Jimmy Connolly, once a saloon-keeper, always a hard-headed politician. When Mr. Record confessed he could not account for it he referred me to Jimmy Connolly, and I asked Connolly:

"How does Mark Fagan do it?"

"You can search me," said he. "I've watched him, and I've listened to him, and I give it up. And you can ast anybody in this town; we've all ast ourselves and that is where you'll end up. You'll ast yourself. I don't know what he says, and I've listened to him, but he doesn't say nothing. Leastways, if you or the likes of me said to a fellar what Mark says, I can just hear the fellar say, 'Say, what ye givin' me, what?' 'Say,' he'd say, 'haven't ye got th' price of a drink in your clothes?' But when Mark says it, what he says, they fall down to it like dead soldiers. Nope, you got to find that out for yerself."

And an idea struck him, "Maybe you can," he said. "Now, maybe you can. I'll get a wagon and we'll go chase Mark out to the railroad yards, and you'll listen to him yerself, and maybe you can tell me."

Out to the yards we went, and we joined the mayor. He was going up to a group of men, who stopped work, wiped their hands on their clothes, and formed a shy group. "I'm Mark Fagan," said the mayor as shyly. "I have tried to serve you honestly and faithfully. I don't know how well, but you know my record. That's the way to judge a man, by his record. And if you don't understand anything in it, I'd like to have you ask me about it. If you think I have done right in most things, I'd like to have your support."

That was all. They shook hands, saying nothing, and he moved on.

"Understand that?" said Connelly at my elbow. "Every one of 'em'll vote for him. Why? What's there to it?"

Mark climbed up into the switch tower and began: "I am Mark Fagan—"

"You needn't waste your time here," said the tower man, looking around steadily. "I know you're Mark Fagan, and I know what you're doing. And I'll vote for you till hell freezes over." He flung over the switch, and Mark retreated, abashed.

"He knows me," he said wonderingly to me when he came down. Of course they all know the mayor, but the mayor can't call them by name; he hasn't a good memory for either names or faces, and I saw him talk to men he had talked to before. So there is no flattery, and no familiarity, and that was one point which missed Connolly, who couldn't understand why those men didn't laugh or josh the mayor. "Why don't they give him a song and dance?" he said.

One man in a group I joined before the mayor reached it did say he was going to "have some fun with Mark," and the others in a mood for horse play, dared the bold one to ask Fagan for "the price of a drink." I thought the man would, but when Mark came up, saying, "I am Mark Fagan; I have been mayor for two terms, and I have tried to serve you," etc., etc., the bold man was silent; they were all respectful, and the psychology was plain enough.

The mayor speaks, what Connolly calls "his little piece," with dignity, with the grave dignity of self-respect, and you feel, and those men feel, the perfect sincerity of Mark Fagan.

But that didn't satisfy Jim Connolly, and it wouldn't satisfy anybody in Jersey City. It didn't satisfy me, and since nobody else could help me, I went to Mark himself. I went to his home with him, and I asked him questions. He squirmed, and it wasn't pleasant for me; but I had a theory I wanted to test.

A Servant of God and the People

Maybe it wasn't right to probe thus into the soul of a man, and maybe it isn't fine to show what you see. It hurt Mark Fagan, that interview, and the report of it will hurt more. But I am thinking of those of us who need to see what I saw when I looked in upon the soul of Mark Fagan.

Why had he done the things that had been done for Jersey City? That was the main question. He said he hadn't done those things, not alone. His cabinet had done them. He gave full credit to his associates, and he gave it honestly, as if he wished to be believed. But, as Record says, whatever of knowledge and resources he and the rest contributed to the mayor, it was the mayor who furnished the courage, the steady will—the transparent character.

"What is your purpose, Mr. Mayor?"

He elaborated his idea of making Jersey City pleasant. He talked about clean streets, good water and light service, and schools. "Now the schools—I think the schools shouldn't be shut up when school is out. Don't you think it would be nice if the mothers could go there, and the girls, and learn to sew and other things? I'd like to have a gymnasium in the schools; and a swimming tank. The schools ought to be the place where the people of the neighborhood go to read and hear lectures, and hold meetings, and for the children to play. Do you think that is foolish?"

"He hadn't read of the efforts elsewhere for these ends. He was glad to know his scheme had struck others as feasible.

"I don't see why things shouldn't be useful, like that, and pretty. Do you think it would be foolish I haven't talked about this to the others, but do you think it would be so foolish to have flowers in the schools?"

"Why do you care about other people?" I asked. "You seem to like men. Do you really?"

His look answered that, but he went on to talk about his boyhood and his experiences as an undertaker. These would make anybody like the people, he thought.

"What do you mean by the people? " I asked. "The poor people? The working people? When you address a crowd, do you appeal to labor as labor, to the unions, for example?"

"Oh, no. I never do that. I mean everybody. The poor need the most, and most people over here work, but by people I mean men and women and children, everybody."

"Railroad presidents? Do you hate the railroads?"

"No," he said, reflecting. "They do a good deal that is wrong. They corrupt young men, and they don't care anything about Jersey City. They should stop corrupting politics, but you can't expect them to look out for us. We must do that." He paused. "I have hated men, almost, some of these corporation men, but I don't any more. I used to hate men that said things about me that weren't true, that weren't just. But I've got over that now."

"How did you get over it?"

"I have a way," he said, evidently meaning not to tell it.

"You must have been tempted often in the four years you have been in office. Have you ever been offered a bribe?"

"Only once, but that was by a man sent by somebody else. He didn't know what he was doing, and I didn't blame him so much as I did those who sent him."

"But the subtler temptations, how did you resist them?"
"I have a way," he said, again.

This time I pressed him for it; he evaded the point, and I urged that if he knew a way, and a good way, to resist political temptations, others should know of it.

He was most uncomfortable. "It's a good way," he said, looking down. Then, looking up, he almost whispered: "I pray. When I take an oath of office, I speak it slowly. I say each word, thinking how it is an oath, and afterward I pray for strength to keep it."

"A silent prayer?"
"Yes."
"And that helps? Against the daily temptations too?"

"Yes, but I—every morning when I go up the steps of City Hall, I ask that I may be given to recognize temptations when they come to me, and to resist them. And at night, I go over every act and I give thanks if I have done no injury to any man."

"When you were considering whether you would give out that letter to Governor Murphy, why did you say, 'Let the consequences go'?"

"Well, when anything is to be done that I think is right, and the rest say it might hurt my political career, I ask myself if such thoughts are tempting me, and if I think they are, I do that thing quick. That was the way of the Murphy letter."

"They say you want to be governor of New Jersey."

"I know that I don't." he said quietly. "I have asked myself that, and I know that I don't. I don't think that I would be able to be the governor; I mean, able to do much for people in that high office."

"What do you want to do, then?"

"Why, what I am doing now."

"Always? Do you mean that you'd like to be mayor of Jersey City all your life?"

He looked up as if I had caught him at some thing foolish or extravagant, but he answered:

"If I could be—if I could go on doing things for the people all my life, as mayor, I should be very happy. But I can't, I suppose, so I shall be satisfied to have done so well that whoever comes after me can't do badly without the people noticing it."

"Well, what do you get out of serving others, Mr. Mayor? Try to tell me that truly."

He did try. "I am getting to be a better man. You know I'm a Catholic."

"Yes, and some people say the Catholics are against the public schools. Why have you done so much for them?"

He was surprised. "I am mayor of all the people, and the schools are good for the people."

"Well, you were saying that you are a Catholic—"

"Yes, and I go to confession ever so often. I try to have less to confess each time, and I find that I have. Gradually, I am getting to be a better man. What I told you about hating men that were unfair to me shows. Some of them were very unfair; from hating them I've got so that I don't feel anything but sorry for them, that they can't understand how I'm trying to be right and just to everybody. Maybe some day I will be able to like them."

"Like them also! What is it, Mr. Mayor, altruism or selfishness\? Is it love for your neighbour or the fear of God that moves you?"

He thought long and hard, and then he was "afraid it was the fear of God."

"What is your favourite book, Mr. Mayor?"

"'The Imitation of Christ.' Did you ever read it ? I read a little in it, anywhere, every day."

I wouldn't tell Jimmy Connolly, nor "Bob" Davis, nor Sam Dickinson, nor, to their faces, could I say it to many men in Jersey City; I'd rather write than speak it anywhere in this hard, selfish world of ours, but I do believe I understand Mark Fagan, how he makes men believe in him, why he wants to: The man is a Christian, a literal Christian; no mere member of a. church, but a follower of Christ; no patron of organized charities, but a giver of kindness, sympathy, love. Like a disciple, he has carried "the greatest of these " out into the streets, through the railroad yards, up to the doors of the homes and factories, where he has knocked, offering only service, honest and true, even in public office. And that is why he is the marvel of a "Christian" community in the year of our Lord, 1909. And, believe me, that is how and why Mark some day will make his Jersey City "pretty." This gentle man has found a way to solve his problems, and ours, graft, railroad rates and the tariff. There may be other ways, but, verily, if we loved our neighbour as ourselves we would not then betray and rob and bribe him. Impracticable? It does sound so -- I wonder why? -- to Christian ears. And maybe we are wrong; maybe Christ was right. Certainly Mark Fagan has proved that the Christianity of Christ not as the scholars "interpret" it, but as the Nazarene taught it, and as you and I and the mayor of Jersey City can understand it -- Christianity, pure and simple, is a force among men and -- a happiness. Anyhow, that is all there is to the mystery of Mark Fagan; that is what he means.

McClure's Magazine
February, 1906

Everett Colby, The Gentleman From Essex

AMONG the new political leaders whom a reviving democracy is raising up to beat the bosses (and perhaps the real rulers) of the republic is Everett Colby, the state senator from Essex County, New Jersey. Born in 1874, he was only thirty-two years old when he "busted" his boss; he shows what a young man can do. The son of Charles L. Colby, builder of the Wisconsin Central Railroad, he inherited wealth and the associations of big business; he shows what a rich young man may do if he rises above his class. And the gentleman from Essex was brought up in a class.

Imperial Kipling has raged at the "flanneled fools" of England. Did you know we had them? We have. There is a constantly growing class of rich men's sons who can throw as much strength, nerve and concentrated intelligence into sport as their fathers put into the game of life; but, having been brought up only to play, they can't work—"can't," not "won't." They don't know how; they don't know anything but games, and they cannot learn. Everett Colby was headed straight for this fate when a man got hold of him—J. A. Browning, a teacher who teaches. He took a small class of boys who had busy fathers and loving mothers: Harold and Stanley McCormick, Percy and John D. Rockefeller, Jr., and Everett Colby. Everett Colby was in the worst condition. The boy could only play. "He played hard," says Mr. Browning, "but it was sport, not work. He couldn't read till he was fifteen; he couldn't fix his attention. I got into his mind through his hands. He liked to play with tools. I let him. It was play till once I set him to making a bookcase for his mother. He finished that, and it was good, and it was work."

Young Colby was prepared for Brown, where he went to college with young John D. He still "played hard." He was a splendid young male when he entered; he went in for all the sports: tennis, golf, baseball; and, making the team, was captain in his senior year of the best football eleven Brown ever put into the field. But he worked, too, and he was graduated with his class, '97. In the next year, after the death of his father, he made a tour around the world; then he studied law and played polo; then he married and settled down in Llewellyn Park, Orange, New Jersey. He didn't mean to stay there, but he got into politics. He became a Wall Street broker, but it was politics that saved Everett Colby.

Now, young Colby meant to go into politics. As a "little shaver" he used to go along with his father, who campaigned in Wisconsin as a railroad man. He dreamed that when he grew up he would be a politician, and, because the dream persisted, he went in for debating in college, and afterward for the law. But it was the scenic side of the game that appealed to him, the crowd and the excitement, the fighting, the speaking and the cheers. He says so himself. He was after glory, and maybe that is all he is after now. He doesn't pretend to know. But there lies the peculiar significance of the career of this rich young gentleman in politics. He simply wanted to go into politics not to accomplish anything in particular; not to reform politics; not even with the thought of being practical in politics. He went in on the machine side, and he served "the party"; he put in his money; he took orders; and he obeyed the boss till he saw what politics meant. Even then he didn't revolt right away; he objected as a gentleman to doing things a gentleman couldn't do, but he "went along" till he discovered as an insider what we have discovered from the outside: that the evils of politics, so-called, were all parts of one system which is perverting our government from a representative democracy to a plutocratic tyranny. When this was beaten into his head, Everett Colby fought like a citizen and a man. Wherefore his experiences are not only the story of a new political leader, but an inside view of the System in action.

When young Colby spoke of going into politics, somebody advised him to see Carl Lentz. This German-American was the Republican boss of Essex County. Bosses were as natural to our young American as the north wind or the road to Newark, and he went to Newark and he saw Carl Lentz.

He says the boss talked to him a long while. Colby doesn't recall what was said, but I can hear the boss drawing out and smacking his lips over an attractive young man of means; free with his money and, therefore, "useful"; the son of a railroad magnate and, therefore, "safe"; attractive and honest, therefore promising as a "good man" candidate, and cheap. All the boy wanted was to "make speeches"; he thought politics was oratory.

"He let me speak," Colby says. "Small meetings for a while, then I held the crowd at larger meetings. I spoke till the advertised speaker came, when, amid the shouts for him, I sat down unnoticed, but well satisfied with myself."

He was in politics, and having got in as many another fool young American has got in, he was taken up and taken in, as the rest are. Lentz flattered Colby; then he passed him on to Governor Voorhees, who flattered him. "Seeing the governor" was honour enough for the year 1901, but when the governor asked him if he wanted to get into politics and the young man said he did, and the governor offered to appoint him to an office, the novice was overwhelmed with gratitude and modesty. He didn't know that to be a commissioner on the state Board of Education was simply to be put to a harmless test—by the machine. Colby thought of his education and worried about his fitness, but he took the place, and he did very well, very well, indeed. Then Boss Lentz made him chairman of the executive committee of the Republican organization of West Orange.

"I thought Lentz was a great fellow," he says now, "a great man." Lentz loomed as large to Colby, probably, as Durham looked to a Philadelphian, Cox to a Cincinnati Republican, Ruef to a San Franciscan, or Murphy to a New Yorker. The bosses live on the images we create of them, out of our own silliness.

The chairmanship—"actual practical politics, with great responsibility"—came in 1902. Of course, young Colby had to spend some of his own money, and he did. He was all right, Colby was. In the next year Lentz offered him the senatorship from Essex. That was too much. The young man, modest now, was sure then that he could not be a senator. In the first place he was under the constitutional age. That didn't matter. Lentz could "have that fixed in the Manual," where the statistics of legislators are kept. This sounded a little queer, like a rather unusual north wind or a bad road to Newark, noticeable, but still a perfectly natural phenomenon. Colby refused to go to the Senate; but he consented to go to the Assembly, so Lentz had him nominated, and elected, an assemblyman from Essex.

The education of this young legislator was begun promptly, and it resembled very closely the course of his education as a boy. He saw things with his eyes long before he saw them with his mind; he saw facts separately, but failed to combine them into the truth. He failed, as so many of us fail, for want of imagination, and his story is the story of thousands of young men who go into politics and go along till some day they wake up and find that they are part of a corrupted government.

One day, early in the session, Sam Dickinson asked Assemblyman Colby to introduce certain excise bills. Dickinson was secretary of state and Republican boss of Hudson County, a "great fellow" like Lentz. And, like Lentz, Dickinson probably saw at once the uses of a fine, upstanding young gentleman to "stand for" a piece of dubious excise legislation. Colby looked over the bills; they seemed to him to be merely a weapon to help the Republican machine take away from the Democrats the control of Democratic Hudson County. He hesitated. He went to see the governor about it. Governor Murphy was a gentleman and the father of a friend of Colby's. The young assemblyman didn't know that governors are usually mere figureheads for the System; he felt only that he could trust the Honourable Franklin Murphy. And when the Honourable Franklin Murphy pronounced the bills "all right," Colby was reassured. He introduced them in the House.

Colby's own pet measure—for every legislator thinks he must put some new law upon the books—was a normal school bill. Then Essex County wanted to have passed a bill providing for the purification of the Passaic River; of course, an Essex assemblyman was for that. But you have to have votes to pass bills, and Colby's two bills lacked a majority. How could some more votes be got for them? Colby and some others of his delegation went to the Democratic assemblymen from Hudson.

Would they help? They would if Colby and his crowd would withdraw his excise bills. Colby would see. He saw the governor. The governor saw Dickinson, and Dickinson consented to the dropping of the excise bills. A bargain was struck; Colby's and Essex County's bills were passed with the help of Democratic votes. And then Dickinson asked Colby to reintroduce his excise bills.

The young legislator was astonished. He had given his word, and he wouldn't break it. Dickinson had somebody else to do it, and when Colby threatened to fight, a caucus was called to bind him to it as a "party measure." Colby appealed to the governor, and the governor spoke to Dickinson, but in vain. The caucus was held. Colby protested that the party was bound by his bargain; not he alone, but the accredited Republican leaders had given their word to the Democrats.

"Your word to a Democrat doesn't mean anything," they told him in those very terms. His did, he answered. There was a scene, and amid cries of "Down with the traitor; up with the flag," Colby bolted the caucus. The party jammed through the excise bills, but Colby voted against them. He didn't see the iniquitous part the caucus plays in the perversion of representative government; he saw only his own honor, but that was enough for a gentleman. Wherefore the word of the gentleman from Essex is good with both parties in Jersey politics.

The boy disappointed his own boss, too, in that first year. George L. Record, the man behind Mayor Fagan, of Jersey City, was in Trenton with a primary election bill. This piece of legislation was to play a decisive part in a crisis of young Colby's career, but Colby didn't know that, of course. He was for it, as Edward C. Stokes was, because his instincts were right. Stokes, though the Pennsylvania Railroad man at Trenton, took charge of the bill and to him, next to Record, belongs the credit for its enactment. Some of the other ring men saw the danger to the System that lurked in the measure; Lentz especially was aroused; he couldn't make Stokes see it, but he ordered his own delegation to fight it. And to his young protégé he gave his orders personally.

"Colby," he said, "you're going to vote against that bill."

"No, Major," said Colby. "It's a good bill, and I shall vote for it."

The Major repeated his command, but the young assemblyman laid down the limitation of his subserviency.

"Major," he said, "you must not interfere with me on any but political bills."

As if a primary bill wasn't political! Bosses have their troubles; it takes time and patience to knock all the decency—or, as they would put it, all the poppycock out of a promising young man. Lentz had to stand by and see Colby vote for the primary bill, and that bill became a law. But the honest young legislator, troublesome as he was, had his uses. For example, they won him easily to the support of a bill to require the consent of 20 percent of the stock of a Jersey corporation to bring a stockholder's suit. "It was an awful bill," he says now. "It was introduced in the interest of the United States Steel Company, and I knew that. But I was told what a great business this was, the steel trust, and how 'strike suits' were being brought against it. Strike suits were bad but that bill was worse. It was so bad, indeed, that even I saw my mistake before the session was over." It was so bad they couldn't raise a majority for it, and it was killed that year.

By the close of the session, young Mr. Colby had few friends among the leaders in his own party; they wouldn't speak to him, and one might have supposed that his political career was over. But this was all part of the game. Since the young man was rich, they couldn't buy him with money, so they were applying a little discipline "just to show him." If they could keep him under for a while, they would get him by and by through his ambition; he should have an office and honors. And as a foretaste of what was in store for him, in the next session the Honourable Everett Colby was made floor leader of the Republican majority in the House.

This was taking a big chance on the boy. This was making him responsible for all the dirty party work of the system, but they counted on "pride" and his "sporting blood" to see him through with it. And they handled him very carefully. They didn't tell him everything, and they didn't give him his orders harshly. They approached him through men he liked.

For instance, early in this session (1904) Percy Rockefeller came to Colby with the United States Steel's same old "20 percent consent" bill which had failed in disgrace the year before. We mustn't blame Percy Rockefeller; he seems not to have known what the bill meant. Indeed, the shocking thought is that he was innocent, and that some of his elders in Wall Street had got this boy to go to his boyfriend, Everett, to ask him to introduce this bill which was so bad that even Francis Lynde Stetson, the great corporation's greatest counsel, told Colby afterward that he did right to keep clear of it. The System will sacrifice its own children to have its dirty work done! Everett Colby, fortunately, was "wise" enough to the purposes of the bill to explain them to Percy Rockefeller, and he sent his chum back to those who had sent him with the message that not only would he not father the thing, he would do his best to kill it if anybody else introduced it. And somebody else did introduce it, and when Colby, the leader, opposed it, the System sent its other messengers to him, not boys this time. No. Governor Murphy and ex-Senator (now governor) Stokes, "the Penn's man." The governor called Colby a "Puritan" for his scruples; he said the great corporations threatened to leave the state unless they were "treated fairly," And Stokes, backing up the governor, said he, Stokes, would be willing to go on the stump and advocate a 50 percent law!

This opened a little the eyes of the young legislator. He didn't see the System yet, but he was learning to. These were the leading men of his state and of his party, and the young assemblyman had great respect for them.

"But," he says, "I saw then that they all were corporation men, and that they represented in politics the interests of corporations."

Seeing this, he opposed and he helped to beat that particular bill, but he said nothing. "What could a fellow say?" He went on, and his education went on.

This was the session when the present issues of New Jersey politics were raised in their present form. Mark Fagan, the mayor of Jersey City, raised them. The Christian mayor went to Trenton with his corporation counsel, George L. Record, to ask in the name of his people for relief from the unendurable burden thrown upon them by the railroads. The railroads, with all the best (terminal, waterfront) property in the city, paid practically no taxes to the city, only to the state, and then, on a valuation fixed by their own state board, at rates lower than the rates on other property. Record had drawn a bill to tax railroad property locally and at local rates. They were Republicans, Fagan and Record, and their party was in control of the state, absolutely; so they applied to the leaders of their party, among them, of course, to the Honorable Everett Colby. He liked Mayor Fagan, he says; he didn't like Record, but Mark Fagan, the "man of the people," intent only upon the needs of his city, walked straight into the heart of the rich young gentleman who, so far as he knew, was bent only upon a political career for personal glory. "I liked that man," he says, "and the condition of Jersey City appealed to me. I wanted to help them, and I couldn't; at least, I didn't."

"Why?" he said, repeating my question thoughtfully. Then he looked me straight in the eye. "I don't know that I can tell you, exactly. I will try to explain, if you will understand that I'm not apologizing for myself. There was no more excuse for what I did in this matter than there was for other things I did and didn't do. The bill was bad; it was crudely drawn."

"Record admits that," I interjected. "Record says that at that time he had never heard of the main stem, and had no right understanding of the situation at all."

"Nor had I," said Colby. "But that doesn't let me out. It served me as an excuse at the time. The big leaders, seeing my bent toward the bill, told me it was badly drawn, and I grasped at this reason as at a straw. But why shouldn't I, the House leader, have amended that bill? The need of the legislation was plain. Why didn't I fix the bill? I couldn't. You understand? I, a lawmaker, hadn't the ability to draw a good bill. Why, then, didn't I have some other, older legislator make the bad bill good? There wasn't a man in that House who could have drawn a sound tax bill to meet the most notorious need of the state. We were incompetent. Perhaps some of us might, once upon a time, have been legislators; but boss rule was so old there that we didn't, we couldn't think for ourselves. We had lost the art of independent thought and work. We were dummies. We took orders, we waited for orders, we depended upon orders. Dummy legislators, that's what we were.

"Oh, I was unhappy! I saw all this, but only dimly; I wouldn't let myself see it clearly. You know how a man jollies himself along with lies to save his face. The Democrats drew a better bill, still not good, and Fagan and Record accepted that; they had no pride in their pet measure; and they didn't care whether the Democrats or the Republicans got the credit of authorship. They wanted an income from railroad property in Jersey City. But the bill was buried in committee and I, the leader, should have got it out. I couldn't have got it out. And when the mayor came to me and asked me why I didn't have it reported, I told him the truth. 'I can't,' I told him. I wasn't really a leader. I was the real leader's dummy.

"You understand that the crime was not that we wouldn't pass the bill, but that we wouldn't consider it. I was willing to vote against it, if there were good reasons. I wasn't against corporations. But why couldn't we have the bill out and debate it? That's what Mayor Fagan couldn't understand, and that's what I asked in the caucus. We had orders, that was all; no reasons, except the one I remember they gave me in caucus a year later on a similar bill. When I asked, 'Why not take it out and beat it in the open if it's so bad?' they answered, in awed tones: 'Why, the Penn would raise hell.' There was the reason, the real reason."

There, too, was the truth about Jersey. When the mayor who represented the people of the second city in the state asked that legislature to consider a bill in their interest, that Jersey legislature couldn't because it represented "the Penn," a foreign corporation. "The Penn" ruled that state, and the ruler would "raise hell." Colby didn't see this. "I didn't want to see it," he says. But Mark Fagan saw it, and he made Everett Colby see it; made him grasp with his mind what his eyes reflected. Mark, the gentle mayor, raised hell. Defeated, with eyes wide open and ears alert, he took in the truth. The thing for a "practical politician" to do was to "take his medicine," and go home and tell his people the lies he heard told to the public. But Mark Fagan had made promises, not only on the stump; he had gone about from house to house and had made his promises man to man, and for keeps. He couldn't go back home to his people with lies. He put the truth to Governor Murphy in an open letter, and this letter was read aloud to the House of Assembly. It was a silent House; the representatives had read in their newspapers what this meek mayor, a Republican himself, had written to the Republican governor about their party and themselves. But they listened again. Colby says that he sat low sunk in his seat, and each separate sentence, as the Democratic leader read it, fell like a whip upon him.

The letter said that the writer spoke "as mayor of Jersey City, and also as a member of the Republican party.... The present session is drawing to a close," he said. "Its record is ... disgraceful. Its control by corporation interests, in the assembly, at least, has been absolute." And those men knew this was true. "For that condition the Republican party is responsible." Everett Colby, leader, knew this was true. And as the letter took up the legislation, bill by bill, to show how everyone that was against a corporation failed, the party leader of the House could recall the orders he had got to make them fail. He heard Governor Murphy's comforting arguments and the bosses' tactful orders. He saw again Major Lentz watching in the lobby. What did it mean? Fagan asked that in his letter to Governor Murphy. "What is the meaning of all this?" And the letter gave the answer, and it is the answer we all must hear as those legislators heard it, writhing. "The answer is plain! A Republican legislature is controlled by the railroad, trolley, and water corporations." So this honest Republican mayor wrote; but he didn't stop there. "And the interests of the people are being betrayed."

After the reading, silence hung on that assembly. "I sat where I was," says Colby, "stunned. It was my duty to reply. I was the leader. The others were waiting for me. And I? I couldn't say a word. It was all true, every bit of it. Nobody moved for a dreadful space of time. Then Tom Hillory got up, and he defended us, all of us. I felt mean. I was sore, sore at myself, you understand; not at the governor, not at the Penn; not at anybody else. I was sore at myself. It was true. We were dummies; we betrayed the people who elected us."

"Do legislators commonly understand that?" I asked.

"They must. I don't know. They must and yet, how can they? It isn't easy to explain. A fellow is moved by a lot of mixed-up considerations. Take my case. I saw it as Mark Fagan described it. I had more facts than he had, knew it better than he, but I didn't go right out and fight. Neither did he. Why didn't we? We both supported the Republican party that fall, and the party was not changed. The truth, falling like that, didn't kill; it didn't even change things essentially."

The governor appointed a commission to investigate taxes, and the platform promised some reform, if reform should prove necessary. But the Republican nominee for governor was "the Penn's man," Edward C. Stokes. And Colby and Fagan supported the ticket; they were "loyal to the party" which one said and the other admitted "represented corporations" and "betrayed the people." Why did they do it? Why do men like John C. Spooner and Edward C. Stokes "go along"? They know, and their friends say, they grieve themselves sick. Why did Mayor Weaver "go along" so long in Philadelphia? Everett Colby says he had excuses for the world, and some for himself. "The commission was to investigate and report," and he, meanwhile, threw himself into a study of taxation. He broke away, finally; like Mayor Weaver and Mark Fagan, he made a stand in the end. And why did he do that? And why did Mayor Weaver and Mark Fagan do it?

The way Everett Colby will try, when you ask him, to lay bare his motives is one of the convincing traits of the man. He is instinctively honest, and his candor is obvious.

"You'll hear," he told me, "that I wanted to be Speaker, and that my defeat made me turn. There is something in that. I think you understand that. I don't want to think that that was all, and, as I recall it, I don't think it was decisive, nor just that alone. That was only one of a score of things that made me see and drove me to act. I simply don't know the exact weight of any one thing."

All he knows is, that from seeing things separately, with his eyes, he came to see them all together with his mind. His friends put into his head the idea of the Speakership in the next session (1905). "I didn't care much," he said. "I felt I hadn't done very well, and I was willing to wait." But he wrote to his colleagues, and enough of "the boys" promised him their support to elect him. When Major Lentz got wind of it, he told Colby he couldn't have the Speakership. This was the System at work; the House leader hadn't "made good"; he was not yet "safe"; but that isn't what the boss said. Lentz said Colby mustn't run because he couldn't be elected. With those letters in his pocket, Colby knew it wasn't his colleagues that would make it impossible to elect him. He didn't mention to Lentz how many pledges he had; but neither did he bow to the boss as bosses like to be bowed to.

Now political bosses are not really bosses; they are the agents of the real bosses, who are businessmen, and when Colby got a telephone message to come to the Newark office of U. S. Senator Dryden, the young man, his eyes wide open now, realized that he was to see one of the men who represented one of the sovereign interests of his state. Senator Dryden, the president of the Prudential Life, was there, and with him was Lentz. The United States senator was the financial head of the Public Service Corporation in New Jersey; not the president; Thomas C. McCarter is that. Dryden is the man back of McCarter as he is the man back of Lentz; and that is why he was a United States senator; he represented one of the two great sources of the corruption of the state. He told Mr. Colby that he couldn't be Speaker. Dryden is a pleasant-spoken man, and he appealed to "his young friend's" good feeling, explaining that since he couldn't get the votes, it would weaken the prestige of their (Essex) delegation to run and fail. But Colby said he could get the votes. How did he know he could? He knew it because he had them in his pocket; and he tapped those letters. This was unexpected, and the senator exclaimed:

"But Tom McCarter says it won't do."

That settled it. Tom McCarter spoke for the trolley business.

Colby consented not to run; he told them it was all right. "But," he said, "I could be elected if I could have the support of my county."

Major Lentz approved, as they went away, the obedience of his young protege. "That's the way to talk," he said. Colby was "mad"; he hated the fraud of it all. "Why didn't they give their real reasons? Why didn't they say they feared that as Speaker I might not represent their trolleys?"

The next session was to be crucial. Colby made up his mind to be a freelance. The Speakership denied him, he would decline the leadership also. Without knowing what he meant to do, he was going to be free to act as he might find it right to act. If Colby had begun his career at the bottom, in local politics, he would have known of two or three separate reform movements that had long been going on in his county, and he could have gone to these, combined and led them against the machine. He does lead them now, but he didn't go to them; they came to him. One of these movements was in Newark, the metropolis of the state. This city belonged absolutely to the business interests grouped about the Prudential Life, the Fidelity Trust Company, and the Public Service Corporation, which, ruling through Major Lentz, gave the city a government in which these special interests came first, the common interest of the city last. The Democratic machine stood in with the Republican ring. Now and then, when James Smith, Jr., the Democratic business boss, had business differences with the Republican business grafters, there was a political fight. But all the opposition that counted at all came from a few young men, with William P. Martin at their head, who, mostly Republicans, got into councils and opposed steadfastly the public utility grabs. Their story is a story by itself, and a good one; suffice it for the present to say these fellows were battling against the enemies of their city, the public service interest, all the while Colby was trying to get along with his party.

Several other movements were underway in the suburbs of Newark—Bloomfield, the Oranges, etc. These were "good-government," "good-men-for-office" reforms till Tom McCarter aroused these "communities" to opposition to the real cause of all their troubles. Tom McCarter is a fiery, red-headed politician, who, as president of the Public Service, believes honestly that any thing that helps business is right. He was extending his trolley system, and, desiring to go through parks and residence streets, needed franchises. Of course, he must have them, and of course he must have them for nothing, and forever. Frederick W. Kelsey, a park commissioner, opposed him till public sentiment was formed and then McCarter undertook, by the methods characteristic of privilege-seekers, to get what he wanted anyhow. There was scandal and mass-meetings. The New England Society took up Kelsey's old fight against business graft. Could the fight have gone on locally, with McCarter's franchises for issues, it might have developed good citizenship in the Oranges. But both sides appealed to the state.

Tom McCarter, finding that the local council, though corrupt enough and willing, lacked the nerve to vote for him what he wanted in the face of "mobs" of good citizens, decided to appeal to the legislature; and his plan was to create a Greater Newark, taking into the city which he could control the suburbs which were giving the trolley "so much trouble." And the men of Orange, finding that their representatives in the local council did not represent them (except when watched), determined not to reform themselves and their voters and their council, but to go also to the legislature. Their petition was a very modest one; they wanted "their" state to forbid "their" council to grant any franchise for a period longer than twenty-five years.

The average Jerseyman thinks his state is well governed. His local government is bad, but politicians run that and he sees the results with his own eyes. The state is a government by lawyers, whom he knows by reputation at least; these lawyers are counsel for businessmen, like senators Dryden and Kean, ex-Governor Murphy, and Tom McCarter—the kind of men he knows as good business men, and they tell him the state is all right. When the good men of Orange, finding that Tom McCarter was back of the politicians who misrepresented Orange, set about getting their good state government to check Tom's chicaneries in Orange, the average Jerseyman learned why Senator Dryden and Governor Murphy and Tom McCarter called the state government "all right." The state government also represented "business," and it did not represent the average citizen of Jersey.

The men of Orange had to approach the state legislature through members of that body, and, naturally, they applied to their own Essex County legislators. What was their surprise to find that their own representatives wouldn't, nay couldn't, represent them! One by one they sounded them only to see that no representative of theirs dared touch their bill.

Why? Everett Colby was learning why. The men of Orange decided to ask him to take up their bill, and the Newark fighters were to support them. Would Colby do it? He didn't know. Before his fellow-citizens asked him, he heard of their intentions and he wasn't sure what he should do. He was aware of the feeling between the corporations and the people, not only in Orange but everywhere, and his disposition was not to take a side, but to listen to both, study the subject, and do the fair thing.

One evening ex-Governor Murphy gave a dinner. "Everybody" was there; all the business and political leaders and others, quite a crowd. When they rose from the table Colby went up to Tom McCarter to get the trolley side of the franchise question. He heard, he said, that the New England Society of Orange had a limited franchise bill to offer to the legislature, and wouldn't McCarter like to talk it over with him (Colby)?

"Now, you know," said Colby to me, "they could have fooled me easily. If they had had any tact, and had given me any reasonable argument, I think, in my ignorance, I would have been taken in. But, no; they ruled and they ruled, not by reason, but by command."

Tom McCarter did not want to talk it over with Colby. Irascible and dictatorial, the trolley boss bent his head forward at the young legislator, and, slapping his hands insultingly in his face, he said that anything but perpetual franchises in Jersey was "talk," "child's play"; and, raising his voice so that all in the room turned to hear, he cried: "We wouldn't touch anything else with a ten-foot pole!" With that he turned his back on Colby, and walked off.

"It wasn't a question," Mr. Colby explained to me, as he recalled this scene, "it wasn't a question of right and wrong as between two interests; it was, and it is, a question of who rules here."

Colby listened to his neighbours. He explained to them how difficult it would be for them to get any relief from their legislature, how little he could do; but they were agreeing on plans when McCarter drove home the lesson Colby was learning. This time it was at a luncheon at Trenton. The legislature had met, and again all the rulers of the state were present, the rulers and their dummies, the office-holders and legislators. This time Tom McCarter went to Colby; that is to say, the business boss beckoned the assemblyman to him.

"Colby," he said, "what's this I hear about you introducing a limited franchise bill?" He didn't wait for an answer. Raising his voice, as before, so that all could hear, he laid down the law of the land for legislators. "You introduce that bill," he bawled in his mad rage, "and you'll lose every friend you have in Essex County."

What did Tom McCarter mean? His brother made that clearer. The financial rings that rule Jersey often have to smooth over the troubles their quick-tempered trolley president causes with his "honest grafter" blunders. Uzel McCarter, Tom's big brother, and the head of the trust company through which (like the Big Three) the Prudential Life Insurance crowd finances its trolley and other schemes—Uzel, a diplomat, joined Colby that day on a train. He talked pleasantly, even flatteringly, to the young man. By and by the franchise subject happened to come up, and that led, naturally, to Colby's connection with the bill to limit trolley grants. Most unfortunate connection, that.

"We," said the banker, "we think you have a political future before you, and we don't want to see you throw it away."

There was more, but that was the point. Uzel McCarter was taking the young man who couldn't be bribed with money, or browbeaten by the bosses, up on the mountain to see the cities of the earth, and the young man understood it.

"It was a promise," says Colby, "and—a threat."

Undaunted, uncorrupted, the young man came down from the mountain to a study of the situation. He knew a limited franchise bill could not be passed, so he hit upon the idea of introducing a resolution to put the legislature on record. He drew one. He spoke of it to no one except Edward Duffield, the House leader, to whom Colby, as an ex-leader, owed that courtesy. Just before he rose he turned to Duffield and said:

"Now, Ed, don't be surprised, but watch. And look out that you don't make the mistake of your life."

And Colby offered a resolution to the effect that it was the sense of this House that perpetual grants of monopolies to corporations should not be made. Everybody looked to the leader. He sat still. The Speaker hesitated, then, with all eyes on the mute leader, he put the motion. Colby says, and I've heard men in other states who know legislatures well say, that if a body of elected Americans are not interfered with by business corruption they will do right nearly every time. That House that night, having no orders from the System and getting no sign from "Ed," adopted that resolution with not one negative vote!

But before the Speaker declared the resolution carried, the lobby woke up. Governor Stokes's Pennsylvania man came rushing in out of breath; wanted to know what the thing meant anyhow. "Can't you give us time?" he begged. Colby knew that A. J. Cassatt would call down Stokes and that Stokes would call down his man, and that the Public Service lobbyist and legislators would catch it; and besides, he didn't want to join in a fluke, so he said: "Surely; we'll make it a special order for Thursday."

The next day a telephone message summoned him to one of the business-political leaders of the state, a man who usually had been able to "handle Colby." "Everett," said this man, "our friends are awfully upset by this resolution of yours." Of course, he said, it had gone too far to be absolutely withdrawn—by Colby—but "our friends will fix up an amendment," and "if you will accept this amendment, they'll let it pass." "They'll let it pass!" "You don't mean to tell me," Colby exclaimed, "that they are to determine what bills shall pass!"

"Now, Everett," said this gentleman, "you ought to know by this time how all these things are." The amendments were absurd, ridiculous, impossible. Colby refused to accept them, and he meanwhile had been busy seeing his colleagues. The Speaker and four-fifths of the members were for the resolution. Yet, when it came up again on Thursday, only ten men voted "yes"!

This was only a preliminary skirmish in the long fight of that session of 1905. It was a defeat, but it was better than a victory since it aroused public interest and attracted to Trenton citizens and committees of citizens to take object lessons in a "good business government" in action. The Orange men on hand in force insisted upon having their limited franchises bill introduced, and Colby presented it. It went to committee for burial, but there were hearings on it, and Colby says the sight of citizens delivering carefully prepared arguments to a committee of legislators whom he knew to be dummies with no will of their own, no minds of their own—no ears for anything but the orders which they already had received to "hang onto that bill"—this spectacle, common as it was, and typical of all our legislatures from the youngest state to Congress itself, the humiliation of it struck deep into the growing intelligence of the young legislator. And evidently it made an impression on Jerseymen; the papers described the scene mercilessly, and the rumble of popular indignation finally scared the rings. Major Lentz is said to have told Governor Stokes that if some bill wasn't reported, "that fellow Colby would make a lot of trouble" for him (Lentz) in Essex. So the Pennsylvania Railroad threw over the Public Service Corporation. Stokes gave orders. A substitute bill was drawn, for a commission to investigate; that was all, but just before final adjournment this old device to gain time was reported and rushed through. And, even then, Tom McCarter told the governor he had no right to let such a thing happen when "our great interests were against it." And Governor Stokes did not sign it for weeks; and then he appointed a commission typified by ex-Governor Murphy, the chairman.

A railroad tax bill, promised in the Republican platform, was introduced with the permission (as I happen to know) of Mr. Cassatt of Philadelphia, but it was in the form prescribed by "the road." It taxed second-class property (buildings and ordinary real estate) at local rates, but not the "main stem" (the roadbed). This would relieve Jersey City somewhat, but it would not satisfy Mayor Fagan or any other citizen who believed in "equal taxation."

And after it was passed, another bill was run out and jammed through, prescribing that the first bill should not materially increase the total tax of the railroads. This was made "the governor's bill," but Colby opposed it and introduced another to tax the main stem like any other real estate. Of course, Colby's bill was beaten, but its defeat left equal taxation an issue in Jersey politics.

Another fight that showed things as they are was over a bill to promote Tom McCarter's scheme to bring into a Greater Newark all the suburbs which did not respond to trolley corruption. Bloomfield was one of these. The people there had held the trolleys at bay; annexation had been proposed to them, and they had voted it down. In this session of 1905 some "leading citizens" of Bloomfield applied to the legislature for another referendum on annexation, and the trolley pretended to have nothing to do with it. But it had. Those leading citizens were stockholders and friends of stockholders in McCarter's company; Major Lentz "steered" them; and for more direct evidence, there was the story of a friend of Colby. This man had been in the employ of the Public Service. He was against the bill, and "they sent for him." This was their bill, they told him. They wrote it, and they needed it as a step in their plan to absorb into Newark all the troublesome suburbs about the city; their employee must get out of the way. Their employee told them he was out of their employ and, being there for free, would continue to fight them with this added information to spur him on.

It was this bill that finally brought about the declaration of war between Boss Lentz and Assemblyman Colby. One day, when Lentz was steering his "citizens' committee" about the Capitol, he introduced Colby to them. And he told Colby in their presence that he must work for their bill. "They contribute to the campaign fund"; that was the reason he gave, and it was bad enough, but Colby knew that the real reason was that Tom McCarter and Senator Dryden wanted to control through Newark the destinies of Bloomfield and the Oranges against the will of the inhabitants of those places.

David Baird came along as they were talking. Baird is the Republican boss of Camden, and the agent there of "the Penn" and the Public Service Corporation. "David," said Lentz, after introducing him, "I want you to get your boys in line for that bill."

"All right, Major," said David, "I will."

Colby wasn't so agreeable. He didn't say much, but Lentz suspected him and his suspicions were promptly confirmed. Colby happened to meet about noon that day the chairman of the committee which had the Bloomfield bill in charge, and they went together to lunch. When they entered the restaurant there sat the major with his citizens. The boss seemed gradually to work himself into a rage, for after staring angrily at Colby a few moments, he got up, stalked over, and "putting his head in between ours," Colby says, "and spluttering in my face, he demanded to know if I was opposing him in this." So far as Colby can recall, he and the chairman hadn't mentioned the bill, but he was opposing Lentz "in this," and he said so.

"That settles it," said the Major.

Not only "that," but everything settled it between Colby and his boss and the bosses of the boss. Tom McCarter had said Colby would lose every friend he had in Essex; Uzel had warned him to take heed for his political future. "It was fight," says Colby now. "I went home from that session burning hot with indignation. But I didn't think about my political future. That had sunk into a small detail of a situation which was bigger than the political ambition of any man. I saw that the legislature, yes, and the government in nearly all of its branches, was ruled absolutely by our Jersey corporations. And despotically, unscrupulously, too; in the interest of their business, they were corrupting all of us. Hadn't they nearly corrupted me?"

The question was what to do. Colby didn't know what to do. He asked me what I would have done, and I pass it on to you who read this: What would you have done? And I ask the question to bring home to you the quandary of this young legislator and of his friends, and of the citizens of Orange and of Newark and of Jersey who wanted to fight. Lentz said Colby should not be renominated for the Assembly, and some of his friends proposed a fight in the party for the county committee. But Colby didn't want to run for boss of Essex; he wanted to make his appeal more to the people. This was an instinct, a democratic instinct which this rich railroad magnate's son has well developed in him. He proposed running an older man

Everett Colby, The Gentleman From Essex 529

for senator, but the older man wouldn't run and the Newark, Bloomfield, and Orange men wanted Colby to lead their common fight. He was in doubt. He wanted to make the fight impersonal, and they adopted his principle to fight the boss, not Lentz; not the man, but the boss as an institution, as an agent of a corrupt oligarchy. But how?

"Then," said Colby, as he told me the story, "then came Record."

There's a good deal of feeling against George L. Record in Jersey. He is the man who came to Mark Fagan when the kindly mayor of Jersey City was at the first crisis of his administration, and Record helped Mark Fagan. From suspecting him, Mayor Mark came to lean upon him for his economic policy, and they and their Jersey City cabinet have influenced Jersey politics and the Jersey legislature more and more healthfully than any other one force in the state. Yet, while none denies the perfect honesty of Mark Fagan, many men distrust George L. Record. And you may recall that Colby, two years before, when he took to Fagan, "disliked" Record. But when "Record came" he told Colby just what to do and how to do it. Colby is very handsome in his acknowledgment of the service Record rendered them in Essex, and his friends confess, though more grudgingly, that Record is a man of resources. But nobody can see what Record gets out of it for Record. They think he wants to go to the United States Senate. I hope he does; this long, lean, thinking Yankee from Jersey City might accomplish something even in the United States Senate. But Record is another story, and it doesn't matter now "what Record is after."

When he came to Colby, he came suggesting that since Colby had made one good fight at Trenton, he should make another; and since he personified all the discontent that opposed the control of the state by the corrupt corporations of the state, he, Colby, was the man to run for senator. How? There was the primary law. Record, the father of that law, suggested the use of it to beat the Republican boss in his own party. "But," he said, "don't stop there. Adopt a platform. Promise specific things and go to the people with these definite promises. And put up a full ticket: senator and assemblymen and county officers, everything."

Mark Fagan has in Jersey City a "group plan" of government. A picked lot of fellows get together, discuss, and agree upon policies and plans. Colby took that idea, and he accepted also the suggestion to join issue with fighters in other counties. So two groups, one from Essex and the other from Hudson, came together and out of their deliberations grew a platform and what is known as "The New Idea Movement."

They adopted Colby's Orange issue: limited franchises; Record's: franchise taxation; Fagan's: equal taxation; and Colby, Record and others added one new one: an expression at legislative elections of a popular choice for United States senators.

It isn't necessary to follow the campaigns, for there were two—the first a fight at the primaries for the nomination for state senator, the second the general election at the polls. Both were anti-boss fights. Colby opened with an announcement of his candidacy, backed by a statement of his programme. The boss and the ringsters laughed. They laughed till the first mass-meeting was held. That was expected to fall flat, but the opera house was filled to overflowing and Fagan, Record, Colby and Martin aroused the crowd to tremendous enthusiasm. But the best thing Colby did was to adopt Fagan's method of meeting the voters face to face. Fagan told him how to do it. Colby asked him. The young club man thought there was some mystery about talking to workingmen, so he invited Mayor Mark to luncheon to get his secret. The mayor was puzzled.

"Why, Mr. Colby," he said, "I can't tell you how to do that. I can tell you when you will find working-men at liberty to listen, and I can tell you how they feel about some of these great questions. But I can't tell you what to say to them. You must say just what you think, and, Mr. Colby, if you don't feel from the bottom of your heart a real interest in people you might as well stay at home."

"And that," says Colby, "is about the best advice I ever got. The instant he said it I knew it was right. After that I went out to my noonday meetings and I didn't try to find out what they thought. I told them what I thought about things."

Colby's class suffers from class consciousness, as much, if not more, than labor does. If he had gone forth as a rich man to the poor, or as a capitalist to labor, or as a business man offering a good business administration to a people incompetent for self-government, he would have had to buy votes or be beaten. But going as he did, as a man to men, and promising things that were directed at the reform, not of politicians and the police, and dirty streets, etc., etc., but of the grosser vices of his own class, even though he did not mention class, those people sized up "this rich young club fellow" as they sized up the ex-gilder and undertaker, Mark Fagan, and they put their faith in him as the Missourians did in Folk, as the people of Wisconsin did in La Follette, and as the people of San Francisco did in Heney. The American people seem not to know the difference between clean streets and dirty streets, but they do know the difference between hypocrisy and sincerity, between plutocracy and democracy. They'll help you beat the boss if you'll show that you see as plainly as they do who is back of the boss.

  The machine blundered. The bosses always blunder when, as they put it, "they go up against a new game," and the New Idea was a new game. Colby made use of Record's primary law to print his name, as candidate for the senate, after the names of his delegates. Lentz wouldn't do that. He wanted to elect his delegates, then dictate as of old, all the candidates to be nominated by the convention. Governor Stokes warned Lentz. Colby thought he saw signs of the governor's interference against him, and he went to Mr. Stokes to ask that "he keep his hands off."

  "Why," said the governor, "all I have done was to tell Lentz that if he didn't name a man against you, you'd beat him."

  Colby's crowd worked early and late. As time went on and the excitement grew, men who never had taken part in politics joined in what they agreed was the "greatest game they ever sat in at," the great game of politics. Everybody was welcome, and everybody was happy. It was a popular election, every man's election, and they won. Won? The completeness of their victory at the primaries astonished them. They carried everything. The next morning Major Lentz told Colby the convention was his, Colby's, and Colby might "run it" to suit himself. Very gracious, indeed, was this defeated boss, but he hoped (and he hopes) to be boss again.

"I've been thinking," he said to the victor, "that maybe I ought to resign. What do you think, Colby?"

"I think you might as well, Major," said Colby, who thought Lentz meant what he said. But Lentz didn't mean anything of the kind.

"Well, I won't," he answered in a huff. "I didn't mean to resign the chairmanship of the county committee; I meant as manager of the campaign." Colby said he and his crowd nearly went to pieces on this very point. They held their convention, and they nominated the whole legislative and county ticket. That had all been planned in advance. But what next? What about managing the campaign? Lentz had the county committee, and the county committee usually ran county campaigns. Colby and his group meant to have their fight made by a joint committee, but their plans were indefinite. "We hadn't thought it out," Colby says, "and we made a bad blunder."

The county committee was to have a meeting, and it was the custom for candidates to go and be presented. Colby left town intending not to recognize the committee, but he was telephoned for by some of his best friends. As a victor he must not show ill-will, etc., etc. So Colby went to the meeting. In the course of the formalities, Lentz said something about the campaign being run as usual, and, Colby says, "I should have jumped up then and there to declare that it would not be run as usual. I didn't. Don't know why I didn't, but I didn't. I just hadn't my wits about me, and I let it pass."

The next day the papers were full of the "Love Feast." "Colby and the boss were together." Colby thinks this was a very "bad break," and so do some of his friends, but mistakes don't count in these criminal days, and he corrected his promptly. He came out with a letter demanding that his own, not the county committee, should run the campaign. This was a repudiation of the organization. Lentz refused to give up, so he ran one campaign, and Colby's committee, with William P. Martin for chairman, ran the other. The machine men cut Colby at the polls, but he won in spite of them. The normal Republican majority in Essex County ranges from ten to twelve thousand. Colby's was 19,986, and some of the other men on his ticket ran a few hundred ahead of him. The election of Everett Colby and his ticket ranked in significance with the victories that fall of Jerome in New York, of Weaver's ticket in Philadelphia, of Judge Dempsy's for mayor of Cincinnati, of Tom Johnson in Cleveland, of Brand Whitlock in Toledo, of Pattison in Ohio, etc. They all were anti-boss fights. Some of them, like Pattison's and Dempsy's, were minority party fights against the majority party boss; some, like Jerome's and Whitlock's, were against "both the bosses" and "all parties"; Colby's, like LaFollette's and Folk's, was within the majority party. No matter how made, these fights were all against the boss, and the boss fell. What next?

The political boss is nothing but an agent of the business bosses back of him. Some of these anti-boss leaders know this; some do not. Those that do may get somewhere; the others won't. Colby is one of those that can see beyond the boss; that is one reason why he would not make his campaign a personal fight against Carl Lentz. He saw, and he sees, and some of the men with him see, the powers behind Lentz, and he is proceeding now deliberately and intelligently against them, the real enemies of the state, its active rulers, the class which corrupts it, and its officials, and its people for the sake of the privileges obtained or to be obtained from the state.

Look at their programme of bills again. In themselves they might not interest you and me very much, but look behind those bills. To "limit franchises" and "to tax them" these will bring these New Jersey leaders in direct, open conflict with the Prudential-Fidelity Trust-Public Service interests. To "tax the roadbed of railroads" like any other real estate is to challenge a most profitable privilege of the Pennsylvania and other railroads. To let voters pledge their legislators to candidates for the United States Senate—that is to make the United States Senate represent the people. All the resources of the railroads, trolleys, and other public utilities, and of all the "protected" businesses of Jersey and of the United States will be called into play to defeat this kind of reform; for this is real reform. It is not a little tap at superficial evils; it is a stab at the source of all evil in all our politics. It aims at democracy, at the restoration of truly representative government. It is "radical"; it is "dangerous." If the corporations do to Colby in Jersey what they have done to LaFollette in Wisconsin, they will stir up envy and hatred against him; they will befool his followers with false arguments or buy them with money or office or "business"; and they will embitter his life, public and private, too, with misrepresentation and slander. If the fight is fought to a finish, every trick known to expert manipulators of legislatures and public opinion will be tried, but the rings didn't believe it would be fought to a finish. Can you guess why? One of them told me what their faith was founded upon.

"We'll get Colby," he said. "We'll get him before the session is over. He wants something. Every man wants something. It's all a matter of finding out what he wants. He may not know what it is himself, but we'll find out; and he'll get it and we'll get him or his crowd, or both."

There is no conceit about Colby, no bluster, and when I told him this, he did not clench his fist and set his jaw. He pondered a moment, then he said:

"I wonder if they will."

Colby knows the tremendous power and the infinite ingenuity of the interests that will oppose him, so he wondered, as you or I may, what is going to happen to him. He is as open-minded to the truth about himself as he is to the truth about corruption, and because he is open-minded, and because he can confess his mistakes when he sees them; because he takes fences as he comes to them, and because he says he "will go any length to put a stop to the corruption of men and government," it is likely that the gentleman from Essex will fight to a finish. What the end will be in Jersey, Jersey men must decide; they will have to watch the struggle and choose between those representatives who represent and those who do not. But the rest of us should watch, too. Everett Colby is a national leader; the Jersey fight is a national fight. The arena is local, but others are making the same fight elsewhere; the fight we all must make, sooner or later: the fight to restore the government of the people to the people.

McClure's Magazine
October – December, 1906

Ben Lindsey, The Just Judge

I "THE KIDS' COURT"

IN the County Court of Denver, one night, a boy was arraigned for larceny. The hour was late; the calendar was long, and the judge was sitting overtime. Weary of the weary work, everybody was forcing the machinery of the law to grind through at top speed the dull routine of justice. All sorts of causes went to this court, grand and petty, civil and criminal, complicated and simple. The petty larceny case was plain; it could be disposed of in no time. A theft had been committed; no doubt of that. Had the prisoner at the bar done it? The sleepy policeman had his witness on hand, and they swore out a case. There was no doubt about it; hardly any denial. The law prescribed precisely what was to be done to such "cases" and the bored judge ordered that that thing be done. That was all. In the same breath with which he pronounced sentence, the court called for the "next case" and the shift was under way, when something happened, something out of the ordinary.

A cry, an old woman's shriek, rang out from the rear of the room. There was nothing so very extraordinary about that. Our courts are held in public; and every now and then somebody makes a disturbance such as this old woman made when she rose now with that cry on her lips, and, tearing her hair and rending her garments, began to beat her head against the wall. It was the duty of the bailiff to put the person out, and that officer in this court moved to do his duty. But the man on the bench was Ben B. Lindsey, the celebrated judge of the Juvenile Court of Denver. He wasn't celebrated then; he had no juvenile court. He was only a young lawyer and politician who, for political services (some aver, falsely, for delivering a vote for a United States senatorship) had been appointed to fill out an unexpired term as county judge. Lindsey didn't want to be a judge; he had asked for the district-attorneyship. His experiences on the inside of politics had shown him that many things were wrong, and he had a private theory that the way to set the evils right was to enforce the law, as the law. But another man, Harry A. Lindsley, had a prior claim on the district-attorneyship, and Ben Lindsey had to take the judgeship or nothing. So he had taken it (January 8, 1901), and he had been administering justice as justice for several weeks when that woman cried out against his "Justice" and his "bailee" moved to uphold the decorum of his court, the dignity of the law. And the judge upheld the woman.

"I had noticed her before," he says now. "As my eye wandered during the evening it had fallen several times on her, crouched there among the back benches, and I remember I thought how like a cave-dweller she looked. I didn't connect her with the case, any case. I didn't think of her in any human relationship whatsoever. For that matter, I hadn't considered the larceny case in any human way. And there's the point: I was a judge, judging 'cases' according to the 'law' till the cave-dweller's mother-cry startled me into humanity. It was an awful cry, a terrible sight, and I was stunned. I looked at the prisoner again, but with new eyes now, and I saw the boy, an Italian boy. A thief? No. A bad boy? Perhaps, but not a lost criminal. I called him back, and I had the old woman brought before me. Comforting and quieting her, I talked with the two together, as mother and son this time, and I found that they had a home. It made me shudder. I had been about to send that boy to a prison among criminals when he had a home and a mother to go to. And that was the law! The fact that that boy had a good home; the circumstances which led him to not steal, but 'swipe' something; the likelihood of his not doing it again, these were 'evidence' pertinent, nay vital, to his case. Yet the law did not require the production of such evidence. The law? Justice? I stopped the machinery of justice to pull that boy out of its grinders. But he was guilty; what was to be done with him? I didn't know. I said I would take care of him myself, but I didn't know what I meant to do except to visit him and his mother at their home. And I did visit them, often, and—well, we—his mother and I, with the boy helping—we saved that boy, and today he is a fine young fellow, industrious, self-respecting, and a friend of the court."

This was the beginning, the judge will tell you, of his practice of putting juvenile offenders, not in prison to be punished, but on probation to be saved. It wasn't. The judge is looking backward, and he sees things in retrospect as he has thought them out since, logically, with his mind. If you should take his word for it, you would get the impression that this first "probation case" was the beginning of his famous Juvenile Court, the most remarkable institution of the kind in all the world. And if you got that impression in just that way, you might do as the reformers some twenty-five states and a few hundred cities have done—you might lose the significance of Judge Lindsey. You might learn his methods and miss the man. You might imitate his "kids' court" and make a mistake with both the "kids" and their "Jedge," as they call him. And you certainly would do, as Denver desires to do, and limit the meaning of Judge Lindsey's life-work to the problem of the children.

Ben Lindsey's "methods" are as applicable to grown-ups as to kids. Man has a way of inventing devices to help him to be a man; a spear, an army, the Church, political parties, business. By and by the aid to his weakness comes to be a fetish with him, a burden, an end in itself, an institution. He decorates his spear, keeping a commoner weapon to hunt with. His army returns from fighting his enemies to conquer him. Priests declare the Church holy and, instead of ministering to men, make men minister to the Church. Political parties, founded to establish principles for the strengthening of the state and its citizenship, betray principles and manhood and the state for the "good of the party." Business, the mere machinery of living, has become in America the purpose of life, the end to which all other goods—honour, religion, politics, men, women and children, the very nation itself—are sacrificed. And so with the laws and the courts. Jurists and legislators note and deplore the passing of respect for the law and of faith in the courts, and they wonder why. It is largely because we laymen think we observe that legislation purporting to be for the common good is bought for the special evils; that laws enacted to help us are manipulated to our hurt;

and that our courts, set up to render justice, either make a worship of the letter of the law or violate the spirit thereof to work deliberate injustice. As for the penal code, nourished by the centuries to prevent crime, it is operated as escapes for the strong criminal or as instruments of society's revenge upon the weak.

Ben Lindsey's great, new, ancient discovery is that men are what we are after, men and women; and that everything else, business and laws, politics, the church, the schools—these are not institutions, but means to those higher ends, character and right living. He began with the laws; the law he was prepared to revere. He saw that the law was capable of stupid injustices and gross wrongs; and setting humanity up on the bench beside his authority, he has reduced the law to its proper, humble function—the service of men and of the state. He has drawn the sting of punishment out of the penal code, stamped out the spirit of vengeance; he has tried to make his court a place where the prisoners at the bar are helped to become good men and useful citizens. His greatest service has been to boys and girls, but that is only because he found in children the most helpless victims of our machine system of "businesslike justice." He has created in his Juvenile Court a new human institution, the beauty and use of which is spreading imitative "movements" all over the land. But, wonderful as his creation is, this man should not be known as the founder of another institution. That might become, like certain societies for the prevention of cruelty to animals or to children, only another "end in itself."

Judge Lindsey is a man, a brave, gentle man, who is re-introducing into life, all life, and into all the institutions which he can influence, the spirit of humanity. As he puts it in his "Problem of the Children," "these great movements for the betterment of our children are simply typical of the noblest spirit of this age, the Christ-spirit of unselfish love, of hope and joy. It has reached its acme in what were formerly the criminal courts. The old process is changed. Instead of coming to destroy, we come to rescue. Instead of coming to punish, we come to uplift. Instead of coming to hate, we come to love."

That the man has this more general significance is shown by the gradual, apparently accidental way in which he developed his "methods" and his court. He didn't think them out with his mind. That isn't the way big, human things are done in this big, human world of ours; they are felt out with the heart. The man Lindsey had heart, and the cave-dweller's cry reached it, and when the judge felt her agony, he found himself. That was all. His judgment in this case was but the beginning of Judge Lindsey's practice of putting heart into his business. He didn't know what probation was when he said he'd take care himself of the cave-dweller's boy. We have seen that he hadn't thought of being a judge, and the idea of a Juvenile Court hadn't dawned upon him. It took other cases to "set him thinking." The other cases came.

One day a "burglary" appeared on his calendar. The judge says he looked around curiously for the burglars. He saw none till the case was called. Then three boys were haled whimpering before him, three ordinary, healthy American boys, from twelve to sixteen. What had they burglarized? A pigeon-loft. A pigeon-loft! Yes, Your Honor, they broke into a pigeon-loft and were caught red-handed stealing pigeons. That was burglary; there was no doubt about the crime. What was to be done with the burglars? They were to be sent to the reformatory, of course; the law prescribed the penalty. The judge shook his head, "No."

He didn't say so in court then, but he tells now how he was recalling the time when he, as a boy, went robbing a pigeon-loft. He didn't actually commit "burglary," but he would have if he hadn't lost his nerve. He was "scared"; the other kids had told him so, and it was true. And they left him, in contempt and ashamed, while they robbed the coop. So he wasn't an ex-convict, not because he was a good boy, no; nor because he was "smaller than them," though that was a plea set up in the gang in his behalf. He wasn't a burglar, like these boys before him now, simply because he didn't have as much "sand" as they had. Was he going to punish them as burglars, "send them up" for crime, to live among criminals? No.

But the complainant had a view to present. A worried, old, persecuted man, he told how boys were forever stealing his pigeons; how he had "laid for them" again and again; how they generally escaped; and how, finally, after many failures, he had caught these three. He wanted them punished; he begged to have them "sent to jail." There was something familiar in the appearance of the poor old pigeon fancier, and the judge questioned him: where he lived; where his barn was; just where the pigeon-loft was; what his name was; whether he had a nickname. The old man answered, peevishly, but fully enough for the judge to learn what he wanted to know. This was the very man, his were the pigeons, his loft was the same old loft which he, the judge, and his gang had burglarized years ago. And now the law expected him, a judge, to send to prison these boys who were no worse than he was; nay, who were better, for they had the "sand" he lacked! If he, the judge, had been sent up for burglary he might not have become county judge, and if he didn't send up these boys as burglars, they might become county judges, or since they had more "sand" something better.

But there was the law; what about that? The boys had committed a crime; what was the judge to do with them? He didn't know; he would have to "think it over." And, he thought it over. He went back to first principles. What did the complainant really want? Only to have his property protected. And what was the law against burglary for? To protect property by preventing burglary. Wasn't there any other way to achieve these common ends except by punishing these boys as burglars? And if he put them in prison might not other boys go on robbing the pigeon-loft? The judge says it is "out of the mouths of babes" that he has learned wisdom. He took the prisoners into his chamber, and he talked with them. Now, the judge's talks with boys and girls are regarded with superstition by some people; he gets such wonderful results—the truth, for example. Children who lie to their parents, their teachers, and the police, tell him everything. The police started a story that Judge Lindsey is a "hypnotist," and others speak wisely of his "method." His "method" is very simple; he employed it before he knew it was a "method," with his Italian "thief" and his first trio of "burglars." Friendship is the key. Judge Lindsey talks to boys as one boy talks to another.

His personal appearance helps him. The "Jedge" is a short, slight, boyish-looking young man, open-faced, direct, sincere, and he lays off the ermine, figuratively speaking, very readily; indeed, he hardly ever puts it on now, even on the bench. In chambers he comes right down to earth, using boy-talk, including slang. For this he has been criticized by good people who think of English as an institution, to be kept pure. The judge answers that he has something else in mind than the purity of the language. He has found "after four years' experience that the judicious use of a few of these slang terms not only does not hurt the boy, but actually helps him, and wins his confidence" and, since the boys are what he is after, he declares he will "continue to talk to the boys to a certain extent much the same as they talk with one another." As a matter of fact, it is an instinct with the judge, a part of his simple naturalness and his native desire to understand others, which prompts him to say "fellers"; " ah, say, kids, let's cut it out." When he called in his burglars, it was no judge that asked them if they belonged to a gang. It was no fatherly elder, wisely pretending to a superior sort of interest in the habits and customs of their "crowd," and the limits of their range or habitat. It was "one feller askin' th' other fellers, on the level now, all about swipin' pigeons." The reason he, the judge, and his gang robbed the coop was to get a certain variety of fantail pigeons which the old man wouldn't sell, and he understood it when the boys explained that what they were after, really, was to get back some of their pigeons which had joined the old man's bigger flock. Also, however, the boys understood the judge when he reflected that it wasn't right to go and "rob back" your pigeon; that it annoyed the old man, wronged him, and hurt the boys. Maybe the old man was grouchy, but, gee, the coop was his, and "swiping" wasn't "square." It was sneaky, it was weak to steal. So he proposed to stop this "weakness" of this gang; not only of the three that had been caught, but of the whole gang.

  Now, the judge teaches respect for grown-up law by himself invariably showing great respect for "kid law." It is against the law of Boyville to "snitch" (tattle). So he wouldn't let them tell him who the other "burglars" were. "But, say, fellers," he said, "you bring in the other kids, and we'll talk it over, and we'll see if we can't agree to cut out stealing altogether, and especially to stop swipin' pigeons off the old man."

That was fair, and it was human. They went away, and they got the gang. And the gang entered into a deal with the "Jedge"; "sure they did." Who wouldn't? And do you think they would go back on a judge like that? Sure they wouldn't, and they wouldn't let any other feller go back on him either; not much; not if they could prevent it; and they thought they could. And they did, as they reported from time to time.

It was this case, which, coming home so personally to him, set the judge thinking. "It seemed to me," he says, "that we were not proceeding just right in such cases. I didn't know anything about it, but it looked wrong to charge these boys with burglary. It was unnecessary under the law, too; the school law of 1899 permitted children to be brought to the County Court as 'juvenile disorderly persons.' And here they were being arraigned as thieves and burglars. We were dealing with the thing the child did, not with the child; and the child was what should concern us. I don't blame anybody in particular. I had been at fault myself. A good many children were brought into my court, and I had been following the thoughtless routine. The fact is, I was pretty free in sending boys to the Industrial School at Golden till these special cases awoke my special interest. Then I began to consider the situation generally. I found that there was no system about juvenile cases. Some were sent to the District Court, others to the Justice Courts, others to mine. We all were 'trying' the boys for the 'crimes' they had committed, finding many of them guilty and sending them away. It was absurd; it was criminal, really. The thing a child had stolen was treated as of more importance than the child. This was carrying the idea of property to an extreme. It was time to get back to the idea of men and women, the men and women of tomorrow, and obviously some system of character-building was needed in the court. Fortunately, there were laws in existence under which juvenile offenders could be brought into court as 'dependent', 'neglected' or 'delinquent' children, and these laws were enough as they stood for the starting of a Juvenile Court. We hoped to get other laws later; but those that we had would enable us to treat the children, rather than the children's crimes."

Judge Lindsey went to District Attorney Lindsley with the request that all children's cases be brought to his court; and that they be accused there of delinquency instead of the particular crimes for which they were arrested. The district attorney was willing. Lindsey's request was regarded as "queer" but nobody wanted the bother of these "kids'" cases, so the judge was permitted to found his "kids' court." And he founded it, and it is the "kids' court," their very own. It is run in the interest of the "bad" boys and girls, and therefore of the state, and the children needed the court, and so did the state.

While the judge was "thinking," the question arose in his mind: "What sort of a place is the Industrial School where I have been sending boys so freely?" He went to Golden to see. Nobody up there remembered ever having been visited before by a judge on the bench, and this judge saw boys with the ball and chain on them. He began a quiet reform of the reformatory. Then he asked himself what kind of places the jails were. One Sunday evening he visited the city jail.

"It was a dirty, filthy place," he says. "The plaster was off the walls, which were crawling with vermin." He went over to the county jail. The conditions were much the same, but what stirred up the judge's "thoughts" to the bottom of his heart was the sight of boys in the same cells with men and women "of the vilest type." A little further inquiry showed him that these children were allowed to associate freely with grown criminals. Locked up with them in the county jail, they visited the men in the bull-pen down in the city jail. The boys liked to listen to the "great criminals," and the great criminals liked to brag to the boys. It was a school of crime. The men told the boys how they "beat the police" and, filling them with criminal ideals, taught them how to commit "great" crimes.

"I found that in the five years before I went on the bench, 2,136 Denver boys had been in these jails for periods varying from a few hours to thirty days, and," the judge adds in his mild way, "I was satisfied the influence was not good. But that was typical. This was being done all over the country, and it is now in many places. Every boy who makes a mistake or, if you will, every child that shows any tendency to crime is sent to a school where crime is taught. Is it any wonder that juvenile crime is on the increase?"

And the judge found that juvenile crime was on the increase generally in the United States. He engaged the services of a clipping bureau, and he quotes, in his "Problem of the Children," some of the results: "Five Thousand Boys Arrested Last Year" (in one city); "4,000 out of 16,000 Arrests Last Year Were Boys Under Twenty" (in a city of less than 150,000); "Bandits Caught Mere Boys" (a frequent head line); "Over Half the Murderers Last Year Were Boys"; " Boy Burglars Getting Common"; "Thieving Increasing Among Children"; "Desperate Boy Bandits Captured" (aged twelve, thirteen, and fifteen). And he cites the Van Wormer boys of New York; the Biddies of Pennsylvania; the car-barn murderers of Illinois; the Collinses of Missouri; the boy murderers of Nebraska; the Youngblood murderers of Denver; the boy train-wreckers of the West, and the reform-school boy murderers of California. The phrase "mere boys" indicated that the news editors regarded juvenile crime as exceptional and remarkable; it isn't. Three-quarters of the crimes committed in the United States, the judge says, are done by boys under twenty-three!

"And why not?" he asks. "The children of parents who die or fail in their duty are taken by the state and sent for their schooling into the streets or jails where they pick up false ideals and criminal arts. With few exceptions, all these boy criminals named above, whom society has sent to the slaughterhouse to be killed, had been sent to jail in their teens by society for other crimes. And most of them were first imprisoned as little children."

In other words, our criminal court system does not prevent, it fosters crime. Our "businesslike" procedure of heartless, thoughtless "justice" makes criminals. What should the state do? The judge says that when the state gets hold of a "bad" child, it takes the place of the parent, and like a good parent, it should try to mould that child into a good citizen. He gives an illustration in his "Problem of the Children."

"We recall the case (and it is one of hundreds)," the judge says there, "of a young man who had been in the criminal courts at the age of thirteen. At twenty he shot down a policeman who was heroically doing his duty. Suppose that at the age of thirteen that boy had been studied, helped, looked after, and carefully handled; would that policeman be maimed for life, or dead, a young wife and child a charge on the community, and a strong, robust young man a charge on the state for life? Perhaps not, and even so we could have felt better about it, and in the sight of God less accountable. Was the state responsible? Yes, even more than the boy, for he was in jail in the plastic stage. The state had him in time, and it did nothing—not even try. The state treated him as a man, this boy. . . Strange that if his money or property were involved he could control none of it; he would need a guardian in that case. A boy's property is important. But his morals—the boy, the man in embryo, the citizen to be—needed no guardian. This boy needed no help. He needed punishment. He needed retribution, and so as a boy he got what men got, that which is often barbarous even for men. I have seen them, eleven to fifteen years of age, in the same bullpen with men and women, with chains about their waists and limbs. And I have seen them crowded together in idleness, in filthy rooms where suggestiveness fills the mind with all things vile and lewd. Such has been too often the first step taken by the great state in the correction of the child."

    Judge Lindsey founded his Juvenile Court to correct and save to the state the children who were caught up in the meshes of the criminal law, and his first step was the correction of himself and of the court. Having to start with only the idea, which was really little more than a sentiment, that the welfare of the child prisoner was the chief consideration, he had to institute proceedings to meet the needs of the child. What were those needs? The judge didn't know, and he had no theory; he had to find out for himself. How did he go about finding out? Very simply, very naturally. He asked the child.

    One of the first, most obvious observations he made was that children came into court with either tears or defiance in their eyes. They hated the policeman, and they feared the judge, and since the "cop" and the court were the personification of justice and the state, these young citizens were being reared in the spirit of dread and hatred of law and authority. This was all wrong, and yet it was perfectly natural.

"The criminal court for child-offenders," writes the judge, "is based on the doctrine of fear, degradation, and punishment. It was, and is, absurd. The Juvenile Court was founded on the principle of love. We assumed that the child had committed, not a crime, but a mistake, and that he deserved correction, not punishment. Of course, there is firmness and justice, for without these there would be danger in leniency. But there is no justice without love."

The judge drove out fear from his court, and hate and brutality; for awe, he substituted confidence and affection. How did he do this? By coming down off the bench to the boy. Since the boy was the center of interest, the judge subordinated his own "dignity" and the whole machinery of the court and even the "stolen property," to win back the prisoner at the bar. The good of the boy, obviously paramount in the mind of the court, was made paramount in the mind of the boy, who was led to feel that everybody cared about him, that everything done was done for him in his interest. "Of course," he says, "the law is important, but the vital thing is the relationship established with the child. The case from the boy's standpoint must be understood." Each case, the judge means. He seeks to get for himself a personal, sympathetic understanding of each separate case. There are no hard and fast rules. No fixed routine will do the work. The judge didn't turn away hate, quiet fear, and dry tears by any "methods." When a child is brought weeping or scowling before him, Ben Lindsey is dragged off that bench by his heartstrings, and when he sits on a stool beside the boy in trouble, or goes for a walk with him, or takes him home to dinner or "out to the show," this is no art thought out by a wise man. This is nothing but a good man putting into his work what he wants to get out of it "faith, hope, and love."

To understand the case of Ben Lindsey, it is necessary to study it as he advises us to study the cases of boys from the boys' standpoint. He tells in one of his articles how a young fellow of twenty, who was under sentence for murder, regarded the old criminal court. This boy had been arrested at the age of twelve for stealing a razor to whittle a stick. "It was this way," he explained to Lindsey. "The guy on the high bench, with the whiskers, says, 'What's the boy done, officer?' And the cop says, says he, 'He's a bad kid, Your Honor, and broke into a store and stole a razor.' And the guy on the high bench says, 'Ten dollars or ten days.' Time, three minutes; one round of a prize-fight."

In Judge Lindsey's court, in the beginning, when boys still came there with sorrow and gnashing of teeth, they saw no "guy with whiskers, on a high bench" asking the "cop" questions. They saw a clean-cut young man come into court, go up to the first boy to be "tried" and ask: "What's the matter, my boy? You been making a mistake? Well, lots of fellers make mistakes. That's nothing. I've made mistakes myself, worse'n yours, I guess." Then turning to the policeman, he asks: "What is it, officer?" The policeman tells about the crime, say theft. "Stealing isn't right," says the judge, and he appeals to the boys in the court room, "Is it, fellers?" Putting his hand on the boy's shoulder, he gives him a shove back and a pull forward. "It's weak to swipe things." That hurts. Boys learn in the street that it's smart and brave to steal, and the only evil thing about it is getting caught. Lots of men take this view, too, but judge Lindsey sets up another standard. "I know how it is," he says. "It's a temptation. It's a chance to get something easy, something you want; or something you can sell to get something you want. Wanted to go to the show, maybe. Well, it takes a pretty strong feller to down the desire to take the chance and see the show. But it's wrong to swipe things. 'Tain't fair; 'tain't brave; it's just mean, and it hurts the feller that steals. Makes him steal again, and by and by he is caught and sent up a thief. Now you ain't a thief, and you don't want to be. Do you? But you were too weak to resist the temptation, so you were caught. Ought to cut it out. Not because you were caught. That isn't the reason a feller oughtn't to steal. It's because it's mean and sneaky, and no feller wants to be mean and sneaky. He wants to be on the square.

"But what are you crying for? You've been crying ever since I began to talk to you. Afraid of being punished? Pshaw, a feller ought to stand up and take his medicine; but we don't punish boys. We just try to help 'em get strong and be square.

Even when we send fellers to Golden, it isn't for punishment; it's only to help a kid that's weak to get strong enough to control himself. So we aren't going to punish you. I believe you can control yourself without going to Golden. We'll see. But first off, a kid ought to be strong enough and sufficiently on the square to tell the truth about himself. Ought to tell not only about this time, when you're caught, but all the other times, too. You wait, and after court we'll go back in chambers and we'll have it all out, just us two."

This is rather reassuring, isn't it? It proved so to the children who sat waiting their turn at the first sessions of the Juvenile Court. There was no terrorism in it, no trace of hardness, there were no awful forms. The children felt the difference. "The judge, he gives a feller a show," said one boy to me. And as they saw the proceedings in court, so the children heard about the scenes in chambers. These were the best of all, best for the kids and best for the judge. There is where Lindsey saw into the hearts of children, and where they saw into his. "Never let a child get away with a lie on his soul," the judge says. "A clean breast is half the battle." Children are wonderful liars, but the judge thinks he can tell when they are lying and they admit that he has an instinct for the truth. One foundation for their respect for him is that with all his kindness he isn't sentimental, and he isn't "easy." "You can't fool the jedge," the boys say, and the police tell, as an illustration, the story of a "tough kid" on whom all the judge's appeals seemed to fail. He "lied straight," and since the judge will not help (try) a boy who will not tell the truth, he told the officer to take the boy away On the way back to jail, the boy changed his mind. He asked to be taken again before the judge. "You're right, judge," he said, "and you're game, too. I lied to you, I lied like a horse thief, and I couldn't fool you a little bit. You've beat me, judge, and I'll tell you th' truth." And he did.

The judge in chambers reasons with the boy that while it is wrong to "snitch" on other fellows, it is all right to "snitch" on yourself. The boys understand this. It is made clear to them that there is no punishment, only "help for a feller if he needs it," and among the most interesting experiences that the judge has to tell, are the discussions he has with boys as to whether they "need to go to Golden."

There's a little, old, young, big man, called "Major" whom I saw in command of the battalion at Golden. He is somewhere between twelve and sixteen, but with an old, old face; very tiny of stature, but very tall in dignity. He never smiles, so sober and sensible is he. But he had what the kids and their judge know as the "movin'-about fever." The Major had come honestly by it. He had no home, and he wanted none, for he could range all over the West, from Chicago up into Idaho and down into New Mexico, and always, everywhere, he was known for his pompous dignity to hoboes, cowboys, miners— to all men as "the Major." The judge gave him trial after trial, and it was no use; the time always came when the Major had to "move on." If they must move, the judge lets boys go, but he expects them to call on him to say good-bye and be pledged to write to him regularly and not to steal. Well, once when the fever was coming upon the Major, he called on the judge. The judge urged the Major to down the temptation. The Major tried, but he couldn't; he confessed that he was too "weak" to resist. Then the judge suggested Golden; they would help him there, all right, to stay. The Major received the suggestion thoughtfully. He raised objections which the judge answered, but they separated without a decision, and the judge says that for a week or two he and the Major weighed ponderously the mighty question, till in the end the Major agreed that perhaps he'd better go up to Golden and be helped to cure that moving-about attack and thus learn to "stay put." That's how the Major came to go to Golden, and that's how he won the rank and title which the "movin'-about" world had given him as a "little shaver." And that's the spirit in which the judge in chambers persuades boys to "snitch up" on themselves and look upon the reformatory as a help. As they begin to tell him things bit by bit, he expresses no horror, only understanding; he sympathizes with a feller. If a kid describes how he saw an easy chance to steal and not get caught, the judge exclaims: "Gee, that was a chance. That's certain. But 'tain't square, Hank." "Mistake" after "mistake" is confessed, "weakness" after "weakness"; no crimes, you understand, for the kid and the judge, they see things through the kid's eyes, with all the mitigating circumstances. And so they come to discuss the question whether the kid can "cut it out." The judge is sure the boy can, surer than the boy, but then, it's up to the boy, because the boy has to do the hard work of resisting. The judge can "only help; th' feller has to do the business himself." "Interest is everything in a boy's life," the judge says sagely. "If you want his loyalty, excite his interest." Well, the game of correction is interesting, especially when you are the center of the game. It's one of the most interesting games "a feller" ever played, and the judge has a fascinating way of playing it. Having done something wrong, you try to do something that's right, positively right. This is the judge's great doctrine. He calls it "overcoming evil with good." There's nothing "sissy-boy" about it. You have done an evil thing; you are not, therefore, bad, only so much weakened. So you go and do a good thing. This not only balances the evil; it "strengthens a feller."

Now then, a good thing a feller can usually do right away is to go out and bring in some other kids that are "swipin' things." You mustn't tell the judge who the other fellers are. That would be snitching. But it's all right to get the other fellers to come in and "snitch up" on themselves just as you have "snitched up" on yourself. That gets them into the game; helps them and, since the more fellers there are in on it, the easier it is for you; it helps you.

One of the early cases in the Juvenile Court was that of seven boys brought before him by a policeman who had caught them wiring up signal-boxes, hopping cars, stoning motormen and conductors, and otherwise interfering with the traffic of the street railway. The boys were either tearful or sullen, and they denied the testimony of the officer and his witnesses. The judge took them into his chambers. There he cleared away all ideas of punishment, and got down to the truth. The judge could see that it was fun, but also he could see that what was fun for the boys was trouble for the conductors and motor-men; it made life hard for them, delayed them, and got them home late. The boys hadn't thought before of these railroad men as human beings, only as "fair game" as "fellers what'd give you a chase if you held 'em up." So the judge gave the boys a good view of the men's side of the fun, then he said:

"'Tain't fair, is it, fellers?"

"No, sir."

"Well, what do you say to cuttin' it out?"

They agreed. But there was more for these boys to do than simply to quit themselves. There was an evil deed done to be overcome with good. There was the gang.

"Will you fellers bring in the rest of the gang tomorrow?"

"Sure they would."

But they didn't. The seven turned up the next day without their "crowd." "The other fellers was askeared to come," they reported.

"Well, what are you going to do?" the judge asked the seven.

They believed that if the judge would write a letter to the gang, they would come.

"A warrant," said the judge, seizing the chance to take the terror out of another instrument of the law. "I'll write you out a warrant, and you shall serve it on the gang. But what'll I write?"

One little fellow spoke up. "You begin it," he said; "begin by saying, 'No kid has snitched, but if you'll come, the judge'll give you a square deal.'"

This showed what the matter was, and it brought home to the judge the force of his own feeling against snitching.

The judge began the "warrant" as the little fellow suggested, and thus he ended it, too. The boys took it, and evidently they served it, for the next day the gang came pouring into the court, fifty-two kids. There was a talk, straight talk, like that which he gave the seven. Only the judge put more faith into it. He was going to see if they couldn't get along out where that gang lived without any policemen. The peace of the neighborhood was to be left to the gang, but the gang had to play fair, and give him a square deal.

"For," said the judge, making a personal appeal to their honour, "I have told the company that I would be responsible for their having no more trouble. The company don't trust you kids; and they say I'll be fooled. They said you'd go back on me. But I said you wouldn't, and I say now that you won't. So I'm depending on you fellers; and I don't believe you'll throw me down. What do you say?"

"We'll stay wit' you, Jedge," they shouted. And they didn't throw the judge down. They organized, then and there, a Kid Citizens' League, and the League played square with the judge.

It will be noticed that Lindsey made effective use in this case of the "gang" which the police and all prematurely old reformers seek only to "break up." The "kids' jedge" never thought of breaking up such organizations. His sense is for essentials, instinctively, and there's nothing wrong about gangs as such. They are as natural as organizations of men. The only trouble with gangs is that they absorb all the loyalty of the members, turning them from and often against the home, the law, and the state. But that happens in grown-ups' gangs, too. Railroad and other corporations are gangs which, in the interest of their "business," corrupt the state. Churches are "gangs" whose members submit to evils because, if they fought them, the church might be hurt. So with universities, and newspapers, and all kinds of business organizations. Tammany Hall is only a gang which, absorbing the loyalty of its members, turns it, for the good of the gang, against the welfare of the city. Judge Lindsey simply taught the members of his kid gang what many gangs of grown-ups have to learn, that they are citizens also, and he turned the loyalty of the Kid Citizens' League back to the city, using the honour of the gang as his lever.

Another similar case came up when two boys were brought in by a policeman from the Union Station. The policeman said they belonged to a gang the members of which stoned him wherever they saw him. Why? Well, he was trying to keep them out of the station and off the grass around the station. What were the boys doing at the station and on the station lawn? They explained, and they explained with many manifestations of hate for the cop. They were there to sell papers. It was their place of business, and everybody had acknowledged it—not only all the other newsboys, but everybody else till, one day, some other bigger boys with red caps appeared there selling papers and things. Then "this cop chased us off." Why? Why had the cop suddenly interfered with their business? It was his turn to explain, and he explained that the railroad company, having come to realize that the trade in newspapers at the station was profitable, had decided to take a share in it. The concession was let to a man who employed the boys with red caps. The man wanted a monopoly. So the policeman had received orders to drive off the other boys. He had obeyed. No explanation was given to the boys; no notice. They suddenly found themselves deprived of their means of livelihood, and resenting it, blamed the cop and stoned him.

Thus it was all a misunderstanding, not a "crime" at all, and the judge undertook to clear it up to the satisfaction of all concerned. Having explained it to the two boys under arrest, he enlisted their services in behalf of the court to bring in the others who were "in it" but had not been caught. The policeman, knowing how hard it had been to catch two, was scornful of the judge's confidence of getting the rest, but he was invited to be present at the hour appointed for the "round up," and he was not a little chagrined when his two prisoners returned with twenty-four other kids. The judge lined up the gang on one side of the room, the policeman and his friends on the other. This was the Juvenile Court in session; let the judge describe what happened:

"I proceeded to explain why it was that the owners of the station had a right to grant 'concessions' to the man who employed the boys with the red caps to sell papers and carry baggage to the exclusion of all others; why, if the company demanded it, they had a right to protection for their lawn; how all of this was justified by the law, which secured the right of every man in the enjoyment of his property; how it was not the officer's doings, but the law that required him to perform his duty; how, therefore, they had no real grievance against the policeman—rather their sympathies should be with him. After the sympathetic admission by both the officer and the court that if it were our station and grounds all boys could play on the grass and sell papers there, there was gained for the policeman sympathy and loyalty. As 'little citizens' interested in a 'decent town of decent kids' they agreed not only to 'keep off' and 'keep out' themselves, but to keep other boys out; and everyone agreed 'on the square' that he would give any kid there leave to 'snitch' to me, if any boy broke his word and was not square. Thus harmony was established between their world and ours, and we all pulled together one way."

As the judge remarked to me, those boys did what few men would do; they gave up their business "just because it was right." All that was necessary was to make them understand the right and their duties, and then to interest them in the "game of correction."

The arena for the great game of correction is the Court of Probation. Held every other Saturday forenoon, it is a picturesque and a very pleasant spectacle. All the "bad" boys in town who have been caught committing mistakes or who have "snitched up" on themselves, assemble there to report. It isn't new. Like the Juvenile Court itself, the "method" of putting children on probation did not originate with judge Lindsey. Yet he discovered it himself. As I quote him as saying above, he didn't know about such things. When he went first to the home of the "cave-dweller" to investigate, he was performing one function of a probation officer; and when he went there again and again, he was holding a court of probation. So with the three pigeon burglars and their gang; he went to see them, but there was no method as yet. It was only as the cases grew that the judge had to ask the boys to come to see him, and then, finally, to appoint a time and place where most of the boys could meet all together with him; and that was the origin of Judge Lindsey's Court of Probation, the institution.

But there is more than that to the story of it. The judge feels that he suffered as "a little shaver" from lack of approbation. He was born in Tennessee and his family, well-to-do southern people, were brought to trouble and to Denver by the war. His father died, and Ben had to work hard as a boy. For a long time he had three jobs: he carried newspapers in the early morning; worked all day in a lawyer's office; and, after hours, served as janitor. Always slight of build, he was often worn out;

and nobody appreciated it. He was only doing his duty, and it nearly killed him—literally. He sank under his load to the very verge of despair; and he learned the value of a kind word of sympathy and good cheer.

Many of the bad boys who came to his court were lonely little fellows. They had no home and no friends, and he found in their hearts a longing which he knew all about. He gave them the sympathetic hearing and the kind word he had wanted, and "they drank" he says, "they drank in my friendship as if they were famished." Right there we have one secret of his "hypnotic" influence over children. The judge is proud now of the fact that he has made himself a friend of every boy in town, or, at least, of every "feller that needs a friend," and he will tell you the philosophy and the use of his method if you care to listen. He will tell you how he learned from the gangs that the members thereof did bad things largely because some big fellow, who was bad, or some leader of their own, suggested to them evil and praised them for its accomplishment. He will reason it all out for you, now, if you wish, showing how by his method he has put himself in the place of the big fellow; made himself the fountain of praise, the source of approbation, "the feller" for whose good words kids do good things now. In short, Ben Lindsey is the actual leader of most of the gangs of Denver. And the loyalty which the boys give to him, he is giving back to the state.

All this, however, is but the unforeseen result of this kind man's native sweetness and strength. The only definitely thought-out method is that of having the boys bring reports from the schools. "If you want a boy's loyalty, excite his interest." It was easy enough for the judge to excite the boy's interest; the problem was to keep it. In the early history of the court, before the new laws, he had no probation officers to follow up his cases, and since there was too much for him to do, he bethought him of the school teachers. The judge has always been clear on the point that his Juvenile Court is merely supplementary, that the home and the school are the places where juvenile character should be molded, and that he had to do only with those children who, for some reason, were not successfully treated in the regular way. Thus he was helping the teachers, and since he needed help, he went to the teachers for it, and he got it. The school teachers of Denver have been his mainstay. All that the judge required of the teachers was a report as to how the boys in his Court of Probation were doing in deportment and studies.

"What I was after," the judge explained, "was something for which I could praise the boy in open court. Believing in approbation as an incentive, I had to have their reports for the boy to show me, in order that I might have a basis for encouraging comment, or, if the reports were not up to the mark, for sympathy. It didn't matter to me very much what the reports were about. Some of the teachers couldn't see at first why they should report on the scholarship of a boy who was good at school and bad—a thief, perhaps, out of school. But you can see that these fortnightly reports were an excuse for keeping up my friendly relationship with the boy, holding his loyalty, and maintaining our common interest in the game of correction he and I were playing together. Since we had a truancy law, the teachers were in touch and thus could keep me in touch with every boy under school age in the city, and their reports were my excuse for praise or appeal."

Judge Lindsey's Court of Probation is thus a Court of Approbation. It serves other purposes; indeed, it is everything to the boys of Denver. It is the state, the law, and justice; it is home, school, club, and society; it is friendship, success, and the scene of triumphs; it is the place also where failure goes for help and for hope renewed. It is all that Judge Lindsey is; all that he means to the minds of the boys. For the judge's personality makes it, his and the boys', and they made it up out of their own needs.

The boys assemble early, two or three hundred of them, of all ages and all sorts, "small kids" and "big fellers"; well-dressed "lads" and ragged "little shavers"; burglars who have entered a store, and burglars who have "robbed back" pigeons; thieves who have stolen bicycles, and thieves who have "swiped" papers; "toughs" who have "sassed" a cop or stoned a conductor, and boys who have talked bad language to little girls, or who "hate their father," or who have been backward at school and played hookey because the teacher doesn't like them.

It isn't generally known, and the judge rarely tells just what a boy has done; the deed doesn't matter, you know, only the boy, and all boys look pretty much alike to the judge and to the boys. So they all come together there, except that boys who work, and newsboys, when there's an extra out, are excused to come at another time. But nine o'clock Saturday morning finds most of the "fellers" in their seats, looking as clean as possible, and happy.

The judge comes in and, passing the bench, which looms up empty and useless behind him, he takes his place, leaning against the clerk's table or sitting on a camp-chair.

"Boys," he begins, "last time I told you about Kid Dawson and some other boys who used to be with us here and who 'made good.' Today I've got a letter from the Kid. He's in Oregon, and he's doing well. I'll read you what he says about himself and his new job."

And he reads the letter, which is full of details roughly set in a general feeling of encouragement and self-confidence.

"Fine, isn't it!" the judge says. "Kid Dawson had a mighty hard time with himself for awhile, but you can see he's got his hand on his throttle now. Well, let's see. The last time, I talked about snitching, didn't? Today I'm going to talk about 'ditching.'" And he is off on the address, with which he opens court. His topics are always interesting to boys, for he handles his subjects boy-fashion. "Snitching," the favourite theme, deals with the difference between "snitching," which is telling on another boy to hurt him; and "snitching on the square," which is intended to help the other fellow. "Ditching" is another popular subject. "To ditch" a thing is to throw it away; and the judge, starting off with stories of boys who have ditched their commitment papers, proceeds to tell about others who, "like Kid Dawson out there in Oregon," have "ditched" their bad habits and "got strong." I heard him on Arbor Day speak on trees; how they grew, some straight, some crooked. There's always a moral in these talks, but the judge makes it plain and blunt; he doesn't "rub it in."

After the address, which is never long, the boys are called up by schools. Each boy is greeted by himself, but the judge uses only his given or nickname. "The boys from the Arapahoe Street School," he calls, and, as the group comes forward, the judge reaches out and seizing one by the shoulder, pulls him up to him, saying:

"Skinny, you've been doing fine lately; had a crackerjack report every time. I just want to see if you have kept it up. Bet you have. Let's see." He opens the report. "And you have. That's great. Shake, Skin. You're all right, you are." Skinny shines.

Pointing at another, he says: "And you, Mumps, you got only 'fair' last time. What you got this time? You promised me 'excellent' and I know you've made good." He tears open the envelope. "Sure," he says. "You've done it. Bully for you." Turning to the room, he tells "the fellers" how Mumps began playing hookey, and was so weak he simply thought he couldn't stay in school. "He blamed the teacher; said she was down on him. She wasn't at all. He was just weak, Mumps was; had no backbone at all. But look at him now. He's bracing right up. You watch Mumps. He's the 'stuff,' Mumps is. Aren't you, Mumps? Teacher likes you now all right, doesn't she? Yes. And she tells me she does. Go on now and keep it up, Mumps. I believe in you."

"Why, Eddie," the judge says, as another boy comes up crying. "What are you crying for? Haven't you made good?" "No, sir," Eddie says, weeping the harder. "Well, I told you I thought you'd better go to Golden. You don't want to go, eh? Get another job, you say? But you can't keep it, Eddie. You know you can't. Give you another chance? What's the use, Eddie? You'll lose it. The best thing for you, Eddie, is Golden. They'll help you up there, make you stick to things, just make you; and so you'll get strong."

Eddie swims in tears, and it seemed to me I'd have to give that boy "another chance," but the judge, who is called "easy," was not moved at all. His mind was on the good of that boy; not on his own feelings, nor yet on the boy's. "You see," said he to me, "he is hysterical, abnormal. The discipline of Golden is just what he needs." And he turned to the room full of boys. "Boys," he said, "I'm going to send Eddie up to Golden. He hasn't done wrong; not a thing. But he's weak. He and I have tried again and again to win out down here in the city, and he wants another trial. But I think a year or so at Golden will brace Eddie right up, and make him a strong, manly fellow. He's not going up there to be punished. That isn't what Eddie needs, and that isn't what Golden is for. Is it, fellers ?"

"No, sir," the room shouted.

"It would be unjust to punish Eddie, but Eddie understands that. Don't you, Eddie?"

"Yes, sir, but" (blubbering), "Judge, I think if I only had one more show I could do all right."

"Eddie, you're wrong about that. I'm sure I'm right. I'm sure that after a year or two you'll be glad I sent you to the school And I'll be up there in a few days to see you, Eddie, myself. What's more, I know some boys up there friends of mine, that'll help you, Eddie; be friends to you. They won't want to like a kid that cries, but I'll tell 'em you need friends to strengthen you, and they'll stay with you."

All forenoon this goes on, the boys coming up in groups to be treated each one by himself. He is known to the court, well known, and the judge, his personal friend, and the officers of the court and the spectators, his fellow-clubmen, all rejoice with him, if he is "making good," and if he is doing badly, they are sorry. And in that case, he may be invited to a private talk with the judge, a talk, mind you, which has no terrors for the boy, only comfort. They often seek such interviews voluntarily. They sneak into the judge's chambers or call at his house to "snitch up" that they are not doing well. And the boys who sit there and see this every two weeks, or hear all about it, they not only have forgotten all their old fear of the law; they go to the court now as to a friend, they and their friends. For Judge Lindsey had not been doing "kid justice to kids" very long before all Boyville knew it. The rumour spread like wildfire. The boys "snitched" on the judge, "snitched on the square"; they told one another that the county judge was all right.

The judge tells many stories to illustrate the change that followed. Once as he approached a group of boys, one of them said: "There's th' Jedge, fellers," and two kids dived down an alley. The others gathered around the judge.

"Who were those boys that ran away?" he asked. "Who? Them? Oh," came the answer, "they're kids from K. C." (Kansas City); "they ain't on to the game here."

Another time the judge was walking along the street arguing with me that stealing isn't a heinous crime in a boy, and that it shouldn't be treated with holy horror. Most boys swipe something at one time or another; and to prove his point, he halted before a "gang." "Say, kids," he said, and, as they looked up, he asked: "how many of you fellers have swiped things?"

Every boy's hand shot up in the air. The judge had proved his point, but he had proved also another thing. Those boys knew he was the judge, yet they were not afraid to tell the truth. Or, to state the situation more completely: those boys knew he was the judge and therefore they were not afraid to tell him the truth. Not all these boys had been in his court; in fact, only one or two had; but that didn't matter. All the boys of Denver know of the judge, and what they know of him is that though he represents the law and the state, he is "all right."

One afternoon, a boy of about ten years stuck his head into the door of the judge's private room.

"Is the judge in?" he asked.

"Yes," said the judge.

"Is this him?" the boy asked.

"Yes, my boy. I'm the judge."

"Well, I'm Johnny Rosenbaum, and I came down here to see you."

"Yes ? I'm glad you've come, John, but what did you come for?"

"Well," he said, "Joe Rosenthal, he used to come down here, and he 'swiped' things once. And I 'swiped' something, and he said I better come down here and see you about it."

"All right, but what have you come to me about it for?"

The tears started. "Well," he said, "I came down here to tell you I'd cut it out and never do it again. And I thought I better get here before the cop did. Joe said the cop 'ud ditch a kid that swiped things, but that you'd help a feller to ditch the swipin'."

"Yes, I'll help you ditch swipin', but you're a mighty little boy; how did you find the way down here alone?"

"Oh," he said, " 'most every kid I seed knew about it, and they passed me down th' line to here."

Johnny Rosenbaum was put on probation, and he began overcoming evil with good, as he proved one day in court. Sometimes the judge will turn to the boys and ask whether any feller has done that week a thing good enough to make up for an evil thing done before. Once, when he asked this question, Johnny rose and said: "Judge, some of the kids I run with was diggin' a cave, and we wanted a shovel, and they said: 'Let's go and swipe one.' So they wanted to put me into Mr. Putnam's barn where the shovel was, through a little hole that nobody but a little kid could crawl through. And I says, 'No, I gotter report down to th' judge, and I told him that I'd cut out swipin' and when I got a chanct I'd do a good thing. Now is my chanct' I says. 'I won't swipe th' shovel,' I says, 'and you mustn't' I says to them. Now I ain't goin' to snitch on who the fellers was because they says 'All right, we won't swipe the shovel.' And I went 'round and I ast Mr. Putnam to borrow us the shovel, and he said he would. So we got the shovel on th' square. But, judge, if I hadn't done that they would have swiped the shovel, wouldn't they?"

"Yes, John," said the judge. "They would have swiped the shovel, and if you ever swiped anything in your life, you have more than made up for it by doing the right thing this time."

Another case of "making good" was that of Eli Carson. Eli told at a meeting how his news gang down in the *Post* alley were going to "swipe a box of cherries off'n Wolf Londoner's grocery store." "I says it wasn't square," said Eli, "and the other kids, they all allowed it wasn't either. Texas was th' kid that said first to swipe th' cherries; and he thought afterwards it was best not to do it. And I wanted to tell you, judge, that I had done a good thing, but Texas he didn't want me to. But by and by Texas changed his mind, and says I could tell you. So I'm not snitchin', am I?"

"An experience like that," the judge said by way of comment, "goes to show that my theory is correct, that all we need is an influence for good to counteract the influence for bad of the gang. For Texas is a well-known newsboy, and had Eli not been a member of our gang, coming to court where he could tell his experiences in the presence of one hundred and fifty other boys, and be praised, why, then, Eli would have wanted to please Texas. As it is, he wants to please me and the court gang; and Texas does, too."

Another instance of faith in the court: The judge had been trying a case all day. It was a grown-up case, difficult and slow, and when the adjournment came late, at six o'clock, the judge was tired. As the courtroom cleared, however, he saw a child in a back seat. "He was so small," the judge says, "that I thought someone must have gone off and forgotten him, and I told 'Uncle John' Murrey (the bailiff) to find out whose child it was. But when Uncle John spoke to him, the little fellow got up, and I saw he was almost ten years old. I called him up to the bench, and he came, and when he reached me he dropped his head on my shoulder and began to sob.

"Judge," he said, "I'm Clifford, and my mamma don't live here, and I stay with my aunt down on Street, so I been swipin' things, I have, and I come here to 'cut it out.'" As the tears flowed more abundantly, he said he was sorry and would never do it again if the judge would "give him a show" as he had another boy he named. The judge took the little fellow back in his chambers; they had a long talk, and the boy, put on probation, reported regularly and well. "He turned out to be a splendid boy," the judge says.

But the best example the judge gives of the difference in results between the old criminal court system of vengeance and fear and the new method of friendship and service, is a story he tells of two brothers. "Both were wayward," he says. "The older was brought to the criminal court for some boyish offence in the days before the establishment of the Juvenile Court. He was flung into a filthy jail and herded with men and women, where he heard and saw vile and obscene things. He was dragged into court by an officer and put through the police court mill. He was only a little boy. He had been sinned against long before his birth. Both by heredity and environment he had been driven to lawlessness. But the state took no account of this. It had its chance to make a good man of him. He wanted bread; the state gave him a stone.

It branded him a criminal, made him a criminal. It made the pressure of evil upon him inexorable. Today he is a man and in the penitentiary. "The younger brother was as wayward as the elder. Four years ago he was brought to the Juvenile Court, defiant and frightened, just as his brother had been taken to another tribunal. The policeman told me the boy was a very Ananias, and I replied that, given the same conditions, he (the cop) would probably have been the same, and the officer went away convinced that there was no use bringing the boys to the Juvenile Court, where the judge 'did nothing to them.' The policeman would count as nothing the many hours during many weeks that I labored for that boy. He told me the truth; he convicted himself, but no stigma of conviction was put upon him, and he was not punished. He was put on probation, and encouraged to do his best. He was made to feel that the state was on his side; that the forces of the law were working for him rather than against him; that the court was his friend, his appeal when he was in trouble. And that Morris, as I will call him, did feel perfect faith in the court, the law, and the state, he proved once in an amusing way.

"One day I was trying an important will case. Millions of dollars were involved. The door opened cautiously, and Morris poked his freckled face in, piping up that he wanted to see the judge. The bailiff started to shoo him away, but I called in the boy. I ordered a recess. No doubt the distinguished counsel were shocked; certainly they looked shocked. But a live boy looms larger than a dead man's millions to me, and when this boy came into my court, unafraid, smiling, and sure of justice, I remembered the flash of fear and hatred that I once had seen on this same freckled face. So I beckoned Morris up to me, and I heard his case then and there. He was in business. He sold newspapers, and his place of business was a certain busy corner where he dealt not only with pedestrians, but with passengers on passing cars. The 'old cop,' it seemed, had let him 'hop the cars,' and all had gone well till a new cop had come there. The 'new guy,' as Morris called him, had ordered the boy off the corner. 'Thinks 'cause he's a cop he owns the whole town,' said Morris, who was losing about fifty cents a day. The case stated, I asked Morris what he would have me do.

"Evidently Morris had been reading, as well as selling, his newspapers, for he was ready with his answer.

" 'Judge,' he said, 'can't you gimme one o' them there things they call 'junctions against de fly cop?'

"I gave him one. Why not? I called for an injunction blank, and on it I wrote a note to the policeman. I told him about Morris; not much, but enough to make him understand that the boy was one of my probationers who was trying to 'make good'; that he was bringing me good reports from his teachers; and that I hoped the officer would give the boy all the leeway possible. To the boy I explained that the officer represented the law, as I did, and must be respected accordingly. Morris went away gleefully with his writ."

And the writ "worked." The judge says that the next time he saw Morris, he asked the boy about it. Morris said he had "served it all right."

" 'An' say, judge," he said, "it worked fine. De cop liked to 'a dropped dead when he read it. He tinks I got a pull wit' de court, so he wants to be my friend. And I don't know but I'll let him in." The judge spoke for the cop. He told Morris he must be a friend of the policeman, and the boy reported later that he had "let the cop in." And he had. The judge learned that they became good friends. In his comment on this incident, the judge attributes the difference between Morris and his brother to one thing: "opportunity." "The state," he says, "surrounded the boy who is in the penitentiary with everything to make him do evil; hence the state must support him now in the penitentiary. The state surrounded Morris with every influence to make him do right; hence he is growing up a good citizen who will support the state." There is a great difference there. But I want to point out another "difference," a "method" of the judge to which he does not refer in anything he ever says about the celebrated injunction case of Morris, the "bad" boy, vs. the new cop on his corner. Recall what the judge wrote into that injunction. How did he make the policeman obey the writ which the boy served on him? The judge simply told the policeman about the boy. Having told the boy about the cop, he related enough of the history of the newsboy to get the cop interested in the boy and in the game of correction which he and the boy were playing together. In other words, Ben Lindsey, the man of heart, reached for the heart of the policeman, and since the heart is a vital spot, it is no wonder "de cop liked to 'a dropped dead,"

This, then, is Judge Lindsey's "method." It is an old method. He didn't discover it. A great religion was founded on "faith, hope, and love" once. That was long ago. The only new and interesting thing about Lindsey's experiment is that he finds that this ancient, neglected method "works" works, too, as I said at the outset, with grown-ups as well as with children, with cops as well as with kids. It has won his fight for him. Yes, he fights. The kids' judge has had to fight, and, as we shall see, he has fought. The fight isn't finished yet. The "bad" men of Colorado haven't been taught by their state and their courts to see things as the bad boys of Colorado are learning to see them. They also go to the courts for injunctions, and some of them get their writs. Ben B. Lindsey is a man with a man's fight for men on his hands, and he is the kind of man that finishes his fights. He will win with good men or he'll wait and win it with bad boys. For his bad boys will grow up some day, and they know what the state can be to a feller and that "there can be no justice without the love of man for man."

II. WHAT MAKES "BAD" CHILDREN BAD

If you care to take the measure of Christian civilization in the United States today, reflect for a moment frankly upon the meaning of this fact: There is opposition to Judge Lindsey. That men like Heney and LaFollette, Everett Colby, and (even) Mark Fagan should have to fight for the right to do right, is significant enough of the power of evil among us; but Ben Lindsey! This man is so just and so gentle; his purposes are so pure, his work is so beautiful, so successful, and you would think so harmless, that no one would expect to see any man's hand raised against the judge of the Juvenile Court of Denver. Callous souls might show indifference, but why opposition? And such opposition?

The two bosses of the two political parties conspired together once to keep Judge Lindsey off the bench. At another time, some men tempted him to disgrace with a woman! Legislation is proposed (and has been passed) to divide his court and thus limit his power as a judge to serve the children of his county. Physically delicate, the only rest this overworked man takes is when he travels, as he does, thousands of miles to tell people what wonders "justice with love" has done for the "bad kids" of Denver. This time-off he justifies on the ground that his lectures further the cause of the children elsewhere, and bring in money to carry on his plans for his own "court gang" at home; and he spends thus all he makes from these lectures, and out of the $4,600 which the county pays him, he retains some other judge to fill his place while he is away. I ask the thousands of men and women who have heard Judge Lindsey tell his stories of boys and girls, to consider what it means, that powerful men in Colorado have drawn a bill that shall "put a stop to this little whipper-snapper's running around all over the country lecturing." This is hate. And the other attacks upon him and his work show a deeper-seated opposition. Why?

There's a reason. There are two reasons. One is that Judge Lindsey does not confine himself to saving the children that are "lost in crime"; he began early to inquire into the causes of juvenile crime. He asked what made bad children bad. That led him to a study of the conditions of child-life; that led him to the conclusion that the typical environment of an average Christian community was such that even little children could not be good; and that led this man to attack those conditions. In other words, Judge Lindsey has sought not merely to cure but to prevent the evils of child-life.

"Don't tear down all the time," men shout at reformers. "What we want is reconstructive work." It was Lindsey's "reconstructive work" that threatened to "hurt business."

There we have one all-sufficient reason why he has to fight; but there's a second: Ben Lindsey does not limit his labors to the cause of the children. He is celebrated for his juvenile system, and in Denver you hear that he is "a philanthropist, and if he would stick to his philanthropic work, he might go on forever." That's a lie. But, as I said, this man should not be known only as the founder of the Juvenile Court; he is doing a man's work for men. The "kids' judge" of Denver was elected as the county judge of Denver, and as such he dealt out justice to bad men as well as to bad boys, and when by accident one day he discovered evidence of graft in his court, Judge Lindsey forced the grafters to trial and to conviction.

Ben Lindsey does his duty, his whole duty as a man, as a citizen, and as a public official, and that's what makes him a menace to Things As They Are in Colorado and in the United States. Like Heney, and LaFollette, and Colby, and (even) Mark Fagan, Ben Lindsey is up against the System, and, therefore, like them and like every honest man you hear of in this land, the just judge has to fight.

A large part of the opposition to Judge Lindsey, especially at first, was honest. It was ignorant, but sincere and natural. For, you understand, Lindsey's methods are applied Christianity. Without thinking much about it he was putting into practice in actual life, and, of all places, in the criminal courts, the doctrine of faith, hope, and charity. In a Christian community this was revolutionary and, "as it was in the beginning" caused a great rumpus. The Bar was shocked. When the judge, searching the juvenile mind for causes of juvenile crime, saw fear of the law and hate of the court in the eyes of the little prisoners and, looking about him, realized that there was reason for this dread, we have seen how he threw off authority, came down off the bench, subordinated the machinery of justice to the good of the boy, and for routine and vengeance substituted sympathy and help. He took the boys' view of boys' "mistakes," and when he sent a "feller" to the reform school at Golden, it was only upon his own confession and for his own good. The boys understood, but the lawyers wagged their heads; the lawyers, I mean, who regard the law as a sacred institution. When they saw a judge who was "a lawyer, and a good lawyer," sweeping aside technicalities and ignoring "good practice" to get at the real, human interest of the prisoner at the bar, they were deeply pained. But the judge, who understands men as well as he does boys, understood this feeling, and he was patient to explain, and, since this was an honest opposition, he overcame it. He tells the story:

"I sent a boy to the Industrial School on the charge of 'needing correction for his own good.' The boy had made a clean breast of it to me, and we had such a perfect understanding, that boy and I, that he had taken his commitment papers and gone off by himself to Golden. Then appeared counsel employed by his parents, declaring that he had been dealt with without due process of law, no jury trial, etc., etc. He (the lawyer) said he would apply for a writ of habeas corpus. I assured him I could make no objection, but that the boy had been guilty of two or three offences constituting technical burglary, so that while he might be released for the purpose of obtaining due process of law, this process would not only make the boy a burglar and a thief, but would return him, so branded by the records, to the place whence he might be brought upon the habeas corpus writ.

"The case," says the judge, "was never brought." Lawyers still lift their brows at Judge Lindsey's "loose practice," but though he has dealt with more than five thousand children's cases, the question of due process has been raised but once since—at home. A Boston judge demurred not long ago. Lindsey lectured there, teaching his doctrine that the boy is more important than the law, and that where justice, blindfolded, made criminals of "bad" boys, justice with love saved them to the state. "God forgive the people who brought that man here!" exclaimed the Boston judge. And the next time a young criminal was brought before him he "showed how to deal with such cases." The boy had thrown a snowball at a man, and the Boston judge sent the prisoner to jail for thirty days "on the evidence." But Lindsey's doctrine had taken hold of the public mind; the newspapers investigated the case very much as Lindsey would have done, and on the facts Boston public opinion reversed the Boston judge. He had made a mistake. He was right, in a way, this law-worshipping judge; it wouldn't do to let men like him exercise their human feelings. But Boston was right, too; such men shouldn't be allowed to deal with the children of men. Even blind justice isn't revenge.

The penal instinct is strong in man, and Denver felt, for a long while, as this pagan judge felt. Grave fears were expressed everywhere of Lindsey's "leniency," as men called his

Christianity, for, of course, no one recognized it for what it was. "What the little devils want is a good licking," said the grown-ups, "or the jail."

"No," the judge replied, "all they lack is a fair show and understanding." And he gave the boys and girls a "show and understanding" and they showed that they understood. He had to fight the doubts of their elders, but he believes in fighting. "The world needs fighting men," he teaches. "Every good, great man was a fighter." So he enlisted the children in his fight for a "decent town of decent kids" by telling them how he was called foolish for putting faith in "bad kids." But also he teaches that "a good example and loving service -- these are the weapons of peace." And this, likewise, the kids understood. The difficulty was to make their elders understand, but he was patient, and the children helped him.

A city official of high degree, exasperated by the outrageous depredations of a "gang up his way," called on the judge once to send to prison three of the boys that were under arrest.

"Born criminals, that's what they are," said the official, and some of their acts were "burglaries."

The judge talked with the boys. He got them to bring in the others, and among them was the son of the official of high degree!

"Your son isn't a born criminal," said the judge, "and neither are the others."

He sent none of the boys to prison. The judge taught them some elementary lessons about crime and, putting them on their honour, let them go "on probation." Their "crimes" ceased. The judge says his service in the Juvenile Court has taught him many things about children, but the information he has gained there about parents he characterizes as "amazing." He ranks fool fathers and incompetent mothers among the first causes of the troubles of children, and if you add vicious and negligent parents you have nine-tenths of all his children's "cases" accounted for. "Children don't rebel at authority," he says, "only at ignorant authority," and there is where many parents fail. "Every father and mother ought to know more about their own children than anyone else. Perhaps, in most cases, they do, but it is amazing how often they don't. And the reason they don't is that they haven't enough love for children to understand them, and not enough character to hold their respect. Their children lie to them, and it is the parents' fault. I recall hardly a single case in the thousands I have dealt with when we did not get the truth from the child; yet in hundreds of these cases the children had lied to the parents. Why? They were afraid of their parents; they were not understood at home."

The reference here is not to the parents of the poor "bad kids"; they also have their faults, and the judge has had his troubles with them. But the poor have in poverty an excuse for neglect, and where one parent is vicious, the other is pathetically glad, usually, of help such as Judge Lindsey gave. The poor are "down on" the Society for the Prevention of Cruelty to Children, of New York; but for Judge Lindsey, of Denver, they will fight even at the polls. He won over the poor easily enough.

His hardest honest battles were with the well-to-do father who "had no time to fuss with his boy," except now and then to "lick him," and the vain and frivolous mother who "just knew that her nice little boy" or her "nicer" little girl "wouldn't do such things." Now, the judge finds that all children are pretty much alike at bottom; they all are "nice," but the Old Harry who is in their parents is in the kids, too; and the judge doesn't mind. The judge has a sneaking, human prejudice against "little prigs"; he rather favours husky lads and mischievous little girls who, if they can do wrong, can do right with equal energy. But the "nice" parents are forever making prigs and snobs of their children or proving to them their elderly asininity.

"I remember a gentleman," the judge relates, "who was most violent in his complaints to me about boys in a certain (fashionable) district who swiped ice-cream and other good things to eat from back-porches, and he declared he had forbidden his boy to go with the suspects. He was the surprised dad of one, the worst of the gang. I had to find it out for him. He should have known it himself. He was too busy downtown all day, and at night too busy denouncing his neighbors' children. He is busier now studying his own son.

"The mother of a very well-to-do family once swept into my chambers, highly indignant that I had sent to the school for her boy who had been, with others, complained against for a serious offence. I had preferred not to send an officer to arrest him. 'I would have you to understand,' she excitedly declared, 'that my boy is no thief; he never did anything wrong in his life.' She knew it because she heard her boy say his prayers every night at her knee. And she knew how he came to be so falsely accused. For she said: 'I know Mrs. A. across the street has been lying about Frank. She is a mean, contemptible old thing. She told Mrs. B. that he did so and so, and I know it is a lie, because Frankie told me so.'

"I had never heard of Mrs. A. before," the judge says; "I had got at the truth from the boys themselves, and Frank had told me all about his part in it. Indeed, we had just finished our talk, and Frank was in the next room waiting for the typewriter to copy a note I had dictated to ask his father not to lick the boy. Frank feared his father, and I knew that the licking would be, not to correct the boy, but to sate the anger of the parent and salve his wounded pride. Children know, and I know, and you know how many a licking is as selfish as that. Well, as the mother ended her tirade, the boy came back with the letter to be signed. His face fell when he saw his mother. 'Now, Frank,' I said, 'tell your mother what you have told me.' He did. She sank into a chair with a frightened little sigh: 'Well, who would have believed it?' Another mother, in an exactly similar situation, after nearly fainting away, suddenly arose and, with the image of Mrs. A. plainly in her mind, persuaded her little Frankie to repudiate his confession and stick to the lie. Her little Frankie didn't turn out as well, but the one I saved from a 'lickin' has been a princely little fellow ever since this, his first real lesson."

Experiences like these would make an ordinary man feel like "licking" Frankie's busy father and humiliating his silly mother, and Judge Lindsey has some very healthy, human feelings about such things, as he shows by the way he writes of them. The man has humor and heat, but also he has charity and infinite patience. He was as gentle with those parents as he was with their children. Having discovered early that many parents thought less of their children than of what their neighbours might say, the judge provided privacy. We have seen him calling up boys in his Probation Court by schools, and addressing them by their first or "nick" names. This he does to spare not only the pride of the boy, but the vanity of his father and mother. And so he abolished criminal records in the Juvenile Court, not only to save a boy from growing up with a rogue's name to burden him, but to shield his family from "disgrace."

But the best example of his practice of privacy and consideration for both parents and children is his method of dealing with girls. He himself seldom speaks of this part of his work, and the reason is that he finds it is a sex-problem. Some women, who themselves are students of delinquent children and who admire Lindsey's service with boys, say that he errs with girls.

"Little girls steal, lie, and do all the other things that boys do," they say. "The police don't arrest them as often, but the problem of the girls is as various and as complex as that of the boys." However that may be, Lindsey finds the sex-problem big enough to alarm him; and he says his observations are borne out by men who know in other cities.

In brief, it is another case of parental ignorance and Anglo-Saxon prudery. Parents do not like to tell their children the essential, natural facts of sex; they think their children too innocent. The result is that their children learn them at school or at play from other people's children, "bad" boys and "forward" girls, who impart all this knowledge in the very vilest form. And the judge, probing into the doings of boys and girls brought before him for other things, discovered that these lessons had taken a practical turn; that in certain schools, where the thing got started, it had spread to include, in one case fifteen, in another nearly all the little girls in the school. What did he do about it?

First, he got the truth. Girls lie more readily and more obstinately than boys, but he persuaded them to tell all about it. And this he accomplished by affecting no horror of the subject. He treated it naturally. He didn't take the course the world would have taken, and especially the women's world—he didn't make the poor little girl feel that she was lost forever and ever.

As with boys, he called it "all a mistake," and a mistake that could be retrieved. Having the truth, he called in the mother. It is a fact for mothers to ponder that no children wanted mamma and papa to know; they would get no such candor and no such sympathetic understanding at home as they got from their judge. But the judge insisted, and after an hour with the child, he often had to spend hours with the mother to prepare her to be motherly. She was horror-stricken; she thought of the disgrace; of what Mrs. A. would say. But the judge had foreseen all that. He had other women calling on him the same day, other mothers and unmarried women. The shocked mother's good name was shielded, and she and her daughter were brought together. For once, no lies, no vanities, no hypocrisies, and no false modesty stood between them, and therefore there was no lack of a perfect understanding. In one case the judge was so stirred by the extent to which the schools had been cursed by this evil that he called a "meeting of mothers." No one knew what it was for; mothers not involved were invited with those that were in trouble; school teachers and other women; some of the "best" women in town. There, all together, the women of Denver were informed, warned, and instructed in private. It was beautifully done. No names were mentioned, of course, not even the name of the school, and no breath of the purpose of that meeting ever leaked out.

The head of one of the public utility companies once marked Lindsey for defeat, and one of his executive staff remonstrated.

"Oh, no," he said, "not Lindsey."

"What!" exclaimed the magnate. "You, too? Everywhere I turn it is, 'Oh, no, not Lindsey.' My wife is for Lindsey, my mother is for Lindsey, my sisters are for Lindsey. And now you are for Lindsey. What is it that makes everybody and everything fight for this judge?" Everybody doesn't fight for Judge Lindsey; only those are for him who know how he has conspired with them in secret to help their little boy or their little girl. But these are legion. Poor and rich, "everybody" has knowledge of private calls made by this man; of hours, days, weeks spent on the case of somebody's bad little boy whom they have seen afterward being "good" to "show 'em that th' jedge is dead right in bankin' on th' honour of a kid." Opposition? That of the parents of Denver melted like one of Denver's summer snows.

All the opposition to faith in mischievous boys soon disappeared, but there remained the fear of this treatment for "really bad" boys. The police represented the old policy of vengeance and prison. When the judge received official permission to deal with all juvenile cases, and they saw what his treatment was faith and hope and love, they snorted. The town snorted with them, and when the police held back its "criminals born," public opinion backed the police. But the judge is a politician, too; he knows the game, and he went after the police. How? He might have exercised his authority, and he has done that since, in his fights with the dishonest opposition of the police. But this was honest opposition, this that came first. It was nothing but the natural conservatism of human nature, and he was patient with it. He reasoned with the police. He "showed them." He got the bad boys to help him "show 'em," just as the "nice" boys had helped him show the "good" people up on the hill. Judge Lindsey came down off the bench to go into the jails and bring into his court the "criminals born"; and he brought them there, and there he gave to them also trust, encouragement, and service, and, like the good boys, the bad ones gave him back faith for faith, hope for hope, and for his love, their loyalty, and his greatest triumph.

That is what most of the admirers of Judge Lindsey call his practice of trusting young "criminals" to go alone to Golden. Other triumphs of his seem to me to be greater, but certainly the sight of "a convict" and a boy convict at that, receiving his commitment papers from the judge and passing through the streets, taking train and changing cars to get to Golden, and there delivering himself up—this is indeed a spectacle to see. And it is a common spectacle in Denver. Judge Lindsey hardly ever sends an officer with a boy now, and out of the hundreds he has trusted, only three have failed him. One of these I saw. He was "Eddie," the boy I told about in the first part of this story, who was hysterical, and the judge had doubts about him; indeed, he put him privately in charge of a "tough kid" who was going also to the school, and it was the tough kid who reported by telephone from the station where they changed cars, that "Eddie can't seem to make it, judge. He don't say he won't, but he cries, and I guess he ain't strong enough."

Another of the three failures was a boy who was started twice, and when the judge reproached him for his weakness, suggested a way to beat himself. "Try me by another road, judge," he said. "This road goes right by my old stamping ground, and when I see th' gang playin' 'round, I can't help it. I just have to drop off th' car." The judge gave him tickets over another route, and that night received word that the boy had "made it." Well, this practice of the judge was begun on an impulse in this first, honest conflict with the police. They had caught two "dangerous young criminals," boys with records for serious crimes and jail breaking, and the judge, having found them in the cells, talked with them. One night the judge telephoned to the warden to send over two of the boys. An officer brought one. "I think," the judge says, "that the warden's idea was that it was dangerous to send two at one time without handcuffs on them, and the police knew it offended me to have them come into my court or my chambers with young fellows handcuffed."

When the officer came in with the boy, he spoke in an undertone to the judge, warning him that the prisoner was the "worst in the bunch," and that every time he had brought him to that room, the boy had eyed the window with the fire-escape.

"Better let me stay here," said the officer. The judge said he would take his chances. "All right," said the officer, and he smiled, "but we shall have to hold you responsible. You know what it has cost the county to catch this prisoner." The judge knew, and he promised to give a written order of court, if necessary, and the officer left. It was ten o'clock at night, dark and cold. The boy, sixteen years old, was strong, and his face was not very prepossessing. The judge is built like a flower, but he had worked hard on this boy, and he believed in his "method." So when the door closed behind the officer, he went straight up to the boy.

"Henry," he said, "the officer who brought you here says you had your eye on the fire-escape, and that you are looking for a chance to 'skip.' He said he wouldn't be responsible for your return to jail if I made him leave you alone in this room with me. He said that you'd be down that fire-escape quicker'n a wink. Now, I don't believe it. I believe in you, Henry, and I hope you believe in me."

With that, the judge went to the window and, throwing it up as high as it would go, he said:

"There, Henry, there's the fire-escape and the night and two hours the best of it, for I'll promise, if you decide to 'duck,' not to report to the warden till twelve o'clock. Now, then, if you think you are not worth saving, not worth helping if all the hours I have spent with you in jail are to go for nothing, you 'scoot,' I'll not interfere. I leave it to you. I can't save a fellow, you know, not by myself; I can only help a fellow to save himself, if he wants to. If he doesn't want to, and I can't convince him that he ought to want to, then I do not see much hope. So, go or stay, as you wish, Henry."

"Do you mean that, judge?" the boy asked, and the judge thinks his impulse was to go.

"You know what I mean," he answered, and for a moment the two looked at each other.

"Then," says the judge, "I thought I saw a peculiar shadow cross his face, and I believed he understood. I went back to my table and sat down. I must confess it was an anxious moment for me. I wasn't sure that I had made on that boy the impression I hoped to make. He looked so hard. And he wavered there. I hardly dared to look at him. I thought of the ridicule of the police, of the failure and what it would mean: the defeat of the policy I was coming to believe in. And there that boy hung, swinging, actually swinging. Well, he had a certain peculiar swinging gait, and when he made a lurch for that window, my heart rose in my throat. His hand went up in the air, and I thought he was gone. But no—the hand that went up seized the window and brought it down with a slam and a bang. Then the boy came and sat down at my table. 'judge,' he said in a very simple, almost boyish way, 'I'll stay with you. I never had nobody talk to me like you. I'll do anything you say for me to do.'"

So they talked. The judge told the boy he might have to go to Buena Vista (the penitentiary), and they discussed that. And they discussed crime and the police, till it was time for Henry to go back to the jail. And then—the judge sent him back alone, and he went back alone, and he took voluntarily his place behind the bars!

It "worked," this "method" did, so the judge adopted it as a method. It would strengthen the boys. He told the police that he proposed thereafter to trust all prisoners to go alone to Golden. The police laughed. It is said that they passed the word to put up a job on the judge. At any rate, the next boy for Golden was Billy B., a chronic little runaway, and with the two policemen who brought him in came two reporters. The officers excused their double patrol by pointing to a brand-new shine-box which Billy carried as evidence that he meant to "skip." That kid had given them a two-weeks' chase, they said, and they weren't taking any chances on him. The judge might, they implied, but there were the two reporters to bear witness that, if Billy skipped, it was no fault of the police. As a matter of fact, one of the reporters told the judge that the papers had been "tipped off to send them out and get a good story on the judge."

When the case was called, everybody was laughing in his sleeve, everybody but the judge and Billy B. The judge was anxious, and the boy was sobbing in a corner with his shine-box hugged to his breast. Billy was only twelve years old. He had no father, and his mother was a washerwoman. He had learned early to tramp. The judge had worked with him, but when the "movin'-about fever" got hold of Billy, Billy had to move. And he had the fever now. He admitted it to the judge, and when the judge said he must go to Golden, the little fellow burst into tears. He had visions of stone walls and iron bars, with a policeman standing over him with a club all the rest of his days. That is what prison means to boys, and Golden was prison to Billy. So he dropped on his knees and begged the judge not to send him away, promising pitifully "never to do it again." Billy was simply afraid.

"Billy," said the judge, "you are crying because you are scared. What are you scared of? Me? Why should you be afraid of me? Haven't I given you a square deal? Haven't I given you every chance I could, helped you every way to be a good boy at home?"

"Yes," Billy sobbed, "but—"

"You can't be a good boy at home. You don't get a fair chance at home. You want to move on all the time, and by and by you'll just be a 'vag.' Now, you don't want to grow up to be a bum; do you? No, you want a chance to learn a trade and be a man."

The judge explained at length that Golden wasn't a reformatory or a prison. It was only a school, a good industrial school, where a poor kid that hadn't a chance at home could learn a trade. "Why," said the judge, "I've been there. I like to go there. And I tell you everybody up there just loves a kid that tries to do his best, and they help him. Nobody hates a kid at Golden. No, siree."

By and by, the tears ceased to flow. The judge described the school, its shops, its military organization, its baseball nines, and then, as the judge relates, "when fear vanished, and interest began, I appealed to the boy's nobility, to his honour, pride, his loyalty to me." Judge Lindsey seized for this purpose the very preparations the police had made for their "joke on the judge." He introduced Billy to the reporters.

"What do you think the cops have told these reporters, Billy?" he said. "They have told them that that fool judge was going to trust little Billy B. to go to the industrial school all by himself, and that they were going to have the laugh on the judge because they knew Billy better than the judge did. They say they know you'll never go, and they are saying what a fine joke it will be to have the reporters write a story tomorrow telling how the judge trusted Billy, and Billy threw the judge down, ditched his papers, and ran away. And, gee whiz, it would be tough if I did get thrown down. But I'm not scared. I believe in you, and I'm going to trust you. I am going to give you these, your commitment papers, and your railroad ticket, and we'll see whether you stay with me or stay with the police. I want these reporters to tell just what happens, so it'll be up to you, Billy, to go to Golden or skip."

As the judge proceeded, Billy's head began to go up in

the air. By and by he pushed the cold tears out of his eyes, and when the judge ceased to speak, those eyes were blazing.

"Judge," he said, "you know John Handing, don't you?"

The judge hesitated.

"You know, judge; the kid th' fellers call Fatty Felix."

"Yes, yes," said the judge.

"Well," said Billy, "he's my chum, Fatty is. Now, here's my shine-box. You give that to Fatty, and you gimme them papers. I'll show 'em. You trust me, and I'll stay wit ye, judge, and we'll fool 'em, all right."

And off went Billy B., twelve years old, out of the courtroom, down through the streets the streets he loved to the car; then over three railroads to the little town of Golden where, asking his way, he climbed the long, lonely hill road to the industrial school just to show a doubting world that "it" works.

Was the world convinced? No. The grown-ups marvelled, and even the boys sneered. The judge "fixed" the boys. He heard that they called Billy B. a "chump" up at Golden, so he went up there, and he told the story in a speech which made Billy B.'s face shine like his old shine-box. That speech, repeated again and again, at Golden and in Denver and all over the state, has made it an honour to go alone to Golden: a test of pluck, loyalty, and self-control. And, on the other hand, to "ditch your papers and run" is a disgrace in Boyville now. A boy called on the judge one day with an offer from the gang to "lick" any kid that ditched his papers or in any other way went back on the judge, and the judge had some difficulty in explaining why that wasn't "square."

Wonderful ? Yes, it's wonderful, if you don't see what "it" is, and Denver didn't at least, official Denver didn't. The judge saw that he had to "win out" with what the world calls "young criminals born," so he watched for a chance; and the chance came. "One morning," he says, "the newspapers reported the capture of Lee Martin and Jack Heimel, two notorious boy burglars known as 'The Eel' and 'Tatters.' They were the leaders of the River-Front Gang of sneak thieves, pickpockets, burglars, etc., and they had done time in the reform school and jails in Colorado and elsewhere. The newspapers, having told all about them and their crimes, went on to say that these criminals had amply qualified for a long term, and they should therefore be tried in the criminal court, not before the new-fangled, grandmotherly juvenile department. Here was my chance and a challenge.

"I visited the jail. The boys were in separate cells, handcuffed to their benches. They had just come out of the sweat-box where the police had been bullying and threatening them for hours in an effort to make them tell on the other members of the gang, and they were bruised and battered. Tatters looked more like a pirate than the fifteen-year-old grammar school boy he was. A picture of uncleanliness, he scowled at me out of sullen black eyes, and the sinister effect was increased by the livid bruises on his swarthy face. I talked with him, but could get nothing out of him. His lips were padlocked, for he was plainly suspicious of me.

"Lee Martin presented a very different appearance. He was slight, fair, and scrupulously neat, despite the unutterable prison filth. About him was an air of childish innocence hard to reconcile with his established reputation as the most expert and reckless boy criminal within a thousand miles. There was something peculiarly winning about him. I have never met so interesting a boy, or one so full of vital, human experiences learned in the hard school of life. He had gentle, blue eyes, just now glaring with hate. It was an expression I was to see in them often during the next few months, for hatred and revenge were then the dominant emotions of his life.

"As I stepped across the cell, he drew himself up with an odd touch of dignified pride peculiar to him. He was only a little boy, hunted and run to earth like a wolf, cuffed and kicked and flung into a dark cell prior to being railroaded through the court to the reformatory, but he was staunch and 'game' still to his comrades. 'I ain't no snitch,' he flung out before I had said a dozen words.

" 'Good for you' I told him. 'There's always good in a fellow that won't snitch on his chums.'

"He looked at me, greatly surprised but still suspicious. He asked me who I was. I told him. 'Are they going to try me in your court?' he asked. I answered that he would probably be tried in the criminal court. 'They'll send me up, all right,' he said with conviction. 'Would you?' he demanded. 'I'd give you a square deal,' I told him. He sneered in my face."

Not a very promising beginning, was it? The judge did not give up. He called again on the boys, and again and again. He told them the truth. He told them he was laboring to have them tried in his court, and why. He talked about his court, and what it meant; how it was opposed, and why. He had no secrets; he kept nothing back. He discussed crime, his view of it, the police view of it, the world's. He didn't know who was right. "Gradually their suspicion of me disappeared," the judge says. "They came to regard me and my court as engaged in a fight for them against the hated police." The judge let them think that. It was true. He explained how it was true, how "the police were not to blame," not the policemen. They were reared in a school that taught them that it was their duty to fight crime with crime, craft with craft, violence with force, and maybe that was the only way. Certainly, "fellers" like Tatters and the Eel made it hard for the police. Hadn't the boys added to the work of the "cops," and to their worries?

They had indeed. The judge laid down the kid law, which was the criminal law, about "snitching"; how snitching on the other fellow was wrong, but snitching on yourself was all right, if you believed what you told was to be used to help you. This they understood, and as their confidence grew, they began to snitch on themselves.

They told the judge their stories, and they were amazing stories of crime and of hate. "The Eel especially hated anything in the nature of legal machinery with a bitterness that amazed me," the judge says, "till I had heard his story." And then the judge tells the Eel's story. His father was foreman in a machine-shop, honest enough, but brutal to the boy, who loved his mother, who loved, but was too weak to help, her son. He "bummed" the streets day and night, dodging his father, who cuffed and cursed him whenever their paths crossed. Lee ran away, and to keep himself became a sneak thief. Before he was ten, he had "bummed" his way from Chicago to Denver and become a "pretty slick thief." Arrested now and then, and railroaded by the law, he was patted on the back in the jails by hardened criminals who taught him to pick pockets. Caught at this, he learned burglary from burglars in the jail and, at the age of twelve, nearly killed himself trying to blow a safe. The "Bull-pen" had shown him how, but he put the powder in the wrong place. He was full of courage. An experienced "hobo," he travelled twenty-five thousand miles in one year on brake-beams till, tiring of that, he learned to sneak into Pullmans and hide and sleep in a vacant upper berth. Once he was awakened by an exclamation from the porter: "Good Lawd, they's a kid in heah!" The Eel tells the rest: "I flew th' coop when the coon guy went to tell th' conductor. That ditched me in a town they call Reno, Nevada. 'Course, I was broke. I touched a guy for a half and bought me a cane and some chewing-gum. I walked into a bank and up to th' guy in th' monkey cage. I says I wanted work, and when he went to see de head guy, I rammed th' gum in de end of my cane, shoved it through the cage, and swiped a twenty that stuck to th' gum. Then I hiked out on th' express that night."

Where did the boy learn that trick? In jail. That's where the state taught him his trade, and, when he had learned a new crime, he could break out and try it. Twice he had broken jail, cleverly, boldly. Once when an officer, Roberts, tried to recapture him, Lee smashed a lantern in the man's face and then led him a chase through a backyard where clotheslines hung in the dark. Caught under the chin by a line, the officer turned a "flip-flop" and the boy got away; not unscathed, however; the officer fired several shots at him, and one hit the boy in the hand.

To kill that policeman was one of the vows the boy had made to himself. "He tried to kill me. I was only a kid, and he tried to kill me. I'm going to kill him one of these nights."

The judge listened to these stories, noted what they meant, and he sympathized with the boys. But that isn't all he did. He sympathized with the law and with the policeman, too. He showed the boys just where he thought things were wrong in the law and in the courts, and the boys came to understand. It wasn't easy to correct the teachings of the jails and the police and the home and the streets, but this man did it with those boys.

He showed them, for example, how the officer, Roberts, was acting in good faith, doing his duty, and how he must have been exasperated with the Eel. And the Eel saw it. And when the judge saw that he saw it, he brought the boy and the officer together, and they are good friends now.

So with the law; the judge explained what the machinery of justice was for. It had been perverted from its true function, justice, to vengeance, but it could help a fellow, and he proved it, the judge did. He got the cases. And he got them with the consent of the police. One captain who was loudest in his protestations, said: "You can't baby Lee Martin, judge. He's been in jail thirteen times, and it hasn't done him any good."

"No," said the judge, "and if I fail, I'll still have twelve times the best of you. You've failed with him your way. It's my turn now. It has cost the city in officers' fees alone $1,036 to make a criminal of him. Let's see what it'll cost to turn him into an honest boy."

The captain ran over a list of his crimes. The judge brought out a longer, more correct, typewritten list.

"How in the world did you get that?" the officer asked, astonished.

"They've confessed to me everything."

"How did you do it ? We couldn't sweat it out of them."

"I made them see that I was their friend," the judge said, "and that I wanted to use the information for and not against them."

It was a strange, new point of view to the police, but they saw that there was something in it, so they tried the boys before the kids' judge.

The evidence was plain. Burglary was the specific charge, and the police proved it; the judge was convinced formally of what he knew (for the boys had told him all about it). What did the judge do to the boys?

He put them on probation. Yes, to the horror of the police and the town, he did by these bad boys just as he did by good boys; he gave them a "show." What was the result?

A day or two later the boys called on the judge. With them were two others, "Red" Mike and Tommy Green. The judge understood; these were members of the River-Front Gang, for whom the police were on the lookout. But nothing was said about that. "We had a general talk about crime," the judge says, "and the principles of the Juvenile Court." The judge was expectant, so were Lee and Tatters, but it was left to the newcomers to do their own snitching, and they did it. After a while, "Red" turned to Tommy. "Don't you think it's about time we were snitchin' up?" he asked. Tommy allowed that it was, and then followed what the judge calls "a snitching bee." "And," the judge adds, "I had two new probationers for my court." A week or so more; and these four called with a fifth "kid," and he, a "soft, mushy one," as the judge describes him, he also "snitched up." Another period, and the five brought in two more. That finished the "criminal" list of the River-Front Gang. "Not one of these boys had snitched on another," the judge says. "Each one had told only on himself."

All those "young criminals" were put on probation, "and," says the judge, "six out of the seven have stuck. The seventh made the pluckiest fight I ever saw before he slipped back, and I still have hopes of his ultimate success."

What does the judge mean by a plucky fight ? "A plucky fight" means what the judge means by probation—the game of correction, the game of overcoming evil with good. These young criminals had not only to be good; they couldn't be good. That's too negative for husky kids, and the River-Front Gang were a husky lot. The judge says boys are bad because, while they have lots of opportunity to do wrong, they have none to do good. So, as in the case of mischievous boys, he gave these criminals opportunities to do good. There were other "fellers" starting on careers of crime. If they were allowed to go on, they would be caught, jailed, and made criminals by the police, who, though they didn't mean to be, were really criminal-manufacturers. The game was to beat the police and beat public opinion by showing the opposition that the judge was right about kids, that "there ain't no bad kids." So the game was for the River-Front Gang to bring in kids that were going wrong, get them into the court gang, and thus prove by the good they all could do together that "it" worked. And "it" did work.

The loyalty of the River-Front Gang to the judge as leader of their new gang was superb. It was mistaken sometimes. Once when Jack Beimel's mother was away, he slept in a cheap boarding-house. A drunken man cried out that he had been robbed, and he accused Jack and a friend of Jack's. The lodging-house keeper knew Jack and, of course, believed the charge, so, sending for the police, he placed himself in the door to bar the way out. Jack made a dash, hit the man behind the ear and, dropping him, leaped out and away with his chum. The police searched for them all night, but couldn't find them. The judge found them. When he went down to court the next morning the boys were "layin' for him." Jack explained:

"We didn't take th' money, judge, but I had to hit de guy, because, you see, if de cops had 'a jugged me, me name would 'a' been in the papers, and then, wouldn't they say that this was de feller what de judge ought to 'a sent up and didn't? And, say, wouldn't dat 'a got you into trouble, and maybe lost you yer job?"

It developed afterward that the drunken man hadn't lost the money at all, so Jack Heimel was cleared, and that was his last "scrape." He got a job as a mechanic in the railroad shops and, loyal always, his last report to the judge was that he had sent East for a book on mechanical engineering. He was rising, and he feels to this day that his success means much, not only to him, but to the judge and the court gang, and the methods thereof.

The Eel had a hard time. "This boy, whom the police called a depraved criminal, has done more to discourage crime," the judge says, "than any ten policemen in the city." He brought in boy after boy to "snitch up," and he helped keep his own gang straight. "Red" Mike slipped back once. Arrested for robbery, he escaped, and the police were after him. The Eel was troubled. He called on the judge, He knew where "Red" was hiding, and he knew the judge knew he knew, but the judge asked no questions. He and Lee simply talked the matter over till they agreed that it would be better for "Red" to come in and surrender than to be driven deeper into crime. And a day or two later "Red" appeared at the judge's house, "ready," as he said, "to take his papers and go to the reformatory."

Lee became an unofficial officer of the court, and the judge used him freely. Once a boy stole a pocketbook from a woman in the store where he worked. The judge sent for Lee. "Something ought to be done," the judge said, "to get that boy back in the right path." Lee went after him. He found him in a cheap theatre, "treating a gang," brought him voluntarily in, and today the boy is a trusted employee in that same store. Another time, Teddy Mack, a fourteen-year-old "criminal," who was arrested for stealing a watch, sawed his way out of jail and got out of Denver. All summer the police searched, and the judge and Lee Martin often talked over the case. One day Lee said:

"I'd like to get that kid for you, judge. I'll bet he's down to the fair at El Paso. You send me down there, and—I won't be a 'snitch cop,' but I believe I kin get him to come in."

The judge gave Lee five dollars, and the boy went across the line to the bull-fight. There was Teddy. The two boys took in the fair together, but Lee talked "crime, and the principles of the Juvenile Court" to Teddy, and back these two came together to the "jedge." Teddy "snitched up." The judge gave him twenty dollars to redeem the watch he had pawned for three dollars, and when Teddy returned with the watch and the exact change, he was sent to deliver the watch to the owner and to admit that he was the thief. That settled the case, and that settled Teddy. "We had no more trouble with Teddy Mack," the judge says, "though he had been one of the worst boy thieves in the city."

The boy with whom Lee Martin had the most trouble was Lee Martin. He could not settle down. The habit of "bumming," developed in him from early childhood, was too strong, and every once in a while that "movin'-about fever" would get him. "It was like a thirst for drink," the judge says, "and I told him that when he felt it he must come to me. Once or twice when I saw that the call of the road was too strong to be resisted, I let him take a ride as far as Colorado Springs and back." But that didn't always satisfy him, and he would throw up his job and "skip." It hurt him to do this; it was regarded as disloyalty to the judge, and that was awful.

"One Sunday evening," the judge relates, "word reached me that Lee was going to 'fly out.' This worried me so much that

I started for his home. I found his mother in tears. The Eel was gone.

" 'He just couldn't stand it any longer, jedge,' she apologized. 'He lay on the floor there and sobbed just like he was in a high fever. "What'll the judge think? What'll the judge think?" he kept saying, an',' the woman added, 'he told me to tell you he'd write.'

"I went home much troubled, but the promised letters reached me, one from Albuquerque, then another from El Paso, a rapid succession of them. They were like wails from a lost soul. He implored me not to think he had 'thrown me down.' That was the burden of them all. He was coming back, he said; he just had to get on the move for a while, but he hadn't thrown me down. I wrote him not to steal, and he didn't. When he came back a month later, he showed me a letter from a man he had worked for to prove it."

There is more of the story, more triumphs, and more disappointments, and there are more stories just like it, of other gangs. For all the time the judge was devoting himself to the "River-Fronts," he was giving himself with the same devotion to his other "cases." And there were failures as well as successes, and the police and the cynics clung to the failures. As the judge says, however, the failures were really weak boys. "The husky kids, the kind the cops call 'dangerous,' they stuck with me; they showed the police that there 'ain't no really bad kids.' Bad? I believe," the judge said, smiling, and he quoted Riley:

> "I believe all childern's good
> Ef they're only understood
> Even bad ones, 'pears to me,
> 'S jes as good as they kin be!"

He smiles as he quotes, then the smile disappears, and he adds, "And that's so of men, too." "Yes, but," you say, "there are criminals born?" "Yes," he replies, "there are criminals born, and there are criminals bred, minors and majors, too. But who bears them, and what breeds them? What makes bad boys bad? What makes bad girls bad? And what makes men and women bad?"

That's his answer, another question: one question; the fortunate, fatal question which got Ben Lindsey into his fights with the dishonest opposition of Denver, the fights which, because he won them, he and the children, and because they led him straight to the cause of crime, juvenile, and grown-up, too have made the "kids' Jedge" of Denver one of the leaders of the great war that is going on in Colorado. The outside world couldn't understand why the people of his state wanted the judge of the juvenile court to run for governor; nor why he was willing to take the nomination. The reason, as we shall see, was that Ben Lindsey is no mere philanthropist, but (in the true sense of the word) a politician; no mere saver of little victims of wrong, but a man leading men to destroy the opportunities for evil-doing, and to give all the children of men a "show" to "do good."

III. BATTLES WITH "BAD" MEN

Early in the history of Denver's Juvenile Court, a boy was arraigned for stealing lumber and sand from a contractor. The contractor was indignant; he "wanted to know whether Judge Lindsey was going to coddle that kid or protect the property of the citizens of Denver from thieves." The judge said he would take the case under advisement. He did. He took the case "for a walk and a talk."

Once out of that stiff old, stuffy old court room, the tears dried up, and the two got acquainted. "What did you want the lumber for, kid?" the judge asked.

"We were building a shack in my back yard, and we needed more boards than we had."

The judge used to build shacks, and he and the kid discussed the different kinds you could build. The judge bragged about some he'd put up. But he never used sand in a shack.

"What did you swipe the sand for?" he asked.

"Well," said the kid, "girls can't build shacks. They can keep house in 'em after they're built, but my sister and the other fellers' sisters, they wanted something to do till the shack was done. So while we was gettin' the boards, we seen the sand, and we swiped a little pile for the girls to play in."

And coming into the back yard, the kid showed the judge the shack and the sand-pile—abandoned now. All work was suspended, pending a decision in their case. The kid wanted to know what the court was going to do to him. The judge said he'd take the case under advisement, and he did. He took a walk down to the contractor, and he told said complainant all about the shack and the sand, and the contractor furnished all the lumber and sand necessary to finish the job in that back yard. As for the children, they "cut out" all "swiping."

The judge kept the case under advisement, however. He kept on walking around in back yards, and talking with young "thieves" and "builders." He saw many signs of energy and enterprise, and nothing to do; nothing good. Everywhere was private; nowhere to play. Everything was property to steal. The grown-ups had "hogged" everything, and children had nowhere to play and nothing to play with.

The judge set about organizing a juvenile association of grown-ups to furnish materials for young builders to build with; playgrounds to build on; water to swim in; jobs in the beet fields for vacation kids that had to work, and mountain trips for the rest. In brief, the judge's Juvenile Association for the Protection and Betterment of Children, which he is trying to make a national organization, originated out of his discovery that society had forgotten to provide children with opportunities for good.

But society provided opportunities for evil. Denver offered plenty of these, and the children knew them all. "I was amazed to hear what children knew," the judge says. "I talked to them, and I walked with and among them; I visited back alleys at night, hung around cheap theatres, visited the tenderloin and the slums. Standing in the shadow just outside of saloons, I saw children come with pitchers in their hands, sent there for beer by their parents, and while they waited, I heard men tell obscene stories. The children listened, boys and little girls. I talked with the boys, and I found that they understood everything that was vile. You see, I was trying to get at the causes of criminality in children, in children whom I found responsive to the noblest sentiments of honor and fair dealing. Well, I thought I saw what the causes were: the problem is one of environment; manifold opportunity for evil and none for good; and then, back of this, certain social and economic conditions. What could I do to relieve these conditions? I asked myself that again and again. My court could correct the evil done, some of it, but how could I prevent the evil from being done?"

Perfectly simple and logical, all this. The judge had no answer ready, but he attacked the worst condition, one that stirred him to his depths. He found that the Denver saloons had wine-rooms, and that not only boys, but girls, were allowed in them and ruined. The law forbade these places to women, but the law wasn't enforced. Why? Everybody knows, in a general way, why. Denver is a typical American city government, and Lindsey, a former member of the Democratic state Executive Committee, knew, in a general way, the reason for a "liberal" excise policy. It helped business. When cowboys and miners and other visitors came to town, they wanted to have a good time, and it was good for all business to help them spend their money. But the judge saw that however good for business it might be to neglect to enforce the wine-room law, it was bad for the children; and he put that view of it before the Police Board. He knew well the president, Frank Adams, and the members of the board. Frank is a Democrat, like Ben, so Ben urged Frank to enforce the law in the interest of the children. The judge also addressed the chief of police. The chief couldn't do anything but refer the letters to the board, which wouldn't or, at any rate, didn't, do anything. The judge then proceeded in his own way to compel the board to enforce this law.

Colorado is a great place for injunctions. The "interests" there use the courts very much as in other states they use legislatures and governors. The brewers own the saloons, and brewing is an interest. It "contributes" to both parties. The brewers and the dive interests got out a writ enjoining the Police Board from enforcing the law. Judge Lindsey says the Police Board got out the writ against itself, and there was some ground for this suspicion. In the first place, the attorney for the brewers was the Democratic state chairman. In the second place, Frank Adams, who is a member of the Adams family, famous in Colorado politics, was the "iceman" in Denver. There were other icemen, but the saloons generally bought of him. So he may have been doing his customers a favor, on the side. But certainly the brewers were interested, for they warned Lindsey that if he went on making trouble for them, they would defeat him for reelection. No matter about that, however. Judge Peter L. Palmer, of whom it has been said that he would "enjoin the birds of the air from flying and the fishes of the sea from swimming," held that since, under the constitution of Colorado, women had the same rights as men, the law forbidding them the wine-rooms was unconstitutional. Wherefore he enjoined the Police Board, and the Police Board obeyed his order. Judge Lindsey didn't. He fined a dive-keeper in the face of it, and the Supreme Court of the United States upheld his ruling.

It takes time to go through the courts, however, and while the case was pending on appeal, girls were being haled into the Juvenile Court as "incorrigible"; and they did look "bad." But the evidence showed that they had been made bad in wine-rooms.

"And I found that these wine-rooms were 'protected' by the police," the judge says. "I tried time and again, with Frank Adams and with the other commissioners and with the chief of police to get the wine-room keepers arrested, and in vain. Children they would bring in, the boys and girls, but no adults. I investigated further. I called on the Humane Society, and the secretary, Mr. E. K. Whitehead, told me of the most horrible details. He also had complained in vain to the police. Then I went out and I saw some of these things. I saw sixteen boys gambling in one place, and when I reported it to the police man on the corner, he insulted me. I wrote about this and about the wine-room to the chief and to the commissioner. No answer.

"One Sunday I went to visit one of my probationers, and I found him cursing his mother vilely, with an amazing command of oaths. Looking about, I saw that it was partly a house of assignation, partly a home for the very poor, and all the children were masters of men's language. Looking further, I saw, ten feet from the door of this house, the rear entrance to a wine-room wide open, though it was a Sunday morning. I went to the mistress of the house of assignation, and she, hardened though she was, told me that this wine-room had supplied more than one bad place with inmates. Only a week before, she said, she saw two girls halt at that wine-room door. One was afraid to go in. The other was urging her, and while they were talking three men came out, seized the reluctant girl, and dragged her in. The next day the woman heard groans and sobs across the way, and she went to see what was the matter. She found the girls in the cellar, naked and drunk!

"My God!" the judge exclaimed, "where was the policeman all this time?"

"Oh!" she said, "he knew all about it. He was in there, too, drinking with them!"

"It would be hard for me to repeat," the judge says, "all the things I saw and heard that harrowed my very soul. But they were the causes, this crime and vice and this police partnership, of many of the woes and troubles that come into my court." What could he do? The judge knew that besides the "ice" and the brewers' contributions, there were other powers back of all these conditions. The railroads ruled the state, the railroads and the mine-owners and the American Smelting Company. Under them, in Denver, and for them, were all the public utility companies which, having grants of privileges, rewarded the people of the city and state by corrupting their government. "It's necessary," they say. Now the corrupt business interests that ruled Denver and Colorado ruled partly by ballot-box stuffing, and it was the dive-keepers, thieves, loafers, all the hangers-on of vice and crime who did the stuffing. Lindsey, who long had known this, realized now that he had nowhere to turn to appeal for some little consideration of the children of his town, except to the people of his town.

He invited the Police Board to visit the Children's Court on Saturday morning, May 24, 1902. He also invited reporters. Frank Adams didn't come, but the other commissioners did, and the bailiff gave them seats in the jury-box. There the children could see them, and they could see the children, and there were some two hundred children on hand that morning: two hundred "bad" boys who knew all about everything, including that Police

Board. When they were all ready, Judge Lindsey entered and took his place on the bench. He looked over his gang of kids, and then he spoke to those officials, typical American officials.

"I have asked you gentlemen to come here and look at these boys," he said. "There are also girls in this city who report on Fridays," he added. The commissioners looked at the boys, and the judge went on to say that while these children were brought there as delinquents, it was not alone the children who were delinquent. "Parents, in many cases, and adults who violate the law, and particularly police officials who refuse to enforce the law, they are more responsible than the children," he said.

He illustrated: "It became the duty of this court recently to send a young girl to the Industrial School. She was not depraved or vicious; she was capable of being a good, pure woman with any kind of favorable environment. But she was subject to temptations. What were these temptations? The wine-rooms; not one, but many. She was induced to enter such places. You knowingly permitted them to run in violation of the law. Yet the child is punished and disgraced. You and the dive-keeper, the real culprits, you go scot-free."

The judge—from the bench, mind you—said this to those commissioners. Then he spoke of a young man who had lost his life in the same place where this girl was ruined. He told the rooming-house woman's story, and he described also her terror lest the police should learn that she had informed on the dive-keepers! Then he described what he knew of gambling by boys.

"I have seen a pitiful, gray-haired old lady, bent with years, her face dimmed with tears, pleading in this court to recover all she had on earth, lost by a son in a gambling hell tolerated by you. And here in broad daylight those who conduct the place come, and they tell of the open game of this young man and the loss of that money, and this they do with the prosecuting officer passing in and out. . . . It is nonsense to talk about these things not being known to your Board. It only subjects you to contempt and ridicule."

Frank Adams had been appealing to the judge in the name of "business" and "the party" not to "rip up" the liquor question. The judge answered that appeal now with another:

"Flesh and blood, body and soul, the future of little children is so sacred," he said, "that it is a monstrous sacrilege to permit any other consideration to interfere. . . . I know it is unusual to speak thus publicly, but all things usual have been done, and something unusual is justifiable. I therefore beg of you in this public manner, in the presence of these children, for their benefit, that you earnestly and diligently war upon these places. . . . I assure you that you will have then the good will and respect which are denied you now. That is worth more than all the vaunted boastings of all the devil's agents in this town. It is to these that you are catering now, and until you break the spell they have over you, you will be storing up misery, hell, and damnation for the present and future generations."

It was a terrible arraignment, there before those children, whose eyes bored into those officials. There was silence for a moment; then one commissioner, Charles F. Wilson, rose to answer. He said the board had closed the place where the judge had seen the boys gambling. The two hundred boys looked at the judge; he hesitated. Didn't he know about that? Some of the boys did, and one of them sprang to his rescue. Leo Batson, twelve years old, rose, and pointing his finger at Commissioner Wilson, he said:

"Yes, you closed it up, but you opened it up again, like you generally do. It was open inside of a week. And it's open now, 'cause I seen boys in there myself."

There was silence when Leo sat down. The boys looked at the commissioner. He was still a moment, then he went on without answering the boy. He referred to Peter L. Palmer's injunction. It was the judge's turn.

"The issuance of that injunction was without sense or precedent," said Judge Lindsey. "And it didn't tie your hands. You could have brought your cases to my court. In this tribunal you will find the whole power of the court on the side of the law."

The newspapers all turned "yellow" with this story, and that settled the matter for the time being. The tip was passed that the police couldn't "stand for wine-rooms where young girls went for a while."

The judge went on walking and talking with the children, and he listened, too, and the things they suffered kept his feelings aroused, while their wisdom "put him wise." It was appalling, what these children knew.

"Huh, business men! They steal, too!" said a cynical little thief one day when the judge held out to him the prospect of growing up to be a "respected business man," if only he would stop stealing. "Don't the street railway swipe franchises? And the gas company and them, don't they steal 'em? Guess I can read. And my boss, that's kicking to have me sent to jail, don't he sell cheap jewelry for eighteen carat fine?"

In this and similar cases the judge had to reach down below the teachings of the world of business to the nobility born in the "born thief" to save him. "It's mean to cheat and steal," he said, and it was the success of this appeal that convinced Ben Lindsey that human nature was good enough to go to war for.

Of course, he didn't realize at first what he was warring against. Brought up in a perfectly conventional way, his notions of life and economics were perfectly commonplace; but when men came to him and in the name of "business," "the party," and "property" besought him not to fight so hard for the children, he began to see that the enemy of men, as of children, was not men, but things. Once he and a police captain had a dispute in chambers over the custody of some boys arrested for stealing bicycles. The police wanted to hold the boys. Why? The judge couldn't make out till the officers said something about the owners of the wheels wanting to "get back their property."

"Oh," said the judge, "I see the difference between you and me: you want to recover the property, while I want to recover the boys."

The judge recovered both.

A cotton mill was set up in Colorado. That was a new industry, and the men who established it were applauded for their "enterprise, which could not but benefit the whole state." To compete with the South, however, this mill had to employ child labor. The kids' judge heard that they were importing large families and setting the little children to work. Colorado had a child-labour law, and the judge went to the mill to see if the law was being violated. It was, and the conditions were pitiful.

"These imported people were practically slaves," he says. "They had come out under contracts, and the children, unschooled, toiled at the machines first to liberate their parents, then to support them."

The judge warned the milling company, but that did no good, so he had criminal proceedings instituted, and not only against the superintendent, but against the higher officers also.

This is not the custom in the United States, and the president of the mill, who was also one of the big men in the Colorado Fuel & Iron Company, called on the judge to explain that he was a respectable citizen. The judge suggested that it wasn't proper to try to influence a judge in a pending case, but the president "didn't want to do anything improper"; all he wanted was to remind the judge that a conviction in the case would make him (the president) a criminal. "And I am no criminal," he said. The judge replied that he was if he broke the law. But the president didn't break the law. If the law was broken, it was by his superintendent, and it was all right to fine his superintendent. But the president was a gentleman and a "big man."

"I'd rather fine you than your superintendent," said the judge. "He is only your agent, and, as you intimate, you wouldn't mind if he were punished. So I'll punish you as I warned you; I told you that if he persisted in violating the law for you, I'd hold you responsible."

"But, judge," he said, "if you are going to keep up this fight, we will close the mill!" And he proceeded to tell what a great industry it was; how many people it gave employment; how much good it was doing to the city (he meant the business) of Denver; and how much money had been invested in it by himself and other capitalists.

"His point of view," the judge says, "was perfectly plain. Money was sacred, men were of no account. If business went well, children could go to—well, let us say, to work. And he blamed me, not the law, not the state; he had no fear of these.

I, personally, with my queer regard for men and women and children—I was a menace to business."

"I warn you right now," he said to the judge, "that if this thing keeps up, we will shut down the mill, and you will have to share the consequences." And Judge Lindsey replied: "We are here to protect the children and to enforce the law, and all I regret is that the penalty isn't imprisonment instead of a fine, so that I could be sure of preventing you from employing young children."

And the Judge persisted, and the mill was closed down. Other causes contributed, but Lindsey never shirked his "share of the responsibility."

What is more, Judge Lindsey had the child-labor law made stricter. He can put "money" in prison now if it hurts children. He had to fight business and politics and the police to do it, but he did it; he and the kids and the men and women of Denver.

We have seen that the judge set out to correct the evils of child life under the laws as they stood. He had been making notes, however, of legislation he wanted, all the while he was walking and talking and trying cases. For example, the Juvenile Court existed by the courtesy of the district attorney, who was a machine man; Lindsey gave himself the legal right to demand all children's cases. He had exercised discretion; he gave himself explicit authority to exercise discretion. He had found adults at fault for the criminality of children; he drew a paragraph making parents, employers, businessmen, and all other grown-ups amenable to the criminal law for neglect, abuse, or temptation of children. This is his now famous "contributory delinquency law against adults." Needing probation officers, he authorized the appointment of them, and since the police and the sheriff and the district attorney were all tied up with the liquor and other business interests, he gave his probation officers certain police powers. The child-labor law was only one item in the legislation Judge Lindsey went after.

The judge's bills were most important legislation, and to put them through he had to proceed most carefully. He began in the convention, by taking a hand in the nomination of legislators.

His enemies fought him there, and they beat his man, but he came up on good terms with the others. They introduced his bills and started them through the mill, very quietly. Hardly any notice was taken of them. Apparently the lobbyists didn't do their work well, for the interests were amazed after it was all over to see in the new laws "What Lindsey had been up to." An officer in one of the telegraph companies said the "interests" would never have let either the child labor or the adult delinquency bill pass if they had known of them. The judge had learned that the messenger service was a degrading influence for boys; they were sent to all sorts of vile places, saw all sorts of vile things, and caught respectable citizens in predicaments the knowledge of which made the boys cynical and vicious. So he advised, and he still advises, both boys and parents against the messenger service. But he wished also to have a club to hold over the companies; wherefore he had drawn into one of his bills a clause including officers of telegraph companies under the "adult delinquency law." The companies, suspecting the judge, twice sent a lawyer to the capital to see "Lindsey's bill," and he saw one bill, an inoffensive one, never the other. He didn't know there was another. It was the other that "hurt our business," he said. Thus beaten, the companies never dared to move for a repeal; they surrendered, and, calling on the judge, came to an understanding with him about what they might and might not do with boys.

There was a fight on these bills, however. It is known among the good citizens and bad kids of Denver as "the fight against the jail." After moving along regularly through the Senate, the judge noticed that his bills suddenly stuck in the House. "What was the matter?" the judge inquired. The clerk couldn't explain. One evening a reporter called at the judge's house.

"Judge," he said, "Frank Adams is fighting your bills. His brother Billy, you know, is a power in the legislature. They don't dare come out in the open and fight you, but they are telling it around that you are crazy on the children subject, and that the boys fill you up with lies!"

"What had I better do?" the Judge asked.

"Stir 'em up," said the reporter. "Give me an interview and tell all about the jail."

"That's grandstand playing," the judge said, smiling.

"It's appealing to public opinion," said the reporter, "and that's against the rule of graft, but what do you care? You aren't a grafter."

The judge made out a statement, but it was too mild. The reporter rejected it, and with the facts the judge told him and what he and all police reporters knew, Harry Wilber (for that was the reporter's name) did what newspaper men love to do when they get the chance: he wrote the truth, and he wrote it to kill. United States Senator Patterson's paper, the *Rocky Mountain News,* printed the interview in red, and it was sensational. The judge says it gave him a sensation himself. But it was true, so he "stood for it." Frank Adams answered it with a denial. The boys were liars, he said, and as for Judge Lindsey, he was crazy.

"I knew then," says the judge, "that I was up against it. I must make good. So I wrote to the Police Board offering to hold an inquiry. They were willing, they answered, but not then. I wanted it then, and I ordered it for two o'clock the next day in my courtroom. And lest the Board, recalling the last time they met the boys, might not come, I invited also the governor, the mayor, the district attorney, other officials, fifteen ministers and rabbis, and others. I didn't expect many to come, but they all accepted, even Governor Peabody, all but Frank Adams and the police commissioners. The board sent a dummy to represent it."

It was Saturday morning when the judge got his acceptances, and he had to hurry. Calling in a friendly deputy sheriff, he asked him to get ten witnesses named on a list he had made of boys who had been in the jails. "I must have them by two o'clock," the judge said. The officer declared it impossible. He should have had two days' notice. The judge was in despair, but he ran over his list till he came to the name "Mickey."

Mickey was a street boy. He had been in jail often, and the last time was only a month or so before. After he got out, he and the boys in with him had called on the judge to complain. They stated their case. They were running through the street when one of them knocked over a sign to which some shoes were attached. The man in the store rushed out and sent the policeman after the boys. They had stolen his shoes, he said, and the policeman arrested them. The boys hadn't taken a shoe, and absolutely the only evidence against them was the fact that one of the boys needed shoes! His feet had come through his old ones. They were thrown into cells among criminals, bums, and drunks, then put all together in one cell next to drunken women of the street. During the evening one of them broke a window, and when the jailer came and cursed and kicked them about, they wouldn't tell who had done it. In a rage, the man knocked down one of them and, when the rest scattered and ran, pursued, and bowled them over with his great keys. They were detained a week and then released without a hearing.

The judge had the boys examined by a physician, who found evidences enough that they had been beaten. But the judge went down to the jail, and he learned the truth there from his regular sources of information. Satisfied of the justice of their complaint, the judge went with the boys to lodge a protest with the Police Board. The commissioner refused to believe the boys' stories. It was this case, and many, many cases like it that had convinced Judge Lindsey that the jails were not only schools where older criminals, male and female, taught boys crime and vice, but places where the police practiced brutal injustices which made the boys hate the police, dread the law, and despise everything that we mean by "civilized society." It was the experiences of boys like Mickey and his gang which had prompted the Judge to write the bill which had been held up, the bill providing a detention school and forbidding juvenile offenders to be held in jail at all.

"This was Mickey's fight that I was making," the judge says, as he tells the story, "and I knew I could count on the little chap. I asked the officer if he could get me Mickey. He said he could, and I begged him to go and tell the boy I needed help."

In a few moments Mickey burst breathlessly into the judge's chamber.

"What's the matter, Judge?" he asked.

"Mickey," the judge said, "I'm in trouble, and you've got to help me. I helped you. I went down and I made a fight for you fellows. Didn't I?"

"That's what you did," said Mickey. "Betcher life you did."

"Well, now you've got to stay with me." And he told Mickey what he wanted—all the kids he could find that had been in jail. "The officer can't get them; says there isn't time enough. Can you?"

"Can I? Well, you watch me! Don't you worry about the kids, judge! Gimme a wheel, and I'll get kids, kids to burn!"

The judge went out, and he and Mickey borrowed a wheel. It didn't fit, but Mickey hopped on and went spinning down the street.

"It was a relief to me to see him go," the judge says, "but my worry wasn't over. The invited officials began to arrive before Mickey returned. At ten minutes before two, when the governor appeared, there was not a kid in sight. The entire company had assembled in my chambers before I saw sign of any witnesses, and I was troubled. It was painful. I knew I could count on Mickey, and the kids generally, but suppose he couldn't find them!"

But Mickey found them. Just at two there was a murmur outside. It grew into a hubbub which, as it came down the hall, developed into an alarm. The judge's guests were startled, and even the judge wasn't sure. It sounded like a mob, and up the stairs it rattled, then down the upper hall toward his chamber. As it approached, the judge knew. He flung open the doors, and there were thirty or forty boys, with Mickey radiant at their head.

"Here's the kids, Judge. Got more'n I thought I would."

"Bully for you, Mickey!" said the judge. "You've saved the day."

"I told ye I'd stay wit' ye, Judge."

The judge took the "mob" into a side room. There he told them what was up. They were to tell the truth about the jails. "The police say you have lied to me," he said. "If you have, I ask you now to tell the truth. But tell it. Tell it as you tell one another. Tell it in your own words. They may be bad words, but these gentlemen want to know the truth. So tell them all. Tell them what you see, the dirty things; tell them what the older prisoners say, and what they do to you."

He put Mickey in charge. "Pick out your best witnesses, Mickey," he instructed him, "and send them in one by one." And Mickey began to sort his witnesses. As the judge left the room, he heard Mickey say, with a shove, "You get back there, Skinny, you've only been in five or six times. Fatty Felix has been in twenty-three times and—"

Mickey led in his witnesses, one by one, Fatty Felix, Teddy Healy, Teddy Mack, and the rest, till the governor and the ministers cried "enough!"

Those boys told what was what. They told of lessons in crime by older criminals; stories they had heard there of injustices by judges and of cruelties by the police. They showed up the world as the criminals see it and as those criminals showed it to the boys. And they also related scenes of vice and foulness too revolting to repeat. And those boys made that company of grown-ups believe them, too. Once or twice the police representative interrupted, but, as the judge says, "Teddy Healy's answer, direct, awful, and yet innocently delivered, made the matter ten times worse." The officials dropped all thought of cross-examination. Once a minister asked Mickey about the visits of the clergy to the jail.

"Never saw one," said Mickey. Then he remembered. "Oh, yes, seen the Salvation Army there once, but they sang 'Praise God from Whom All Blessings Flow,' and we'd heard that before, and besides, there didn't seem to be no blessings flowing our way."

It was the officials' turn to smile, and the ministers, they also ceased to cross-examine. The boys were left to talk, watched by Mickey and frankly guided by the judge. It went on for an hour or two, then a preacher rose.

"My God," he said, "this has gone far enough! It is too, too horrible!" And, as he left, Governor Peabody got up.

"Gentlemen," he said, "I never in my life heard or knew of so much rot, corruption, and vileness as I have learned this day from these babes—almost—and I want to say that nothing in my administration will be so important to me as signing Judge Lindsey's bills, I don't care to read those bills. If he says they are designed to correct these conditions, I am satisfied. And," turning to the representative of Frank Adams, he added, "if Judge Lindsey is crazy, I want my name written right under his as one of the crazy people. And as to those boys lying, any one who says they have been lying today must be himself a liar."

With that the meeting broke up. The judge went back to the boys, and he thanked them and Mickey. He was careful to explain again what it was all about. "Skill in handling marble is as nothing to skill in handling men," he quotes, and he wished to be sure that no false impressions were left in these boys' minds. "I am fighting for a decent place to keep kids that are too weak to be on the level," he said. "The jails are not decent; and Mickey, you boys have beaten the jail today, you and all the good kids in Denver. Go out and tell them so, for it is their victory."

That was true. It was a victory. The pulpits rang with the story the next day. The men and women of Denver heard, and so did the grafters, and the grafters felt the effect in public opinion. Lindsey's bills came up from the bottom and were passed and signed and made part of the laws of Colorado within a week. And now other states are copying them.

Reformers, whose notion of reform consists in "getting a law passed," are often amazed to find that their good law does no good. The reason is that neither public opinion nor public officials enforce the new laws. Lindsey had waited for his legislation till he had the support of public opinion, and then he enforced his new laws; he, and the boys and girls, and public opinion.

They were effective laws. They gave the judge control of the whole children's case. He proceeded gently to the enforcement of his power. He had written into the laws full authority to exercise his discretion, with adults as with children, and he did this because he meant to be human and charitable to men as he had been to children. It had worked with the children; he would try it on their elders. So he was firm but not unkind.

When the police brought in a boy for getting drunk, the judge asked for the man who sold the boy the liquor, and the police had to fetch the man. Sometimes the judge fined him; sometimes he imprisoned him; sometimes he suspended sentence. For he talked to the men as he did to the boys, and if he found that they hadn't thought of the evil they did by carelessly serving boys and girls with tobacco and liquor, the judge explained it to these saloon-keepers. And if he thought they were impressed, he put them also "on probation." That gave him a hold on them, which prevented crime and vice. For the judge knew what was going on. He had thousands of eyes. The boys and girls watched for him. When the judge had got his legislation, he told the children that the new laws were their laws, enacted for them and by them; for Mickey and his "gang of jailbirds" who carried the day, represented the children of Denver. The children, therefore, must obey these laws and help enforce them. He broadened the doctrine of "snitching on the square." It was mean to spy; it was wrong under the law to "get a man to break the law and then peach on him." No child was to be "smart" and hunt for evil. But when a man sold cigarettes and liquor to children, that man was "making kids bad" and for a pitifully small profit, too. Wherefore, the thing for a kid to do was, first, to warn the man, then, if he didn't "cut it out," to tell the judge.

This was a very delicate part of the judge's policy, and many a man will shake his head over it. We all despise spying. But boys despise it more than men, and I know no better way to prove that the judge made it clear and right than by stating that the boys of Denver, the "big fellers," approved the doctrine and practiced it. Take the Battle-Axe gang of Globeville, for example. Globeville is a suburb of Denver, and the Battle-Axes were the toughest "fellers" over there. Their leaders were three brothers, known as the Cahoots—"Big Cahoot," "Middle Cahoot," and "Little Cahoot." The whole gang frequented dives, drank, smoked, chewed (they were named after their favorite brand of plug tobacco); they did everything that men did, and other things besides. The judge got hold of this gang, in the usual way; one or two were arrested, won over, and persuaded to bring in the rest. They all came, and were interested in the game of correction. The good they could do, the judge told them, was to help enforce the laws of the kids' court. They did it, too. They had trouble at first. One day Big Cahoot went to a saloon where some of the little fellers in his gang had bought tobacco.

He told the man about the law and asked him not to sell to any Battle-Axes. The saloon-keeper, taken aback, became angry, and started for the boy. Big Cahoot wasn't afraid. He stood his ground; there was a fight, and the young tough was kicked out into the street. But he told the judge, and the judge sent the man to jail for fifteen days. After that it was easier for the boys, who are still reporting to the judge that the law is respected "over in Globeville" and that "the Battle-Axes are doin' all right."

One curious development of this policy was that many of the liquor dealers, having been made to understand what all this meant to the children, came to like the judge and to help him to carry out his policy. The Baker case will illustrate.

One day a girl was brought in. She told her story; it was a wine-room story, and the judge had the wine-room keeper, Baker, arrested. He tried him in the Juvenile Court, and sent him up for sixty days.

"The girl I kept on probation," he says, "and I was talking to her one day—the day before Christmas—when I was told that a boy, Paul Baker, wanted to see me. Putting the girl in a side room, I had the boy in. He was a handsome, wholesome little fellow, and he came up to my table, halting, but with a frank look on his face.

" 'Judge,' he said, 'you put my papa in jail, but everybody says that you like boys and do all you can to help a boy. So I came to ask you to let my father come home for Christmas.' "

He began to cry, and the Judge spoke.

"Yes, I like boys," he said, "and I like men, too. Do you think I dislike your father? Not a bit! I was sorry to put him in jail. And did it never occur to you that it wasn't I that put him in jail? It was the law. And the law is right. Do you know what your father did?"

The boy knew. "Well, I like little girls as well as I like boys, and you know that wine-rooms are bad places for little girls. This little girl and her mother, they are suffering just as you and your father are suffering; all because he broke the law." The judge sent for the girl, and he introduced the two children. He drew the girl on to tell what "trouble" the violation of the law had caused her and her mother. The judge explained why she should not hate, but be sorry for the man, since he was only thoughtless, as she was, and was in trouble, too.

"Here is his son, Paul, who has come to ask that his father may be allowed to come home for Christmas to see his family. His mother suffers as yours does; his sister has wept as you have wept. It is all, all trouble, and no one is worse than another. Now, what shall I do about letting Mr. Baker go home for Christmas?"

"Let him go," the girl said, and she and the boy joined in the plea. The judge consented.

When Paul brought in his father to see the judge, on the day after Christmas, the judge sent the boy out of the room, then, he praised the son to the father. It was a pity, he said, to bring up that boy in such a business.

"Judge," the man said, "you are right. I've been thinking it all over in jail, and I've made up my mind to get rid of this business and go back to the mountains where I came from."

The judge did not send Baker back to jail; he suspended sentence, as his law authorized him to do, and the man did sell out and go back to the mountains. Now, when they come to town, he and his boy always call on the judge, their "best friend."

"You see," the judge says, "Baker wasn't a bad man. He did a bad thing, and that bad thing made a little girl bad. But what made him do the bad thing? To make his business good; to increase his profits. But there was the law and the power of the state to compel him to restrict his enterprise within limits where it wouldn't hurt anybody else. That's where the System broke down; that's where it breaks down all the time. Why?"

Baker told him why. He said that he broke the law because the bosses told him he might. He contributed to their campaign funds, paid blackmail, and furnished "stuffers" to vote, so they told him he was "protected." "Then you came along, judge, and you sent me up. I don't blame you. I blamed them, and I went to them for their protection. They said they couldn't handle you. They said they didn't mean I could break juvenile laws, but they didn't tell me that. I paid them, and they couldn't deliver the goods. That's why I blame them."

Baker blamed the bosses, and so did the other saloon-keepers. So did the people of Denver; most of us blame the political bosses. The judge himself blamed them for a long while, and he ought to have known better. One of his first political services was to help Governor Thomas destroy the power of Boss Thomas J. Mahoney, famous in Denver politics. And they did destroy Mahoney's power. But that made no difference. Only the man was down and out; the boss lived. Who was the boss of the political boss? For whom was blackmail collected from the saloon-keepers in return for which they were permitted to break the law, sell liquor to boys, and keep wine-rooms where girls might be ruined? The parties? For whom did the parties work? The parties worked for the big business interests of Denver and Colorado, as the judge found out.

You hear in Denver that "the trouble with Ben Lindsey is that he 'butts into' everything." He does and he must. His critics mean that Judge Lindsey might solve the problem of the children, if, for their sake, he would not interfere with other evils. Many good men and women adopt that policy. Temperance reformers, to get their prohibition laws through, trade votes with the railroads; and charities and churches, colleges and all sorts of benevolent and reform groups, to say nothing of businesses, professions, and interests generally. We, all of us, are standing in with Evil, in the hope of destroying the particular little evils against which we are fighting. Lindsey won't. This is the institutional idea; this is the fallacy which makes men sacrifice civilization, for no less is at stake for their church, their party, or their grocery store. If Lindsey should make this common, almost universal mistake he might build up his Juvenile Court, they tell him, into a national, yes, an international institution, and send his name reverberating down through the ages. But Ben Lindsey won't do it; and he won't because he sees that he can't.

He can't for two reasons. One, as he soon learned, is that the problem of the children isn't a separate problem. Ben Lindsey discovered that bad children are made bad by the conditions which men create. And he went after some of those conditions, and when it was found that his legislation gave him power over adults that hurt children, as well as over the children, the leading citizens of Denver were incensed. Why? His authority over saloon and other vice interests loosened the hold the machines had over the vicious elements of society, and menaced the election frauds on which the business and political system of the state was built. And Lindsey saw, and he was told (though not in these words) that the big men of his state would prefer to see children hurt than business. So they fought him, and when he beat them, as we have seen, with the help of the men, women, and children of the city, they declared that he "had too much work to do" and that therefore they would take away from his court jurisdiction over adults who contributed to the delinquency of children. In other words, they are indeed willing to let him do what he can for the kids after the harm is done, but he must not undermine the vice of the city, however much it may injure youth, the foundation of "prosperity."

Thus the first reason why he can't let all the other evils go to correct the one he is after, was his discovery that our apparently separate evils are all tied up together; they are all one evil; they are a System, as he calls it, of Evil.

The second reason is that Lindsey is so constituted that he must attack any wrong with which he comes in personal contact. We have seen how, accidentally, the county judge drifted into the case of the children. That was characteristic. When he was a young lawyer he was beaten in a damage suit against the street railway by a "fixed" jury. Inquiring into the matter, he learned that jury-fixing was a common practice, and he attacked that practice. He drew a bill to enable a majority of jurors to render a verdict. The company offered his firm an annual retainer, but Lindsey declared that it was a bribe and refused it. "This was my first sight of the grand System," he says, "but I didn't recognize it as such. I've learned since that this is the way the interests get their first hold on promising or troublesome young lawyers." Lindsey put his bill through. Challenged as unconstitutional, it was first upheld, then thrown out by the Supreme Court of Colorado; "which gave me my first sight of the Supreme Court as a part of the System," he says.

His practice developed along probate lines, and he found the laws obscure and unfair. He revised them, and his revision, enacted, has been highly praised by the law journals. Indeed, his knowledge of probate law was one of the justifications for putting so young a man on the county bench. Lindsey is the author of the present election laws of his state. Everybody was complaining of the old laws, but nothing was done about them till Lindsey went to work and got them changed. I could go on for a page with practical reforms taken up by this man, all of them suggested by his accidental, personal contact with evils, and all having nothing to do with children. If Judge Lindsey had never heard of the problem of the children he would have been known as a man doing a man's work for men.

But the incident in his career which will show this best is his exposure of the county commissioners. That also was begun by accident.

At the close of the Juvenile Court one Saturday afternoon, the judge picked up idly from the clerk's desk a paper, which, as he talked, he glanced at. "To 1,000 sheets paper, $280." It was a bill, and the price interested the Judge. He asked the clerk about it. The clerk hadn't seen the bill. He "guessed" it was there by mistake; bills didn't come to him; "must have been meant for the clerk of the county board." Lindsey sent the clerk to "see Mr. Smith, of the Smith-Brooks Publishing Company (which furnished the paper), and ask if the bill was correct." The clerk brought the answer that his (Smith's) "damned boy had taken the bill to the wrong place, and the price was none of our business." The judge sent to the county clerk for other bills charged to the county court.

"I was amazed at the charges," he says. "Six letter files at $6 apiece; these cost me personally twenty-eight and thirty cents apiece. Paper which was charged for at the rate of $48 a thousand I could get for $6. I spent the night on those bills, and the next (Sunday) morning I took expert advice. I found that the county was paying several hundred percent too much for all supplies to my court." As with the children and as with the Police Board, the judge wished to give the county commissioners a hearing, so he wrote them a letter containing the facts. "I thought probably they didn't know about these overcharges. I didn't want to misjudge them, and I wanted to examine into the situation with them privately and personally. I believe if they had come up with the truth, I'd have been satisfied if they had promised to cut it out."

The judge received no reply to his letter. He sent another, and still no response; that is to say, none that was direct. There was an indirect response, however, which interested the judge profoundly. Both the police and the county boards of Denver were bi-partisan, but the fighting line in the politics of the city was a machine, not a party line, and the police and the county boards were at odds. The county board had appointed Lindsey a judge. When he went after the police board, Frank Adams, the president, unable to believe in honesty and sincerity, had looked around for an explanation of "Lindsey's enmity" to him; and the theory he fixed upon was that Lindsey, out of gratitude to the county board for his job, was "hurting the party" to help Frank Bishop, the president of the county board, who was a candidate for the nomination for governor of Colorado. So now, when Ben "got after Frank Bishop's board," he puzzled Frank Adams and all the other men in Denver who, to account for the conduct of others, read their own souls.

"What does Ben mean? Is he an ingrate? You go ask him what the hell he means." This was said by Commissioner Watts to the judge's clerk, whom the board had also "given his job." Cass Harrington called; the attorney to the county board, this man had resigned to be "of counsel" to the Colorado Fuel & Iron Company. Others called, many prominent men. "This stealing," the judge says, "had friends, political and business friends, and they were powerful men, all of them." He saw that he would also need friends, so the judge paid some visits. He called on some other judges; he told them the facts, and he asked them to move with him for an investigation. They wouldn't.

"Why, judge," said one of them, "you have your hands full now. You are doing more than two or three men can do. You oughtn't to want to know about this. I don't. That would make me responsible, and I don't want to have anything to do with it. Go to the district attorney. . . . Well, then, that means that you know what politics is in this town. My advice to you is, let the whole thing alone." This from a judge! And other officials took the same view or a similar view: "You can't do anything"; or "The county board appointed you; I believe in sticking by your friends"; or "It will ruin you, judge"; or "It will spoil your work for the children."

The judge went on investigating, and the evidence he discovered and the things his "friends" told him to stop him, showed him that this county graft was well known, and that it was but a small part of a system of graft. For example, business men were in on the deals; each commissioner had merchants for graft-partners. And besides, the county board was a board of tax revision; it had remitted the taxes of public service corporations, and it could "hurt" or "help" property-holders generally. But the judge got help. Some of the early commissioners "snitched" to the judge; they didn't snitch like the boys, "on the square"—they "squealed" to save themselves, and the others squealed on the squealers to get even. Oh, he got the facts! He appointed a committee to investigate, and the committee reported the facts to the judge.

A concerted effort was made to have the judge suppress his report. Many respectable friends of the grafters went to the front for graft. They pretended to represent "business," the "party," "the fair fame of Denver," etc. They used the names of United States Senators Patterson and Teller. They were panic-stricken. As for the judge, he was awed at the show of influence. "And," he says, "I was really in doubt lest I might be doing a great harm to accomplish a little good." But he was reassured. He sounded the United States senators, and both Mr. Patterson and Mr. Teller sent back word to "go ahead and show up the grafters regardless of party." That was the first encouragement the judge got. Finally, three of the county commissioners called, and their pleadings decided him. They also prayed in the name of "the party," the "credit of business," Denver, gratitude, their families; but there was no word about stopping the stealing! The judge published the report in the Democratic newspaper, the *News*.

The county board had to act; and it began with an investigation of its own—a farce, of course. "One thing I learned from it, however," the judge says, "and that was that many men of business are cowards. The same experts who had told me that the commissioners were thieves, went on the stand and perjured themselves. And their perjury was all in vain. District-attorney Lindsley had to act. Lindsley is the man who got his office when Lindsey wanted it, and the judge urged him now to do what he, himself, had thought of doing: use the power of the public prosecutor to prosecute public criminals and clean up the city. Lindsley wouldn't; he was in the gang, and other gangsters said he didn't dare. He proposed that the judge meet with a committee of the party leaders and discuss what should be done. The judge refused. And the newspapers made demands. So Lindsley had to make a show of action. He called on the judge and talked about doing his duty. He has a peculiar whine, Lindsley has, and in that whining way he protested to the judge that while he didn't believe the commissioners could be convicted, he would do his duty. Judge Lindsey happened to go down to the Democratic Club right after this talk, and he found Lindsley there drinking with one of the accused commissioners. And the information that this district attorney drew was under a statute which limited the penalty to $300 fine and removal from office.

The newspapers, principally Senator Patterson's, forced this case to trial. District-attorney Lindsley refused to appear in it himself; he appointed a deputy, George Allan Smith, who, the Judge says, was faithful. (And evidently he was, for he was forced to resign after the trial.) No local judge cared to sit on the case, so a judge of the Pueblo district (controlled by the Colorado Fuel & Iron Company) was called in. For the grafters appeared Charles J. Hughes, a leading attorney for the corrupt corporations of Colorado (since elected a United States senator). The story of the trial is a story of "jury work," stolen papers, conspiracies and plots, and an attempt to brand Judge Lindsey as "an ingrate" (to the System), a "reformer" and a "grand-stand player." (How they do hate to have a man serve and appeal to the people!) Nobody expected anything but a verdict of acquittal, and then Judge Lindsey was to have been put on trial.

But the jury convicted those grafters. How it happened I couldn't learn. Somebody blundered, I heard. The jurors apologized; the district attorney apologized; the very judge apologized. Judge Voorheis delivered from the bench to those prisoners at the bar a speech which was eulogistic of them. He spoke of their standing and usefulness as Christian gentlemen and good citizens. He said they were victims of an evil System. He regretted that he had to impose any punishment, but he must; so he gave the smallest penalty provided by the law: "Ten dollars and costs!"

The learned judge was right: there is a System, and the penalties that System imposed upon Judge Lindsey were not light. His sentence was destruction. Knowing that money couldn't prostitute him, women were tried. The janitor of the County Court House wouldn't clean Lindsey's court-room and so neglected his closet that the Board of Health had to interfere. He was cut on the street by other officials and, to avoid hearing himself called insulting names, had to stay away from his club. His party council allowed the convicted county commissioners to name their successors and to reject from the platform a plank declaring for honesty in office.

This persecution continued for a year or two and, it must be confessed, the judge was aggravating. He not only refused to surrender; he went right on fearlessly supporting in public every good reform measure and movement that anybody proposed. For example, a convention, called for by the so-called Rush Amendment to the state constitution, drew for Denver a good, new, home-rule charter. The big business interests "had to" beat it, however, because it gave the people a vote on all franchise grants and permitted municipal ownership. The only way to beat it was to have the ballot-boxes stuffed. Yet, when some inexperienced young men organized a League for Honest Elections, this county judge came down off the bench to help the league. And, as usual, his speech was no mere perfunctory address on the sacredness of the ballot-box; he named names, and he named not merely the despised agents who did the dirty work; Judge Lindsey called the roll of the officials who employed and protected the ballot-box stuffers ! The people, already aroused, became so inflamed that finally their rulers had to elect a pretty good charter themselves.

Do you see the situation? Do you see Ben Lindsey doing his duty, all of it, not only as a judge of children, but as County judge, and not only as a judge on the bench, but as a man on the bench and off it? and fighting all the while for his life; cheerfully, without malice, but without fear? Paul Thieman in the *Denver Post* once called Ben Lindsey "the first citizen of Colorado," and declared that, not the mines and the mills, not the railroads, the farms, and the banks, but Ben Lindsey's work was "the greatest thing the state has produced." And from the point of view of the history of man, this is true. It looks absurd from a shop window, but Paul Thieman was seeing things through the eyes of a little boy he mentions, who, sitting silent one day watching the judge deal out justice, suddenly rushed up and kissed him on the cheek. "I love you!" the child said.

    The test came at the elections of 1904. The judge had to run then, and he sought the office. "I had to," he says apologetically; "my work was only just begun." His enemies meant to defeat him. Who were his enemies? There was Frank Adams and his police board, whose co-partnership with vice and crime he had exposed and disturbed; they were still in office and powerful in his party. Then there were the county commissioners whom he had driven to trial for grafting; they controlled the county board, and the party machinery. These two groups with all their followers hated the just judge, of course, and they proposed to beat him openly for the nomination. But wiser counsels prevailed. Other, cooler enemies, passed the word to beat him quietly. Lindsey was "popular" with the women and children, the leaders said, and women vote in Colorado. The big leaders advised caution, and the scheme was to make him decline the nomination himself. They proposed to nominate as his associate on the county bench a man who was "going to knock out all this kid business." They expected the judge to revolt, and he did; he said he would "denounce his fellow-candidate from the stump." This was the excuse the Democrats wanted, and they decided to drop the judge.

    But a hitch occurred. There was a row in the Republican party, and the dominant state leader, to affront the Denver boss, William G. Evans, nominated Judge Lindsey on the Republican ticket. This put the Democrats in an awkward attitude. They demanded that Lindsey be loyal to his own party and decline the Republican nomination. He refused. They offered him a better associate judge, if he would run only on the Democratic ticket. But the judge knew that they meant to knife him, so he accepted their associate, but declared he would accept any and all nominations from all parties. And he did. And his party decided again not to nominate him. This was three days before the convention, but that was time enough for the judge.

He went to the people. He published an open letter in the Denver Post. The newsboys, all friends of the judge, cried it as news, and not only that, they sent kids as couriers to raise the gangs. Men took the letter home, and mothers turned out. But the children were before them. They poured out into the streets and, collected and organized by the newsboys, marched up and down the main streets, yelling for Lindsey. By the time the procession had reached the Democratic Club, the cries of the children had developed into a song which they sang as they marched and countermarched and halted before the club:

> "Who, which, when?
> Wish we was men,
> So we could vote for our little Ben."

And they kept it up all that night and all the next day. It was most embarrassing to the politicians. "Little sons of —!" exclaimed a leader in the club, "they are doing more than anybody else to beat us." But the answer was that cry from the street, "Who, which, when?" All day long, everywhere, the boys kept at it. And then the mothers of the city held a mass-meeting at the Women's Club. And then there was a mass-meeting of men, women, and children in the Opera House.

Ben Lindsey was nominated, "amid howls and curses" and on his own terms, on his own party ticket, and all other tickets, excepting only that of the Socialists. Nominated by the people, he was elected by their unanimous vote; but that didn't settle it.

The judge believed that the election of two county judges was unconstitutional; if it was, the mayor of the city would have to choose between him and his colleague. The mayor, Robert Speer, was a Democrat and the leader of Lindsey's party. The judge asked him whom he would choose. This Democratic mayor said he would have to consult with

William G. Evans, the Republican boss, before he could answer, and he did see Mr. Evans and the answer was that there would be no choice; the spring election was legal and would stand. But if it should not be held legal, then, the mayor made plain, Judge Lindsey would not be the judge.

"That's enough for me," said Lindsey. "I fight."
And he went forth to fight. He went to the editors of Senator Patterson's two papers, the *News* and the *Times*, and to the *Denver Post*. They sounded the alarm, and they kept it up, too. Paul Thieman rehearsed the whole story of the kid's judge as a serial. The people began to be interested, but they were too late; the conventions of both parties met and adjourned without nominating the judge, and "Bill" Evans left for New York.

Mayor Speer, the Democrat, was in charge of this business for both parties, but he could not control the younger Republicans. They made such a fuss that the older leaders consented to recall the convention. It was to nominate Lindsey, of course, but this "matter of course" was so insisted upon by the System's organ, the Republican, that Lindsey became suspicious. He inquired, and he heard the night before the convention that all this talk was part of the game to keep the young Republicans away from the convention; another man was to be nominated in the judge's place.

Lindsey called up his friends among the delegates, and the young men wanted to give up. The caucus had been held; the slate was fixed; it was too late to make a fight. The judge wouldn't hear of quitting, however, so, in their desperation, one of them suggested seeing David H. Moffatt. Mr. Moffatt is the leading banker and financier of Colorado, and to go to him was to appeal over the heads of all the political bosses and the apparent business bosses to the very head of the System. Moffatt was the man to go to, but Lindsey didn't know Moffatt.

"Well, you know Walter Cheesman; go to him."

Walter Cheesman was a religious man, very rich and benevolent and an active supporter of the Humane Society and of Lindsey's Juvenile Improvement Society. So the judge knew Mr. Cheesman, but it was not because of his benevolence that those young men suggested seeing him. Walter Cheesman was president of the Denver Water Company, and therefore "had to" be part of the System which causes the corruption and the evils that, as a philanthropist, he "had to" contribute money to ameliorate.

The judge went to see the philanthropist. He told Mr. Cheesman about the plot and the caucus.

"You, Mr. Cheesman, you know," he said, "what I have done in that office. You know I have slaved and worked and fought; that it has been often a hell on earth. You know, too, that I have saved the county very much money, in many ways; that I have tried to walk straight and do right; and that I have begun for the children a work that must not stop now."

"Judge," said Mr. Cheesman, "I am sorry, and I have just been talking to Mr. Field about your case." Mr. Field? Mr. Field was the president of the Telephone Company, another privileged business. The judge was seeing the System plainly.

"Mr. Field and I discussed the case, judge," said Mr. Cheesman, "and we are very sorry, but we can do nothing. With us, politics is business and business comes first. You might as well understand it. My advice to you is to let go the judgeship, and the Children's Court. Mr. Shattock will be nominated by the Republican convention; Mr. Johnson will be nominated by the Democratic convention. That's certain. And I want to give you one bit of advice. Don't you run independent. I know what I'm talking about. You can't be elected."

So that was the situation; that was the System. The judge rose:

"I'm going to fight," he said, "and I'm going to fight till I'm licked good and hard."

He went back and he told his young men. There was no time to appeal to the voters, but it wasn't necessary. Those young men scoured the town; they filled the streets and the convention hall. The excitement was intense. Speer, the Democrat, wired to Evans, the Republican, that the Republicans were pulling away, and that if they did, the Democrats would have to quit, too. Evans wired his orders back, but Lindsey was nominated by the Republicans, and the Democrats had to nominate him. They had to nominate and run their whole county ticket over again, and (this is the funniest thing that I know in politics) the Democratic gang that had hatched this scheme to "lose Lindsey somehow in the mix-up"—these grafters, elected in the spring and settled at their graft, were defeated in the fall! Lindsey alone was re-elected. And the Supreme Court did declare the spring election void. The gang had beaten themselves. And the people—the women, the children, the honest men of Denver—they had saved Ben Lindsey.

American Magazine
February, 1908

Rudolph Spreckels: A Business Reformer

IT IS important to know Rudolph Spreckels. He is a businessman. He never has been anything but a business man. He did not go to college and, except for some interrupted private schooling and tutoring, all the education he ever had was in business. That was thorough and practical. It began when, as a boy, he sat, silent, listening to his father and older brothers talking business at home. And he caught the spirit of modern business. His boyish ambition, confessed to the amusement of the family, was to be a millionaire. That was all. He didn't mean to run a locomotive, find the North Pole, write a sonnet, or set the world on fire. He didn't dream even of the management of some great business. No, young Rudolph looked past the work to the end thereof; he was "for results." He wanted millions. And he succeeded; before he was twenty-six he was able to retire a millionaire, self-made.

Certain events in the business world called him back to life in a year or two, and—to get to the point—this rich young man of business went in for political reform in his city. That alone is important, but that doesn't half express Rudolph Spreckels's mind. He has said that he will devote the rest of his life—and, if need be, his fortune—to reform: general reform. For when he has "made good" in San Francisco, he proposes to try some other cities. New York attracts him; so do Chicago and Denver.

New York will arch its brows and smile; Chicago may laugh. But Rudolph Spreckels has tackled big men and big jobs; he never has failed; he is unlicked. He has "hate of hate, scorn of scorn." He doesn't care who laughs first. With his quizzical, winning smile, he says:

"I don't care who sneers in the beginning, or who doubts. I don't doubt. I fix my eyes on a purpose, and I'm sure of the end."

It won't do to waive this man lightly aside. He has health and youth, will-power, and persistence, and ability. This young captain of industry is the kind of man that has done so much evil in this country. He was born and bred to the type that has built and robbed railroads, "made" and unmade states; corrupting business and courts and governments, but accomplishing its end. When the goal of such a man is the creation of a monopoly of all the food or all the oil or all the steel in our world, we take him seriously too late. I think that Rudolph Spreckels—capitalist, bank president, captain of industry who at thirty-five has devoted his knowledge of men and business methods good and bad; his patient impatience; his talent for organization and his executive ability to reform in the united cities of America—such a man is worth our study.

At any rate, he is the political ideal of the business world. All over the country I have heard business men say that what we want is some good business man who will apply good business methods to politics and government and give us a good, businesslike administration. The efficacy of this solution is dubious, but never mind. Here we have the business men's dream come true; here we have the business man "sacrificing his money and his still more valuable time" to the public service. How do business men receive the devotion of Rudolph Spreckels? Do they like and applaud and support him?

No. Business men do not like and applaud and support Mr. Spreckels. They denounce him and they oppose him and they oppose his reform. The leading business men of San Francisco hate and vilify him, and they oppose his prosecution of criminals. They and their organs fight on the side of graft against this young business man who has gone in for politics. And not only the San Franciscans; the business men of the East, and especially of New York, have turned their newspapers against him. And Mr. Spreckels smiles; he expected all this. Why?

There was no doubt about the badness of politics in San Francisco. "Labor ruled there," and the business world has been "long" with pity for "poor old Frisco." Why then this opposition of the San Francisco business men to Mr. Spreckels? What do they say against him? Not very much. They attribute political ambition and, in the same breath, a business motive to his efforts for political reform; they say he wanted a street railway franchise and sought to "get in on" the United (Street) Railways of San Francisco. Patrick Calhoun offered him an interest in that company, and Spreckels declined it; and he has promised publicly that he will never own, directly or indirectly, a share in any public utility company and that he will take no office in the city government. Nothing has been produced from his business record against him. That must be well known, and since it was a record of "success," I expected to hear of sharp deals and queer turns; but, no, nothing of the sort. Mr. Spreckels must indeed be a good business man. You will hear, as I did, that "Spreckels got a lot of people into a railroad and then sold it out to the Santa Fe." That is true. Spreckels did that, but not Rudolph Spreckels. That was an act of his father, Claus Spreckels. Again, they asked me if I didn't know that the public utility system of San Diego was a Spreckels monopoly. I did, but I happened to know what many Californians seem not to know, that the Spreckels of San Diego are not Rudolph, but a brother of his and a personal enemy. Claus Spreckels is interesting; the whole Spreckels family may be well worth knowing, but most of them are in business or private life. Our subject is Rudolph Spreckels, the business reformer; not his family except as "blood will tell."

  The Spreckels family is an institution in California and, generally regarded as a unit, is not popular. The Spreckelses fight. They fight hard. But they don't fight together. They are not a unit. The family fights inside as well as out, and not all the members speak to one another. They differ among themselves in character, tastes, methods, purposes and, apparently, in morals. All they seem to have in common is a certain aggressive independence. They are in business what Labor would call "scabs." They work by themselves and each by himself. They play with others, and the family "stands well" both downtown and up, but there is more fear than affection in their social and financial reception. They are a family of individuals, and individuality is offensive not alone to organized labor; organized capital hates it, too. And the Spreckelses are capitalists.

Claus Spreckels, the sugar magnate, was the head of the family. A German peasant, he came to this country when he was about eighteen years old, with two German thalers in his pocket. But he had the capitalist's instinct in his heart. After clerking one year in a grocery store, he bought the business on credit; and he extended both. In a few years he sent home to the village next to his for the young girl who became the mother of his family.

The Spreckelses moved to California in 1856, opened a grocery store in San Francisco and extended the business. Seeing that there was money in beer, Claus Spreckels built a brewery. Seeing that there was money in sugar, he built a refinery. There were other refineries; Claus Spreckels beat his competitors, but when the American Sugar Refining Company came along and, buying them up, offered to buy him out or, as Labor says of "scabs," "beat him up," he fought. And he fought not only in self-defence—he took the offensive; he built an independent refinery at Philadelphia and, carrying the war thus into the enemy's own field, Claus Spreckels compelled a division of the territory, the Pacific Coast, for his. Because of a personal affront by the president of the Gas Company in San Francisco, he started a rival concern and he marked down the price of gas so low that it never did get all the way back. And because he was dependent in business on the Southern Pacific Railroad monopoly, he did not "lie down"; he helped build that competing line which became a part of the Santa Fe system.

"He sold out," they say. Yes, he sold out, but at his price, and he never "stood in"; he never was " satisfied," "safe," "reasonable." And that's why "they" are down on Claus Spreckels. If he had been "satisfied" with his grocery-store, he might have become a patient grocer. If money was all he was after, he might have been a rich brewer. If he had been "reasonable" with the sugar trust, "fair" to the gas company and had stood "in" with the railroad, he might have become an "organized capitalist" and a dummy director in these and in many other businesses. But he must dominate whatever he took part in. Impatient, implacable, ruthless, his "Dutch obstinacy" made him fight, and the result was that Claus Spreckels was a captain of industry, retired, but victorious; not only rich, but an independent financial power. You hear that his methods were—those of big business. I don't know anything about them, nor do I care. It isn't the father that is trying to clean up San Francisco, it's the son.

And Rudolph Spreckels is the son of Claus; not only of his loins, but of his spirit. He was the eleventh or twelfth child; he couldn't recall which, offhand, and it does not matter, for now he is the first. This masterful father tried to dominate his masterful son, and they clinched. It was a long, bitter business fight and, in the course of it, Rudolph Spreckels discovered that there is such a thing as Organized Capital. He learned that a financial power like Claus Spreckels can close all the banks and shut off credit to his "scab" enemies. But Claus Spreckels learned some things, too, among them the character and resources of his own son.

"I never was beaten but once in my life," he is quoted as saying not long before his death, "and that was by my own boy."

This sounds like pride, and it was known in financial circles downtown that when the head of the Spreckels family went away, he left his affairs in the hands of Rudolph, his eleventh or twelfth child, the president of the First National Bank.

Rudolph is only thirty-five years old, but he began his career early. He was, like Roosevelt, an asthmatic child, and when the attacks were upon him he used to go off by himself on his pony, seeking relief "on the ranch" or in the woods. When he first disappeared in this sudden way, the family was alarmed, but as he continued to do it, no further protests were offered. Self-reliant by birth, this boyish practice developed that trait in him, and some power of reflection, too. For solitude is good for the mind. But Rudolph could not go regularly to school, and his progress seemed to be irregular and aimless.

When he was seventeen, his father walked into the library one day and bade him choose on the spot one of three courses: college; a trip around the world with his tutor; or business. Rudolph chose business on the spot. And, on the spot, the father directed him to go to Philadelphia and help his brother, Claus Augustus, run the independent refinery that was fighting the Trust. The boy went and, advanced rapidly from department to department, he learned early the principles of business and the lack of them.

Young Rudolph saw machinery destroyed by his father's employees. Sticks, stones, tools were thrown in among the parts, which were broken, of course. Watching, the boy caught the vandals and learned that they were bribed by agents of the Trust to do what they did!

He saw, in the morning, pans of sugar spoiled during the night. Staying up one night, the boy tried to find out who was to blame, but he saw no workman neglect his duty. Nevertheless, in the morning there was the same old trouble with the vacuum pans. Rudolph discharged the night superintendent, and, taking the place himself, filled it for four to six months, and he did the work well or, at any rate, honestly. No more sugar was spoiled at night.

In the course of this fight, it became manifest that the Trust knew the secrets of their rivals' business. They seemed to have each day the exact condition of the independent's stock, orders and finances. There was a period of mystery till suspicion settled upon the chief accountant. Shadowing him, they saw him copy the figures and take them to a certain cigar-dealer, who carried them in the morning to the Trust.

Thus it was that before he was twenty years old, Rudolph Spreckels learned at first-hand that capital "throws bricks"; that it "destroys property" and "hurts business"; and that it bribes men, not alone in politics, but in business. This schooling did not make a cynic of him, however, nor a "crook." He fought these methods, and he beat them and the Trust.

At one great crisis in the fight, when his brother Gus was away sick, Rudolph carried through a coup which is remembered yet in the trade. The Spreckelses were overstocked with sugar; all their warehouses were filled; great purchases of raw were coming forward and, because the price was being cut every few days, the dealers were living from hand to mouth. One night Rudolph (age eighteen, remember) told his city and outside salesmen to meet him the next morning at seven o'clock. When they reported, he bade them wire all brokers that sugar was to be advanced 1-16th of a cent a pound. The older men were aghast.

Rudolph Spreckels: A Business Reformer

What if the Trust kept the price down?

"Never mind," said the boy. "Say we will fill immediate orders at the old price, but after that —"

The orders came in with a rush. Rudolph watched the Trust. He knew that he had this advantage: he was in command in his refinery. In the Trust the principals were probably away from town or not yet up; subordinates were in command, and subordinates cannot take chances on losing their jobs. They would hardly dare take the initiative and keep prices down. So he reasoned, and he was right. The Trust followed Rudolph Spreckels's lead, and three times that day he advanced the price. And he sold out all his stock and all that he had in sight. The cutting of prices was resumed, but once again the boy beat the Trust by this same trick. And so, before he was twenty, Rudolph Spreckels measured himself with great captains of industry and—became sure of himself.

At any rate, he was bold enough to fight his father, and he knew what that meant. This quarrel, alluded to above, broke out during their struggle with the Trust. On one side were Gus and Rudolph; on the other, the father and his other sons. It was a general business row at first, but as it grew the Spreckels sugar plantations on the Hawaiian Islands became the bone of contention. A losing business, Rudolph visited them; he saw neglect, mismanagement, extravagance and stealing, and he declared that the plantations could be made to pay. He and Gus bought them; Rudolph took charge and, cutting out the graft and introducing method and discipline, was getting things on a paying basis, when a crisis occurred. They needed more time and money. The rest of the family wouldn't give them either. Very well, Gus and Rudolph would borrow of the banks. Their security was good, the plantations were sure payers, but the banks refused any " accommodation." The young men went from one bank to another till they realized that there was an understanding among these Organized Capitalists; the word had been passed not to let the two Spreckels boys have a cent. For a while they stared at ruin, but they hustled around and finally found a private capitalist who backed them; and they made good. They sold the plantation at a price which netted them a fortune each.

Rudolph thought he was through with business. Investing his money in real estate and gas stock, he retired to the country and, content with his rents and dividends, was neglecting his duty as a stockholder to develop a beautiful estate in Sonoma County, when bad news came. His father had started the gas war in San Francisco. It seemed that the gas works were blowing smoke in the old man's windows. He protested, in vain, and one noon at the Pacific Union Club he met the president, Joe Crockett.

"Look here, Joe," he said, "I've had enough of that smoke of yours. You'd better do something." "The Club is no place to discuss business," said Crockett, and he turned on his heel and walked off. Claus Spreckels was amazed, and angry. "I'll make you regret this!" he said, and in twenty-four hours he had organized the Independent Gas and Electric Company. Rudolph Spreckels knew that a fight with Claus Spreckels meant economy and able management for the old company. Gas was $1.25, and the Independent proposed to sell it at 75 cents. When Rudolph saw his stock drop from 85 to 60, he came to town to attend to his duties as a stockholder and to learn what graft is in business; and what politics is in business; and what the relation of said business corruption is to political corruption.

Rudolph Spreckels made some swift, superficial inquiries about the gas company, and he heard that it had a big floating debt. There were other signs of neglect in the management, yes, and of inefficiency. The directors were all "leading citizens," "prominent business men," "veterans in finance." They were just the sort of men that business men would put upon a board of aldermen or supervisors to give good business government. Yet this young man found that these picked business directors were neglecting their duty to him as a stockholder, very much as his supervisors neglected their duty to him as a citizen and property holder. And that wasn't all: the company wasn't earning the dividends it was paying to him! Why? The price of gas was high enough; gas companies elsewhere earned big dividends at a much lower rate, and his father was proposing to reduce the price from $1.25 to 75 cents. Young Mr. Spreckels couldn't get answers to his questions from the officers and directors; they wouldn't listen to him. So he did as reformers do in politics; he appealed "to the people," and the people heard him gladly. In other words, the stockholders to whom he addressed a circular elected Rudolph Spreckels to the board of directors. Then he found out what the matter was.

Those respectable old business men on the board were dummy directors. They took orders like our dummy legislators, and, like these despised politicians, were organized by a boss who ran this business as our political bosses run cities and states, inefficiently and dishonestly. Mr. Spreckels sent to Chicago for a chief accountant; and he sent so far because he needed a man who would be free from local reverence for the standing of the officers and directors of the San Francisco Gas Company. He feared "pull" and "corruption." And the Chicago man came; and he soon was keen on the scent. He became excited. He was on the track, he told Mr. Spreckels, of "something sensational."

"Go ahead and get it!" Mr. Spreckels ordered.

"But, no"; the accountant said it was so big that he must first have a talk with his Chicago chief about it. The Chicago chief came; there were a few days of mystery, then the accountant and his chief both left the coast together.

"I never got that something big," Mr. Spreckels says now, with a smile. He wasn't balked, however. He put other investigators to work and, though they found nothing "big," they did find something small, very small. Besides general confusion, mismanagement, unearned dividends and inefficiency, there was graft. The directors got gas, electric light, gas ranges, coke, and other supplies free. That was their price, perhaps. That was the way the boss, Joe Crockett, bribed them, but the business boss had another political method of control. He gave places to relatives and friends of the directors and other influential men. The payroll was "padded" like a city payroll, to make jobs for persons with pull.

How can business men despise politics so? How can they pretend to dread the inefficiency, the pulls and the graft of public ownership of public utilities, when they know that this San Francisco Gas Company is a typical example of "private" or business management of this class of business? And Mr.

Spreckels didn't find out for whom and for what Joe Crockett wanted to run the company; but the rest of us have. We learned in the life insurance and railroad investigations what that "something big" is.

Mr. Spreckels was busy. He reported to that board of directors what he had discovered, and he suggested that they cut out all this "dry rot"—the financial term for corruption. There was a scene. There was just such a howl at this reform in business as there is in politics, and more hypocrisy. Those old directors were indigant. To think that they, gentlemen, men of business standing and years of experience, were to be insulted and dictated to by a boy of twenty-eight! He should learn that he couldn't dominate them. They were having troubles enough from one Spreckels already; they wouldn't put up with another "in their midst."

But that boy of twenty-eight was, indeed, a Spreckels. Independent, willful, he was sure of the end. He had the facts. He appealed again to the stockholders, who, like him, had been allowing themselves to be voted by "the party in power." He reported to them the condition of things and, offering a ticket in opposition to the regular ticket, he won. Enough of Spreckels's directors were elected to give him control. He did not take the presidency. Because his father was fighting the company, he put up W. B. Bourn for president, but Rudolph was boss. And he cut off more than $300,000 of useless expenses (graft, politics, and inefficiency) in the first year!

It was while he was in control of the gas company that young Spreckels got his first insight into the government of the city. He found upon the padded payroll a man employed at $500 a month to collect the bills against the city for public lighting. Inquiring why, Mr. Spreckels was told that "this arrangement facilitated" the collections; that the collector was a politician, with a following and a pull; he could get the money without delay, and—besides—was "useful in many ways." Mr. Spreckels understood. He discharged the man.

"What was the result?" I asked Mr. Spreckels, when he told me of this incident.

"Some delay; that was all," he said.

One day an employee brought Mr. Spreckels the bill for gas furnished to the city gas inspector. This official had always ignored his bills and the company had never cut off his gas. What would Mr. Spreckpls do about it?

"Treat him like anybody else," was the answer. When Mr. Spreckels told me of these incidents, I explained to him that such things happened in most cities; that this was part of what business men called political blackmail; that business men, especially those in public service corporations, commonly submitted to and excused this corruption on the ground that, to protect the interests of their business and stockholders, they "had to." They were "held up."

"What do you say to that, Mr. Spreckels?"

"I say that you don't have to be blackmailed, even if you are in the public service business. A little backbone is all that is needed unless you want things you shouldn't have."

"And that is true even as against a Labor government?"

Mr. Spreckels smiled. He knew that the "Labor" government was no more "labor" than the Republican party was "republican" and the Democratic party "democratic." He knew that the boss and the leaders of the Labor party, and the officials of the Labor administration, were willing to sell out their followers and the city to capital. And this he knew at first-hand. Soon after he and the Labor boss came into power, Spreckels in the San Francisco Gas Company and Ruef in San Francisco, they met. Mr. Spreckels has told under oath the story of that meeting. He says:

"Ruef was brought into my office by Mr. Charles Sutro and introduced and left there, and he stated to me that he thought he had legal ability and could be of service to the corporation 'otherwise.' He suggested that he be employed as counsel for the company."

To have the political representative of Labor offer to represent a "hated capitalistic" corporation shocked Mr. Spreckels, the capitalist, no more than it did citizens or the workingmen themselves. That was old and, as newspaper men understand, it is news, not evil, that stirs men. Mr. Spreckels declined Ruef's offer, but let it pass without a protest. When, however, a little later, the boss came back and proposed to him to use organized Labor as a "capitalistic club" in the interest of a capitalist, Mr. Spreckels was aroused. That was news. Mr. Spreckels has recounted this experience also under oath:

"Mr. Ruef called on me at the time of the issuing of the city bonds," Mr. Spreckels's affidavit reads, "and he asked me to get up a syndicate for the purpose of taking them over. He said it could be guaranteed that the bonds would be sold to my syndicate. I asked him how he could possibly guarantee such a thing when it (the bond issue) was open to public bidding. Ruef said that was easy. They could call a strike on the streetcar system of San Francisco, and with every streetcar line tied up, he would like to see the capitalists or bankers, other than the (inside) syndicate, that would bid."

That was the incident which fixed the determined mind of Rudolph Spreckels upon political reform. His present enemies—business men who cannot conceive of a business man taking part in public affairs except for a business motive—date Mr. Spreckels's interest in his city from 1906, when, they say, he failed to get a certain street railway franchise that he wanted. But this bond issue experience was two years before that, in 1904, and from his interview with Ruef that day, he went straight to a luncheon where to several men of his acquaintance (who remember) he told the story and declared he was going to employ detectives, investigate the government and present evidence to convict the men that ran the city and Labor. He talked to others about it. Professor Loeb, the biologist, recalls that Mr. Spreckels talked of his plan to him on an overland train in September, 1904. So there are witnesses for those who doubt, but I happen to know from conversations with Older and Heney in Washington, before the franchise matter came up, that Spreckels was the man who was to back their investigation in San Francisco.

The franchise matter is, however, a most important incident in the development of the public character, interest, and ideas of Rudolph Spreckels; and, likewise, in the history of the corruption and reformation of the city. Brown Bros., bankers, of New York, managed the consolidation of the San

Francisco street railways. These had been held separately by the Southern Pacific crowd and by other groups of capitalists. As the earnings increased, the fare had to be reduced, higher dividends paid, or the stock watered, and, of course, the stock had been watered. The consolidation meant more watering, and the result was a capitalization amounting to several times the cost of construction.

This over-capitalized consolidation was taken over by Mr. Patrick Calhoun, of New York, Cleveland, St. Louis, and Pittsburgh. And genial San Francisco merchants, in conversation with me, sympathized with this very charming gentleman, "because," they said, "he really was cheated by our Mr. Huntington." But Mr. Calhoun has left everywhere the reputation of a very astute financier; he probably knew what he was about; he knew how he could make San Francisco pay dividends on his watered stock. At any rate, he added about one-third more water.

His scheme was to take out the old cables and put in the overhead trolley. He knew how people object to that system, but in an easygoing community like San Francisco and with a "Labor" government, anything should go. He was so sure of success that he recommended his stock to his friends and to the bankers who direct the investments of widows and orphans. Moreover, he filled solid with cement some of the cable conduits, which might have served for the underground wires. Mr. Calhoun was sure of himself and of San Francisco.

But one day, while the scheme was fresh, Rudolph Spreckels was invited by Charles Page, an attorney, to join with some other property owners on Pacific Avenue to consider the proposed overhead trolley. He went to the meeting and he heard them decide to oppose the change as to Pacific Avenue. A petition to the supervisors had been drawn to that effect. Mr. Spreckels remonstrated. He said that he, too, objected to overhead wires, but he thought it wasn't right to fight for their own street in the interest of their property alone.

"I don't want an overhead trolley in front of my property," he said, "but I suppose that other people don't want it in front of their property, either. Certainly the city's supervisors should treat all streets alike, and we shouldn't ask them to favour us particularly." He moved that they oppose the overhead trolley on the whole Sutter Street (cable) system. That was agreed to; the old petition was torn up and a new one drawn. Solicitors were engaged to get signatures, and with 75 percent of the property-owners' names upon it, the paper was presented to the board of supervisors. And the supervisors refused the grant. But this was the old, so-called Phelan Board, which held over into the Schmitz administration. In 1905, when "Labor" came into complete control, the outlook for Mr. Calhoun and his street railways was better. It was known that the "Labor" supervisors would sell out to "Capital." And it was supposed that, of course, Capital would sell out to Capital.

The United Railways Company tried to "get" Rudolph Spreckels. I mean that Patrick Calhoun offered Rudolph Spreckels a bribe. Let me hasten to add that business men may not call it bribery; such as Mr. Calhoun would call his proposition to Mr. Spreckels "business"; and it was "business." But one of the evidences that have gone to persuade me that the ethics of American politics is higher than the ethics of business, is that this typical piece of business would be called bribery and corruption in politics, even by the low-down politicians themselves. They might take the bribe, but they would take it knowing that it was a bribe.

The company tried "reason" first. Arthur Holland, the then president of the United Railways, and Chapman, the general manager, called upon Mr. Spreckels. He had become the head and front of the opposition, and they asked him to withdraw. His reply was that he had read all the published arguments of the company against underground trolleys. There was nothing in them, he said, and he asked if they had any others. They said no, that the engineering impossibilities were all they had to offer. There were some sixteen deep depressions on the proposed lines, and in the rainy season these could not be drained.

"That, then, is your only reason?" Mr. Spreckels asked.

That was all, they said.

"There is no other?" Mr. Spreckels made sure. "You don't mind the difference in cost?"

Not at all; they were sure.

"Very well," Mr. Spreckels said. "Then I have a solution. I will put drains on the present (cable) conduits, and keep them dry. I will keep them so dry that you will yourselves admit that they are dry. But, if I do that, I shall expect you to install the underground trolley in those conduits." They refused this proposition, and Mr. Spreckels told them why.

"You haven't given me your real reason, and I will continue to fight."

Then came Mr. Patrick Calhoun talking "business." There were three meetings. The first was a general, pleasant chat at the Bohemian Club between Messrs. Calhoun, R. B. Hale, James D. Phelan, Rufus B. Jennings, and others. They couldn't get very far without Mr. Spreckels, so he was sent for, and Mr. Calhoun soon saw that Spreckels was the man. He was keen, firm, amiable, but not to be charmed or fooled. Evidently Patrick Calhoun made up his mind then to "get" Spreckels, for, after the meeting, he asked for a second meeting with him alone.

They met at the Canadian Bank and went to a private room in the Mercantile Club upstairs. After some preliminaries, Calhoun offered to modify his overhead trolley plans to this extent: he would except Pacific Avenue. That was the street on which Spreckels lived. Mr. Calhoun would leave the cable there for the present, at least, and, if he ever did apply electricity to that line, would use the underground conduit. Mr. Spreckels understood the proposition perfectly, as his reply showed. He said that no concession to him or to his street could break his allegiance to the other property owners. Mr. Calhoun went away disappointed. But he tried again.

The third meeting was again in the Canadian Bank building, and Mr. Calhoun had a witness present, his brother-in-law and manager. Mr. Spreckels had none, so I must be careful. Mr. Spreckels says that Mr. Calhoun explained that he couldn't put in conduits all over the city. But he could put in some, and he told where. Also, however, he would tunnel the Powell Street hill and make Powell and Sutter the most valuable transfer-point in the city.

"Is that because I own property at that point?" Mr. Spreckels asked.

"Why, no," Calhoun answered. "Are you interested? I didn't know that."

Besides this offer, Mr. Calhoun bid to remove streetcars altogether from Pacific Avenue and take the parallel street, Broadway. That would make Mr. Spreckels's street more attractive, and as for the convenience, Mr. Spreckels and his friends used automobiles and carriages. And Mr. Calhoun went on to tell Mr. Spreckels in a very flattering way that he was the kind of man he wished to have with him, and he suggested that Mr. Spreckels take a stock interest in the United Railways. Mr. Spreckels put the whole business aside with a reference to "people that didn't live on Pacific Avenue and did not ride in automobiles and carriages." He was quiet about it, but he understood it. He was being offered personal inducements to betray the other property owners with whom he had associated himself and of whom he was the leader; the price held out to him was expected to bribe him over to the side of the United Railways.

"Did you understand this to be bribery?" I asked Mr. Spreckels.

"Of course it was bribery," he answered. "Bribes aren't always offered in cash, and corruption isn't confined to politics. Anything that tempts any man from what he thinks to be his duty is corruption."

Mr. Spreckels resisted the temptation easily. He told Calhoun, as he told Calhoun's predecessors, that he would fight, and he went out and organized a company to build and operate an underground trolley line in Bush Street. That is the offence charged up to him by his fellow-capitalists now. At the time he proposed his scheme it was not regarded as bad. On the contrary, it was spoken of as public-spirited. It was perfectly understood then that Rudolph Spreckels sought only to prove on Bush Street that the underground trolley was feasible. He expected to incur no loss; he must make the road pay to prove his point. But there was to be "no big money in it," either. One of the terms stated in the papers and to be fixed in the franchise grant from the city was an agreement that the city was to take over the plant at cost plus interest, at any time it pleased after the demonstration had been made. The scheme was conceived neither as a self-sacrifice nor as selfish; it was only a weapon made for a particular fight, the fight for the city beautiful as against Patrick Calhoun and dividends on the watered stock of the street railway company.

But the earthquake knocked that weapon out of Rudolph Spreckels's hand. The articles of incorporation were filed a day or two before the disaster of April 18, 1906, and Rudolph Spreckels, invited by Mayor Schmitz to join the Committee of Fifty that was to rehabilitate San Francisco and govern it, at last, as it should be governed, by its best citizens in its own best interest, as a community of men and women Mr. Spreckels left his company in the air and devoted himself to this bigger, finer task. And he was absorbed for a while. It was an inspiring spectacle, that of those fifty leading men leading a whole city of men and women in the work for the common good. But Spreckels was the first to see that the grafters smelt the graft and that the fifty, reduced to forty, caught the smell, whiffed, and dashed all together low politicians, high financiers, and dignified attorneys for the graft. Herrin was on hand; Harriman came flying to the rescue and to get his rails farther into the city. Calhoun came out to get, while the city was down, the franchise held up before but "arranged for," and he got it. But Rudolph Spreckels saw now that the fight wasn't with Mr. Calhoun; and neither was it with Schmitz and Ruef. It was with some sort of a big, general condition. So he went back to the big, general war he had planned with Heney and Burns—before the earthquake; before that franchise for Calhoun came up—his plan as outlined years before to his friends at lunch, the day Ruef offered to lend him Organized Labour to knock out Organized Capital and seize a bond issue. Rudolph Spreckels went on with his plan for such an investigation of the corruption in San Francisco as he had made and won in San Francisco gas.

That's Rudolph Spreckels's story, in brief. Can you see the man? Stress has been laid upon his youth and his self-reliance, his fearless readiness to fight. But there is an amiability about the man that is very winning. He is hard, hard as youth, both in conflict and in his judgments of men. "Are you with me?" he asked a friend, and when the friend began to "explain,"

Spreckels cut him short: "Then you're against me. That's all I wanted to know." And his friend didn't like that; none of the men that know him do; Spreckels is so cold-blooded in opposition. But he is reasonable, most generous, and even charming as an ally. When Heney's friends learned that he was "with Spreckels," they warned him.

"Look out, Frank! You want to run yourself and all your own undertakings. So does Spreckels, and Spreckels will run this prosecution of yours. He must dominate." "I know," said one banker; "I've gone into business schemes with him, but I never do now any more unless I'm willing to have him be the whole show. It's safe to let him—he is a master manager; but I found out that if anybody opposed him, he would bust the scheme, you, and himself rather than not have his own way."

So Heney expected to have trouble with Spreckels, and the two have clashed sharply, as only two such men can. But Spreckels, aggressive though he is, and positive, is not quick tempered like Heney. He is serene and, when Heney storms, he waits. Heney is just and—he has humor. So Spreckels smiles till Heney laughs. Then, whoever is right wins, and whoever is wrong doesn't care, for there isn't a petty trait in either of these men. If they ever fall out, it will be because they ought to, for the big difference between them is fundamental.

Heney is a democrat; Spreckels is an aristocrat, and an autocrat. Both of them have been too active all their lives to have thought out their philosophies to the definiteness of policy, and they should be able to go far together before they split. For they both are, and probably long will be, fighting what both of them detest, a rotten plutocracy, founded on class hate. But by and by, when they come to build up where they have torn down, either Heney or Spreckels will go asunder or Spreckels will go on learning what Heney knows by heart.

I say "go on" learning because I think I never have seen a man learn so fast as Mr. Spreckels has. That is why I believe in him. Since the first time I met the man, I have never doubted his integrity; nor the singleness of his unselfish purpose; nor his capacity to do great deeds. All the stated objections of his fellow-business men to this business man in politics are silly

Rudolph Spreckels: A Business Reformer 637

and all their real objections are nothing but the symptoms of the corruption of the commercial mind and its class-conscious folly. The trouble with Mr. Spreckels is that he is, like his critics, a business man and that his scheme for political reform is a business scheme.

He believes that all men are divided into two classes: good men and bad men. Anybody who has thought about actual life knows that there is something in the plea of railroad and public utility men, that they "have to" be bad; that there are certain businesses which no man can "succeed" at and be honest. But Mr. Spreckels has that great fault of the self-made man; he has learned not from the experience of others, but only from his own, and what he doesn't know isn't known. He is unacquainted with the literature and the history of politics and government; he has no economic enlightenment at all. He is truly a practical man, and his practical experience is exceptional. He knows that he, as a gas magnate, did not bribe anybody and that he didn't "have to." If you call his attention to the salient fact that he didn't make a "success" of gas; that he didn't "finance" the company, but only managed it in the interest of the stockholders, he smiles. "That is all any public utility man should be allowed to do," he says. So Mr. Spreckels proposes to put the bad men of San Francisco in jail. But what then? What is to prevent the generation of other bad men?

There is where Mr Spreckels thinks his scheme excels all others. He knows it won't suffice to have Heney "put away" the few "bad men" Burns can catch. He knows that eternal vigilance is the price of good government. So he proposes, after this prosecution is over, to establish a permanent bureau, a staff composed of an expert accountant, to keep watch of the city's books, contracts, etc.; a detective to shadow forever the men in public office; and an attorney to receive, order, complete, and present the evidence in court. This has been done before, but never mind; it has never been done as Rudolph Spreckels is proving that he means to do it. There may be some objection to spying, but Mr. Spreckels says such a watch is the common, everyday practice in banks and in other business. So let that pass.

But what is to prevent Mr. Spreckels's accountant from "selling out"; his detective from "standing in"; his attorney from "taking perfectly proper fees" from other clients? The vigilance of Mr. Spreckels. He will watch his watchers. So it comes down, finally, to the character of Mr. Spreckels. That happens to be about as sound a foundation as any one man can furnish, but it is a one-man scheme. It isn't democratic. The democratic theory is founded on the expectation that self-government, by its very abuses, will tend gradually to develop in all men such a concern for the common good that human nature will become intelligent and considerate of others. That sounds almost Christian, and it isn't business. In business the old autocratic practice prevails; one man is boss, and he runs everything and everybody.

That is why business men's reform movements seek to abolish or subordinate the board of aldermen and to concentrate all power in the mayor. They want a good, responsible king. And if they would only elect men who would be king, they might be satisfied, but the "good" business man they choose is usually of the sort that looks up to "big" business men; he has the prejudice of his class against the political boss, but when he discovers that this low-down politician is the mouthpiece of the high-up business men, he takes orders as well as the ordinary heeler. "Better," says ex-Boss Buckley, of San Francisco, who tried him out. Business men ought to elect a "big" business man mayor. Rudolph Spreckels is the very type. He wouldn't look up to anyone and no politician, no matter whom he represented, could get Mayor Spreckels to "take programme," as they say in the West. But big business men "despise politics" and scorn office-holding; they are too proud, or something, to "appeal to the people," and they have a class aversion to publicity. Mr. Spreckels, possessed of the virtues, has some of the faults of his class. He, too, despises politics; he told me he never had voted in his life; and he promises, with pride, not to take office. It is sometimes a duty to take office; it is as ridiculous for a citizen in a republic to boast that he won't as it would be to announce with pride that he will not go to the front in time of war. As for the fine instinct of your sensitive gentlemen for privacy, criminals have that. And as for rendering an account to the people, somebody has to; and Mr. Spreckels lets Heney issue the statements of the prosecution to the public.

Now I have shown, I think, why business men should be for Rudolph Spreckels. Why haven't I shown why real democrats should be against him? There are two good reasons: one is that while he has some of the faults of his kind, he hasn't all; he lacks those that are dangerous. The other is that he is getting over those that he has. His original idea was to let whosoever would nominate and elect whomsoever they pleased. But politics is interesting, and I noticed that Mr. Spreckels could not keep his hands off. He regretted it, but he had to help run the board of aldermen after the members confessed; and he had to help name a mayor when Schmitz was convicted. And in doing these things, he had to consider the wishes of the public, as he wanted to. Well, this was politics, and it was amusing to observe that Mr. Spreckels showed a native talent for the game. He says he won't, but he will play it, as he should.

And he will be boss. He thinks not, of course; he hates the word. We all do. But he will have the power. Since he is back of the prosecution, and will be back of his vigilantes, men do, and they will continue to come to him for advice. His advice may be good, and he may be, therefore, a good boss. But a boss he is and a boss he must be. But his scheme, like the whole idea of the San Francisco prosecution, is extralegal and unsafe.

Mr. Spreckels now, like any other boss, is working through agents: Heney, Langdon, etc. They are doing well; they may do better; but they may do something that Mr. Spreckels would not have done. Mr. Langdon may become jealous of his prerogatives; the mayor may adopt a policy that is repugnant to Mr. Spreckels, and yet not criminal. Mr. Spreckels will see then that he can't, and that he shouldn't, carry out his ideas, no matter how good they are, except in a legal office where he has himself the power and is, in his own person, responsible to the other citizens of the city, who should be free to elect or defeat him.

That means going to the people, yes, but Mr. Spreckels has learned something about the people. When I first met and heard him talk about "business," I said:

"But, Mr. Spreckels, business won't help you. You'll find, if you go far enough into this political corruption, that business graft is at the bottom of it. And when you touch that, your own class, the business men of San Francisco will go back on you."

He smiled; he knew all that. But what he didn't know, and what I saw him find out when his own class did go back on him, was that the people, yes, even Labour, would listen. Organized Labour, led by the same kind of selfish grafters that lead Organized Capital, held off like its capitalistic twin, but the rank and file were reasonable and capable of some little self-sacrifice. And Mr. Spreckels's personal experiences were private, with a few men. He won't address a crowd, but Heney does and he sees that Heney rarely fails to get a response from his juries and from "the masses" generally. Well, the masses decide in this country and their decisions are good, and the reason they are good is not because the people are better than their "betters," but because they are disinterested. They are not in on any graft, so they can be fair.

But the best hope of Spreckels lies in this rare trait: he has mental as well as moral integrity. He has class prejudices, but they take a peculiar form. A capitalist, he can see the beam in the eye of capital as clearly as he can the mote in the eye of labour; and the only sense of class that he shows is in his real scorn for the workingman's brick and the politician's petty blackmail. He would let them go to get the big, real deviltry of his own class, which is the source of our corruption, political, business, and labour, too. And he did.

Mr. Spreckels was fair. He gave his own class a chance. He passed the word in business circles that he was going after grafters; that he knew business men were held up; he argued that they couldn't like to be held up and therefore would undoubtedly be glad to help expose and destroy the whole blackmail system. He invited the business men of San Francisco to turn state's witnesses and help him "get" the politicians. But no business man accepted his hospitality. They all stood pat; some of them went on being held up by the politicians who did accept Mr. Spreckels's invitation. For he sent it to them also.

And when they turned state's witnesses, there was clamour downtown. A strike was impending, the car-men's strike, and Spreckels himself has suffered from labour's tyranny. "Everybody" wanted the unions smashed and Patrick Calhoun promised to smash them. No matter. A whole lot of leading business men, the very leaders of the city, were indicted for bribery or corruption and Calhoun was among them. Spreckels "went back on his class." That's what was said, and he was "cut"; his family was punished; his bank suffered a (rich depositors') run. Spreckels was unmoved; he was getting publicity, but he took it. He called at his bank; lunched at "the" Club; and he appeared constantly in court. He was following the evidence.

This is all that is necessary. Let such a man as this, honest, fearless, young and open-eyed let Rudolph Spreckels but follow the facts; they will teach him the truth, and, no matter what the truth may be, he will tackle it; and he will tackle it right or quit. "And Spreckels can't quit," Heney says. "I don't say he won't; he can't."

American Magazine
March, 1908

W. S. U'Ren, The Lawgiver

OREGON has more fundamental legislation than any other state in the union excepting only Oklahoma, and Oklahoma is new. Oregon is not new; it is and it long has been corrupt, yet it has enacted laws which enable its people to govern themselves when they want to. How did this happen? How did this state of graft get all her tools for democracy? And, since it has them, why don't her people use them more? The answer to these questions lies buried deep in the character and in the story of W. S. U'Ren (accent the last syllable), the lawgiver.

They call this man the father of the initiative and referendum in Oregon, but that title isn't big enough. U'Ren has fathered other Oregon laws, and his own state isn't the limit of his influence. The Dakotas have some similar legislation. Meeting on a western train one day a politician who seemed to know all about things there, I inquired into the origin of the Dakota laws.

"There's a fellow over in Oregon," he answered—"funny name—he tipped us off and steered us; sent drafts of bills and pamphlets containing arguments. I can't recall his name."

"U'Ren?"

"That's it; that's the man."

They are getting good laws in the state of Washington, also. I asked in Seattle where they came from. Very few knew, but those that did said: "U'Ren of Oregon." The first time I heard this name was in Rhode Island. Ex-governor Garvin, the advocate of democratic legislation for that law-bound state, knew about U'Ren. After that I used to come upon his influence in many states and cities where men were tinkering with the sacred constitutional machinery that won't let democracy go. But my last encounter with the mysterious ubiquity of this singular man's influence was amusing. Spreckels, Heney, and the other fighters for San Francisco thought of going to the people on a certain proposition and, seeing thus the uses of the referendum, wanted it. I suggested writing to U'Ren. They never had heard of him, but they wrote, and he came. And he heard them out on their need of the referendum.

"But I think," said U'Ren, "that you have it in your city charter." Everybody looked incredulous. "Where is the book?" U'Ren asked. "I think I can find it. I certainly had some correspondence with the makers of that charter; I think I drafted a section—yes, here it is. [He read it to himself.] It isn't mine—not very clear but—[handing back the book] good enough for your purpose, you see."

William Simon U'Ren, the lawgiver, was born January 10, 1859, at Lancaster, Wisconsin. His father is a blacksmith, and his father's seven brothers were blacksmiths; their father was a blacksmith, and their father's father, and his father, and his. As far as the family can trace from Cornwall, England, back into Holland, they see an unbroken line of blacksmiths. And preachers. Five of U'Ren's seven uncles preached and, among their ancestors, other blacksmiths preached. And William U'Ren himself is both a blacksmith and a preacher in a way; in a very essential way.

"Blacksmithing is my trade," he says. "And it has always given colour to my view of things. For example, when I was very young, I saw some of the evils in the conditions of life, and I wanted to fix them. I couldn't. There were no tools. We had tools to do almost anything with in the shop, beautiful tools, wonderful. And so in other trades, arts and professions; in everything but government. In government, the common trade of all men and the basis of all social life, men worked still with old tools, with old laws, with constitutions and charters which hindered more than they helped. Men suffered from this. There were lawyers enough; many of our ablest men were lawyers. Why didn't some of them invent legislative implements to help the people govern themselves? Why had we no tool makers for democracy?

U'Ren is a very quiet man. He never would strike one as a blacksmith. He never would strike one at all. Slight of figure, silent in motion, he speaks softly, evenly, as he walks; and they call him, therefore, the "pussy cat."

"You see," he purred now, "I saw it all in terms of the mechanic." But he feels it all in the terms of religion. His mother, also Cornish, also of the class that labours hard, was also religious—a Methodist. She taught her children from the Bible. Jehovah, Moses, and Jesus were the ideals of this humble family, and, for some reason, Moses caught the imagination of her oldest boy, William. He always wanted to hear about Moses, the lawgiver, and when he could read for himself, Exodus and Numbers were the books he loved best. And just as some boys want to be Napoleon, so young U'Ren dreamed that when he grew up he would be like Moses, the giver of laws that should lead the people out of Darkness into the land of Promise. But, of course, the Biblical hero-worship, taught him first by that pious woman, his good mother, made it a religious influence, as it still is, for when U'Ren, the blacksmith, is fashioning his legislative tools he works not alone with the affection of the true mechanic, but with the devotion of a faith that his laws will indeed deliver the people from bondage.

All his life William U'Ren had heard of liberty. His father's father lived in Cornwall on land leased for ninety-nine years; his mother's father on land leased for "three lives." That's why his father emigrated at seventeen, and his mother at ten, to the "land of the free." And one of William's first recollections of "American liberty" is of our war against slavery. His mother told stories of "poor little black children sold away from their mothers," and his father pointed out the power of the "slave interest." He realized the Power of Evil, that father did.

A strong, independent spirit, he wanted to work for himself. He was an expert mechanic. The son tells how once when they got a job together, he boasted of his father's skill, and the next time a piece of work came along calling for a master workman, the elder U'Ren was put to it. He did it to a turn "in one heat." So he was in demand as "a hand," but he had a head and he "hated a boss." He wouldn't stick to a good job, no matter how good it was. He must "move on," seeking liberty—freedom to do his own work in his own way. He couldn't. The best pay for a blacksmith was in big organizations like the copper mines of Lake Superior. He tried farming. He led his family West, from Wisconsin to Nebraska; over into Colorado; back to Wisconsin; down again to Wyoming and Colorado. It was no use. Father and sons, they all worked as only border farmers work; they couldn't earn enough ahead to buy their liberty; or, if they got a start, something set them back.

U'Ren visualized one tragic day out of this life for me. His father had taken up a homestead in Nebraska, and they had made a farm of it. William remembers halting, on his way to town one morning, to look back from a hill over the rich, yellow level of their crops spread out under the sun. When he came home that afternoon, he stopped, stunned, on that same hilltop. The sun still shone, but the homestead, the whole country, was bare and brown. The boy understood then what one of the plagues of Egypt was. The grasshoppers had passed, a cyclone of them, and in four hours the U'Rens were ruined.

"I was brought up in the fear of the poor," U'Ren says, "the terrible fear of poverty." But not in hate; at least, not in the hatred of men. "Things make men do bad things," he says. He does not believe in bad men and good men, and, as we shall see, he deals placidly with both kinds. "Conditions are to blame for all evil," he pleads patiently, "conditions that can be changed." His father, who pointed out conditions to him, taught him also to fight. But he was to fight for justice, not for hate.

Since the family moved about so much, William seemed always to be "the new boy" at school. The others picked on him. He was still a child, quick-tempered, but not aggressive. And the first time he was tempted to fight, when he was seven years old, he took his mother's counsel that only

"Dogs delight to bark and bite;
It is their nature to."

William didn't fight. But when, not long after that, at Nevadaville, Colorado, Davie Radcliffe called Willie U'Ren a liar, Willie consulted his father. The father reflected a moment, then said in a way the boy never forgot:

"Never hunt a fight, boy, but never run from one; never suffer wrong or injustice."

The next day Willie U'Ren hunted the fight he had avoided. He found Davie; Davie didn't care to fight then. But another boy accommodated Willie. Johnnie Badger, the fighter of the school, licked Willie that day; and the next; and the next. Willie came back for his daily licking till his father happened to hear of it. "What's the matter, William?" he asked. "Can't you lick that boy?"

"Not yet," said William, "but I will some day."

The father took his boy in hand, taught him how to use his fists and Willie went to school and licked Johnnie Badger. "And then," U'Ren says, "we became good friends."

A salient trait of U'Ren, the man, is his perfect self-possession. His father developed that in him. One day William was sent to a neighbour's for a set of double-trees for a wagon. He hitched a trace to it and, letting his horse drag it home, lost one of the clevis pins. His father rebuked him sharply, and William flew into one of his violent but infrequent passions. His father was silent. He didn't want to break the boy's spirit; he waited till William "felt bad." They were haying together then, and at one of the pauses to rest the father talked quietly about self-control. One must learn to govern one's self, he said, and he concluded: "If you don't, William, you might kill."

No one who meets W. S. U'Ren now could believe that he ever had a temper. It took time, but the character-building done for the boy both by his parents and by himself was good work well done. And his mental development was still more interesting. Though his father's discontent kept the conditions of their life critically before him, there was no understanding of causes. The family read "Greeley's Paper," and both father and son followed politics. But the first definite sense of the economic problems underlying politics came to William himself when he was hardly thirteen. The farmers in the Nebraska district where his father had his homestead, needing a school, met to devise ways of making the absentee landowners pay for it.

"It seemed to me, as a boy," U'Ren says now, "that something was wrong in this. If it was right for those non-voting landholders to own the land, it was wrong to tax them for the school they did not use. Or, if it was right to tax them, it was wrong for them to hold the land they did not use. I puzzled over this, but I could not put my finger on the injustice I felt lurking somewhere."

He never spoke of this. He was a solitary soul, as his sports show. He didn't dance, nor even play much. He liked to hunt and think, to work and think, to read and—dream. While he learned his trade, and learned to love it, and while he worked the farm and took pride in his straight rows of corn, his ambition ran off to politics. But not to the game. Congress was his goal. That was where the lawgivers gathered. To fit himself to make laws, he must study law and, in Denver, he entered an office as a student, but not with the idea of making law his career. One of the firm, Merrick A. Rogers, encouraged U'Ren there. "Money-getting isn't a very high object, not for a life," he used to say. And despite his terror of poverty, U'Ren has always regarded the practice of his profession as a secondary consideration. He is a legislator.

Politics comes first with U'Ren. He makes his living with his left hand; his right is for the state. And that such citizenship can be effective is demonstrated by this remarkable fact: the father of the initiative and referendum, the first legislator of Oregon, has held office but once in his career. He has done what he has done as a citizen in politics.

His first experience of the game was in Denver when he was a law student. The presidential campaign of 1880 was on and U'Ren had just come of age. The Republican party needed the help of all good men and true, and first-voters were invited to work. U'Ren volunteered. He offered his services with the enthusiasm of youth and the fervour of that secret inspiration of Moses. And the leaders welcomed the boy. They put him to work. They directed him to aid in colonizing voters in a doubtful ward! U'Ren was stunned. He did not know such things were done. He was horrified, but fascinated. He said nothing; he didn't do the work, but he hung about watching it done. The dreamer was allowed to see the inside. There were anti-Chinese riots in the town. The mob marched through the streets crying "The

Chinese must go!" and threatening to kill them. U'Ren became excited. Here was oppression of the weak. At his request, he was appointed a deputy to "protect the poor Chinamen," and he served in all earnestness till an insider explained to him that the mob was organized and the riots were faked to get the good citizens out to the polls to vote for "law and order and the Republican party."

The elders forget how young people feel when they first discover that the world isn't what schools and grown-ups have taught them. It would be better to teach the truth; then the new citizens would be prepared for the fray. As it is, the sudden shock carries away not only the "illusions" but more often the character of youth. Not so with U'Ren, however. His dream of Congress vanished, but his hope of inventing laws to make such evils less easy and profitable stayed. Indeed, this was the time when the dominant idea of his life took its first definite form. "As I watched this fraud, and saw that it was the means by which the other evils were maintained, I felt clearly that a modicum of the thought and ingenuity which had been devoted to machinery, if given to government, would make this a pleasant world to live in. That men were all right at bottom, I was convinced, for I noticed that we young men were honest and capable of some unselfish service. It was the older men that were 'bad.'"

Sickness befell U'Ren, a long, lingering, weakening illness, that took all the sand out of him. He was admitted to the bar, and practised long enough to see the trickery and the injustice of the law. He edited a newspaper at Tin Cup, a mining town, but he saw that that business had its frauds, too, and that the editor is no freer than his father, the blacksmith, was. So he quit, and began just such a wandering life as his father had led. In pursuit of liberty and health, he moved about from Denver to Iowa, back to Colorado, on to California, the Hawaiian Islands, and Oregon, and back, getting better and worse till 1889-90, when something happened; something for which these wander-years and his whole life and his father's had prepared him. He read "Progress and Poverty." It is wonderful how many of the men who are working for political reform got their inspiration from Henry George. "I am for men," George said, and he made men. No matter what the world may decide to do about his single tax, some day it will have to acknowledge that Henry George brought into the service of man more men of more different kinds than any other man of his day. U'Ren is not an orthodox single-taxer today; U'Ren cannot be classified economically at all; he thinks for himself. He read other books then; he reads other books now. Open-minded in the period when, as he says, "the hard conditions and selfish interests of life are ossifying most men," he never has been able to close up his mind. He is wide open to any truth from any source.

The way he started on his career as a legislator shows this. One day toward the end of his wander-years, as he was changing from the train to the boat on the Oakland (California) mole, somebody thrust into his hand a leaflet on the "initiative." There was nothing about the "referendum," and U'Ren had never heard of either. But he had noticed that all the political evils of all the cities and states, where he had idly watched men defeat themselves, culminated in the betrayal of the people by their representatives. And this leaflet showed how the people themselves, outside of and over the heads of their elected representatives, might initiate and pass laws. Here was a tool for democracy; here was a means to achieve the reforms Henry George indicated. U'Ren determined then and there to hammer this leaflet into a bill and pass it somewhere.

U'Ren didn't care where. The need of it was universal in the United States. He thought how useful it would be in Denver, in Iowa, in Wisconsin; it was needed right there in California. But he happened to be going to Oregon and that's how U'Ren came to be the lawgiver "of Oregon."

The initiative—as a tool, remember; as a means to an end; as a first political step toward changing our economic conditions—this idea gave purpose to his life. His health improved. He went to Portland and, mousing around for books and men, came upon E. W. Bingham. "Ed. Bingham," U'Ren says, "was a law-maker. He had the most wonderful constructive talent for law-building that I ever encountered." Bingham was working with an Australian Ballot League. He was secretary, and he taught U'Ren to be secretary of things. "Never be president," he said. "Never be conspicuous. Get a president and a committee; and let them go to the front. The worker must work behind them, out of sight. Be secretary."

U'Ren has always been secretary; clerical, impersonal, but busy, like Bingham. He has given credit for all his work to other men. The first time I met him, he talked of leagues and committees of leading citizens—bankers, railroad men, corporation attorneys, corrupt politicians—whom he named. But I noticed that while the members of U'Ren's several committees knew something about their own work, they seldom knew anything about that of the other committees of which U'Ren was secretary; and when it came to precise information, they all would say, "You must see our secretary, a Mr. U'Ren, for that." A Mr. U'Ren was the one man in Oregon who knew all about all this legislation.

Well, Bingham had drawn the Australian ballot law for his league, and he talked it over, section by section, with U'Ren, who thus got from an expert his first lesson in law-building. The next thing was to pass it. U'Ren asked why they didn't get the platform committee of the Republican Convention to endorse the bill. Bingham laughed, and so did a senator who was present, but the dreamer "rushed in where angels feared to tread." You will hear today in Oregon that U'Ren is "the smoothest lobbyist" in the state, and he is. He is calm, conciliating, persistent; and he fits his argument to his man. He talked politics to that platform committee; he gave, not his reasons for wanting the Australian ballot, but arguments which appealed to these party politicians. And they listened. Then Bingham appeared. Unlike U'Ren, Bingham was aggressive. He came into the committee room with fire in his eye, bulldozing, begging, reasoning, and threatening. They could put off U'Ren; Bingham hung on like a bulldog, and in the end, they got his bill endorsed by the Republicans. Then they went to the Democratic Convention and there also they won. And the legislature, thus pledged, adopted Bingham's Australian ballot.

Started thus first in the public service, U'Ren had still to make his living. About that time he fell in with an interesting group of people, the Luellings of Milwaukee (Oregon), orchardists and nurserymen. Seth developed the well-known cherries, "Bing" and the "Black Republican," which latter the South re-named the "Luelling." Seth and his wife, and Alfred Luelling, were live-minded people, and they gathered about them other active brains. They thought, and they read; they had lectures and they recited from the English poets. Lacking orthodox teachers, they guided themselves through studies ranging from economics to spiritualism. Unafraid of any new idea, they gave a welcome and a hearing to any apostle of any ism. U'Ren was well received among them. He was taken into partnership in the business. When that failed in the panic of 1893, there was a quarrel, and bitter feelings which endure to this day, but U'Ren says that his health, his heart, and his mind all were better for this life among these people.

It was here that he heard first of the referendum. They were all members of the Farmers' Alliance, and Alfred Luelling brought to a meeting one night J. W. Sullivan's book on direct legislation in Switzerland. It contained the whole set of tools of which, hitherto, U'Ren had heard of but one, the initiative. This would enable the people to make laws; the referendum would enable them to stop legislation initiated by their legislators. U'Ren was enthusiastic; the whole alliance was. With these tools, the people could really govern themselves. And that is what these people wanted; they were Populists.

We of the East despised the "Pops"; but their movement was to the reform movement of today what the "extreme" Abolitionists of New England were to the great movement that produced Lincoln and the Republican party. U'Ren became a Populist. But that party was to him—what the Republican party is to him now; what any party must be to any man who has in mind the good, not of an organization, but of a people—a means to an end, an instrument, a political tool. The "Pops" were sincere people who wanted to change things for the better. There was a use for them, and U'Ren, who saw it, joined them and soon was secretary of the Populist state Committee.

And when, as secretary of the Populists, he had worked the initiative and referendum plank into their platform, he went forth as secretary of a Direct Legislation League to the conventions of the other parties. And he lobbied initiative and referendum planks into the platforms of all of them, excepting only the Prohibitionists, who, like the Socialists, "won't play" with anybody else. Having the parties pledged, he set about making them keep their promises. He lighted a fire behind them.

U'Ren went to the people. They were ready for him. The year was 1893. Discontent was widespread. Agitation had taken the form of a demand that the legislature to be elected in 1894 should call a constitutional convention to rectify all evils, and U'Ren was one of the many workers who went about pledging candidates. But he and the Luellings concentrated on the "I. & R.," as they called the initiative and referendum. As secretary of the Direct Legislation League he got up a folder stating simply the democratic principle underlying the initiative and referendum and the results to be expected from it. Direct legislation was an acknowledgment of the right of the people to govern themselves and a device to enable them to do so. The "I. & R." would put it in the power of the voters to start or stop any legislation, just like a boss. In other words, it would make the people boss; the legislators would have to represent the voters who elected them, not railroads and not any other "interest." Nobody could object (openly) to this; at least, nobody would out there in that western state where the failures of democracy were ascribed, not as in the East, to the people, but to the business and political interests that actually are to blame.

Everybody worked. The women sewed the folders; two-thirds of the houses in Milwaukee were thus engaged that winter (1893-94); they prepared 50,000 folders in English and 18,000 in German; and the alliances and labour unions saw that the voters got and read them. The effect was such that when the politicians pleaded ignorance of the initiative and referendum, U'Ren could answer: "The people know about them." And that was true. After the election, these same workers, men and women, circulated a petition which, with 14,000 signatures, was presented to the legislature.

Now, that is as far as a reform movement usually goes. U'Ren went further. Knowing that the representatives elected by the people are organized in the legislature to represent somebody else, U'Ren went to Salem as a lobbyist, a lobbyist for the people, and he talked to every member of that legislature. He saw the chicanery, fraud, and the politics of it all, but he wrung from a clear majority promises to keep their pledge.

"And we lost," he told me quietly. "We lost by one vote in the House and in the Senate also by one vote."

"Fooled?" I asked.

"Fooled," said U'Ren. "It was done in the Senate by a wink, a wink from Joe Simon" (president of the Senate and boss of Portland).

"You understood. How did you feel?"

"We were angry," U'Ren answered. "I completely lost my self-control and I said and did things that were wrong. And when I saw my mistake, I remembered what my father used to say about self-control, and I tied a string on my finger to remind me. That device of the children worked with me. I think I never afterward completely lost my temper."

The act which U'Ren calls his mistake was to go out from that legislature to punish the members who had broken their pledges; and that is what I can't help believing must be done. But U'Ren is one of those very, very few men that believe, after these 2,000 years, in the Christian spirit as a practical force.

"Alfred Luelling first questioned the wisdom," he said, "of punishing faithless legislators. We talked it over and I thought a lot about it. And I decided that he was right. After that, we never again punished men. Of course, we voted against a delinquent, if the parties gave us a choice; but our policy was to publish, not a man's delinquencies, but his promises."

Coming from a practical politician, this is a most important tip for reformers. And U'Ren is a practical politician. He learned something from that legislature. Watching it as, when a boy, he watched Denver politics, open-eyed, he saw what he saw, and his mind, never taught to blink the facts, took in what his ears and eyes perceived. When he came home, he organized his county, and he organized it well. The "dreamer" became the boss of his (Clackamas) county, but he was not a selfish boss. This was his chance to realize his young dream of Congress. The Populists wanted him to go, but he knew now what Congress was, and "What could I have done against the combine that ran it?" he asked. "I could do nothing but protest at Washington," he added. "In Oregon I could get the initiative and referendum through."

So he ran for the Assembly and was elected. This was in 1896. Bryan was running for president, and Oregon was a free silver state. Even Republicans like Senator Mitchell were for silver; they were called "Silver Republicans" just as in the East we had "Gold Democrats." The Populists elected thirteen assemblymen, the Democrats three, the Republicans forty-four; in the Senate the Populists had three votes, the Democrats three, the Republicans twenty-four. And this is important because that legislature never was organized; it was the famous hold-up session, a scandal yet in Oregon. And U'Ren was one of the managers of that hold-up. Oh, he had learned a lot of politics!

The demand for a constitutional convention was waning. Leaders like U'Ren realized that a convention might not be so amenable to public opinion as the legislature, so he was for the initiative and referendum by legislative amendment. That would require the passage of the resolution through two legislatures in succession and then a vote by the people. This way looked long, but U'Ren, as a boy, had proven on Johnnie Badger that he was built to fight till he won. And he had a plan. He had seen in the last session how a delegation such as the "Pops" had now could be used to play politics with, and U'Ren had made up his mind to play politics—for the people. He began right after election.

Oregon at the time was in that primitive stage of corruption where personalities still played a part and any cash briber had a chance for high office. The railroads ruled, but the dominant road, the Southern Pacific, was a foreign corporation. Its bosses might have gone to the United States Senate from Oregon if they had lived there, but they were elected by California, so Oregon was open to its own rich men. And many of them sought the "honour." They paid out great sums trying to get it. The politicians told me that these bankers, editors and business men were "played for suckers" year after year; and any Oregonian will tell you with a laugh the names of the victims of this long-drawn-out comedy.

U'Ren understood this. In 1897 Senator Mitchell was to be re-elected; U'Ren had no doubt of that, and he called on him to trade "Pop" votes for his help on the initiative and referendum. Politician as he was, Mitchell talked favourably in August, not at all in November, and just before the session "went back on" the measure entirely. He told U'Ren why.

"I've got three "Pop" votes that nobody can get away," he said.

"Are you sure?" asked U'Ren, who could hardly believe that the Populists, so new and so enthusiastic, would surrender so soon to "the conditions that make men bad."

Mitchell was sure; he advised U'Ren not to introduce the bill. "My people won't stand for it," the senator said.

Mitchell had made one other shift of position. A Silver Republican all through the Oregon campaign (which ended in the June election), he came out after it for McKinley and gold. Some of his lieutenants left him, among them Jonathan Bourne, Jr., a man we must know. He is now a United States senator from Oregon. You have heard of black sheep? Well, Jonathan Bourne was the black ram of a rich old New England family. After a wild time at Harvard University and a wilder time "about town," he went West and had the wildest time of all. I think U'Ren will not charge him up to conditions; I've heard him say that Bourne was improved by age. Bourne learned his game from Mitchell, who learned his from Quay in Pennsylvania, whence Mitchell came (after a change of name). And the lesson of the Quay school of politics was not to organize like Tammany for the year around, but to "let her rip" till just before a campaign, then make a new "combine."

When Mitchell made his gold "combine," Bourne made his new silver "combine" and U'Ren joined Bourne. Mitchell didn't have the three Pop votes. U'Ren found that his delegation was solid, and ready to trade. All they wanted was (1) the initiative and referendum, (2) a good registration law (Ed Bingham's), and (3) Pop judges and clerks of elections. Bourne wanted to be Speaker. He was willing to swing his delegation to the Pop bills in return for their votes for his speakership. This settled the House; they looked to the Senate. The president, Joe

Simon, was the man who beat the constitutional convention with a wink. No matter. U'Ren wasn't punishing men. He called on Simon. He knew Simon wanted to go to the United States Senate. Simon didn't say so. No. Simon's conversation suggested that President Corbett of the First National Bank would make a good senator, but the politicians understood that Corbett was "only Simon's rich sucker." And so it turned out, for when, later, Simon did control a legislature for Corbett, Simon, not Corbett, was elected to the United States Senate. But U'Ren wasn't interested in senatorships. He believed that Simon would go into a strong combine to beat Mitchell. And he was right. Since the terms—U'Ren's "fool" legislation and Bourne's speakership—were satisfactory, Simon delivered the Senate.

Does it begin to appear now how U'Ren got his good laws in the bad state of Oregon? Do you begin to understand why it was that "leading citizens" and "corrupt politicians," the very men who are against reform elsewhere, "passed all these reform measures ascribed to U'Ren?" Most of these men didn't know what they were doing, and they didn't care. They wanted something for themselves; U'Ren wanted something for the people. On that basis, William U'Ren went into every political deal that he could get into.

And that he was a factor to be reckoned with, he proved right away. Quick, quiet, industrious, he had his "combine" organized before Mitchell woke up. The Simon-Bourne-Pop crowd captured the temporary organization of the House. This they did by a snap. They weren't ready to elect a United States senator, and since the election must be held, by law, on the second Tuesday after the permanent organization was effected, their play was to put off the election of a Speaker. U'Ren himself made that play. There was a contest over one seat in the House. U'Ren was on the committee and he controlled three of the five votes. He wouldn't report. The minority, seeing the game, rushed back and, reporting a row in the committee, caused a row in the House. And a mad scene it was. The Mitchell men rose in a rage and, all on their feet, were crying "Fraud!" and demanding "Action." When U'Ren arrived, his side, uninformed and without a leader, was in a state of confusion. They greeted him with a cheer and he took the floor. Quietly, with great courtesy and unexepected ability, he met the attack. Everybody else was excited. U'Ren alone was cool and, as man after man arose to accuse him, he, with the papers they wanted in his pocket, answered with reason and with tact. And his self-possession soon possessed the House. "It is wonderful!" a woman spectator exclaimed. "Whenever that man speaks, you can feel a sense of quiet settle upon the whole House." Little known in the state and known to the politicians as "the dreamer," U'Ren's debate that night made him a reputation. The recollection of everybody present was vivid ten years afterward, when I inquired, but when I mentioned it to U'Ren, he smiled; he never fools himself.

"It is easy to make a reputation as a parliamentarian," he said, "when you have the chairman on your side."

He won out; that is what he recalls. He beat permanent organization that Monday night, and thus put off the senatorial vote for two weeks. And then followed, not two weeks, but a session, of bribery, drunkenness, hate, and deadlock. Men were bought, sold, and bought back again. Both sides used money fiercely; and since there was no appropriation bill, the members got from the state no salary, no mileage, nothing; they had to have money. Well, they got it. Bourne set up a private house, somewhat like the "House of Mirth" at Albany, N. Y., where he "kept" men on his side. Mitchell ran the price of votes up to thousands of dollars, and he and his lieutenant, Charlie Fulton (later a United States senator from Oregon), paid out the money in cash. The Pops caught them at it.

Johnson Smith, assistant warden of the penitentiary, then a Pop assemblyman, proposed to go to Mitchell and take some of his money for evidence.

"Go ahead," said U'Ren. "We'll vouch for your purpose in doing it."

So Smith got from Mitchell and Fulton $1,500 as for himself, and $250 as for the go-between. The next day, when the Mitchell men were trying to gather a quorum, Smith stood outside in the lobby. Rushing up to him, Fulton ordered him to his seat. Smith laughed. "Why! Aren't you going in?" said

Fulton. And when Smith said he wasn't, Fulton flew into a rage. "Didn't you take our money and promise to go in?"

"Yes," said Smith, "I took your money. You were so damn fresh and free with it, I thought I'd take a piece. But it's you that's sold, not me."

There was more to this dialogue, but the sequel will interest the people of the United States who want to know about their United States senators, Governor (now U. S. senator) Chamberlain of Oregon made an affidavit for Francis J. Heney to send to President Roosevelt, deposing and swearing that when Smith was under consideration for appointment to the penitentiary, Fulton protested on the ground, not that Smith had taken Mitchell's money, but that, having taken it, he had not stayed bought! Charles W. Fulton is fundamentally corrupt.

"No," says U'Ren. "That was in war time, and we mustn't judge men in the heat of battle by the standards of cold blood." But U'Ren is excusing the bribery of 1897; the senator's protest to Governor Chamberlain was in 1903—in cold blood. But never mind Fulton. How about U'Ren? That deadlock, which he helped to manage, lasted to the end. Nothing was accomplished; no senator was elected, no legislation passed, and everybody concerned was under suspicion. U'Ren himself had charges to answer. He was accused of taking money from Bourne, and calling together the Pop committee, he admitted that he had borrowed $80. He had to, he pleaded. He had opened a law office in Oregon City, but a "country lawyer" in politics earns very little, and since there was no appropriation bill, he got no pay as an assemblyman. He earned none, he admitted, and he abided by that. For when the next legislature voted full salaries and mileage to its predecessor, U'Ren and one other member, George Ogle, sent back their warrants. So he never did get any money for that time and, to exist, he had to borrow from Bourne. But the $80 was a loan, not a bribe; he has long since paid it back and, since he suggested the whole deal, the money did not affect his conduct. His committee exonerated U'Ren, but the transaction hurt him, and so did some letters of his which, published later, showed how he traded with the powers of evil; as he did and as he went on doing deliberately, in cold blood, as George Ogle knows.

George Ogle, farmer and Populist, is notoriously honest. He was U'Ren's best friend, and when in the fall of 1898 Ogle's mother died, he asked U'Ren to deliver the funeral address. The next day Ogle mounted his horse and rode back to town with U'Ren. It was a cold ride in the rain through slush, but they had a warm talk, those two. U'Ren had run for the Senate that summer against George C. Brownell, the senator from Clackamas who, as chairman on the committee on railroads, had represented for years the corrupt system of Oregon in the Senate. He beat U'Ren, who turned right around and made a deal with him, U'Ren promised to help elect Brownell to any office he might choose to run for next time, if the senator would work in good faith for the initiative and referendum. Ogle knew this because he was one of the "Pops" U'Ren had asked to join in his bargain. And Ogle had been thinking it over ever since, and now, out there in the mud and sleet of that country road, he asked U'Ren what the fight was to cost him.

U'Ren understood, and he answered, "I am going to get the initiative and referendum in Oregon," he said, "if it costs me my soul. I'll do nothing selfish, dishonest, or dishonourable, but I'll trade off parties, offices, bills anything for that."

Ogle objected. "Good things are not worth that price," he said.

They were both thinking of Brownell, of course, and U'Ren said he had to deal with the men in office. "We can't choose our human instruments," he argued, "and we can't change political methods till we have passed some legal tools to do it with." And he recalled a story Ogle had told him once of a cattleman who discharged a cowboy because he returned from a search for some cattle with an explanation of his failure to find them. "I want my cattle, not your excuses," the cattleman said, and "that," said U'Ren, "is what the people say to us." It was the old question whether the end justifies the means.

They quarrelled over it, those two good friends. It was a quiet quarrel and it is being made up now, but they parted then for many years, Ogle returning to his farm, U'Ren to the lobby at Salem.

And U'Ren used the lobbyist's means to attain his end. He and Frank Williams watched their "friends" and made new ones. Brownell was true; also he was clever. He didn't pretend to believe in the "crank" measure. "I've got to vote for it," he would say to his "practical" colleagues. "My district is chock-full of 'Pops' and I have to placate them. And what does the initiative and referendum amount to anyway? It's got to go through two sessions. Pass it now and we can beat it next time." But Brownell's best service was in trading. Once, for example, Williams, one of Lincoln's old secret-service men, learned that two senators were quarrelling over an appropriation for a normal school. U'Ren arranged through Brownell to get appropriations for both. Two normal schools for two "I. & R." votes! And it was either at this session or the next that U'Ren and his friends connived at what he calls a "vicious gerrymander."

"We helped through measures we didn't believe in," U'Ren says in his plain way, "to get help for our measures from members who didn't believe in them. That's corruption, yes; that's a kind of corruption, but our measures were to make corruption impossible in the end."

The "I. & R." passed in 1899, 44 to 8 in the House, 22 to 6 in the Senate. And U'Ren went on working. The moment the session closed, the Direct Legislation League (W. S. U'Ren, secretary) set about making it impossible for Brownell's friends to "beat it next time." U'Ren instructed the voters. The propaganda was systematic, thorough, complete, and the politicians knew it. And the politicians knew now that U'Ren's word was good, and his support worth having. So in 1901, when the measure came up for second passage, U'Ren, from the lobby and after more dickering, saw it go through unanimously. And at the next general election (1902) the people approved it, 11 to 1.

Thus it was, then, that the people of Oregon achieved actual sovereignty over their corrupted state by the methods of corruption. What good has it done them? They have the power to change their constitution at will; to make laws and to veto acts of their legislature, but laws and machinery are of no use to a people unless there are leaders to apply them. The referendum which U'Ren found in the charter of San Francisco was a dead letter; Heney didn't even know it was there. And Heney's exposure of Oregon came two years after U'Ren had his "I. &

R." In brief, to repeat the question raised at the beginning of our story, Why don't the people of Oregon use their power to change the system?

The answer is, as before, "W. S. U'Ren." He knows the "I. & R." is nothing but a tool; that it is worthwhile only as it can be used to change the "conditions that make men do bad things"; and he means to use it. Indeed, he proposed, when he got it, to proceed at once to economic reforms. But wiser heads counselled that, until the new instrument had been tempered by custom, it would be better to use the "I. & R." only to get other new tools. So the Direct Legislation League gave way to a Direct Primary League, and W. S. U'Ren, secretary, drew a bill for the people to initiate that should enable them to make their own nominations for office and thus knock out the party machines. While this was doing, a railroad planned a referendum to delay a state road which the Chamber of Commerce wanted, and the Chamber, in alarm, threatened an initiative for a maximum rate bill. That settled the railroad, pleased the business men and showed them the use of the new tool. And when, in July, 1903, a circuit court declared the "I. & R." unconstitutional, there was backing for the tool. U'Ren was able to get Senator Mitchell, Brownell, and eight other political and influential corporation attorneys to appear before the Supreme Court, to defend the "I. & R.," which was sweepingly upheld.

The Direct Primary Bill was passed by the people in June, 1904, 56,000 to 16,000. A local option liquor bill was passed by initiative at the same time, and in November several counties and many precincts went "dry." U'Ren had nothing to do with this last, but he did have very much to do with another important enactment—the choice of United States senators by direct vote of the people.

This radical reform was achieved without secrecy, but yet without much public discussion. It was a bomb planted deep in the Direct Primary Bill, and U'Ren planted it with the help of Mitchell, Brownell, Bourne and two or three editors of newspapers. The idea occurred to U'Ren to write into the Primary bill a clause: that candidates for nomination for the legislature "may" pledge themselves to vote for or against the people's choice for United States senators, "regardless of personal or party preference." Mitchell helped to draw the clause, now famous as statement No. 1, which legislators might sign, and he expected to be and, if Heney hadn't caught him grafting, he would have been elected on it without having to bribe legislators. U'Ren would have helped him. As it happened, Mulkey (for a short term of six weeks) and Bourne were the first senators elected under the amazing law which hardly anybody but U'Ren realized beforehand the full effect of.

That Jonathan Bourne, Jr., should have been the first product of the popular election of senators has been used to disparage this whole Oregon movement, but Bourne had backed all these reforms with work and money, and U'Ren says he is sincerely for them. But U'Ren tried to get another man to run, and turned to Bourne only when he was convinced that, to establish statement No. 1 as a custom in Oregon, the first candidate must be a man rich enough to fight fire with fire if the legislators should be bribed to go back on their pledges. So, you see, U'Ren was still thinking only of the tool, and he won again. For the knowledge of Bourne's resources and character (and, also, a warning from the back country that the men with guns would come to Salem if their legislature broke its pledge) did have its effect. The legislature confirmed Bourne without bribery and with only four votes against him.

The Direct Primary Law settled, a People's Power League was organized (W. S. U'Ren, secretary) to use the people's power, but U'Ren still stuck to toolmaking. Other reformers used the "I. &. R." for particular reforms. The Anti-Saloon League passed a local option bill; the state Grange enacted two franchise tax acts, which the legislature had failed on; and U'Ren's league put through a constitutional amendment to cut out the state printer's graft. On the other hand, a graft bill to sell the state a toll road, another for woman's suffrage, and a liquor dealers' amendment to the local option bill were all beaten by referendum. But U'Ren and the League worked hardest for and passed, by initiative, bills extending the "I. & R." to cities and towns, and giving municipalities complete home rule—more tools. And so—next year, initiative bills were passed to let the people discharge any public officer of the state and choose his successor by a special election (this is the famous " recall"); a corrupt practice act; to make the people's choice of United States senators mandatory; and, deepest reaching of all, proportional representation. All tools. There were referendum petitions out, also; two against appropriations, one to make passes for public officials compulsory, another to beat a sheriff's graft. But U'Ren was still after the tools.

But will this tool-making never be over ? "Yes," said U'Ren; and he added very definitely, "Reform begins in 1910." And one proposition in the list for 1908 showed what we may expect. This was a bill "to exempt from taxation factory buildings and machinery; homes and home improvements, but not the lots nor the farms." Quietly worded though this was, the reform involved is economic, and economic reforms are, as we have seen, what U'Ren is after. And he will get them, he and the people of Oregon. I believe that that state will appear before long as the leader of reform in the United States, and if it is, W. S. U'Ren will rank in history as the greatest lawgiver of his day and country.

But what about the man? What about reforms got as he has got his? It must be remembered, before passing judgment, that Oregon was in that stage of corruption where the methods were loose, crude and spontaneous. Perhaps the condition I mean can best be brought home by citing an agreement written by Harvey W. Scott, the really great editor of that really great newspaper, the *Oregonian* (and of its afternoon edition, the *Telegram*), one night in 1903. There was a contest on for United States senator. Scott had hopes. Bourne had had them, but he had nothing left but a small minority of legislators. These he owned, however; they had cost him $25,000. Scott wanted Bourne's legislators, so on the last night of the session he wrote the agreement printed below, and Wm. M. Ladd, the leading banker of Portland, wired it (hence the verbal errors) to Salem. Here it is:

"In case I receive Jonathan Bourne, Jr.'s support for United States senator at the joint session of the legislature tonight, I hereby agree to use the full power of the *Morning Oregonian* and the *Evening Telegram* to defeat John H. Mitchell at the next senatorial election, and elect Jonathan Bourne, Jr., in his place.

"I further agree that if I receive the support of Jonathan Bourne, Jr., for United States Senate in the joint session of the legislature tonight, that if elected I will turn all the federal patronage over to Jonathan Bourne, Jr.

"I hereby further agree in lieu [view] of receiving the support of Jonathan Bourne tonight at the joint session of the legislature, that whether elected or not, I will pay to Jonathan Bourne $25,000 in United States gold coin."

Scott didn't get his senatorship; Brownell threw it to Fulton, but that is neither here nor there. Other contracts like this are in the the safe-deposit vaults of Portland, and they illustrate the state of corruption W. S. U'Ren worked his reforms through. And all U'Ren did was to trade, dicker, and connive. I've told the worst of it yes, practically all of it; and it may not be considered as very bad; certainly it never was selfish; but it was corruption. So I ask:

"Isn't U'Ren only our damned rascal?"

I put the question to U'Ren himself one day. I was at his home, a small cottage on a point of land that looks up the Willamettte River to the famous falls. One afternoon, when the country lawyer was telling me his story, the "wrong as well as the right of it," and we were in the midst of one of his deals, his wife looked into the parlour and asked him if he wouldn't get her some wood. He rose and we went out to the woodshed; and, as he chopped, I said:

"How well off, are you, U'Ren?"

He rested his axe to answer: "I think," he said, "that I am one of the richest men in Oregon."

"How is that? Have you made money?"

"My earnings average about $1,800 a year. But that isn't what I mean. I haven't any money, but I haven't any wants either, not for myself."

"What about your conscience?" I persisted. "What have those compromises with corruption cost you?"

"Nothing," he said. "I never have done a dishonest or a dishonourable thing."

"No, but you have made bargains with the devil to get him to pass your laws. You remember Moses? He also broke the covenants of the Lord, and you know what happened to him. He was taken up where he could see the Land of Promise, but he wasn't allowed to go over into it. Why won't it be so with you? You may have saved the people of Oregon, but haven't you lost your own soul? Won't you go to hell?"

He was looking down while I spoke, and he didn't see that I was speaking half in fun. Evidently he considered the prospect seriously, for after a moment, he looked up steadily at me, and in even tones answered out of his deliberation.

"Well," he said, "I would go to hell for the people of Oregon!"

McClure's Magazine
May, 1918

Midnight in Russia

Sitting before our hot American fire that night in our cold Petrograd hotel, we were marveling that we could not remember to say "Come in" in Russian. We knew the word, we wanted to learn the language, and we believed that if we used the little we had of it all the time, we might speak the impossible someday. Others did. But let a knock come and we both called "Come in!" It had just happened. It was most humiliating, machinelike. So we agreed that it would not occur again; we were making a solemn compact that thereafter we would wait when someone knocked—wait till we had presence of mind enough to say it in Russian, when there was a knock.

"Come in," I called, and Benton echoed, "Come—."

We were staring, disgusted, at each other as the door opened and a young soldier stepped in. He saved us from ourselves. A dark, handsome Jewish boy, in a blue uniform coat and cap, he cracked his heels together, military fashion, saluted with his left hand (his right arm was gone), and he smiled happily.

"Come in!" he repeated. "Good words, good American words. They are music to me. And you are Americans, real Americans; born there. And reporters!"

We had stood up. He shot his hand to us, one after the other, and a glad hand it was. I could feel the joy in his grip. It made us glad to see him, and Benton reached for his overcoat to help him off with it.

"No," he protested, with a gesture of pride. "I can do it alone. See?" And he threw off the coat and tossed it on the great lounge.

"I wish never to miss my lost arm," he explained. "I gave it to Russia. I gave it willingly to Russia, and Russia may have the other, also; and my legs, my head—my life.

"But I am glad to see you Americans. From New York? Sure. New York. What that means to me! And you are reporters, so you know it all: New York, Chicago, Frisco—the United States? And you know it as we know it, we immigrants; as I know it. I—"

His voice softened, and I guessed: "Homesick for the states?"

Benton was keener. "Miscue," he warned me, and the soldier, hearing, looked at him, amused, admiring. But he put out his hand deprecatingly to me.

"No," he said, "not that; not homesick. I am home here, now. But America means so much to me, so much. I was brought up there and I learned there—You will not misunderstand? It was in America that I learned to know and to love Russia."

Benton laughed. I started to explain how I had come to misinterpret the soldier's melancholy gladness, but—

"Let's sit down," said Benton, and we drew chairs close in around the fire.

"I was so glad," the soldier said, "and so sad, because I thought that you, as correspondents, you might help America to learn to understand and—and to love Russia and the Russians, this beautiful revolution and the people who are making it, the beautiful Russian people."

"Beautiful?" I questioned. "Hark," said Benton sharply. "There they are now, a mob of them."

Listening, we heard the unmistakable sounds of a Russian mob: a low, slow clatter as of many hoofs on the pavement. That's all. No murmur of voices, no cries, no noise. We knew it well.

It was May, our calendar, the first week. The Revolution was young, about two months old. Milyukov was still at the head of the first Provisional Government, and all seemed well. But the people, who really reigned, had been growing restless. They were deeply troubled. We didn't know what the matter was; nobody seemed to, not exactly; not Milyukov—we had asked him; and not the mobs, either. They turned out, as the fire engines do at home, upon alarms we did not hear; at all hours; day and night. Only the mobs came out quietly, slowly, moving leaderless through the streets to head into the great squares, where the main herd stood still or, if excited, quietly milled, stamping but speechless.

"Yes," said Benton, getting up, "that's the mob, all right, the damned Russian mob."

"No," the soldier answered softly from his place at the fire, "that's the people, the beautiful Russian people."

I had gone to the window, and making out dimly in the dark the dull, moving mass of them, I remarked:

"Just like a herd of cattle."

"Exactly," Benton agreed, "the beasts."

"No," the soldier corrected, "beast. Some Russian poet called the Russian people a beast. 'That gentle beast,' he said, 'the Russian people.'"

I knew what ailed Benton. He had to go out and follow and report that mob; and it was cold, late, and probably useless. I boosted his great fur coat onto his bucking back.

"You've got a story there," he muttered covetously, jerking his head at the soldier. "Me for mere news." And aloud he grumbled. "Good night," and was gone.

I sat down beside the fire and the soldier—and his story.

"That isn't the way to feel about the Russian people," the soldier said gently. I explained that Benton, on a daily, had to "cover" all these mobs and report what they did.

The soldier chuckled. "He needn't," he said. "They won't do anything; not a thing that's news. They haven't killed anybody; they haven't looted anything. The soldiers did; not the mob. On the contrary, the mob saved policemen—even policemen—from the soldiers, and they wouldn't let the revolutionist leaders kill their prisoners, the terrible old ministers of the czar who had killed so many of them. No, the Russian people do not kill."

He said this plainly, like a Russian; slowly, without emphasis or sentiment, as if it was merely a natural fact. Which it is. I recalled that the first official act of the Russian Revolution was the abolition of capital punishment.

"Sure," he said, "and they won't do anything tonight that an American reporter would report."

"But what are they out for?" I asked, a bit impatiently.

"They don't know," he answered. "That's why it was no use for your friend to bother. We know; I know what takes them out, but they don't, not the people. And that's one of the things I want to explain to you."

He didn't explain right away. He stared into the fire, and to keep him in mind of me, I got down the cigarettes, put them near him, and myself filled and lighted a pipe. The maneuver succeeded. He took and lighted a cigarette.

"You don't know the Russians at all, do you?" he began. "We do, we Jews. We're not Russians ourselves, not though we have lived here for generations. We're Jews. You call us Russian-Jews, and that's half right. We're Jews, but we know and we love Russia and the Russians, we Russian-Jews do. Isn't that queer?"

It was a sudden question, this, and he glanced up suddenly at me.

"Why queer?"

"Well," he answered, like a flash that casts a shadow, "we have suffered, my people have—we have known little else than injustice, cruelty, terror in Russia, and yet we love Russia and her people."

He stared steadily at me, repeating:

"Love, I say. That's what the hyphen stands for in Russian-Jew: love. Isn't that strange; and stranger still, all strange people that live here and know the Russians are the same. They also suffer and they also love Russia."

He was emphatic now, not Russian; a Jew again, he had a feeling about what he was saying.

"Take my case," he sprang on. "My grandparents were murdered in a pogrom—both my grandfather and my grandmother—by a Russian mob. . . ."

He expected something from me. I said it.

"By the beautiful Russian mob that does not kill."

"That's it," he said. And he saw what he was going to add. "They were torn to pieces, limb from limb, by this people which is against all killing. And my father was driven out of Russia; he ran away to America, ran away from Russia. Yet—I must make you understand."

Carefully, watchfully he went into his story.

"I was a child when my father took me to America. I remember the terror of the flight and the tragedy: he had to leave my mother and sister behind. And I remember the seaport and the sea; the ship that swallowed us down into its belly, and then heaved with us; sick, as we were, sick for days and days and nights. I remember the whole of that terrible, dark, long, heaving voyage in the stinking steerage of that dizzy ship across the clouds of the Atlantic—that's what I saw from the steerage: the clouds, not the sea—across the world of sky to the land of—"

He halted. He put his hand on my knee. "May I?" he pleaded. "May I tell the truth about it all, the raw Russian facts. It's important."

I divined what he was going to say, and I wanted to hear it. I wanted to hear just what the Russians who had been to the United States and gone back to Russia—I needed professionally to know—were telling the other Russians about us. It was affecting our relations with our ally; it was counting in war and peace and the Revolution.

"Go right ahead," I urged him. "Go on to the land of . . ."

He wanted me to finish, but I wouldn't. He did at last, in a low tone.

"Liberty," he said, and he hurried. "The land of liberty. You don't know, you Americans who are born there, you don't know what a vision we immigrants have of your country. And you don't know, and you don't use, the inspired spirit of willingness we bring to your shores. All immigrants are good men when they sail up your harbor; all are citizens, patriots; all. They are loyal Americans; especially the Jews. For we have imagination. We have had a vision for thousands of years; our minds can see, we can almost map, the land of promise.

"It was ahead of our dark ship on that voyage, that vision. It was America. That was the light that kept us alive, guided our ship. I was sure. My father told us about it. All the grownups did; yes, and the children. We were all telling one another about America, describing, picturing it. It seems to me now as I look back that we were all worshiping our vision of the land of promise: America.

"And do you know?" he asked, turning to me directly, "I believe that that vision we flashed in upon one another's minds, that vision of the United States—not what you are; no, but what we dreamed that you were—that vision, brought back here by the thousands of us who have returned, that is the vision which is inspiring this Russian Revolution."

"Why not?" I said. "That vision is only the dream of all mankind. It's nothing but heaven on earth. And not only the Jews; our fathers, the Puritan fathers who found and founded the American colonies, they also saw it ahead of them when they crossed the Atlantic. And they thought they would create it; they meant to. All pioneers and all revolutionists mean to, and someday some of them will."

"That's it," the soldier said, passionately. "And this is that day. The Russians will do it. That's what I must make you believe and report to America. The Russians will really do it. No? Yes. It isn't so impossible, that dream. Take mine: take the picture they painted of America for me in that ship. There would be no pogroms; no cruelties; no brutal police; no need of a police; because there would be no unjust government. You think we thought of picking up gold in the street? No, no. We thought of work, plenty of work, and we wanted to do it, well; but it was to be well paid for, we dreamed; so that a man by working all his life could live well all his life, live well, and be safe, he and his family. Yes, work. Workmen want work, and so that was in our dream. Work. And a chance. A fair chance. Equal opportunity, you call it. Not a chance to graft, and get rich, and live without working; no; but only to get on as well as you worked, as well as everybody. Hope, you see. Not despair, not misery and fighting and meanness. No suffering of the soul, but only working, whistling and—hope. That's all. Is that so impossible? No. Not as I saw it; not as we saw it. The land of promise we saw was not gold; it was green. And I ached for the green, for the green grass and the blue sky, sunshine, and—work, work and no fear.

"And it was green." He laughed. He laughed as he must have laughed when he sighted land. "It was spring when we arrived. Long Island was fresh with new leaves, and the breakers on the shore seemed to make it smile. And then, staten Island!

Do you know what a part staten Island plays as the foreground of ten million pictures of America in ten million memories? It is —it looks like the threshold of heaven: so green, and kind, so earthy, and—home, after the waste of water and—Europe."

He picked out another cigarette, but he didn't light it. He didn't look at it. He was looking at me.

"We were herded ashore at the Immigrant Station. We were hustled in contempt by harsh, strange voices. Anxious, we were confused; uninformed, we were frightened; in a panic, we were driven like cattle and jammed. And," very slowly, he added, "we were robbed." He stopped.

"Go on," I said. "I 'covered' Ellis Island as a reporter once. I know."

"That's what I meant," he cried, "when I was so glad you were reporters; that you knew what we immigrants know. You know how we were robbed there. We were poor, and we were robbed on the Island, and again on shore. And we were distracted; strangers, without the language, we were misled, misdirected—robbed, till we had nothing. Nothing. It was an awakening—from the dream.

"We found our own people at last—those that had gone before us—on the East Side, in the ghetto, as in Russia. Oh, I know. No police, no written law kept the Jews there; only poverty, misery, and the need of friends. And such misery, such darkness, dirt, and the stink, and the crowd. America . . .

"It began right away. My father had been well-to-do, a merchant tailor of known skill, but he couldn't get work in New York, not for weeks—weeks of worry for him, of terror for me: I felt, I saw his despair. And then when he got a job, at last, then he might have risen fast, he was so clever, but the bosses ground him down, him and all labor; the bosses or the competition for work. Then the unions began to organize. . . ."

Again he hesitated, apologized. "I know," he said. "I didn't then, but now I understand that if you start a country off wrong underneath—economically wrong; not as a commonwealth for the common good, but each for himself and the mines and the lands for the firstcomer—then, of course, labor must organize to force the workers to unite for the good of all. A wrong to fight a wrong, a monopoly of labor to meet the monopoly of—I understand, we Russian-American-Jews, we know now, and we've warned the Russians here in Russia, and—But they understood before. That's why they despise the organized labor of America, and want to prevent the evils that make labor unions necessary.

"My father, I, we Jews are individualists. He didn't want to combine. He only wanted to work, by himself, and he could have risen fast, out of his class, the labor class, so—labor beat him up, the leaders did. He never got over it; he lost his job; he lost his skill. His hand was hurt, and his head! Permanently.

"He peddled. He had a cart on Hester Street. You know? The police came. It was against the law, blocked traffic, but—you know. Blackmail. My father was a bearded, orthodox Jew, honest. He would not bribe. One day there was a raid and the policeman on post picked him out; split the scalp off his skull. I saw that! His skull was cracked. He died.

"He died in the hospital. A Hebrew society protested; no good; but the head of it took to me. He liked me, sent me to school, college; you know—College of the City of New York. I was bright, quick, eager to learn—everything. I chose law. I had ideals; can't help it. That vision—it stuck; it sticks. My best friend got me into a Wall Street law firm, clerk, but I was advanced and—I saw what the law is, and the courts; heard it and saw it, and—I did things myself, too, little things, but I know about the big things. You know. And I was willing.

"And politics. Our crowd, the young fellows in our ward, we all went into politics. The old Irish leader, Tim; you know him? Sure. Well, Tim showed us the game, and we—I played it. 'Peanut politics,' we called it, but we knew the big game, we heard all about it; from the inside. I was going in for it, when—but wait.

"I heard the socialists talk on the corners, the fellows that didn't go to college. They knew something, too; they had a science of their own, history, political economy, literature, plays; they had a culture. Absurd, it sounded, at first, so different from what the college taught, and I was fixed against it, I thought. But—that vision, that old vision. They had it. They saw something better, the promised land, heaven on earth. I didn't join. No, but I would have. Sure. I listened. And I saw. I saw the whole thing, the wrong of it, the right. But—

"The war came, Russia's war, the czar's. I didn't care. It was Russia in need. Maybe it was my mother, and home, too; I don't know. I think it was just Russia that I loved, but maybe it was because America was—was not what we thought. I used to remember, as I learned your ways, the ways of Russia, and not so different! Not so bad, but not so hard, either; not so—so businesslike. I had begun to—love Russia, and to think that, not yet free, it would be really free someday; not yet democratic, it would know what democracy was. We knew how bad Russia was, and how good, and in New York—we didn't. How can you be free if you think you are free; how can you become a democracy if you think you are one?

"Anyway, when the Kaiser struck at Russia, I ran—yes, ran—I ran to the Russian consul; I ran to the ship; to Russia. To fight. I had to fight for Russia. I wanted to.

"Well, I did. They let me. Even a Jew could do that. I went home to our old village. Terrible. I saw my old mother, and my—my sister, old, too, with poverty. They had been living on the little I had sent them, living and lying to me; telling me they had enough! No matter. I enlisted. I marched. . . ."

He stood up, and his face glowed with the sight he was seeing.

"That was good. That was the best I had ever known, the march and the battle. It was in the Carpathians, way up in the air; that's where—there in the clouds—they turned us loose.

"I fought for the land I loved. I fought for Russia. I led that charge, yes, I did; I couldn't help it. It was all wrong, they said, but when they showed us the enemy of Russia and said, 'Go.'

"I went. I laughed, I think; I know I was glad, I ran and I—I fought for Russia, the country I found I had been looking back to from America all those years. It was good; it was good. I lost my arm, you see, hardly knowing it; I know I fought after it was hit. It didn't hurt, then. I fought on, and well, you can see—they gave me this decoration on the field." He tapped the ribbon I hadn't noticed before in his buttonhole.

"I wear it," he said, "not because I'm proud. No, I wear it because Russia gave it to me."

He leaned against the mantelpiece, lit his cigarette and smoked, thinking, smiling at first, then he frowned.

"When I came out of the hospital," he said in the slow Russian way, "I had a leave to go home. At the station where we changed cars, most of us, we got out and the train for Petrograd was late. We hung around the station, all us invalids; hours. About ten o'clock at night, it happened, the thing I want to tell you first. A freight train came up to the station, a train of cattle cars. It didn't belong on that track, not at the station, and I remember vaguely that I wondered. But it came there, and stopped. It stopped at the station platform.

"I smelled it. I was leaning against the corner of the station with some friends, other wounded men, and we looked at one another. That smell! What was it? Then they opened the doors, the brakemen did, running up and down; and out came people.

"Yes, there were people in those cars, Jews. They were being deported, in wartime, to the border and dropped there—nowhere. While I was fighting for Russia at the front—I, a Jew—Russia had cleared out my people from many towns, and was shipping them off, like that, men, women, and children. I was stunned. I was hurt, deep down. It was a pain, a sharper, more piercing pain than the shot in my arm. But I leaned there, watching, helpless till—"

He threw his cigarette into the fire.

"Out of the car, right in front of me, out of that stink, with the crowd, came my mother, yes, my own, old mother weeping, scared. She was supported on one side by my sister, who was so young, younger than I, and so old-looking. On the other side, holding her other arm, came a woman of the town that I had known as a girl and seen at her trade when I went home. And I had . . . ! She saw me first. It was she who told my mother.
. . .

"Who did that?" he demanded—of me. He demanded it so suddenly, and in a voice that startled me. "Russia, you say? You say Russia did that? It's a lie. Government did that, the thing that killed my father in America, and my grandfather, my grandmother in Russia; and in Germany made this war. And you come over here, you Americans, you Allies, and you advise us to hurry up and set up—government; and a police; and labor unions; and an army. And you wonder that we won't do it, that the Russians say no?"

He walked away. He was in a rage. He crossed the room, turned, and he flew back.

"You say the Russian people tore my grandfather and my grandmother and—many more, many, many—before my eyes? You think the Russian mob did that?"

He sat down, flaming, and he reached for me with hands and eyes, as he said, hissing:

"Yes, the Russian mob did that, the Russians did it. You are right. But that was the Russian people drunk, made drunk and told to do it, by officers of the law, government. Not sober people, like your mobs that burn Negroes. Oh, no. The Russians would not burn Negroes; not in their sober senses. Only drunken Russians would do that. Only drunken Russians, who have orders, and only drunken Russians will take orders to kill—drunken or beaten—and that's why the czar, and the government, and the master Russians, all of them, kept the Russian people drunk, drunk, drunk all the time. They had to."

He sat back, quietly, silent a moment. Then he bolted upright, and fired at me:

"They had to. They had to. That was the only way to rule the Russian people; with vodka. Yes, the czar caused the Revolution when he abolished vodka. That's what started it, and—Listen, if this Revolution fails, if those mobs out there do violence; murder and burn; and so have to be put down by force—listen—it will be because the Dark Forces remember and reintroduce—vodka."

Mobs had been passing all the time we were talking there, in waves—no, more like rollers. They rose and fell, as the mass increased and diminished, but they didn't break. It was a heaving, noiseless flood. The soldier's reference to them reminded me of the question he had set out to answer. I recalled it, partly to change his tone.

"I wonder what they are all out for?"

"They don't know," he said. "I'll tell you. They are governing Petrograd—Russia. Yes, oh, yes. They don't know just what it is, but they know things are not going right under Milyukov. Therefore they are out to make it right."

"At night?"

He smiled. "Yes. The Russian people are young, you know. You call them children, you foreigners here. They have been kept children by their rulers. They are ignorant; kept so, by the government which kept them drunk for the same reason. And the reason is that they are, naturally, like children—free; ungovernable. They can govern themselves, oh, very well; they understand that. But they don't understand being governed by others. They're like your Indians, free spirits, hopelessly free; but unlike your Indians, they are a people, one people."

Puzzled, my face must have shown my failure to understand.

"I mean," he said, "that they have a mass sense. They are farmers, not hunters like the Indians. They are just one step higher up off the ground. They live and do work in communities, and they think and they feel as they hold their land, as communities. And their minds were saved. Kept ignorant and sodden with drink, their minds were not taught, not written upon. You understand? They were clean, like the baby's. When the czar made war, he sent them in, drunk, and then he stopped the drink, and they looked up, sober, clean, clear-eyed. It was an awakening; like being born at the age of eighteen or twenty-five; and it was like looking out for the first time upon the world. They saw. They saw it, not as you and I do; not out of our education, which teaches us to see wrong, and—accept wrong. They saw it just as it is.

"Hence the Revolution! Somebody told the soldiers to shoot into the crowd in Petersburg. And the soldiers weren't drunk. So they wouldn't. They wouldn't shoot their own people. They would not kill. That was all, except that at the front, too, they would not kill, even Germans."

He laughed, but he ceased laughing; cut it sharp, short.

"It wasn't a decision, you understand," he said. "They

didn't say, those Russian soldiers, they didn't agree together not to fire any more on the Germans. They merely didn't. They forgot to, when the Revolution broke. You can see why?

"Imagine a people, an army of people, who had lived always—always in the dark; pitch dark, inside their souls and outside. No hope, no light—nothing, nothing but a sound. They had heard in their drunken ignorance a whisper, the secret whisper of the propagandists: 'someday, the revolution.' And then—imagine it—one day in the trenches, the filthy, frozen, dark and deadly trenches, they saw a light, and they heard that sound, the glad cry of the revolution. Do you wonder they turned to look at that light; that they forgot the Germans, turned their backs on them and watched the fight in the east, from Petrograd. It was the dawn; it was the break, the morning of their day.

"And not only for the Russians. They called the good news to the Germans across the trenches. 'The revolution has come,' they said, and they thought it was for the Germans, too. They think so now. That's why they still won't fight. They are telling the Germans that the revolution has come, for the Germans, for all the people of all the earth; that we don't any of us have to kill one another any more."

"The brotherhood of man," I sentimentalized.

"No," said the Jew, "that's Christian; Jewish. That's acquired. We got it from not having it. We think that we ought to be brothers. The Russians can't think that; only an educated Russian like Tolstoi can preach that. Turgenev and Dostoevski couldn't; nor the others. They were it. The Russians never thought we were not; they think we are brothers. Not the czar, and the kings, and kaisers—they're only cousins; hence they fight, and make us fight, but we, the people, we are brothers."

"Literal," I said.

"The very word," he jumped, "literal; that's what they are, the children. It's that community sense. Having it for the village, they have it for the world, and it goes deep. That's the hope of this Revolution. For what's the matter with us everywhere? We are like my old father, out to make a success of our own lives, each one, a successful grab for—for things; things we all must have. So some get too much; most of us not enough.

And the Russians had begun to get that spirit. The old reformers had been giving it to them with the vodka and the superstition. They had been breaking up the communal land holdings and establishing private property in the earth. So the peasants were learning to grab hold and hang on, each for himself. But most of them, the mass of this 180 million of newborn men, they are for community success, the common good, the welfare of man. They don't have to learn it; they are human nature in the raw. They have never unlearned it; so they and their Revolution have and will teach it to the rest of the world." "Let us hope," I breathed.

"Hope?" he said. "Well, hope is something in this world of despair, of mass despair. But I can give you faith, too. The Russians are literal, you say, and I say right. They mean it; they mean just what they say; yes, and they mean what you, what all the rest of the world merely say. You say, you Americans, for example, you say 'free speech.' They have it, absolutely."

I nodded. "Anybody can say anything here."

"Literally," he said. "Anybody, good or bad, can say anything, right or wrong. And then you say democracy," he said, "and you mean political democracy."

"Government of the people by the politicians for the businessmen," I quoted, smiling. "What does it mean here?" I challenged.

"Look out of the window," he said. "Listen. What do you hear?"

We both listened; we both heard the mob.

"What the deuce are they out for?" I asked, remembering that he hadn't answered, after all, the question I had started him with.

"That beast out there," he said, "that gentle beast is made up of the Russian people, just folks, lots of simple workingmen and peasants. When the Revolution came here in Petrograd, and won, it meant to them that the czar was gone and that they, the people, were to govern. They began to govern at once, naturally; they didn't, they don't know just how to take hold, or where; they don't know just what to do. But they took over, and they feel, each one of those two millions out there, they are carrying the sense of responsibility for Petrograd, Russia. They are trying soberly, anxiously, conscientiously to govern Russia right, for themselves, for all of them, all. And that's democracy, isn't it?"

"Well, yes," I admitted, "in a very, very literal sense."

"Well," he answered, "that's the Russian sense. That's the sense in which they mean to get to the promised land, the literal sense; that's what heaven on earth means to them. It means paradise here, now, for all. And that's what the revolution means here, and now, and everywhere for all time, according to the Russians. It means literally no private property in land or oil or coal—literally; it means that each man and woman is to get what he produces, no more and no less; it means no loafers, not even rich loafers; no leisure class; it means no classes at all. Literally."

"Literally?" I spurred.

"Literally," he said, "literally. That's the only difference there is between the Russians and—the rest of us. They practice what we preach."

"All right," I said, "but you said when Benton went out that he wouldn't find out what the mobs were about, and that you knew. What is it?"

"I'll tell you," he said, "now that I have made you able to understand. There's trouble in our relations with the other allies. It's the secret treaties. They're wrong. Milyukov knows it; but he thinks they are contracts which must be kept till finally abrogated by the signers of them. The mob doesn't see that. All the mob knows is that there is something wrong with our side of the war; that Russia is up to something wrong, and—so the people are troubled. They don't understand; but they're worried, and since they govern—they, not Milyukov—since he is only their representative, and is not representing them, he must do right or go down. In other words, since he is wrong, they are wrong, or, as they would put it, if they could speak, it isn't Milyukov at all, it's they, the people, the responsible Russian nation that is wrong. But they can't speak; they won't say it. You'll see, when your friend gets back, all they will have understood is that there's something wrong and that they, literally, must make it right, gently, but—literally."

We sat there silent awhile, a long while. I was thinking over what the handsome boy had been saying; studying him there, the Jew, the Russian-American-Jew; and his aristocratic comprehension and his artistic appreciation of—other peoples, when there was a knock.

"Come in!" I exclaimed.

And, grinning in triumph, Benton came in. "Come in"—he laughed. "You'll never learn Russian."

"And how about you?" I asked. "Will you? What did you learn tonight?"

He pitched out of his coat, pitched it and his hat on the bed, and with an intimate American smile at the soldier, pushed in between us up to the fire.

"What did you find out?" the soldier asked. "Did the mob know why it was out?"

"The beast? No," said Benton. "It's a scream. Really. I'll tell you just how it was. I hooked up with Wallace, from the embassy; he speaks Russian, and we interviewed the mob—the mobs. We laid for 'em, at the corner of the Nevski there, as they'd come down the street, each herd of 'em; we'd go out and I'd say, 'Whoa,' and they'd stop. The cattle! Anybody could stop them, or drive them, or—but nobody does. No leaders at all; none."

"Not yet," said the soldier. 'Whom did you interview?"

"Just the mob," said Benton, "anybody. When we'd hold 'em, so, we'd say, through Wallace:

" 'What's the matter?' and they'd consult—you know—talk it over with one another. Finally—

" 'Don't know,' they'd say.

"Who does know?' I'd shout, and Wallace would translate, 'Who does know?'

" 'Don't know,' they'd answer. 'Maybe those people up in front know.'

"So we'd go up in front. Same questions. Same answers. 'Didn't know.' I got mad. I got hot at Wallace.

" 'Ask 'em, then,' I bawled, 'why the hell they're out here, a million of 'em, at midnight.'

"Wallace put it to them, and they consulted. You've seen 'em consult one another? They all talked, each one, in turn; all quiet; all listening; all so sober, so-patient, so-so gentle. Gee, but they certainly are what that poet said; I kept thinking of it: 'That gentle beast.' Took an hour or, anyhow, half an hour, and then Wallace turned to me and said:

" 'They say,' he said, 'they say that they don't know what the matter is, but that it's something; that there is a rumor that there's something wrong in Petrograd and so, they said, they, the people, had to come out to see about it.'"

Benton looked from me to the soldier, and back to me; and back to the soldier.

"Do you get it?" he asked. "They think that they are the government. All of 'em. One mob after another. They all said the same thing; they all think the same things. . . ."

"From here to Vladivostok," the soldier said, "they all say, think, and do the same things in the same way."

Benton stared open-mouthed. "They think that they, the people, govern."

"What did they do?" the soldier asked.

"Nothing," said Benton. "Not a thing. The Russian reporters said there'd be speeches by about tomorrow afternoon. Can you beat it? They meet tonight at midnight, stand there silent all night, all morning, all forenoon, begin the debate at 2 p.m., and maybe the next day decide what to do."

"And it will be done," said the soldier. "Milyukov will abrogate the Russian secret treaty or be dismissed—by that mob which doesn't know now that it will do that. And then, when they do it, all the communities, all the people of Russia and Siberia will, hearing of it, nod and say, 'That is right,' and, by and by, all the peoples of the world also will say, 'That was right.'"

"And it will be right," said Benton. "That stupid mob out there is the tightest, gentlest, justest—safest Thing I ever—felt."

"Safe!" the Jew exclaimed. "Do you feel that, too—that you are safe with them? That's the way we Jews feel now, safe. New Russia is the safest place in the world for us Jews. So you feel that!"

"Yes," said Benton. "But—but what the deuce does it mean? Why is it right?"

"Because"—I laughed—"it has no education—"

"Sure," said Benton, not laughing at all. "I see that. And it has no interest, no selfish interest."

"No interest," I quoted, "that is not a common, a community interest."

"And no leaders," said the Russian soldier. Benton stared at us, first at the soldier, then at me, and he said to me:

"You got the story, I see."

"So did you," I answered.

"Y-e-ss," he said, "but the mob is the hero of my story."

"Mine, too," I said.

"And mine," said the Russian-American-Jewish soldier.

The Nation
October 4, 1919

Report of Lincoln Steffens

Politically, the Soviet Union has reached a state of equilibrium; internally; for the present at least.

I think the revolution there is ended; that it has run its course. There will be changes. There may be advances; there will surely be reactions, but these will be regular, I think; politically and economic, but parliamentary. A new centre of gravity seems to have been found.

Certainly, the destructive phase of the revolution in Russia is over. Constructive work has begun. We saw this everywhere. And we saw order, and though we inquired for them, we heard of no disorders. Prohibition is universal and absolute. Robberies have been reduced in Petrograd below normal of large cities. Warned against danger before we went in, we felt safe. Prostitution has disappeared with its clientele, who have been driven out by the "no-work-no-food law," enforced by the general want and the labor-card system. Loafing on-the-job by workers and sabotage by upper-class directors, managers, experts and clerks have been overcome. Russia has settled down to work.

The soviet form of government, which sprang so spontaneously all over Russia, is established.

This is not a paper thing; not an invention. Never planned, it has not yet been written into the forms of law. It is not even uniform. It is full of faults and difficulties; clumsy, and in its final development it is not democratic. The present Russian government is the most autocratic government I have ever seen. Lenin, head of the soviet government, is farther removed from the people than the tsar was, than any actual ruler in Europe is.

The people in a shop or an industry are a soviet. These little informal soviets elect a local soviet; which elects delegates to the city or country (community) soviet; which elects delegates to the (state) soviet. The government soviets together elect delegates to the All-Russian Soviet; which elects commissionaires (who correspond to our cabinet, to a European minority). And these commissionaries finally elect Lenin. He is thus five or six removes from the people. To form an idea of his stability, independence, and power, think of the process that would have to be gone through by the people to remove him and elect a successor. A majority of all the soviets in all Russia would have to be changed in personnel opinion, recalled, brought somehow to recognize and represent the altered will of the people.

No student of government likes the soviet as it has developed. Lenin himself doesn't. He calls it a dictatorship, and he opposed it at first. When I was in Russia in the days of Milyoukov and Kerensky, Lenin and the Bolsheviks were demanding the general election of the constituent assembly. But the soviets existed then; they had the power, and I saw foreign ambassadors blunder, and the world saw Milyoukov and Kerensky fall, partly because they would not, could not, comprehend the nature of the soviet; as Lenin did finally, when, against his theory, he joined in and expressed the popular repudiation of the constituent assembly and went over to work with the soviet, the actual power in Russia. The constituent assembly, elected by the people, represented the upper class and the old system. The soviet was the lower class.

The soviet, at bottom, is a natural gathering of the working people, peasants, in their working and accustomed groupings, instead of, as with us, by artificial geographical sections.

Labor unions and soldiers' messes made up the soviets in the cities; poorer peasants and soldiers at the village inn were the first soviets in the country; and in the beginning, two years ago, these lower class delegates used to explain to me that the "rich peasants" and the "rich people" had their own meetings and meeting places. The popular intention then was not to exclude the upper classes from the government, but only from the soviets, which were not yet the same. But the soviets, once in existence, absorbed in their own class tasks and their own problems, which the upper class had either not understood, solved, ignored—no; they simply forgot the council of empire and the Duma. And so they discovered (to be more exact, their leaders discovered) that they had actually all the power. All that Lenin and the other Socialist leaders had to do to carry through their class-struggle theory was to recognize this fact of power and teach the soviets to continue to ignore the assemblies and the institutions of the upper classes, which, with their "governments," ministries, and local assemblies, fell, powerless from neglect.

The soviet government sprouted and grew out of the habits, the psychology, and the condition of the Russian people. It fitted them. They understand it. They find they can work it and they like it. Every effort to put something else in its place (including Lenin's) has failed. It will have to be modified, I think, but not in essentials, and it cannot be utterly set aside. The tsar himself, if he should come back, would have to keep the Russian Soviet, and somehow rule over and through it.

The Communist Party (dubbed "Bolshevik") is in power now in the Soviet government. I think it will stay there a long time. What I have shown of the machinery of change is one guaranty of communist dominance. There are others.

All opposition to the communist government has practically ceased inside of Russia. . . .

All Russia has turned to the labor of reconstruction; sees the idea in the plans proposed for the future; and is interested—imaginatively.

Destruction was fun for a while and a satisfaction to a suppressed, betrayed, to an almost destroyed people. Violence was not in their character, however. The Russian people, sober, are said to be a gentle people. One of their poets speaks of then as "that gentle beast, the Russian people," and I noticed and described in my reports of the first revolution how patient, peaceable, and "safe" the mobs of Petrograd were. The violence came later, with Bolshevism, after the many attempts at counterrevolution, and with vodka. The Bolshevik leaders regret and are ashamed of their red terror. They do not excuse it. It was others, you remember, who traced the worst of the Russian atrocities and the terror itself to the adoption by the counterrevolutionists of the method of assassination (of Lenin and others), and most of all to the discovery by the mobs of wine cellars and vodka stills. That the Russian drunk and the Russian sober are two utterly different animals is well known to the Jews, to the reactionaries, and to the Russians themselves. And that is why this people lately have not only obeyed; they have themselves ruthlessly enforced the revolutionary prohibition decrees in every part of Russia that we would inquire about and hear from.

The destructive spirit, sated, exhausted, suppressed, has done its work. The leaders say so—the leaders of all parties.

There is a close relationship between the Russian people and the new Russian leaders, in power and out. New men in politics are commonly fresh, progressive, representative; it's the later statesmen that damp the enthusiasm and sober the idealism of legislators. In Russia all legislators, all, are young, new. It is as if we should elect in the United States a brand-new set of men to all offices, from the lowest county to the highest federal position, and as if the election should occur in a great crisis, when all men are full of faith. The new leaders of the local soviets of Russia were, and they still are, of the people, really. That is one reason why their autocratic dictatorship is acceptable. They have felt, they shared the passion of the mob to destroy, but they had something in mind to destroy.

The Soviet leaders used the revolution to destroy the system of organized Russian life.

While the mobs broke windows, smashed cellars, and pillaged buildings to express their rage, their leaders directed their efforts to the annihilation of the system itself. They pulled down the tsar and his officers; they abolished the courts, which had been used to oppress them; they closed shops, stopped business generally, and especially all competitive and speculative business; and they took over all the great industries, monopolies, concessions, and natural resources. This was their purpose. This is their religion. This is what the lower-class culture has been slowly teaching the people of the world for fifty years: that it is not some particular evil, but the whole system of running business and railroads, shops, banks, and exchanges, for speculation and profit that must be changed. This is what causes poverty and riches, they teach, misery, corruption, vice, and war. The people, the workers, their state, must own and run these things "for service."

Not political democracy, as with us; economic democracy is the idea; democracy in the shop, factory, business. Bolshevism is a literal interpretation, the actual application of this theory, policy program. And so, in the destructive period of the Russian revolution, the Bolshevik leaders led the people to destroy the old system, root and branch, fruit and blossom, too. And apparently this was done. The blocks we saw in Petrograd and Moscow of retail shops nailed up were but one sign of it. When we looked back of these dismal fronts and inquired more deeply into the work of the revolution we were convinced that the Russians have literally and completely done their job. And it was this that shocked us. It is this that has startled the world; not the atrocities of the revolution, but the revolution itself.

The organization of life as we know it in America, in the rest of Europe, in the rest of the world, is wrecked and abolished in Russia.

The revolution didn't abolish it. The tsar's governnlent had rotted it. The war broke down the worn-out machinery of it; the revolution has merely scrapped it finally.

The effect is hunger, cold, misery, anguish, disease—death to millions. But worse than these I mean this—was the confusion of mind among the well and the strong. We do not realize, any of us—even those of us who have imagination—how fixed our minds and habits are by the ways of living that we know. So with the Russians. They understood how to work and live under their old system; it was not a pretty one; it was dark, crooked, and dangerous, but they had groped around in it all their lives from childhood up. They could find their way in it. And now they can remember how it was, and they sigh for the old ways. The rich emigrés knew whom to see to bribe for a verdict, a safe-conduct, or a concession; and the poor, in their hunger, think now how it would be to go down to the market and haggle, and bargain, from one booth to another, making their daily purchases, reckoning up their defeats and victories over the traders. And they did get food then. And now—it is all gone. They have destroyed all this, and having destroyed it they were lost, strangers in their own land.

This tragedy of transition was anticipated by the leaders of the revolution, and the present needs were prepared for in the plans laid for reconstruction.

Lenin has imagination. He is an idealist, but he is a scholar, too, and a very grim realist. Lenin was a statistician by profession. He had long been trying to foresee the future of society under socialism, and he had marked definitely the resources, the machinery, and the institutions existing under the old order, which could be used in the new. There was the old Russian communal land system, passing, but standing in spots with its peasants accustomed to it. That was to be revived; it is his solution of the problem of the great estates. They are not to be broken up, but worked by the peasants in common. Then there was the great Russian Cooperative (trading) Society, with its 11,000,000 families before the war; now with 17,000,000 members. He kept that. There was a conflict; it was in bourgeoise hands but it was an essential part of the projected system of distribution, so Lenin compromised and communist Russia has it. He had the railroads, telegraph, telephone already; the workers seized the factories, the local soviets, the mines; the All-Russian Soviet, the banks. The new government set up shops—one in each neighborhood—to dole out not money, but on work tickets, whatever food, fuel, and clothing this complete government monopoly had to distribute. No bargaining, no display, no advertising, and no speculation. Everything one has earned by labor the right to buy at the cooperative and soviet shops is at a fixed, low price, at the established (too small) profit—to the government, to the members of the cooperative.

Money is to be abolished gradually. It does not count much now. Private capital has been confiscated, most of the rich have left Russia, but there are still many people there who have hidden away money or valuables, and live on them without working. They can buy food and even luxuries, but only illegally from peasants and speculators at the risk of punishment and very high prices. They can buy, also, at the government stores, at the low prices, but they can get only their share there, and only on their class or work tickets. The class arrangement, though transitory and temporary—the aim is to have but one class—is the key to the idea of the whole new system.

There are three classes. The first can buy, for example, one and a half pounds of bread a day; the second, three-quarters of a pound; the third, only one-quarter of a pound; no matter how much money they may have. The first class includes soldiers, workers in war, and other essential industries, actors, teachers, writers, experts and government workers of all sorts. The second class is of all other sorts of workers. The third is of people who do not work the leisure class. Their allowance is, under present circumstances, not enough to live on, but they are allowed to buy surreptitiously from speculators on the theory that the principal of their capital will soon be exhausted, and, since interest, rent, and profits—all forms of unearned money—are abolished, they will soon be forced to go to work.

The shock of this, and the confusion due to the strange details of it, were, and they still are, painful to many minds, and not only to the rich. For a long time there was widespread discontent with this new system. The peasants rebelled, and the workers were suspicious. They blamed the new system for the food shortage, the fuel shortage, the lack of raw materials for the factories. But his also was anticipated by that very remarkable mind and will—Lenin. He used the state monopoly and control of the press, and the old army of revolutionary propagandists, to shift the blame for the sufferings of Russia from the revolutionary government to the war, the blockade, and the lack of transportation. Also, he and his executive organization were careful to see that when the government did get hold of a supply of anything, its arrival was heralded, and the next day it appeared at the community shops, where everybody (that worked) got his share at the low government price. The two American prisoners we saw had noticed this, remember. "We don't get much to eat," they said, "but neither do our guards and the other Russians. We all get the same. And when they get more, we get our share."

The fairness of the new system, as it works so far, has won over to it the working class and the poorer peasants. The well-to-do still complain, and very bitterly sometimes. Their hoardings are broken into by the government and by the poverty committees, and they are severely punished for speculative trading. But even these classes are moved somewhat by the treatment of children. They are in a class by themselves: class A-1. They get all the few delicacies—milk, eggs, fruit, game, that come to the government monopoly—at school, where they all are fed, regardless of class. "Even the rich children," they told us, "they have as much as the poor children." And the children, like the workers, now see the operas, too, the plays, the ballets, the art galleries—all with instructors.

The Bolsheviks—all the Russian parties—regard the communists' attitude toward children as the symbol of their new civilization. "It is to be for the good of humanity, not business," one of them, an American, said, "and the kids represent the future. Our generation is to have only the labor and the misery of the struggle. We will get none of the material benefits of the new system, and we will probably never all understand and like it. But the children—it is for them and their children that we are fighting, so we are giving them the best of it from the start, and teaching them to take it all naturally. They are getting the idea. They are to be our new propagandists."

And this is what is making Lenin and his sobered communist government ask for peace. They think they have carried a revolution through for once to the logical conclusion. All other revolutions have stopped when they had revolved through the political phase to political democracy. This one has turned once more clear through the economic phase to econoinc democracy; to self-government in the factory, shop, and on the land, and has laid a foundation for universal profit sharing, for the universal division of food, clothes, and all goods, equally among all. And they think their civilization is working on this foundation. They want time to go on and build it higher and better. They want to spread it all over the world, but only as it works. As they told us when we reminded them that the world dreaded their propaganda:

"We are through with the old propaganda of argument. All we ask now is to be allowed to prove by the examples of things well done here in Russia, that the new system is good. We are so sure we shall make good, that we are willing to stop saying so, to stop reasoning, stop the haranguing, and all that old stuff. And especially are we sick of the propaganda by the sword. We want to stop fighting. We know that each country must evolve its own revolution out of its own conditions and in its own imagination. To force it by war is not scientific, not democratic, not socialistic. And we are fighting now only in self-defense. We will stop fighting, if you will let us stop. We will call back our troops, if you will withdraw yours. We will demobilize. We need the picked organizers and the skilled workers now in the army for our shops, factories, and farms. We would love to recall them to all this needed work, and use their troop trains to distribute our goods and harvests, if only you will call off your soldiers and your moral, financial, and material support from enemies, and the enemies of ideals. Let every country in dispute on our borders self-determine its own form of government and its own allegiance.

"But you must not treat us a conquered nation. We are not conquered. We are prepared to join in a revolutionary civil war all over all of Europe and the world, if this good thing has to be done in this bad way of force. But we would prefer to have our time and our energy to work to make sure that our young, good thing is good. We have proved that we can share misery, and sickness, and poverty; it has helped us to have these things to share, and we think we shall be able to share the wealth of Russia as we gradually develop it. But we are not sure of that; the world is not sure. Let us Russians pay the price of the experiment; do the hard, hard work of it; make the sacrifice—then people can follow us, slowly, as they decide for themselves that what we have is worth having."

That is the message you bring back, Mr. Bullitt. It is your duty to deliver it. It is mine to enforce it by my conception of the situation as it stands in Russia and Europe today. . . .

Freeman
November 3, 1920

John Reed: Under the Kremlin

John Reed, American poet, died, a Communist, in Moscow, the capital of the future state, of the disease of the revolutionary present: typhus; he was bitten by a sick louse, a doomed parasite.

Jack could have made a song of that, a laughing song, in the days when he sang and laughed. He was a joyous spirit then; I tried to keep him glad. His father asked me to. Jack's father was my friend, and a brilliant man he was; a wit. He was the leading spirit of the leading club of Portland, Oregon; and he played himself, as he wished his boy to play, till he was bitten, as the boy was, by those same deadly, dying things.

Francis J. Heney came to Oregon, prosecuting timber frauds, seeking with William J. Burns for the proofs of the process by which our forests fell into private hands. The evidence reached up among the commanding men of Oregon, and they controlled, among other things, the machinery of the law. Their U.S. marshal picked the juries. Heney asked Reed—Jack's father—to be U.S. marshal and so see that the panels were free and fair. Reed laughed. He guessed what it meant to him, but he took the job; and he did the job. There were convictions and there were hates. Reed's club hated Reed, who faced the hate and bit it with his wit. He had a tongue, as Jack had. It is a story of breed I'm telling.

One day, several years after the timber-fraud scandal, ex-U.S. Marshal Reed invited me to his club. He led me into the main dining room up to the center table, where "the crowd" lunched. It was the noon hour; most of the crowd were there.

"There they are," said Reed to me, but for them to hear. "That's the crowd that got the timber and tried to get me. And there, at the head of the table, that vacant chair, that's my place. That's where I sat. That's where I stood them off, for fun, for years, and then for months in deadly earnest; but gaily, always gaily. I haven't sat in that place since the day I rose and left it, saying I'd never come back to it and saying that I would like to see which one of them would have the nerve to think that he could take and hold and fill my place. I have heard, and I am glad to see, that it is vacant yet, my vacant chair."

That was Jack Reed's father: tall, handsome, audacious, and a wit; a gay and, later, a bitten, bitter wit. He told me about his boy at Harvard and he asked me "to look out for Jack" when he came out of college into life in New York.

"He is a gay spirit," the father said, "a joyous thing. Keep him so. He is a poet, I think; keep him singing. Let him see everything, but don't—don't let him get like me."

I couldn't. I tried, and not for his father's sake only. When John Reed came, big and growing, handsome outside and beautiful inside, when that boy came down from Cambridge to New York, it seemed to me that I had never seen anything so near to pure joy. No ray of sunshine, no drop of foam, no young animal, bird, or fish, and no star, was as happy as that boy was. If only we could keep him so, we might have a poet at last who would see and sing nothing but joy. Convictions were what I was afraid of. I tried to steer him away from convictions, that he might play; that he might play with life; and see it all, love it all, live it all; tell it all; that he might be it all; but all, not any one thing. And why not? A poet is more revolutionary than any radical. Great days they were, or rather nights, when the boy would bang home late and wake me up to tell me what he had been and seen that day; the most wonderful thing in the world. Yes. Each night he had been and seen the most wonderful thing in the world.

He wrote some of those things. He became all of those things. He fell head over heels in love with every single one of those most wonderful things: with his job; with his friends; with labor; with girls; with strikes; with the I.W.W.; with socialism; with the anarchists; with the bums in the Bowery; with the theatre; with God and Man and Being. I pulled him out of each such love affair anxiously at first, but so easily and so often that I soon felt he was safe. I thought I could trust the next most wonderful thing to save him from the last most wonderful thing, so I went off on a long journey, to Mexico. So did Jack, but Jack went, as a poet, to Villa, the bandit, while I went, as U.S. Marshal Reed would have gone, to Carranza's side.

I don't know just what it was that finally caught and took the joy out of this poet and turned him into a poem. He loved a girl, one girl, but Louise is a poet, too, and a vagabond, or she was when she left here in boy's clothes last summer to follow Jack to Russia. And he loved the I.W.W. faithfully and the Red Left of the Socialist Party, and like his father, he hated hate and—all that. I really think it was in the breed. Anyhow, he got a conviction and so, the revolutionary spirit got him. He became a fighter; out for a cause; a revolutionist at home here, and in Russia a Communist. He didn't smile any more.

A friend of his and of mine, who traveled and worked with Jack in Russia last summer, said that Jack was "like the other Communists in there": he was hard, intolerant, ruthless, clinched for the fight. I could see that Jack had hurt our friend, who, having said this, brooded a moment. But then said his friend:

"I wish I could be a Communist."

You see, in Moscow, in Soviet Russia, where there are lice and hunger and discipline and death; where it is hell now; they see—even a non-Communist can see something to live or to die for. They can see that life isn't always going to be as it is now. The future is coming; it is in sight; it is coming, really and truly coming, and soon. And it is good. They can see this with their naked eyes, common men can; I did, for example. So, to a poet, to a spirit like Jack Reed, the Communist, death in Moscow must have been a vision of the resurrection and the life of man.

Sources

Carnegie Library of Pittsburgh
http://www.clpgh.org/exhibit/steffens.html

Hathitrust Digital Library
http://www.hathitrust.org/

History Matters: The U.S. Survey Course on the Web
http://historymatters.gmu.edu/d/5733/

Internet Archive
https://archive.org/

Unz.org
http://www.unz.org/

Further Reading

Applegate, Edd. *Muckrakers: A Biographical Dictionary of Writers and Editors.* Scarecrow Press, 2008.

Behrens, John C. *The Typewriter Guerrillas: Closeups of 20 Top Investigative Reports.* Nelson-Hall, 1977.

Brasch, Walter M. *Forerunners of Revolution: Muckrakers and the American Social Conscience.* University Press of America, 1990.

Brendon, Piers. *The Life and Death of the Press Barons.* Atheneum, 1983.

Cather, Willa and Robert Thacker. *The Autobiography of S. S. McClure.* University of Nebraska Press, 1997.

Chalmers, David Mark. *The Muckrake Years.* Norstrand, 1974.

Chalmers, David Mark. *The Social and Political Ideas of the Muckrakers.* Citadel Press, 1964.

Chamberlain, John. *Farewell to Reform.* Quadrangle, 1965.

Cook, Fred J. *The Muckrakers: Crusading Journalists Who Changed America.* Doubleday, 1972.

Cooper, Jr., Milton J. *Pivotal Decades: The United States, 1900 - 1920.* W. W. Norton, 1990.

Faulkner, H.U. *The Quest for Social Justice.* Macmillan, 1954.

Faulkner, Harold U. *Politics, Reform and Expansion, 1890 - 1900.* Harper & Row, 1963.

Filler, Louis. *Crusaders for American Liberalism.* Harcourt, Brace and Co., 1932.

Filler, Louis. *The Muckrakers.* Penn State University Press, 1975.

Geiger, Louis G. *Joseph W. Folk of Missouri.* University Press of Missouri, 1953.

Goodwin, Doris Kearns. *The Bully Pulpit: Theodore Roosevelt, William Howard Taft, And The Golden Age of Journalism.* Simon & Schuster, 2014.

Graham, Otis L. *An Encore for Reform: The Old Progressives and the New Deal.* Oxford University Press, 1967.

Harrison, John and Harry Stein, eds. *Muckraking: Past, Present and Future.* Pennsylvania State University Press, 1973.

Hartshorn, Peter. *I Have Seen the Future: A Life of Lincoln Steffens.* Counterpoint, 2011.

Hofstadter, Richard. *The Age of Reform.* Vintage Books, 1960.

Kaplan, Justin *Lincoln Steffens: Portrait of a Great American Journalist.* Simon & Schuster, 2013.

Kolko, Gabriel. *The Triumph of Conservatism: A Reinterpretation of American History 1900 - 1916.* Quadrangle Books, 1967.

Link, William A. (ed.) and Susannah J. Link (ed.). *The Gilded Age and Progressive Era: A Documentary Reader.* Wiley-Blackwell, 2012.

Lyon, Peter. *Success Story: The Life and Times of S. S. McClure.* Scribner, 1963.

McGerr, Michael. *A Fierce Discontent: The Rise and Fall of the Progressive Movement in America, 1870 - 1920.* Oxford University Press, 2005.

McKean, Dayton D. *The Boss: The Hague Machine in Action.* Houghton Mifflin, 1940.

Noble, Ransome E. *New Jersey Progressivism Before Wilson.* Princeton University Press, 1946.

Patton, Clifford W. *The Battle of Municipal Reform.* Greenwood, 1981.

Prestitto, Robert J. and William J. Atto. *American Progressivism: A Reader* Lexington Books, 2008.

Steffens, Lincoln. *The Autobiography of Lincoln Steffens.* Heyday, 2005.

Sullivan, Mark. *Our Times: The United States 1900 - 1925.* Scribners, 1962.

Thomas, Evan. *The War Lovers: Roosevelt, Lodge, Hearts, and the Rush to Empire, 1898.* Little, Brown 2010.

Tolman. William H. *Municipal Reform Movements in the United States.* Ulan Press, 2012.

Traxel, David. *1898: The Birth of the American Century.* Alfred A. Knopf, 1998.

Wiinfield, Betty Hochin, ed. *Journalism 1908: Birth of a Profession.* University of Missouri Press, 2008.

Wolraich, Michael. *Unreasonable Men: Theodore Roosevelt and the Republican Rebels Who Created Progressive Politics.* Palgrave Macmillan, 2014.

Online Collections/ Current Journalism

Chronicling America: Historic American Newspapers
http://chroniclingamerica.loc.gov/

HathiTrust Digital Library
http://www.hathitrust.org/

Internet Archive
https://archive.org/

New England Center for Investigative Reporting
http://necir.org/usa-muckraking-archive/

Project Gutenberg
http://www.gutenberg.org/

ProPublica
http://www.propublica.org/

The Center for Public Integrity
http://www.publicintegrity.org/

The Fund for Investigative Journalism
http://fij.org/

Unz.org
http://www.unz.org/Home/Introduction

from The Archive

**Theodore Roosevelt
Wilderness, Vol. 1
ISBN: 978-0-9907137-1-5**
List Price: $24.95
In the western territories a young Theodore Roosevelt found inspiring loneliness and a hunter's paradise. Out here TR enjoyed tough physical challenges and a pleasing distance from the half-formed men of the East, who grasped so desperately for money and power. As the "open season" on buffalo, antelope, mountain goat and white-tailed deer brought these species close to extinction, however, he began to understand the meaning and value of conservation-a progression expressed eloquently in the articles he penned for Century, The Outlook, Outing, Forest and Stream and other journals. This volume is the first of two offering Roosevelt's complete and unabridged articles on the great western outdoors which inspired one of his most important legacies: the preservation of vast swaths of America's frontier in its natural state. Presented in chronological order, the articles reveal TR's personal progression from dedicated hunter and rancher to determined environmentalist, who came to understand the threat to western flora and fauna from unchecked development and decimating "recreational" sports. The collection includes writings on ranching and the cowboy life that appeared in contemporary juvenile magazines, including Youth's Companion and St. Nicholas.

Richard Harding Davis
The Great War: Reporting 1914 - 1916
ISBN: 978-0-9907137-4-6
List Price: $24.95
A skilled foreign correspondent with a wide public following, Richard Harding Davis represented a new generation of adventurous journalists, for whom no battle zone, revolution or political turmoil posed too great a danger for the pursuit of news. By the time of World War I, Davis was a literary star for hundreds of evocative articles written from the front lines as well as his (now-forgotten) novels and plays. Dispatched to France, he covered the major early battles of the war, the brutal occupation of Belgian cities, the horrors of trench warfare, the war-time escapades of American civilians and officers, and his own arrest by the Germans on a capital charge of espionage. This collection of newspaper and magazine reports, complete and unabridged, offers the reader a front page seat to the compelling events of the Great War, and newspaper reporting as done with literary skill, social conscience and a flair for the dramatic.

Nellie Bly
Undercover: Reporting for *The New York World* **1887-1894**
ISBN: 978-0-9907137-2-2
List Price: $24.95
Nellie Bly's convincing disguises gained her admission to oppressive sweatshops, underground gambling parlors, illicit adoption agencies and creepy mesmerists' parlors, all in the service of sensational headlines and the steadily rising circulation numbers boasted by the New York World. This fascinating collection of original, unabridged articles—compiled for the first time since their original publication--traces Bly's brief yet astounding career as an undercover journalist.

Reporting: The Tulsa Riots, 1921
ISBN: 978-0-9907137-6-0
List Price: $19.95

An awkward encoounter between a young black man and a white woman in the elevator of a Tulsa office building sparked the deadliest and most destructive riot in American history. Within 24 hours, the looting, arson and general mayhem reduced the Greenwood neighborhood, home to a thriving African-American community, to smoking ruins. Thousands of black residents fled for their lives as killers roamed their streets, the local police stayed indoors and biplanes sent up by law enforcement bombed and strafed them from just above the rooftops. Designed for the use of students, teachers, and researchers, this innovative collection from The Archive includes all of the major newspaper and magazine coverage of the event, along with a detailed introduction., timeline, glossary, bibliography and index.

Future Volumes: Reporting

Reporting: The Ludlow Massacre, 1914
Reporting: The Triangle Shirtwaist Factory Fire, 1911
Reporting: The Black Sox Scandal, 1921
Reporting: The Great Spanish Influenza Pandemic, 1918

Notes

www.ingramcontent.com/pod-product-compliance
Lightning Source LLC
Chambersburg PA
CBHW031356290426
44110CB00011B/190